COLD HARBOR

COLD HARBOR

Grant and Lee
MAY 26–JUNE 3, 1864

Gordon C. Rhea

LOUISIANA STATE UNIVERSITY PRESS *Baton Rouge*

Copyright © 2002 by Louisiana State University Press
All rights reserved
Manufactured in the United States of America
First printing
11   10   09   08   07   06   05   04   03   02
5   4   3   2   1

Typeface: Cochin, Times Roman
Typesetter: Coghill Composition, Inc.

LIBRARY OF CONGRESS CATALOGING-IN-PUBLICATION DATA:

Rhea, Gordon C.
   Cold Harbor : Grant and Lee, May 26–June 3, 1864 / Gordon C. Rhea.
       p.   cm.
Includes bibliographical references and index.
   ISBN 0-8071-2803-1 (alk. paper)
   1. Cold Harbor (Va.), Battle of, 1864.   I. Title.
   E476.52 .R475   2002
   973.7′36—dc21   2002006017

Contents

Illustrations

Maps

Preface

FOR FORTY-SIX DAYS in May and June 1864, the American Civil War's foremost commanders, Ulysses S. Grant and Robert E. Lee, fought a grinding campaign through Virginia from the Rapidan River to Petersburg. Encompassed in that brief span were several of the war's bloodiest engagements—the Wilderness, Spotsylvania Court House, Totopotomoy Creek, Bethesda Church, and Cold Harbor. Maneuver stepped to center stage as Grant tried to flank Lee out of fortified lines with turning movements across the Rapidan, the North Anna, the Pamunkey, and finally the James. Ingenuity also figured in the tale as the Confederates countered Grant's every move and magnified their defensive power several fold with cleverly sited earthworks. Adding spice and color were cavalry brawls among the likes of Philip Sheridan, George Custer, "Jeb" Stuart, and Wade Hampton. History never gets more exciting.

No two military figures have stirred popular imagination more than Grant and Lee, and none have been more thoroughly misunderstood. The ghost of "Grant the Butcher" still haunts Civil War lore. The Union general, the story goes, was fond of attacking earthworks, averse to maneuver, and unmoved at the prospect of massive casualties. "General Meade, I wish you to understand that this army is not to maneuver for position," Grant is said to have announced before crossing the Rapidan and to have inflexibly adhered to that dogma throughout the campaign. Grant "avowedly despised maneuvering," according to northern journalist William Swinton, and relied "exclusively on the application of brute masses, in rapid and remorseless blows." After the war, Virginia newspaperman Edward Pollard took up the cry, asserting in his popular book *The Lost Cause* that Grant "contained no spark of military genius; his idea of war was to the last degree rude—no strategy, the mere application of the vis inertia; he had none of that quick perception on the field of action which decides it by sudden strokes; he had no conception of battle beyond the momentum of numbers." Northern historians followed suit. Grant, John C. Ropes informed the prestigious Military Historical Society of Massachusetts, suffered from a "burning, persistent desire to fight, to attack, in season and out of season, against intrenchments, natural obstacles, what not." In the mid-1970s the noted Grant scholar E. B. Long decried the popular depiction of the general as an "unfeeling martinet who ruthlessly threw thousands of men into the belching death of the cannon." Long conceded, however, that "Grant the butcher is a hard myth to extinguish."[1]

Contrary to the image urged by Grant's detractors, the general's campaign against Lee reveals a warrior every bit as talented as his famous Confederate counterpart. Grant understood the importance of seizing the initiative and holding tight to his offensive edge to keep Lee off balance and prevent him from going on the offensive. The very nature of Grant's assignment guaranteed severe casualties. He made mistakes, many attributable to awkward command relationships within his army. Sometimes he acted precipitously, launching the Union force on operations with inadequate preparation. Other times he moved lethargically, frittering away advantages won by hard fighting and maneuver. He rarely used cavalry to advantage and tolerated laxness in the army's command structure that plagued his operations. But despite Grant's stumbling, the overall pattern of his warring showed an innovative general attempting to employ combinations of maneuver and force to bring a difficult adversary to bay. In its larger features, Grant's operations belie his "butcher" caricature.

Judging from Lee's record, the rebel commander should have shared in Grant's "butcher" reputation. After all, Lee lost more soldiers than any other Civil War general, including Grant, and his casualties in three days at Gettysburg exceeded Union casualties for any three consecutive days under Grant's orders. Yet Lee's public image is the opposite of Grant's. The Confederate general, his many admirers have argued, possessed Olympian qualities. Lee's aide Colonel Walter H. Taylor noted that the "faculty of General Lee, of discovering, as if by intuition, the intention of his opponent, was a very remarkable one." Nowhere, southerners claimed, were Lee's talents better displayed than in his campaign against Grant. Even while the campaign was under way, a Confederate newspaper correspondent expressed amazement at the "way in which [Lee] unravels the most intricate combination of his antagonist, the instinctive knowledge he seems to possess of all his plans and designs."[2]

The real Lee, however, fell considerably short of the infallible icon depicted by Taylor and others, even when he was battling Grant. Several times, Lee was unsure or plainly wrong about Grant's intentions. He misapprehended Grant's rapid march into the Wilderness, was surprised by Grant's shift to Spotsylvania Court House, and courted disaster by withdrawing artillery from the very sector of his Spotsylvania line that Grant had targeted for attack. The Confederate movement to the North Anna River almost backfired when Lee unwittingly marched within a mile of Union camps. Lee's true strength was his remarkable ability to rescue his army from seemingly irremediable predicaments, often of his own making, and to turn unfavorable situations to his advantage. He was a master at improvising, and the pressure of crisis only sharpened his wits.

Now four books into a multivolume study of the Overland campaign, I have come to view Grant and Lee as different in personal style but similar in military temperament. Both men favored offensive operations and took fearless courses of action that left traditional generals aghast. Grant predicated his campaign on maneuver, attempting to turn Lee out of a series of strong positions. And Lee used maneuver boldly as well, taking the offensive in the Wilderness by attacking Grant's juggernaut like a terrier assailing a bulldog. Each general made brilliant moves, and each made glaring mistakes and miscalculations. Each labored under handicaps, although of different sorts, and each was bedeviled by subordinates who often seemed incapable of getting things right. Grant and Lee were about as evenly matched in military talent as any two opposing generals have ever been.

Grant's and Lee's battles spawned persistent legends almost as farfetched as the parodies of the generals themselves. Grant's critics hold up the early-morning assault of June 3 at Cold Harbor as Exhibit 1 in their brief, deriding the offensive as a senseless undertaking fueled by Grant's bloodlust. "The decisive action was over in eight minutes," a popular author claimed, intoning the mantra that generations of historians have repeated without question. "Within less than an hour seven thousand men fell, killed or wounded, in moving against a fire power so uniform in its destructiveness that no living thing could advance in the face of it." A reviewer in the prestigious *New York Times Book Review* recently opined that Grant's frontal assault at Cold Harbor "lost 7,000 men in an hour, most in the first ten minutes," perpetuating for modern readers a picture of the battle and of Grant that has no basis in reality.[3]

The Cold Harbor in these pages differs sharply from the Cold Harbor of popular lore. Grant is not an unthinking automaton shoveling bodies into the maw of Lee's earthworks. And Lee does not fight a perfect battle. Grant begins the campaign by executing one of his best moves, pulling his army across the North Anna and stealing a march on Lee. Discovering Grant's deception, Lee takes up a strong defensive line along Totopotomoy Creek, countering the Union ploy. Grant sends out feelers, and Lee responds, sparking battles across woods and fields northeast of Richmond. By accident rather than by design, the military center of gravity shifts to an obscure Virginia crossroads called Old Cold Harbor. Lee's line seems stretched thin. The rebel army, its back to a river and on its last legs by Grant's reckoning, defiantly faces the Federals. Grant senses a chance—a long shot perhaps—to end the war and orders an army-wide assault.

This narrative is about Grant's Cold Harbor offensive and events leading up to the major attack on June 3, 1864. It is a campaign study about commanders and armies. So much happened from May 25 to June 3, 1864, and so little has been written about those momentous days, that the telling fills this book. I ask forbearance from those seeking expositions about the campaign's political and social ramifications. My next book, covering the last week of operations at Cold Harbor and Grant's crossing of the James River, attempts to place the Overland campaign in a broader context.

The cavalry battles at Haw's Shop, Matadequin Creek, Hanover Court House, and Ashland, the infantry fights at Totopotomoy Creek and Bethesda Church, and even the big assaults of June 1 and 3 at Cold Harbor have received little serious attention from historians. To this day, details of the Cold Harbor operation and its antecedents are familiar to most readers of Civil War history in only a general—and frequently distorted—way. Two historians have helped me separate fact from fiction and tell the real story of Cold Harbor. Patrick S. Brady of Seattle, who knows more about the battle than any other living student, is completing a book that will doubtless serve as the last word on the fight. I, along with the rest of the community of Civil War scholars and buffs, eagerly await the completion of his project. Mr. Brady selflessly shared information and insights and reviewed my manuscript, saving me from several pitfalls and vastly improving the final product. I am also deeply indebted to Robert E. L. Krick of the Richmond National Battlefield Park. Over the years, Mr. Krick has assembled a superb collection of material on the battles around Richmond. He, too, read my manuscript, endured my many telephone calls, and offered a host of valuable suggestions.

A veritable army of historians and collectors has sent me material about various units and stages of operations. I give special thanks to Dorothy Francis Atkinson, Daniel J. Beattie, Todd Berkoff, Keith S. Bohannon, Michael S. Cavanaugh, Thomas Clemens, W. Eric Emerson, John J. Hennessy, Robert Keating, Dr. Kenneth L. Lawrence, Eric Mink, Kevin O'Beirne, Scott C. Patchen, Robert G. Poirier, Michael T. Russert, Rosanne Groat Shalf, Marc and Beth Storch, Bruce Trinque, Robert J. Trout, David Ward, Zack C. Waters, and Eric J. Wittenberg, who generously shared with me their knowledge and resources. Bryce A. Suderow, as always, helped greatly in my research, particularly with Civil War–era newspapers and casualty returns. Mr. Suderow also read my manuscript with care and offered his usual pithy comments. Donald C. Pfanz of the Fredericksburg and Spotsylvania National Military Park and Michael T. Snyder of Pottstown, Pa., also read the entire manuscript, rescuing me from several embarrassing errors. And Keith Poulter, of *North and South,* published three chapters in abridged form in his fine magazine, affording me a chance to rethink material and benefit from his editorial skills.

Several people assisted in the tedious and near-impossible task of calculating casualties. Alfred C. Young has spent years of laborious research documenting Confederate losses. His general conclusions appeared recently in "Numbers and Losses in the Army of Northern Virginia," *North and South* 3 (March 2000), 14–29. Mr. Young's backup material permits fairly accurate reconstruction of Confederate losses to company and regimental levels, opening a revealing window onto the fights between Grant and Lee. Determining Union losses is also a difficult task complicated by conflicting and often irreconcilable reports. I was aided by Mr. Suderow, who copied handwritten Union regimental returns in the National Archives, and by Henry P. Elliott of the Fredericksburg and Spotsylvania National Military Park, who drew the dreary assignment of entering those returns into a computer program. I hasten to add that the National Archive returns, while helpful, are not definitive. Returns for some units are not extant, and some categories of loss, such as missing soldiers, appear to have been omitted. Union loss figures cited in this work represent simply my best estimates after considering all sources.

Finally, of course, I am deeply indebted to George F. Skoch, who once again translated my scribbling into fine maps that go hand-in-hand with the narrative and hopefully render it comprehensible. I am also grateful to Gerry Anders of LSU Press, whose finely honed editorial skills put the final polish on the manuscript. And as with all of my endeavors, this book would not have been possible without the understanding, support, and encouragement of my wife, Catherine, and our two sons, Campbell and Carter, who are integral parts of everything I do.

Abbreviations

B&L	Buel, Clarence C., and Robert U. Johnson, eds. *Battles and Leaders of the Civil War.* 4 vols. New York, 1884–88.
BL	Bentley Historical Library, University of Michigan
CL	William L. Clements Library, University of Michigan
DU	William R. Perkins Library, Duke University
FSNMP	Fredericksburg and Spotsylvania National Military Park Library
GDAH	Georgia Department of Archives and History, Atlanta
HSP	Historical Society of Pennsylvania, Philadelphia
LC	Manuscript Division, Library of Congress
MC	Eleanor S. Brockenbrough Library, Museum of the Confederacy, Richmond
MHS	Massachusetts Historical Society, Boston
MSU	Michigan State University Libraries
NA	National Archives, Washington, D.C.
NYSLA	New York State Library and Archives, Albany
OR	*The War of the Rebellion: A Compilation of Official Records of the Union and Confederate Armies.* 130 vols. Washington, D.C., 1880–1901. Unless otherwise stated, references are to Series I.
PMHSM	*Papers of the Military Historical Society of Massachusetts.* 14 vols. Boston, 1881–1918.

RNBP   Richmond National Battlefield Park

SCL   South Caroliniana Library, University of South Carolina

SHC   Southern Historical Collection, University of North Carolina

SHSP   *Southern Historical Society Papers.* 49 vols. Richmond, 1876–1944.

USAMHI   United States Army Military History Institute, Carlisle, Pa.

UV   Alderman Library, University of Virginia

VHS   Virginia Historical Society, Richmond

VSL   Virginia State Library, Richmond

WRHS   Western Reserve Historical Society, Cleveland

COLD HARBOR

I

MAY 25, 1864

Lee Deadlocks Grant on the North Anna

"We are getting well used to the whizzing of bullets and the whirring of shell."

LIEUTENANT GENERAL ULYSSES S. GRANT parted the flaps of his head-quarters tent. Spring had painted Central Virginia lush shades of green. Trees loomed like misshapen figures in the early morning drizzle. The field at Grant's feet fell sharply to the North Anna River, hidden in mist and campfire smoke. Two days of rain had swollen the normally placid stream to a torrent bobbing with splintered limbs and tree trunks. Grant's pontoon bridges—tenuous lifelines linking the Union army south of the river with its base to the north—were in danger of breaking free and floating downstream. Even the makeshift corduroy log span at Quarles's Mill, near Grant's headquarters, risked destruction. Slightly stooped in the early morning fog, cigar clenched firmly in his mouth, Grant pondered this latest crisis. For the third time in a month, his campaign against Robert E. Lee had reached impasse.

The story of Grant's meteoric rise from clerk in his father's leather-goods store in Galena, Illinois, to commanding general of the Union armies had all the drama of a nineteenth-century penny novel. The year 1861 began with the plainspoken midwesterner hopelessly mired in failure and bad luck. War wrought a dramatic reversal of fortune. Grant won the North's first major victory by taking Forts Henry and Donelson, compelling the Confederates to abandon Kentucky and much of Tennessee. He followed Donelson with an-other success at Shiloh and topped both battles with a brilliant campaign of maneuver and siege that captured Vicksburg and ensured Union domination of the Mississippi River. For an encore, he masterminded a bold attack that drove a Confederate army from its mountain fastness above Chattanooga. Union forces were winning the war in the West, and Grant was the architect of their success.

The Eastern theater—the band of farm and forest stretching from the Appalachian Mountains to the Atlantic Ocean—presented a very different picture. The flag of rebellion still fluttered defiantly over Charleston, South Carolina, the seat of secession, but it was Virginia that riveted the nation's attention. The hundred miles between Washington, D.C., and Richmond was the domain of General Robert E. Lee and his Army of Northern Virginia, and the graveyard of Union hopes. Since assuming command of the rebel host in June 1862, Lee had defeated every Union general sent against him in the Old Dominion. Successive commanders of the Union Army of the Potomac—Major Generals George B. McClellan, Ambrose E. Burnside, and Joseph Hooker—had felt Lee's sting. Their successor, dour Major General George G. Meade, had won the nation's applause by repelling Lee's foray into northern territory with a resounding victory at Gettysburg in July 1863. But Meade had remained content with following Lee back to Virginia. Summer, fall, and winter had come and gone, leaving Meade little to show for his Gettysburg triumph. In the spring of 1864, the Army of Northern Virginia and the Army of the Potomac glared at each other from camps on opposite sides of the Rapidan River, midway between Washington and Richmond. Battle lines were not appreciably different from where they had been when the war began three long years ago.

Politics raised the stakes in Virginia to new heights in 1864. It was a federal election year, and ballots cast in November were expected to serve as referenda on President Abraham Lincoln's conduct of the war. Dissatisfaction was sweeping the North after three years of bloodshed. Troops had quelled draft riots in New York, and copperhead politicians strode brazenly across the public stage. Lincoln needed military success, not just in the West, but in Virginia as well. The Confederacy's president, Jefferson Davis, contemplating the North's edge in manpower and industry and its conquests so far, concluded that his fledgling nation's best hope lay in the political arena. If Confederate armies could prevent Union victories—or better yet, if they could score telling victories of their own—the burgeoning peace movement in the North might prosper and bring about Lincoln's defeat at the polls. Lincoln's successor, Davis speculated, might see his way to negotiating a settlement with the South to bring the slaughter to a close. Simply put, a war-weary North might let its wayward sister go, delivering to the South through political means the freedom that it could not win militarily.

Lincoln anticipated the spring of 1864 with trepidation. Union armies had advanced on Richmond the previous two springs with high hopes, only to suffer defeat at the hands of Lee and his tatterdemalions. This year had to be different, or the North risked losing the war. And so, in March, Lincoln summoned Grant to Washington to oversee the Union war effort. The general from Galena reached the nation's capital on March 8 and discovered to his dismay that he was a celebrity. A surprise visit to the White House climaxed with an embarrassed Grant standing on a couch so spectators could see him over the mob. Afterward he met privately with Lincoln. The president promised Grant a free hand running the war, and Grant promised Lincoln victories.

Grant fundamentally changed the North's conduct of the war. As he saw it, Union generals had squandered their massive advantage in men and material by running the two theaters like independent fiefdoms. In Grant's homespun language, armies east and west had behaved like balky mules, each pulling without regard to the other. The uneven pace of combat also made little sense. The armies would fight for a few days, then break off and rest, sometimes for months, enabling the rebels to repair their losses. Northern generals also frittered away resources trying to conquer and hold Confederate territory.

Grant's plans for the spring offensive avoided these pitfalls. Union armies were to move in tandem and bring the major Confederate forces to battle at one fell swoop. The days of short clashes were over. Henceforth, Union armies would engage rebel armies and hold on like bulldogs, fighting every step of the way. And no longer would Union armies waste time and resources capturing and garrisoning territory. Some sites, of course, remained important. Richmond had psychological value and worth as a rail and manufacturing center, as did Atlanta. But Grant's chief objective was the Confederate armies. Only their destruction would end the rebellion. Grant gave his friend and trusted subordinate Major General William T. Sherman the assignment of pounding General Joseph E. Johnston's Confederate Army of Tennessee into submission in the West. The destruction of Lee and the Army of Northern Virginia he kept for himself.

Grant positioned three Federal forces to converge on Lee. Meade's Army of the Potomac, swelled to 118,000 soldiers by the addition of Major General Ambrose E. Burnside's independent 9th Corps, was to cross the Rapidan River and engage Lee in battle. At the same time, Major General Benjamin F. Butler, a contentious Massachusetts Democrat, was to take his 30,000-man Army of the James upriver from Fortress Monroe, threaten the Confederate capital at Richmond, cut Lee's supply lines, and harass the rebel army's rear. A third force—one prong under Major General Franz Sigel and another under Brigadier General George Crook, totaling over 15,000 men—was to invade the Shenandoah Valley, playing havoc with Lee's supplies and threatening him from yet another direction. After pushing aside minor Confederate forces

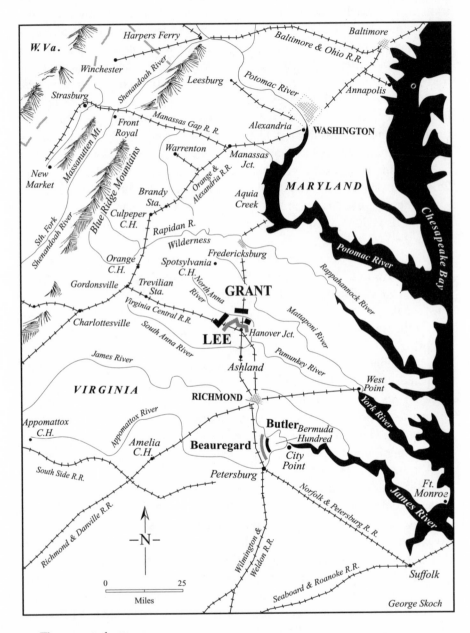

The eastern theater

in the Valley and below Richmond, altogether 165,000 Federals were to hold Lee's 66,000 Confederates in a massive three-jawed vice and crush them.[1]

Grant's scheme, seemingly flawless on paper, proved elusive in execution. Hoping to flank Lee from his stronghold south of the Rapidan, Grant crossed the Army of the Potomac east of Lee on May 4 and overnighted in tangled woodland known as the Wilderness. Lee attacked, cleverly exploiting the dense forest. Two days of brutal combat ended in stalemate, with Lee holding well-entrenched lines along high ground. Realizing the futility of fighting on such ground, Grant broke off the engagement and maneuvered south, hoping to draw Lee from the Wilderness by interposing between the Confederate army and Richmond. Lee swung across Grant's route and dug in above the village of Spotsylvania Court House, where Grant renewed his hammering with a flurry of assaults against Lee's fortified position. Exploiting advantages in terrain and constructing a formidable array of earthworks, Lee repulsed the attacks with relative ease. Slaughter escalated to a bloody climax on May 12, when Grant assailed a bulge in Lee's line called the Mule Shoe. All day, in heavy rain, the armies fought for control of the Mule Shoe, their foremost elements plastered against opposite sides of the same earthworks. Fighting reached a bloodthirsty frenzy at a bend in the Mule Shoe that participants later christened the Bloody Angle. Lee's objective was to hold this stretch of line until he could construct a defensible position to the rear. Grant's goal was to break through. Combat raged until 3:00 A.M. on May 13, when Lee completed his new line and withdrew the Mule Shoe's defenders. The sun rose on a Confederate army more strongly entrenched than ever.[2]

Grant refused to concede defeat and planned a succession of attacks. Rain, mud, and uncertainty about Lee's troop dispositions forced him to withhold his blows. When the weather cleared on May 18, Grant sent ten thousand men across the abandoned Mule Shoe in an attack against Lee's new line. Rebel artillery broke the assault with ease. Once again, as after the Wilderness, Grant resorted to maneuver to break a deadlock, dispatching part of his army southeast on a looping march aimed at enticing Lee from his earthworks. The Confederates declined Grant's bait and instead made for the North Anna River, twenty-five miles south. Grant followed, expecting Lee to fortify the river's south bank and confront him there. This time the rebel commander misjudged Grant's intentions and neglected to defend the river line. Late on May 23, part of Grant's army crossed the North Anna upriver from Lee at Jericho Mills, repulsed a belated Confederate attack, and dug in. All along the North Anna, Lee's soldiers seemed to be falling back. Grant prepared to follow.

Lee, an aide later noted, possessed a "remarkable capacity for using the accidents of ground." Never was Lee's grasp of terrain more evident than on the North Anna. Caught below the river, he prepared a trap that exploited Grant's offensive bent. During the night, the Army of Northern Virginia deployed into a wedge-shaped formation south of the river, its apex resting on the stream. Grant played into Lee's hand the next morning by advancing across the river and dividing his force on either side of the Confederate wedge. Lee, a Federal later conceded, had "one of those opportunities that occur but rarely in war, but which, in the grasp of a master, make or mar the fortunes of armies and decide the result of campaigns." For a few breathless hours, the divided Federal army stood stranded below the river, isolated from supplies and vulnerable to attack. The crisis deepened when violent thunderstorms threatened to sweep away Grant's pontoon bridges. Buffeted by current to their armpits, engineers at Quarles's Mill pounded posts into the riverbed, stacked boulders as anchors, laid timber cribs lengthwise to the flow, covered the cribs with logs, and placed smaller logs crosswise to form a corduroy road. "Occasional flashes of lightning revealed the men hard at work in the rolling torrent," an engineer remembered, "the noise of which drowned the voices of the officers and made altogether one of the most weird-like scenes that can be imagined."[3]

To Grant's surprise and considerable relief, Lee did not attack. Unknown to the Federals, Lee had become too ill too command and lay confined in his tent. "We must strike them a blow," he intoned. "We must never let them pass us again. We must strike them a blow." Lacking a trusted subordinate to manage the army in his stead, Lee had no choice but to forfeit his opportunity. By morning on May 25, the Federals had thrown makeshift bridges across the North Anna, opening lifelines to the north. Union soldiers lay behind hastily dug earthworks that conformed to the outer contours of the rebel position. Unless the rising river washed away the bridges, the Federals were out of immediate danger. But Lee's innovative deployment had drained the momentum from Grant's offensive. For the third time in the campaign, in a pattern dismally familiar to the men in blue, Lee had thwarted the Federal juggernaut and maneuvered it to stalemate.[4]

"Meade's position proved embarrassing to me if not to him."

After three weeks of fighting, the Union's premier combat force had been unable to defeat an ill-equipped Confederate army half its size. What was wrong with the Army of the Potomac?

The answer lay partially in a defensive mindset. The army operated close to Washington. Its goal was not only to quell the rebellion, but to protect the nation's capital. Politics and fear of failure had led it onto a cautious path. George McClellan, the army's first commander, was a political animal of the highest order, and his deep distrust for the Lincoln administration created a paranoid mentality that persisted long after his departure. An officer aptly noted that McClellan and his successors had "dissipated war's best elixir by training [the army] into a life of caution." Caution had become a Federal tradition in the eastern theater and the Union army's timidity when confronting Lee was deeply ingrained. Every time the Federals had met Lee in Virginia, they had lost, and they did not see why 1864 should be different. The Confederates were fighting for hearth and home, knew every trail and byway, and possessed in Lee a commander whose reputation loomed larger than life. "Nothing I could do or say could make the army move," Lincoln complained after Meade's lethargic pursuit of the Confederates following Gettysburg. Grant voiced similar sentiment in the Wilderness. "Think what we are going to do ourselves," he enjoined a panicky aide, "instead of what Lee is going to do."[5]

Friction within the Army of the Potomac's leadership was also responsible. On March 10, the day after his appointment as commanding general, Grant had visited Meade at the Army of the Potomac's winter quarters near Brandy Station. Meade offered to resign, expecting Grant to replace him with either Sherman or Major General William F. "Baldy" Smith, a former Army of the Potomac general who had recently won Grant's approval during the Chattanooga campaign. Impressed by Meade's selfless gesture, Grant decided to keep him on. As commander, Grant hoped to concentrate on national strategy and leave tactical details to army heads. He intended to travel with the Army of the Potomac—to "keep out of Washington as much as possible," he assured Meade—but wanted to avoid being drawn into the minutiae of managing the army. "Grant has not given an order, or in the slightest degree interfered with the administration of this army since he arrived," Meade confided to his wife, Margaretta, in mid-April, "and I doubt if he knows much more about it now than he did before coming here." But signs of future difficulties were apparent. Meade fretted that his "share of the credit" would be "less than if [Grant] were not present." He also worried that the press, and perhaps even the public, might "lose sight of me in *him*." Meade's temperamental chief-of-staff, Major General Andrew A. Humphreys, shared his boss's concern. "General Grant will reap all the glory," Humphreys predicted, "all the reputation of success, and share none of the obloquy of disaster if such should befall us."[6]

Grant and Meade were cut from different cloth. The forty-two-year-old

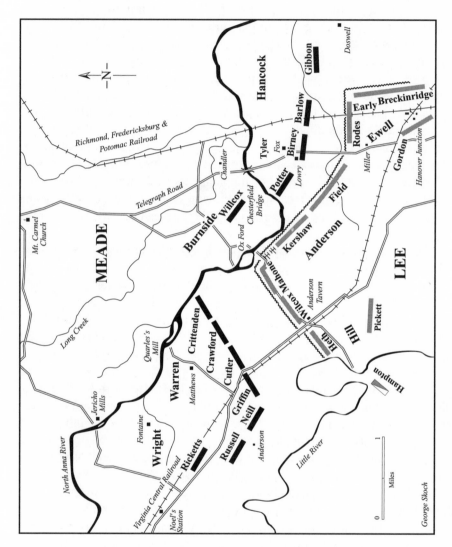

Stalemate on the North Anna River

George Skoch

commanding general seemed "stumpy, unmilitary, slouchy, and Western looking," according to an easterner. Meade, in contrast, had the air of an aristocrat, complete with hooked nose, piercing eyes, and marriage to the daughter of a prominent Philadelphia lawyer, congressman, and socialite. Compared to the even-tempered Grant, Meade struck one observer as "irritable, petulant and dyspeptic." Assistant War Secretary Charles A. Dana, who accompanied the army into Virginia, declared the Pennsylvanian "totally lacking in cordiality toward those with whom he had business [and] generally disliked by his subordinates." Grant's and Meade's staffs mirrored their bosses' divergent styles. Grant's chief aide, Brigadier General John A. Rawlins, was a small-town lawyer, and Grant's staff included the likes of his brother-in-law Frederick T. Dent and a Seneca Indian from Galena named Ely S. Parker. Meade's staff boasted figures such as Lieutenant Colonel Theodore Lyman and Major James C. Biddle, scions of prominent eastern families. A small incident dramatized the difference between the two generals. As the army moved against Lee, Meade adopted for his headquarters flag a magenta, swallow-tailed affair sporting a golden eagle inside a silver wreath. "What's this?" Grant inquired when he first spied the banner. "Is Imperial Caesar anywhere about here?"[7]

Most important, the two generals possessed starkly different military temperaments. Grant was an innovative warrior wedded to aggressive tactics. The Vicksburg campaign showcased his ingenuity and tenacity, qualities notoriously lacking among Union commanders in Virginia. "He has the grit of a bulldog," President Lincoln reportedly remarked of Grant. "Once let him get his 'teeth' in, and nothing can shake him off." Meade, seven years Grant's senior, epitomized the Army of the Potomac's cautious bent. He loathed risks, and offensive operations were foreign to his makeup. The ten months from Gettysburg to Grant's coming witnessed no major Union offensive in Virginia. Meade was a major reason that Lincoln brought Grant east.[8]

As the spring campaign unfolded, Grant became frustrated by Meade's caution and meddled increasingly in tactical details. He devised the plan of attack for May 6 and designated the route each corps was to take out of the Wilderness on May 7. The battles at Spotsylvania Court House were Grant's doing, with Meade serving as Grant's de facto chief-of-staff. "At first I had maneuvered the army," Meade candidly admitted to a group of visiting senators, "but gradually, and from the very nature of things, Grant had taken control." Meade remained composed in public but privately seethed at his diminished role. Newspapers, he confided to Margaretta, wrote daily of Grant's successes but "counted me out entirely." If he could find "any honorable way of retiring from my present false position," Meade lamented, "I should undoubtedly adopt it, but there is none and all I can do is patiently submit and bear with resignation the humiliation." Grant agreed that Meade's position "proved embarrassing to me if not to him."[9]

The generals were barely on speaking terms by the time they reached the North Anna River. Meade had opposed the move in the first place, preferring to swing well east of Lee. Grant, however, did not want to maneuver Lee out of one heavily fortified position simply to confront him on equally unfavorable terms elsewhere. He vetoed Meade's suggestion and went straight for the Confederates, underscoring the gulf between his aggressive approach and Meade's more deliberate style. "Meade was opposed to our crossing the North Anna, but Grant ordered it, over his head," Provost Marshal Brigadier General Marsena R. Patrick recorded in his diary. "Grant was put out with Meade," ran the rumor at headquarters, "and Meade proposed that next time [Grant] should take charge of things and do the fighting himself."[10]

Although Grant and Meade tried to keep their differences private, their staffers feuded with unbridled partisanship. Meade's aide Biddle derided Grant as a "rough, unpolished man" of only "average ability, whom fortune has favored." Rawlins, he fumed, understood "no more of military affairs than an old cat." Biddle found it "perfectly disgusting" to see Grant "lauded to the skies as being the greatest military man of the age." Grant's aides for their part urged him to remove Meade, alleging that he was incapable of acting in the spirit of Grant's hard-hitting style. Conceding that Meade was an embarrassment, Grant insisted that he had to keep him on. "By tending to the details," Grant explained, "he relieves me of much unnecessary work, and gives me more time to think and mature my general plans." Meade's reaction to a message from Sherman underscored the tension at headquarters. "If Grant could inspire the Potomac army to do a proper degree of fighting," Sherman wrote from Georgia, "the final success could not be doubted." Meade was furious. "I consider that dispatch an insult to the army I command, and to me personally," he announced in a huff. "The Army of the Potomac does not require General Grant's inspiration or anybody else's inspiration to make it fight!" He groused the rest of the day about the "armed rabble" that passed for Sherman's western army. Grant's and Meade's command arrangement, Meade's chief-of-staff Humphreys tartly observed, "was not calculated to produce the best result that either [general] singly was capable of bringing about."[11]

Burnside added another distracting level of complexity. The burly general had formerly headed the Army of the Potomac, and his major general's commission predated Meade's. Since Meade could not properly give orders to the senior Burnside, Grant designated the 9th Corps an independent command

and assigned himself the job of coordinating Burnside and Meade. The result was a military tangle of gargantuan proportions. From the Wilderness to Spotsylvania Court House, Burnside stumbled like a wayward stepchild, in part because of the awkward chain of command and in part because of his own ineptitude. Grant ended the ambiguous relationship at the North Anna River and directed Burnside to report to Meade. Burnside professed satisfaction over his diminished status, but how he would perform as Meade's subordinate remained to be seen.

The appointment of Major General Philip H. Sheridan, Grant's protégé from the West, to head Meade's cavalry set the volatile high command boiling. The strong-willed thirty-three-year-old son of Irish immigrants was bereft of social graces and possessed a temper every bit the equal of Meade's. The two generals despised each other from the start. Meade viewed the scrappy little man—Sheridan was only five feet five inches tall and 115 pounds—as an upstart imposed on him by Grant. Sheridan considered Meade an effete Philadelphia snob without the slightest idea how to manage cavalry. Meade wanted the horsemen to reconnoiter enemy positions and shield his infantry, while Sheridan wanted to mass his troopers and fight enemy cavalry. The philosophical rift played out dramatically during the first weeks of the campaign. Sheridan performed abysmally in the Wilderness and botched the move to Spotsylvania Court House by failing to clear the road south. Outraged, Meade ordered Sheridan to his tent, and the two obstinate men quarreled. Meade accused Sheridan of failing at every turn, and Sheridan charged Meade with meddling in the management of his cavalry. The meeting ended with Sheridan demanding permission to fight the rebel cavalry. Meade reported Sheridan's remarks to Grant, expecting Grant to reprimand the insolent subordinate. Grant, however, was frustrated over Meade's inaction. To Meade's chagrin, he backed Sheridan and instructed Meade to let the plucky cavalryman try his hand.

The next morning—May 9—Sheridan took the Army of the Potomac's cavalry toward Richmond, intending to draw out the Confederate horsemen and defeat them. Lee's cavalry chief, Major General James Ewell Brown "Jeb" Stuart, reacted as Sheridan had predicted and accepted the challenge. Seven miles north of Richmond, near the ruins of an abandoned hostelry called Yellow Tavern, Sheridan defeated the Confederate riders and mortally wounded Stuart. Following another victory at Meadow Bridge, near Richmond, he returned triumphantly to the Army of the Potomac. Reports of his exploits rankled the sullen Meade. In less than a week, Sheridan had won two stunning victories, killed the vaunted Jeb Stuart, and administered a staggering blow to Confederate cavalry in Virginia. Morale in the Union mounted arm had never been higher. "Many of our generals were more warmly loved by the soldiers, some perhaps ranked higher in their esteem as able soldiers, but none, to the best of my belief, carried such a convincing air of success to the minds of his men, or could get the last drop of strength out of their bodies, when the effort was demanded," an admirer asserted of Sheridan. "They simply believed he was going to win, and every man apparently was determined to be on hand and see him do it." Sheridan's star was rising, and Meade, who felt increasingly like a stranger in his own army, was not happy about it.[12]

Aside from Sheridan, none of the Potomac army's corps commanders had measured up to Grant's expectations. Forty-year-old Major General Winfield Scott Hancock, widely touted as Meade's ablest subordinate, looked every inch a general, but his performance heading the Union 2nd Corps had been mixed. He had unaccountably left his flank unguarded in the Wilderness and had failed to exploit his attacks at Spotsylvania Court House. A painful wound inflicted at Gettysburg kept Hancock bedridden and helped explain mistakes that would have been unthinkable in earlier years. But despite Hancock's lapses, Grant considered him his steadiest infantry commander and used the 2nd Corps to spearhead the army's offensives.

Major General Gouverneur K. Warren, heading the Union 5th Corps, was the army's youngest corps commander. Initially he had impressed Grant, but three weeks of combat had disclosed serious flaws. The gangly New Yorker could be unmerciful to subordinates, brazenly confrontational to superiors, and given to outbursts so vituperative that they filled one spectator "with wonder at the ingenuity of invention and desperate blackguardism they displayed." Meade complained that Warren could not "execute an order without modifying it," and Grant finally pronounced the opinionated young general's meddlesome streak "constitutional and beyond his control." Warren demonstrated welcome initiative during the North Anna operations by repelling determined rebel attacks at Jericho Mills, but Grant still questioned his fitness. Grant had similar qualms about Major General Horatio G. Wright, commanding the Union 6th Corps since May 9, when a Confederate sharpshooter killed his predecessor, Major General John Sedgwick. Six feet tall, with chubby cheeks and a pointed goatee, Wright was having difficulty filling Sedgwick's shoes. Coming days would show whether he, like Warren, had been promoted beyond his capabilities.[13]

Three weeks of brutal combat had profoundly affected the army's fighting capacity. Roughly 1,800 officers had been killed, severely wounded, or captured, and attrition in foot soldiers was terrific. The Wilderness, Spotsylvania Court House, and the North Anna River had cost Grant close to 40,000 men, about a third of the soldiers he had taken across the Rapidan. Some units, such as Hancock's 2nd Corps, bore a disproportionate share of casualties. Major General John Gibbon, commanding a division under Hancock, had entered the campaign with nearly 6,800 officers and men. Thus far, the fighting had cost him 44 officers and 454 men killed, 144 officers and 2,399 men wounded, and 4 officers and 517 men missing, an aggregate loss approximating half his original strength. "The quality of the loss was what made it almost disastrous, for the very best officers, and the bravest men were those who fell," Gibbon lamented. "When they were gone the number who served as leaders was fearfully reduced and this, of course, immensely to the detriment of the fighting force of the division." The effect of combat subtractions, along with exhaustion from relentless campaigning, seemed to Gibbon "very marked, and was the subject of general comment throughout the army." Exacerbating the problem was the influx of drafted men and "many of a class afterwards known as 'bounty jumpers,'" Gibbon wrote, "whose motive in entering the ranks was simply sordid gain unmixed with any sentiment of patriotism or loyalty to the government."[14]

Adding to Grant's woes, many of the army's veterans had volunteered in 1861, and their three-year terms of enlistment were due to expire. Thus far, only the 1st Massachusetts, 79th New York, and 84th New York had left. The floodgates, however, were about to open. Slated to leave during the last week of May were thirteen Pennsylvania regiments—including the crack Pennsylvania Reserves—and two New Jersey regiments, to be followed in June by nineteen more regiments. Some veterans, of course, would reenlist, but many would not, and their departures reduced Grant's numbers as surely as Confederate bullets.[15]

To replace the mounting subtractions, Grant petitioned Washington for all the men it could "rake and scrape." With Grant firmly positioned between Lee and the nation's capital, Lincoln felt comfortable releasing large numbers of garrison troops, many of whom belonged to heavy artillery regiments with no combat experience. The prospect of marching into central Virginia's killing fields elicited strong protests from the greenhorns, but off they went. On May 15, the 2nd New York Mounted Rifles (dismounted) and the 1st Vermont Heavy Artillery reached the front. Close on their heels came Colonel Mathew Murphy's Corcoran Legion of four New York Regiments, followed two days later by Brigadier General Robert O. Tyler's division of five heavy artillery regiments. The next few days saw the 2nd Connecticut Heavy Artillery, the 9th New York Heavy Artillery, the 2nd Pennsylvania Heavy Artillery, and a hodgepodge of regular infantry and cavalry regiments joining Grant. By May 25, some 33,000 reinforcements had reached the Army of the Potomac or were on the way, bringing Grant's strength to approximately 111,000 men, almost the size of his army at the beginning of the campaign.[16]

Much to Grant's disappointment, his subsidiary armies had failed miserably. On May 15, Major General John C. Breckinridge defeated Sigel at New Market and drove him back toward the Potomac River. The next day, Lieutenant General Pierre G. T. Beauregard defeated Butler at Drewry's Bluff, south of Richmond. Butler withdrew to Bermuda Hundred, a triangle of land formed by the confluence of the James and Appomattox Rivers. Corked in Bermuda Hundred, Butler could contribute little to the Union war effort, and Grant toyed with shifting part of Butler's force to join him. Grant's chief-of-staff in Washington, Major General Henry W. Halleck, sent Brigadier Generals Montgomery C. Meigs and John G. Barnard to Bermuda Hundred to determine how many troops Butler could spare. Learning on May 22 that Beauregard had dispatched soldiers to reinforce Lee, Grant directed Halleck to leave Butler only enough troops to man his earthworks at Bermuda Hundred and to send him the rest. Meigs and Barnard reported that Butler could maintain his position with 10,000 soldiers, freeing 20,000 more troops to join Grant.[17]

The Union army's mood was mixed. Three weeks of relentless fighting and hardship had numbed men's spirits. Everyone was exhausted. "We are getting well used to the whizzing of bullets and the whirring of shells, for it is an every day's music for us now," an aide wrote home. "A campaign with so much marching and fighting is unequaled in history and our men are nearly worn out with fatigue and want of sleep." According to Gibbon, troops had come to appreciate two truths. First, the Union army "had never succeeded in forcing Lee, by battle, from any position he assumed, nor had he succeeded in forcing us from any." Second, a few hours of digging would "render any position so strong by breastworks that the opposing party was unable to carry it." Consequently, Gibbon noted, "it became a recognized fact amongst the men themselves that when the enemy had occupied a position six or eight hours ahead of us, it was useless to attempt to take it." Acceptance of these principles as immutable was to influence the campaign's next stage profoundly. "I'm getting a little tired of this work and hope that General Grant will shove things as fast as possible," a New Yorker wrote his wife. "I think that it is his intention to get Lee out of his works by flanking rather than by storming him, which I like better," he added, echoing a near universal sentiment. "As a general thing charging costs a good many lives while flanking does not."[18]

But the overall tenor was upbeat. For the first time since crossing the Rapidan, Union soldiers sensed that the end might be near. Grant had broken each deadlock, not by retreating like his predecessors, but by maneuvering south. Now Richmond was only twenty-five miles away. One more turning movement, it seemed, and the Army of Northern Virginia would be backed against its capital. Unable to maneuver, Lee would have no choice but to surrender or submit to a siege. Union soldiers watched Grant carefully for signs of the impending offensive. "Grant takes it perfectly cool and smokes his cigars," a soldier assigned to headquarters had noticed. "When he whittles his stick down from him he is a 'little mixed,' but when he whittles towards him it is all O.K."[19]

"Grant with his minions will be hurled back much faster than he came."

The mood in Lee's camps was also cautiously optimistic. "We have undergone the most arduous and toilsome duties that ever the human race was exposed to," a South Carolinian wrote home from the North Anna River. Lee's men considered the campaign's hardships worthwhile, having defeated Grant in the Wilderness, at Spotsylvania Court House, and now again on the North Anna. They had sound reason for optimism. For two years, the fifty-seven-year-old patriarch had won victories against seemingly insurmountable odds. Soldiers and their general had forged a close bond, and jaunty optimism was their hallmark. "Our boys are well fortified," a Virginian assured his family, "and I think Mr. Grant with his minions will be hurled back much faster than he came." Lee's adjutant Walter H. Taylor described the prevailing mood to his fiancée. "Our army is in excellent condition—as good as it was when we met Grant, two weeks since for the first time," he explained. "He will feel us again before he reaches his prize."[20]

But a disconcerting pattern was emerging. Union commanders in the past had retreated after Lee's thrashings. Grant, however, kept sidling south to resume battle nearer to Richmond. A North Carolinian fretted that Grant was "twice as badly whipped now as was Burnside or Hooker but he is so determined he will not acknowledge it." Even Lee's aide Taylor could not suppress grudging admiration for his opponent. "He certainly holds on longer than [his predecessors]," he observed. "At this point we enjoy many military advantages which we did not possess at the Wilderness or on our line at Spotsylvania Court House," a Georgian noted in trying to put a positive face on Lee's drift southward. "Here we have two railroads from Richmond and being so near our depot of supplies, we will run no risk of being annoyed by raiding parties of the enemy." Grant, the Georgian reflected as he warmed to his subject, was "inhuman" in his disregard for his own soldiers' lives. "Lee has been waiting for such a man and Lincoln has found him," he concluded. "Poor Grant, your road is a rough one." Southern newspapers compared the Union commander's performance unfavorably with Major General George B. McClellan's advance on Richmond two years before. "If it has been a part of [Grant's] original design to make . . . the lower James his base of operations," the correspondent Peter W. Alexander opined in May 1864, "then he has committed a great blunder in marching across the country from Culpeper at a cost of forty or fifty thousand men, when by following McClellan's route he might have reached the same destination without the loss of a single man." Alexander's criticism, which has reverberated through the years in various guises, misapprehended Grant's objective. His central goal was not the capture of Richmond, although the Confederate capital loomed increasingly important as Lee retired toward it. The focus of his efforts was the destruction of Lee's army, a costly venture under the best of circumstances.[21]

Cocky rhetoric could not mend the damage that Grant's pounding had inflicted. The Wilderness had cost Lee 11,000 men, Spotsylvania 13,000 more, and the North Anna another 1,500, for a total of 25,500 casualties, or nearly 40 percent of the Confederate force. Lee's ability to replace losses was limited, although by May 25 he, like Grant, had managed to get his numbers surprisingly close to where they had been when the campaign began. After defeating Sigel, Breckinridge hurried to join Lee with his army, and Beauregard's victory over Butler freed up Major General George E. Pickett's veteran division. Lee also picked up an agglomeration of infantry, cavalry, and artillery known as the Maryland Line, increasing his total reinforcements to 8,500 men. As many as 15,000 additional soldiers returned to their commands during the first three weeks of fighting, bringing Lee's numbers on the North Anna to approximately 64,000. The only additional reinforcements on the horizon included a division under Major General Robert F. Hoke, a cavalry brigade under Brigadier General Matthew C. Butler from South Carolina, several Florida regiments under Brigadier General Joseph Finegan, and a handful of miscellaneous regiments and battalions from Georgia and North Carolina. The lot totaled at most another 11,000 men, many of them novices. Any further reinforcements would have to come from Beauregard, whose willingness to release soldiers to Lee turned on his estimation of the strength of the Federal force opposing him.[22]

The campaign had played havoc with the Army of Northern Virginia's command structure. Lee had started with four corps commanders. By the end of May, all were dead, gravely wounded, or ill. Lieutenant General James Longstreet, commanding Lee's 1st Corps, was seriously injured on May 6; the next day, Lieutenant General Ambrose P. Hill, heading the Confederate

3rd Corps, became ill; Jeb Stuart, Lee's cavalry commander, fell mortally wounded on May 11; and Lieutenant General Richard S. Ewell, head of the Confederate 2nd Corps, exhibited growing signs of sickness and instability throughout the month.

Lee was left with an assemblage of senior commanders that was far from ideal. Major General Richard H. Anderson, a stolid, undistinguished professional soldier from South Carolina, commanded the 1st Corps following Longstreet's wounding. His best days had been May 7 and 8, when he fled the Wilderness to escape smoke and stench from decaying corpses and inadvertently camped at precisely the right spot to block Grant's advance to Spotsylvania Court House. He had remained largely untested since then. Two of Anderson's division heads—Brigadier General Joseph B. Kershaw and Major General Charles W. Field—were talented and aggressive, but his third top subordinate, Pickett, had only recently rejoined the corps and was considered a weak leader.

Ewell, heading the Confederate 2nd Corps, had performed admirably early in the war, but ill health seemed to have sapped his aptitude for Lee's aggressive style. He overlooked offensive opportunities in the Wilderness, lost his composure during Grant's massive attack on the Mule Shoe, and bungled a reconnaissance-in-force at Harris Farm a few days later. Now, at the North Anna, he was suffering from dysentery. The eccentric Virginian's days in command were numbered, but Lee took heart from the 2nd Corps's strong set of division commanders. Major General Jubal A. Early, a headstrong bachelor and former prosecutor, possessed the gift for aggressive warring conspicuously absent in Ewell. So did Brigadier General John B. Gordon, a lanky young Georgia lawyer with an irrepressible love for combat, and Major General Robert E. Rodes, a grandly mustached Virginian whose steadiness was legendary.

Feisty A. P. Hill, called "Little Powell" by his men, had excelled as a division commander early in the war but failed to meet Lee's expectations when elevated in 1863 to head the Confederate 3rd Corps. Hill was frequently sick and remained bedridden for much of the spring campaign, returning to active service on May 21 only to suffer an embarrassing reverse at Jericho Mills. "Why didn't you throw your whole force on them," Lee scolded Hill on learning of his defeat, "and drive them back as [Stonewall] Jackson would have done." A strong set of division commanders—Major General Henry Heth, Major General Cadmus M. Wilcox, and Brigadier General William Mahone—helped compensate for Hill's shortcomings.[23]

Attrition had gutted the lower echelons of Lee's command structure. The Wilderness and Spotsylvania Court House cost him a major general and fifteen brigadier generals. The loss in colonels was staggering. Hardest hit was Ewell's corps. Beginning the campaign with 17,000 soldiers, Ewell had lost better than 60 percent of his strength. Gone also were thirteen of his fifteen brigade commanders and one of his three division commanders. The Stonewall Brigade and Colonel William A. Witcher's Virginia brigade were so decimated that Ewell consolidated their remnants, along with other stray Virginia regiments, into a new brigade under Brigadier General William Terry. Grant's relentless pounding was fast reducing the Army of Northern Virginia to a ghost of its former self.

Of all May's losses, Stuart's death cut Lee deepest. The plumed cavalier had embodied the Confederate army's youthful, daring spirit, running circles around Sheridan in the Wilderness and waging a stirring defense on the road to Spotsylvania Court House. Sheridan's Richmond raid had killed Stuart and Brigadier General James B. Gordon, one of Stuart's best brigade heads. Three weeks of campaigning had also cost the Confederate mounted arm six colonels, 1,200 troopers, and thousands of horses, a serious loss since southern cavalrymen had to provide their own mounts. Lee had decided to wait before naming a replacement for Stuart. The senior division chief, Major General Wade Hampton, was a South Carolina planter; next in seniority was General Lee's nephew, Major General Fitzhugh Lee, a Virginian; and heading a third division was another Virginian, General Lee's son, Major General William H. F. "Rooney" Lee. "Until further order," Lee directed, "the three divisions of cavalry serving with this army will constitute separate commands and will report directly to and receive orders from these headquarters of the army."[24]

Lee compensated for attrition in his top command by changing his style of leadership. Formerly, when his chief subordinates had been the likes of Lieutenant General Thomas J. "Stonewall" Jackson and James Longstreet, Lee had liberally delegated tactical responsibility. But Jackson and Longstreet were gone, and the new complement of corps commanders seemed incapable of executing discretionary orders to Lee's satisfaction. The standoff at the North Anna underscored the Army of Northern Virginia's leadership crisis. Lacking a trusted subordinate to manage the army while he was ill, Lee had no choice but to forfeit his best opportunity yet to assume the offensive.

Tactically, Lee had deftly fended off Grant's blows and maneuvered his opponent to stalemate. But strategically, he was in trouble. At the beginning of the campaign, he had instructed President Davis on the importance of holding the line of the Rapidan River. If Grant forced him back on Richmond, Lee predicted, the Army of Northern Virginia would lose its ability to maneuver and the campaign would become a siege. In that event, warned Lee, "great misfortune will befall us." With the front only twenty-five miles from Richmond, disaster seemed dangerously near.[25]

In former years, Lee had won battles by outwitting his enemies. But in Grant he faced an opponent as aggressive, tenacious, and resourceful as himself. The three weeks of fighting and maneuvers from the Rapidan to the North Anna had resembled a high-stakes chess match played by two masters. Several times, Lee had misjudged Grant's intentions and placed his own army in serious peril. Now that the armies were close to Richmond, Lee's margin for error was thin. A single serious misstep could spell disaster. Simply put, Lee had to play his next move right or risk losing the game.

Aggressive as ever, Lee longed to take the initiative and strike out against Grant. At this juncture, however, offensive action was impossible. Lee's army stood ensconced in its wedge below the North Anna, hemmed in on three sides by the Union army. Pressed closely together, the opposing forces reminded Grant of "two armies besieging." The only direction Lee could shift was south, toward Richmond. Retreat, of course, was out of the question. Having no other choice, Lee awaited Grant's next move, reluctantly forfeiting the initiative to his enemy.

"Our success over Lee's army is already insured."

May 25 saw Grant's soldiers perfecting their entrenchments south of the North Anna. Rebel earthworks loomed only a few hundred yards away, visible across open fields. The Confederates had mastered the art of field fortifications, and the North Anna position was their most accomplished effort yet. The rebel line appeared as a raw mound of red dirt atop commanding ground that looked across killing fields cleared of brush and trees. Entanglements lay heaped along the face of the fortifications, sharpened branches facing outward. Dirt and wood ramparts rose several feet, surmounted by headlogs that protected the defenders while firing. Trenches behind the earthworks gave the rebels safe places to load, and short, stubby earthen walls called traverses ran rearward every fifteen feet to provide havens from flanking fire. Carefully sited artillery lunettes rendered the position impregnable. Grant's men were acquainted with Lee's fortifications from Spotsylvania Court House. They had no stomach for testing them here on the North Anna.

Union scouts and pickets gave Grant an accurate picture of the rebel line's layout. Lee's army formed a wedge, its broad tip resting on the North Anna at Ox Ford. The Union force was arrayed in a larger V that wrapped loosely around the perimeter of Lee's wedge. The left, or western, leg of the rebel formation slanted southwest from Ox Ford along a prominent ridge, crossed the Virginia Central Railroad at Anderson's Tavern, and continued another half mile to anchor on Little River. Hill's 3rd Corps had crafted this sector into a formidable bastion. Facing him were Wright's 6th Corps, Warren's 5th Corps, and Major General Thomas L. Crittenden's division of the 9th Corps. The right, or eastern, leg of Lee's wedge slanted southeast to Telegraph Road, paralleled the river for a mile or so along the lower fringe of Major Doswell's plantation, then dropped south to guard against Federal attempts to outflank the line. Anderson's 1st Corps held imposing earthworks from Ox Ford to Telegraph Road, where Ewell's 2nd Corps picked up and completed the formation past the Doswell place. Confederates holding the right wing had unobstructed fields of fire that rendered the sector every bit as menacing as Hill's wing on their left. Facing them was Hancock's 2nd Corps, augmented by Brigadier General Robert B. Potter's 9th Corps division.

Linking the eastern and western legs of the Confederate inverted V was a broad apex extending half a mile along the North Anna's southern bank. High, brush-covered bluffs crowned with Confederate artillery made the position unassailable. Portions of Hill's Confederate 3rd Corps occupied the heights and looked across the river at Brigadier General Orlando B. Willcox's 9th Corps division. Union guns lined the northern bank.

Grant pondered his options. The present situation was untenable. Lee had the advantage of interior lines and could shift troops at will to various parts of his wedge. Federal troops moving from one wing of the Union army to the other had to cross to the north side of the river, traverse three muddy miles past Ox Ford, and then cross the river again. "Lee's position to Grant was similar to that of Meade's to Lee's at Gettysburg, with this additional disadvantage here to Grant of a necessity of crossing the river twice to reinforce either wing," a northerner observed. Grant was not concerned that Lee would attack, since both Federal wings south of the river were well entrenched. But he was anxious to get on with the campaign, which he could not do while pinioned on Lee's inverted V. The two armies reminded the 5th Corps aide Major Washington A. Roebling "very much of two schoolboys trying to stare each other out of countenance." Unless the Confederates committed "some great error," concluded Roebling, "they hold us in check until kingdom come." Attacking was impossible. Trying to push south made no sense, either, as doing so would only force the divided wings of the Union army farther apart. For all practical purposes, the campaign had reached deadlock. Grant agreed. "To make a direct attack from either wing" of his divided army, he noted, "would cause a slaughter of our men that even success would not justify."[26]

At noon on May 25, Grant wrote Halleck in Washington. "The enemy are evidently making a determined stand between the two Anna's," he reported, predicting that he would need "probably two days to get into position for a general attack or to turn their position, as may prove best." Persuaded that the Confederates intended to concentrate their forces to oppose him, Grant instructed Halleck to send as many of Butler's troops as possible right away. "Baldy" Smith, earlier touted as Meade's replacement, commanded the 18th Corps in Butler's army. Grant wanted Smith to bring his corps and any additional troops Butler could spare up the Pamunkey River to White House and march them along the north bank to the Army of the Potomac. Grant also directed Halleck to step up Union operations in the Shenandoah Valley, where he had put Major General David Hunter in charge after Sigel's defeat. "If General Hunter can possibly get to Charlottesville and Lynchburg he should do so, living on the country," Grant urged.[27]

On the evening of May 25, Grant met with Meade and other generals to discuss ways to break the impasse on the North Anna. Everyone agreed that Lee was too firmly entrenched to attack head-on. Warren and the Army of the Potomac's artillery chief, Brigadier General Henry J. Hunt, favored maneuvering the Federal force west of Lee, pressing south across Little River and turning Lee's western flank. Fully half of the Union army—Warren's and Wright's corps, and a division of Burnside's corps—was already below the North Anna and west of Lee, they pointed out. Grant needed only to shift Hancock's corps and Burnside's other two divisions to position the entire army for the maneuver. All of Grant's turning movements thus far, they added, had been around Lee's right. A maneuver around Lee's left might catch the Confederates by surprise.

Grant was concerned that concentrating his entire force around Lee's western flank might cause more problems than it solved. First was the question of supply. Provisioning the Army of the Potomac and its 50,000 animals was no easy matter, particularly in war-ravaged central Virginia. During the winter of 1863–1864, Meade had drawn sustenance from vast warehouses in Alexandria, Virginia, bringing provisions south along the Orange and Alexandria Railroad to camps around Brandy Station and Culpeper Court House. When Grant set out against Lee, he abandoned the rail line and adopted a new system of supply relying on Virginia's tidal rivers. Ships carried supplies from Alexandria down the Potomac River, moved inland along rivers closest to the army, and unloaded at temporary depots. Wagons hauled provisions and ammunition the rest of the way to the army, while wounded Union soldiers and captured rebels made the trip in reverse. As Grant moved south, he opened new depots to keep abreast of his progress.

This network of "flying depots," as the progressive transport hubs were called, required Grant to keep his army east of Lee or risk being cut off from his supplies. Sensitive to logistical concerns, Grant had initiated the campaign by crossing the Rapidan River east of Lee, and he kept east of Lee during his turning movement to Spotsylvania Court House. By May 8, he had opened a supply line that ran from Alexandria down the Potomac to Belle Plain, then overland to Fredericksburg. Logistics also shaped Grant's shift to the North Anna River; he stayed safely east of Lee and established a new "flying depot" at Port Royal, on the Rappahannock River. Warren's and Hunt's proposal that Grant change his practice and place Lee between the Union army and its supplies troubled Grant. If the campaign lasted longer than a few days—an eventuality that seemed extremely likely—the Federals might find themselves stranded without food or supplies.

Grant also worried that a westward maneuver might cut him off from reinforcements. Smith, too, would have difficulty reaching Grant and might fall prey to a superior rebel force. Virginia's geography also raised daunting obstacles to a westward move. Below the North Anna, the Union army would face three formidable streams—Little River, New Found River, and the South Anna River, each running west to east only a few miles apart. High-banked and swollen from recent rains, the rivers afforded Lee prime defensive positions. Each time Grant turned Lee's flank, the rebels could drop behind the next river, rendering the Union army's advance a bloody and tedious process.

Both Meade and Grant's aide Lieutenant Colonel Cyrus B. Comstock urged Grant to follow his practice and maneuver east of Lee. Pursuing his usual course, they argued, would avoid the problems raised by Warren's and Hunt's proposal. Geography would help, rather than hinder, the Union movement. The North Anna, Little River, New Found River, and the South Anna merged a few miles southeast of the Confederate army to form the Pamunkey River. By sidling east along the Pamunkey's northern bank and crossing downstream, Grant could put all the bothersome waterways behind him at one stroke. A few miles farther east, the Pamunkey and the Mattaponi combined to form the York, which in turn emptied into Chesapeake Bay. White House, the highest navigable point on the Pamunkey, was ideally situated as the next of Grant's "flying depots" and coincidentally the place where Smith's reinforcements were slated to disembark.

Another consideration favored swinging east. As the Federals followed the Pamunkey's southeastward course, they would slant progressively nearer to Richmond. At Grant's most likely crossing point—the fords near Hanovertown, about twenty-eight miles southeast of Ox Ford—he would be only eighteen miles from Richmond. Once the Army of the Potomac was over the

Pamunkey, only Totopotomoy Creek and the Chickahominy River would stand between Grant and the Confederate capital.

Grant's audacious streak at first inclined him toward Warren's and Hunt's position. At the end of the conference, he voiced his preference for a "bold stroke, viz: to cut clear of our communications altogether, and push to get around Lee's left, shoving right on for Richmond." That evening he changed his mind. Better to swing east, he concluded, and go with a sure thing, than to maneuver west and risk the campaign. He emphasized Meade's and Comstock's point: moving east would put the Union army across "all these streams at once, and [leave] us still where we can draw supplies." Lee, Grant surmised, would have no choice but to abandon his stronghold below the North Anna and hurry southeastward to confront the Federal army. The decisive battle of the war, Grant concluded, would be fought along the Chickahominy, on the outskirts of Richmond. He did not fear the outcome, as recent events persuaded him that the fight was gone from Lee's army. After all, Lee had caught him at serious disadvantage on the North Anna but had failed to attack. "Lee's army is really whipped," he assured Halleck. "The prisoners we now take show it, and the actions of his army show it unmistakably. A battle with them outside of entrenchments cannot be had. Our men feel that they have gained the morale over the enemy and attack with confidence. I may be mistaken, but I feel that our success over Lee's army is already insured."[28]

Grant spent much of the night with his maps, studying the Pamunkey crossings. A short distance east of the armies, the North Anna turned sharply south and flowed past the right end of Lee's formation. Five miles farther on, the North Anna became the Pamunkey and bent southeastward to loop and twist above the small town of Hanover Court House. Two roads crossed the river near Hanover Court House, at Littlepage Bridge and Taylor's Ford, but Grant rejected these crossings as impracticable. Because of the river's meandering course, they were actually considerably closer to Lee's army than to his own. As soon as Lee discovered him moving, Grant reasoned, he would shift troops to contest Littlepage Bridge and Taylor's Ford.

The situation improved downstream. A major road crossed the Pamunkey at Nelson's Bridge, eight miles east of Hanover Court House. Union soldiers had destroyed the bridge two years before, but the river was relatively narrow at the site, and Meade's engineers could easily throw across a pontoon span. Two miles east of Nelson's Bridge, near the hamlet of Hanovertown, was another crossing called Dabney Ferry. And three more twisting miles downriver was yet another crossing at New Castle Ferry. These three sites—Nelson's Bridge, Dabney Ferry, and New Castle Ferry—seemed ideal for Grant's purpose and were close enough for the Federals to reach them in less than a day of hard marching. In fact, if Grant got a jump on Lee by starting under cover of darkness, he could be across the Pamunkey before Lee could react. The three crossings were accessible from a main road, called Ridge Road, that paralleled the Pamunkey's northern bank from Chesterfield, behind Grant's North Anna line, and continued east to White House, facilitating the maneuver. Another road—called Hanover River Road—ran along the southern bank from Hanover Court House to White House, connecting the three crossings with Grant's new flying depot.

Grant decided to start his maneuver at night to increase the chances for success. To speed the march, he elected to advance in two columns, one crossing at Dabney Ferry and the other downriver at New Castle Ferry.

By far the most hazardous part of the operation would be disengaging from Lee. Breaking away from an enemy was tricky in the best of circumstances. Grant had pulled away from Lee in the Wilderness and at Spotsylvania Court House with only slight loss, but the situation on the North Anna was vastly more difficult. Not only were the contending armies pressed tightly together, but they were both on the same side of the North Anna, with Grant backed against the stream. As soon as Lee discovered Grant leaving, he was certain to attack, and the consequences could be catastrophic. The Union army would have to funnel across on Chesterfield Bridge and on temporary bridges constructed by Meade's engineers over the rain-swollen river. How long these spans would survive the rising, debris-filled water was anyone's guess. "This movement was one of great delicacy, requiring the utmost caution and care," a Union engineer emphasized. "Could the enemy once know of our intention and discover of the least weakness in his front, he would of course advance in force and drive the remainder of the army into the river." Grant's immediate nightmare involved Lee catching the Federal force astride the river, away from its earthworks and unable to defend itself.[29]

Grant's solution to the tricky problem of disengagement was a deception, followed by a phased withdrawal. On the morning of May 26, Sheridan was to dispatch Brigadier General James H. Wilson's cavalry division to Little River, west of Lee, to probe the rebel defenses and create the impression that he was preparing the way for an army-wide movement. At the same time, elements from Brigadier Generals Alfred T. A. Torbert's and David McM. Gregg's cavalry divisions were to ride east to Littlepage Bridge and Taylor's Ford on the Pamunkey. Their mission was to further confuse Lee about Grant's intentions by making it appear that the Federals were considering crossing there as well.

While Sheridan's cavalry practiced its diversions, Brigadier General David

A. Russell's division of Wright's corps, along with two four-gun batteries, was to withdraw from its entrenchments, cross to the north side of the North Anna River, and bivouac at Chesterfield Station, three miles north of the river and well behind the Union army's eastern wing. At dark, Russell, accompanied by cavalry and engineers with pontoons, was to march swiftly along the Pamunkey toward Dabney Ferry while cavalry demonstrations at Littlepage Bridge and Taylor's Ford concealed his movement from Confederate scouts on the southern shore. Under Grant's timetable, Russell and his cavalry escort were to reach Dabney Ferry at Hanovertown shortly after daylight on May 27 and secure the Pamunkey crossing. The rest of the Potomac army was to steal from its entrenchments the night of May 26–27 in a carefully orchestrated sequence. Screened by pickets, Wright was to withdraw the rest of his corps from its earthworks on Grant's western wing, cross to the north side of the North Anna, and follow Russell's route to Dabney Ferry. Warren was to take a second route a few miles to the left of Wright that would bring him to New Castle Ferry. In the meantime Burnside and Hancock, Grant's eastern wing, were to cross the North Anna, screen Wright's and Warren's departure, and follow behind them. If everything went according to plan, the Army of the Potomac's main body would stream across the Pamunkey at Dabney and New Castle Ferries late on May 27 or early on May 28.[30]

Not everyone was happy about Grant's latest scheme. Meade had advocated a maneuver across the Pamunkey several days before, but Grant had overruled him and gone to the North Anna instead. Meade was smugly satisfied now that Grant saw things his way, although the satisfaction scarcely compensated for the initial slight. Colonel Charles S. Wainwright, the 5th Corps's artillery chief, was flabbergasted at Grant's lack of originality. "Can it be that this is the sum of our lieutenant general's abilities?" asked Wainwright, who had been unimpressed with Grant from the start. "Has he no other resource in tactics? Or is it sheer obstinacy? Three times he has tried this move, around Lee's right, and three times been foiled."[31]

Grant's plan, bold in conception, had a critical weakness. For the Union host to successfully turn Lee's flank, Lee had to remain stationary while the Union army maneuvered. The best way for Grant to ensure Lee's quiescence was to leave a force at the North Anna to occupy him. Grant, however, intended to pull his entire army away from the North Anna, freeing Lee to maneuver. The problem was not new to the campaign. The Army of the Potomac had initiated its spring offensive with a wide swing past Lee's right flank that took the Federals into the Wilderness. Union commanders had neglected to leave a force to keep Lee busy, enabling him to catch them in the dense thickets. Grant's army-wide shift to the Pamunkey ran comparable risks. Even if the particulars of the plan went right and Grant successfully crossed the Pamunkey, he might still find himself facing Lee on a field selected by his wily opponent.

The chess game was about to resume with a vengeance.

II

MAY 26–27, 1864

Grant Shifts to the Pamunkey

"Sticky as shoemaker's wax on a hot day."

MAY 26 BROUGHT another deluge. The North Anna crept higher in its banks. Anxiety at Grant's and Meade's headquarters near Quarles's Mill became palpable. Sheridan's cavalry corps, recuperating from its raid toward Richmond, was slated to initiate the army-wide sweep to the Pamunkey. One mounted division was to demonstrate upriver of Lee to create the impression that Grant intended to move west. Sheridan's other two divisions were to spearhead the actual movement by riding east, spreading a screen of riders along the Pamunkey's north bank, and securing the crossing at Dabney Ferry by Hanovertown. Russell's infantry division was to follow Sheridan on his eastward jaunt. If preparations kept on schedule—and if rising floodwaters did not sweep away the bridges across the North Anna—nightfall would see the entire Union force slipping from its entrenchments and setting off to steal a march on Lee. Should the rebels get wind of the disengagement, or should the river rise too quickly, the maneuver might well end in disaster.

Grant busied himself with logistical details. A new "flying depot" had to be established, and he ordered a change in the army's supply base "at once" from Port Royal on the Rappahannock to White House on the Pamunkey. Wounded and sick men were to be loaded onto wagons, taken to Port Royal, and evacuated by ship. When the wagons were empty, the quartermaster at Port Royal was to load them with supplies and drive them overland to White House, escorted by a cavalry detachment. The Federals would then abandon Port Royal and begin shipping supplies from Alexandria directly up the Pamunkey to White House.[1]

Blue and Gray spent a miserable morning on the North Anna. Rain pelted down unabated, flooding soldiers from their trenches. Men close to the front hunkered low behind earthworks slippery with mud and knee-deep in water to avoid exposure to enemy snipers. Sharpshooters plied their deadly trade with unusual malice, adding to the discomfort. Lieutenant Colonel Rufus R. Dawes of the 6th Wisconsin counted a dozen rounds clipping by each minute. "It is raining steadily," he wrote home around 7:00 A.M. "I have a little shelter tent with logs piled up at the end toward the enemy to stop bullets, and I lie on the ground as I write." Dripping forms huddled under rubber blankets—"satirically denominated 'waterproof,'" a disgusted officer quipped— and shivered in the rain. "The picket fire and sharpshooting at North Anna was exceedingly severe and murderous," a Federal complained. "We were greatly annoyed by it. There was an unwritten code of honor among the infantry that forbade the shooting of men while attending the imperative calls of nature, and these sharpshooting brutes were constantly violating that rule. I hated sharpshooters, both Confederate and Union, in those days, and I was always glad to see them killed."[2]

James Wilson's cavalrymen saddled up at 6:00 A.M. for their demonstration against Lee's left flank. The selection of the twenty-six-year-old to head one of Sheridan's three cavalry divisions had come as a surprise. Sporting a dashing mustache and goatee, Wilson had no combat experience, having served in the west as an aide to Grant; his only experience with cavalry was a ten-week stint running the Cavalry Bureau in Washington, a desk job that had nothing to do with leading men in battle. Wilson was smart and adept at bureaucratic maneuvers, but whether his desk savvy would translate on battlefields remained an open question. The Illinois native got off to an embarrassing start in the Wilderness by failing to picket roads toward the rebel army, permitting Lee to catch Grant in the dense thickets by surprise. Then his former friend and classmate, Brigadier General Thomas L. Rosser, stampeded his division with a brigade. Troubled by Wilson's poor showing in the Wilderness, Sheridan relegated the young brigadier general to supporting roles, with only minor parts in the victories at Yellow Tavern and Meadow Bridge. Sheridan seems not to have liked Wilson. The brash subordinate, a biographer observed, "was often imperious and outspoken, to the extent that he fully alienated as many people as he attracted."[3]

Wilson's route took him by Grant's headquarters at Quarles's Mill. He stopped near noon to visit Grant, Rawlins, and other staffers with whom he had recently served in the west. "Greetings warm and cordial," Wilson noted in his diary. He was surprised to hear from his former colleagues that Sheridan's adjutant, Lieutenant Colonel Charles Kingsbury Jr., had written reports critical of his performance. Outraged, Wilson fired off a formal protest to Sheridan urging Kingsbury's dismissal. After lunch, Wilson continued on to

Jericho Mills, crossed the North Anna on pontoon bridges, and passed behind Wright's 6th Corps to Little River. Colonel John Hammond's 5th New York Cavalry had been reconnoitering off the 6th Corps's flank and joined Wilson for the diversion. "I examined the country for means of crossing Little River, so as to strike well in toward Hanover Junction," Wilson reported, "but I found the bridges all destroyed and the streams so much swollen that the fords were impracticable." Wilson put on a conspicuous show, firing artillery and sending troopers over Little River on a fallen tree. "To complete the deception," one of Wilson's men recounted, "fences, boards, and everything inflammable within our reach were set fire to give the appearance of a vast force, just building its bivouac fires."[4]

Russell's infantry meanwhile slipped quietly from its camp near the Virginia Central Railroad and started north. Accompanying the column were Captain William E. Rhodes's Battery E, 1st Rhode Island Light, and Captain Stephen W. Dorsey's Battery H, 1st Ohio Light. Russell's men tramped across pontoon bridges at Jericho Mills and marched five miles east to Chesterfield Station, the jumping-off point for their march that evening to Dabney Ferry. Supply trains arrived, but provisions were thin, and Russell limited his men to half rations. Loath to start a long march on empty stomachs, the hungry Federals looted neighboring farms. "Some of the inhabitants professed to be Unionists but I think this was only put on," one of Russell's troops declared. "They hoped that by doing this they would save their property."[5]

All day, wagons carried the Union army's baggage across the river and returned for fresh loads. The North Anna crossings at Jericho Mills and Quarles's Mill, behind the Union right wing, were hidden from the Confederates, and workers spread boughs across the flooring of the pontoon bridges to muffle the wagon sounds. Some of Hancock's crossings—Chesterfield Bridge and the adjacent pontoon bridges—were visible to Ewell's and Anderson's pickets. Unusually heavy wagon traffic behind Hancock's lines alerted the rebels that something was brewing, and they forwarded the information to their superiors.

Ill and confined to his tent, Lee scrutinized reports from the front for keys to Grant's intentions. Kershaw, holding the left of Anderson's line, had a clear view along the river and reported the comings and goings of the Union wagons. Lee was not at all sure what the stepped-up activity meant. Was Grant withdrawing, was he concentrating troops and supplies for an attack, or was he preparing to maneuver with all or part of his army?

Lee needed more information. At midmorning he directed Anderson and Ewell, whose two corps occupied the eastern leg of his wedge, to advance skirmishers and find out what Hancock was doing. He also alerted his cavalry to remain vigilant. Elements from Wade Hampton's division—predominantly Georgians from Cobb's Legion—patrolled off the rebel left along Little River, where they skirmished heatedly with Wilson. Fitzhugh Lee's division kept watch off the Confederate right, toward Hanover Court House, and sent scouting parties east along the Pamunkey to Hanovertown. Recognizing that he might have to fall back to counter Grant's next move, Lee directed his engineers to prepare a footbridge over the South Anna River. He also instructed his chief engineer, Major General Martin L. Smith, to reconnoiter the South Anna for a new defensive line. Having done everything possible to anticipate Grant's moves, Lee awaited fresh news from the front.[6]

In response to Lee's request for intelligence, Anderson directed Kershaw to send out skirmishers. The troops facing Kershaw belonged to Potter's division of the 9th Corps, temporarily assigned to Hancock. As rebels swarmed along his line, Potter organized a foray to drive them off. He also decided to seize a grove a few hundred yards south of his position as a buffer against Kershaw's probes. Soldiers from the 7th Rhode Island slipped from Potter's fortifications and emerged into a field across from the grove. Kershaw's pickets opened from rifle pits, but the Rhode Islanders charged across the field, repulsed the Confederates, and secured the ground that Potter wanted. The operation's chief casualty was Lieutenant Colonel Henry H. Pearson of the 6th New Hampshire. Alerted that Confederates were bringing up artillery, Pearson climbed onto a stump for a better look. He had just lifted his binoculars when a sharpshooter shot him in his right temple, catapulting him backward into the arms of his horrified soldiers. "He never spoke," a man who caught Pearson recalled, "and was unconscious till he died at eight o'clock in the evening."[7]

Lee was concerned about Potter's show of aggression. "From the report of the enemy advancing his pickets," he warned Anderson, "an attack on that part of our line may be intended." Lee instructed Anderson to remain "alert and ready," and Ewell to send troops to support him. Firing sputtered in Kershaw's sector all day, but the attack that Lee thought likely did not materialize.[8]

The western side of the Confederate wedge, where Warren and Wright faced Hill, saw little action on May 26. Warren's men remained in their entrenchments, trading shots with Hill's pickets. Wright's soldiers toiled at destroying the Virginia Central Railroad, building bonfires from cross ties, heating rails, and bending them around trees into decorative loops. By evening, they had wrecked the railway ten miles west to Beaver Dam Station. The Confederates felt certain that a Union move was imminent and debated Grant's destination. "Supposed they are moving not generally known where," a rebel noted. "We have been in this position several days and Grant shows no disposition to attack," another observed. "I imagine his object is to flank us and get closer to Richmond before he does any more fighting, but he will find General Lee a match for him in maneuvering."[9]

Toward the end of the day, the persistent rumble of wagons behind Hancock's fortifications convinced Ewell that Hancock was girding to assault. At 6:00 P.M., Ewell probed the center of Hancock's line, but Hancock's pickets repelled the attackers. Undeterred, Ewell an hour later advanced troops along Hancock's front. No sooner had Hancock beaten back Ewell's second feeler than Kershaw renewed his forays against Potter's advanced position at the grove. Those attacks, too, were repulsed, but the pattern troubled Union commanders. Hancock was slated to withdraw the army's eastern wing shortly after dark, something he could not easily do with Confederates pressed close against his entrenchments. Near dark, in an effort to clear his front of rebels, Hancock directed Colonel Thomas A. Smyth to advance the 69th Pennsylvania, 170th New York, and two companies of the 14th Connecticut. Smyth's force worked into the no-man's land between Hancock's and Ewell's earthworks and captured a commanding rise on Major Doswell's farm. Companion forays by the 12th New Jersey and 1st Delaware cleared enemy skirmishers from the rest of the Doswell fields. These small actions gave Hancock breathing room to prepare for his evacuation. They also made possible the rescue of wounded soldiers who had been lying between the hostile lines for nearly two days.[10]

Lee pored over reports from his field commanders all afternoon, searching for patterns that would reveal Grant's intentions. Sightings of constant wagon traffic behind Hancock's lines confirmed him in his suspicion that Grant was planning some sort of movement. Federal efforts aimed at keeping Ewell's and Anderson's pickets at arm's length provided more evidence that Grant was anxious to conceal an impending deployment. Wilson's activity along Little River struck Lee as especially important. Union cavalry seemed to be preparing the way for a major push past the Confederate left. Lee must also have noticed that the weight of Grant's army was already concentrated on the Confederate left, toward Little River. Wagons moving behind Hancock and Potter might well be transporting troops and supplies from Grant's eastern wing to reinforce the western wing. Assembling all of these clues, Lee discerned a pattern. From "present indications," he wrote Confederate War Secretary James A. Seddon, Grant "seems to contemplate a movement on our left flank." The maneuver, Lee recognized, would render his wedge-shaped formation untenable and compel him to take up a new line along the South Anna River. The timing of his retreat, Lee concluded, depended on the pace of Grant's movement. As soon as it became clear that Hancock was shifting across the North Anna, Lee would order the Army of Northern Virginia to begin its retrograde movement.[11]

Throughout the campaign, Lee had misjudged Grant's intentions. His uncertainty over Grant's movements after the Wilderness had almost cost him the race to Spotsylvania Court House. His mistaken belief on May 11 that Grant was retreating had led him to withdraw artillery from the Mule Shoe at the very time Grant was attacking, again imperiling the rebel army. Lee had even misunderstood Grant's shift to the North Anna River, enabling Grant to get a portion of his army across at Jericho Mills and turn Lee's left flank.

Now, once again, Lee guessed wrong about Grant's plan. Falling for Wilson's ruse, he expected Grant to assail his left. In fact, Grant was initiating an army-wide move around Lee's right. Lee's misapprehension of Grant's maneuver helped the risky Union disengagement off to a remarkably good start.

The second stage of Grant's plan was also falling neatly into place. Toward dark on May 26, Torbert's and Gregg's cavalry divisions started south from Chesterfield Station. Their mission was to seize the Pamunkey River crossings and establish a bridgehead at Hanovertown. Sheridan and his entourage led the mounted column south along Ridge Road and turned east toward Concord Church. The way threaded along the watershed between the Mattaponi to the north and the Pamunkey to the south. Trotting past the stately columns of Concord Church, Sheridan reached the road to Littlepage Bridge. The crossing afforded the rebels an avenue for intercepting Grant's march, so controlling Littlepage Bridge—or rather the bridge site, as Federals had destroyed the span earlier in the war—was important. Sheridan dispatched elements from Gregg's division to Littlepage Bridge and continued east with his main body. A few miles farther along Ridge Road came the road to Taylor's Ford, designated on some wartime maps as Norman's Ford. Sheridan sent Lieutenant Colonel James Q. Anderson's 17th Pennsylvania Cavalry south to control that crossing. The rest of the Union horsemen—Torbert's division, Brigadier General George A. Custer's Michigan brigade leading—continued east along Ridge Road to Mangohick Church. There they turned south on the road to Dabney Ferry and Hanovertown.

Confederate cavalry operating out of Hanover Court House was keeping watch along the Pamunkey. Virginians from Brigadier General Lunsford L. Lomax's brigade of Fitzhugh Lee's division were camped in the courthouse town. Two Maryland outfits—the 1st Maryland Cavalry and the Baltimore Light Artillery, both under Colonel Bradley T. Johnson—were temporarily attached to Lomax's command, along with a brigade of North Carolina cavalry under Colonel John A. Baker. That evening, the 5th Virginia Cavalry was patrolling the river near Hanover Court House. Elements from the 5th

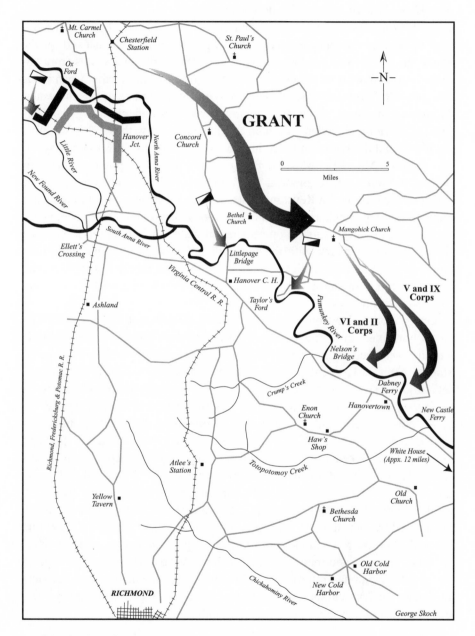

Grant's plan of maneuver

North Carolina Cavalry of Baker's brigade watched the remote crossing sites near Hanovertown, eight miles downstream.

Anderson's Pennsylvanians reached Taylor's Ford about dark and discovered some fifty troopers from the 5th Virginia Cavalry bivouacked on the south shore. The Southerners mistook the Federals for rebel scouts from another regiment who were supposed to be patrolling the northern bank. "Is that you, 9th Virginia?" they called to the indistinct figures across the water. "Camp on that side," a Pennsylvanian answered in a mock drawl, "and lay low till morning." Anderson's men felt camaraderie with the 5th Virginia, having routed the regiment twice in two days—at Yellow Tavern on May 11, and again on May 12 at Meadow Bridge. They were disappointed when Anderson ordered them to shoot at the Virginians. "Look out, rebels, we are going to fire on you," a Keystone State soldier called out as he and his companions shot a volley harmlessly into the woods. Separated by the river, Pennsylvanians and Virginians "soon became intimate," a Federal reported, "and the rascals made merry with their defeats and losses," shouting across the water about recent escapades. Comfortable that the rebels posed no threat, Anderson left a squadron at the ford and rode off with the rest of his regiment to catch up with the main column.[12]

Gregg's blue-clad troopers had a similar experience at Littlepage Bridge. Rebel horsemen on the far bank—apparently from Company I, 2nd Virginia Cavalry—showed no interest in fording the river, which was high from recent storms. After dark, Gregg posted a few men to maintain a show of force and left to join the rest of the cavalry. All night, Federals and rebels threw up temporary earthworks on opposite sides of the river at Littlepage Bridge.[13]

At 9:00 P.M., Russell's infantrymen set the buildings at Chesterfield Station ablaze and started off, following Torbert and Gregg. "We marched at a very rapid rate in order to keep near the cavalry," a soldier from Maine recollected. "Soon some of the men began to fall out and lay down beside the road and go to sleep. They were all worn out with hard marching and fighting." Soldiers straggled in large numbers. "It seems impossible that so much can be endured by mortal man," a surgeon jotted in his diary. "It is fight and run, run and fight, move to the left all the while—get whipped sometimes when we don't know it, and then turn in and whip the rebs the very worst way. So we go." Sheridan had returned from his Richmond raid along the same route two days earlier, and putrefying horse carcasses lined the roadway. The march, a Union man observed, was memorable for the stench.[14]

Shortly after dark—Sheridan had already posted troopers at Taylor's Ford and Littlepage Bridge, and Russell was starting from Chesterfield Station on his long march east—Meade began evacuating his North Anna entrenchments in earnest. "Toward afternoon it cleared off and gave us the coveted opportunity to dry all our things," a 5th Corps officer wrote. "Having succeeded in drying everything, and congratulating ourselves on the decreased weight, and getting supper, imagine our disgust at finding another storm brewing, which shortly burst over us as furiously as before, and all were drenched again."[15]

Bringing the western wing of the army over the North Anna was a "delicate move," Grant noted. Crittenden's 9th Corps division anchored the wing's left end on the river at Quarles's Mill. The 5th Corps divisions of Brigadier Generals Samuel W. Crawford, Lysander Cutler, and Charles Griffin ranged south in that order, completing the line to Little River. The 6th Corps—consisting since Russell's departure of Brigadier Generals Thomas H. Neill's and James B. Ricketts's divisions—was concentrated behind the 5th Corps near Noel's Station on the Virginia Central Railroad. All of these troops had to cross the North Anna on the corduroy bridge at Quarles's Mill or on two pontoon bridges upstream at Jericho Mills. Warren, Wright, and Crittenden had to coordinate their movements closely. Wright was to begin by passing north behind Warren, crossing at Jericho Mills, then continuing through Mt. Carmel Church to Chesterfield Station and on to Dabney Ferry, following Russell's route. Then Warren was to pull out in stages, sliding his southernmost units northward one after another behind the rest of his line. Griffin, next to Little River, was to initiate the 5th Corps's withdrawal, followed by Colonel Wainwright's artillery, then by Cutler, then by the Maryland Brigade, and finally by Crawford. Crittenden, closest to the North Anna, was to cross last. Once across he was to keep one brigade, under Colonel Joseph M. Sudsburg, on the northern bank at Quarles's Mill and to dispatch his other brigade under Brigadier General James H. Ledlie to guard Jericho Mills. When everyone else was across, pickets left behind south of the river were to slip quietly from the empty earthworks and dash across, leaving the engineers to dismantle the bridges. Warren would follow behind Wright to Mt. Carmel Church, then proceed to New Castle Ferry along roads running east of Wright's route.[16]

Confusion there was, but the evacuation went surprisingly well, particularly when measured against the Potomac army's dismal performance on night marches thus far in the campaign. Warren and Wright concealed their departure by throwing out clouds of pickets and instructing their soldiers to mimic the appearance of routine camp life. "Such bands as there were had been vigorously playing patriotic music, always soliciting responses from the rebs with Dixie, My Maryland, or other favorites of theirs," a Federal noted. The 6th Corps stole away undetected, Ricketts leading, the corps's artillery following, and Neill closing up behind. Rearguard elements from the 110th

Ohio and 10th Vermont under Lieutenant Colonel Otho H. Binkley screened Wright's departure at Jericho Mills, then crossed the river without loss. Warren began withdrawing his units as planned. "Roads heavy and slippery with mud and approaches to stream bad," Warren noted of the Quarles's Mill crossing. The water was so high that many soldiers feared the corduroy bridge might float away.[17]

The commander of the 5th Corps's picket line, Lieutenant Colonel William A. Throop, did a masterful job covering the withdrawal. Once the infantry had pulled out, Throop's skeleton force was left occupying two miles of entrenchments from the North Anna to Little River. The rebels had no inkling that Wright and Warren were gone, and Throop wanted to keep it that way. He began surreptitiously removing men from the southern end of his line and placing them in a "moving line," as he called it, rolling north toward the fords. Toward morning, he brought most of his pickets across the river, leaving only a small contingent on the southern bank, where a herd of "half-wild and savage-looking hogs" kept them anxious until dawn. After the last of Throop's pickets had darted across, engineers dismantled the bridges. "There was an immense sense of relief," a soldier explained. Throop took roll call and was pleased to discover that not a man was missing. The 5th and 6th Corps had gotten cleanly away.[18]

Evacuating the Union army's eastern wing presented more of a challenge. Hancock's line bowed in a two-mile arc below the North Anna, both flanks touching the river. Brigadier General John Gibbon's division held the left, extending across Major Doswell's farm to the Richmond, Fredericksburg, and Potomac Railroad. Brigadier General Francis C. Barlow's division picked up near the tracks and continued westward across Telegraph Road to the Lowry and Fox properties. Major General David B. Birney's division began there and bent back toward the river. Potter's 9th Corps division anchored the right on the river, and elements from Brigadier General Robert O. Tyler's fresh heavy artillery division remained on the north bank as a reserve.

Most of Hancock's line traversed open fields in full view of the Confederates. The rebels were sure to attack when they discovered Hancock leaving, and his escape routes were limited. On May 23, Confederates had burned the Richmond, Fredericksburg, and Potomac Railroad trestle in Hancock's rear, and the only other permanent bridge—Chesterfield Bridge, carrying Telegraph Road—was dangerously exposed to rebel artillery at Ox Ford. The span had endured three days of shelling, and how long it would hold up was anyone's guess. Hancock's other crossings were temporary bridges erected by Union engineers. On May 24, Captain William W. Folwell of the 50th New York Engineers, supervised by Major Wesley Brainerd, had constructed two canvas pontoon bridges downriver from the burned railway trestle, behind Gibbon. The next day, Union engineers had built a third canvas pontoon bridge above the railway, behind Barlow and Birney, which they replaced on May 26 with a stronger wooden pontoon bridge. Attempts were made to construct a floating wooden footbridge, but swift current tore it loose, reminding everyone how vulnerable the bridges were. "That was an anxious minute," recollected Brainerd, who lassoed the end of the span to keep it from floating off. "Had that rope broken then," the engineer noted, "our bridges would have been swept away and the 2nd Corps left on the opposite bank of the stream with no means of escape."[19]

Hancock started pulling out around 9:00 P.M. "How we longed to get away from the North Anna, where we had not the slightest chance of success," an artillerist recalled. Bands played to drown out the tramp of marching feet and pickets concealed the movement as 2nd Corps infantrymen filed from their earthworks. Gibbon started across the lower pontoon bridge at 10:00 P.M., taking with him Captain Edwin B. Dow's and Captain J. Henry Sleeper's batteries. Barlow, along with Captain T. Frederick Brown's and Captain Frederick M. Edgell's batteries, took the bridge above Gibbon. Potter, on the right of Hancock's line, began feeding men across both Chesterfield Bridge and the upper pontoon bridge. Birney covered Potter's withdrawal by shuttling troops to fill Potter's vacancies. Once Potter was gone, Birney, along with Captain George F. McKnight's and Lieutenant James Gillis's batteries, crossed the upper pontoon bridge. Last to cross were some of Tyler's regiments, posted below the river.[20]

Burnside meanwhile labored to unite his scattered elements to protect the upstream fords. Willcox's division—the only 9th Corps division already on the northern bank directly under Burnside's command—stood guard over the stretch of river abutting Ox Ford. Potter was over well before midnight and shifted west along the riverbank to link with Willcox's left, covering the shoreline from Ox Ford to Chesterfield Bridge. Crittenden's division stood guard over Quarles's Mill and Jericho Mills to form Burnside's right.[21]

Despite Hancock's precautions, rebel pickets along the Union 2nd Corps's front suspected something was afoot. "Our retreat was closely followed by a heavy picket line of the enemy," a Federal recollected, "which made things lively for us with their whizzing, spattering bullets, both before and after our crossing." A New Jersey man remembered passing "from end to end of our line under a constant picket fire." Sometime after midnight, one of Ewell's scouts penetrated Hancock's picket line and hid in Union earthworks along the Doswell fields. He heard men prying open boxes, wagons coming and going, and the rumble of artillery crossing a bridge in the rear. "There was a great deal of talk and commotion in their lines," the scout reported to Ewell, adding that he was "satisfied the enemy is moving." Lee received the intelligence around 3:00 A.M. and directed Ewell and Anderson to step up their probes. "If you discover the enemy is leaving you," Lee cautioned, "be prepared to move your command promptly to the south side of the South Anna River."[22]

The last of Hancock's soldiers was across by daylight. Engineers pulled up the pontoon bridges, and Birney's rearguard set fire to Chesterfield Bridge. When a downpour extinguished the flames, a detachment from the 7th New York Heavy Artillery ran back to rekindle the fire. Rebel pickets at the south end of the bridge shot at the New Yorkers to keep them away. A party under Lieutenant Benjamin Ashley of the 7th New York Heavy Artillery managed to rip up the bridge's decking and get the fire going again. Soon flames engulfed the wooden structure. Only then was it discovered that several Union pickets, including a contingent from the 32nd Maine, had failed to receive notice to withdraw and were still south of the river. "When they emerged from the forest upon the river bank," the Maine regiment's historian recounted, "the flames were already curling around brace and stringer, and blazing above plank and piling, and their retreat was cut off." Marooned, the Maine men surrendered to their Confederate pursuers.[23]

Hancock's troops rested about a mile north of the river, waiting for the roads behind them to clear of Wright's and Warren's men. Union pickets lined the northern bank to keep the rebels from coming across. Soldiers from Lieutenant Samuel S. Kerr's Company K, of the 140th Pennsylvania, dug holes with bayonets and tin plates and hid behind trees, "which they hugged tighter than they did their sweethearts as they bid them adieu when first off for war," a Pennsylvanian recalled. The chief excitement was a "sharp artillery duel" between Hancock's guns and Anderson's Confederate pieces to the south. "The rebs got a good range on us and dropped a few shells amongst us," a Federal reported, "but we soon got under cover." Sergeant Eli Cook's squad of Berdan's Sharpshooters maintained harassing fire from behind stumps and rocks to keep the rebels from firing their artillery. "They tried every possible way to get in a shot," a Federal noted of the Confederate gunners, "but as the sharpshooters had orders not to let them load again, their cannon became subject to the will of Sergeant Cook's force, who kept them quiet until our passing troops had gone by." Union pickets watched rebels fiercely charge the earthworks south of the river only to find them empty.[24]

All morning, Wright's and Warren's troops, screened from inquisitive Confederates by Hancock and Burnside, filed along the narrow road from Jericho Mills to Mt. Carmel Church. "For several miles, the mud was nearly knee-deep, a little thicker than soup," a soldier from Maine recounted, "and the horses, weak from their hard service and lack of forage, were constantly stumbling and falling and required the assistance of the men to get them up." A Massachusetts Yankee remembered mud "knee deep and as sticky as shoemaker's wax on a hot day." The muck, another Federal swore, was "so deep and liquid, that the course was rather a stream than a road." Soldiers amused themselves waiting beside holes in the road and watching unsuspecting men fall in. Several soldiers lost their shoes in mire. One hole sucked men in to their waists, and another seemed virtually bottomless. Rumor had it that a few unfortunates disappeared over their heads in viscous ooze and suffocated.[25]

Mix-ups were inevitable, and tempers flared. Wright fell behind schedule, forcing Warren to wait several hours on the northern bank, near Quarles's Mill, where he issued rations and fired off scathing missives accusing Burnside of cutting the 5th Corps's line of march. "Where are these troops going?" Meade's chief-of-staff Humphreys asked Burnside in an attempt to correct the tangle. "Have the brigades for Jericho Mills ford and Quarles's Mills ford been directed to move on the south side of the river?" Burnside, not yet reconciled to his new position as Meade's subordinate, responded testily. "It does not seem possible that any of my troops are on the south side of the river," he snapped back. "My information as to the position of the troops is necessarily obtained from officers in charge of the movement, and I deem it quite as reliable as that received by the commanding general from like sources until the certainty is established. I am not in the habit of making reports inconsistent with the facts of the case, and cannot permit any person to make such insinuations." Meade and his staff visited Burnside to investigate. Burnside, Lyman related, came out of his tent "pretty angry, and stood by Meade's horse and complained indignantly of being told his men were not in position." Concluded Lyman: "The impression is that Burnside was nearly, or quite, right."[26]

Grant and Meade breakfasted at their headquarters by Quarles's Mill. Despite delays and confusion, the withdrawal was ticking along tolerably well, and spirits were high. The generals waited to leave until the last Union troops south of the river came across the corduroy bridge. "We had to be pretty lively in getting off," Meade's aide Lyman wrote, "for there we were, right on the bank of the river, and the enemy's skirmishers expected down at any moment." No sooner had engineers dismantled the bridge than rebels appeared on the south bank. They fired at the headquarters entourage and hit a telegraph wagon, "wounding the side of the same," Lyman quipped.[27]

Grant had pulled off a difficult evacuation with no appreciable loss. Most

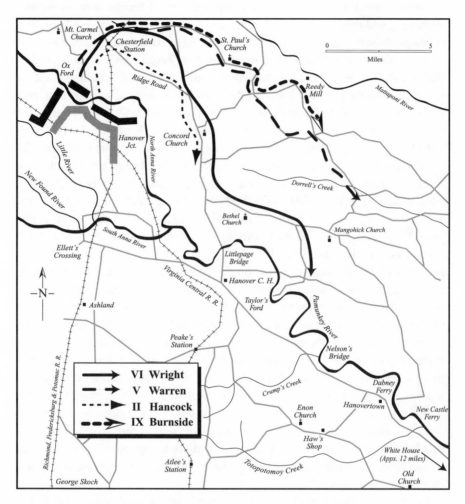

Union routes from the North Anna on May 27

important, Lee had not attacked. Here, wise heads at Union headquarters concurred, was more proof that the Confederate army had lost its will to fight.

"The enemy retired to the north side of the North Anna last night."

Shortly before daybreak on May 27, nearly thirty miles east of the North Anna entrenchments, George Custer's Michigan cavalry brigade of Torbert's division rode into a dense fogbank. The chill, moist air was refreshing. Dabney Ferry lay just ahead. Torbert, who was riding at the head of the column with Sheridan and Custer, pressed to the river's edge. Sheridan directed him to secure both banks so that engineers traveling with the cavalry could construct a pontoon bridge for the army to cross.

Pontoon bridges simplified campaigning in central Virginia, where rivers raised formidable barriers. The wooden pontoon frames and their skin of tightly woven waterproof canvas called "duck" were easily disassembled and carried in wagons. Trained engineers could put the frames together in minutes and stretch the "duck" into place just as quickly. The result was a watertight boat twenty-one feet long, five feet wide, and two and a half feet deep. To construct a bridge, engineers anchored a row of pontoons across the river to form piers, connected the pontoons with stringers, then lay down flooring, all of which was carried in the wagons. Properly built, a pontoon bridge could hold wagons, field guns, and a troop column marching four abreast. Accompanying Sheridan to Dabney Ferry were two pontoon trains and workers from the 50th New York Engineers proficient in bridge building. During the march, the New Yorkers had passed the time plundering farms. "From nearly every wagon dangled poultry, some alive, some dead," a bridge builder recorded. "Most conspicuous was a big rooster, standing on an anchor, and crowing with a spirit such as few but a rooster can maintain under adverse circumstances— ignoring the fact that he was tied to the anchor and couldn't get off."[28]

Custer joined Sheridan and Torbert at the Pamunkey. Sheridan regarded the twenty-three-year-old Michigander as his most dependable subordinate, and for good reason. The intense young general had led the Union cavalry attack down Brock Road after the Wilderness; he had broken Stuart's line at Yellow Tavern; and he had rescued the cavalry corps from an especially tight spot at Meadow Bridge. Reckless and exuding confidence, he dressed to match his devil-may-care attitude. Long golden locks spilled from under a black felt hat set at a jaunty angle. A black velveteen jacket laced with gold piping, top boots with gilt spurs, and a scarlet neck scarf completed the outfit. Lyman, who had a knack for caricature, described Custer as "one of the funniest-looking beings you ever saw . . . like a circus rider gone mad!" A more sympathetic observer thought he resembled a "Viking of old." Custer was especially fond of leading mounted charges to strains of "Yankee Doodle" played by his brigade band. Critics differed over his military acumen, but no one accused him of being boring.[29]

Custer contemplated the current, murky and fast from recent rains. No rebels were evident, so he decided to swim across on horseback. He turned his mount into the stream, but rushing water spooked the animal, and it began to buck. Jerking the reins hard, Custer sent himself somersaulting into the water. The horse swam back to shore while the nattily attired general bobbed precariously downstream. Finally he splashed his way back to the northern bank, looking, an onlooker chuckled, "like a drowned rat." Bemused, Sheridan asked the dripping Custer if he had enjoyed his bath. "I always take a bath in the morning when convenient," Custer replied with a smile, "and have paid a quarter for many not so good as this."[30]

Custer directed Colonel Peter Stagg to quietly assemble his 1st Michigan Cavalry on the north bank in preparation for crossing. As Stagg's men gathered beside the river, a detachment of some sixty troopers from the 5th North Carolina Cavalry opened fire from the south shore. Soldiers from Company C, 1st Michigan Cavalry, returned the fire with repeating carbines and drove the Tar Heels back. In the meantime Captain M. Van Brocklin, commanding the lead pontoon train, set his engineers to assembling two pontoon boats. The boats were completed in short order, and Van Brocklin's men heaved them onto their backs and hauled them to the river. While the rest of Stagg's regiment laid down heavy covering fire, the men of Company C jumped into the two pontoon boats and rowed across the Pamunkey. Landing on the far bank, they cleared the immediate area of rebels and established a bridgehead. Working feverishly under sporadic long-range fire from the Tar Heels, Van Brocklin began pushing pontoon boats into the water, connecting them with stringers, and laying down flooring. A rebel sniper killed one of Van Brocklin's sergeants when the span was midway across, but Company C kept the rebels sufficiently back from the shore for the bridge team to complete their work. The finished structure floated on eight pontoons and spanned 180 feet of river. As soon as the flooring was hammered down, the rest of Stagg's regiment galloped over the bridge. Custer's remaining regiments quickly followed, as did Torbert's other two brigades, under Brigadier General Wesley Merritt and Colonel Thomas C. Devin. Captain Folwell, commanding Sheridan's second pontoon train, began work on a 164-foot pontoon bridge a few yards upriver from Van Brocklin's handiwork. When the engineers had finished, they celebrated with a meal of poultry soup.[31]

Torbert's immediate objective was to secure the landing at Hanovertown and prepare the way for the Army of the Potomac to cross later in the day. Originally named Page's Warehouse, Hanovertown in colonial times had been the Pamunkey's highest transshipment point for tobacco awaiting transport downriver. In the settlement's heyday, warehouses had groaned with leaf from neighboring plantations. But history had passed Hanovertown by. In 1864, nothing remained of the place but memories of its past and a few tumbledown houses occupying a broad, flat expanse of bottomland near the river. From Hanovertown, Hanover River Road ran west toward Hanover Court House and east to New Castle Ferry, roughly paralleling the Pamunkey's southern bank. The floodplain extended about a mile from the river and was ringed by hills. Torbert considered the hills key to holding the army's prospective assembly area at the river and directed Custer to capture them. Two mansions perched grandly on opposite sides of Hanover River Road where it crossed the cusp of the ridge west of Hanovertown. "Summer Hill," on the Pamunkey side of the road, had been home to Captain William Brockenbrough Newton of the 4th Virginia Cavalry. The captain had been killed at Kelly's Ford in 1863, and his widow Mary and their three children now occupied the property. South of the road stood "Westwood," residence of Dr. William S. R. Brockenbrough and his family. Custer's lead elements drove the pesky North Carolina troopers west along Hanover River Road and set up temporary headquarters in the doctor's yard.[32]

Hanover River Road at the Brockenbrough house jogged slightly to the right, passed through a mile of woods, and emerged into the cleared fields of the Hundley family. From there, another road ran a quarter mile north to the Pamunkey crossing at Nelson's Bridge. Torbert recognized that securing Nelson's Bridge would afford the Union army another way across the river and reduce the marching distance from the North Anna by several miles. He instructed Custer to send two regiments—Stagg's 1st Michigan Cavalry and the 6th Michigan Cavalry, under Major James H. Kidd—west along the river road to clear the Hundley property of Confederates and uncover Nelson's Bridge.

A road forked left at Dr. Brockenbrough's house and meandered southwest two and a half miles to the little settlement of Haw's Shop. John Haw III had established a shop there well before the war to manufacture farming and milling machinery. After McClellan's brief occupation of the surrounding countryside in the summer of 1862, Haw sold his machinery to Tredegar Iron Works in Richmond. By 1864, the shop was in ruins. Salem Presbyterian Church, a schoolhouse, and a scattering of residences constituted the remainder of the settlement. Haw's Shop was important to the Federals because five roads converged there, two of them leading to Richmond. Torbert directed Custer to take his remaining two regiments—the 5th Michigan Cavalry, temporarily commanded by Captain William T. Magoffin, and the 7th Michigan Cavalry, under Major Alexander Walker—out the left fork at Dr. Brockenbrough's farm and secure the critical Haw's Shop intersection. The rest of Torbert's division was to support the divided sections of Custer's command, Devin's brigade following Stagg and Kidd along the river road, and Merritt's brigade veering left at Dr. Brockenbrough's farm toward Haw's Shop, behind Magoffin and Walker.[33]

Lee had received conclusive evidence by sunup on May 27 that the Federals had left their earthworks below the North Anna. His artillery chief, Brigadier General William N. Pendleton, reported that troops formerly in front of Ewell were gone. Pendleton could see blue-clad soldiers on the far side of the river to the right, moving toward Telegraph Road and disappearing from view off to the east. Kershaw reported that the Union works facing him were empty as well. A considerable force—Hancock's corps—remained on the northern bank, but the enemy all seemed to have left the southern bank.[34]

Shortly after 6:00 A.M., a report arrived that Union cavalry and infantry were streaming across the Pamunkey at Dabney Ferry. Grant's purpose was now clear. Wilson's cavalry demonstration at Little River had been a ruse. Grant was sticking to his usual pattern and maneuvering past the right end of the Confederate position.

Lee quickly settled on a course of action. Grant had a significant head start. Part of the Union army was already across the Pamunkey at Dabney Ferry, breaching the river line and securing a bridgehead at Hanovertown. From Hanovertown, Grant could move in any of several directions. He might advance west along Hanover River Road, emerge in Lee's rear, and sever the Army of Northern Virginia's escape routes. Or he might move west only to Hanover Court House, then descend to Richmond along the Virginia Central Railroad and its companion wagon roads. He might even take an entirely different tack and march south to Haw's Shop. From there he could follow Atlee Station Road west to Virginia Central Railroad, cut the rail line, and march south to Richmond; he could descend a few miles to Old Church Road, follow that route to Mechanicsville, and cross into Richmond; or he could pursue one of several roads threading south to a little settlement known as Old Cold Harbor and gain access to yet another road network feeding into the capital or across the James River.

Lee could not predict what route Grant would take. As a hedge against the several potential courses, he decided to abandon the North Anna line and shift fifteen miles southeast to a point near Atlee's Station, on the Virginia Central Railroad. This would place him southwest of Grant's concentration at Hanovertown, in position to block the likely avenues of Union advance. Grant, by his move to the Pamunkey, had turned Lee out of his North Anna line in much the same manner that he had maneuvered Lee from his strongholds in the Wilderness and at Spotsylvania Court House. But Lee's response was equally cunning, as it would enable him to confront Grant head-on along a new line of his own selection.[35]

The Army of Northern Virginia was under way by 10:00 A.M., marching south along parallel routes. Ewell's troops followed Telegraph Road to Taylorsville, crossed Little River, then cut across on another road to the Virginia Central Railroad. There they crossed the South Anna River on a trestle and wound along a patchwork of country roads through a thinly populated region of dense woods to the Wickham plantation. The fine estate was a "splendid looking cool place," a soldier noted as he marched past, with slave quarters "laid off like a town, each square having a house and garden to itself." It was also the ancestral home of Brigadier General Williams C. Wickham, commanding a cavalry brigade under Fitzhugh Lee. Captain Henry W. Wingfield, who guided Ewell's corps along the maze of back roads, had grown up close by. Whether by accident or design, Wingfield led the army sufficiently near his home that he was able to slip away for a meal. Winding south through Merry Oaks, Ewell's corps reached Hughes' Crossroads, halfway between Ashland and Atlee's Station, near dark.[36]

Breckinridge's little army, followed by Anderson's 1st Corps, dropped due south along the Richmond, Fredericksburg, and Potomac Railroad. The column crossed Little River and the South Anna River on railway bridges, passed through Ashland, then turned east toward Hughes' Crossroads. Breckinridge camped at the crossroads, near Ewell, and Anderson bivouacked a few miles away, between Hughes' Crossroads and Half Sink. The army's wagons and artillery evacuated along Telegraph Road, the major north-south road passing between the two railroads. Hill held his corps and Pickett's division of Anderson's Corps at the North Anna until everyone else had left, then brought up the rear, following behind Anderson and camping near Ashland. Lee, who was still sick and rode all day in a carriage, set up headquarters at the Jenkins house, near Hughes' Crossroads and in close communication with the various elements of his army.[37]

At midmorning on May 27, as Lee's men left their earthworks and marched south, Grant and Meade wended their way to Mt. Carmel Church through dense masses of troops. Infantry and wagons mingled on narrow, muddy

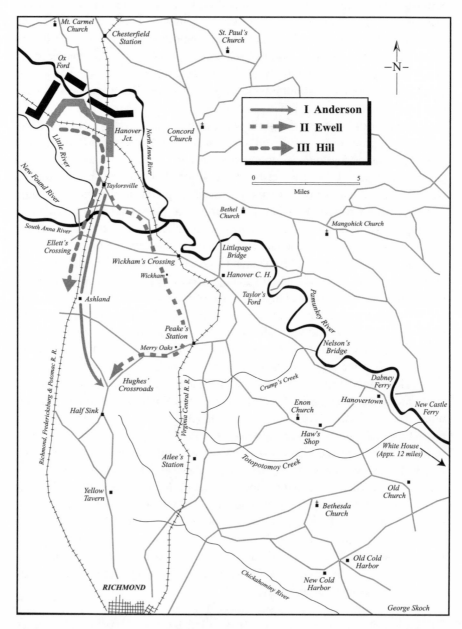

Confederate routes from the North Anna on May 27

roads in a horrific traffic jam. At places, Wright's and Warren's corps, the vanguards of Grant's two columns heading toward the Pamunkey, marched side by side on the same road. A few of Hancock's soldiers mixed in as well, although most of the 2nd Corps still waited near the river, marking time until Wright and Warren moved on. "It seemed to me inextricable confusion," Warren's artillery chief Wainwright observed.[38]

East of Mt. Carmel Church, Grant and Meade turned off on the road to Chesterfield Station. They planned to ride in front of Wright, staying near the Pamunkey so as to be close to the fords when the columns arrived. The greater part of Ricketts's and Neill's divisions had stopped at the smoldering ruins of Chesterfield Station, bone tired after their all-night march from the North Anna. Soldiers lounged beside the road, nibbling rations. Grant rode a small black pony named Jeff Davis. Next to him was his aide Parker, mounted on an immense black charger. The contrast between the general and his staffer sometimes sparked merriment, but this was no such moment. Men congregated along the roadside, standing in silence and lifting their caps as Grant passed. "Citizens would have split their throats with cheers," an onlooker remembered, "but soldiers who fight for him every day and pour out their blood receive him thus quietly." Grant acknowledged the salutes with a smile. "He looked calm, satisfied, and resolute," a colonel from Pennsylvania recorded. "The cold relentless energy with which he is pursuing Lee is actually sublime."[39]

Sending the Army of the Potomac's headquarters guard ahead to brush away stray rebels, the generals followed Ridge Road, the route that Sheridan and Russell had taken a few hours before. The way ran along high ground. Little water was available, and festering horse carcasses from Sheridan's earlier passage were beginning to split open. The party stopped at a house, and a woman came out, children clinging to her skirts. Spotting beets in her garden, Lyman inquired if she would sell him some. "We shall starve," the children cried, and the woman protested that Sheridan's cavalrymen had already taken most of their food. Meade, apparently thinking of his own offspring, became so upset that he gave them his entire lunch and five dollars. An hour later, the generals stopped to eat by the home of a Mr. Jeter. "Is it fair now, when we are obliged to contribute a large part of our crops to support our army," Mr. Jeter inquired accusingly, "that you should come and take still more from us?"[40]

Wright left Chesterfield Station around 7:00 A.M. and followed a few miles behind the headquarters entourage. Shortly after noon, the 6th Corps marched past Concord Church. The late-spring sun had burned off the morning mist and bore down on the thirsty, wool-clad men toiling along the road.

"The sun came out of the clouds, and the grease came out of us as we trudged along," a soldier wisecracked. A Vermonter regarded the experience "the severest trial of its stamina the regiment ever had." A Massachusetts man found his endurance "taxed almost to its limit." Everyone seemed "as good natured as a wasp," a New Yorker commented.[41]

Warren got off from Mt. Carmel Church about the same time as Wright. Meade had instructed him to follow roads to the left of Wright but had neglected to identify the precise route. Warren's aide Roebling spent "considerable work in finding the shortest and most direct route" and finally patched together a course through St. Paul's Church that came into Wright's projected path at Mangohick Church. On the initial stages of its trek, the 5th Corps slogged through "characteristic Virginia mud, so thick and adhesive that many a footgear is left in its tenacious clutches," a Bay Stater remembered. Part of Warren's artillery became separated in the jumble around Mt. Carmel Church and took the wrong road. Discovering that he was heading toward Bowling Green, away from his proper destination, Colonel Wainwright tried to pick his way back along country roads, trusting to his "Yankeeism to find a new way around." The artillerist's instincts proved accurate, and he rejoined the 5th Corps at St. Paul's Church, where Warren had stopped his column to rest and brew coffee.[42]

Veterans never forgot the ordeal. "What language will convey to those who were not there, the least idea of the murderous cruelty of that march?" a chronicler later asked. "We had already suffered all that flesh and blood seemed able to bear, on the road from Spotsylvania to the North Anna, and the future had in store for us many other marches that were grievous beyond expression; but I am persuaded that if all the regiment were to be summoned—the living and the dead—and notified that all their marches except one must be performed over again, and that they might choose which one should be omitted, the almost unanimous cry would be, 'Deliver us from the accursed march along the Pamunkey!'" Some, however, saw grandeur in the movement. "Few people can witness the spectacle unless they belong to it, and no one can imagine how vast is the exhibition unless they witness it," a Connecticut man wrote home. "A single division seems to fill the country, and an army corps with its masses of men—batteries, supply trains, cavalry, etc.,—as it goes swarming over all the roads and byroads, and through the fields and woods, really does cover the entire area within its horizon. At least the whole of it is seldom under the eye at one time. Imagine several of these army corps in motion at once."[43]

Warren's route traversed prime Virginia plantation country. Pillars and porticoes overlooked splendid lawns and verdant fields untouched by marauding armies. Temptation was great for fagged-out soldiers. "Droves of pigs, flocks of turkeys and sheep, and plenty of poultry, etc., offered tantalizing inducements to the passing multitude, not to be set aside, and there was more foraging that day than we had witnessed for many months," a man in the 22nd Massachusetts recounted. "As the dreadful heat and the severity of the march caused unprecedented straggling, the whole immediate route was swept clean of living animal things," he added. "Rich and poor suffered alike." Another Federal agreed that "at no time had we ever seen such unstinted foraging. Everything disappeared before the knife and gun, until the whole immediate country was swept clean." One plantation—the property of John B. Floyd, former secretary of state of the Confederacy—was larger and grander than the rest, with richer appointments. Floyd's gardens and pens "paid handsome tribute to the Yankee hosts, who were now the lordly masters of the soil," a Pennsylvanian reported. Floyd's widow impressed a Massachusetts soldier as a "fine lady." Her entreaties, however, did not deter him and his companions from supplementing their coffee and hardtack with her pork.[44]

Local slaveowners cautioned their wards to stay clear of the Federals—"the Johnnies told them we had horns, would cut off their arms, etc.," an officer recorded in his diary—but slaves soon got over their fright and greeted the blue-clad troops as liberators. "We saw two or three cart loads of big blacks and little blacks with all their motley worldly effects, drawn by oxen, following in the wake of the army," the artillerist George Breck wrote home. One woman reported that her master had beaten her with a hoe and kicked her sick child to death. Soldiers found the infant's decomposing body in the master's barn. The owner claimed to be a Union man, but slaves whispered that he had been supplying the Confederate army. "We took all his butter, milk, meal, in fact, every thing eatable, burned all his outhouses, and left him a wiser, certainly a poorer man," a Federal remembered with satisfaction.[45]

Roads from the North Anna had not cleared enough for Hancock to start until 10:30 A.M. His corps fell in behind Wright and marched in two lines, halting every hour for a short rest. Once, everyone in Gibbon's rearmost brigade fell asleep and did not wake up until the rest of the division had moved out of sight. "We now had been marching and fighting day and night almost constantly for 25 days," Gibbon observed, "and officers and men began to show very decided evidences of the wear and tear of this hard and continuous work." It was afternoon before Burnside could gather his divisions at Mt. Carmel Church and set off in Warren's path. A short way past St. Paul's Church, Warren's stragglers became so dense that Burnside sought an alternative route. Turning east to Reedy Mill, near the Mattaponi, he took a longer route over difficult roads a few miles to the left of Warren. Some of his green regiments ran out of food and paid veterans a dollar for a piece of hardtack. "Had plenty of money," a seasoned New Hampshire man gloated.[46]

Wilson's cavalry brought up the Union army's rear. Wilson had abandoned his demonstrations along Little River shortly before midnight and ridden north, crossing the North Anna at Butler's Bridge, upstream from Jericho Mills. After destroying the span, he bivouacked nearby at the Canfield house. "Three or four hours only had the weary boys to rest," a trooper remembered, "and the bugles sounded the advance." Leaving Colonel George H. Chapman's brigade to watch the North Anna fords, Wilson pushed on with Colonel John B. McIntosh's brigade to Mt. Carmel Church. At 2:00 P.M., after the last of Burnside's infantry had passed by, McIntosh moved out, "bringing up the rear and picking up stragglers," according to a Connecticut man.[47]

"The command then struck a gallop."

Sheridan sent an upbeat dispatch to Meade at 9:00 A.M. He had crossed at Dabney Ferry with little opposition and had thrown two pontoon bridges over the Pamunkey. Torbert, he added, was advancing to clear the roads leading from Hanovertown, and Gregg was preparing to bring his cavalry division across the river. Russell's infantry was following close behind.[48]

Torbert, it developed, was having a busier morning than he had expected. He had set about reconnoitering the neighboring roads by dividing his lead brigade, under Custer, into two parts. Stagg's and Kidd's regiments rode west along Hanover River Road, driving stray pockets of Confederate horsemen before them, while Magoffin's and Walker's regiments, accompanied by Custer, rode south toward Haw's Shop. About a mile out from Hanovertown, Stagg's and Kidd's troopers neared Mrs. Hundley's property. Resistance from rebel cavalrymen intensified. Fitzhugh Lee had been alerted to Torbert's appearance at Hanovertown and had dispatched the rest of his North Carolina cavalry brigade to contain the interlopers. A hard-fighting outfit, the Tar Heels had incurred serious losses in the campaign, including the death of their talented commander James Gordon. On May 26, the 3rd North Carolina Cavalry, fresh from eastern North Carolina and commanded by Colonel John A. Baker, had joined the 1st, 2nd, and 5th North Carolina Cavalry formerly under Gordon. Now the senior North Carolina colonel, Baker assumed command of the brigade. This would be his first fight heading these troops.[49]

Dismounting three regiments, Baker deployed them behind makeshift log and dirt barricades in woods east of Mrs. Hundley's farm. The 3rd North

Carolina Cavalry, now commanded by Lieutenant Colonel Alfred M. Waddell, probed east along Hanover River Road until it ran into Stagg's and Kidd's Michiganders headed its way. Fighting stubbornly, Waddell retired to Baker's main line, drawing the Federals after him. Surprise volleys from Baker's entrenchments bought the Michigan men up short. Kidd dismounted his 6th Michigan and formed the troopers north of the road. Stagg deployed his 1st Michigan, also dismounted, to the south, extending the line perpendicular to the road through thick woods. Kidd tried to advance, but carbine fire off his right flank caused him to stop. Sounds of a band playing behind the North Carolina troopers led Kidd to suspect that he faced a full rebel brigade. Tar Heels, it seemed, were slipping through the woods around the right end of his line.[50]

Kidd sent an officer back for reinforcements. Devin's brigade was close behind, and the officer found Colonel Devin and explained that Kidd was about to be flanked. "Who in hell is this who is talking about being flanked?" roared Torbert, who was riding with Devin and overheard the officer's remarks. While Devin ordered his lead regiment to hurry ahead, the officer returned and reported Torbert's outburst. "I was mortified at this," Kidd reminisced, "and resolved never again to admit to a superior officer that the idea of being flanked had any terrors."[51]

Torbert, however, did not press his grievance with Kidd. The thirty-one-year-old division commander was a novice at commanding cavalry. A painful spinal abscess had bedridden him during the first weeks of the campaign, forcing him to sit out Sheridan's Richmond raid. He was anxious to prove himself, and he thought he saw an excellent opportunity to capture Baker's entire brigade. Custer had reached Haw's Shop with his 5th and 7th Michigan. From there, a road sliced northwest across Dr. George W. Pollard's farm "Williamsville" and entered Hanover River Road a short distance west of Mrs. Hundley's fields. It would be a simple matter, Torbert reasoned, for Custer to take the 5th and 7th Michigan past Dr. Pollard's place, emerge behind the North Carolinians, and bag the entire lot. Torbert dispatched a courier to Custer with instructions to initiate the movement right away.[52]

At the same time, Fitzhugh Lee at Hanover Court House began pumping more Confederate horsemen into the fray. As fighting heated in front of Baker, Colonel Bradley T. Johnson arrived from Hanover Court House with the 1st Maryland Cavalry, some 250 strong, and horse artillery. Passing across Mrs. Hundley's fields and into the adjoining woods, Johnson found Baker holding his own. Underestimating the strength of the Federal force in front of them—only two of Custer's regiments were engaged with the Tar Heels at this juncture, Devin not yet having made his presence felt—Baker and Johnson hit upon a plan to capture the Wolverines. While Baker held the Federals in place, Johnson was to take his own command and a squadron from the 5th North Carolina Cavalry, proceed southeast past Dr. Pollard's farm to Haw's Shop, then veer north and come up at Dr. Brockenbrough's place in the enemy's rear. "After a conference Johnson agreed that if Baker could hold the Federals while he, Johnson, could get at them, the two would capture the whole party," a Marylander recalled of the scheme. Coincidentally, the ploy was almost a mirror image of the pincer movement Torbert was trying to achieve with the two halves of Custer's brigade.[53]

No sooner had Johnson started down the farm road toward Haw's Shop than Devin's lead regiments—the 17th Pennsylvania Cavalry and 9th New York Cavalry—arrived on Hanover River Road to reinforce Stagg and Kidd. Devin sent his Pennsylvanians and a squadron of New Yorkers north, past Kidd's fragile right flank, and posted a section of Lieutenant Edward Heaton's horse artillery to command the road. Feeling the weight of Devin's reinforcements, Baker retired west across Mrs. Hundley's farm, contesting every inch of ground. Pennsylvanians aggressively pressed North Carolinians, capturing two officers and twenty men.[54]

Johnson and his Marylanders were also in for a rude surprise. Starting along the road toward Haw's Shop, Johnson sent the 5th North Carolina squadron ahead to scout for Federals. About a mile out, the Tar Heels ran headlong into Custer with his 5th and 7th Michigan coming from the opposite direction. The North Carolinians spurred back to alert Johnson, who found himself at considerable disadvantage. His horsemen were jammed into a narrow stretch of roadway with swampy timberland on their left and a stout woven cedar fence on their right. To gain maneuvering room, Johnson directed his troopers to rip out part of the fence and ride through the gap into Dr. Pollard's adjacent fields. Johnson sent his adjutant George W. Booth back along his column to prepare the rest of his men for the impending fight and ordered his horse artillery back to Mrs. Hundley's to avoid capture.[55]

Custer, aggressive as always, moved to attack. Magoffin's 5th Michigan rode to the woven cedar fence, dismounted, and fired multiple volleys into the Confederates, who were hurriedly trying to form in the flatland. A shot felled Colonel Johnson's horse, and another clipped the saber from his hand. "We were under heavy fire," adjutant Booth recounted, "but for some twenty minutes or more held our ground, suffering considerable loss."[56]

Custer meanwhile swung Walker's 7th Michigan into the field in preparation for one of those blistering mounted attacks that had become his stock in trade. Dr. Pollard's six-year-old son, Harry, looked on from his house. "I never saw a more striking figure than General George Custer," Harry wrote years later. "I thought he was a very young looking man for a general. He was faultlessly dressed in a uniform covered with gold embroidery. He had long yellow hair, yellow mustache, a long thin nose, and deep blue eyes." Harry would see many Yankees over the next few days, but the image of Custer remained special. "The memory of him lingered in my mind more than that of any other general," he reminisced.[57]

"Charge!" Custer shouted, and Walker's troopers thundered across the field, hooves pounding and sabers flashing overhead. "Their dense masses came toward us as if to swallow up the little command," Booth related. Johnson's formation disintegrated, and the Maryland troopers scattered. Many attempted to escape through a gate that Lieutenant Colonel Ridgely Brown, commanding the 1st Maryland, held open. "A dreadful hand-to-hand fight ensued," a southerner recounted. Brown stayed at the gate as long as possible, fending off Custer's slashing Wolverines in hand-to-hand combat while his men escaped. Seriously wounded by saber blows to his head, Brown had to give up his vigil at the gate but managed to get away. Johnson also escaped, riding a mount one of his men gave him. "The command then struck a gallop," a Marylander reported, "and the retreat was made with all rapidity, the order being passed down the line to the men to scatter and take care of themselves." Another rebel recorded that "we attempted to withdraw decently and in order, and as we found this impossible we were ordered to get out the best we could." In the melee, a bullet knocked Booth's costly gilt-corded, black-plumed hat to the ground. Stopping to pick it up, Booth saw Federal troopers riding hell-bent toward him. "I looked at the hat and then at these people and decided to try for it," Booth reminisced. Leaping from his horse, he scooped up his headgear, threw himself back on his mount, and sped away in a blaze of bullets.[58]

A road turned off northwest of Dr. Pollard's farm and ran generally west, parallel to Hanover River Road and a half mile or so below it, past the farm of the Sledd family. This side road afforded the Marylanders an escape route, and they streamed down it. A short distance west, they crossed Crump's Creek, a rambling stream that flowed north into the Pamunkey. Johnson tried to rally his command behind the creek, but Walker's 7th Michigan drove them back before they could form. Wolverines harassed the rear of Johnson's disorganized mob for about three miles and captured thirty-six prisoners. Finally Custer called off the pursuit. "My diminished numbers and exhaustion of both men and horses," the general later explained, "prevented me from making a vigorous attack on the enemy's rear."[59]

Custer recognized, however, that he was ideally situated to carry out Torbert's initial plan to capture Baker's North Carolinians. Leaving Johnson to

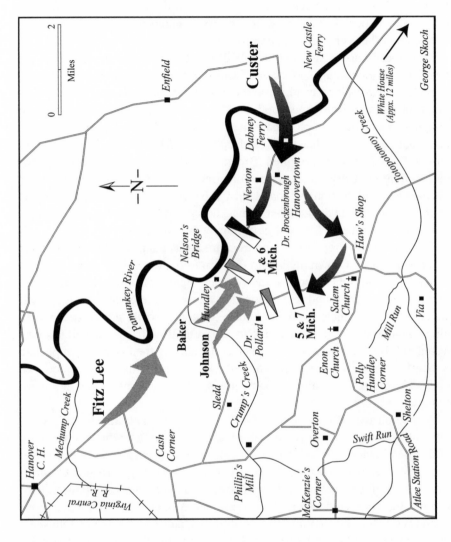

Custer's fight against Baker and Johnson on May 27

escape, he hurried his Wolverines northwest toward Mrs. Hundley's farm. Baker, meantime, had fallen back to woods along Hanover River Road west of the farm, his band still playing loudly in the rear. "The last note of the 'Bonnie Blue Flag' had scarcely died on the air," recollected Kidd of the 6th Michigan, "when far to the left and front were heard the cheery strains of 'Yankee Doodle.'" Custer was coming along the Pollard farm road with Magoffin's and Walker's regiments.[60]

Baker, learning of Johnson's rout, sent Major William H. H. Cowles with detachments from the 1st and 3rd North Carolina Cavalry to try and fend off the threat to his flank. The situation, however, was past redeeming. Johnson's collapse had rendered the Tar Heels' position untenable, leaving them no course but to retire as quickly as possible. Pressed by Federals from front and right, Baker's North Carolinians dashed west along the river road, trying to reach Hanover Court House and Lomax's cavalry brigade stationed there. "We were forced to fall back and came well nigh being stampeded," a North Carolina officer admitted. "Even the best officers and men seemed to be demoralized," another Confederate conceded.[61]

Kidd, Stagg, and Devin sliced insistently forward, like wolves closing for a kill. Baker tried to make a stand where Hanover River Road crossed Crump's Creek, but Captain Raymond L. Wright, Devin's brigade inspector, led part of the 9th New York Cavalry on a charge that drove the Confederates from the bridge and captured high ground beyond. Devin was anxious to pursue, but Torbert called him off in favor of consolidating his position along Crump's Creek. His mission, after all, was to secure the Pamunkey crossings for the Union army, not to chase after Confederate cavalry. Devin's 9th New York deployed near the bridge, and his 17th Pennsylvania and 6th New York formed in a field north of the road, supported by Heaton's artillery. Custer formed his brigade along Crump's Creek south of Devin. At a loss of four men, Devin had captured forty-one Confederates.[62]

Tar Heels and Marylanders blamed each other for the rout. Baker's soldiers justly maintained that Johnson's collapse had left their rear unprotected and had mandated their precipitate withdrawal. "We had lost heavily in this encounter, about fifty or sixty men killed and wounded and prisoners, but we undoubtedly saved [Baker's] brigade from destruction," a Marylander countered. A recent tabulation indicates that Baker and Johnson lost about ninety soldiers in all. A Confederate noted that the Federals took "special pains in shooting and killing the horses of our men . . . in the hope of disabling that arm of the service." Considering the dearth of available horses in the South, the tactic, if accurately reported, had much to commend it.[63]

Johnson's and Baker's dejected troopers agreed that their compatriots' jibes stung almost as painfully as Custer's and Devin's bullets. "This is a pretty how-de-do for the Maryland Cavalry—let the Yankees run you off the face of the earth," Fitzhugh Lee shouted in jest as the Marylanders rode past his tent. Booth, his coveted hat firmly on his head, had a perfect retort. Lee, he knew, was still smarting from a recent defeat at the hands of black troops at Wilson's Wharf, on the James. "Well general, one thing is certain," was Booth's repartee. "The people who have been after us were white; we stayed long enough to find that out, anyway." Johnson wrote his wife that he had "lost horse, saddle, bridle, overcoat, oil cloth, and that elegant dressing case, but thank God I escaped with my life."[64]

With Hanovertown securely in Federal hands, Russell's division began crossing at Dabney Ferry before noon. The infantrymen camped on the flats around Hanovertown while Russell sent artillery to the nearby ridge to guard the approaches. "We have marched about thirty-three miles since 9:00 last night," one of Russell's soldiers scrawled in his diary. "Boys are very tired, dirty and sleepy." Foraging, of course, took precedence over rest, and men gleefully appropriated a supply of fresh pork that a trooper joked "was seen traveling about on four legs." Sheridan, however, was not ready to relax his guard. His scouts reported Breckinridge's Confederates, estimated by Union sources at 10,000 men, at Hanover Court House, an easy march from Hanovertown. The intelligence was wrong—Breckinridge had only 2,200 men, and he was nowhere near Hanover Court House—but Sheridan had no reason to doubt the report. Torbert, whose brigades under Custer and Devin lined Crump's Creek, held a strong defensive position across Breckinridge's prospective route. Gregg's cavalry division went into bivouac along Hanover River Road in support of Torbert. But Sheridan was, after all, on the same side of the river as Lee's army with only two cavalry divisions and a single division of infantry. "Any other portion of the [6th Corps] which is intended to be sent here," he reminded Meade in a dispatch, "should be pushed forward as rapidly as possible."[65]

Sheridan's horsemen, basking in the glory of recent triumphs at Yellow Tavern and Meadow Bridge, felt invincible. They had secured Dabney Ferry and Nelson's Bridge with negligible loss. The ease with which they had overrun Baker and Johnson further persuaded them that the fight had gone out of the Confederate horsemen. "Rebel cavalry is exceedingly demoralized, and flees before ours on every occasion," Assistant War Secretary Dana noted in his summary of the day's work.[66]

The Pollard family and neighboring farmers carried wounded soldiers to the front yard of "Williamsville" and stripped them to take stock of their injuries. Dr. Pollard, a physician, did his best to care for the invalids. "The

Yankee soldiers who were brought in were fearfully wounded," young Harry Pollard remembered. "I saw two that had been shot through and through, and every time they breathed, blood would come out from front and back." For three months, Harry's sister Ellen nursed a Confederate who had been shot through the hip. When he was finally able to leave, he thanked Ellen and shocked everyone by proposing marriage to her sister Fanny, who according to Harry had "not lifted a hand to help him."[67]

"Our longest and hardest pull."

Grant, Meade, and their staffs reached Mangohick Church near 1:00 P.M. and stopped for the day. Two stores, a few houses, and Mr. Cardwell's plantation were nearby. The church had been a popular meeting place for rebel volunteers early in the war. Built of old brick brought from England during colonial times, it was a prominent landmark perfectly located for supervising the army's crossing of the Pamunkey. Roads fanned south to Nelson's Bridge, Dabney Ferry, and New Castle Ferry. Wright and Hancock were approaching from the west, and Warren and Burnside were arriving on roads from the north.[68]

Grant settled into his tent by the church. He was suffering from a migraine headache and used chloroform to relieve the pain. Meade set up shop next door at the home of a Mr. Thompson, described by Lyman as a "singular being with light hair and a squeaky voice, who talked just like a nigger." Mr. Thompson complained that foragers had stripped his home bare, but staffers managed to find a large quantity of concealed corn. His spring proved especially refreshing. The army's provost marshal, Marsena Patrick, had his hands busy with soldiers "plundering and destroying everything in houses," Patrick noted in his journal, remarking with satisfaction that "I gave one of them a good hiding, whom I found in the act."[69]

In order to swing well clear of Lee, Grant had planned to cross Wright and Hancock at Dabney Ferry, and Warren and Burnside at New Castle Ferry. Torbert's movement from Hanovertown to Crump's Creek, however, gave the Federals possession of Nelson's Bridge. By crossing there and at Dabney Ferry, Grant could eliminate the longer march to New Castle Ferry and move his entire force below the Pamunkey more quickly. At 4:15 P.M., Meade issued new orders. Wright was to turn south at Calno, a short distance west of Mangohick Church, march partway to Nelson's Bridge, and camp for the night. Hancock was to camp on Ridge Road near Concord Church, and Warren and Burnside were to proceed to a point near Mangohick Church as ini-

tially planned. The next morning, Wright and Hancock were to cross the
Pamunkey at Nelson's Bridge, and Warren and Burnside were to go over at
Dabney Ferry. By afternoon on May 28, if all went as planned, the Union
army would be below the Pamunkey and girding for its next—and possibly
final—battle against Lee.

Evening of May 27 saw the Army of the Potomac going into camp. Wright
halted a few miles short of Nelson's Bridge in flatland along Hornquarter
Creek. Hancock's lead elements reached Concord Church at 4:30 P.M. and
bivouacked in fields near the building. Warren stopped around 7:00 P.M. on
high ground south of Dorrell's Creek, a mile north of Mangohick Church,
where prosperous farms—Sallie Tuck's "Catalpa Grove" and land owned by
a Mrs. Orman and a Dr. Cunningham—provided ample provender. "The
weather was very warm, and ripe strawberries peeped out and blushed at us
from the thick grass that covered the land of the traitor," a Maine man noted
with satisfaction. Only Burnside, whose 9th Corps had been the last Union
infantry force to leave the North Anna, was still on the move after dark. "It
was emphatically a forced march," a 9th Corps soldier remembered. "The
roads were ablaze with burning rails, and the tall pines on fire presented a
most picturesque and brilliant scene for those who could keep their eyes open
long enough to enjoy it." Wilson's brigade under McIntosh, bringing up the
Union rear, camped a short distance past the smoking ruins of Chesterfield
Station. Wilson's other brigade, under Chapman, after a busy day of skirmishing at the North Anna fords, joined Wilson late in the night.[70]

Headquarters was upbeat. "Everything going well," Assistant Secretary
Dana summarized in his evening dispatch. "Whole army was withdrawn
north of the North Anna during the night without loss or disturbance. All the
corps are now far on their way to crossing of the Pamunkey." Even newspaper
reporters traveling with the army were impressed. "The heart of the nation will
be thrilled when the news of today reaches it," the *Philadelphia Inquirer*'s
correspondent gushed, "for the tidings will prove that this Virginia campaign
of Grant's, in its finality, is destined to rival those glories which, just a year
ago, he was conferring upon his country upon the heights of Vicksburg."[71]

Grant's soldiers, however, were in no mood for celebrating. "I was pretty
well used up," a Federal admitted. The prospect of starting off again in the
morning set tired men grumbling, although one Yankee took "some comfort
in the thought that the Johnnies had to get up just as early." Another soldier
philosophically noted that this flank movement, "like all the others, is because
we can't walk over Lee's army and must therefore go round it." A Bay Stater
rubbed his blistered feet and reflected that "Virginia distances always were
disappointing." Troops fell asleep without bothering to eat. "We had not had

our clothes off in 24 days," remembered one grimy warrior. "Not a man thought of washing his face, much less of taking a bath; nor is the strain over yet." What made the hardships bearable for many was the possibility that the end might be in sight. "All felt this was about our longest and hardest pull," a tired Union man penned hopefully, "and probably one of the last." A New Yorker seconded the thought. "We believe Lee is outgeneraled," he jotted in his diary, "and his army is soon to be whipped effectively and finally."[72]

Lee's soldiers poured into fields around Hughes' Crossroads all evening, exhausted after their hot and grueling fifteen-mile trek from the North Anna. "Marched very rapidly but few rests and got very tired before night," a footsore rebel noted. The army's artillery pushed on all night to catch up. Portions of road were flooded from recent rains, and an artillerist with the Richmond Howitzers remembered wading for miles through standing water. "And the mud holes!" he wrote. "After a time our gun wheels went up to the hub, and we had to turn to, there in the dark, and prize our guns out; nearly lift them bodily out of the mud. I suppose we did not go more than five or six miles, in that all-night march, and by the time day dawned we were as wet and muddy as the roads, and felt as flat, and were tired to death."[73]

The effort, however, had paid off. The Army of Northern Virginia was positioned precisely as Lee had intended. The head of Ewell's Corps was only three miles from Atlee's Station, and the rest of the army stood massed nearby at Hughes' Crossroads. Confederate cavalry controlled the roads leading east, with Hampton's division at Atlee's Station, Wickham's brigade north of the station at Oakwell, Lomax's brigade at Hanover Court House, and Baker's brigade on Hanover River Road, facing Torbert.[74]

From his headquarters at the Jenkins house, Lee contemplated his next move. Baker's and Johnson's cavalry spats along Hanover River Road and at Dr. Pollard's farm established that Federal cavalry had crossed the Pamunkey in strength. Union infantry was not yet reported, but Lee expected them soon. Intelligence about Grant's likely route after he crossed the Pamunkey remained scanty. Around noon, Fitzhugh Lee reported that Federal cavalry had called off its pursuit and was showing no signs of advancing past Crump's Creek. "I think perhaps it is a demonstration to cover a movement toward Mechanicsville," he ventured, "or by Haw's Shop across both railroads in the direction of Ashland." Later in the day, he reported Union cavalry congregating near Haw's Shop, on Atlee Station Road. This intelligence supported General Lee's suspicion that Grant meant to proceed west from Haw's Shop to Atlee's Station. By evening, rebel scouts still could not confirm whether any Union infantry had crossed the Pamunkey, but Lee had no doubt that a crossing was imminent.[75]

Lee agreed with his nephew's assessment that Grant would most likely come by way of Haw's Shop, but it was still possible that the cavalry buildup there was a diversion to screen a Union advance by way of Hanover Court House. Lee wanted to keep his options open, and he believed that he could best preserve flexibility by shifting the Army of Northern Virginia behind Totopotomoy Creek. Originating northwest of Atlee's Station, the creek flowed generally east and emptied into the Pamunkey southeast of Hanovertown. Along much of its course, the slow-moving creek created broad, marshy floodplains, rendering it eminently defensible. High ground south of the creek—the watershed between Totopotomoy Creek and Beaver Dam Creek—provided a natural line from Shady Grove to Pole Green Church along which to deploy defenses covering not only Atlee Station Road but Grant's other probable routes.

Lee's evening orders directed his soldiers to rest until 3:00 A.M., then start for Atlee's Station. Their object, he stressed, was to "get possession of the ridge between Totopotomoy and Beaver Dam Creek, upon which stands Pole Green Church." Lee also directed Fitzhugh Lee to leave Lomax's brigade at Hanover Court House to cover Hanover River Road and to take his other brigade, under Wickham, to Atlee's Station, uniting with Hampton and concentrating the Confederate cavalry across Atlee Station Road. "I think that we will have enough force to check any cavalry demonstrations the enemy might make," Fitzhugh Lee assured his uncle, adding that he and Hampton would push toward Haw's Shop the next morning to find out what the Federals were doing. While Lee's infantry marched into place along Totopotomoy Creek, his cavalry was to launch a massive reconnaissance-in-force to break Sheridan's cavalry screen and ascertain Grant's precise whereabouts.[76]

That evening, dysentery claimed another highly placed Confederate. Ewell, the mercurial head of Lee's 2nd Corps, became so ill that he had to relinquish command to Jubal Early, his senior division head. Planning to remain near his troops until he recovered, Ewell took up residence at the Satterwaite house, near Hughes' Crossroads. If Lee could sympathize with Ewell on his illness, it nevertheless afforded him a graceful way to be rid of the man. Early was considerably more aggressive than Ewell and had done a commendable job handling the 3rd Corps when Hill was sick. Advancing Early created an opening at the head of a division. Lee awarded the post to Brigadier General Stephen D. Ramseur, a North Carolinian and one of his most promising brigade commanders. He would soon have reason to question the wisdom of the appointment.[77]

III

MAY 28

Sheridan and Hampton Meet at Haw's Shop

"Great is the shovel and spade."

SUNRISE ON SATURDAY, May 28, revealed two armies in motion, each reaching blindly toward the other. Grant's goal was to finish crossing the Pamunkey. An advance force—Torbert's and Gregg's cavalry divisions and Russell's division of infantry—had already secured a bridgehead below the river, extending from Hanovertown to Crump's Creek. The rest of the Union host was preparing to cross at Nelson's Bridge and at Dabney Ferry. A little over ten miles southwest, Lee's soldiers were starting from Hughes' Crossroads. Their objective was Totopotomoy Creek, the first natural barrier below the Pamunkey, where they hoped to draw a defensive line and halt Grant's progress. The fate of Richmond was at stake.

North of the Pamunkey, Wright's men pried themselves from camps around Hornquarter Creek shortly after sunup, marched past McDowell's Millpond, and started southeast toward Nelson's Bridge. Several miles back, near Concord Church on Ridge Road, Hancock's troops shouldered muskets and stepped off, following behind Wright. Warren's men were also on the move, covering the mile from their Dorrell Creek campgrounds to Mangohick Church, then taking the road leading through Enfield and on to Dabney Ferry. In the army's rear, filling the roads behind Warren, came Burnside's soldiers. "The troops moved in three parallel columns, one in and one on each side of the road," an engineer reported, "like three blue rivers sweeping on in their irresistible course towards their destination." Dana's morning report was ecstatic. "Everything goes finely," he informed Washington. "Weather splendid, clear and cool. Troops coming up very rapidly, and in great numbers. The whole army will be beyond the Pamunkey by noon."[1]

Marching men clogged the way to Nelson's Bridge, bringing Wright's col-

umn to a halt. The Vermonter Wilbur Fisk and his comrades took advantage
of the stop to light a roadside fire. "I had just begun to cook my meat when
the order came again to fall in," Fisk recounted. "I loved my breakfast better
than I did the order and concluded to remain and eat it." The regiment's provost marshal took pity on Fisk and his compatriots and let them finish eating.
Threading through a maze of farm roads and shortcuts, the 6th Corps passed
Wyoming Plantation, home of the widow Henrietta Nelson—"a large,
wooden, tumble-down house with a considerable garden and some fine beech
trees nearby," an onlooker noted—and descended a sharp little bluff to the
broad flatland by the river.[2]

The indefatigable bridge-builder Captain William Folwell had received orders at midnight to bring construction materials and workers from Dabney
Ferry to the Nelson's Bridge site and assemble a serviceable pontoon bridge
there by sunup. Folwell reached the crossing at 6:00 A.M. with his trains and
immediately went to work. He had already used most of his decking at Hanovertown and improvised by spacing canvas pontoons on his new bridge farther apart than usual, making an unsteady but functional structure. The head
of Wright's column reached the river around 7:00 A.M. and watched the engineers complete their work. Within the hour, a 146-foot bridge spanned the
river and the 6th Corps was treading across the frail-looking contraption.
Officers ordered men to march out-of-step to keep the bridge from swaying.
A second and sturdier wooden pontoon bridge was erected later in the day.[3]

Warren was also making good time. Griffin's division led the 5th Corps,
followed by Cutler, Crawford, Wainwright's artillery, and the corps's wagons. "Battle flags, equipments, and rifles, reflecting in the light, spoke of the
martial array of war," a soldier remembered. Warren ordered officers to shoot
stragglers and prohibited foraging "upon penalty of death." The 5th Corps
passed Mangohick Church at 6:30 A.M. "with bands playing and men in good
spirits cheering," Lyman noted. Winding south, Warren's soldiers reached
Dabney Ferry at 9:00 A.M. and filed across the two pontoon bridges erected
the previous day.[4]

The movement across the Pamunkey was progressing without incident, but
Meade was worried. Intelligence about the location of the Confederate army
was scant. Meade was confident that Lee had evacuated his North Anna
stronghold, but where he had gone remained a mystery. Sheridan reported
Breckinridge's division at Hanover Court House—erroneously, it developed,
as only cavalry was there—but no information had arrived concerning the
whereabouts of the rest of the rebel force. Frustrated over the absence of concrete intelligence, Meade directed Sheridan to "demonstrate" south toward
Mechanicsville and the Chickahominy River in search of the rebels.[5]

Most of Sheridan's cavalry was occupied protecting the movement of troops across the Pamunkey. Wilson was north of the river, watching the Union army's rear, and Torbert was entrenched along Crump's Creek, guarding against an attack from the direction of Hanover Court House. This left only Gregg, bivouacked near Dr. Brockenbrough's farm, available to reconnoiter. One of Merritt's regiments—the 1st New York Dragoons—was already at Haw's Shop, and Sheridan decided to use the fields around the shop as his staging area. Around 8:00 A.M., he directed Gregg to shift his division to Haw's Shop and hold it there in "readiness to make a reconnaissance."[6]

Gregg, a quiet, heavily bearded Pennsylvanian and professional military man, decided to lead with a brigade under Brigadier General Henry E. Davies, a twenty-eight-year-old New York lawyer with no formal military training who had evolved into a sterling combat officer. During the previous months, Davies had welded a hodgepodge collection of cavalry regiments— the 1st Massachusetts, 1st New Jersey, 1st Pennsylvania, 6th Ohio, and 10th New York—into a formidable force. Accompanying Davies were the 1st Maine, 4th Pennsylvania, and 13th Pennsylvania Cavalry of General Gregg's other brigade, commanded by his first cousin, the hard-case colonel J. Irvin Gregg. Captain Joseph W. Martin's 6th New York Light Artillery also went along. The force numbered slightly over 3,500 men.[7]

General Lee, at his encampment near Hughes' Crossroads, was having second thoughts about how best to deploy the Army of Northern Virginia. Fitzhugh Lee's reports persuaded him that Grant's main thrust would come from Hanovertown through Haw's Shop, then push west to Atlee's Station or south to Mechanicsville. To counter, Lee planned to shift his army into a defensive line along Totopotomoy Creek and its tributaries. News of increased Union activity along Hanover River Road, however, troubled him. Sheridan's advance on May 27 had come west along Hanover River Road, in the direction of Hanover Court House and Peake's Station, on the Virginia Central Railroad. During the evening, rebel scouts had spotted Union infantry—Russell's division—on Hanover River Road as well. This intelligence increased the likelihood in Lee's mind that Grant was planning to move west along Hanover River Road to Hanover Court House, sever the Virginia Central Railroad, then descend south along either the rail line or one of several roads leading toward Richmond. It was also possible, as Fitzhugh Lee continued to argue, that Grant was simply blocking Hanover River Road with cavalry to protect the flank of his moving columns as they passed south to Haw's Shop and on toward Richmond.

Lee decided to continue his army-wide movement through Atlee's Station to Totopotomoy Creek but to make no final deployment until he learned more about Grant's design. He directed Early, now commanding Ewell's corps, to take up a position near Pole Green Church, below Totopotomoy Creek and across the route to Mechanicsville. The rest of the army was to deploy west of Early along Shady Grove Road, ready to shift north or south to block Grant's other possible moves. "In either event," Lee stressed in an early morning dispatch to President Davis, "I shall endeavor to engage [Grant] as soon as possible, and will be near enough to Richmond for General Beauregard to unite with me if possible."[8]

At 3:00 A.M. on May 28, the Army of Northern Virginia started toward Totopotomoy Creek. "I noticed on the march today that the whole column of infantry seem to feel that a battle was immediately impending," a Confederate wrote home. "They marched in such deep silence that a man with his eyes shut would only have known that anyone was on the road by the occasional rattle of a canteen." Early crossed the Virginia Central tracks at Atlee's Station, marched south to Shady Grove, and continued east along Shady Grove Road to high ground around Pole Green Church. Anderson, marching close behind, camped along Shady Grove Road west of Early. Breckinridge and Hill, bringing up the rear, massed near Shady Grove. Part of Hill's corps strung back toward Atlee's Station. The arrangement gave considerable flexibility. If Grant came toward Atlee's Station or Mechanicsville, Lee could shift his army along Totopotomoy Creek in line with Early. If Grant continued along Hanover River Road, Hill and Breckinridge could turn north to counter him there.[9]

Lee, like Grant and Meade, needed reliable intelligence. And like his Union counterparts, he looked to cavalry to get it. While the Army of Northern Virginia marched into place along Totopotomoy Creek, its mounted arm prepared to reconnoiter east from Atlee's Station toward Haw's Shop, seeking to penetrate Sheridan's cavalry screen. Fate had placed the opposing cavalry forces on a collision course.

The venture was the Confederate cavalry's first offensive since Jeb Stuart's death a little over two weeks before. Lee had left his mounted corps without a head while he considered a successor to Stuart. The top contenders were Wade Hampton and Fitzhugh Lee. The forty-six-year-old Hampton was a South Carolina planter and politician with no formal military training. He had organized the Hampton Legion at his own expense at the outbreak of the war and had amassed an impressive combat record. Leadership came naturally to Hampton, he intuitively understood the rhythm of battle, and his grasp of terrain was phenomenal. Handsome, gregarious, and extraordinarily wealthy—he was reputedly one of the richest men in the South—he was con-

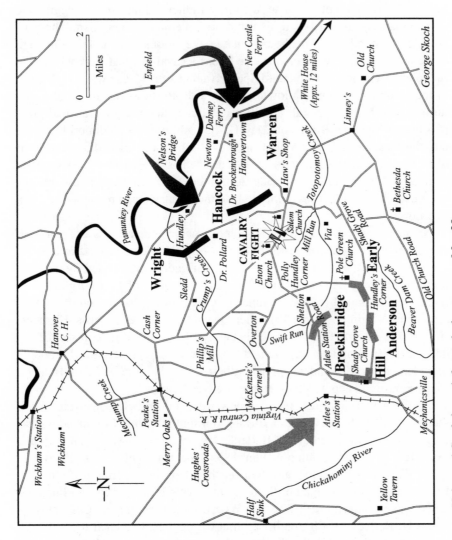

Union and Confederate infantry deployments on May 28

George Skoch

sidered an outsider by the Virginia faction, but his patriotism and martial talents were beyond reproach.

Twenty-eight years old, a massive beard spilling down his chest, Fitzhugh Lee was a West Point graduate, a former Indian fighter, and an aggressive cavalryman. Wags attributed his rapid advancement to nepotism—he was, after all, General Lee's nephew—but the allegations were unfair. Fitzhugh Lee embodied more than anyone else Stuart's cavalier spirit, and his masterful delay of Grant's movement to Spotsylvania Court House was a high point in the campaign. Events following Stuart's death, however, revealed a disturbing side to the general. His flings at independent command had gone poorly—at Meadow Bridge on May 12, he had failed to hold a critical river crossing, and at Wilson's Wharf on May 24, he had attacked a garrison of black troops in an unsuccessful episode derided as "the most useless sacrifice of time and men and horses made during the war." Fitzhugh Lee's bravery was never in doubt, but his ability to lead the cavalry corps remained an open question.[10]

Hampton, as the cavalry corps's senior major general, was nominally in charge of the expedition toward Haw's Shop. He decided to take along a seasoned Virginia outfit called the Laurel Brigade, commanded by Thomas Rosser. Fitzhugh Lee came with Wickham's brigade of four Virginia regiments, and Rooney Lee, also commanding a cavalry division, contributed his brigade of Virginians under Brigadier General John R. Chambliss. Elements from Baker's North Carolina brigade tagged along, as did several sections of horse artillery. Lomax's brigade and Brigadier General Pierce M. B. Young's brigade, temporarily under Colonel Gilbert J. Wright, remained near Hanover Court House to keep watch on Hanover River Road.[11]

Southern recruiters had raised a new mounted brigade consisting of the 4th, 5th, and 6th South Carolina Cavalry during the spring. Commanding was Brigadier General Matthew C. Butler, a lawyer turned cavalryman who had lost a foot at Brandy Station in June 1863. The 5th South Carolina Cavalry, under Colonel John Dunovant, had reached Virginia in time to fight with Beauregard against Benjamin Butler at Drewry's Bluff and to join Fitzhugh Lee on his misadventure at Wilson's Wharf. Its sister regiment, Colonel Benjamin H. Rutledge's 4th South Carolina Cavalry, had reached the Army of Northern Virginia on May 27 and had yet to see combat. Many new men harbored second thoughts about army life. "In Virginia the usual daily allowance to a man was one-third of a pound of bacon and some corn meal, occasionally varied by some wheat flour, there being no coffee, tea, or other stimulant," an officer accustomed to the bounty of South Carolina's Lowcountry complained. Most of the 4th South Carolina Cavalry's camp followers and servants had deserted on the way to Virginia, and the regiment's horses had broken down in distressing numbers, predominantly from galled backs. On May 27, when the regiment reached Atlee's Station, 987 men were present, but only 400 mounts were fit to carry them. Onlookers mistook the 4th South Carolina for a brigade. "South Carolina is a little state," the Carolinians retorted, "but she gets up big regiments."[12]

The night's bivouac at Atlee's Station provided Rutledge's greenhorns occasion to rub elbows with the Army of Northern Virginia's veterans. Seasoned troopers, a soldier in the Charleston Light Dragoons of the 4th South Carolina Cavalry noted, wore gray jackets and generally carried breech-loading carbines captured from their Union opponents. New men, by contrast, wore coarse brown uniforms woven from "homespun" and wielded muzzle-loading Enfield rifles nearly as long as infantry muskets. Veterans ridiculed the Enfield "Long Toms" and joked about how best to adapt the oversized pieces to fighting on horseback. "I say," a Virginian volunteered, "let me have your long shooter and I'll bite off the end." The Charleston Light Dragoons, nattily outfitted in white kid gloves, drew particular ridicule from the hardened warriors.[13]

Early on May 28, Lieutenant Colonel John M. Millen's 20th Georgia Cavalry Battalion reported to Atlee's Station. This 600-man unit had spent most of the war on guard duty in the Deep South and was every bit as green as Butler's South Carolinians. Assuming that Hampton planned to review his troops, Millen showed up at Atlee's Station wearing a new uniform and sash.

Hampton banded the new regiments together for the reconnaissance. General Butler had not arrived, nor had the 6th South Carolina Cavalry. That made Colonel Rutledge senior officer, and Hampton gave him command of the makeshift brigade, consisting of Rutledge's 4th South Carolina Cavalry—headed temporarily by Lieutenant Colonel William Stokes—Dunovant's 5th South Carolina Cavalry, and Millen's 20th Georgia Battalion. Precisely where Rutledge fit into the cavalry corps's chain of command was far from clear. Butler's brigade was formally part of Hampton's division. Hampton, however, exercised general command over the corps and delegated his duties as division commander to his senior brigade head, Thomas Rosser. Rosser assumed that he was in charge of Rutledge, but Fitzhugh Lee, who ranked Rosser, was under the impression that Rutledge was to report to him. The novice Rutledge had no inkling who his boss was and also seemed unsure about his relationship with Millen. Although Hampton had temporarily assigned Millen's Georgians to Rutledge's brigade, the battalion's sergeant Charles P. Hansell recollected that "we seemed then and all through the fight that followed to be acting independently." The ill-defined chain of command was to cause considerable confusion. [14]

Mounting up, Hampton's column, about 4,500 strong, started from Atlee's Station around 8:00 A.M. A few miles east, the road descended to Totopotomoy Creek, then climbed gently to the far crest, passing the gabled home of Colonel Edwin Shelton. Wickham led, followed by Rosser, then by Rutledge's jury-rigged command. Chambliss's brigade brought up the rear. Haw's Shop lay two and a half miles ahead.[15]

"We've got the Yankees where we want them now."

John Haw and his family lived in a well-appointed two-story home called Oak Grove, on Atlee Station Road half a mile west of Haw's Shop. Half a mile farther west stood Enon Methodist Church. The relatively flat terrain from Haw's Shop to Enon Church was prime Virginia farmland crisscrossed by rail fences. Atlee Station Road, bordered on both sides by fences, ran along the backbone of the watershed between Pamunkey River to the north and Totopotomoy Creek to the south. Most of the region's able-bodied men were off fighting Yankees, and weeds choked the once-prosperous fields. The three Haw boys had joined the Army of Northern Virginia, leaving the aged Mr. Haw, his wife, and their twenty-four-year-old daughter at home. Little did the Haws suspect, as the sun rose on May 28, that their farm and the dense stand of woods around Enon Church were about to become the site of a bitterly fought cavalry battle.[16]

At 8:00 A.M., Gregg started his horsemen south from the Brockenbrough farm toward Haw's Shop. Major M. Henry Avery's 10th New York Cavalry, reduced by heavy campaigning to 380 men, led the way. Behind came Colonel John P. Taylor's 1st Pennsylvania Cavalry. At ten o'clock, Avery's troopers reached Haw's Shop and turned west onto Atlee Station Road. Colonel Davies, commanding the brigade, rode ahead and set up headquarters in a grove around the Haw residence, where he busily drafted orders while waiting for the rest of the brigade to arrive. Avery's men dismounted near the house, leaving space nearby for Taylor's Pennsylvanians. As a precaution, Avery directed Captain Martin H. Blynn of the 10th New York to scout west with his squadron. Blynn followed Atlee Station Road through Mr. Haw's wheat field and halted in woods near Enon Church. Forming his troopers into a loose battle line perpendicular to the road, he instructed Lieutenant Truman C. White to continue west with Company D. White rode half a mile to another set of fields, posted a picket line under Sergeant Alfred J. Edson, and continued on toward Atlee's Station with the rest of Company D.[17]

Hampton's Confederates were fast approaching from the opposite direction. Leading was Wickham's brigade, the 2nd Virginia Cavalry in front. Colonel Thomas T. Munford, commanding the regiment, instructed Lieutenant Robert C. Wilson to scout ahead with the regiment's 1st Squadron, an outfit now reduced to some twenty men. Forming his hardened veterans into a compact body, Wilson trotted east.[18]

Sergeant Edson, heading the New Yorkers, caught sight of Lieutenant Wilson's approaching riders in gray. Hurriedly firing a few shots, Edson fled back to White's outpost at the woodline and deployed across the road in hopes of stopping the Confederates. When the southerners rode into view, the New Yorkers opened fire with their seven-shot carbines. Wilson's Virginians raised the rebel yell and charged gamely toward the thin blue line at the edge of the trees. Uncertain about the strength of Wilson's force and unwilling to provoke a full-fledged fight this far from reinforcements, White ordered his men to fall back on Blynn's squadron at Enon Church.[19]

Emboldened, Wilson pursued White back to Blynn's battle line, where the sight of more Yankees brought him up short. Soon, however, Munford and the rest of the 2nd Virginia Cavalry caught up, skewing the numbers in favor of the Confederates. Munford ordered his men to charge the New Yorkers, who retired toward Davies's headquarters at the Haw residence.[20]

The spectacle of Blynn's New Yorkers stampeding into the Haw fields galvanized Davies. Colonel Taylor was just then arriving with his 1st Pennsylvania Cavalry, and Davies ordered him to drive Munford back. "Draw saber!" Taylor shouted to his men. Quickly he deployed his 1st Battalion, under Major R. J. Falls, on the right of the road, and his 3rd Battalion, under Captain William Litzenberg, in the roadway itself. Sharpshooters from the 10th New York steadied themselves against fence posts along the road. "Charge!" Taylor cried as remnants of Blynn's broken command tumbled past. New York sharpshooters opened fire on Munford's advancing column, picking off the foremost riders, and Litzenberg's Pennsylvanians spurred their mounts furiously ahead, intent on meeting the approaching Confederates head-on in the narrow road. The scene, a witness recounted, was "spirited in the extreme."[21]

Taylor's ferocious counterattack caught the Virginians by surprise. Rail fences along both sides of the road funneled the rebels into a tightly packed formation, leaving them no room to maneuver. "Our men, with cheers, were dashing forward, their sabers gleaming in the sunlight," a Union man remembered. The foremost Confederates tried to brace for the impact, but the press of troopers coming from behind pushed them on. Frantic Virginians began tearing down fence rails to get away, but it was too late. Taylor's warriors from the Keystone State slammed into Munford's vanguard in a bloody hand-to-hand melee. "The 1st Pennsylvania never wielded the saber with better effect," an observer claimed. It was the Virginians' turn to break. Crashing through fence rails and over fallen comrades, Munford's riders scattered into the woods west of Enon Church. There they regrouped, dismounting and forming a line across the road. Stacking limbs and fence rails into barriers, they waited for the rest of Wickham's regiments to arrive.[22]

Davies hurried dismounted troopers into line east of Enon Church and placed them perpendicular to Atlee Station Road, facing the Virginians. The 10th New York formed north of the road, its left resting near Enon Church. The 1st Pennsylvania spread south from the 10th New York's left, Litzenberg holding the road and the rest of the regiment extending from his left. Rebels picked off Davies's men with well-directed fire as they moved into place.[23]

Hampton rode up with Fitzhugh Lee and the rest of Wickham's brigade. Scanning the field, he decided to accept Davies's challenge. Wickham's remaining regiments—the 1st, 3rd, and 4th Virginia Cavalry—hurried into place on both sides of the 2nd Virginia, extending the Confederate line well past the ends of the two Union regiments. Rosser arrived next, dismounted his troopers, and marched them northwest along a farm road that ran past Wickham's left flank. Halting, he directed his senior colonel, Richard H. Dulany, to graft the 7th and 11th Virginia Cavalry onto Wickham's formation, running the Confederate line farther north still. Rosser led the rest of his brigade—the 12th Virginia Cavalry and Colonel Elijah V. White's 35th Virginia Battalion, called the "Comanches"—into a clearing near the northern end of his formation. Here he posted Captain William M. McGregor's and Captain Philip P. Johnston's batteries, and a section of John J. Shoemaker's battery.[24]

Hampton had chosen his position well. His dismounted troopers occupied a north-south line perpendicular to Atlee Station Road a short distance west of Enon Church. His left wing, held by Rosser and buttressed by artillery, was anchored on a tree-lined tributary of Crump's Creek half a mile north of Atlee Station Road. Immediately east of Rosser, the tributary veered north and its lowlands formed an impassable marsh. Similarly, half a mile south of the road, a branch of Totopotomoy Creek called Mill Creek provided a firm anchor for the Confederate right wing, held by Wickham. Employing lessons learned in the Wilderness and at Spotsylvania Court House, the Confederates scooped out shallow rifle pits and stacked tree limbs and fence rails into serviceable breastworks. Hampton meant to fight entrenched, inviting the enemy to attack.[25]

The South Carolina grandee examined his formation with approval. Most of the line was hidden in woods, and streams covered both flanks. "The Confederates had the advantage of the forest almost the entire length of the battle line," one of the Haw boys explained years later, "while the Yankees had forest on the right of the road, but field and small scrub pines on the left." Hampton rode up to Colonel White of the 35th Virginia Battalion. "Good morning, Colonel," he announced. "We've got the Yankees where we want them now."[26]

Davies meanwhile sent the 4th and 13th Pennsylvania Cavalry to the northern end of his formation, countering Rosser. The Union line now consisted of the 13th Pennsylvania, 4th Pennsylvania, and 10th New York, right to left north of Atlee Station Road in that order, and the 1st Pennsylvania south of the road. To offset rebel artillery, Gregg stationed Captain Martin's battery north of the road, slightly west of the Haw house, supported by the 1st Massachusetts Cavalry. A second battery, supported by the 1st Maine Cavalry, deployed on Martin's left, near a large, abandoned brick kiln.[27]

The battle taking shape on Mr. Haw's property reflected a tactical development that had revolutionized cavalry warfare in the eastern theater. Mounted charges replete with flashing sabers and pistols had formerly been the order of the day. Close-in combat on horseback still had its place, as the 1st Pennsylvania's repulse of Munford's Virginians had demonstrated. But increasingly, cavalry was acting like infantry, erecting breastworks and fighting dismounted, every fourth man serving as a horse-holder, taking his own horse and three others to the rear. The battle in the wooded, brush-filled terrain around Enon Church looked more like an infantry fight than a traditional cavalry clash.

Davies ordered an advance, but scathing fire from Wickham's and Rosser's Virginians drove the Federals back. Confederates ventured from their barricades in pursuit, only to be repulsed in turn. Isolated battles between small groups of men seesawed back and forth in woods north of the road and in scrubby fields to the south. "It was clearly an unequal contest, so far as numbers were concerned, but never did the regiment display better staying qualities or exhibit more gallantry than on this occasion," a New Yorker claimed. Soldiers crouched behind breastworks, shooting through dense foliage. "The murderous missiles flew so thick and fast that it did not appear possible for anyone to survive," a New Yorker recollected. "The fighting at once assumed the most desperate character," a Pennsylvanian seconded. Troopers fought "at point-blank range, neither able to carry the other's position, but each determined to hold its own." Artillery fired blindly, adding to the chaos.[28]

Resolved to break the impasse, Davies threw the 6th Ohio into the fray.

The fresh troops formed north of the road, between the 10th New York and 4th Pennsylvania, and charged through the woods. Opposing them was Colonel Thomas Marshall's 7th Virginia, of the Laurel Brigade. Captain Delos R. Northway of the 6th Ohio was immediately shot down at the head of his squadron. Two soldiers ran to where he lay—"flat on his back, his feet to the foe, straight as an Indian," an Ohio man recalled—and fell severely wounded. Five more Ohio troopers were hit climbing over a fence, including Lieutenant Josiah E. Wood, who was shot in the chest as he mounted the top rail. A soldier braved the leaden inferno to grab the lieutenant and drag him back. Opening the stricken officer's blouse, he discovered that a ball had struck Wood's breastbone and glanced off, inflicting only a minor wound.[29]

Concerned about the safety of his northern flank, Rosser sent a staff officer to find the 7th Virginia's Colonel Marshall. Locating the colonel in the thick of the battle, the staffer inquired how long he thought he could hold. "Until my last man falls," answered the twenty-eight-year-old grandson of former U.S. Supreme Court chief justice John Marshall. "These Virginians," wrote an observer, "fell back, refilled their cartridge boxes and returned to the front without hesitation."[30]

The battle had degenerated into a brawl where tactics played no discernible part. Troopers on both sides simply hugged the ground and traded fire across a shallow no-man's land, in places only a few hundred yards across, while opposing artillerists waged heated duels. One of White's men guarding the Confederate guns testified that the "storm of shot and shell that howled madly over and around was terrific." George Baylor of the 12th Virginia Cavalry playfully tossed a shell fragment onto a compatriot quivering in terror on the ground. "With a cry of anguish he leaped up, left his horse, ran back through the pines, and all my efforts to stop his retreat were futile," Baylor remembered of the man, who thought he had been hit. Union artillerymen and their supports suffered severely. A shell slammed into the 1st Massachusetts's color bearer and killed him instantly. Cavalrymen from the 1st Maine crouching next to the abandoned kiln watched projectiles whizz past the chimney, threatening to hit it and shower them with bricks. "Shells never scream so fiercely or sound so wickedly as under those conditions," a Maine soldier reminisced. "Men can only think and hope, and their nerves are sorely tried." One of Martin's gunners termed the battle "the hottest musketry fire I have yet been under." The battery lobbed shots over the 10th New York, and a shell exploded prematurely, killing several horses and shattering the leg of the 10th New York's Sergeant James S. Reynolds. "The fellows of that regiment talked hard against us," an artillerist admitted.[31]

Gregg commandeered the Haw house as a hospital. Elderly Mr. Haw, his aged wife, and their daughter Mary huddled in the cellar as the yard filled with wounded Federals and a lone Confederate from the 2nd Virginia shot early in the engagement. Rebel gunners soon found the range. A ball passed through three horses tied to a fence. Another severed an officer's leg and skewered his horse, pitching rider and mount to the ground. "The officer caught hold of the stump of his leg and called to the men to take him to the surgeons," a witness recounted. "Blood spurted in large streams from the stump for a distance of three or four feet."[32]

Surgeon H. K. Clarke of the 10th New York Cavalry set up an emergency ward in one of the Haw outbuildings. Orderlies carried in the regiment's Sergeant Reynolds, whose leg had been badly mangled. As the surgeon began amputating the leg, a shell tore through the door, ricocheted into an overhead beam, dropped to the floor, and rolled under the operating table. Orderlies held their breaths and turned white, expecting an explosion. Clarke had reached a critical stage of the amputation and stood frozen at the table, holding a severed artery. To everyone's relief, the shell's fuse had burned out and the projectile did not explode. "Take that shell out!" Clarke shouted and returned to his work. Concluding that the Haw grounds were too exposed, medical officers ordered the wounded men—except for the Confederate—moved back to Salem Church, which became the new hospital.[33]

Around 11:00 A.M.—the battle had been blazing for an hour—Hampton stepped up the pressure. He had held Rutledge's brigade in reserve on Atlee Station Road, behind Wickham. Stokes's 4th South Carolina was closest to the front, with Millen's Georgians and Dunovant's 5th South Carolina stretched west behind them. It was the first time most of these men had seen combat, and they watched in horror as wounded soldiers hobbled back. Then came a dead lieutenant, his body draped over his horse, blood oozing from a gaping wound. The mood lightened when a shell exploded near a courier and catapulted him into the air. "Getting on his feet in a somewhat dazed condition," a soldier reminisced, "the man looked furtively first on one side and then on the other, as a rabbit might do before springing up, and then bolted back in the direction from which he had ridden, with incredible swiftness, his sabre trailing out behind him almost horizontally." Sergeant Hansell, commanding a platoon in the 20th Georgia Battalion, glanced up to see a cannonball hurtling toward him. Ordering his men down, Hansell gritted his teeth in anticipation of the impact. The shell smacked into a horse and nearly severed the hand of a soldier holding the bridle.[34]

Buffeted by Davies's relentless pounding, some of Wickham's men began dropping out of line. Wickham dashed over and coaxed them back. Fitzhugh Lee, concerned that a concerted Union push might break through, and asked

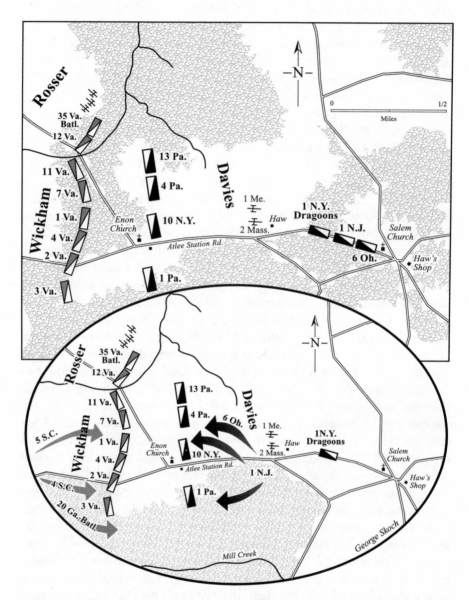

Battle of Haw's Shop, first stage

Hampton for permission to send the 4th South Carolina into the fight. Hampton agreed, and instructions went to Stokes to march across Wickham's rear and form on the Confederate right. Leaving its horse-holders near the road, the 4th South Carolina—reduced now to three hundred men—started off in "good style," a rebel reported, "giving a splendid Confederate battle yell." Union sharpshooters spotted the soldiers marching across a clearing and fired at them, killing three men. One casualty, Percival Porcher, writhed in the trail as his fellow Carolinians stepped over him.[35]

Stokes formed his troopers in woods below Wickham's flank, keeping them low to avoid fire from Union sharpshooters. Hampton, however, decided that Wickham's crisis was over and ordered Stokes back to Atlee Station Road. The South Carolinians retraced their steps under heavy fire and rejoined Millen's and Dunovant's men. "We lay down behind a few scattered rails—not enough to be called a rail pile" a Georgian wrote. "Here [Colonel Millen] walked up and down the line and encouraged the men to keep cool and be ready to receive the enemy warmly."[36]

All morning, while Gregg dueled Hampton, Union infantry filed across the Pamunkey. Wright's soldiers crossed at Nelson's Bridge and traversed Mrs. Hundley's fields, where signs of Custer's and Baker's fight of the previous day were still evident. Turning west on Hanover River Road, Wright formed a defensive line along Crump's Creek, anchoring his corps's northern end on the Pamunkey and bending its southern end back to Dr. Pollard's farm. Neill held the upper portion of the line across Hanover River Road, placing two brigades and three batteries on high ground west of the creek and two brigades east of the stream. Russell came up from his camp at Hanovertown and formed on Neill's left, plugging the road to the Sledd farm, where Colonel Johnson's Marylanders had escaped the previous day. Ricketts's division camped on Dr. Pollard's farm, "Williamsville." Its opulence impressed the Northerners. "We approached this place through long avenues, shaded by the magnolia and catalpa," a Vermonter wrote home, "and the large egg-shaped flowers of the former, and the clusters of smaller trumpet-shaped blossoms of the other, variegated with yellow and purple, loaded the air with delicious fragrance, and filled the scene with the most tranquil beauty, strangely contrasting with the smell of powder."[37]

Entrenching by now had become second nature to the Federals, and they set about ripping down Dr. Pollard's stables, carriage house, and wagon shed, incorporating the lumber into their fortifications. "Great is the shovel and spade," a northerner exclaimed. "I would as soon dig the Rebels out as to fight them." Colonel William H. Moody of the 139th Pennsylvania attributed the digging to cowardice. "The soldiers whose time is nearly out don't like to face the enemy," he fumed. "I know of one regiment whose term expires in a few days, which broke twice during recent battles—a thing it was not accustomed to do. Said one of these men in my hearing, 'I have only eight days to serve, and it will take a long range gun to hit me.'" Most of Wright's soldiers had consumed their rations, and provision wagons had not yet arrived. Everyone complained of hunger.[38]

Through the midmorning, Warren's corps streamed across at Dabney Ferry and deployed in double lines of earthworks on high ground reaching from Mrs. Newton's property by the Pamunkey two miles south to a branch of Totopotomoy Creek. Griffin held the 5th Corps's right, Cutler the middle, and Crawford the left. After inspecting the layout, Warren set up headquarters at Mrs. Newton's house.[39]

Over at Haw's Shop, Gregg was growing concerned. Wickham's Confederates were pressing hard against the center of his line. In desperation, he committed his final reserve—the 1st New Jersey Cavalry of Davies's brigade. Now every available Federal horseman was engaged. Still hoping to wrest the initiative from Hampton, Gregg petitioned for reinforcements. "I sent [Sheridan] word as to how we stood," Gregg reported, "and stated that with some additional force I could destroy the equilibrium and go forward."[40]

Reinforcements were available, but they were not the kind that suited Sheridan's style. Wright's men occupied Dr. Pollard's fields, no more than a mile from the fighting. And the lower end of Warren's line passed just east of Haw's Shop. "All day the sounds of battle raged but a short distance beyond the lines," a 5th Corps soldier confirmed, "so close that occasionally shells intended for the active combatants fell among the unoffending soldiers of Griffin's division." Sheridan, however, was confident that his troopers could whip the rebel horsemen by themselves. He did not want to dilute their accomplishment by bringing foot soldiers into the fray and declined to ask for assistance.[41]

Sheridan's reluctance to accept infantry reinforcements meant that Gregg had to do his best with the men at hand. Sheridan's other division, under Wilson, was still north of the Pamunkey, and Torbert's division was in the process of turning over its Crump's Creek defenses to Wright. Rather than give the rebels more time to dig in, Gregg decided to renew his assaults. He ordered Colonel John W. Kester, commanding the 1st New Jersey, to dispatch a company to each end of the Union line as videttes and divided the rest of his regiment into two wings. Captain Walter R. Robbins took four New Jersey companies north of Atlee Station Road to support the 10th New York, and

Captain Hugh H. Janeway deployed the rest of the regiment south of the road, supporting Taylor's Pennsylvanians.[42]

Gregg's troopers were understandably cool to the idea of charging Hampton's entrenchments. "I stood in the midst of the dead and dying while the little missiles battered against the trees and logs and cut the twigs on every side," Captain Noble D. Preston of the 10th New York remembered. "An aide arrived from General Gregg, saying the line must be advanced. He ducked his head while the bullets whistled past, and shrugged his shoulders as he started for the rear, stating, 'Those are the orders.'"[43]

Robbins went forward under a hail of artillery and musketry. Reaching the front, he discovered a disturbing situation. Confederates had punched ahead north of Atlee Station Road, forcing the 10th New York to bend back its upper flank a few hundred yards. This created a gap between the New Yorkers and the 4th Pennsylvania to the north that endangered the entire Union position. Robbins set about trying to recover lost ground and rectify the Union line. Dense woods and gunsmoke hid the Confederates, but Robbins estimated their location by the sound of their firing. Riding through thick foliage, he found scattered pockets of refugees from the 10th New York and ordered them back into formation. Ruthlessly he pushed men into the maelstrom, venting his "towering rage" on anyone who fell behind, striking skulkers and berating them for cowardice. When a "tremendous volley" erupted in front, one of Robbins's subordinates, Captain Garrett V. Beekman, turned as though he intended to retreat. "Back to your place, Captain," Robbins roared, and the Jersey troopers charged ahead, driving the Confederates over a fence, across a gully, and back to another fence along the farm road slanting northwest from Enon Church. "It was every man for himself," a New Jersey soldier remembered, "and from behind trees, stumps and the fence we poured a heavy fire upon the rebels behind a fence scarcely 30 yards away." Hoping to redeem his standing with Robbins, Beekman led a party into the gully in front of the Confederates. Discharging their breech-loading carbines as fast as they could squeeze the triggers, they silenced the rebels at the fence and charged exultantly into Wickham's line. The advance faltered as Virginians fired from the front and both sides. Falling back across the gully, Beekman's men rallied at their own fence. "Thus the time passed on," stated the 1st New Jersey's historian, "both parties holding their own, and neither gaining ground upon the other."[44]

Robbins's offensive north of Atlee Station Road persuaded Fitzhugh Lee that the Federals had weakened the southern portion of their line. Turning to Stokes, Lee ordered him to "relieve that Virginia brigade and hold that wood." Colonel Rutledge, nominally in charge of the South Carolina brigade, later complained that he was "left literally without command except of the led horses."[45]

Once again the 4th South Carolina Cavalry marched behind Wickham, raised the rebel yell, and charged east. A ravine split the regiment. Stokes remained with the larger section on Wickham's right flank, adjoining the 3rd Virginia, and began trading volleys with Taylor's Pennsylvanians no more than fifty yards away. Captain Thomas Pinckney led the 4th South Carolina's smaller wing—comprising the 2nd Squadron and the Charleston Light Dragoons, under 1st Lieutenant Lionell C. Nowell—into a branch of the ravine south of Stokes. In places, Virginians and South Carolinians fought intermixed. The battle degenerated into brutal blind-fighting in the forest. Smoke and trees hid the antagonists from view. "Most of the shots had to be snaps, fired at faces only for a second thrust from behind a tree, or peering round a bush," a dragoon recounted, "or at the rifle flashes, which were sending the lead zipping and singing through the air like devil's bumblebees." The dismounted South Carolinians held their own against the Union veterans. "This continued for three-quarters of an hour," a witness recorded, "the battle raging at its highest pitch conceivable, without intermission or cessation, but one continual roar of musketry, it seeming impossible that a man could escape."[46]

Hampton ratcheted up his firepower by committing Dunovant's 5th South Carolina to the fight. Dunovant's men joined Wickham's troopers north of Atlee Station Road and fired at patches of blue uniform visible through the pall. "The storm of lead became terrible," a New Yorker recalled. "It was at times the hottest place I ever was in. I had participated in engagements of greater magnitude, but never did I encounter in so short a space of time so much of desperate fighting." Dense undergrowth, a southerner noted, "served as a screen but not as a shelter." He remembered a "rough-and-tumble affair, frequently carried on in thick cover, much in the Indian style." Killing Yankees, a Carolina boy mused, resembled hunting squirrels and birds back home. Dunovant suffered a debilitating hand wound, but his men fought on.[47]

Judging that Taylor's Pennsylvanians could keep Stokes occupied, Colonel Kester shifted Major Janeway north of Atlee Station Road to stem Dunovant's onslaught. The battle now swirled around the New Jersey troops and Avery's New Yorkers. Jersey men fired as fast as they could load, ran low on ammunition, and sent back for more. Union officers fell at an alarming pace. Captain Beekman passed out cartridges along the firing line until a rebel bullet ripped two fingers from his right hand. Lieutenants John W. Bellis and Alexander Stewart fell mortally wounded. A New Jersey private, nursing a grudge against Robbins for accusing him of cowardice, shot the captain in the shoulder as he stood to lead a countercharge. A ball grazed Janeway's forehead, and Lieutenant Joseph Brooks, whose New Jersey squadron was north of the road with Janeway, stood to lead a charge when a ball tore through his belly and knocked him thirty feet. Ignoring the gaping hole in his abdomen, Brooks stood, ordered his men forward, advanced a short distance, and collapsed. Unaccustomed to combat Virginia-style, Dunovant's soldiers also took serious casualties. A Jersey man later remarked that they "showed their inexperience by continually half-rising to fire or to look at our line, thus giving our men an opportunity of which our marksmen took instant and fatal advantage." A combination of bravery and inexperience, he noted, turned the South Carolinians' position into a "perfect slaughter house, preventing them from making any dash at our weaker front."[48]

South of the road, Taylor's Pennsylvanians buckled under Wickham's and Stokes's pounding. Kester rode to Taylor's assistance with a three-company squadron of Jersey men under Captain Moses M. Maulsbury. Reinforced, the 1st Pennsylvania attacked and broke part of Wickham's line. Virginians streamed rearward "so fast as to be almost a run," a witness observed. Fitzhugh Lee ordered Millen's 20th Georgia Battalion into the fight south of the road, where it mixed with Stokes's and Wickham's commands. "I had a fine opportunity of looking around and noting the effect of this first taste of battle on the men," the Georgian Hansell recollected. "Most of them stood it all right, but some few were so badly rattled that they had no idea where they were going or what they were doing." Hansell noted that "in one or two instances no attention was paid to the calls, commands, or curses of their officers." Bullets from Pennsylvania and New Jersey soldiers converged on the Georgians, but they stubbornly stood their ground. "Our line did not give way," asserted Hansell, "but halted to face the fire and took advantage of every shelter they could." The New Jersey troopers took fearful losses. Captain Maulsbury fell mortally wounded, his successor Lieutenant Vorhees Dye was killed, and command devolved on Sergeant Thomas S. Cox, who fought on despite a wound to his back.[49]

Davies was at his stirring best, riding along the battle line with his staff and "animating the men and so disposing the forces as to strengthen the weakest portions of the line." A ball clipped his saber in half, and another shot sliced off part of his horse's tail. Two of Davies's aides were wounded in a volley that also killed the popular Lieutenant W. W. Wardell of his staff. Colonel Gregg also plunged into the thick of the fight, keeping his composure even when a shell bored into the ground under his horse. "The musketry was very heavy," a correspondent wrote, "and as incessant for a time as the volleys between infantry in regular line of battle."[50]

Still Hampton held. Sheridan's attempts to break through, a New Yorker noted, had met with "sickening failure."[51]

"Had to cut our way out."

Shortly after noon, Hancock's 2nd Corps started over the twin pontoon spans at the Nelson's Bridge site. Grant and Meade, who had crossed during the morning at Dabney Ferry, came to watch. "Grant looked tired," an artillerist noted. "He was sallow. He held a dead cigar firmly between his teeth. His face was as expressionless as a pine board. He gazed steadily at the enlisted men as they marched by, as though trying to read their thoughts, and they gazed intently at him. He had the power to send us to our deaths, and we were curious to see him. But the men did not evince the slightest enthusiasm. None cheered him, none saluted him."[52]

Turning onto the road to Dr. Pollard's farm, Hancock's corps marched behind Wright's entrenchments and took up a line on the 6th Corps's left. Gibbon's division occupied Dr. Pollard's farm, sharing the fields with Ricketts. Barlow formed on Gibbon's left, and Birney carried the line to its terminus behind Salem Church, following a ridge that paralleled the road from Dr. Pollard's place to Haw's Shop. Union engineers designated earthworks to run through the Pollard family cemetery. Dr. Pollard's wife was buried there, and the doctor asked the engineers to avoid disturbing her grave. When they ignored his entreaties, he appealed to Hancock, who had set up headquarters in his yard. "Certainly I will have [the line] changed," the general promised, and he directed the engineers to curve the breastworks around the cemetery. Little Harry Pollard later called the sector of entrenchments adjoining the cemetery a "monument to General Hancock's kindness."[53]

On the far side of Totopotomoy Creek, Lee was rearranging his troops. At 10:30, Early had reached Hundley's Corner, at the intersection of Shady Grove Road and the road running north to Totopotomoy Creek and Polly Hundley Corner (not to be confused with Hundley's Corner, two miles south on Shady Grove Road). "This is the point from which General Jackson commenced his famous attack on McClellan's flank and rear, in 1862, and it was very important that it should be occupied, as it intercepted Grant's direct march toward Richmond," Early later observed. Lee was becoming increasingly concerned that Grant might be massing his army behind Sheridan's cavalry screen at Haw's Shop. If that were the case, Federal troops would be poised to march south from Haw's Shop, cross Totopotomoy Creek well east of Early, and swing southwest toward Richmond along roads leading through

Mechanicsville. To block such a move, Lee directed Early to string his corps south across Old Church Road, a major route paralleling Shady Grove Road about a mile to the south.[54]

Early's proximity at Pole Green Church intrigued Hampton. It would be a simple matter, the cavalryman surmised, for Early to cross Totopotomoy Creek and join the battle at Haw's Shop. "Whilst the fight was going on," Hampton later wrote, "I suggested to General Early, who was stationed at Pole Green Church, to move down in the direction of Old Church [east] and there by turning to his left to gain the rear of the force opposed to me." Early rejected Hampton's plan. By crossing Totopotomoy Creek, he would put himself on the same side of the stream as the Federals, isolated like Hampton from the rest of the Confederate army. He was not about to lead his corps to destruction.[55]

Now that most of the Union army was across the Pamunkey, Torbert could leave his defensive line along Crump's Creek to the 6th Corps and assist Gregg. Sheridan immediately ordered him to Haw's Shop. Threading past Dr. Pollard's farm, Torbert's three brigades rode into the Haw intersection and turned right on Atlee Station Road. Merritt's Reserve Brigade massed behind Gregg's right. Devin sent the 17th Pennsylvania to Gregg's right and deployed the rest of his brigade at Haw's Shop as a reserve. Near four o'clock—the nasty brawl around Enon Church and the Haw fields had been continuing unabated for six hours—Custer rode into Haw's Shop at the head of his Wolverines.[56]

Hampton was also receiving reinforcements. As Torbert moved into place behind Gregg, Rooney Lee arrived with John Chambliss's brigade of three Virginia regiments. To counter the Union buildup, Hampton directed Rooney Lee to dismount Chambliss's men, march them to the northern Confederate flank, throw out skirmishers, and "turn the right flank of the enemy if he could do so." Accompanied by McGregor's artillery, Chambliss's fresh Confederates formed north of the tributary of Crump's Creek, on Rosser's left, and headed east, careering into Merritt's troopers moving onto the northern end of the Union line. Dismounted horsemen from the 6th Pennsylvania Cavalry—Rush's Lancers—attacked Chambliss's skirmishers and drove them back, but McGregor's guns held the Pennsylvanians at bay while Chambliss fortified his position. Union guns—Lieutenant Edward B. Williston's Battery D, 2nd United States Artillery—pulled up in support of Merritt, and a fierce artillery barrage shook the battlefield's northern sector. Mistaking dismounted Pennsylvanians for infantry, Rooney Lee informed Hampton that an overwhelming Federal infantry force had attacked him. He was in no shape to fight infantry, he added, and he feared that the enemy might turn his flank. He requested permission to withdraw.[57]

Custer's Michiganders—they mustered just under a thousand men for the fight—came under Confederate artillery fire as they turned west onto Atlee Station Road. Halting behind Gregg, Custer dismounted his troopers and formed two battle lines perpendicular to the road, facing the Confederates. Colonel Stagg's 1st Michigan and Major Kidd's 6th Michigan spread north of the road, while Captain Magoffin's 5th Michigan and Major Walker's 7th Michigan deployed to the south. Custer was at his flamboyant best. "Cannon were raining grape and canister into our ranks and fresh troops pushing forward with a shock," Kidd remembered of those moments. Galloping in front of the 6th Michigan, the golden-haired general waved his hat overhead and called for three cheers. His men shouted back loudly, the brigade band struck up "Yankee Doodle," and Custer gave the order to charge.[58]

Colonel Kester was still with his New Jersey troopers south of the road. As Custer's Wolverines marched up, Kester swung back the right of his line to open a gap for them to pass through. Thinking Kester was retreating, a detachment of Millen's Georgians charged east along the road, took cover behind fences, and began shooting into Kester's flank. Their fire also tore into the 5th and 7th Michigan, whose advance south of the road had been slowed by a stand of small pines. "A perfect hell of fire and smoke broke from the rebel works," Sergeant James H. Avery of the 5th Michigan recollected. "Even the air we breathed seemed thick with lead and sulphur. It did not seem possible for balls to fly thicker." The 5th Michigan lost fifty men in minutes.[59]

Blistered by volleys from Wickham and Stokes in front and Millen's deadly enfilade from the road, the Michigan troopers halted and began raking the Georgians with their seven-shot carbines. Several New Jersey soldiers between the Wolverines and Georgians got caught in the fire. Mistaking the mounted Kester for a Confederate officer, Custer's troopers shot his horse and riddled his coat with bullets. Kester emerged unscathed. The regimental chaplain reported the colonel's coat "so torn that his escape appeared miraculous." The Georgians on the road were all killed, wounded, or captured, according to the 1st New Jersey's historian.[60]

Custer made a conspicuous figure on horseback leading the dismounted 6th Michigan in an impetuous charge north of Atlee Station Road. The Wolverines laid down a carpet of bullets that dramatically magnified their numbers. "Each of these Spencer breech-loading rifles would shoot seven times without reloading, and they could be fired all seven times and reloaded while

the Confederate cavalryman was reloading his musketoon with just one cartridge," a southerner complained. "Long Tom" Enfields, however, had better
range than the carbines, and the South Carolinians ruthlessly exploited this
advantage. "The sound of their bullets sweeping the undergrowth was like
that of hot flames crackling through dry timber," a Federal recalled. Custer's
horse was shot from under him, for the seventh time in battle. His aide-de-
camp, Lieutenant James I. Christiancy, was wounded twice and lost his horse,
and a spent bullet hit his acting assistant adjutant general, Captain James L.
Green, on the head. The 6th Michigan was reduced by a quarter in ten minutes.[61]

Just when the Wolverines faced extinction at the hands of the Lowcountry
marksmen, the Confederate defense faltered. Persuaded by Rooney Lee that
Union infantry was massing near his northern flank, Hampton authorized
Chambliss's withdrawal. As Chambliss fell back, the 6th Pennsylvania Cavalry and the 1st New York Dragoons moved into the vacuum, placing a strong
Federal force across Rosser's left flank. Enfiladed, Rosser had to withdraw.
which in turn exposed Wickham's northern flank, compelling him to retire.
Most of Wickham's men retreated in good order, as did the 5th South Carolina and the 4th South Carolina's left wing, under Colonel Stokes. Couriers
sent to warn Millen's Georgians, the portion of the 4th South Carolinian
under Pinckney, and elements of the 2nd Virginia of Wickham's brigade,
failed to get through. A captain in the 2nd Virginia exacerbated the confusion
by emerging through swirling gunsmoke to assure Pinckney—incorrectly, it
developed—that Wickham was still in place and that there was "no danger of
our being flanked." While Confederates north of Atlee Station Road dropped
back, pockets of unsuspecting rebels south of the road maintained their bitter
fight against rapidly mounting odds.[62]

Slackening fire north of the roadway alerted Custer that Hampton was
pulling out, and he immediately ordered the 1st and 6th Michigan to advance.
Charging ahead, Stagg's and Kidd's troopers overran the remaining Confederates in their front. The move placed Custer north of Millen and Pinckney.
"Balls came singing by, not only from the front but from the left flank, and
the line to our left began to double back until it was nearly at right angles to
us," a Georgian related. "We were outflanked and exposed to a terrific crossfire," a South Carolinian agreed. To snuff out this last pocket of resistance,
Custer ordered the rest of his brigade to charge. The 5th and 7th Michigan
punched headlong into Millen's and Pinckney's isolated fragments.[63]

Lieutenant Nowell of the Charleston Light Dragoons first realized his predicament when a frantic Confederate officer reported Federals streaming past
the Dragoons' left flank. Fitzhugh Lee discovered what had happened and

sent a courier, Sergeant John Gill, into the melee to alert Millen and Pinckney to leave. Spurring his horse through a torrent of bullets, Gill rode into the ranks of the Charleston Light Dragoons. "Right about face," he screamed. "Double quick, march!" Hampton also ventured into the woods to help lead the men out. Under his guidance, they fell back into a field and temporarily rallied behind a rail fence. "The presence of Hampton, calm, cool, and reassuring, had braced everyone up," a participant stated. "I rode in and brought them out," Hampton wrote simply, "but not without a heavy loss." Some Georgians stubbornly stood their ground and were captured. Others worked rearward from tree to tree to avoid detection. "We all gave back," a Georgian reminisced, "were rallied to the old line, but could not hold it." Millen tried to shore up his formation by directing a detachment of mounted soldiers into the fight but was shot and killed. "There was a scarcity of officers at this point," observed Sergeant Hansell, who remembered a lone Virginia colonel passing along the line.[64]

Propelled by the momentum of their breakthrough, Custer's victorious Wolverines pressed ahead, shooting into fleeing Confederates. Gregg's fought-out troopers joined the chase. Captain Charles F. Wolcott of the 6th Ohio Cavalry saw a felt hat lying on the ground and picked it up. The left rim was looped up against the crown and fastened with a metal South Carolina button displaying a palmetto tree, a coiled serpent, and a Latin inscription. A bullet had passed through the crown, and pieces of dark hair clotted the exit hole. Wolcott tried on the hat. It fit, so he wiped the former owner's hair from the bullethole, cut off the button, and resumed the pursuit wearing his new headgear.[65]

Hampton's withdrawal dissolved into a rout. "On their hands and knees, afraid to stand upright, [Confederates] scrambled with wonderful rapidity through the grass and underbrush," a New Jersey man claimed. "Had to cut our way out," a soldier in the 2nd Virginia confirmed. Sergeant Hansell of the Georgia Battalion saw Lee Bacon of his platoon tearing through trees, blood streaming from an ugly chest wound. Bacon's brother was trying to get the wounded man to safety and beseeched Hansell to "make a stand" to buy time for them to escape. "The idea of one man making a stand when the whole Battalion had been unable to do so struck me as so ridiculous that I could hardly keep from laughing," recounted Hansell. Discovering popular Sergeant Ben Huger missing, soldiers from the Charleston Light Dragoons rode back and found him wounded in the shoulder. They helped him to a field hospital, where he refused to relinquish his pistol, claiming he might need it to fend off surgeons if they tried to amputate his arm.[66]

Zigzagging through trees, Captain Pinckney found himself staring into

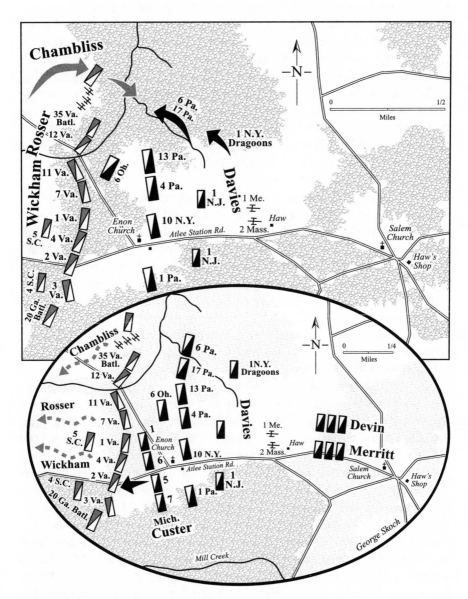

Battle of Haw's Shop, second stage

carbines held by two officers and a private from the 7th Michigan Cavalry. Pinckney surrendered to Lieutenant James H. Ingersoll, who demanded his sword. The sword had belonged to Pinckney's grandfather, a Revolutionary War hero and signer of the Declaration of Independence, and he refused to surrender the heirloom. Unclasping Pinckney's belt, Ingersoll drew out the sword and examined it. Noticing the weapon's curved blade, Ingersoll announced his preference for a straight blade and handed his own sword to Pinckney to heft. Ingersoll added that he would keep Pinckney's sword and return it after the war. The southerner rejoined that he hoped to meet Ingersoll before then and get his sword back. "It must have afforded an interesting sight to lookers on," Pinckney later mused, "to observe us during this parley, brandishing each other's sabres."[67]

At 5:00 P.M., as Hampton's line was unraveling, General Lee sent an urgent dispatch to Breckinridge. "I wish you would place your troops on the road from [Atlee's Station] to Haw's Shop (or Salem Church) to guard that road," he directed. "The enemy is at Haw's Shop, and may take our troops in reverse." Breckinridge marched onto Atlee Station Road, deployed along Totopotomoy Creek across the road, and began digging entrenchments. "There were few, if any spades or shovels," one of Breckinridge's soldiers remembered, "but the men split their canteens, making scoops of them, and, together with the bayonets and their hands, for the soil was light and sandy, soon had a very respectable earthwork thrown up." Hampton would have strong support to fall back on.[68]

Any organized semblance of combat was over by 6:00 P.M. Hampton's frazzled troopers retraced their morning's march, crossed Totopotomoy Creek, and passed through Breckinridge's line to safety. Breckinridge's formidable position curtailed further pursuit. Stray muzzle flashes sparked through the night, reminding a soldier in the 9th Virginia Cavalry of fireflies. A Union artillerist visiting the Haw fields near dark remarked on the large number of dead cavalrymen. "The poverty of the south was plainly shown by the clothing and equipment of her dead," he reflected. "There were ancient and ferocious-looking horse-pistols, such as used to grace the Bowery stage, lying by the dead Confederates." That night, while looking for water, the artillerist stumbled on corpses in the woods. "I struck a match so as to see one of these men plainly, and was greatly shocked to see large black beetles eating the corpse," he wrote. "I looked at no more dead men that night."[69]

The Battle of Haw's Shop, as the fight around Enon Church came to be called, had been a vicious affair. Sheridan considered it a "hard contested engagement, with heavy loss, for the number of troops engaged, to both sides." Numbers bore him out. The battle cost the Confederates about 378 men. Some veteran brigades got off lightly, Rosser losing 33 men and Chambliss 25. Wickham, who was more heavily engaged, reported 12 killed, 64 wounded, and 10 missing, for a total of 86 losses. The new regiments paid a heavy price. The 5th South Carolina recorded 31 casualties. The 4th South Carolina was gutted, losing 127 of the 300 troopers who went into action, including, Stokes lamented, "some of our most valuable and gallant officers and men." The 20th Georgia Battalion lost its colonel, its major, a captain, two lieutenants, and about 80 soldiers. "Most of our loss is attributable to the fact that nearly all the force engaged on our part were new men," a Richmond reporter observed, "whose only idea was to go in and fight, which they [did] most gallantly and creditably." Sheridan's casualties were almost identical to Hampton's. Gregg's division, which bore the brunt of the fighting, lost 30 officers and 220 men. Custer, who was engaged only a short time, lost 6 officers and 109 men. "Our loss in this battle," Custer conceded in his report, "was greater than in any other engagement of the campaign."[70]

Everyone praised the South Carolinians. Acknowledging their "desperate courage," Davies thought they had been simply "too inexperienced to know when they had suffered defeat, and continued to resist long after it was apparent that the position they held was turned and efforts to maintain it were hopeless." One of Gregg's troopers saluted them as the "most desperate fighters that we had encountered among the Southern cavalry." The Charleston Light Dragoons, derided by veterans as effete dandies just the day before, had proved their worth. "No more was heard about that 'kid-gloved company,'" a Confederate asserted, "and often delicate little compliments were paid in yielding to the 'Drags' particularly hot spots and lonely picket posts."[71]

Both sides claimed victory. Sheridan boasted that he had broken Hampton's line and driven him from the field. Jubilant Union cavalrymen viewed the battle as affirmation of their superiority, another victory in an unbroken string of successes since Yellow Tavern. Northern newspapers praised Sheridan. "He appears to keep himself so thoroughly informed as to know just how many men to send in to win a fight," a correspondent effused, "or else he is endowed with intuitive judgment in this respect, for he always wins." But in important respects, Hampton had come out ahead. He had thwarted Sheridan's objective of locating Lee's army and had achieved his own goal of determining Grant's whereabouts. He had also scooped up prisoners from the Union 5th and 6th Corps—probably scouts or pickets, since the cavalry battle did not reach Union infantry lines—confirming Lee's hunch that Grant was across the Pamunkey in strength. The battle "resulted in unmasking and locating the enemy's infantry at a very critical period of the campaign," a southern writer argued, "inflicted severe losses upon [the enemy's] cavalry, which materially checked them for the future, and above all had convinced friend and foe that dismounted Confederate troopers would fight against vastly superior numbers with the stubborn tenacity of infantry."[72]

Commanders on both sides had stumbled badly. The Union high command had missed a superb opportunity. For eight hours, the cream of the Confederate cavalry stood isolated on the Union side of Totopotomoy Creek, ripe for plucking. Several roads circled behind Hampton, yet Sheridan eschewed maneuver and concentrated on frontal assaults, leaving the Confederates a clear escape route. Incredible as it may seem, Grant and Meade never dispatched infantry to snag the rebel cavalry, even though portions of the Union 2nd, 5th, and 6th Corps were entrenched within a mile of the battle. "I could not convince Meade that anything but the enemy's horse was fighting us," Sheridan claimed years later in his memoirs, "and he declined to push out the foot-troops, who were much wearied by night marches." Sheridan's official report mentions nothing about requesting infantry support, however, and no such request written by Sheridan during the battle exists. Sheridan's postwar claim smacks of fabrication inspired by his contempt for Meade and perhaps by second thoughts about whether he had missed the chance for a more decisive victory.[73]

Hampton also made mistakes. His determination to stand and fight on the Union side of Totopotomoy Creek, miles from reinforcements, unnecessarily risked the destruction or capture of his force. Had Sheridan thrown in his entire corps, he would have outnumbered Hampton better than two to one. As the day progressed and the Army of the Potomac filed across the Pamunkey, Hampton's situation became breathtakingly precarious. In retrospect, Hampton got away only because the Federals failed to exploit the opportunity he afforded them. A Georgian wrote home that Butler (who himself never made it to the battle) later "cursed Fitzhugh Lee, who commanded the fight in person, for everything he could think of—told him he was a fool for making the fight with so few men." In fact, Hampton had been in charge, not Fitzhugh Lee, and Butler's curses more appropriately applied to him. "I did not then and do not now see that there was any point in pushing the attack as our cavalry did," the Confederate army's chief engineer, Martin Smith, wrote his wife the next day, "as all that is required of them is to warn of the enemy's approach or movements."[74]

Hampton had managed the details of the fight with an unsure hand. The battle was a slugging match between closely entrenched forces, bereft of grand strategy and tactics. Content with holding a defensive line and inviting attack, Hampton missed superb opportunities to turn Davies's flanks early on, when he held a comfortable numerical edge. And he gave subordinate commanders too much latitude. His acquiescence in Rooney Lee's ill-advised request to withdraw almost proved his undoing, as it forced brigades on Lee's right to retire seriatim, rendering the entire Confederate line untenable. "We had a strong position and could have held it until now," Rosser told one of the Haw boys fifteen years after the battle, "but 'Rooney' Lee reported that the infantry was coming up on his flank and he could not hold his position longer, and the whole line was, therefore, ordered to withdraw." Hampton blamed his line's collapse on the "too sudden withdrawal of Wickham's Brigade, by which a gap was left in the center of the line and the flank brigades were thus exposed." Neither scenario casts him in a favorable light. He alone was responsible for deciding which brigades to pull back and for ensuring the integrity of his formation. His unintentional abandonment of units on the southern end of his line spoke poorly of his stewardship.[75]

Despite Hampton's fumbling, his troopers were impressed. He understood the efficacy of earthworks and he stood up to Sheridan, giving as good as he took, falling back only when no other choice remained. Confederates could speak of the fight at Haw's Shop with pride, something they could not do of their recent drubbings at Yellow Tavern, Meadow Bridge, and Wilson's Wharf. The Army of Northern Virginia's cavalry corps needed a commander who gave it prospects of winning. Haw's Shop suggested that Hampton was that general. "The men of his corps soon had the same unwavering confidence in him that the 'Stonewall Brigade' entertained for their general," a cavalryman later observed. Haw's Shop was a learning experience for Hampton. He was an attentive student, and time would show that he had learned well.[76]

A weary Union army settled into camp. Except for Burnside's corps, slated to arrive late that night, the Army of the Potomac was across the Pamunkey. "There was much suffering among the troops," a Pennsylvanian noted. "Hundreds of private soldiers could be seen the previous two or three days wending their way over the scorching, sandy roads with sorely blistered bare feet, unable to wear shoes, caused by wading the streams and marching over the sand and stones, and the bruises incident to the severe campaign." A man in the Iron Brigade observed simply that "men are nearly dead from pure exhaustion."[77]

Near dark, Meade ordered Brigadier General Nelson A. Miles to move his 2nd Corps brigade "as rapidly as possible" to Haw's Shop. The cavalry battle was over by then, and the gesture was meaningless. Miles's aide, Captain Robert S. Robertson, rode to Haw's Shop and spied Sheridan's headquarters flag in a fence corner. Officers in shirtsleeves were discussing the merits of boiled chicken. Robertson asked for Sheridan. "I am your man," volunteered a short figure brandishing a chicken leg. Robertson explained that Miles was on his way. "Glad to see you, with that news," Sheridan replied. "Get down and have some chicken." Miles's brigade shuffled up, relieved Sheridan's pickets, and began entrenching. Sheridan's troopers retired several miles east toward Old Church to recuperate from the day's fight.[78]

Grant and Meade made their headquarters near Dr. Nelson's home, next to Nelson's Bridge. Grant's aide Comstock remarked that several young ladies lived there—"strongly secesh," he recorded, "but polite." That evening, Grant and Meade visited Warren at Mrs. Newton's house, a two-story frame building with porches on both sides. The widow Newton was there—Lyman judged her to be thirty-five—as was her aunt, Mrs. Brockenbrough, who struck Lyman as a "conceited, curious, sallow, middle-aged woman itching to 'tackle' a Northerner." She tried to "catechize" Grant, Lyman noted, "with an eager relish—who replied with entire calmness and candor, whereat she was plainly taken aback, as she looked for a volley of gasconade!" Wounded cavalrymen filled Mrs. Newton's slave quarters and spilled into Dr. Brockenbrough's yard next door. The good doctor had been away when the Federals came, and his wife and daughter Judith found themselves unwilling hosts to the invaders. He finally got a pass from a Union surgeon authorizing him to return home. A Pennsylvanian declared him a "real specimen of Secesh." Settling into a hilltop encampment near Mrs. Newton's house, an aide took in the scene. "White tents are scattered here and there, and, occasionally, the flashing of long lines of steel, reflecting the rays of the sun, betray the march of columns from point to point," he wrote. "Success to our arms, a beautiful spring day, lovely scenery, unusually good music by the band at headquarters, and a happy heart make this a red-letter day."[79]

It was also a red-letter day for Mrs. Newton's slaves. During McClellan's occupation in 1862, three Newton slaves—a father and two sons—had escaped to the Union army. The younger son stayed with the army as a headquarters servant and now found himself once again at the plantation. His mother, grandmother, and innumerable relatives were overjoyed to see him. News spread of the Federals' arrival, and slaves poured in from surrounding plantations. "Hundreds of contrabands of all sexes, ages, and condition flock into our lines like crows, and beg our protection," a correspondent observed.[80]

Union soldiers, tired as they were, considered Grant's bold maneuver across the Pamunkey a ringing success. "I expect we have stolen quite a march on Mr. Lee, as we are only about 18 miles from Richmond and we left him quietly in the night, very busy fortifying himself on the Little River and at last accounts he was still at work at it," a Massachusetts man wrote home. Grant's turning movement, an officer concluded, "forces Lee to give up his position on the Anna, avoids the after works on the South Anna, and is twelve miles nearer Richmond, without a fight or the loss of a single life." Grant, he effused, "has proven a match for Lee, and if prisoners are to be credited, the latter is at a loss to know how to keep himself before Grant." Writing home to Wisconsin, another officer proclaimed the march a "glorious achievement" and expressed "admiration and gratitude for the man who has pushed back the rebel army thirty miles without a general battle." An artillerist applauded Grant's objective of destroying Lee's army rather than wasting time trying to take Richmond. "It is the rat we are after," he explained, "not so much the rat hole."[81]

Had the tired soldiers reflected further, they might have tempered their enthusiasm over Grant's accomplishment. Grant had expected to regain the initiative by shifting from the North Anna to the Pamunkey, but the opposite had occurred. "Instead of immobilizing Lee's army at the North Anna while carrying on the turning movement, the Union commander moved his whole army away from the enemy, leaving [Lee] free to maneuver," a student of the campaign aptly noted. "The result of this movement was as might well have been expected, that there was no flank to turn." Most importantly, Grant had left Lee free to dictate where the next battle would occur. Once again, Federal commanders would have to feel blindly for Lee and fight him at a place of his selection, not of theirs.[82]

At 6:00 P.M., from his headquarters at the Clarke house, near Atlee's Station, Lee sent a message apprising War Secretary Seddon of the day's developments. "The army is in front of this position extending toward Totopotomoy Creek," he wrote. "As far as I can ascertain none of the enemy have advanced south of that creek. I believe he is assembling his army behind it." Confederate cavalry, Lee added, had engaged Grant's cavalry near Haw's Shop and had captured prisoners from the Union 5th and 6th Corps. "I have not, however," Lee concluded, "received very definite information as yet either as regards their position or numbers." He would continue to wait in his strong defensive line until Grant revealed his hand.[83]

IV

MAY 29

Grant Searches for Lee

"The next move on the chessboard by General Grant."

SUNDAY, MAY 29, saw the Union army safely across the Pamunkey. "Thus far General Grant has succeeded in flanking Lee in every strong position taken by him until finally the enemy is pushed back into the works of [Richmond]," an Indiana man crowed. "We are very confident of success and I think there is no doubt but Richmond will be in our hands very shortly," an Ohioan agreed. Warren's aide Roebling expressed smug satisfaction. "We are now seventeen miles from Richmond," he wrote his fiancée, Emily Warren, the general's sister. "The joke of it is the Johnnies thought we were retreating and I dare say they were a little surprised to find us after them so soon." Even newspapermen gushed. "The flanking movement of the Army of the Potomac from the south bank of the North Anna to the south side of the Pamunkey, accomplished by daybreak this morning, deserves to be called the most remarkable and creditable performance of this campaign," a Boston correspondent boasted. In less than two days, he added, "the army marched a distance of nearly forty miles, over good but dusty and unknown roads, effected the passage of two large rivers, and was brought within an easy day's march of Richmond. Of all our immense transportation not a wagon was lost. Of men only [a few pickets] were lost—a few stragglers who were captured by the enemy."[1]

Dana's morning dispatch to Washington was glowing. "Movement of the army across the Pamunkey is complete, and has been executed with admirable celerity and success," the assistant war secretary advised his boss. "Our present position is one of exceeding strength, extending from Pamunkey, above Nelson's Ferry, to Totopotomoy Creek." Officers and men, Dana assured Stanton, were "in high spirits at the successful execution of this last long and difficult flank movement." A single cloud darkened the horizon. Union scouts reported that Lee had left the North Anna the morning of May 27, Dana related, but the rebel force's precise location remained unclear. "It is certain Lee was prepared to resist our crossing at Littlepage's [Bridge]," Dana speculated, "but had no idea of our coming here."[2]

The weather turned unexpectedly cool, raising spirits even more, and soldiers caught up on diaries and letters. "A stunning night's rest," the 6th Corps aide Oliver Wendell Holmes Jr. penned in his diary. Roebling composed a letter to Emily extolling the local laurel, which he believed more beautiful than the variety found in their native New York. A few outfits held Sunday services. The main complaint involved food. Supply wagons had still not arrived, and rations were exhausted. "All day nothing to eat," a soldier groused. "This was a Lonesome Sabbath to us."[3]

Lewis H. Steiner, the Sanitary Commission's chief inspector for the Army of the Potomac, visited Mrs. Newton's house. He counted three hundred wounded cavalrymen—fifty of them rebels—sprawling about the grounds. Wandering over to Warren's headquarters at Dr. Brockenbrough's house, he discovered that soldiers had ransacked the place. Curious officers examined letters by Thomas Jefferson strewn in an outhouse. Officers had also commandeered the first floor of Dr. Pollard's home, forcing the family to move upstairs. Little Harry Pollard surprised a Federal stealing cigars from the guestroom and scooped up a handful for safekeeping. "The Yankee was amused, but he did not try to take them away from me," Harry recalled. "He stole a lot of fine towels, and I saw him stuffing them in his coat pocket as he came down the steps." Harry's brother discovered that a soldier had stolen his pet hen to make chicken pie. He scoured the yard with a brickbat threatening to "kill that Yankee," but hen and captor were nowhere to be found. Troops continued dismantling Dr. Pollard's outbuildings. The lumber, a soldier noted, was handy for strengthening earthworks and made "good material under coffeepots." An Ohioan observed that destroying private property had become commonplace. "Some said it was cruel, others that it was no more cruel than to kill a traitor to our flag," he ruminated. "The writer holds that the former is too often needlessly cruel and that both are simply the outgrowth of barbarism yet sticking somewhere."[4]

Slaves kept arriving from surrounding plantations. The reporter Charles C. Coffin sympathized with their plight. "Old men with venerable beards, horny hands, crippled with hard work and harder usage," he noted in describing the endless procession. "Aged women, toothless, almost blind, steadying their steps with sticks; little Negro boys, driving a team of skeleton steers, mere bones and tendons covered with hide, or wall-eyed horses, spavined, foundered, and lame, attached to rickety carts and wagons piled with beds, tables, chairs, pots and kettles, hens, turkeys, ducks; women came with infants in their arms, and a sable cloud of children trotting by their side." Hard-pressed to supply its own needs, the Union army was in no condition to care for refugees. Provost Marshal Patrick temporarily solved the problem by sending them on to White House with a load of Confederate prisoners. By his estimate, six hundred blacks of all ages traveled in the caravan.[5]

Meade's first order of business was to assemble the Army of the Potomac in a continuous north-south line from the Pamunkey to Totopotomoy Creek. Wright's 6th Corps was already ensconced in earthworks along Crump's Creek, its right on the Pamunkey and its left at Dr. Pollard's place. Hancock's 2nd Corps also held a good line, picking up on Wright's left and following a ridge paralleling the road from Dr. Pollard's farm to Haw's Shop. Burnside's 9th Corps and Warren's 5th Corps, however, had to move to complete the army-wide deployment. Burnside's troops had crossed at Dabney Ferry after midnight and filled the floodplain around Hanovertown. Meade directed Burnside to push on to Dr. Brockenbrough's home, take the left fork to Haw's Shop, and hook onto Hancock's left flank, continuing the fortified line south to the Norment family farm. Warren, whose corps dangled south from Mrs. Newton's place, was to move onto Burnside's left and reach south to Totopotomoy Creek. When the shuffling was over, Wright, Hancock, Burnside, and Warren would be strung along a north-south axis in that order.

Meade's directives were straightforward, but they spawned a logistical nightmare. Much of Burnside's route was identical to Warren's. Burnside got off first, leaving Warren to move onto roads clogged with 9th Corps troops, and the tie-up set Warren fuming. "My command has been ready to move since daylight," he griped to Humphreys. On arriving at Haw's Shop, bleary-eyed Burnside found things very different than he had expected. Hancock's line did not end at Haw's Shop as Meade had said, but rather terminated a half mile east of the place. "Shall I connect with him?" Burnside inquired of Meade, gently reminding the army commander that his men were "very weary, being almost constantly on the road for two days and nights." Meade resolved the discrepancy by ordering Hancock to advance the lower end of his line to Haw's Shop and for Burnside to link with him there.[6]

By midmorning, Meade had changed his mind. Instead of moving into line, Burnside was to mass east of Haw's Shop as a reserve, and Warren was to hook his right onto Hancock's left and extend south, forming behind little Mill Creek. By noon, Warren had pasted together a temporary line along Mill Creek, Cutler's right touching the 2nd Corps near Haw's Shop and Crawford's left resting on Totopotomoy Creek at the confluence of Mill Creek.

Part of Warren's line crossed the farm where Patrick Henry was born. A Federal thought the contrast between Henry's patriotism and the populace's current rebellious spirit "may forcibly have suggested to the thoughtful men in the ranks of the Confederacy of how far they were astray from the teachings of this most eminent of Southern statesmen."[7]

Grant was undecided about what to do next. The fight at Haw's Shop confirmed that Confederate cavalry was up in force, and Lee's infantry was doubtless close behind. Hampton's horsemen, however, were doing a fine job of screening Lee's troop dispositions, leaving Federal leaders to speculate about the Confederate army's actual location. "Present indications are that the rebels are beyond the Chickahominy," was Dana's best guess, and Grant's aide Comstock concurred. Grant, however, suspected that his opponent was closer, perhaps on Totopotomoy Creek, and he felt uncomfortable committing to a course of action until he solved the mystery of Lee's whereabouts. He may have had in mind his movement across the North Anna a few days before, when he had advanced precipitously and stepped into Lee's trap. Certainly he was in no mood to repeat that mistake by charging blindly across Totopotomoy Creek. "This army has been successfully crossed over the Pamunkey and occupies a front about three miles south of the river," Grant explained his thinking to Halleck. "Yesterday two divisions of our cavalry had a severe engagement with the enemy south of Haw's Shop, driving him about 1 mile on what appears to be his new line. We will find out all about it today." Meade shared Grant's caution and ventured only that Lee was "somewhere between us and Richmond." Now that the army was safely below the Pamunkey, the next step, he informed his wife, was to "move forward today to feel for [the Confederates]."[8]

Finding the enemy was ordinarily cavalry's job. After the fighting at Haw's Shop had quieted, however, Sheridan had taken his troopers east to rest, effectively removing them from the immediate operations. Gregg camped near Old Church, Torbert settled downstream along the Pamunkey, and Wilson remained north of the river, rounding up stragglers and patrolling back roads to Port Royal. Sheridan's ostensible assignment was to keep the sector safe for supplies and for Baldy Smith's arrival. But with Lee's army several miles in the opposite direction, Sheridan had little to do. His horsemen looted plantations, giving special attention to Marlbourne, home of the fiery secessionist Edmund Ruffin. The Ruffin family was away, and Federal riders helped themselves to livestock and food, broke windows, and made off with Ruffin's prized paleontology collection.[9]

Grant had made poor use of cavalry throughout the campaign. On May 8, he had permitted Sheridan to take virtually all of the army's horsemen on his

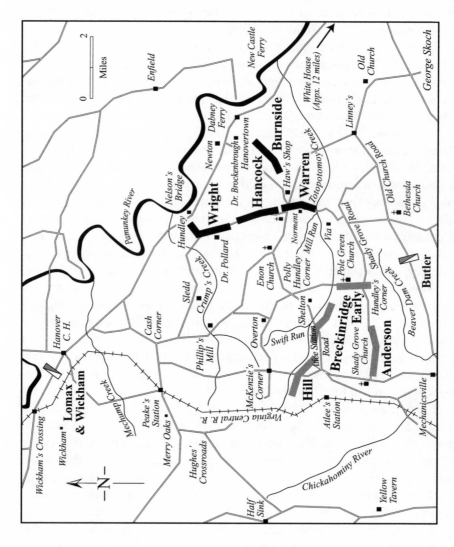

Union and Confederate deployments by noon on May 29

Richmond raid, leaving the Federal commanders blind during the battles at Spotsylvania Court House and on the maneuver to the North Anna River. He made the same mistake again on May 29, permitting Sheridan to bivouac behind the Army of the Potomac instead of actively seeking out Lee. Meade, who was not on speaking terms with Sheridan, voiced no complaint.

The decision to do without cavalry left the Union high command no choice but to send infantry to find Lee. Late in the morning, Meade formulated a plan to advance large bodies of foot soldiers along three main routes radiating from his position. Wright was to send Russell's division northwest along Hanover River Road, heading for Hanover Court House; Hancock was to dispatch Barlow's division west along Atlee Station Road, making for Totopotomoy Creek; and Warren was to push Griffin's division south across Totopotomoy Creek, strike Shady Grove Road, and probe west toward Pole Green Church and Hundley's Corner. Burnside was to hold his corps ready to support Hancock or Warren and to reconnoiter the roads between their two corps if need arose.[10]

Letting Sheridan recuperate in the army's rear was a bad idea, and dispersing three Union divisions in three directions misused the infantry as well. Grant was forfeiting his advantage of mass simply to gather intelligence. As Russell, Barlow, and Griffin progressed along their assigned routes, diverging roads would spread them increasingly farther apart, making each prong vulnerable to attack and virtually impossible to reinforce. "What is to be the next move on the chess board by Genl. Grant I don't know," a colonel wrote as he watched troops make ready for the three-pronged reconnaissance. "They can't go far to the front before they encounter the enemy."[11]

Lee was indeed ready and awaiting Grant's move. He had arrayed the Army of Northern Virginia along Totopotomoy Creek's south bank, covering Grant's possible approaches. Early's 2nd Corps stood on Shady Grove Road, its left near Pole Green Church and its right passing south toward Beaver Dam Creek and Old Church Road. Breckinridge was still entrenched across Atlee Station Road at Totopotomoy Creek, and Hill's 3rd Corps had shifted from reserve into line on Breckinridge's left, facing north to cover the Virginia Central Railroad and the road from Hanover Court House. Confederate cavalry—Gilbert Wright's brigade, backed by Lomax's Virginians—was at Hanover Court House, watching Hanover River Road, and Butler's cavalry patrolled the country off the Confederate right, below Totopotomoy Creek. Anderson's 1st Corps, posted on Shady Grove Road behind Early, could support Early, Breckinridge, or Hill as needed. Lee was adept at drawing defensive lines, and his formation along Totopotomoy Creek was a masterpiece, reminiscent of the line he had taken along Mine Run the previous fall. To attack, the Federals would have to cross the creek and its swampy lowlands and charge uphill across cleared land and entanglements into the teeth of the rebel entrenchments. Each sector of the Confederate line was positioned to support the others, and ample troops stood in reserve.[12]

Lee expected Grant to come along Atlee Station Road. "I do not propose to move the troops today unless it become necessary," he wrote Breckinridge early in the morning. "I think it probable that should the enemy intend to advance from his present position on Richmond it will be by Haw's Shop to Atlee's Station. I have directed General Hill to be ready to support you. Take a position to resist his advance, acquaint yourself with the roads and country in your vicinity, and post your pickets to insure your security."[13]

The three Union divisions started along their assigned routes at noon. Russell left his encampments on Crump's Creek and headed northwest along Hanover River Road, taking with him Captain Charles W. White's 4th Maine Battery. Meade's chief engineer, Major Nathaniel Michler, led the way. Rebel cavalry—predominantly Cobb's Legion of Wright's brigade, generously estimated by one Federal at about 400 men—"gave us only a running fight," a New Yorker related, and was easily driven off. Confederate horsemen also pecked at the column's rear, shooting stragglers. "This had a good effect," a Federal noted, "as [the stragglers] very soon joined their several commands." Around 3:00 P.M., the 15th New Jersey, leading Russell's march, approached Mechump's Creek. Confederate horsemen were visible on the far bank, and behind them, on high ground, rose Hanover Court House. Terms of service for many New Jersey troops were about to expire, and officers questioned whether the short-timers could be trusted to fight. The Jersey men set doubts to rest by splashing across Mechump's Creek and driving the rebel horsemen from Hanover Court House. Russell bivouacked south of town along the creek, skirmishers well out, covering the Virginia Central Railroad and the wagon road to Richmond. Soldiers ripped up rails, heated and bent them, burned the train station, and tore down two railway bridges. "A sign post on the main road says 17 miles to Richmond," Russell enthusiastically reported to Meade.[14]

Barlow, accompanied by Captain Frederick M. Edgell's 1st New Hampshire Battery, started west along Atlee Station Road from Haw's Shop. Nelson Miles's brigade led. "Instead of a march by the flank," an aide remembered, "the whole brigade, with the exception of the color companies of each regiment, was deployed in a skirmish line nearly a mile in length, with its center on the road." Barlow's men passed Enon Church, site of the previous day's cavalry fight, and saw the dead bodies of men and horses.

"The trees were torn by the shells," a Pennsylvanian recollected, "fences leveled and farm houses and barns filled with the wounded." Hancock's aide-de-camp William G. Mitchell remarked that some corpses—doubtless Carolinians and Georgians—had "shining new uniforms and clean shirts, a rarity to our eyes now." A soldier in the 7th New York Heavy Artillery saw other bodies so caked with dust and dirt that he could "scarcely distinguish the blue from the gray."[15]

A mile and a half out, Barlow reached Polly Hundley Corner, where Atlee Station Road intersected the road running south from Hanover Court House to Pole Green Church. A handful of rebel cavalrymen disputed the way but hastily retired when they realized they faced infantry. A local lady told Barlow that Confederates—Breckinridge's division—were entrenched a mile ahead at Totopotomoy Creek. To guard his flanks, Barlow sent the 125th New York to the left out Pole Green Church Road and Colonel John R. Brooke's brigade to the right, out the road leading north toward Hanover Court House. The rest of Barlow's division continued on, Miles's brigade leading, Major Nathan Church's 26th Michigan skirmishing in front. Musketry became brisk around 3:00 as Church approached Colonel Shelton's fine brick mansion. A broad field descended from the Shelton place almost half a mile to Totopotomoy Creek. The stream made a short jog to the south where Atlee Station Road crossed, and Breckinridge's troops held both banks. Barlow and Hancock's aide Mitchell passed through Church's skirmish line for a better look and were nearly killed by Breckinridge's pickets. Another hail of bullets, accompanied by rounds of cannon fire, persuaded Barlow that he could go no farther. Forming his division across the Shelton property perpendicular to the road, he sent back for Brooke's brigade. He also dispatched Mitchell to alert Hancock that he had run up against substantial rebel infantry and needed support.[16]

Griffin, comprising the Union probe's third element, moved south toward Totopotomoy Creek, pickets and flankers extended. "The advance continued slowly," a Pennsylvanian recounted, "several times forming line and again breaking into column." Around 3:00 P.M., Griffin's lead elements descended into marshes around Totopotomoy Creek, waded across, and ascended the far bank into the fields of the Via family. Mrs. Via's house—a large home in the Georgian style constructed in the 1700s—stood in a fifteen-acre clearing carved from surrounding woods. Confederate cavalrymen were there—apparently scouts from Butler's South Carolina brigade—and sounded the alarm. Soon skirmishers from Early's 2nd Corps—veterans from Pegram's Brigade of Ramseur's division—began pecking away at the intruders. The brigades of Brigadier General Joseph J. Bartlett and Colonel Jacob B.

Sweitzer threw up entrenchments on the Via farm facing south. Brigadier General Romeyn B. Ayres's brigade continued across the Via fields and followed a small farm road south three-quarters of a mile. Driving back a thin line of rebels, Ayres's lead elements broke onto Shady Grove Road.[17]

Early rushed the rest of Pegram's Brigade east to meet the intruders, and heated fights sparked in swampy woods below Totopotomoy Creek. At 3:30 P.M., Warren advised Meade that he was fighting skirmishers. Negroes reported the enemy in force at Shady Grove, he added, and he set out for the front to study the situation. Warren's appearance troubled Ayres's men, as the general had recklessly exposed himself several times in the campaign. Once an aide had pulled him into a ditch to keep him from being killed. Sergeant John C. White of the 12th United States Regulars watched Warren lean against a rail fence, "scrutinizing the situation through his glasses." White had "come to rather dread seeing [Warren] come out to the front, as it seemed to be, usually, a prelude to some desperate work for us."[18]

A courier from the cavalryman Lomax reached Lee's headquarters at the Clarke house around 3:30 P.M. The general was writing his wife and paused to receive the visitor. Union infantry and cavalry had passed through Hanover Court House, the courier explained. If the Federals—Russell's men—kept on their present course, they would reach the Virginia Central Railroad near Peake's Station. The intelligence suggested that Grant was doubling back below the river. "The enemy is moving again this afternoon, apparently to our left on the line which they came from," Lee continued the letter to his wife. "I am writing in the midst of many things," he informed her, hastily closed, and instructed his adjutant Taylor to pen a note to Anderson. "General Lee directs me to inform you that the enemy appear to be moving toward [the Virginia Central Railroad]," it read. "Be prepared to move in any direction."[19]

Before a messenger could leave with Taylor's dispatch, a report came in from Breckinridge. Federals were advancing on Atlee Station Road and had reached Colonel Shelton's property. The force seemed to be cavalry—it was actually Barlow's infantry division—and there was no telling what was behind it. On the heels of Breckinridge's message came a dispatch from Early. More Federals—Griffin's division—had crossed Totopotomoy Creek, and Early had thrust out skirmishers to meet them. Early was concerned about a half-mile gap between his left at Pole Green Church and Breckinridge's right, near Atlee Station Road. The sector was marshy, and prospects that Federal troops would exploit the gap were remote, but the void troubled Early. Out of an abundance of caution, Lee directed Anderson to stand ready to support Early and move into the swampy breach if necessary.[20]

More couriers dashed into Lee's headquarters an hour later. Butler's cavalry reported a heavy infantry column—Ayres's brigade—pushing west along Shady Grove Road. More Union cavalry and infantry seemed to be advancing west on Old Church Road, parallel to Shady Grove Road and three-quarters of a mile south of it. To counter, Early was shifting Rodes south, toward Old Church Road, leaving Ramseur across Shady Grove Road and Gordon on the northern end of the 2nd Corps's line at Pole Green Church. Word also arrived from Fitzhugh Lee at McKenzie's Corner, on the left end of the Confederate line near Atlee's Station. Federals—Brooke's brigade of Barlow's division—had marched northwest from Polly Hundley Corner past Samuel Overton's plantation, Oak Forest. Their lead elements were only three-quarters of a mile from McKenzie's Corner, on the road from Hanover Court House south to Mechanicsville. Hill had advanced Brigadier General Ambrose R. Wright's brigade of Georgians north of Totopotomoy Creek to intercept them.[21]

Federals were materializing across the entire Confederate entire front. Lee had no way of telling whether they were probes or vanguards of major attacks. The only course open to him was to remain vigilant, shifting to meet the enemy as they approached and staying alert to exploit mistakes.

The Union generals, of course, had no intention of initiating battle at this juncture. Grant and Meade were fully cognizant of their reconnoitering parties' vulnerability and were every bit as anxious as Lee. Grant monitored reports at his headquarters by Mr. Nelson's house. "It will be well to keep the troops that have gone in search of the enemy to the front and close up on them in the morning," he wrote Meade at 4:00. "If you think their position unsafe, strengthen the front tonight." Reports that Barlow had met an uncertain number of rebels near Totopotomoy Creek troubled Grant. "If the enemy is found in the position described by General Barlow, he had better be supported before making the attack," Grant cautioned. "They are probably only covering whilst getting everything well ready to receive us on the south side of the creek."[22]

A flurry of dispatches reached Union headquarters shortly before 5:00. "General Barlow has met the enemy in force," Meade notified Grant. "He reports artillery in position and infantry in rifle pits." Meade immediately authorized Hancock to forward Barlow support. News from Warren's front was equally unsettling. "General Griffin met the enemy about 1 mile from the Totopotomoy on the road to Shady Grove, and is now skirmishing with him," Meade informed Grant, adding: "General Warren is prepared to support him." Only Russell seemed unopposed. "General Wright reports his reconnaissance being within one-fourth mile of the railroad," scribbled Meade. "Hanover Court House is in sight; only cavalry pickets encountered. He will be directed to hold his advance position and support them if necessary."[23]

Russell, however, was worried. He had no idea how many Confederates faced him, he was isolated several miles from the army, and he was out of food—"Our rations have run out and don't know when we will get any," a commissary sergeant fretted. Wright, who was also uneasy about Russell's precarious situation, decided at 6:00 P.M. to send Brigadier General Frank Wheaton's predominantly Pennsylvania brigade and a mixed Massachusetts and Rhode Island brigade under Colonel Oliver Edwards, both of Neill's division, to Hanover Court House. They were to take the more southerly road past the Sledd farm under the guidance of the engineer George H. Mendell.[24]

Wright's aide Holmes rode to alert Russell that reinforcements were on the way. "Don't spare your horse," Wright advised Holmes. Galloping toward Hanover Court House, Holmes saw twenty men across the road in front of him. "Friend!" he called out, assuming they were Yankees. Then he saw their gray jackets and spurred his horse. A Confederate rode straight at Holmes, hollering, "Halt! Surrender!" Holmes thrust his pistol into the man's chest and pulled the trigger, but the weapon misfired. Lying close against his horse "Comanche fashion," Holmes ran the gauntlet of rebels and broke free on the far side. "Got my dispatch through," he stated proudly in his diary.[25]

Wheaton's and Edwards's men were unhappy about their assignment. They had been digging earthworks all day at Crump's Creek and were looking forward to a safe evening's rest. And they were hungry. "We were supposed to have two days' rations on hand, and did, by the commissary's figures," a Massachusetts soldier complained, "but we had been up so many nights, that the ten crackers, small piece of fresh beef, and a spoonful of coffee and sugar, per day, was too scant a supply to satisfy the demands of the stomach." Leaving before the supply wagons arrived seemed especially cruel. Tightening their belts a notch and grumbling "over the carelessness of quartermasters and the great length of the day," Wheaton's and Edwards's troops set off. They reached Hanover Court House after dark and formed two lines on Russell's left, facing south across Richmond Pike. Jones's Church, near the courthouse town, doubled as Edwards's headquarters.[26]

Barlow meanwhile arrayed his division across the yard of Colonel Shelton's historic home, Rural Plains. Reputedly the county's oldest dwelling and certainly one of its wealthiest, it had been built in 1670 from glazed brick brought from England as ballast in trading ships. In 1754, Rural Plains had hosted Patrick Henry's marriage to Sarah Shelton, whose family owned the porticoed mansion. Now sixty-six years of age, Colonel Shelton presided over a thousand acres of prime Virginia farmland and some fifty slaves. "The colonel had his body servant, like every fine old Virginia planter of his times, and the mistress' work basket was carried from chair to chair by a dusky little maid, who also waved a lilac brush in fly time," the colonel's son William H. Shelton reminisced after the war. "Each of the daughters had her maid and there were old mammies and cooks and house servants swarming about the out-kitchen under the plum trees, a hundred feet back of the house." Colonel Shelton had opposed secession but, like many of his contemporaries, became an ardent Confederate when his state left the Union.[27]

Screams and wails from the house prompted Miles's aide Robertson to go inside and investigate. Colonel Shelton knew General Breckinridge and had gone to seek protection for his family, leaving his wife Sarah, their five daughters, a son, a grandchild, and some servants at the house. Barlow's arrival and the outbreak of fighting in the front yard prevented Shelton from returning, and his terror-stricken family had hidden in the basement. Bullets from the distant rebel line spattered against the house. "You will not harm my little darling, will you?" a Shelton daughter asked Robertson, clutching her infant. "It was a scene which compelled sympathy," Robertson recalled, "and awakened all the humanity in our natures." The aide took the baby, cradled it in his arms, kissed it, and handed it back to the frightened mother, urging them all to leave. One of the Shelton daughters was pregnant and lying on a couch in the dining room, and Sarah refused to disturb her. When Robertson's entreaties failed, he and other aides carried beds into the basement and barricaded the windows with logs, giving the Sheltons a relatively safe place to weather the battle.[28]

Robertson went upstairs with Miles and Church and looked out a window. A tributary named Swift Run entered Totopotomoy Creek a short distance upstream, and the combined creeks formed a wide, marshy ravine five hundred yards away. Confederate infantrymen were stationed along the treeline in the bottomland. Barlow advanced his skirmishers, who hastily threw up light earthworks and settled down to the sound of rebels chopping trees across the stream.[29]

Soon Birney's division and Captain John E. Burton's 11th New York Battery arrived, joined onto Barlow's right, and began extending the 2nd Corps's new line a mile north along Swift Run to Oak Forest, home of the Overton family. "Not being able to procure shovels or picks," one of Birney's soldiers recollected, "bayonets and tin plates were used." More 2nd Corps artillery rolled into place along the lip of ground looking across Swift Creek. The 1st Rhode Island Light, Battery B, took up position near the Shelton house.[30]

Hancock rode out late in the day and warned Mrs. Shelton that a battle would probably be fought in her yard. She and her family still refused to budge, even after he offered to let them pass into Confederate lines. Failing to persuade the Sheltons to leave, Hancock strolled into the yard. Barlow opined that Breckinridge's entrenchments were "too strong to attack," but the corps commander insisted on getting a closer view. "I subsequently went down to the skirmish line and examined the position very carefully," Hancock reported. A field of waist-high wheat covered the gently slopping terrain from the Shelton place to the creek. The banks were steep, except where the road crossed, and Breckinridge's rebels on the other side of the creek had constructed epaulements for their guns and two lines of rifle pits. Hancock estimated a brigade of Confederates in his front and, judging from smoke rising from cookfires, more to the left and right. "Our whole open space is swept by their artillery," he noted with concern, although he was comforted to see that high ground behind the Shelton house overlooked the Confederate side. Barlow's men were busy erecting earthworks and posting artillery. "The movements of the corps, to unite," Hancock informed Meade, "ought to be made at the earliest hour; for if the enemy choose to cross and attack our isolated commands, it looks to me as if it could easily be done; the country is very open."[31]

Over on Warren's front, Ayres, pressed hard by Pegram's Confederates, broke off his foray along Shady Grove Road and retired to the Via farm. Griffin arranged his three brigades across the grounds, Ayres on the left, Sweitzer in the middle, and Bartlett on the right, reaching to the neighboring property of the Talley family. Lieutenant Benjamin F. Rittenhouse's 5th United States, Battery D, Lieutenant Lester I. Richardson's 1st New York Light, Battery D, and Captain Charles E. Mink's 1st New York Light, Battery H rolled across Totopotomoy Creek and onto the Via grounds, supporting Griffin. A Virginian who had been fighting in the swampy bottom described the Union line as "piles of rails and in an open field."[32]

At 6:00 P.M., Meade informed Warren of the fate of the other reconnoitering parties. "Barlow meets the enemy in position and force 4 miles from here," he wrote. "[Russell] has got within one-fourth of a mile of the railroad. Hanover Court House in sight, only meeting cavalry. Keep Griffin up to the enemy and support him," Meade directed. "Burnside is in reserve on your right flank and rear to assist you if necessary." Expecting a fight the next morning, Warren sent a newly constituted division under Brigadier General Henry H. Lockwood to the Via farm to support Griffin. Warren was also concerned about the country off his left flank, toward Old Church. He understood that Sheridan was supposed to cover the roads east of his corps but had yet to see any horsemen there. To prevent rebels from slipping behind Griffin's left, he dispatched Colonel Peter Lyle's brigade to Linney's Corner, two miles east of the Via farm on Shady Grove Road. Lyle's men reached Linney's Corner near dark and began throwing up earthworks.[33]

Warren established headquarters for the night at the Norment family's house, north of Totopotomoy Creek on the road from Haw's Shop to the Via farm. Griffin had stirred up rebels south of Totopotomoy Creek, he advised Meade, and the enemy seemed to be concentrated to the west, along Shady Grove Road. "If the enemy should be tomorrow as we have found him today it would require my whole corps south of the Totopotomoy," Warren concluded. The terrain also gave him pause. Totopotomoy Creek's shallow valley was marshy and thickly overgrown, reminiscent of the Wilderness and every bit as hostile to troop movements. Burnside, Warren suggested, should cover the interval between the 5th Corps and Hancock, "and connection be kept up over the bad country by strong skirmish lines well supported."[34]

Soldiers in blue and gray settled along Totopotomoy Creek for the night. "What a busy scene," a Union man remembered. "The clatter of picks and shovels, the tramp of cavalry, the ringing orders from brigade officers and the hum of voices of the tired troops as they were gathered around campfires for their evening coffee and hardtack." Barlow's soldiers in the Shelton yard listened to Confederates felling trees across the creek and predicted that a "great battle was close at hand." Russell's troops spent a hungry night at Hanover Court House. "No supper and no blankets," a surgeon complained. Black women at the Bickerton Winston house cooked hoecakes and sold them to Russell's hungry soldiers, and pickets rounded up sheep, which they slaughtered and distributed. On Warren's front, a Massachusetts soldier raided the Talley plantation for bacon, sweet potatoes, and ripe strawberries. Musketry crackled from opposing skirmish lines, and some of Ayres's outposts got separated from the main body and spent an anxious night "completely surrounded and cut off," according to Sergeant White.[35]

Late in the day, Meade left Dr. Nelson's yard by the Pamunkey and rode south. Passing through Haw's Shop, he turned west onto Atlee Station Road. The aide Lyman stopped to inspect Salem Church, at Haw's Shop intersection. Troopers wounded in the fight of May 28 had been evacuated, but the building still showed signs of service as a hospital. "The church was small, rather neatly painted within," Lyman noted, "but the pulpit and pews were stained with blood."[36]

A short distance west of Salem Church, the headquarters cavalcade reached the northern end of Warren's line, held by Cutler. A slow patter of musketry could be heard off to the south, where Ayres's skirmishers were

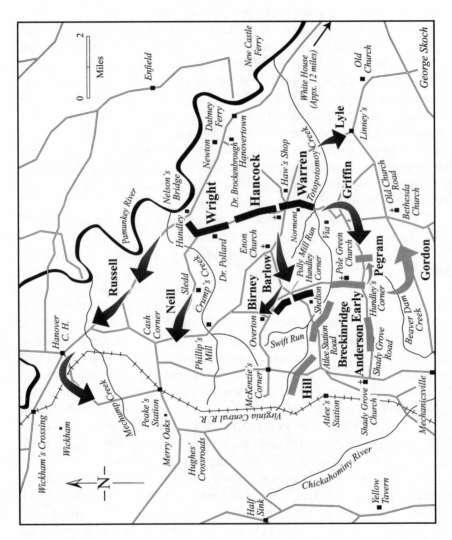

Union probes and Confederate responses during afternoon of May 29

dueling Pegram's Confederates. Meade was aghast to discover that Cutler had neglected to post pickets and demanded an explanation. Warren, who had ridden over from the Norment house, was in a bad mood. "Well," he interjected, "all I can say is this. If General Cutler doesn't know enough to throw out pickets without my telling him, the only thing is for me to get rid of General Cutler." Firing Cutler, of course, was not in the cards. Meade rode back onto Atlee Station Road and set up headquarters near Enon Church to be close to the developing battlefront. Engineers ran telegraph lines from headquarters to the various corps.[37]

After dark, the aide Robertson checked on the Shelton family in their basement. Mrs. Shelton had come to regard Robertson as her protector and insisted on cooking dinner for him. She apologized for the absence of tea, sugar, and coffee but offered fresh vegetables from her garden. Robertson and his friends donated the contents of their haversacks, and soon Mrs. Shelton was spreading white linen over a table and serving the first civilized meal Robertson and his companions had seen for a long time. "It was a bright bit of green in the desert of war," Robertson reminisced.[38]

The Union army had displayed impressive energy and initiative in maneuvering from the North Anna to the Pamunkey. Once across the Pamunkey, however, Federal commanders had frittered away the advantages their quick march had gained them. Exhaustion was partly to blame, as was Grant's uncertainty about Lee's location and his decision to wait for Baldy Smith's reinforcements. But at the core of the army's lethargy was Grant's and Meade's failure to devise a plan in advance to guide them once they were over the Pamunkey. The consequence was a series of improvised movements that forfeited the initiative to the rebels.

At least May 29th's reconnaissances had given the Union commanders a fair picture of Lee's location. The Army of Northern Virginia held the far side of Totopotomoy Creek on a line from Atlee Station through Pole Green Church. "They seem to have a line covering the railroad," Meade announced after reviewing the latest reports. The intelligence, Grant's aide Lieutenant Colonel Horace Porter noted, "disclosed the fact that all of Lee's troops were in position on the north side of the Chickahominy, and were well entrenched."[39]

The next step was to press the rebel line. First thing in the morning, Hancock was to advance the rest of his corps to the Shelton home and pin Breckinridge in place, locking down the center of the Confederate position on Atlee Station Road. At the same time, Wright was to shift the entire 6th Corps south, moving athwart the rebel army's left flank and linking with Hancock's right. Warren was to resume Griffin's movement with his entire corps, testing the Confederate right flank on Shady Grove Road. Burnside was to move forward as well, slipping between Hancock's left and Warren's right to bridge the gap between the 2nd and 5th Corps. The idea was for the Union 5th and 6th Corps to strike opposite ends of Lee's formation while the 2nd and 9th Corps advanced frontally, preventing Lee from reinforcing his beleaguered flanks.[40]

Lee expected Grant to attack in the morning but was uncertain where the blow would fall. He felt secure behind Totopotomoy Creek. Hill held the Confederate left, facing north across the stream, ready to receive an attack from the direction of Hanover Court House. Breckinridge remained across Atlee Station Road, supported on his left by Lieutenant Colonel David G. McIntosh's 3rd Corps artillery battalion and on his right by William McLaughlin's battalion of his own division. Anderson advanced Colonel Henry C. Cabell's and Lieutenant Colonel Frank Huger's battalions on Breckinridge's right, posting them to enfilade the Federal approaches along Atlee Station Road and the Shelton fields. Early, from his entrenchments at Hundley's Corner, was situated to block Union advances on both Pole Green Church Road and Shady Grove Road. Anderson's corps remained in reserve, Kershaw's division supporting Breckinridge south of Atlee Station Road, Pickett's division backstopping Early along the stretch of creek north of Pole Green Church, and Field's division covering the swampy marshland between Breckinridge and Early. If Grant wanted to fight on Totopotomoy Creek, Lee was ready to oblige him.[41]

That night, Lee's chief engineer assessed the military situation. "The Yankees have lost all the boldness and dash which characterized their first movements and are now proceeding with extreme caution," Martin Smith wrote his wife. "This is the fourth position in which we have confronted [Grant] and it remains to be seen whether he will draw off from this without a fight as he did from the last at [the North Anna River]." As far as Smith could tell, Grant had "fortified himself strongly in his camp with a view to inducing Lee to attack him." The engineer did not expect Lee to accept Grant's invitation. The Confederate commander, he predicted, would wait for Grant's "columns to show themselves in the open ground to make an onslaught upon them."[42]

"We are going up to help Grant finish up the job with Lee."

Following Grant's instructions, Halleck had directed Butler to reinforce the Army of the Potomac, keeping back only those troops "absolutely neces-

sary" to hold his line at Bermuda Hundred, "acting purely on the defensive."
Halleck was relieved at the prospect of consolidating the two armies. "I wish
everything was away from the south side of the James with you," he assured
Grant. "I do not like these divided commands, with the enemy intervening. I
would rather use them altogether under your own eye."[43]

Butler was understandably reluctant to preside over his army's dismem-
berment, but Halleck's order left him no choice. The reinforcements were to
be incorporated into the 18th Corps and placed under Baldy Smith's command. A West Point graduate and professional engineer, Smith had fought
with distinction under McClellan, had briefly commanded the 6th Corps at
Fredericksburg, and had served in the west following an army-wide shakeup
early in 1863. He had impressed Grant by solving formidable supply problems at Chattanooga, and Grant had sought Smith's counsel in planning his
spring campaign. McClellan, who valued the Vermont native for his "great
personal courage and a wonderfully quick eye for ground and for handling
troops," noted that Smith was "too quick tempered towards those under him,
very selfish, and had a most bitter tongue which often ran away with him and
got him into trouble." Grant was well aware of the forty-seven-year-old New
Englander's shortcomings. "General Smith, whilst a very able officer, is obstinate," he warned Halleck, "and is likely to condemn whatever is not suggested by himself." Lyman, who could sum up a person in a few words,
described Smith as a "short, quite portly looking man, with a light-brown
imperial and shaggy mustache, a round, military head, and the look of a German officer."[44]

How Smith and Meade would mesh was anyone's guess. During Smith's
tenure with the Potomac army, Meade had played a lesser role. In March
1864, when Grant visited Meade for the first time as commander of the Union
armies, he took Smith with him. "It is rumored, and there are strong reasons
for believing it true," Provost Marshal Patrick had written, "that Baldy Smith
is to replace Meade in command of this army, backed by Grant." Meade
could not help looking askance at Smith's return. And Smith must have bridled at serving under Meade, whom he had recently expected to replace.
Army wags speculated that sparks would fly when these two obstinate men
butted heads.[45]

Smith was to command the two 18th Corps divisions under Brigadier Generals William T. H. Brooks and John H. Martindale, supplemented by a 10th
Corps division under Brigadier General Charles Devens Jr. and an artillery
brigade under Captain Samuel S. Elder. The plan was for Smith's 17,000 soldiers to steam down the James River, round the point at Fortress Monroe, and
ascend the York and Pamunkey Rivers to White House, where they would

disembark and march the rest of the way to join Grant. Smith began pulling troops from Bermuda Hundred late on May 27 while a flotilla of twenty ships and several barges assembled at Bermuda Hundred Landing and City Point. The next day—Hampton and Sheridan were fighting at Haw's Shop—Smith's men boarded transports and set off. "Am now embarking," Smith wrote Grant at 10:30 P.M. on May 28. "I will proceed as rapidly as possible to West Point or White House, according as I find it best to land." [46]

Smith's men were relieved to be leaving. "Our army feels that there is no need of the predicament we have been in, here at Bermuda Hundred," a soldier wrote, "and the men are neither slow nor mild in their expression of opinion and feeling concerning the vexatious situation." Speculation was rife over their objective. "Some thought it meant a change of base for the whole army that had so signally failed to accomplish its mission, and that Bermuda Hundred and City Point were to be evacuated," a soldier recollected. "Others thought that Washington was again threatened by another rebel raid, and that the 18th Corps was on its way to the rescue; while others still guessed rightly and exclaimed, 'We are going up to help Grant finish up the job with Lee.'"[47]

The cruise down the James raised the men's spirits. Ruined mansions drifted past, as did formerly splendid fields, once tended by slaves and now overgrown with weeds. Men who had fought in McClellan's army two years before pointed out Harrison's Landing and other familiar sites. Jamestown, Virginia's earliest settlement, came into view. Near dark, the lead ships reached Newport News and Fort Monroe, where they anchored for the night. The novelty of the journey had worn off by then, and Smith's men took critical stock of their surroundings. "The [steamer] is crowded to excess, and is very filthy from long use in transporting horses, mules, war materiel, and men," a New Hampshire soldier noted. "We have in tow an old leaky barge on board of which is a portion of the men of the 8th Connecticut who are in a rage because of their bad accommodations." Barges drifted loose and boats ran aground on sandbars during the windy night. The New Hampshire troops had an exciting time when their overcrowded bunks collapsed, spilling sleeping soldiers across the deck.[48]

Since early spring, Lee had been urging President Davis to send him troops from the Richmond defenses. Butler, however, had launched his offensive against the Confederate capital the same day that Grant moved across the Rapidan against Lee, compelling Davis to engage in a delicate balancing act. If he weakened Beauregard to strengthen Lee, Butler might take Richmond. If he left troops with Beauregard that Lee needed, Grant might defeat Lee.

Lee and Beauregard had explored the idea of joint movements by their armies, but they entertained very different notions about who should cooperate with whom. On May 14, when Lee was at Spotsylvania Court House, Beauregard suggested that Lee retire to Richmond, place the Army of Northern Virginia behind the Chickahominy River, and reinforce Beauregard. Thus strengthened, Beauregard contended, he would defeat Butler, then join Lee in a combined operation against Grant. Key to Beauregard's plan was the massing of both Confederate armies near the capital. "Without such concentration nothing can be effected, and the picture is one of ultimate starvation," the Louisianian stressed. Beauregard's plan was anathema to Lee, whose overriding concern was to keep Grant from pinning him against Richmond. Lee preferred that Beauregard simply send him troops.

Beauregard's defeat of Butler at Drewry's Bluff on May 16 dramatically changed the situation. Beauregard manifestly needed fewer troops to keep Butler corked at Bermuda Hundred than he had required to defend Richmond against an aggressive and mobile foe. Davis accordingly took 5,000 soldiers—Pickett's division—from Beauregard and sent them to Lee. He also permitted Matthew Butler's new cavalry regiments arriving from South Carolina to leave Richmond and join the Army of Northern Virginia. He felt uneasy, however, about further weakening Beauregard.

Beauregard continued to urge Lee to drop back to Richmond, arguing that it would be better for the southerners to combine their forces and defeat Federal armies piecemeal than to wage separate holding actions. His argument got a frosty reception in Richmond. Requiring Lee to withdraw, Davis's military adviser General Braxton Bragg pointed out, would mean abandoning the Virginia Central Railroad and the Shenandoah Valley, dangerously exposing Lee's army and undermining Confederate morale. Davis left the decision to Lee, who not surprisingly rejected Beauregard's plan.

The strategic picture changed again with Lee's withdrawal to the North Anna. The move brought the Army of Northern Virginia within twenty-five miles of Richmond and revived prospects of cooperation between the two Confederate forces. He was now near enough to the capital, Lee wrote Davis on May 23, "to combine the operations of this army with that under General Beauregard." Lee continued to view Grant's army as the appropriate target and insisted that Beauregard do the reinforcing. Grant's shift across the Pamunkey and Lee's movement to meet him at Totopotomoy Creek altered the military equation yet again. Grant had closed the distance to Richmond even more, limiting the Confederates' options for maneuver. Circumstances, however, were now ideal for shifting troops between the two rebel armies, and Lee was quick to remind Davis of that fact. Writing from Hughes' Crossroads on the morning of May 28, Lee again pointed out that he was "near enough to Richmond for General Beauregard to unite with me if possible."[49]

Davis's response, delivered that same day, was not encouraging. Beauregard, the president stressed, claimed to be occupying an enemy force twice the size of his own army. "If he be holding nearly double his number inactive," Davis observed, "and at the same time protecting our line of communication, along which we are bringing up supplies, it is doubtful whether he could be better employed at this time." Before making up his mind, Davis wanted more information about Butler's intentions. Confederate scouts had spotted ships steaming up the James. "There are two reports in town," Davis told Lee, "one that General Butler was withdrawing, and another, mentioned to me at this instant, that reinforcements to the extent of 4,000 to 5,000 men had joined Butler last night." Until Davis determined whether Butler was leaving or being reinforced, he did not want to risk weakening Beauregard.[50]

Beauregard erroneously discounted the notion that Butler was sending troops to Grant. "The report you refer to of Butler breaking up his encampments in my front," he informed the president, "is only partly true, and indicates probably a change of position, not a withdrawal of part of his forces." At best, Beauregard thought, Butler had lost no more than four thousand soldiers. "My force is so small at present," he went on, "that to divide it for the purpose of reinforcing Lee would jeopardize the safety of the part left to guard my lines, and would greatly endanger Richmond itself." His recommendation remained firm. "The question of abandoning in part or in whole my present position from Drewry's Bluff to Petersburg is a momentous one," Beauregard insisted, "which requires the most earnest consideration of the Government before it is adopted."[51]

On the morning of May 29, Lee invited Beauregard to Atlee's Station, and a meeting was arranged later that day. During the afternoon, President Davis visited Lee. Their conversation was not recorded, but it is certain that Lee pressed his case for reinforcements. Beauregard arrived after the president had departed. Details of his talk with Lee have also been lost to history, but the outcome was disappointing to Lee. "In conference with General Beauregard he states that he has only twelve thousand infantry and can spare none," Lee telegraphed Davis at 9:00 P.M. "If General Grant advances tomorrow I will engage him with my present force."[52]

Lee later briefed Davis more fully on his conference with Beauregard. The Louisianian had insisted, Lee explained, that he faced superior numbers and could spare no troops to reinforce the Army of Northern Virginia. Accepting Beauregard's contention at face value, Lee suggested that Davis release soldiers from the Richmond defenses, retaining only sufficient men to ward off sudden cavalry attacks against the city's outer fortifications.

"If this army is unable to resist Grant," Lee reminded the president, "the troops under General Beauregard and in the city will be unable to defend it."[53]

V

May 30

The Armies Clash at Bethesda Church and Matadequin Creek

"This is just a repetition of their former movements."

MAY 30 DAWNED warm and pleasant. Lee rose early as usual. His illness persisted, but he felt stronger than he had in days. He was pleased with his defensive line along Totopotomoy Creek and confident he could hold it. His chief concern was that Grant might turn his flanks. Confederate cavalry— Fitzhugh Lee's division stationed at McKenzie's Corner and Gilbert Wright's brigade near Hanover Court House—had saturated the country to the north. Along with Hill's infantry, they kept the approaches from that direction well covered. The situation off the southern end of the Confederate line, however, troubled Lee. Early could fend off attacks along Shady Grove Road and Old Church Road, but the next road network south was unprotected. Four miles southeast of Early, five roads converged at a star-shaped junction called Old Cold Harbor. From Sheridan's encampment at Old Church, the Federals had an unobstructed four-mile march to the strategic crossroads. Once there, they could spread onto several routes leading to the Confederate capital. They would also be ideally situated to slip past the Confederate right and into Lee's rear. Butler's South Carolina cavalry, reinforced by a newly arrived South Carolina cavalry brigade under Brigadier General Martin W. Gary, was watching the roads south of Early. All day, Lee remained alert for signs that Grant might be shifting toward Cold Harbor or generally toward the Confederate right flank.

Despite Cold Harbor's potential importance, the intersection played no significant part in Grant's thinking. The Union commander's three-pronged reconnaissance had found Lee's army at Totopotomoy Creek. Aggressive as ever, Grant intended to feel for weak spots and then to attack. Meade's order for the day called for Hancock's 2nd Corps, holding the Union center along

Atlee Station Road, to probe Breckinridge. Wright's 6th Corps was to move down from Hanover Court House, link with Hancock's northern flank, and lap westward across the northern sector of the Confederate line, held by Hill. Warren was to bring the 5th Corps across Totopotomoy Creek at Mrs. Via's farm and advance west along Shady Grove Road, confronting Early at Hundley's Corner. And Burnside was to slip into the gap between Hancock and Warren, facing Anderson. When these maneuvers were complete, the Army of the Potomac would form a continuous five-mile line from McKenzie's Corner to Shady Grove Road. Sheridan's cavalry was to keep watch in the army's rear near Old Church, protecting supply lines and preventing the Confederates from interfering with Baldy Smith's arrival.

Hancock's morning started off well. Birney held the northern sector of the 2nd Corps's line, reaching southeast from the Overton farm at Oak Forest to a point near Atlee Station Road. Barlow had dug in on Birney's left. His right wing covered Atlee Station Road and the Shelton house, stringing through wheat fields overlooking Totopotomoy Creek. His left tracked a bend in the creek and arced almost east to anchor on Pole Green Church Road half a mile south of Polly Hundley Corner.

Hancock's final division under Gibbon reached Polly Hundley Corner from Haw's Shop near daylight. Hancock directed Gibbon to attach his right to Barlow's left and reach east, facing south toward Totopotomoy Creek. Gibbon's lead brigade, under Colonel H. Boyd McKeen, made the connection with Barlow, and the brigades of Brigadier General Joshua T. Owen and Colonel Thomas A. Smyth extended the line east along a farm road to Washington Jones's place. After sharp skirmishing, Smyth occupied the Jones farm and drove Confederate pickets across Totopotomoy Creek. The 7th West Virginia of Smyth's brigade captured a hill that provided a superb observation post above the leafy green expanse. Gibbon posted Sleeper's battery on the western edge of the Jones clearing, nailing down the 2nd Corps's left flank. Mr. Jones's pantry, it developed, contained a profusion of onions, flour, bacon, and wines made from currants and ginger, much to the satisfaction of Gibbon's men. Union skirmishers pressed to Totopotomoy Creek and found Confederates strongly posted on the south bank. Bitter firefights sparked and flared in dark thickets between snipers hiding behind trunks and logs and in hastily constructed rifle pits.[1]

Breckinridge's Confederates had been busy all night putting finishing touches on earthworks across from the Shelton farm. Daylight disclosed the strength of their fortifications. "We could almost look into the mouths of several field pieces in position, and protected by lunettes," Miles's aide Robertson observed. Already old hands at this sort of work, the Federals began digging in earnest. The wheat field between the Shelton house and the creek afforded little protection, and southern sharpshooters were posted too close for comfort. Miles's men, Robertson noted, "would cast up a shovel of dirt and then lie down in the wheat until the bullets which the throwing up of the earth had attracted had passed over, then resumed their labor." Soldiers heaped dirt into low shelters, then shoveled lying down behind the mounds. Colonel Church and Robertson entertained themselves by picking off rebels popping up from rifle pits. The artist Alfred R. Waud sketched the scene from his perch by the Shelton house. "The [Confederate] works seen from this point consist of a double row of rifle pits on the crest above the stream called Totopotomoy, with epaulements for guns, not more than 600 yards away," he wrote. "The guns, flags, and men are distinctly visible from this mansion." During the desultory skirmishing, Colonel Miles received formal notice of his appointment as brigadier general, to date from May 12.[2]

The previous night, Hancock had directed his artillery chief, Colonel John C. Tidball, to post the 2nd Corps's guns along the crest behind the Shelton house. Tidball misunderstood his assignment and placed the pieces a quarter mile back. Hancock discovered the error soon after sunup. Concluding that the guns would be "useless" where they were, he ordered Tidball to move them up. Using two battalions of the 4th New York Heavy Artillery as laborers, Tidball prepared new artillery positions by the Shelton house. Rebel sharpshooters along the wooded fringe of Totopotomoy Creek took potshots at the soldiers as they worked, and McLaughlin's artillery on Breckinridge's front maintained a harassing fire. "This was a dangerous operation," a New Yorker recollected, "and several of the men were hit." By midmorning, despite a "constant shower of bullets," Tidball had repositioned his artillery along the Shelton house ridge. Captain R. Bruce Ricketts's Battery F, 1st Pennsylvania Light, and Captain A. Judson Clark's Battery B, 1st New Jersey Light, were on the right side of Atlee Station Road; Lieutenant John W. Roder's Battery K, 4th United States, and Captain William A. Arnold's Battery A, 1st Rhode Island Light, were left of the road; and a battery of six Coehorn mortars stood in front of the house. Their digging done, the men of the 4th New York Heavy Artillery took position in support of the guns.[3]

Colonel Shelton's fourteen-year-old son, Walter, could scarcely believe his eyes when he walked out of his home to look around during a lull. "I didn't know where I was—I might have been in Europe for any familiar object I saw," he wrote years later. "The soldiers had cut down two orchards and built a fortification across the yard back of the house from the Negro graveyard to the road and filled it with guns. All the beautiful palings and arched gates that enclosed the front yard were gone." He was also upset to learn that the family's butler, Jo, had run away. "I had to black my own shoes after Jo left," he reminisced.[4]

Hancock tried to gauge the strength of Breckinridge's position across the creek. A signal officer stationed on top of the Shelton house reported Confederates "engaged at present in completing works on their right (as visible), but very few show themselves above their works, although their sharpshooters are busy firing on our skirmishers." At 9:00, Barlow sent troops probing along Atlee Station Road, and Gibbon skirmished south from the Jones farm. Neither foray made much headway, although Gibbon's men did manage to scoop up a prisoner from a North Carolina regiment in Hoke's Brigade of Anderson's corps. The captive said that the main rebel line was a mile away, behind a swamp, and "pretty strong." Barlow's skirmishers drove Breckinridge's pickets across the creek and threw up an advance line of entrenchments, even though ravines emptying into the creek made it difficult in places to determine precisely where the main stream ran. Barlow ventured a more spirited probe around 11:00. Two regiments from Miles's brigade—the 61st New York and a battalion from the 2nd New York Heavy Artillery—splashed across the creek and captured a small ridge immediately beyond. Breckinridge's main line was visible on the next ridge, and the New Yorkers found themselves trapped under "severe fire from the enemy of musketry and some artillery," according to Miles.[5]

The right wing of Hancock's line, under Birney, suffered through a bitter morning. Birney's earthworks traversed a belt of high ground roughly paralleling the road from Polly Hundley Corner to the Overton plantation. The land in front sloped down to a veritable jungle cut by Swift Run, Totopotomoy Creek, and countless rivulets and sluggish streams. The lowlands were miserable. Air hung hot and steamy in dense foliage, and clouds of insects buzzed incessantly. Confederates from Mahone's 3rd Corps division had dug rifle pits in bluffs lining the far side of Totopotomoy Creek's main branch and kept up constant musketry from their hidden perches. Birney's soldiers had seen nothing like these thickets since their assault along Orange Plank Road in the Wilderness more than three weeks before. Nasty little battles flared between isolated pockets of skirmishers. "The picket lines were but a few rods apart and the videttes kept up a deadly fire," a New Yorker related. "Worse and more dreaded than all else were the sharpshooters' bullets which kept picking off a man, first here and then there." Death came unexpectedly and frequently. "They were bloody days," one of Birney's soldiers remembered of his sojourn on Totopotomoy Creek, "in which, though no general engagement took place, many names were added to the death rolls of the 2nd Corps." Water was foul and rations nonexistent, adding to the discomfort.

When Meade, Hancock, and their staffs rode out to visit Birney's line, a crowd of filthy blue-clad soldiers greeted them chanting, "Hardtack! Hardtack!"[6]

Meade's plan for the morning envisioned Warren and Burnside moving onto Hancock's left flank to extend the Union line south. Griffin's division of Warren's 5th Corps was already entrenched below Totopotomoy Creek at Mrs. Via's farm. Warren planned to start Griffin west along Shady Grove Road early in the morning, then bring the rest of the 5th Corps across the creek to follow behind him. Burnside was supposed to advance across Totopotomoy Creek and hook his left onto Warren's right, protecting the 5th Corps's flank, while fastening his own right onto Hancock's left somewhere north of the creek. Since the location of Hancock's left could not be known until Gibbon moved into place, and since the right of Warren's line would be constantly shifting through trackless swampland, Burnside's assignment required clairvoyance and the split-second timing of an acrobat. The portly 9th Corps commander possessed neither quality.

Warren kept a wary eye on Old Church Road off his left flank, where Sheridan was supposed to be patrolling. Sheridan's horsemen, however, were still encamped well to the east, leaving Old Church Road in the hands of Confederate cavalry. Warren had a low opinion of Sheridan, whom he blamed for failing to clear the way to Spotsylvania Court House on May 7. He was also still fuming over Sheridan's failure to cover Griffin's left during his movement to Mrs. Via's property the previous day. Sheridan's latest dereliction was the last straw. Taking matters into his own hands, Warren asked Burnside to shift a division south to Shady Grove Road while Griffin, who was slated to lead the 5th Corps's advance, slipped over to Old Church Road. "It is my wish that your troops might take up the position occupied by General Griffin," Warren wrote Burnside at 5:00 A.M., "and allow of his being moved farther to the left."[7]

Burnside was already flustered. His instructions required him to grasp two moving targets. Riding out Atlee Station Road to get a better sense of his task, he learned that Gibbon was in the process of extending the 2nd Corps's line. Until Gibbon got into place, there would be no terminus for Burnside to hang on to. Leaving his aide Major James St. Claire Morton with Hancock to discern when and where the 2nd Corps's flank finally came to rest, Burnside rode back to find a way to cross Totopotomoy Creek and link up with Warren. The prospects were daunting. Fastening onto the 2nd Corps's nonexistent flank was hard enough, but maintaining connection with the 5th Corps as it slogged through the creek bottom's tangles had the earmark of a major disaster.[8]

Time was passing. Finally Warren decided he could wait no longer and at 7:00 A.M. directed Griffin to send a brigade west along Shady Grove Road "till you find the enemy." Griffin selected Sweitzer to conduct the reconnaissance, and Sweitzer led with his crack regiment, Colonel William S. Tilton's 22nd Massachusetts. Tilton's men had performed admirable skirmish duty at Jericho Mills during the North Anna operations and seemed perfect for the job. Tilton deployed them along both sides of Shady Grove Road, massed the 4th Michigan in support, and sent the two regiments marching west. Passing through Ayres's skirmish line, they immediately began sparring with Confederate pickets from Pegram's Brigade. Tilton's troops were stretched thin—their line was one rank deep, and men were spaced five paces apart—and the Confederates put up stiff resistance, falling slowly back into a clearing. When the Bay Staters marched into the field, the rebels opened fire from north and south, catching them in a crossfire and killing the first five who tried to sprint across the clearing. Tilton resorted to stratagem and sent troops to the left "so as to enfilade some of those giving us the crossfire," he later explained. Pegram's rebels retired grudgingly to the next field, formed on the far side, and resumed their delaying tactics, shooting from behind trees. Major Mason W. Burt of the 22nd Massachusetts, commanding a wing of Tilton's skirmish line, ordered a charge. Fixing bayonets, his soldiers attacked in a body. "We went bounding out of the woods with a yell and soon drove them in every direction," a Massachusetts man reported. Rebel sharpshooters hiding in a building picked off several of the attackers, then fled.[9]

Late in the morning—after hours of "steady, constant, and heavy skirmishing"—the 32nd Massachusetts and 62nd Pennsylvania relieved Tilton's line. The fresh regiments formed across Shady Grove Road and nudged west along the roadway and north into thickets leading to Totopotomoy Creek. Ayres's brigade followed close behind, trailed by Bartlett's soldiers. "This advance through the woods was very toilsome," a Federal recorded. "Briars, fallen trees, and similar obstructions impeding our progress, made it difficult to preserve the line of battle."[10]

While Griffin's division labored west along Shady Grove Road, Warren interrogated Confederate prisoners. A fifteen-year-old boy from the 31st Virginia was especially informative and divulged that Pegram's Brigade had moved out the previous day in support of cavalry. Warren now knew he was facing the Confederate 2nd Corps on the right of Lee's formation and directed Griffin to press west until he found the main rebel line. He also sent Captain Charles E. Mink's Battery H and Lieutenant Lester I. Richardson's

Battery D, both of the 1st New York Light, to help. Warren informed head-quarters that he planned to hold the rest of his corps in reserve, "waiting developments before taking up a position."[11]

Eleven o'clock came and went. Burnside had still not linked with Griffin, who was inching forward along Shady Grove Road. Cutler's division moved into place behind Griffin and marked time while Sweitzer's brigade painstakingly pushed back rebel skirmishers. Concerned that Griffin was becoming dangerously isolated, Warren directed him to halt and wait until Burnside appeared on his right. To facilitate the connection, Griffin sent pickets in search of the 9th Corps with instructions to "feel and learn the country." To Warren's relief, pickets from Burnside's leftmost division, under Crittenden, emerged from the greenery on Griffin's right. "Griffin's skirmishers connect with Burnside's, and I have given directions to press back the enemy's skirmishers," Warren wrote headquarters at noon. A new batch of prisoners—North Carolinians from Rodes's division—revealed that the Confederate 2nd Corps was entrenched less than half a mile ahead.[12]

Wright, on the Union army's right flank, was also having an exasperating morning. His twofold assignment was to connect with Hancock's right flank at the Overton farm and also to place himself "on the enemy's flank." It was not immediately apparent how best to do either of those things. Half of the 6th Corps—Ricketts's division and two of Neill's brigades—was still camped along Crump's Creek, reaching over to Dr. Pollard's farm. The other half—Russell's division and Neill's other two brigades—was five miles west of Crump's Creek at Hanover Court House. Wright decided to move his troops south along two parallel routes. Russell's men were to follow the Virginia Central Railroad through Peake's Station and continue on toward Atlee's Station. Ricketts's portion of the corps was to march west from Crump's Creek along Hanover River Road, turn left on the road to Cash Corner, and follow the Richmond Pike due south to the Overton place. By the end of the day, Wright hoped to have the 6th Corps's two halves united along Totopotomoy Creek in a line facing south toward Hill.[13]

Russell's men were up before daylight. Commissary wagons had not arrived, inspiring a Massachusetts soldier to wisecrack that he was subsisting on "suppositions," meaning that the "generals and commissaries supposed we had rations in our haversacks, but we didn't." Foraging was disappointing, as the country had been stripped bare. A Pennsylvanian ignored his own hunger long enough to feel sorry for the civilians. "Not a piece of bread nor any kind of foodstuff is left anyone in the county for their next meal," he observed. "This is not right of soldiers, but rather a cruel act."[14]

At 5:00 A.M., Russell's troops started south along the rail line to Peake's Station, where the tracks crossed a major east-west route three miles south of Hanover Court House. Gilbert Wright's brigade of Confederate cavalry tried to slow Russell's progress but proved little more than an annoyance. "Our force was too small to even contend with their sharpshooters," a Confederate admitted, "and they drove us before them as chaff before the wind." Russell reached Peake's Station at 9:00 and deployed his division across the railroad. Soldiers were delighted to find plenty of pigs, chickens, and corn, the latter badly needed as subsistence for artillery horses. A New Englander scrounged up cornmeal and cooked it into bread that he later proclaimed "as nutritious and palatable as from a cup full of white straw dust." To everyone's relief, commissary wagons finally caught up, and the men rested and ate. "We drew a day's ration," a soldier reported, "and burnt two new buildings and a boarding car belong to the railroad, a small barn and a deserted negro shanty."[15]

While Russell's troops wolfed down food at Peake's Station, his scouts explored east. Halfway between the station and Cash Corner they stumbled on Mechanicsville Road, a major route that surprisingly did not appear on their maps. Mechanicsville Road descended south through McKenzie's Corner, crossed Totopotomoy Creek, and continued on to Mechanicsville, paralleling the Virginia Central Railroad. Russell instructed Brigadier General Emory Upton, his most aggressive subordinate, to reconnoiter. Upton peeled off the 95th and 96th Pennsylvania and sent them south along Mechanicsville Road.[16]

As they neared McKenzie's Corner, Upton's Pennsylvanians became embroiled in a heated action with elements from Fitzhugh Lee's cavalry patrolling the approaches to Totopotomoy Creek. Hill's 3rd Corps was arrayed along the far side of the stream to guard against the very flank attack that Wright was contemplating, and some of Hill's skirmishers—probably Georgians from Ambrose Wright's brigade—assisted the cavalry in keeping the Pennsylvanians back. Portions of the 96th Pennsylvania deployed as skirmishers while the rest of Upton's contingent spread in line of battle across Mechanicsville Road. The Union force was too small to make a stand, however, and retired as rebels edged around its flanks.[17]

The other half of Wright's corps—Ricketts's augmented division—started from Crump's Creek around 5:00 A.M., marched most of the way to Hanover Court House, and turned south to Cash Corner. This placed Ricketts a mile east of Russell at Peake's Station. Ricketts's road forked at Cash Corner—the right prong led west to Peake's Station, and the left fork, locally called the Richmond Pike, proceeded south to the Overton farm. Around 10:00, Wright caught up with Russell and Ricketts and learned about the Mechanicsville

Road that Russell's scouts had found. The route sounded promising, and Ricketts started some of his men toward it, expecting them to follow the Pennsylvanians. Intelligence soon came back, however, that the Pennsylvanians had run into Hill's skirmishers. Wagons brought up rations while Wright mulled over his options. Ricketts's soldiers ate, and Wright dispatched scouts down Richmond Pike to locate Hancock's right flank and advise him how best to get there.[18]

Lee carefully reviewed information as it came in, trying to divine Grant's intentions. "I have nothing new to report in my front," Hill informed him. Breckinridge's sector also remained relatively dormant. "I can see the enemy sending pretty strong lines of skirmishers across the meadow to the Totopotomoy on Breckinridge's right," Hill advised after visiting Atlee Station Road. "They are throwing up rifle pits and batteries in front of Breckinridge's, near Shelton's house." No sign of a major offensive was evident.[19]

News also streamed in from cavalry pickets off Lee's left flank. Bradley Johnson, whose 1st Maryland Cavalry was keeping close tabs on Russell's movements, reported that the Federals had left Hanover Court House at 7:00 A.M. Capturing a few 6th Corps pickets, the Marylanders gleaned details. Russell's force, Johnson learned, had moved "by the left flank as skirmishers over the road parallel to the railroad." Their purpose, he informed Lee, was to cover the 6th Corps's movement in the vicinity of Peake's Station. Fitz Lee also noted Wright's withdrawal. Concerned that Grant might be removing soldiers from his northern flank in preparation for a turning movement to the south, General Lee at 8:00 A.M. directed a message to Matthew Butler, whose cavalry was centered near Mechanicsville. "The General thinks the enemy is moving around our right, and desires that you will push some bold scouting parties up the road in which your command is and endeavor to ascertain which way they are going," wrote Lee's adjutant Charles Marshall. "Use every prudent means to find out which way the enemy are going." Within the hour, Butler's command, augmented by Gary's recent arrivals, were trotting toward Cold Harbor.[20]

As Butler was getting under way, critical information reached Lee from another source. S. Franklin Stringfellow, a trusted scout, was investigating developments in the direction of Old Church. Union cavalry, Stringfellow advised, had occupied Old Church and was moving south toward Cold Harbor. "Judging from what I hear and see," Stringfellow went on, "I think that General Grant is concentrating a large force on his left, and contemplates a move in this direction very soon." Such a move was the very development

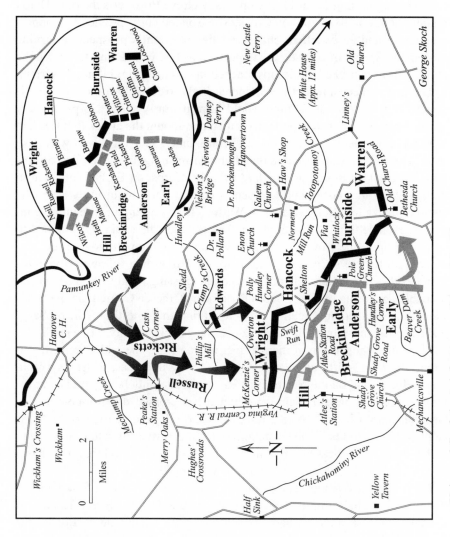

Union and Confederate infantry operations on May 30

that Lee feared. Grant, it seemed, was preparing to shift substantial portions of his army toward Cold Harbor.[21]

Aggressive as ever, Lee longed to take the initiative. At this juncture, Warren's corps, pressing toward Early on Shady Grove Road, was the only Union infantry south of Totopotomoy Creek. The isolated corps provided an opportune target and an excellent chance to disrupt Grant's prospective turning movement. Speed, of course, was important, as Lee would have to launch the attack before more Federal troops reached the sector and reinforced Warren.

Lee had looked in recent weeks increasingly to Jubal Early to lead his offensive thrusts. And as fortune would have it, Early's 2nd Corps, already across Warren's front, was perfectly situated to mount the attack that Lee had in mind. Confederate reinforcements from Anderson's 1st Corps were also readily available. Nothing more than light skirmishing had developed on Anderson's front all morning, which left the 1st Corps, on Early's left, free to participate in the movement. Lee sent a note to Early inquiring whether he could organize an offensive against Warren. Then he sent a companion letter to Anderson setting out his thinking. The Federals, he explained, seemed to be taking up a line from Crump's Creek south to Totopotomoy Creek, embracing McKenzie's Corner. From there, the Union line followed Totopotomoy Creek's north bank and dropped south, crossing Shady Grove Road and probably anchoring on Old Church Road near Bethesda Church, on the headwaters of Matadequin Creek. "After fortifying this line they will probably make another move by their left flank over the Chickahominy," Lee predicted. "This is just a repetition of their former movements," he added, referring to Grant's similar shifts after stalemates in the Wilderness, at Spotsylvania Court House, and on the North Anna River. "It can only be arrested by striking at once that part of their force which has crossed the Totopotomoy in General Early's front," he emphasized. "I have desired [Early] to do this if he thought it could be done advantageously, and have written to him that you will support him. Please communicate with him at once. Whatever is determined on should be done as soon as practicable."[22]

Early penned a response at noon. Warren had advanced on Shady Grove Road to within half a mile of the Confederate 2nd Corps's line at Hundley's Corner. Union skirmishers had also materialized on Old Church Road, near Bethesda Church, but Early had no information about what was behind them. A considerable enemy force—Gibbon's division of Hancock's corps—had moved onto heights across Totopotomoy Creek facing his left, threatening Pole Green Church Road. Early proposed advancing Rodes's division east along Old Church Road "to see what the enemy has." If necessary, he would shuttle his remaining two divisions, under Ramseur and Gordon, to Old

Church Road in support. To free up troops for the fight, Early arranged for Anderson to cover Shady Grove Road. "Field's division is taking the place of my left division," Early informed Lee. If the entire 2nd Corps needed to swing south onto Old Church Road, Anderson was to "take the place of my other divisions." And should Early's foray out Old Church Road prove successful, Anderson was to pitch in as well. "I am inclined to the opinion that no large force is on this side of the Totopotomoy," Early observed, and closed by assuring Lee that he would "not go too far from the rest of our troops."[23]

Lee forwarded Early's letter to Anderson. "I approve what is therein suggested," he told the 1st Corps's commander, "and have authorized General Early to carry out what is proposed, if his judgment approves. I desire you, if circumstances permit, to carry out your part."[24]

The Union high command had no inkling that Lee was girding to attack. The chief debate at the Potomac army's headquarters revolved around whether Lee's entire army held the Totopotomoy line or Lee had withdrawn and left behind only a skeleton force to delay the Federals while he constructed a new line below the Chickahominy. With Union cavalry still massed at Old Church, east of the Federal army, Grant had no way to obtain reliable intelligence. "It still remains doubtful whether his main body remains north or south of the Chickahominy," Dana wrote Washington at 1:00 P.M., predicting that the point would "probably be settled before dark." The day had seen little more than skirmishing, and Dana believed a major battle unlikely. "General Grant means to fight here if there is a fair chance," Dana related, "but he will not run his head against heavy works."[25]

"There seems to be some mistake about cavalry covering my left."

Shortly after noon, Confederate guns along Breckinridge's line focused on Tidball's batteries across the creek on Colonel Shelton's farm. Portions of Cabell's and Huger's Confederate 1st Corps battalions on Breckinridge's right chimed in, escalating the duel. The fire, Tidball thought, was "terrific." Union pieces responded, and woods and fields around Atlee Station Road reverberated from the din. Accurate Confederate artillery fire burst over the Union batteries, preventing Tidball's gunners from loading and sighting their pieces. Standing near one of the guns, Barlow, Miles, and Robertson were showered with dirt and debris when a shell exploded close by.[26]

Then Union Coehorn mortars opened. Shells arced high into the air and fell behind the Confederate earthworks five hundred yards away. Mortars were a novelty, having first been used by the Army of the Potomac at the

Bloody Angle on May 12. A soldier seeing them at the Shelton farm noted that the "precision with which they dropped their shells behind breastworks impervious to direct cannon shots had a most demoralizing effect upon the troops against whom they were directed, causing them to 'get up and dust' with surprising alacrity." Mortar shells silenced the closest rebel pieces— those of McLaughlin's battery—and sent gray-clad artillerists scurrying. Union rifled guns also opened, Roder's battery alone firing 223 rounds of shot and shell.[27]

Breckinridge's men could only hug close against their entrenchments and hope for the best. The 26th Virginia Battalion held a tongue of land considerably in advance of the rest of the Confederate troops, its left resting on a bend in the creek and exposed to enfilading fire. "A score or more siege guns swept, with their deadly fire, the entire plateau upon which our division was entrenched," wrote Colonel George M. Edgar, commanding the battalion. "The enemy's skirmishers, at the base of the hill, with their improved rifles, held ours in strenuous combat, making it extremely perilous for a head to rise above the crest of our entrenchments." Recollected Edgar: "Nothing but the speedy construction of 'bombproofs,' thickly covered with timber and earth, made it possible for us to hold our ground."[28]

John Ford of the 26th Virginia Battalion was crouching behind an uprooted tree near the creek when a mortar shell landed a few feet away, its fuse still burning. Ford dug feverishly in the sand, seeking shelter from the blast. "Scratch, John, scratch," soldiers called out. "She's going off!" Burrowing like a gopher, Ford covered himself with sand. An explosion shook the ground. As smoke and dust lifted, Ford's compatriots were relieved to see him rise slowly out of his hole, look around with a grin, and sing out, "Who-eeh." Not so fortunate was Joe Flint of the same outfit. Assigned to cooking detail, he was returning to the picket line with a pot of corn bread and beef when the shelling started. A projectile exploded in front of him just as he reached his company. "When the smoke cleared away the bloody fragments of the man and the scattered contents of the camp kettle lay mingled together," a compatriot recollected. A soldier eyed the remains of his meal with disgust. "Lor' boys, just look," he exclaimed. "Joe Flint is all mixed up with our breakfast, and it ain't for nothing!"[29]

Signal officers on the Shelton house roof helped direct Tidball's fire. To drive them away, rebel guns focused on the house. Colonel Shelton, who was with Breckinridge on the Confederate side of the creek, asked the general to spare his home. Shelton told a Union officer after the war that Breckinridge assured him his family had left the dwelling. The house must be leveled, Breckinridge insisted, because Federals were using it as an observation post and massing troops behind it. The hapless Shelton looked on as Breckinridge set about systematically destroying his ancestral home, little suspecting that his family was still inside. "Shells were striking the house, bricks were falling from the chimney," young Walter Shelton remembered. "One shell went through a cedar chest of bedding before it exploded. The roar of the guns was deafening; we could hardly breathe for the smoke." In the midst of the bombardment, Robertson and several staff officers ate lunch under the front porch. "A shell came through to the wall and exploded, blowing out the windows, and filling our lunch basket with broken glass and mortar, effectively ruining our dinner," Robertson related. Worried that the house had caught fire, Robertson ran upstairs. The room was in shambles, with everything broken except a large mirror that hung miraculously unharmed. Robertson checked in the basement where the Shelton family huddled, "alternately shrieking and praying." No one was hurt, although one of the ladies suffered so severely from fright that Robertson sent a doctor to attend her.[30]

Artillery caissons stood parked near a row of slave cabins by the main house. At the height of the cannonading, an aged black woman came out of a cabin and dumped a pan of hot coals near a limber chest filled with ammunition. The coals ignited cartridges and the limber chest exploded, killing several soldiers and burning out the eyes of others. The side of a barn also blew out, letting loose a cloud of geese and hens. Hancock's aide Mitchell arrived as the sightless men were being led away. "It was not supposed that the negress had any intention of doing such mischief," he reported. "She was so crazy that none believed she knew what she had done." Hancock's aide Walker was under the impression that the old lady had escaped uninjured and griped that "in the army it always *was* the fool doing the mischief who got off safe." Walter Shelton, who was looking out the basement window with his sister Francis, gave a different version. According to Shelton, the old lady had nothing to do with the explosion. He claimed that a shell hit the limber chest, and that the woman just happened to be standing nearby.[31]

Confederate fire slackened after an hour of Tidball's pounding. The artillery duel left several Union and Confederate soldiers dead or maimed. It did nothing, however, to advance either side's prospects. Rebels and Yankees stared across the creek at one another and girded for the next round. "The Shelton House is riddled by shot of enemy," a signal officer informed Hancock at 3:30 P.M. "Our batteries and mortars in front of the house have silenced for the present enemy's guns, our batteries doing splendid work, almost every shot striking where aimed. Slight skirmishing going on now." Around 4:00, artillerymen from Captain Nelson Ames's Battery G, 1st New York Light, lined up and marched into the Shelton field, accompanied by a hundred or so soldiers from the 4th New York Heavy Artillery acting as laborers. Each man carried a shovel and rails. Reaching a point near Arnold's guns, they stacked their rails and began shoveling dirt into a line of works. Bullets from rebel sharpshooters whistled through the wheat around them. "No one who has not seen men shovel dirt under fire can imagine the quantity of soil that can be heaved in a short time," Ames later claimed. Once Ames's gunners were in place, Edgell's 1st New Hampshire battery and Brown's 1st Rhode Island battery rolled into line next to them, giving Barlow impressive artillery support.[32]

Wright had garnered a fairly accurate picture of the road network below Hanover Court House. Totopotomoy Creek was a little over five miles due south of the courthouse town, and there were three ways to get to the stream. One choice was to follow the Virginia Central Railroad through Peake's Station and on toward Atlee's Station. A second option was to take Mechanicsville Road, which originated a short distance east of Peake's Station and paralleled the railroad south through McKenzie's Corner. A third way was the Richmond Pike, a major road that originated at Cash Corner—about a mile east of Peake's Station—and jogged south roughly parallel to Mechanicsville Road and about a half mile east of it. About a mile north of Totopotomoy Creek, a road ran east to west, paralleling the creek's northern bank and connecting Mechanicsville Road at McKenzie's Corner with the Richmond Pike at the Overton place. Wright decided to form his final line along this east-west road. To accomplish this result, Ricketts was to follow the Richmond Pike to the Overton property on Hancock's right flank and deploy westward. Russell was to remain a while at Peake's Station to screen Ricketts's movement, then shift over to Mechanicsville Road and march south, following the route of Upton's Pennsylvania regiments. When Russell reached the east-west road at McKenzie Corner, he was to extend east, linking with Ricketts. After the maneuver was complete, the 6th Corps would be oriented on an east-west axis along the northern bank of Totopotomoy Creek, facing south and connecting with Hancock on its left.[33]

Ricketts's portion of the 6th Corps started south from Cash Corner around 2:00 P.M. Some troops had advanced toward Peake's Station and had to backtrack. To make up for lost time, Wright authorized them to cut cross-country. Streams and rivulets forming the headwaters of Crump's Creek threaded through the region, creating, the staffer Humphreys later remarked, "a swamp and tangle of the worst character." Shortcuts turned into tortuous detours. At 5:00—nearly twelve hours after the 6th Corps had set out from its camps that morning—Ricketts's lead elements marched into the Overton yard and

merged with the right end of Birney's line. Birney, who had fretted all afternoon about his exposed flank, complained that Wright "wasted hours in getting into position." When Meade questioned Wright's diligence and implied
that he might have halted too long for lunch, the 6th Corps commander fired
back angrily. "I am mortified to learn from your note," he told Meade's aide
Humphreys, "that the major general commanding should suppose that anything short of impossibility should delay me in taking position." Short tempers were much in evidence that hot and sticky afternoon.[34]

Russell remained at Peake's Station until 3:00 P.M., shifted over to Mechanicsville Road, and started south. Colonel Oliver Edwards's brigade
served as rear guard. As soon as Russell's main body was under way, Edwards's men crossed to Richmond Pike and provided cover for Ricketts's
rear. "The rebels followed us up closely with cavalry and two pieces of artillery," Charles Harvey Brewster of the 10th Massachusetts wrote home, "and
we had rare fun and considerable adventure in lying in wait and blazing at the
Johnnies as they followed us up." White's Maine battery, temporarily
attached to Edwards's brigade, dueled effectively with rebel horse artillery.
Edwards camped at Phillip's Mill—also known as Taliaferro's Mill—and
protected Ricketts's rear from harassment by Confederate cavalrymen.[35]

Wright's corps was in place shortly after 5:00 P.M. Neill formed the right,
near McKenzie's Corner, Russell held the middle, and Ricketts deployed on
the left, at the Overton farm. Captain William A. Harn's 3rd Battery, New
York Light, and Stephen W. Dorsey's Battery H, 1st Ohio Light, went into
position near the Overton house, facing Swift Run. Wright's soldiers hoped
for rest, but headquarters would not permit it. At 5:00 P.M., Meade directed
Wright to push forward skirmishers, develop the Confederate position in his
front, "and, if practicable, attack the enemy in case he appears weak."[36]

The situation on the 5th Corps's left continued to irritate Warren. Despite his
protests, Sheridan had done precious little to clear rebel cavalry from Old
Church Road. To quiet Warren, Sheridan sent three squadrons from the 17th
Pennsylvania Cavalry late in the morning, but they were patently insufficient
to cover the 5th Corps's flank. Crawford's division had now massed in the
Via fields. The term of service for Crawford's two brigades of Pennsylvania
Reserves was due to expire the next day, and Warren had no desire to send
them into combat. Helping to drive rebel cavalry from Old Church Road
seemed an innocuous assignment, however, and Warren directed Crawford to
send a brigade south to handle the job. Then he vented his spleen to Humphreys. "There seems to be some mistake about the cavalry covering my
left," he wrote headquarters at 2:10 P.M. Crawford, he added, was preparing

to march onto Old Church Road. As soon as Burnside could bring sufficient troops across Totopotomoy Creek to relieve Griffin, he intended to shift his whole force south. "General Sheridan's cavalry," he noted in a closing jab, "is I believe lying in the vicinity of New Castle Ferry."[37]

Crawford started Colonel Martin D. Hardin's brigade of Pennsylvania Reserves from the Via farm around 2:30. Advancing to Shady Grove Road, the Pennsylvanians marched a short distance west to the farm of the Bowles family—"a man, his wife, and a large brood of young rebels," one Federal described the inhabitants. A road turned off at the Bowles farm and ran three-quarters of a mile south to Old Church Road, striking it at Bethesda Church. While Hardin continued toward Bethesda Church, Crawford held his other brigade of Pennsylvania Reserves, under Colonel Joseph W. Fisher, at the Bowles farm. That morning, a brigade consisting of the 6th and 15th New York Heavy Artillery, under Colonel G. Howard Kitching, had joined Crawford. Containing many soldiers of German descent, Kitching's brigade had made a name for itself by waging a determined delaying action at Harris farm on May 19. Crawford sent Kitching south toward Bethesda Church and halted him in line facing west, loosely linking Hardin's brigade on Old Church Road with the rest of the 5th Corps on Shady Grove Road.[38]

To the west, Warren's main body was still inching ahead on Shady Grove Road, Griffin leading, Cutler filing in behind. Early's skirmishers delayed their progress by hiding and firing from behind sawdust piles at an abandoned sawmill on Totopotomoy Creek. Griffin finally drove the rebels from their mounds and pushed on, breaking contact with 9th Corps skirmishers trying to keep up on his right. Burnside was beside himself. He had extended troops over to Warren earlier in the day, he wrote headquarters, only to discover that Warren had moved on. "As soon as I learned this I sent in another division," he fumed, "and before that was in position Warren's right had swung off at least a mile and was represented as being hard pressed." Now he understood that Warren's rightmost division, under Griffin, was "moving off by the left flank, thus making a gap and leaving our left entirely exposed." Burnside suggested a simple solution. "If General Warren would fall back to our line and connect with our left we could, I think, hold the line, and I can send him 3,000 or 4,000 men," he wrote headquarters.[39]

Headquarters, it developed, was on the move again. Gathering up a handful of aides, Meade had ridden out to go "confabbing with the generals and spying round the country roads," as Lyman put it. Reaching the Shelton yard, he stopped to visit Hancock. The 2nd Corps commander was dressed as usual in a spotless white shirt—his man Shaw, formerly a British butler, made sure that he had an ample supply—and greeted the visitors with a cheerful smile.

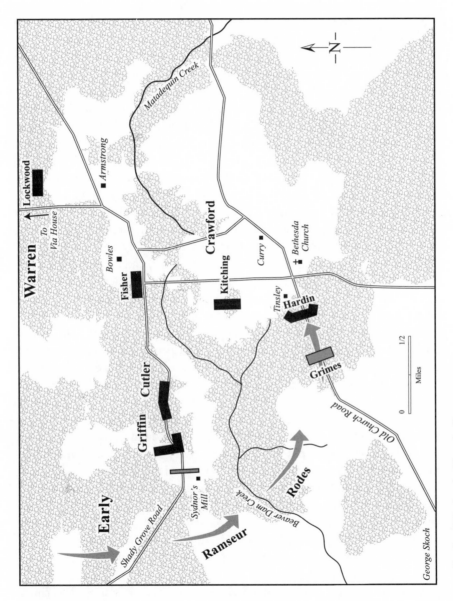

Battle of Bethesda Church, first stage

George Skoch

Several aides were asleep in their tents, oblivious to the constant musketry and artillery fire. "There are a great many wood ticks eating me," the aide Mitchell complained, "but I haven't the strength to fight them." While Meade and Hancock chatted, Lyman examined the flora, noting that the "swamp magnolias are in flower and the azaleas, looking very pretty and making a strong fragrance." After scrutinizing the Confederate position on the other side of the creek, Meade sent a dispatch to Warren. Breckinridge held a strong position across Atlee Station Road, Meade wrote, "and it would not seem probable that much can be done here." He wanted Warren to develop the main rebel line in his front. "If, on examination, you think it expedient to attack the enemy you may do so," he instructed. If Warren needed reinforcements, Meade emphasized, he was authorized to draw on Burnside's reserves.[40]

Warren's skirmishers fought their way west along Shady Grove Road to a small tributary of Totopotomoy Creek. The tributary and its feeders carved out a wooded, swampy ravine. On the far side loomed earthworks, slicing across Shady Grove Road a short distance east of Hundley's Corner. The Federals had found Early's main defensive fortifications, and the line looked formidable. "We could not take them," a Bay Stater concluded, "so kept back as much as we could, out of range." Ayres's men began throwing up earthworks, digging with hands, bayonets, and plates. Sweitzer supported Ayres, and Bartlett sent two regiments—the 83rd Pennsylvania and 16th Michigan—onto Sweitzer's left, extending the 5th Corps's burgeoning line well south of Shady Grove Road. Early's riflemen kept the Federals pinned in place and mortally wounded Major Robert T. Elliott, commanding the 16th Michigan.[41]

Warren fired off a missive to headquarters. "General Griffin reports to me that he had struck the enemy's line with rifled cannon in position," he wrote. "The orders last night contemplated the cavalry covering my left," he reminded Meade. "They have not done it." He noted that Sheridan's dereliction had required him to "send a large infantry force off my line of march to drive away the enemy's cavalry and support it." His right, Warren added, was now ahead of Burnside and isolated. "I think [Burnside's] whole force should cross over and let me move to the left if I am to go farther," Warren recommended, "as I now have to advance on two diverging roads."[42]

Sheridan, it was true, had ignored Warren's cries for assistance. The Union cavalry commander never explained why he turned a deaf ear to Warren's entreaties, but his reasons are easy to surmise. He had no use for Warren, whom he had disliked since their clash on the movement to Spotsylvania Court House three weeks earlier. Besides, Sheridan was charged with guarding the approaches to White House and New Castle Ferry to protect the army's new supply depot and to keep rebels from interfering with Baldy Smith's arrival. Protecting the 5th Corps's flank was simply not high on his list of priorities, and Warren would have to fend for himself. Meade, who wanted nothing to do with Sheridan and was fed up with Warren's complaining, refused to get drawn into their quarrel. Grant stayed out of it as well.

During the morning, Sheridan had moved his headquarters from New Castle Ferry to the Ruffin plantation near Old Church. Wilson's division remained north of the Pamunkey, guarding river crossings and the route back to Port Royal. Gregg's division patrolled the Pamunkey downriver to New Castle Ferry, and Torbert's division camped in fields around Old Church. The old church that gave the crossroads its name was long gone. Nearby Emanuel Church and James A. Lipscomb's ramshackle inn, grandly named Old Church Hotel, were the region's most notable surviving structures. Old Church was important because of the roads that radiated from it. One road ran southeast twelve miles to White House and served as the main artery between the Union army and its supply depot. Another route—Old Church Road—ran west to Bethesda Church and on to Mechanicsville, passing below Warren's left flank. And a third road, Bottoms Bridge Road, ran south toward Bottoms Bridge on the Chickahominy. A mile and a half south of Old Church, Bottoms Bridge Road intersected the road running west to Old Cold Harbor. This junction accounted in part for the concentration of Union cavalry at Old Church. "As our occupation of this point was essential to secure our lines to the White House, which was to be our base," Sheridan later observed, "its possession became a matter of deep interest."[43]

As Warren's protests grew increasingly urgent, Sheridan ordered Torbert to cover the roads off the 5th Corps's left flank. Torbert passed the assignment on to Colonel Thomas C. Devin, whose brigade was camped near the Old Church intersection. Warren's concern was for cavalry to patrol Old Church Road, but the message somehow got garbled, leading Devin to understand that his primary objective was to picket the road toward Cold Harbor. Riding out Bottoms Bridge Road, he reconnoitered the ground. Three-quarters of a mile south of Old Church, Bottoms Bridge Road crossed Matadequin Creek. The creek's high banks made ideal defensive positions, and Devin decided to post part of his brigade there. He placed a reserve at the creek and advanced a squadron from the 17th Pennsylvania Cavalry another three-quarters of a mile south to where the road from Cold Harbor came into Bottoms Bridge Road. The squadron settled down on the Barker family farm, in the northwest quadrant formed by Cold Harbor Road and Bottoms Bridge

Road. "My orders," Devin wrote, "were, if attacked, the reserve should hold [Matadequin Creek] in any event until support arrived."[44]

Around midmorning, unknown to the Union commanders, Butler's Confederate cavalry had left Mechanicsville on its probe to determine whether Grant was concentrating toward Cold Harbor. Butler himself had arrived with the 6th South Carolina Cavalry shortly after the fight at Haw's Shop. Since then, he and his brigade—the 4th, 5th, and 6th South Carolina Cavalry—had operated out of Mechanicsville, watching the roads off Lee's right flank. For his expedition, the one-legged war hero decided to leave the novice 6th at Mechanicsville and take with him the 4th, under Colonel Rutledge, and the 5th, now under Lieutenant Colonel Robert J. Jeffords. Joining Butler was Martin Gary's small brigade. A lawyer and politician like Butler, the thin, balding Gary was an engaging orator and a natural leader of men. His available troops—the 7th South Carolina Cavalry—were greenhorns. This was the first time that the various companies composing the regiment, commanded by Major Alexander C. Haskell, had been joined together.[45]

Two thousand Confederate cavalrymen jangled through Old Cold Harbor and approached the Barker farm along Cold Harbor Road between 1:00 and 2:00 P.M. Butler's skirmishers in the fore of the rebel column easily dislodged the squadron of Pennsylvania troopers and drove them north across the Barker fields to Matadequin Creek. Devin immediately committed two more squadrons to the fight from the 17th Pennsylvania, under Major Coe Durland. Mounting a countercharge, Durland drove Butler's lead elements back across the Barker farm and reestablished the picket line. Having repulsed Butler with little effort, Devin assumed that he faced a light enemy force and did nothing to reinforce his pickets.[46]

An hour later—about 3:00—Butler's Confederates swarmed into the Barker fields in overwhelming numbers. More Confederates poured west, crossed Bottoms Bridge Road, and occupied the fields of Spottswood Liggan's family farm. Severely outnumbered, the Pennsylvania pickets retired north to Matadequin Creek and formed along the stream's northern bank, waging a desperate delaying action to prevent the South Carolinians from getting across. Realizing that he faced more Confederates than he had thought, Devin hurried his 6th and 9th New York from Old Church to Matadequin Creek. Dismounting, the New Yorkers deployed in a line along the creek facing south, the 6th New York to the right of the beleaguered Pennsylvanians, west of Bottoms Bridge Road, and the 9th New York to the Pennsylvanians' left, east of the road.[47]

Butler responded by pumping more troopers into the fray. Bottoms Bridge Road, running along a north-south axis, defined the direction of his attack.

The 4th South Carolina deployed on the Barker farm, west of the road, facing north toward the 6th New York and part of the 17th Pennsylvania. The 5th South Carolina continued the Confederate line east across the Liggan farm, facing the 9th New York and the remaining elements of the 17th Pennsylvania. Butler and Gary ordered their troopers into place "by squadrons, as they were needed," a southerner recollected. The 7th South Carolina remained in reserve well south of the creek, probably along Cold Harbor Road.

Torbert rode up and surveyed his line. Three regiments were patently insufficient to fend off Butler, so he ordered the rest of his division to move up from its camp at Old Church and spread along the creek. The reinforcements came up at a trot. First to arrive was Merritt's Reserve Brigade, advancing "elegantly," Merritt wrote in his report, and supported by Williston's artillery battery. "As we hove into sight, the Johnnies were socking it to Devin's boys at a lively rate," one of Merritt's men remembered. Merritt's arrival tipped the balance in favor of the Federals. The troopers of the 17th Pennsylvania retired—they had run out of ammunition—and the 2nd United States Regulars took their place in line across Bottoms Bridge Road. Advancing in tandem with the 6th New York Cavalry, the Regulars pushed back the 4th South Carolina and threatened to breach a portion of the Confederate line crossing Mr. Liggan's farm abutting the roadway. The Charleston Light Dragoons rushed into the Liggan yard to stem the breakthrough. Hurriedly tearing down a fence, the Charleston men constructed field works. New Yorkers and Regulars sought cover in the nearby Liggan family home and outbuildings.[48]

On the left wing of Devin's formation, the 9th New York drove the foremost rebel skirmishers back across two ravines to the main course of Matadequin Creek. The stream had cut a deep swale east of Bottoms Bridge Road. The banks were steep, rising some forty feet above the water, and Jeffords's soldiers from the 5th South Carolina waited behind fence rails three hundred feet back on the south bank. Colonel William Sackett, commanding the 9th New York, tried to force a crossing over the natural moat, but rebel riflemen picked off his men with ease and persuaded him to abandon the attempt. In an effort to outflank the position, Merritt ordered Captain Charles L. Leiper's 6th Pennsylvania Cavalry to pass around the 9th New York's left and find a place to cross. The Pennsylvanians managed to get over the creek but bogged down in a brutal hand-to-hand fight against Jeffords's men. Leiper fell severely wounded, and his adjutant, Lieutenant Stephen W. Martin, was killed. "Our brave boys fought with desperation, though losing heavily," a Pennsylvanian wrote.[49]

Just when it seemed that the sides were stalemated, Custer and his Wolverines rode up. Ordering his troopers to dismount, Custer placed Colonel Russell A. Alger's 5th Michigan on the right of Bottoms Bridge Road, Magoffin's 1st Michigan and Walker's 7th Michigan on the left of the road, and Kidd's 6th Michigan in reserve. The plan was for the 5th Michigan to swing around the western end of the Confederate line while the 1st and 7th Michigan drove straight down Bottoms Bridge Road. "Jumping off our horses, we formed a line by the side of the column," a sergeant in the 5th Michigan wrote, "then marching by the right flank, we moved out to a field in which there was a rise of ground." While Alger's 5th Michigan threatened the Confederate left, Magoffin's 1st Michigan and Walker's 7th Michigan muscled south along Bottoms Bridge Road. The results were dramatic. Flanked on its left by the 5th Michigan, Rutledge's 4th South Carolina began retiring south across the Barker fields. And as Magoffin's and Walker's troopers pressed across Matadequin Creek on Bottoms Bridge Road, Rutledge found his right flank turned as well. The 4th South Carolina broke, and the 6th New York, which had been facing Rutledge across Matadequin Creek, charged into the mass of fleeing rebels. "Coming out of this Hell was a terrible matter," one of Rutledge's men wrote. "Thicker and thicker came the bullets, and it looked as if every blade of grass and each weed in the field were being cut down as they skimmed past humming their devilish tunes."[50]

The Charleston Light Dragoons found themselves in an impossible situation as Magoffin's and Walker's troopers passed their left flank. "Before long the bullets began to come from the left, and the fence ceased to be of much service as a protection" a Charleston man recollected. "Then every private knew, as well as if each had been the commanding general, that the line was flanked." Taking advantage of the Michiganders' turning movement, the Regulars ensconced in Mr. Liggan's buildings charged and broke the Charleston line. Lieutenant Nowell, commanding the Charlestonians, tried to organize a countercharge, but only a few soldiers responded. The rest of the Charleston Light Dragoons ran rearward across Mr. Liggan's field. "It is needless to say that before we knew it we were badly whipped," a Charleston private later admitted. Nowell was captured, and fourteen of the twenty-eight men who went into battle with him were killed, wounded, or captured.[51]

The going was tough for the northerners east of Bottoms Bridge Road, where deep gullies afforded Jeffords's rebels excellent protection. That changed when the Liggan farm fell to the Federals. Turned out of their stronghold, Jeffords's Confederates joined Rutledge's men in retreat. "I had to run myself near to death to keep from being captured," attested a man in the 5th South Carolina. Custer was in the process of bringing up Kidd's 6th Michigan when Butler's entire front collapsed, making it unnecessary for Custer to

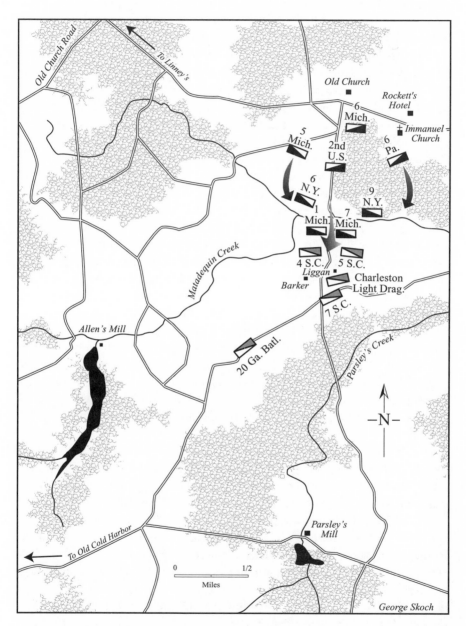

Cavalry fight at Matadequin Creek on May 30

commit his final regiment. The Confederates "fled precipitously on all parts of the field," a Pennsylvanian recalled, "leaving a large number of dead and wounded and prisoners in our hands." Colonel Jeffords, commanding the 5th South Carolina, was painfully wounded in the thigh.[52]

The 7th South Carolina had remained in reserve south of Matadequin Creek. It now counterattacked in an attempt to stem the Union tide. "Our eight companies were ordered to charge dismounted across an open wheat-field [of the Barker and Liggan farms] to try and check the advance, which was overlapping Butler's brigade, and give them an opportunity to with-draw," William G. Hinson of the 7th South Carolina recorded in his diary. Colonel Haskell and Major Edward M. Boykin—cousin of the prolific Con-federate diarist Mary Boykin Chesnut—led the charge on horseback. The results were predictable. The Wolverines' repeating carbines cut down Haskell's greenhorns in droves. Haskell and Boykin were seriously wounded, and six of their captains fell dead or injured. The 20th Georgia Battalion, which had shared the 4th and 5th South Carolina's misfortunes at Haw's Shop, came up as the fight was ending. A mob of horsemen, everyone "riding as fast as his horse could go," almost swamped them. A bareheaded officer, "apparently frightened out of his wits," stopped long enough to identify him-self as belonging to Butler's staff and to warn that Federal infantry—probably Crawford's force on Old Church Road, to the north—was advancing on an-other route and threatened to cut them off. Panic seized Butler's ranks when men falling back from the battle line discovered their horse-holders had dis-appeared, taking the mounts with them. Fields and woods below Matadequin Creek leaked dismounted Confederate cavalrymen for hours. Some of Has-kell's men fled south along Bottoms Bridge Road all the way to the Chicka-hominy.[53]

Butler's main body retreated west along Cold Harbor Road. Torbert's troopers followed in exuberant pursuit. The 5th Michigan "completely routed them," an officer recollected, "firing our Spencers and yelling as only Michi-gan men can yell, Wolverines sure." Butler rallied his stricken command near Old Cold Harbor. Torbert called off the chase and bivouacked firmly across the route to Old Church, with Devin at the Cold Harbor Road–Bottoms Bridge Road intersection and Custer to the south at Parsley's Mill. The Wol-verines felt invincible. Once again, in a dramatic repeat of Haw's Shop, they had turned impasse into victory, driven the enemy from the field, and won the day for Sheridan. And once again, the South Carolinians had earned their respect. "They fight better than Stuart's cavalry can or at least better than they have done this spring," a soldier in the 9th New York Cavalry con-cluded.[54]

Butler could claim a small success, having gathered the information that General Lee requested. "I do not think [the Federals] had infantry," he informed the rebel commander, "and from all I could learn I do not think they have infantry moving down this side the Pamunkey River." By any other standard, Butler's reconnaissance had been a costly failure. The 4th South Carolina lost 52 men, the 5th South Carolina 16, the 7th South Carolina 82, and the 20th Georgia Battalion 38. Butler's troopers were downcast over the debacle, particularly since it followed closely on the heels of their mauling at Haw's Shop. Adjutant Gabriel E. Manigault of the 4th South Carolina thought Butler should have called off the fight when the Federals brought up artillery. Lieutenant Colonel Stokes of the same regiment agreed that Butler had unnecessarily prolonged the battle. "The fight was a very unfortunate one," he wrote home, "and nothing was gained by continuing it for so long."[55]

"A swath of dead and dying."

Jubal Early was also having a busy afternoon. At 2:00 P.M.—Butler's lead elements were pushing Devin's pickets back to Matadequin Creek, Breckinridge was sparring with Hancock at Colonel Shelton's farm, and Fitzhugh Lee was monitoring Wright's southward drift from Hanover Court House— Early began shifting Rodes's division onto Old Church Road, using two trails he had cut over from Shady Grove Road. As Rodes moved out, Early sent Ramseur's division behind him, holding Gordon's division in reserve to exploit Rodes's and Ramseur's foray if opportunity arose. Early expected Anderson to bring a 1st Corps division onto Shady Grove Road to fill the gap created by his corps's withdrawal. The plan was for Anderson to attack the head of Warren's column on Shady Grove Road while Early pushed east along Old Church Road, slipping past the Union 5th Corps's left flank, then turning north. Simultaneously slamming into Warren from west and south, Early hoped that he and Anderson would inflict a devastating defeat on the isolated Union force.[56]

Around 3:00 P.M.—Butler's attack along Matadequin Creek was hitting full stride—Hardin's brigade of Pennsylvania Reserves reached Old Church Road. Bethesda Church, described by a correspondent as "an old, unpainted, dilapidated building," stood in a nearby grove. The Tinsley family farm was immediately west of Bethesda Church on Old Church Road. Perched on the 5th Corps's extreme left flank, Hardin was understandably concerned about his safety. Halting on the Tinsley farm, he set his men to erecting earthworks. Their thoughts already turned toward home, the Reserves grumbled and worked without enthusiasm, perfunctorily stacking fence rails, digging shallow trenches, and throwing dirt onto the rails. When their labors were done, they lay down under the shade of a tall hedge.[57]

While most of Hardin's men lounged on the Tinsley farm, Major W. Ross Hartshorne rounded up elements from the 1st and 13th Pennsylvania Reserves, called "Bucktails" after their distinctive headgear, and reconnoitered west along Old Church Road. Passing through a stand of woods, the Bucktails emerged into a large field. A dense pine thicket rose on the far side. The Pennsylvanians reached the forest, crossed a swampy ravine, and halted, expecting to remain there until the rest of the brigade came up. Unexpectedly, Rodes's Confederates attacked, coming from the west and holding back their skirmishers to conceal their approach. First to strike were Tar Heels commanded by Brigadier General Bryan Grimes. "To retire was impossible because the ravine was at our back," one of Hartshorne's soldiers related. Fighting from behind trees, the 1st Pennsylvania Reserves briefly held its ground, then broke before Grimes's superior numbers. Hartshorne sent word back to Hardin that he was surrounded and began retiring to the barricades at the Tinsley farm.[58]

Grimes's men captured several Bucktails and sent them to the rear for questioning. A Confederate colonel quizzed a captive, Sergeant James B. Thompson, about the strength of the Union force in his front. Thompson answered that he had never made a count, "Any fool knows that," the Confederate responded. "You didn't count them, but how many do you think there are?" Thompson remained obdurate. "If any fool knows I didn't count them, what did you ask me for?" he fired back. "As to thinking, we don't think," he added. "We have generals who think for us."[59]

While Thompson and his fellow prisoners bandied with their captors, Grimes's North Carolinians marched east toward the Tinsley farm, driving the Pennsylvanians before them. Undeterred by Hardin's fieldworks—the entrenchments, a soldier in the 11th Pennsylvania Reserves conceded, were of "poor contriving"—Grimes sent part of his brigade ahead and swooped portions around both sides of the fence-rail fort. "The situation was of course an awful one," a soldier in the 2nd Pennsylvania Reserves remembered, "for the rebels were now in our works on both flanks." Some dozing Reserves did not wake up until the Tar Heels were upon them. "Each hurriedly took in the situation," a Pennsylvanian admitted, "then, such skedadling to the rear was never seen before." The rout was complete, and Hardin's troops streamed north along the road leading back to the Bowles farm. "The volley or two delivered by our feeble force made no impression on the enemy," a Federal recalled. Rodes's division "ran over and around the piles of rails, and his division headquarters arrived amidst the headquarters of [Hardin's brigade] before the latter could extricate itself." Grimes had won a clean little victory, but it had cost him 118 men.[60]

Colonel Wainwright, chief of the 5th Corps's artillery, had ridden down to inspect Hardin's position when Grimes's Confederates appeared. The sight transfixed him. "I waited to see how much of an attack it was," he recorded later that day, "which I soon found out, for in five minutes Hardin's brigade was running." Wainwright joined the stampede back toward Shady Grove Road. The situation, he feared, looked "very squally for a complete turning of our left."[61]

Hardin's closest support was Crawford's other two brigades, under Fisher and Kitching. Kitching's men were already south of the Bowles farm, on the road to Bethesda Church. Learning of the attack on Hardin, Crawford ordered Kitching to start south immediately. Fisher, who was at the Bowles farm, prepared to follow. By this time, masses of Confederates were accumulating at Bethesda Church. Rodes continued a short distance east along Old Church Road, and Ramseur deployed on Rodes's left, facing north toward the rear of the fleeing Pennsylvanians. Captain Thomas B. Massie's four-gun Confederate battery rolled into place near the church and opened on the Reserves.[62]

Kitching had covered about half the distance to Bethesda Church when Hardin's troops stampeded up the road and through fields on both sides of his marching column. North Carolinians followed close on their heels. Kitching had no time to form a battle line before the southerners opened fire. A volley ripped through Kitching's staff at the head of the column, killing four officers and aides. Miraculously, Kitching was unharmed. "This terrible fire right into the head of my column broke the men, many of whom had fallen, killed or wounded," Kitching wrote home the next day. Uninjured soldiers, Kitching recounted, went "sailing across the plain" to the north. Wainwright, who also witnessed the debacle, reported that Kitching's troops "rather indiscriminately hurr[ied] back to the Shady Grove Road." Kitching managed to rally a battalion and waged a brave delaying action, stalling the rebels while Warren patched together a defensive line at the Bowles place. "Handled pretty rough," a soldier in the 6th New York Heavy Artillery wrote of the fight. "Came all very near being captured."[63]

Warren hurried to concentrate his corps along Shady Grove Road and face it south toward the Confederates boiling up from Bethesda Church. "The enemy may have got in force around my left flank," he warned Meade at 4:00. "Any troops that can be sent to the Via house are desirable." Headquarters answered right away. Burnside now had two divisions below Totopotomoy Creek—Crittenden's, sporadically linking with Griffin's left, and

Potter's, on Crittenden's right—and he was directed to send Warren reinforcements. It would take a while for Burnside's soldiers to find their way over to Shady Grove Road. In the meantime, Warren had to fend for himself. The speed with which the Confederates had overrun Hardin, however, now worked to Warren's advantage. Rodes's and Ramseur's divisions had become intermixed during their advance and were bunched up around Bethesda Church. Early needed time to straighten them out and reorient them to attack northward. While Early organized his troops, Warren got the breathing spell he needed.[64]

Riding over from the Via house, Warren met Wainwright, who gave him firsthand news of the disaster at Bethesda Church. Musketry and cannon fire confirmed reports that a formidable enemy force was gathering off the 5th Corps's southern flank. "The volleys sounded to me like throwing down boards that I have heard in a lumber yard," a bandsman noticed, followed by "more scattered firing, as though a number of persons were running on a tin roof." Warren responded by shifting his column of march on Shady Grove Road into a line facing south. Griffin, alerted by sharp musketry that something was amiss, rushed Mink's and Richardson's batteries back to the Bowles farm. Mink posted his guns in front of the Bowles house at the junction of Shady Grove Road and the Bethesda Church road. Richardson advanced his pieces to a shallow ridge where Hardin's retreating troops were forming. Warren instructed Wainwright to bring up more artillery and set up temporary headquarters at the Armstrong farm, where the road from Mrs. Via's place entered Shady Grove Road. Hurrying back to the Via farm, Wainwright started the batteries of Rittenhouse, Lieutenant Aaron F. Walcott, and Captain John Bigelow for Shady Grove Road. Posted at the Armstrong property, the guns had clear views across the Bowles fields and commanded the road to Bethesda Church. Wainwright placed Bigelow to sweep the open ground to the Bowles house and put Rittenhouse and Walcott next to the Armstrong house, facing south.[65]

Warren had been holding his division under Brigadier General Lockwood in reserve at the Via farm. Lockwood was a newcomer to the Army of the Potomac. At forty-nine years of age, he was old for a division commander, and he was also inexperienced, having spent most of the war commanding garrison troops in Maryland. Whether he could make the transition to combat as practiced in Virginia remained to be seen. Major Abner R. Small of the 16th Maine had doubts. Lockwood, Small remarked, resembled a "crabbed schoolmaster," and with his "batch of green aides was running things in a feeble way." Warren, however, needed all the help he could get. Cursing liberally, he shifted Lockwood to the Armstrong fields and supervised the troops as they constructed a line linking with Crawford's left.[66]

From Kitching's position, Warren's officers watched the Confederates at Bethesda Church change front and prepare to march north. Hardin had retired to Shady Grove Road and was forming on Fisher's left. Kitching was still holding a small ridge in advance, his soldiers standing on the crest to fire at the Confederate skirmishers. Confederate musketry, Hardin later noted, "was dealing destruction amongst them, [but] no amount of persuasion or orders could make them lie down." It was folly for Kitching to continue holding his position, and Hardin ordered him to drop back.[67]

Kitching slipped onto Hardin's left, completing Crawford's line. Crawford's three brigades—Fisher's, Hardin's, and Kitching's—were now arranged from west to east in that order, paralleling Shady Grove Road along a shallow ridge that covered the approaches from Bethesda Church. Woods and a deep hollow protected much of the position. Hardin's brigade, in the center, was arrayed along Shady Grove Road or a short distance north of the road, behind a row of slave huts and the Bowles family garden. Richardson had deployed his guns in two sections, one holding high ground on Hardin's right, the other on Hardin's left. Fisher's and Kitching's brigades were south of the road, giving the line a crescent shape, its ends pointing south. A slight breastwork Fisher's soldiers had started earlier in the day was completed—"better ones than those before," a Federal wryly noted—and the Bucktails deployed in a skirmish line to close the gap between Crawford's right and Griffin's left. The troops on the ends of Crawford's crescent had the road from Bethesda Church in a crossfire, and a thick hedge concealed much of the Union position. Altogether, Warren had constructed a formidable trap.[68]

Griffin arrived at the Bowles farm during Warren's preparations. Skirmish fire had quieted, prompting Griffin to inquire why so many troops were concentrated at this point. Hardin offered to take him to the ridge that Kitching's rear guard had been defending to see for himself. Riding to the vantage point, Hardin and Griffin spotted a Confederate headquarters flag at Bethesda Church and ranks of rebel soldiers preparing to charge north. "I'm satisfied," Griffin called as he spurred his horse and rode to bring his division to Crawford's aid. Leaving enough men to hold his earthworks facing Hundley's Corner and Anderson's burgeoning force, he shifted part of his division east along Shady Grove Road. "The men threw up a rifle pit of rails with marvelous rapidity," a Federal recollected. "Aladdin could not have raised a house quicker." The entire 5th Corps was now arrayed to support Crawford, with Lockwood on his left, Griffin on his right, and Cutler in reserve.[69]

Early, anxious to press his advantage, instructed Ramseur to advance a

brigade to "feel the enemy, and ascertain his strength." Ramseur chose Pegram's Brigade, five hundred strong, for the assignment. Comprising five Virginia regiments, the veteran outfit had been Early's former command. It had
seen heavy fighting in the Wilderness, where its namesake, Brigadier General
John Pegram, had been wounded and temporarily replaced by Colonel John
S. Hoffman. Recently, Early had selected Colonel Edward Willis to head the
brigade. A cadet at West Point at the beginning of the war, the slight twenty-
three-year-old had served on Stonewall Jackson's staff and was a favorite of
Lee's. He was from Washington, Georgia, and had commanded the 12th
Georgia until his recent promotion. Wounded in the thigh in the Wilderness,
he had insisted on staying with the army. Richmond had approved his brigadier generalcy, although the papers had not yet arrived.[70]

Colonel Charles B. Christian of the 49th Virginia passed among his men
to select a flag bearer. He had lost nine flag bearers thus far in the campaign,
and with fighting imminent needed another. He stopped in front of a lanky
lad from Amherst, Virginia, who was wearing a red cap. "Orendorf, will you
carry the colors?" Christian asked. "Yes Colonel, I will carry them," the boy
replied. "They killed my brother the other day. Now, damn them, let them
kill me too." The 49th Virginia moved to the head of Willis's column and
started north.[71]

Richardson advanced his pieces somewhat to give him a "splendid view,"
as he later put it, of the ground toward Bethesda Church. He glimpsed Willis's approaching brigade and initiated long-range fire into the far woods,
shooting at different points to feel for the enemy. By this time, Captain John
Milledge's Confederate battery had reached Bethesda Church and began
shooting north, along with Massie's guns. The rebel pieces, Wainwright
thought, fired "remarkably well." Richardson sent back for more ammunition
and tried to silence the rebel guns. The Confederate pieces, however, found
his range, and case shot and shell burst over and around Richardson's men.
Confederate shells also landed on the Bowles farm, and one burst inside the
Bowles house, setting it on fire. A woman ran from the burning home carrying a baby in one arm and leading a child with the other. Confused, she ran
along the Union line until a soldier pointed her to the rear.[72]

After losing three men and four horses to the rebel guns, Richardson asked
Crawford for permission to withdraw his right section and consolidate it with
his left. Crawford ordered Richardson to hold his position "at all hazards,"
but Richardson, who was getting the worst of the duel, directed his gunners
to stop firing. "I never saw the enemy's artillery used to a better advantage
than here," he later admitted. Massie's and Milledge's artillery quieted, and
word arrived from Union scouts that Confederates—Pegram's Brigade, under

Willis—were moving to attack. Richardson pulled back his guns and waited, husbanding ammunition. Warren seemed to be everywhere—"one moment found him at one end of the line and the next at the other," a correspondent noted.[73]

Richardson's fire had attracted Ramseur's attention. The twenty-six-year-old North Carolinian was an ardent secessionist who had made his reputation with hard-hitting attacks. He was also ambitious. He had commanded the division for only a few days and was anxious to prove himself. Pointing toward Richardson's pieces, he asked Early for permission to take the guns out of action. Colonel Christian later claimed that Early "vigorously advised and protested against it," but Ramseur remained obdurate. "Ramseur insisting," Christian wrote, "General Early finally acquiesced in the move."[74]

Pegram's Brigade, the 49th Virginia in front, pressed across a stream and onto the level field extending north to the Bowles farm. Rebel yells broke the calm as Virginians marched in perfect alignment toward the Union guns. "Look! Here they come!" a Federal called. "Never was a more gallant charge made," the Union artillerist Lieutenant David F. Ritchie remembered.[75]

Still Richardson held his fire. Crawford's soldiers sighted down their muskets, taking careful aim at the forms marching into their crescent-shaped line's open arms. "Orders were given not to fire one shot until the enemy reached the line of an old fence half-way across the open space between us," one of Hardin's soldiers recounted. Hartshorne directed his Bucktails to wait until the Confederates were close enough to distinguish their faces. "We never saw so deliberate an advance by the enemy," a Pennsylvanian attested, "in all our three years experience, as this was."[76]

It was 6:00 P.M. The front of the rebel line crossed Shady Grove Road and marched into the Bowles field, toward the slave huts. They were irretrievably in Crawford's sights. Hardin's men aimed straight ahead while Fisher's and Kitching's soldiers looked down their barrels from the curving flanks, ready to unleash a blistering crossfire. When the Confederates were two hundred yards away, Richardson opened with canister, and volleys erupted from the Union entrenchments. "There was a sudden flash of light from the crescent," a reporter observed, "the rattle of a thousand muskets, the booming of a dozen pieces of artillery." Pegram's Brigade reeled, and Richardson shifted to case shot, blasting the gray-clad ranks from both of his sections. "Our line melted away as if by magic," Colonel Christian later wrote. "Every brigade, staff and field officer was cut down (mostly killed outright) in an incredibly short time." It was, he claimed "the heaviest and most murderous fire I had ever seen with grape, canister, and musketry."[77]

The rebels rallied and pressed forward under deadly sheets of lead. Mink,

Battle of Bethesda Church, second stage

George Skoch

in Richardson's rear, opened with solid shot. Concerned that the Confederates might break through, Wainwright ordered Breck onto Richardson's left with his 1st New York, Battery L. Moving up "at the double quick," Breck's battery "did splendid service with its rifled guns," according to a witness. Crawford, worried that Virginians might overrun Richardson's guns, ordered the pieces withdrawn. "I sent word back to the general that it was too late to move my guns," Richardson wrote, "and besides I could not get them out." Confederates advanced to within fifty yards of Richardson's artillery.[78]

"The carnage was terrific," a Federal recounted. Shrapnel tore into rebel ranks, "mowing them down." Canister ripped into Colonel Willis's abdomen, mortally wounding him—"one of the noblest spirits in the Confederate army," the 2nd Corps's topographer Jedediah Hotchkiss said of him. Willis's staff officer, Lieutenant J. Tucker Randolph, was killed, as was Colonel J. B. Terrill, commanding the 13th Virginia, and Lieutenant Colonel Thomas H. Watkins, commanding the 52nd Virginia. Rapid attrition in officers created a leadership vacuum. "No orders were given to fall back," a Confederate asserted, "and nearly the whole brigade were killed or wounded." Colonel Christian, on the brigade's right, brought his men to a "right shoulder shift arms" and sent them forward "at a run through this maelstrom of death and carnage," he later explained. His soldiers were accustomed to yelling when they charged, but they ran silently this time, conscious they were doomed to fail. Musketry tore gaps in Christian's line, but men closed up and kept going. Clawing through a clump of bushes, they emerged in front of one of Richardson's sections. Cannon exploded in their faces, "crashing, tearing, grinding, enfilading their lines, leaving in its track a swath of dead and dying," a Union man recorded. Some of Christian's troops mounted the enemy parapets only to be killed. Their bodies, the colonel later claimed, tumbled into the entrenchments. Color bearer John W. Orendorf defiantly waved his flag twenty feet in front of a Union cannon. "His little red cap flew up ten feet, one arm went up one way, the other another—fragments of his flesh were dashed in our faces," recollected Christian. The regiment's survivors had nowhere to go. "Many dared not go back but threw down their muskets and gave themselves up," a Pennsylvanian related. A few Virginians sought shelter behind the remains of a fence the Federals had stacked in front of their earthworks. They lay under howling sheets of lead, "hoping for support that never came," according to Christian. Whenever a Confederate rose, Federals shot him.[79]

A Union officer finally made an offer. If the Virginians "threw down their arms, came in, and surrendered, they would be spared." A soldier whose leg had been torn off raised a white cloth, and the Pennsylvanians stopped firing. As the remnants of the 49th Virginia stood, Christian ran for the rear, hoping to escape. Muskets barked behind him. Bullets clipped off a piece of his ear, tore through his throat, and hit each of his shoulders. He crumpled into a gully, more bullets whizzing harmlessly over him.[80]

Elements from Lockwood's division crossed the Armstrong fields into a thick stand of woods east of Pegram's Brigade. Bullets from the fight kicked up clouds of dust around the soldiers as they advanced. Lyle's brigade closed in on the Confederate flank and became slightly engaged, suffering some twenty-five casualties. Crawford leapt onto the breastworks and ordered a counterattack. It was nearly dark, however, and the remains of Pegram's Brigade no longer posed a threat. Pennsylvanians wandered into the field to bring in prisoners and succor the wounded. The effect of canister at short range appalled even hardened veterans. "The ground was strewn with the dead, presenting one of war's most horrible sights," an artillerist remembered. A soldier in the 11th Pennsylvania Reserves saw a man whose body "from the knees to the neck was crushed and torn into an indistinguishable mass." Corpses lay heaped in the Bowles garden. "There were mangled forms, bloody and ghastly; men without heads, heads without bodies, hands wanting arms," a Union man recollected. "There were fragments of human flesh hanging to the lattice fence, thrown there by cannon shot." Federal soldiers brought Colonel Christian in on a stretcher. He was the ranking Confederate to survive, and Crawford had him taken to his headquarters. He gave Christian whisky and told the injured colonel that he had "never seen men come up at a 'right shoulder shift arms' and meet death like mine did before," Christian reminisced. The next morning, Christian was taken to Dr. Brockenbrough's house, where the physician's young daughter tended to him.[81]

Early's plan had depended on Anderson attacking along Shady Grove Road at the same time that Early initiated his turning movement on Old Church Road. As fighting intensified in front of Early, Anderson shifted Pickett's division onto Shady Grove Road. Pickett sent his men against Griffin's entrenchments, decided he could accomplish nothing, and abandoned the attempt. Anderson apparently dispatched Field's division to Shady Grove Road as well, but the troops did not arrive until near dark and did not participate in the attack. Anderson's feeble assaults failed completely, dooming any chance that Early might have entertained of breaking Warren. Not only did Anderson make no headway against the head of Warren's column, but his offensive was so inconsequential that Warren was able to ignore it and concentrate on defeating Early. It had been a sad day for the Confederate 1st Corps.

Union details started the grisly business of clearing corpses from in front of Crawford's works. "Buried all the dead," noted Frank H. Elvidge of the

150th Pennsylvania. "That is, the pieces, for they were all blown to atoms by canister."[82]

At the height of Early's assault, Warren informed headquarters that he was holding his own. Meade, however, was worried and tried to spur the rest of the army into action. "You will attack the enemy in your front if you have pushed up men enough to develop his position," he directed Wright. "To relieve Warren you attack whenever you can find a point suitable for it," he ordered Hancock, reminding him that Wright had been told to attack "if practicable." A companion missive went to Burnside. "Hurry up the reinforcements you are sending Warren," Meade chided the 9th Corps's commander, "and attack the enemy wherever you can to relieve Warren." Headquarters's concerns, however, were soon allayed. At 7:30, Warren reported Early's offensive had "quieted down with the repulse of the enemy." Ten minutes later, Meade called off the diversionary assaults by the other corps.[83]

Virtually none of the attacks requested by Meade had come off. Wright's artillery had opened, and his skirmishers had pushed through a thick oaken forest, down a bluff, and into swampy low ground around Swift Run and Totopotomoy Creek. Confederate pickets contested the movement, and Federals who made it to the creek saw a chillingly familiar sight. Visible through the trees was a "high, steep ridge, timber slashed on the slope, and abatis immediately in front of the entrenchments." Wright pronounced the rebel position unassailable. "The country through which the troops moved from road is a swamp and tangle of the very worst character," he wrote, "and no possible effort could have got the troops sooner in position." He had advanced his skirmish line, he notified Meade, "but it is too late to follow it up by an attack tonight."[84]

Bad terrain and inconsistent orders had stumped Burnside. Warren's aide Roebling had found the 9th Corps's commander and had directed him to relieve Griffin. Burnside, however, had already ordered Crittenden's division toward the Via farm to reinforce Warren in accord with Meade's earlier instructions. By the time he reversed Crittenden and started him back to link up with Griffin, Meade's orders arrived canceling the attack. Crittenden pushed ahead anyway and moved into Griffin's entrenchments across Shady Grove Road under brisk fire from Early's skirmishers. Potter's division, on Burnside's right, completed the 9th Corps's linkage with Hancock. The 48th Pennsylvania, after a vigorous firefight with Early's skirmishers, drove the rebels from the Whitlock farm on Totopotomoy Creek's south bank, adjoining the Jones farm. The best general in the 9th Corps, Potter personally supervised his division's deployment. Soon his men were firmly entrenched with a strong line of skirmishers in front, their right joining Gibbon's 2nd Corps division and their left reaching across Totopotomoy Creek. Willcox's division ran the 9th Corps's line to Shady Grove Road, and Crittenden's division continued it southward, joining Griffin. "The entire line of this part of the Union army seems to have become transformed to diggers," a Federal wrote home.[85]

Hancock had done his best to get the 2nd Corps moving by directing each of his division heads to "assault at such point of his line as he may deem best." Tidball's artillery had opened with a "deafening cannonade," but in the brief interval between Meade's order initiating the attack and the dispatch rescinding it, the 2nd Corps lacked time to mount a coordinated assault. Birney, on the right of Hancock's line, instructed his rightmost brigade under Brigadier General Gershom R. Mott to attack without delay, supported by Colonel Thomas R. Tannatt's brigade. Mott threw out pickets but received orders canceling the attack before he could get the rest of his brigade moving. Gibbon, on Hancock's left, managed to advance the right of his skirmish line. A few of his soldiers crossed Totopotomoy Creek, but Early's pickets in rifle pits on bluffs prevented them from going farther. Gibbon, an experienced artillerist, had Sleeper run a section of guns to the front and post them behind a low earthen embankment. "In front there was considerable skirmishing, and on our left [toward Warren] it assumed the magnitude of a general engagement," an Ohio man noted, "whilst the cannon were active in silencing the guns of the enemy, making us think that we were getting into the very midst of affairs." Sleeper's artillerists were enraged when a rebel sharpshooter killed a gunner with an explosive bullet, a "barbarous missile," a Federal put it, "designed to explode shortly after fired and inflict a gruesome wound." Workers from the 4th New York Heavy Artillery built breastworks for Sleeper's guns and scattered brush on top as a screen against sharpshooters.[86]

Action was spirited in Hancock's center, where Barlow directed Brooke to attack. Colonel Lewis O. Morris's 7th New York Heavy Artillery had joined Brooke's brigade that morning. The soldiers were novices, but Brooke placed the regiment, numbering some 1,700 men, in his front line and ordered it forward, supported by the 148th Pennsylvania. Morris's men marched through the Shelton wheat field to the creek under heavy fire, leaving the ground behind them dotted with dead and wounded men. The banks were perpendicular and six feet high in places, but the water ran only a foot deep. Splashing across, the New Yorkers clawed up the far bluff and formed along a fence. Breckinridge's pickets shot down at them from the wooded ridge. "The rails were splintered and cartridge boxes cut from some of the men, and we hugged the ground close," a Federal recollected. Firing a volley, Morris's men charged the crest and drove the rebels from their works. Clambering into the abandoned entrenchments, the New Yorkers "reversed" them by piling dirt on the side facing the main rebel line about a quarter of a mile to the west. Pennsylvanians came up in support, and Miles's foremost regiments reached over from their lodgment and fastened onto Brooke's right. Brooke's soldiers held their advanced position well into the night, then quietly disengaged and retired to the Union side of the creek. Morris's regiment suffered slightly over a hundred casualties.[87]

Hancock was impressed with Barlow's performance. The aggressive young general, he reported, "moved as usual with the most commendable promptness." Brooke's brigade, he added, had progressed "over obstacles which would have stopped a less energetic commander, and carried the enemy's advanced line of rifle pits." The evening's assaults, however, did nothing to change the overall strategic situation. Lee's chief engineer, Smith, visited Breckinridge's sector and marked out a new line farther back to rectify the ground lost to Miles and Brooke. "We had artillery firing and skirmishing today, inflicting more damage than we received, but not much on either side," Breckinridge assessed the day's fighting. "Enemy shelled heavily this evening," he noted, "but little harm done."[88]

"The result of this delay will be disaster."

Fighting had quieted by 8:00 P.M. On the darkening Liggan farm, family members walked among wounded men and corpses. Oliver H. Middleton, a young soldier in the Charleston Light Dragoons, lay in excruciating pain. A ball had entered his shoulder, passed through his lungs, and exited near his backbone. One of the Liggan boys and a Union soldier carried him into the house, where Mrs. Liggan tended to him. He was weak and in pain but related his name and his father's address. "The reason we asked him those questions, we could see that he would die," the Liggan boy later wrote Middleton's family. "Just a little while before he became delirious, he said, 'Oh! My dear mother if I could only see you once more before I die.'" The family wrapped his body in a blanket and buried him in the family graveyard. An officer who knew the Middleton family stuck a board at the head of the grave and carved Oliver's initials on it. To make sure that he could later find the site, he also carved "O. H. M." on a large apple tree near the grave.[89]

Meade kept his headquarters near Enon Church, on Atlee Station Road. Lyman bought peas and beets from a gentleman named Tyler, "an unfortunate cuss," wrote the aide, "who lives the other side of the way with a parcel of children and a wife." Forty-eight years old and crippled with rheumatism, Tyler had recently been conscripted into Confederate service and had escaped by hiding in bushes. Lyman gave him salt pork in return for vegetables, which pleased him greatly. "Here was a man, of poor health, with a family that it would be hard to support in peacetimes, stripped to the bone by Rebel and Union, with no hope from any side, and yet he almost laughed when he described his position, and presently came back with a smile to tell me that the only two cows he had, had strayed off, got into a Government herd, and 'gone up the road,'" Lyman marveled. "In Europe, a man so situated would be on his knees, tearing out handfuls of hair, and calling on the Virgin and on several saints." Concluded Lyman: "The poorest people seem usually more or less indifferent or adverse to the war, but their bitterness increases in direct ratio to their social position. Find a well-dressed lady, and you will find one whose hatred will end only with death—it is unmistakable, though they treat you with more or less courtesy."[90]

Nightfall saw the armies pressed tightly together, pickets in places only a stone's throw apart. Wright held a line along Totopotomoy Creek from McKenzie's Corner to the Overton house, facing Hill. Hancock picked up on Wright's left, bent south along Swift Run, and wound east along Totopotomoy Creek, facing Breckinridge and Anderson. Burnside extended south from his junction with Hancock at the Whitlock place across Totopotomoy Creek to Shady Grove Road, facing Anderson. After the Bowles farm debacle, Early withdrew west of Bethesda Church, placing Rodes across Old Church Road at the Dickinson and Johnson farms, Gordon on the right, and Ramseur in reserve. Warren advanced to fill the vacuum left by Early, holding his right on Burnside's left at Shady Grove Road and anchoring his own left a short distance south of Bethesda Church on a millpond at the head of Matadequin Creek.

Musketry crackled through the night as pickets clashed in the no-man's land between the lines. On Shady Grove Road, Crittenden's soldiers threw up entrenchments to rattling sounds of gunfire. "The pickets seemed only a few steps in front of us and were firing away like mad," a soldier remembered. A rebel sharpshooter killed the 124th New York's popular Captain David Crist in Hancock's sector. The bereaved company placed Crist's remains in a cracker-box coffin and lowered them into a shallow grave. The service was interrupted, a participant recollected, by "one of those terrible night scares on the picket lines in which each side imagined that the other was advancing, and the batteries all along that portion of the works added their thunder peels to the rattle of riflery." For many Union soldiers, the evening's high point was the arrival of rations. "Their fasting was immediately turned into feasting, if such a thing could be done on army rations," a sergeant noted. "I never relished anything better than some boiled beef, hardtack and coffee we had tonight," Major Henry S. Murray of the 124th New York confided to his diary.[91]

Warren's soldiers were elated over their victory at Bethesda Church. "We punished the enemy badly tonight," Warren wrote Meade. "The repulse was quite as decisive as that at the crossing of the North Anna River," a Union artillerist claimed. "It filled our men with the wildest enthusiasm." A soldier thought that Early's rebels had been "handsomely repulsed and severely punished for their audacity." Lieutenant Colonel Dawes of the 6th Wisconsin opined that the failed rebel attack augured well for the campaign. "We cannot help hoping the worst is over, now that our great leader has pushed the enemy almost to the wall, without a general battle since Spotsylvania," he wrote home. "If we can force the enemy to attack us in entrenchments, we shall feel quite happy over the prospect."[92]

Fifth Corps losses turned out remarkably light. Crawford counted 417 men killed, wounded, and missing. More than half his casualties were in Kitching's brigade. Warren praised Wainwright's artillery for "excellent service," and a correspondent congratulated Kitching's troops, whom he wrongly understood to have "stood their ground with the resoluteness of veteran campaigners." The Pennsylvania Reserves considered the engagement a fitting conclusion to their three years of service. By most measures, the 5th Corps had handled itself well, and Warren must have breathed a sigh of relief. He had stumbled badly in the Wilderness and at Spotsylvania Court House. But on May 23 at Jericho Mills and today at Bethesda Church, he had won two victories, both in a week. Wainwright, who always took a skeptical view of Warren, attributed the 5th Corps's success to Early's pause at Bethesda Church after routing the Pennsylvania Reserves. "Had the enemy been in position to follow up their first advantage," Wainwright speculated, "they would have been successful."[93]

Wainwright's nitpicking notwithstanding, May 30 had gone marvelously for the Federals. Warren had repulsed a turning movement by the Confederate 2nd Corps—Stonewall Jackson's former command—and Sheridan had worked his magic again at Matadequin Creek, routing Butler and driving him back to Old Cold Harbor. "It was a very handsome affair," Sheridan crowed in informing headquarters of his latest exploit, "and very creditable to General Torbert and his division." Twice this day the Confederates had assumed the offensive, and twice they had failed. The lesson must have seemed plain to Grant and his generals. Lee's army was a defeated force.[94]

* * *

Grant's plans for the next day revolved around Baldy Smith's reinforcements. Daybreak on May 30 saw Smith's ships rounding the point at Fort Monroe and steaming up the York River. Passing Yorktown and Williamsburg, the boats continued to West Point, where the York split into the Mattaponi and Pamunkey. Two regiments from Colonel Jeremiah C. Drake's brigade, temporarily commanded by Brigadier General Adelbert Ames, disembarked and marched along the northern bank toward White House, fifteen miles away. Brooks unloaded his troops into small boats, intending to ferry them ashore, but instructions arrived to continue up the Pamunkey by boat. "For this order the men were not sorry," one of Brooks's men remembered, "for, had we landed at West Point, we would have had to make a forced march of [15] miles through heat and dust."[95]

Smith's ships steamed slowly into the Pamunkey. Broad marshland framed by distant wooded bluffs lined both sides of the river. The Pamunkey twisted in broad loops and bends, often nearly doubling back on itself and affording the soldiers no end of amusement. "The name 'Pamunkey' must have been suggested by the innumerable curves, bends, doubles, and twists possible to the tail of a prehensile-tailed monkey," a New Hampshire man surmised, "although for crookedness the river beats the monkey tail altogether." Following the river's contortions through low marshes, boats seemed to glide over the land. "At times," a Massachusetts soldier noted, "three steamers could be seen seemingly steering in opposite directions." Rumor had it that a local farmer "maintained a fruitless lawsuit for twenty years to determine upon which bank of the stream his farm lay." Barges, schooners, and steamboats kept running aground. "Some got hung up on snags or stuck in the mud, and had to back out, side off, lighten up, or be pulled along by tugs and other boats until they got into deep water again," a New Englander wrote. "The soldiers, not being used to either salt or fresh water navigation, were both interested and amused in the ways and means employed to overcome all obstacles that the river was so well supplied with." One ship ran aground two miles short of White House and had to wait until the next day before a ferryboat could come back for the soldiers.[96]

The lead transports in Smith's flotilla reached White House around noon. All day, boats disgorged soldiers understandably grateful to feel dry land underfoot. "We have been crowded together, on this nasty steamer, with nothing fit to drink and little to eat, and a broiling sun over our heads," a New Hampshire man complained. "The first thing I did after landing was to drink about a quart of brook water, and it tasted perfectly delicious."[97]

By afternoon, White House Landing resembled a bustling port city. Soldiers repaired the railway trestle across the Pamunkey and camped on surrounding fields. "Coming to White House Landing, we passed, on both sides, a number of vessels of all descriptions, some of them with four, five, and six lights of different colors," a soldier reminisced. "It was a grand and beautiful spectacle, reminding one more of the entering of one of the greatest ports of the new or old world, instead of approaching of a nearly unknown place which, previous to the war, could hardly be found on any map." Officers clustered under a large tree near the ruins of the Custis mansion. Many were mindful of the plantation's history. This was where George Washington had courted the Widow Custis. More recently, it had been the home of Rooney Lee, and had been burned to the ground by Union troops during McClellan's occupation in 1862. Sheridan had also passed through during his Richmond raid, adding to the destruction. A New Hampshire soldier met an aged black man who claimed to be 113 years old and to have served as George Washington's body servant when the general visited White House many years before. "The impression is gaining ground that no man in the United States ever had so many colored servants as George Washington," the incredulous Federal noted, "and serving him seems to have had a very salutary effect on their longevity."[98]

Grant hoped Smith could finish unloading during the night and join the Army of the Potomac the next day. At 7:30 P.M., he instructed Smith to "march up the south bank of the Pamunkey to New Castle, there to await further orders." Confederates, he warned, might attempt to slip between the 18th Corps and the Army of the Potomac. But Grant was not worried, as he was prepared to attack the Confederates if they tried to move past his left flank and strike in the direction of Old Church. "They will be so closely watched that nothing would suit me better than such a move," he assured Smith.[99]

Grant took steps that night to safeguard Smith's arrival. "It is not improbable that the enemy, being aware of Smith's movement, will be feeling to get on our left flank for the purpose of cutting him off, or by a dash to crush him before we are aware of it," he cautioned Meade. Sheridan was to keep close watch toward Cold Harbor and send a brigade to White House to accompany Smith. Hancock was to prepare to shift east to support Smith if necessary, and Wright was to mass close against Hancock to facilitate his occupation of the 2nd Corps's line in the event Hancock had to leave. Alerting Warren to "strengthen your position," Meade explicated the next day's plan. "It is not intended to take the offensive tomorrow," he warned, "unless the enemy should attempt to interpose between you and General W. F. Smith, now at White House and moving tomorrow to New Castle." The Potomac army would remain on the defense, buying time for a massive infusion of fresh troops.[100]

As evening settled over Totopotomoy Creek, Butler's cavalry spread blankets at Cold Harbor in anticipation of a night's rest. Two squadrons from the 20th Georgia Battalion felt east along Cold Harbor Road toward Torbert's picket outposts. The night was black, and the Georgians rode cautiously, in column of four. Shots broke the silence, and horses started coming their way. "The afternoon's experience had made this sound very familiar to us," Sergeant Hansell related, "and every man felt he must get out of there." Panicking, the Georgians started back toward Old Cold Harbor "in a wild stampede," a soldier recollected, "through tree limbs, over fences, ditches, and everything in their path." Partway back, they careened into a squadron of South Carolinians who mistook them for Yankees and opened fire. "I was wounded slightly in the left temple by a minnie ball," a Georgian wrote home the next day, adding that nearly every horse in his squadron had been knocked down. "Then ensued a scene that baffles description," a witness recounted. "Horses became perfectly frantic with terror, and each for himself strove madly to break through and get away." Men and mounts jammed together in a defile where years of use had worn the road into a narrow trench. "It was a frightening scene," a Charleston man explained, "for the poor victims pulled out from beneath the horses were literally covered from head to foot with blood." Several men were seriously injured in the fracas, and one was killed.[101]

Presuming from the racket that Federals were attacking, Butler ordered his staff across the road, pistols in hand, to restore order. Confusion compounded when a loose horse stormed through Butler's camp and a pistol strapped to the animal went off. Several men, including a sergeant, from the 4th South Carolina were trampled to death, and the rest, according to Colonel Rutledge, "were swept along by the resistless rush of the horror stricken." Only after the 5th South Carolina formed across the road did the ruckus subside. One of Butler's officers considered the episode "the most inexcusable, unaccountable performance" he had witnessed. Sergeant Hansell admitted that the Georgians were a "sight to behold the next morning, bloody faces, dirty clothes, no hats, etc."[102]

Early's failure at Bethesda Church caused no end of recrimination in Confederate circles. Richmond newspapers estimated casualties at 300 men wounded and 50 killed. A modern analysis places Early's losses closer to 450 soldiers. Pegram's Brigade, perhaps the cream of the Confederate 2nd Corps, was decimated, sustaining 270 casualties. The 49th Virginia was hit especially hard and lost two-thirds of its strength. Four of the brigade's colonels were dead or seriously wounded, and not a single field officer escaped unhurt. In and of themselves, the losses were not catastrophic, particularly by 1864 standards. What made them upsetting, the *Richmond Sentinel* carped, was that "nothing was accomplished." The lesson, the newspaper suggested, was clear. "It is felt that blame is justly due somewhere for this disastrous affair," a correspondent opined. The *Sentinel* declined to single anyone out, although it suggested that responsibility might lay with an unnamed officer who had selfishly hoped to win "renown for himself by a brilliant achievement."[103]

There was ample blame to go around. Lieutenant Colonel G. Moxley Sorrel, a respected 1st Corps staff officer, had been Willis's neighbor and friend in Savannah. When soldiers brought Willis in, Sorrel rushed to his side. "He died on my arm," Sorrel was to write. Sorrel blamed Early, whom he thought "much given to forced reconnaissances." As Sorrel saw it, information about the enemy's position and strength "could be gathered by scouts and picked men without sacrificing the ranks, but Early thought differently."[104]

Early faulted Anderson for the failed offensive. "I gained the position I mentioned to you, drove the enemy back, and established the batteries, from which I opened on him," Early complained to the 1st Corps's commander. "I met with no cooperation from your force except the artillery, which opened on my request. I could find neither General Pickett nor yourself on the line." He also wrote Lee that "hearing nothing from Anderson, I desisted from the effort to break the enemy's line, as it was evident it would be attended with considerable loss and the attack had to be made under great disadvantages." Early was still angry the next morning. "If Anderson had moved down the road from Hundley's Corner," he wrote Lee, "I think we could have struck the enemy a severe blow."[105]

Early's pique is understandable. Anderson played an important part in his plan of attack, and by Early's estimation, Anderson failed him. Anderson, however, did not suffer Early's complaints in silence. "If you mean by cooperation, committing equal folly with yourself, I grant that I did not cooperate; but if you mean that I did not proceed to carry out the instructions of General Lee, your statement is false," Anderson wrote Early a few days later. "Your opinion as to the best point for attacking the enemy, and the manner of conducting the attack, is very obligingly given," he added. "I have not, however, a high appreciation of your judgment, and I decline to be guided by it." If Early wanted to attempt any more cooperative movements, Anderson recommended that he "communicate it to the Commanding General, instead of me."[106]

At this distance in time, it is impossible to judge whether a more spirited assault by the Confederate 1st Corps could have ruptured Warren's entrenchments across Shady Grove Road. Such an attack, however, would certainly have assisted Early by forcing Warren to pull troops from Early's front to counter Anderson. The outcome might not have changed, but Confederate prospects for success would doubtless have brightened. Anderson's half-hearted showing on May 30 poisoned his future relations with Early and raised serious questions about his fitness for corps command.

Whatever the prospects for Early's enterprise, the decision to send Pe-gram's lone brigade against Warren's position was foolish. Early was in charge, but the soldiers faulted Ramseur, who had "bossed" the expedition, as Colonel Christian later put it. The North Carolinian had a history of impet-uous attacks, most recently at Harris Farm on May 19, and his foray against Warren's position at the Bowles farm fit that pattern. "Ramseur was to blame for the whole thing and ought to have [been] shot for the part he played in it," a soldier from Pegram's Brigade complained to his diary. "A murder for ambition's sake," concluded Captain Buckner Randolph of the 49th Virginia, pointing to Ramseur. The ambitious young general's failing, a 2nd Corps of-ficer opined, was "not putting his whole division in the charge, instead of sending up one small brigade to be cut to pieces by a largely superior force behind strong breastworks." In retrospect, sending more troops against War-ren's stronghold on the Bowles farm would not have changed the outcome. Willis's charge was a forlorn enterprise, and a larger Confederate assault would likely have resulted only in greater Confederate casualties.[107]

The day's reverses at Bethesda Church and Matadequin Creek, although disappointing, did little to dampen the spirits of Lee's soldiers. Grant, Charles Minor Blackford of Anderson's staff wrote home that evening, "has lost fifty thousand men and Lee and his army are before him, full of fight and uncon-querable." As Blackford saw it, the Army of Northern Virginia had forced Grant to abandon his plan to march to Richmond along the rail lines. "He is now making for a new position which McClellan held," predicted Blackford, "and which he could have reached by coming safely up the James under cover of his gunboats." Lee continued to win battles, Blackford observed, inflicting great loss on the Federals. But Grant could replace losses, and Lee could not. "We are being conquered by the splendor of our victories," thought Blackford, "and Grant accepts defeat with that consolation."[108]

Thus far, Lee had managed to extend his army to cover Grant's ap-proaches. Early's failure to repulse Warren, however, complicated Lee's task. Grant now had a firm hold south of Totopotomoy Creek and controlled both Shady Grove Road and Old Church Road. This latest Federal extension com-pelled Lee to reach six miles from the Virginia Central Railroad to Old Church Road. And the concentration of Union cavalry on Cold Harbor Road suggested that Grant planned to shift portions of his army to the intersection at Cold Harbor. To respond, Lee would have to pull troops from his line and send them there, or stretch south another two miles. If Grant meant to tax Lee to the breaking point, he was very near succeeding.

Distressing news reached Lee during the afternoon. Confederate scouts near Old Church had overheard Custer and his junior officers discussing the expected arrival of "Butler's fleet" later in the day. "This may be the fleet reported going down the James yesterday and probably conveying Smith's corps to Grant," Lee telegraphed Richmond. If the intelligence proved correct—and Lee had no reason to doubt its accuracy—Grant stood to receive massive reinforcements. The consequence would be catastrophic, as Grant could send Smith to Cold Harbor without weakening his line along Totopotomoy Creek. Lacking sufficient troops to counter Smith and hold the Army of the Potomac at bay, Lee would have to forfeit the critical road junction, enabling Grant to turn his right flank. Lee was accustomed to daunting odds, but he had no antidote to Grant's next blow with the troops at hand. Reinforcements were Lee's sole hope.[109]

Fortunately for Lee, Beauregard was beginning to see things his way. During the morning, Beauregard had received intelligence from Confederate signal officers on the lower James who counted seventeen transports moving downriver, carrying at least 7,000 men, along with cavalry, artillery, and wagons. The import was clear. Large portions of Butler's army were reinforcing Grant. "I will order Hoke's division to hold itself ready to move at a moment's notice," Beauregard wrote Bragg, who forwarded the information to Lee shortly after noon. Intelligence confirming the signal officer's first alarm poured in. "Several transports went down last night," Beauregard advised, "and more today, heavily loaded with troops, are coming down as far as [can be seen]." Additional confirmation arrived from a *New York World* correspondent, captured by Confederate pickets, bearing letters stating that Smith's corps was expected soon at White House.[110]

Lee needed reinforcements immediately. He telegraphed Beauregard, but the Louisianan refused to send troops on his own initiative. He kept the War Department informed of developments, Beauregard stressed, and it was up to the bureaucrats to decide what troops he should send. Lee at 7:30 P.M. directed a pointed telegram to President Davis. "General Beauregard says the department must determine what troops to send for him," Lee began, outlining his communications with the Louisianian. "The result of this delay will be disaster. Butler's troops (Smith's corps) will be with Grant tomorrow. Hoke's division, at least, should be with me by light tomorrow."[111]

Disaster was a word Lee never used in official communications, and its invocation produced the results he hoped. "By direction of the President," Davis's adviser Braxton Bragg instructed Beauregard in a telegraph marked 10:30 P.M., "you will send Hoke's division, which you reported ready, immediately to this point by railroad. The trains will be ordered to report near your headquarters. Move with the utmost expedition, but with as much secrecy as possible." Beauregard had independently reached the same conclusion. "General Lee having called on me for reinforcements," he wrote in a dispatched dated 10:15, predating Bragg's telegraph by fifteen minutes, "and feeling authorized by the President's letter of 28th instant to send them, I have ordered Hoke's division to report to him."[112]

The race was on, and the Confederacy's fate depended on the outcome.

VI

MAY 31

The Armies Drift toward Cold Harbor

"No man could live a moment unless he lay close to the ground."

AT 6:00 A.M. on May 31, Dana sent a dispatch to War Secretary Stanton describing the Army of the Potomac's dispositions. Wright held the northern, or right, end of the Union line, threatening Lee's left. Hancock still covered Atlee Station Road, joining with Burnside on his left. Burnside was now mostly south of Totopotomoy Creek, reaching across Shady Grove Road, and Warren extended still farther south through Bethesda Church to the headwaters of Matadequin Creek. Baldy Smith, Dana reported, "ought to arrive at New Castle by noon, where he can support Warren and Burnside if necessary." Torbert and Gregg watched the country off the Union left, and Wilson patrolled off the right. "The indications this morning," Dana noted optimistically, "are that the enemy has fallen back south of the Chickahominy." Convinced that Lee was on the ropes—Early's failed offensive at Bethesda Church seemed but the most recent of a series of Confederate debacles—the Union generals remained content with buying time for Smith to arrive. Augmented by the 18th Corps, they reasoned, the Army of the Potomac would be nigh invincible and fully prepared to root Lee out of his last defensive line. Little did they suspect that Lee intended to stand fast. By delaying, the Federal commanders were unintentionally affording him time to bring up reinforcements he so desperately needed.[1]

Cold Harbor still played no significant part in Union plans. The road junction loomed large, however, in Lee's thinking. The Confederate commander was not worried about his Totopotomoy line. His entrenchments overlooking the creek were masterpieces of defensive engineering. Lee's concern involved a Federal force slicing through Cold Harbor, turning his right flank, and pressing on to Mechanicsville or across the Chickahominy into Richmond.

The only Confederates holding the strategic intersection were Butler's and Gary's fought-out South Carolina cavalrymen. Around 4:00 A.M., Butler, acutely aware of his forces' limitations, asked Early to send him a regiment. Reluctant to weaken his line facing Warren, Early declined. Informing Lee of his action, Early estimated that the right of his corps "cannot be more than three miles from Cold Harbor, perhaps not that." He was positioned "to protect Mechanicsville," Early stressed, "and will do so." Light from distant fires persuaded Early that Grant had moved a large part of his army below Totopotomoy Creek onto Shady Grove Road and Old Church Road. He also reported "considerable light farther to south, perhaps on the Matadequin lower down." Lee could not help worrying that the fires marked Smith's encampments brimming with soldiers poised to move on Cold Harbor.[2]

Lee felt uncomfortable pulling infantrymen from Totopotomoy Creek and sending them to Cold Harbor. He could ill afford to weaken his defenses, as Grant might attack anywhere along the six-mile front. Lee's salvation lay in Hoke. At 2:00 A.M., Hoke's division, 6,800 strong, had started from Bermuda Hundred. First to depart was Brigadier General Thomas L. Clingman's brigade. A fifty-one-year-old attorney and politician from western North Carolina, Clingman had resigned his U.S. Senate seat at the outbreak of war and had quickly achieved military prominence. Leaving the 61st North Carolina to hold the sector formerly covered by his brigade, Clingman loaded his 8th, 31st, and 51st North Carolina onto rail cars at Chester Station. Sunrise saw these 1,200 soldiers rolling into Richmond, where Bragg ordered them to continue up the Virginia Central line to Atlee's Station. Lee, however, needed reinforcements, not at Atlee's Station, but at Cold Harbor to help fend off Baldy Smith's expected advance. Learning of Bragg's instructions, he sent his quartermaster to intercept Clingman with new orders. The North Carolinian was to leave the train and march by way of Mechanicsville to Cold Harbor. Lee's message reached Clingman in time. The train ground to a halt, and Clingman started by road toward Mechanicsville on the first stage of his new route.[3]

At midmorning, and three miles shy of Old Cold Harbor, Clingman received orders from Hoke to stop and await instructions. The rest of Hoke's division—three brigades under Brigadier Generals James G. Martin, Alfred Colquitt, and Johnson Hagood—was lagging far behind, making Hoke understandably nervous. By 9:00 A.M., five trains carrying Hoke's men had left Chester. Another train—the last—was loading and was expected to depart within an hour. While Clingman's troops rested by the roadside, Hoke's remaining brigades poured into Richmond and started the grueling march out Mechanicsville Turnpike toward Cold Harbor. "The day was excessively hot, the pike entirely without shade, and the men suffering for water," recollected Hagood, whose brigade brought up the rear of the column. Wagons, artillery, and clusters of fagged-out troops slowed progress to a crawl.[4]

The South Carolina cavalrymen that Hoke was supposed to reinforce—Butler's and Gary's troopers—were in terrible shape from their previous day's fight along Matadequin Creek. A Charleston man surveyed his companions' bruised faces and torn clothes and admitted that they "were certainly very unlike the idea given in fiction of the 'dashing Dragoon.'" The battered Carolinians gamely threw fence-rail barricades across Cold Harbor Road in anticipation of Sheridan's return, but Lee considered Cold Harbor too important to leave to novices and ordered his nephew to relieve them with his veteran division. At midmorning—about the same time that Clingman's men were resting on the same roads—Fitzhugh Lee led his two brigades from their encampment near Mechanicsville to Cold Harbor. They reached the intersection around noon. "Road strewn with cavalry equipment and hatless dragoons," Lee's adjutant, Major J. D. Ferguson, noted in derision. His services no longer needed, Butler took most of his troops south to recuperate near Bottoms Bridge on the Chickahominy. Fitz Lee deployed his division to defend the intersection, apparently facing Lomax's brigade east across Cold Harbor Road to block the approaches from Old Church and forming Wickham's brigade across a road that angled southeast toward Black Creek Church, on Bottoms Bridge Road. Major James Breathed, commanding the horse artillery, arranged Captain John J. Shoemaker's and Captain Philip P. Johnston's batteries to support the entrenched line. Confederate cavalry and ordnance now plugged the approaches from Sheridan's direction.[5]

Most of Grant's and Lee's soldiers spent a miserable day of active but fruitless skirmishing along Totopotomoy Creek. "We are now within 13 miles of Richmond, and we expect to celebrate the 4th of July in Richmond," Sergeant Daniel Godkin of the 17th Maine wrote his wife. "We entrench ourselves as we go along," he explained. "It is one continuous line of breastworks all the way we have come, about 75 miles through blood and fatigue. Pencil will fail me to describe anything like the reality."[6]

The Union commanders did not contemplate a major offensive. They simply wanted to maintain pressure against the Confederates to ensure that Lee did not slip away without their knowing it. At 7:30 A.M., Meade directed his generals to "press forward their skirmishers up against the enemy and ascertain whether any change has taken place in their front, and report the result." Details of the day's fighting varied from sector to sector, but everywhere the result was the same. Lee's line could not be broken.[7]

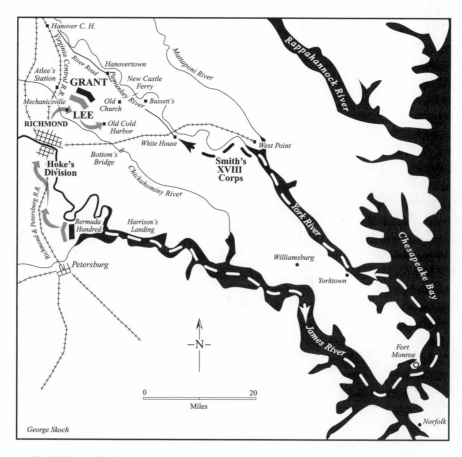

Smith's and Hoke's routes to reinforce Grant and Lee

Wright, on the Union right, ordered skirmishers into lowlands around To-topotomoy Creek. Thickly wooded swamp three hundred feet wide traversed the 6th Corps's front, Hill's sharpshooters held the far side, and behind the rebel rifle pits rose a high ridge, "difficult of ascent, and in some places per-pendicular," Wright reported. Slashed timber covered the slope, abatis ran along the top, and Hill's main entrenchments cut a ragged furrow a short distance behind the brow. Hill had described his position to Lee as a "good line," and Wright said as much in his report. "It is impracticable to attack along my front," a 6th Corps officer agreed. Determined to try, Brigadier General Gershom R. Mott's 2nd Corps brigade on Wright's immediate left pushed across Totopotomoy Creek near the Overton plantation and drove Hill's skirmishers from their rifle pits. Mott's men could proceed no farther, however; throwing up three lines of earthworks, they lay "under a broiling sun and a most uncomfortable shell fire the rest of the day," a soldier from Maine reported. George H. Coffin of the 1st Maine Heavy Artillery and his compatriots found themselves in plain view of Hill's guns. "I think I recall the next two hours as the most trying two hours that I experienced in the army," Coffin reminisced. "It was a very hot day, there was no shade and the sun beat down upon us." Coffin and his companions hugged the sandy soil while rebel gunners sought their range. "There was one [shell] that they cut the fuse just right and it burst directly over the company," recollected Coffin. A fragment hit Sergeant F. C. Plummer on the head, killing him instantly, and soldiers buried him in a captured rifle pit. "The outposts kept up a constant firing, while every now and then, a furious cannonading would commence and continue for a short time; and sharpshooters stationed on the surrounding heights were picking off the men who exposed themselves," a New Yorker recounted. "Though we were not in any heavy engagement, quite a number was added to our list of killed and wounded." The lowlands of Totopotomoy Creek were as miserable a hellhole as the Potomac army's long-suffering troops had experienced.[8]

The Union 2nd Corps's main push came near Atlee Station Road. At 8:00 A.M., Colonel Thomas W. Egan's brigade and Miles's brigade attacked in tan-dem, Egan north of the road and Miles south of it. The 2nd United States Sharpshooters crossed Totopotomoy Creek in skirmish formation and overran rifle pits manned by Brigadier General John R. Cooke's brigade of Heth's 3rd Corps division. The rest of Egan's brigade piled into the abandoned works "under a severe artillery fire," a Pennsylvanian reported, and pickets stalked cautiously ahead. "The sharpshooting was brisk and murderous," Sergeant Wyman S. White of the Sharpshooters remembered. When two of his companions fell seriously wounded, White crawled back for help—"to rise up or to half rise up meant a rebel bullet," he related—and dragged in-jured men to safety.[9]

Birney sent Colonel Tannatt's brigade to reinforce Egan. The 17th Maine drifted to the right and captured part of the advance Confederate line only to find itself stranded. "We very soon discovered that we had no business on that side of the stream, and that if we didn't get back we should arrive in Richmond several days in advance of the army," a Maine man related. "Our movement to the rear was executed with great dash," he admitted, expressing joy at "getting out of this scrape without getting gobbled." The rest of Tan-natt's brigade hunkered down with Egan's men under heavy Confederate ar-tillery fire. McKnight's battery crossed the creek and did "good execution," Tidball reported, until its ammunition ran out. Roder also sent over a gun and did "good work." The 1st United States Sharpshooters joined Egan's Sharpshooters on the picket line and captured several Confederates from the 27th North Carolina of Cooke's brigade. Sharpshooters also fanned to the left, got onto Atlee Station Road, and scooped up some of Breckinridge's men. Despite heavy firing from the main Confederate works—"close shoot-ing and much danger," a Federal recollected—the plucky Yankees held their ground.[10]

Barlow tried to coordinate his movements with those of Birney on his right. Breckinridge had pulled back from the creek during the night, leaving some two hundred men at the creek as pickets, and Barlow thought he could break through. Miles's aide Robertson was to take the 183rd Pennsylvania and a battalion from the novice 2nd New York Heavy Artillery and charge straight ahead while the rest of the New York regiment, along with the 140th Pennsylvania and 26th Michigan, charged obliquely to the right. Robertson dutifully led his soldiers into bushy marshland along the creek. Well-manned earthworks were visible on a sharp bluff across the stream. Colonel Edgar's 26th Virginia Battalion, whose pickets lined the far bank, were under orders to hold the creek as long as possible. "We'll all be in hell or Boston before tomorrow night," one of Edgar's officers predicted. "We won't be missed over here. General Lee will report tomorrow night that in the morning he had had a skirmish in his front, his pickets engaging the enemy on [Shelton's] farm, and only lost about two hundred killed and missing. That's all of us, you know, but we aren't hardly worth counting down here among all these men."[11]

Although vastly outnumbered, Breckinridge's pickets had the advantage of cover and enjoyed clear shots at Robertson's Federals advancing across the Shelton farm. "When they got nearly to the brush which lined the creek's banks," Captain T. C. Morton of the 26th Virginia Battalion recounted, "a well-directed fire blazed all along our line of rifle pits. Every man had taken dead aim, and almost the whole front rank of the enemy went down." Pressing into the marsh lining the creek, Union soldiers sunk to their waists in ooze, which held them fast while Confederates fired down on them. "The men could not get a foothold to leap from the stream, and as we had but short bushes to screen us from a deadly fire at short range, the men fell like sheep, with no opportunity to return the fire," Robertson related. "It was more than new troops could stand, and probably more than older troops could be expected to stand." Colonel Joseph N. G. Whistler, commanding the 2nd New York Heavy Artillery, encouraged his men to seek shelter behind bushes. It was "utterly impossible," he protested, to continue on. Robertson's horse settled to its belly in mire, forcing the aide to dismount to help the animal out. Instructing Whistler to keep his men protected behind bushes, Robertson rode back for further orders.[12]

Robertson found Barlow and Miles watching the movement. "Go back and tell Colonel Whistler there must be no impossibilities," Barlow snapped. "His regiment must charge the works in his front. Tell him to do it with a yell." Robertson started to repeat Whistler's qualms, but Barlow refused to listen. "You are losing valuable time," he interrupted. "They must push forward at once."

Robertson rode down the slope, bullets singing past him. A minié ball ripped into his right hip, passed through his abdomen, and lodged in his left hip. Briefly losing consciousness, he came around to realize that he was lying on the ground, his horse licking his face. "Men singly and in groups were rushing by me up the slope hoping to gain a place of safety, numbers of them falling," he remembered, "until the slope was dotted with their writhing or silent forms." Soldiers tried to stop and assist the stricken aide, but renewed volleys from the Confederate side drove them away. Finally Tidball turned a gun on the Confederates across from Robertson, and the 26th Michigan's adjutant came to Robertson's rescue, wrapping him in a blanket and carrying him back. A second charge finally overran the Confederate pickets and drove them back to Breckinridge's main earthworks. "I thought it was the dearest pile of logs and dirt I ever beheld," remembered the Confederate Morton, who managed to escape back into the rebel entrenchments. Whistler sustained ninety-four casualties in the fight, dubbed afterward by his regiment as the "Battle of Totopotomoy."[13]

The attack by Miles's other contingent—the body of men charging obliquely to the right—met no better success. Rushing toward the creek, the troops came under blistering musket and artillery fire. Captain John F. McCullough, commanding the 140th Pennsylvania, fell mortally wounded, and his soldiers sought cover behind a rise. "We had to lie flat on the ground all the time," Lieutenant Charles T. Hedge of the regiment recollected. "Every man that raised his head was shot by sharpshooters." Confederates positioned a gun to sweep the Pennsylvanians' position. Its first shots tore two men to pieces and wounded several others. Union batteries silenced the rebel piece, but the Pennsylvanians remained pinned down until dark. The 26th Michigan, which advanced with McCullough's men, had better luck and effected a lodgment in Breckinridge's advance works. Byrnes's brigade, on Miles's left, got across the creek and pressed close to Breckinridge but could not break through. "The skirmishing and fighting on the picket line was heavy and incessant," a Pennsylvanian remembered, "and amounted almost to a battle." Colonel St. Clair A. Mulholland, commanding the 116th Pennsylvania, was shot through the body. "We can hear the locomotives whistling on the Richmond Railroad," Daniel Chisholm of the 116th Pennsylvania wrote as he huddled behind earthworks. "It is thought they are running up reinforcements." On Barlow's far left, Brooke moved forward and reoccupied the picket post across Totopotomoy Creek that the 7th New York Heavy Artillery had captured the previous evening.[14]

Around 8:00 A.M., Gibbon advanced McKeen's and Owen's brigades south along Pole Green Church Road and southwest from the Jones farm. The 19th Massachusetts served as McKeen's skirmishers, on the right of Gibbon's formation. They crossed Totopotomoy Creek with little difficulty only to become embroiled in a nasty fight against Kershaw's pickets. The rebels had dug rifle pits through the woods and were almost impossible to dislodge. In a hotly contested advance, the Federals drove Kershaw's men from pit to pit to the main rebel line. The 19th Massachusetts's Captain Dudley C. Mumford was killed by a ball through his head, and Kershaw's men set fire to the woods, retarding the Bay Staters' progress. "No man could live a moment unless he lay close to the ground," according to Captain John G. B. Adams of the 19th Massachusetts. The 36th Wisconsin, a new regiment, came under serious fire for the first time. A soldier recollected crossing a field where rebel bullets "as they struck the ground would throw up the dust as it does when heavy drops of rain fall on a dusty road." Colonel Frank A. Haskell admonished the Wisconsin men to stop dodging whenever they heard gunshots, explaining that the bullets reached them before the sound. A bullet zipped past, and Haskell unconsciously ducked. "Excuse me, gentlemen," he announced, sheepishly raising his hat.[15]

On McKeen's left, Owen's Philadelphia Brigade crossed the creek and skirmished up a gentle wooded rise to a cultivated field. Imposing earthworks ran along the south edge of the clearing, covering Pole Green Church Road.

Soldiers from the 69th Pennsylvania fired at Confederates marching along the road but soon retired into the woods under heavy musketry and "a drenching fire of canister," according to a participant. After several hours of "bush-fighting," Owen managed to drive rebels hiding in the woods back to their works. An old wood-framed structure—possibly one of the buildings associated with Pole Green Church, although not the church itself—stood in the field between the lines, and rebel sharpshooters used the building as cover from which to pick off Owen's men. Private Denton G. Lindley of the 106th Pennsylvania volunteered to burn the structure. While a detail led by the 69th Pennsylvania's Lieutenant Charles McAnally drew the sharpshooters' fire, Lindley crept to the building and set it ablaze. Still unable to cross the field, McKeen's and Owen's men began digging in. Gibbon sent Smyth's brigade in support, but Confederate artillery ruled out further attacks. "The enemy had a battery of five or six guns in front and a little to the right of our division," a Maine man remembered, "which swept the ground between the lines with canister and shell."[16]

Around ten o'clock, Meade drew slight encouragement from Hancock's limited success and urged Wright, on Hancock's right, and Burnside, on Hancock's left, to pitch in. More specifically, Wright was to "continue your examination by your skirmishers as far as possible to the right, and endeavor to find some assailable point." Every effort must be made to "advance in conjunction with General Hancock," Meade urged, "and send to him any of your surplus troops he may ask for that you can spare."[17]

Wright was not sanguine about his prospects. The ground in front of Ricketts and Russell was "nearly impracticable," and scouts reported that Hill's corps overlapped Wright's right flank. Near noon, Ricketts and Russell advanced into the swampy lowlands around Totopotomoy Creek. Much to Ricketts's surprise, his division crossed the creek, drove Confederate pickets from their rifle pits, and seized the advance line of enemy entrenchments, aided by vigorous artillery fire from Birney's guns on their left. Further progress, however, was out of the question, as Hill's rebels remained firmly ensconced in their main line a short distance away. Ricketts's men dug in while projectiles shrieked overhead from both directions. "Our own batteries have been shelling the enemy over us," a Vermonter complained, "but have wounded more of our men than the enemy." Venturesome Federals in the front line reported a rebel flag flying atop earthworks a few hundred yards away. Russell, on Ricketts's right, got no farther than the marsh. "Beyond that was the stream," a New Jersey man recollected, "and across the stream the enemy, in a fortified and impregnable position." Russell decided against trying to cross and entrenched along the "miserable swamp," as a Maine man termed the Totopotomoy lowlands. Constant picket fire flared between opposing lines—"not pleasant," a soldier from Connecticut remembered, "for if you attempted a perpendicular position you paid a forfeit, with your life." Russell's men were close enough to the Confederate lines to hear "their bands playing and bugle calls."[18]

A little after one o'clock, Wright informed headquarters that Ricketts had occupied enemy rifle pits across the creek and that Russell would connect with Ricketts's right "if he can possibly cross the swamp in this vicinity." The prospects were not encouraging, and Confederates were rumored to be approaching the western end of Wright's line. Wright promised to keep a close eye on his flank and not to move Neill's division "without pressing necessity, as he is all we have on the right of the army." An hour later, Wright gave up any pretense of advancing. "General Russell says it is quite impossible to cross the swamp in his front under the enemy's fire, and my own examination confirms it," he informed Meade. "I don't think it advisable to attempt crossing here, and shall hold [Ricketts and Russell] ready to support Hancock, if needed." After inspecting his lines, Wright forwarded the glum news to Hancock. "I can't cross Russell without serious loss," he concluded, "and believe it best in case an attack is to be made to develop it from your front with your force and mine."[19]

Burnside was under orders to advance his right in conjunction with Hancock and to keep his left on Shady Grove Road, maintaining his link with the 5th Corps. "Generals Potter and Willcox will at once take measures to advance their lines so as to connect on the left with the extreme advance of General Griffin's line of yesterday," Burnside gamely instructed, "and on the right with General Owen, of the Second Corps." He also ordered Crittenden, on the 9th Corps's left, to "immediately take steps to relieve the remainder of General Griffin's division, or certainly all of it that he has troops for."[20]

Crittenden's leftmost brigade, under Colonel Joseph M. Sudsburg, had spent a trying night on Shady Grove Road. "By morning, very respectable breastworks had been thrown up, although the work had been done under difficulties," a Federal recorded. "Continual firing and whiz of bullets made us willing to keep our heads down." Brigadier General James H. Ledlie's brigade, on Crittenden's right, tried to occupy abandoned entrenchments in woods to its front but fell back as Confederates slipped around its flanks. Reforming, Ledlie's men moved into the woods again, the 56th Massachusetts leading. Soldiers spoke in whispers and stepped carefully to avoid breaking branches. "It was a beautiful summer's day, birds were singing and the sun shimmering and shining through the trees," the 56th Massachusetts's Colonel

Stephen M. Weld remembered. "Everything as far as nature was concerned was as far removed from the idea or appearance of war as it possibly could be." Ledlie's troops captured the pits again only to conclude that the position was untenable and retire for a final time to their former line. "Between the dirty underclothing, wood ticks, and minie balls singing around you all the time, it is very uncomfortable," Lieutenant Samuel G. Leasure wrote home. "The ticks I cannot get used to, but the minnies come so constantly you can sorter get used to them, but still I would rather hear them sing in the other direction."[21]

Willcox, in the 9th Corps's center, labored slowly along Totopotomoy Creek's bottomlands, Colonel John F. Hartranft's brigade leading, supported by Benjamin C. Christ's brigade. Interminable firefights brought Willcox's men to tableland south of the creek. "We fought all day, steadily, and making a heap of noise," a Michigan soldier recollected. Unable to gain any appreciable headway, the division entrenched two hundred yards from the main Confederate line. Potter, on the 9th Corps's right, pushed skirmishers into a densely wooded marsh. Brigadier General Simon G. Griffin's brigade led, supported by Colonel John I. Curtin's brigade, although at times elements from both brigades slogged in front. Gullies and tributaries knifed across the route, affording rebel skirmishers excellent hiding places. "The worst ground I ever knew," Potter complained. The 48th Pennsylvania stumbled into a nest of sharpshooters, losing the popular Major Joseph A. Gilmour and two lieutenants. "Owing to the nature of the ground" Potter reported, "we cannot move forward a line of battle."[22]

In the midafternoon, after forging across an "almost impassable ravine," Potter linked with Owen on his right to form a continuous line facing the main Confederate works along Pole Green Church Road. "My men are exposed to fire of artillery from their left, and also from the right," Potter informed Burnside. "The nature of the ground makes the lines very irregular." He added that he could not "do anything with skirmishers in my front, however strong." A wagon road behind Burnside's line ran from the Whitlock farm to Shady Grove Road, affording a route between the 2nd and 5th Corps for troops and supplies. Burnside posted Captain Joseph W. B. Wright's 14th Massachusetts Battery and Captain Albert F. Thomas's 2nd Maine Light Artillery, Battery B, behind Crittenden to safeguard the road.[23]

The 5th Corps, on the Union left, spent May 31 consolidating its position and resting from the previous day's fight at Bethesda Church. As soon as Crittenden occupied the 5th Corps's earthworks on Shady Grove Road facing Hundley's Corner, Griffin pulled his division to the rear. The rest of the 5th Corps pivoted west, forming a line reaching south from Crittenden's left.

When the shifting was complete, Cutler stood on Crittenden's left, then Lockwood, crossing Old Church Road near Bethesda Church. Skirmishers from
Lyle's brigade pushed west of the church and spent the day sparring with
Early's skirmishers. Soldiers from the 88th Pennsylvania stood guard over
farmhouses to protect the occupants. When Confederates overran the Union
skirmish line, the occupants of one house turned the guards over to the southerners, who shot them. "The sight of these men, killed while in the discharge
of a benevolent duty, greatly incensed the soldiers," a Pennsylvanian recounted, "and going through the houses, they smashed the furniture, took the
provisions, and broke up house-keeping generally, in spite of the piteous ap-
peals of the owners."[24]

The Pennsylvania Reserves finished burying dead rebels in front of their
entrenchments and started home. "It's a happy day to them," observed a sergeant who watched them go, "the band playing 'Home Sweet Home' and a
sad one to us that we can't go along." Passing through the Via farm, the
Reserves took formal leave of Warren, then continued across Totopotomoy
Creek on their way to White House. "Every regiment and battery as they
passed them gave them cheers and a good sendoff," a soldier remembered.
The repulse of Early's attack at Bethesda Church was a fitting close to the
Reserves' three years of service. In 1862, they had broken a determined Con-
federate assault against their entrenched position on Beaver Dam Creek, only
six miles away. Yet now, even though their obligation had ended, only 1,200
Reserves went back to Pennsylvania and were mustered out of service; 1,759
men reenlisted and were organized into the 190th and 191st Pennsylvania.
They would remain with the Army of the Potomac until the war ended.[25]

Warren's soldiers spent the day writing letters and boiling clothes to get
rid of lice, which they called "gray backs." The hot water shrank the woolen
clothing, and the men struggled to climb back into their garments. "Once a
man brought to me one of his shrunken up shirts in a package, to be franked
by mail," Dawes of the 6th Wisconsin remembered. "He said he thought it
would about fit the baby." Letters home reflected a consistent theme. "Talk
about campaigning and war—this is a huge one it just take the rag off the
bush as far as anything I have experienced before," Lieutenant James B.
Thomas of the 107th Pennsylvania wrote his wife. "Dig, picket, skirmish,
fight, so it goes day and night."[26]

By the end of the day, opposing infantry lines had changed but little. Elements from the 6th Corps had dug in on the Confederate side of Totopotomoy
Creek, as had some of the 2nd Corps and all of the 9th Corps. But there had
been no prospect of a breakthrough anywhere. The cost of the day's skirmishing was high. The Potomac Army's medical director recorded 732 men

wounded in the 2nd Corps alone, although whether all of these casualties were from that day's operations is not clear. Meade's chief-of-staff, Humphreys, aptly summarized the situation: "The infantry corps were pressed up against the enemy as close as practicable without assaulting, but the position was so strong naturally, and so well entrenched, and the entrenchments so strongly held that an assault was not attempted."[27]

*"We could distinctly see our foes upon the opposite plain,
loading and firing upon us."*

As combat heated along Totopotomoy Creek, Federal commanders became concerned about the safety of their army's rear. Five miles of open countryside extended north from the Union line's northern terminus at McKenzie's Corner to the Pamunkey. By sending a force into this unprotected interval, Lee could play havoc with Union supply lines and attack Grant's Totopotomoy Creek defenses from behind. Heightening Grant's concern was the presence of a sizable body of Confederate cavalry at Hanover Court House. The courthouse town was about five miles north of McKenzie's Corner and a short distance below the Pamunkey. From there, rebels could strike south along the Mechanicsville Pike into the rear of the Union line. Or they could proceed southeast along Hanover River Road, following the Pamunkey's southern bank across the army's rear and attacking Grant's main supply depot at White House. In short, leaving the gap between the Union army and the Pamunkey unprotected invited all manner of mischief. Grant resolved to close it with cavalry.

Two of Sheridan's three divisions—Torbert's and Gregg's—were encamped downriver, guarding the approaches to White House and keeping Baldy Smith's line of march free of rebels. That left Sheridan's third division, under Wilson, to plug the bothersome gap between the army and the Pamunkey. Wilson was handily positioned north of the river rounding up stragglers, guarding crossings, and accompanying supply trains. Around noon on May 30, Meade directed him to cross to the south bank and deploy his division on Hanover River Road behind Crump's Creek, four miles southeast of Hanover Court House.[28]

Wilson commanded two brigades. The larger, under Colonel John B. McIntosh, contained the 1st Connecticut, 3rd New Jersey, 2nd and 5th New York, 2nd Ohio, and 18th Pennsylvania Cavalry. The smaller, under Colonel George H. Chapman, consisted of the 3rd Indiana, 8th New York, and 1st Vermont Cavalry. McIntosh and Chapman, both in their mid-thirties, were capable commanders and shared the unusual distinction of having served before the war as midshipmen. Accompanying Wilson was Lieutenant Alexander C. M. Pennington Jr.'s 2nd United States, Battery M, and Lieutenant Charles L. Fitzhugh's 4th United States, Batteries C and E.

As Wilson prepared to wind up his wagon-guarding assignment and head across the river, headquarters decided to expand his mission. The Virginia Central Railroad passed through Hanover Court House on its way from the Shenandoah Valley to Richmond. A short distance west of the Virginia Central and running parallel to it was the Richmond, Fredericksburg, and Potomac Railroad, also a major Confederate supply line. Union cavalry raids had cut the railroads several times, but rebels had repaired the damage in short order. Not so easily repaired, however, were the spans across the South Anna River, both easily accessible from Hanover Court House. Two miles northwest of town, the river road crossed the Virginia Central at Wickham's Station, near General Wickham's plantation. Three miles farther west, Hanover River Road intersected the Richmond, Fredericksburg, and Potomac at Ellett's Crossing. From Wickham's Station and Ellett's Crossing, it was but a short distance to the railroad bridges.

When the Army of the Potomac had first crossed the Pamunkey, the Union 6th Corps had erected earthworks east of the creek to guard against an attack from Hanover Court House. The entrenchments, vacant now, were to serve as the staging area for Wilson's advance on Hanover Court House. Under Meade's final formulation, Wilson was to protect the interval between the army and the Pamunkey and destroy the two rail bridges over the South Anna. Wilson received Meade's orders to "hold the line of Crump's [Creek], between the right of the army and the river." He did not, however, get word of Meade's additional charge to tear up the railroad bridges.[29]

Around noon on May 30, Wilson relieved Chapman and sent him across the Pamunkey to Crump's Creek. Chapman settled into the abandoned earthworks by late afternoon. To guard against a surprise attack, he sent Major William Patton's 3rd Indiana Cavalry west along Hanover River Road to scout for rebels. Patton encountered pickets from Gilbert Wright's brigade of Confederate cavalry. Commanded until recently by Brigadier General Pierce M. B. Young, the brigade consisted of the 7th Georgia, Cobb's (Georgia) Legion, Phillips (Georgia) Legion, and the Jeff Davis (Mississippi) Legion. Wright cut an imposing figure—he stood six feet four and had reputedly killed a friend in a drunken brawl before the war—and his troopers skirmished vigorously with the Indiana men all afternoon. Unable to reach Hanover Court House, Patton returned to Crump's Creek at dark and rejoined Chapman's other two regiments. They remained on picket duty all night, "saddled and bridled and sleeping in overcoat and boots," a Hoosier recollected.[30]

Sometime after midnight, Wilson verified that the wagons were safely across the Pamunkey and set off with McIntosh's brigade to join Chapman. Crossing the river at Dabney Ferry, they reached Crump's Creek at 5:00 A.M. on May 31. Wilson now had his division united. Anxious to get under way, he started west on Hanover River Road with McIntosh's brigade, holding Chapman's brigade in reserve at Crump's Creek.[31]

Hanover River Road forked two miles west of Crump's Creek. The main route continued northwest to Hanover Court House. The left branch ran southeast to Cash Corner and provided ready access to Richmond Pike, Mechanicsville Road, and the rear of the 6th Corps at Totopotomoy Creek. Dr. Lucien Price's fine home—"a large and magnificent mansion house of brick, painted brown, embowered in a forest of oak trees"—stood on a knoll near the fork. Named Dundee, the Price home had numbered among Jeb Stuart's favorite haunts in the war's earlier years and was familiar to veterans of both armies who had passed there during McClellan's campaign in 1862. Wright had posted the Cobb Legion near the house to hold the road fork, and soon the Georgians and McIntosh's lead elements—Colonel George A. Purington's 2nd Ohio Cavalry, and the 18th Pennsylvania Cavalry under Lieutenant Colonel William P. Brinton—were embroiled in a fierce little fight. On discovering the strength of McIntosh's force, Wright sent his Jeff Davis Legion to support the Cobb Legion, and together they waged a stubborn delaying action in thick woods and underbrush along the roadside.[32]

Backed by Fitzhugh's artillery, McIntosh drove Wright's Confederates some two miles along Hanover River Road to an overgrown field, where the rebels took cover in tall grass. "A Johnnie dropped down just ahead of me, and calling to the lieutenant to know if I should go after him, and receiving no answer, I concluded to make an effort anyway," Isaac Gause of the 2nd Ohio reminisced. "On rising to my knees I discovered it was too much like attracting a nest of hornets. With the shower of lead falling about, I experienced a sudden change of mind, and concluded that we did not want any Johnnies."[33]

Hanover Court House was plainly visible a short distance west, across Mechump Creek. The slow-moving tributary to the Pamunkey cut a wide, marshy floodplain that served as a moat barring the way to the courthouse town. Confederates could be seen deploying on a broad plain west of the creek, around the courthouse buildings. Captain William M. McGregor's Confederate Horse Artillery rolled up in support of Wright's brigade and began trading shots with Fitzhugh's artillery. The range was short, and artillerists on both sides had clear targets. "I have been in a heap of fights but that was the closest place I ever was in," a Georgian wrote home. "The balls just plowed up the ground [and] skinned the trees." Buffeted by musketry and artillery fire, McIntosh decided against trying to cross Mechump Creek and pulled most of his men back to the Price farm, where they began cooking supper. A Union contingent remained near the creek's swampy ravine, "watching the movements of the enemy cavalry, dismounted and ready to receive us, on the hill on the opposite side," a trooper in the 1st Connecticut Cavalry remembered.[34]

Dr. Price's place served as Wilson's headquarters, McIntosh's campground, and a field hospital for wounded cavalrymen. Bickerton L. Winston's farm, spreading across nearby Signal Hill, also hosted some of McIntosh's men. The Winston place was familiar to Union veterans, as part of McClellan's army had camped there during a reconnaissance toward Hanover Court House in 1862. Wilson sent troopers south to Cash Corner and on to Phillip's Mill, where they communicated with infantrymen guarding the 6th Corps's rear. Chapman's brigade remained at Crump's Creek, ready to pitch in if Wilson needed it. So far as Wilson was concerned, he had completed his assignment to plug the interval between the army and the river.[35]

Settling into camp at Dr. Price's house around 1:30 P.M., Wilson received a message from Humphreys, Meade's chief-of-staff. The note was ten hours old. "The order for the destruction of the bridges has not been countermanded," Humphreys wrote, advising Wilson that he was not only to cover the army's right flank but to wreck the railroad bridges across the South Anna River as well. Wilson was taken aback. This was the first that he had heard about destroying bridges. "I have now one brigade holding the forks of the roads near Winston's house, and occupying the Richmond Road in force to [Cash Corner], covering its junction with the Mechanicsville Road, with orders to patrol to the right of the army," he wrote in reply to Humphreys. "The other brigade is at the crossing of Crump's Creek, but, if you think necessary, it might be moved to the vicinity of Enon Church." He asked Humphreys to "inform me of your wishes by return courier."[36]

Humphreys's response did not reach Wilson until 7:00 P.M. The cavalryman was to continue to Hanover Court House with his division. From there, he was to dispatch parties to destroy the Virginia Central and the Richmond, Fredericksburg, and Potomac railroad bridges across the South Anna west of town. After wrecking the bridges, Wilson was to move "in the direction of Richmond till [he] should encounter the enemy in such strength that [he] could no longer contend with them successfully." Wilson had reservations about the assignment, believing the far-flung expedition proposed by Humphreys required the entire cavalry corps. His lone division would become increasingly vulnerable as it moved away from the Federal army. Despite misgivings, Wilson directed McIntosh to "get ready to advance at once."[37]

Wilson's first step was to capture Hanover Court House, a formidable task in itself. Confederate cavalry and artillery now occupied the village in force and lined Mechump Creek's west bank. "Before us was a narrow belt of timber on the extreme verge of a steep bluff," one of Colonel Purington's Ohioans recorded, "and at the foot of the bluff a narrow meadow, cut up with deep ditches full of running water, and girdled by a thick, matted growth of brush, briars, and blackberry bushes—and on the opposite side of the meadow the bluffs of Hanover, on which were stationed two brigades of rebels with four pieces of artillery." Wilson's only practicable avenues over the marshy floodplain were two bridges. One carried Hanover River Road. The Virginia Central Railroad crossed about a mile south on the other. The spans would be difficult to take, as the rebels had them well posted.[38]

A close examination of the terrain persuaded Wilson that McIntosh should launch his main assault west and attempt to seize the road bridge by storm. McIntosh dismounted his brigade and formed it in line east of Mechump Creek, perpendicular to the river road. Purington's 2nd Ohio Cavalry lined up across the roadway, with Major Dudley Seward's 1st Battalion north of the road and Major A. Bayard Nettleton's 2nd and 3rd Battalions extending south. Brinton's 18th Pennsylvania Cavalry formed on Purington's right, pushing the line north across the field, and Lieutenant Colonel Erastus Blakeslee's 1st Connecticut deployed on Purington's left, reaching south to the railroad. The 2nd New York Cavalry under Colonel Otto Harhaus remained mounted in reserve behind the Ohio troopers, ready to follow up the dismounted attack with a saber charge across the road bridge.[39]

While Wilson laid his plans and deployed McIntosh's troopers, Confederate reinforcements in the form of Rooney Lee's division poured into Hanover Court House. Wright's troopers, exhausted from their day's sparring with McIntosh, relinquished the field and retired several miles west. Lee dismounted his North Carolina Brigade, formerly under Colonel Baker but now temporarily under Pierce Young, and arranged the troopers along high ground lining Mechump Creek's western bank. The 2nd North Carolina Cavalry anchored the left of Young's line near the courthouse buildings, the 3rd North Carolina Cavalry extended south, and the 5th North Carolina Cavalry held the Confederate right at the Virginia Central Railway depot. The 1st North Carolina Cavalry remained mounted and spread along the front as skirmishers. Lee's other brigade under Brigadier General John R. Chambliss—the 9th,

10th, and 13th Virginia Cavalry—served as a reserve and covered the field north of the court buildings.[40]

Wilson instructed McIntosh to attack at dusk. "The sun was almost down, and we could distinctly see our foes upon the opposite plain, loading and firing upon us," an Ohio man remembered. "Their artillery was in position and every movement made was plainly visible. The clear, unclouded sky placed them in such position that they resembled monuments moving about and changing places before us."[41]

At Wilson's command, McIntosh's troopers marched forward, descended a steep bluff to Mechump Creek, and began sloshing across. Ditches laced the floodplain, and rebels had cleared the area of trees, eliminating any cover. North Carolinians on the ravine's western lip fired into McIntosh's men as soon as they realized that the attack was under way. "By the aid of grape vines, brush and rocks, we gained the valley below and charged over the meadow, but the ditches and briars checked our progress, and after crossing each ditch were obliged to halt and reform under a heavy fire," a Federal recalled. McIntosh had instructed his men to hold their fire to get across more quickly, and many of them were well over before the Confederates fully comprehended what had happened. "We charged right across this valley," a Connecticut soldier remembered, "in the face of grape and canister, waded the creek, [and] went steadily through the bushes that lined its side."[42]

The 2nd Ohio, advancing along the roadway, faced Tar Heels shooting from behind fence-rail breastworks on the western bank. "At short range infantry were pouring small shot on us, while the artillery commenced using up their surplus grape and canister and threw it toward us," a Buckeye recollected. After pressing across the creek north and south of the Hanover River Road bridge, the Ohio men dodged behind the protective roll of the creek's western bank and huddled tightly against the ground. Mistakenly assuming that Young's rebels had broken his charge, McIntosh ordered his bugler to call the men back. "Many of the officers in the other regiments thought it applied to the whole line and ordered a retreat," an Ohioan related, "which left the line with gaps in it, some going back and some advancing." Major Nettleton, commanding the portion of the 2nd Ohio south of the road, decided that advancing was safer than falling back and ordered everyone with five or more rounds to charge. "About one hundred were found 'not wanting,'" an Ohioan reported, "and we moved off on the double quick." When Nettleton's troopers reached the far crest, the 2nd New York thundered across the bridge in support. Ohio men screamed at the top of their lungs and charged the Tar Heels behind their fence. "Our ammunition failed," Purington reported, "and

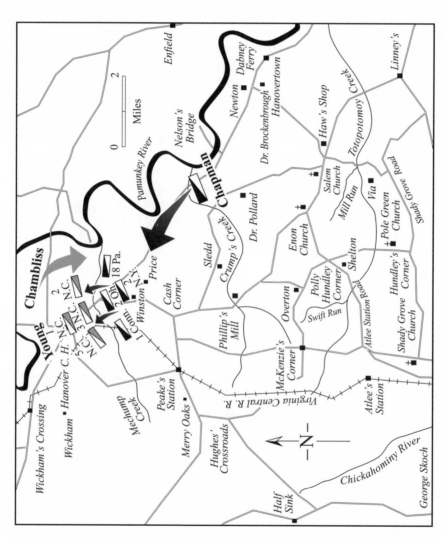

Wilson's capture of Hanover Court House on May 31

in some part of the line the enemy were actually driven from their position with stones and clubs."[43]

The going was tough for the portion of Purington's regiment north of the road bridge. "When we came to the top of the bank, we were met with a fresh volley reserved for our reception, but fired too soon to do any damage," the Ohioan Gause recollected. "We dropped flat between the rows of dead corn stalks, and they had a woeful sound when struck by bullets." Gause and his companions hugged the ground as dirt kicked up by rebel bullets spattered against them. "It appeared to me as if every cornstalk in that field was hit," Gause reminisced.[44]

The 1st Connecticut, on the left wing of McIntosh's line, charged into the creek bed under heavy fire and drove Young's Tar Heels back along the railway. Major McNeill of the 5th North Carolina took cover in the railroad depot and waged a tenacious defense. Young's line became untenable, however, as the 18th Pennsylvania, on McIntosh's right, left the protection of a fence east of the creek, braved Mechump Creek's lowlands, and clambered onto the tableland north of the courthouse buildings, turning the Tar Heels' northern flank. "Our line never wavered," a Pennsylvanian claimed, "and in fifteen minutes from the time we left the fence the enemy were leaving the village in confusion." Major John W. Phillips, who led the Pennsylvanians in the charge, fell wounded.[45]

As Young's line of dismounted cavalry collapsed under the pressure of McIntosh's attack, Chambliss sent his mounted Virginians into the melee, sabers swinging, attempting to cover the retreat. "In passing over open country to our position on the line of battle, the shells screamed and the minnie balls whistled, but passed harmlessly over our heads," Richard L. T. Beale of the 9th Virginia Cavalry recollected. "Give 'em hell, boys!" the Confederate artillerist McGregor admonished his gunners. "Pour it in, boys!" But McIntosh's Federals were streaming across the plain into Hanover Court House and could not be stopped. "They finally gave way before the galling fire from the Spencer carbines and the battery," the Ohioan Gause recollected of the rebels, "which had a fine range on them." A Connecticut man noted simply, "They were routed completely." Mounted troopers from the 2nd New York almost captured McGregor's pieces, but quick-thinking Confederates spirited off the guns in the nick of time.[46]

It was too dark to pursue, so McIntosh occupied the courthouse grounds, posted pickets, and rested his soldiers. Chapman's brigade moved up from Crump's Creek to join them. Wilson considered the fight a "very handsome affair," and jotted in his diary: "Whipped rebels easily." He wrote Humphreys that his men were "fatigued from their fighting today, and ammunition exhausted. I have therefore concluded to halt for the night, recruit men and horses, get ammunition and provisions, so as to push out at the first dawn of day." His objective would be the railway bridges. "It was so dark when we were through the days work," an Ohioan recollected, "that we could not distinguish between our uniform and that of the rebels, so when we awoke at daylight we were surprised to find we had been sleeping by the side of a dead rebel."[47]

"They could shoot us down like turkeys in a pen."

For most of May 31, the only Federals interested in Cold Harbor were cavalrymen. The crossroads held significance for Grant and Meade only as a way station to prevent rebels from interfering with Smith's march to join the Army of the Potomac. Smith, for his part, had no idea that the place might be important. His sole communication with headquarters had been three copies of an order Rawlins had sent from Hanovertown on May 28 directing him to leave a garrison at White House and to take the remainder of his command to New Castle. He had heard nothing from headquarters since reaching White House and had no idea what weight to give Rawlins's three-day-old message. As none of the 18th Corps's wagons or reserve ammunition had arrived, Smith was reluctant to leave White House. To determine whether Rawlins's note was current, Smith sent an aide to find Meade and get fresh orders. The soldiers of the 18th Corps milled about White House reading, writing letters, and as one man recalled, escaping the "fervid heat [by making] the shore gay with bathers."[48]

As the hours passed, Smith developed second thoughts. "Fearing that there might be some urgent reason for the appearance at New Castle of such a force as I could gather, and in such condition as I could move it," he later explained, "I decided not to wait an answer to my letter but to move at once." Leaving Ames with 2,500 men to garrison White House, Smith at 3:30 P.M. started west with the remainder of his force, minus supplies and ammunition. Along the way, he received a letter that Grant had forwarded to him the previous evening confirming Rawlins's earlier missive. "Triplicate orders have been sent to you to march up the south bank of the Pamunkey to New Castle, there to await further orders," it stated. The document breathed not a hint of urgency and said nothing about Cold Harbor.

At 9:00 P.M., Smith reached Washington Bassett's farm, two miles east of Old Church. New Castle Ferry was a mile and a half north, and Smith sent scouts there to determine the state of affairs. They reported that Federal troops—probably elements from Wilson's cavalry—were already picketing the ferry. Smith was reluctant to march his men any farther than necessary and decided to camp at the Bassett home, Clover Lea, until he received definite information about where he was to go.[49]

Ella Moore Bassett Washington was staying with her parents at Clover Lea, as her husband had left to fight in the Confederate army. She was nursing her baby to sleep when a large body of cavalrymen rode up and asked permission to spend the night. Her mother had just sent them away when an aide appeared and inquired if she could furnish a room for General Smith. Mrs. Bassett reluctantly complied, and soon some twenty officers stood packed into her parlor—"the most unmitigated Yankees in manner and appearance I ever saw," her daughter later wrote. Smith asked for a candle, then spread his map on the piano and began studying it. Mrs. Washington looked closely at the intruder. "He did not improve at all upon inspection," she wrote in her diary, "looked very much like a stall fed beef, heavy in the face and figure, sandy hair and beard, worn pointed on the chin." Concluded Mrs. Washington: "I can't think he is smart or be much of an officer unless appearances lie greatly."[50]

While his soldiers arrived and went into bivouac, Smith penned a dispatch informing Grant that he was stopping for the night at the Bassett place. "Finding the New Castle Ferry picketed," he explained, "I shall save the command the extra march unless I receive orders from you to go there."[51]

The idea of attacking Fitzhugh Lee's cavalry at Cold Harbor originated with Torbert and Custer. Both feared that the Confederates intended to renew their previous day's offensive, and both wanted to take the initiative first. Torbert met during the morning with Custer near Parsley's Mill and devised a two-pronged attack. Merritt, followed by Custer, was to launch the main assault west along Cold Harbor Road. Devin meantime was to initiate a companion attack along Black Creek Church Road, slicing northwest into Cold Harbor. If possible, Devin would slip part of his force below Cold Harbor and capture Fitzhugh Lee's horses, presumably tethered behind the Confederate line. Sheridan reviewed the scheme and approved its "immediate execution," he wrote in his memoirs. Devin expressed reservations about the plan, but Torbert insisted that it posed "an excellent opportunity to strike the enemy a severe blow" and ordered the joint offensive for 3:00 that afternoon.[52]

Torbert's division set off at the designated time, Merritt pressing west on Cold Harbor Road, followed by Custer, and Devin angling toward Cold Harbor from the southeast on Black Creek Church Road. Merritt soon encountered rebel scouts, who hurried back to Cold Harbor and warned of the enemy's approach. Fitzhugh Lee immediately dashed off an urgent dispatch to General Lee. "The enemy are advancing on this place," he wrote. "Nothing but cavalry discovered so far." Assuring his uncle that he was "prepared to dispute their progress," the cavalryman went on to note that Clingman's brigade of Hoke's division had halted about three miles away. "Had they not better be ordered on to assist in securing this place?" he inquired. A courier rushed the message to the Clarke house, where General Lee had his headquarters. The general had been expecting a Federal offensive toward Cold Harbor all day and responded immediately. Orders went out for Hoke to get Clingman moving.[53]

Merritt meanwhile pushed strongly ahead, driving rebel pickets west along Cold Harbor Road. As the Union troopers neared Cold Harbor, Lomax's dismounted horsemen, posted behind fence-rail barricades and backed by horse artillery, brought them up short. Merritt dismounted his soldiers and arrayed them facing Lomax, the 5th United States Cavalry on the right, the 1st New York Dragoons in the center, and the 6th Pennsylvania on the left. The Confederate defenses appeared daunting. "They had constructed strong breastworks of logs across each of the roads, and had artillery in a favorable position to sweep the road," a Michigan trooper remembered. "Our men had to advance up a steep rise of ground entirely unprotected and attack infantry and dismounted cavalry behind works with about equal numbers."[54]

Devin, leading the lower portion of the Union pincer movement, had started along Black Creek Church Road at the same time that Merritt set off on Cold Harbor Road. The two roads angled closer together as they approached Cold Harbor, facilitating communication between the advancing forces. To connect Merritt's and Devin's separate columns, Custer dispatched Kidd's 6th Michigan across the interval between the two roads. About two miles from Cold Harbor, Devin made contact with Kidd's troopers and continued on. Soon he encountered Confederate pickets, drove them back, and finally reached Wickham's advanced line. The Confederates had thrown a barricade of logs and brush across Black Creek Church Road, and gunfire from Merritt's and Lomax's fight off to the north imparted an air of urgency. Dismounting the 17th Pennsylvania, Devin sent the regiment around the southern end of the roadblock. After a brief fight, they enfiladed the rebel defenders, forced them back, and opened a gap through the obstruction for the rest of Devin's brigade to ride through. Pressing on, Devin soon reached Wickham's main barricades and halted. The 17th Pennsylvania and 9th New York waged a bitter fight against Wickham's rebels, who, like Lomax's men to their north, held advantageous terrain. "This engagement was one of the most hotly contested fights we ever had, the command losing heavily," a

Pennsylvanian remembered. Adhering to Torbert's plan, Devin tried to send the 6th New York around the lower end of the rebel line to capture Fitz Lee's horses, but the position was too strongly defended.[55]

Hoke, meantime, had reached Cold Harbor, taken stock of the situation, and summoned Clingman. As Clingman's Tar Heels marched into the little settlement, Hoke directed them to form on Fitzhugh Lee's left and extend his line north toward Beulah Church. Lieutenant Colonel Charles W. Knight's 31st North Carolina deployed next to Lomax, Lieutenant Colonel John R. Murchison's 8th North Carolina moved onto Knight's left, and Colonel Hector McKethan's 51st North Carolina formed Clingman's far left flank. After inspecting the deployment, Hoke directed Clingman to advance McKethan five hundred yards to the front and left of the main Confederate line so as to support a body of dismounted cavalry Lomax had posted there. Clingman remained with McKethan out of concern that the regiment was dangerously exposed.[56]

Custer arrived about this time, adding his brigade's weight to Merritt and reaching south to cement the connection with Devin. At this juncture, Clingman held the left of the Confederate line, facing Merritt; Lomax occupied the center, facing Merritt and elements from Custer; and Wickham stood on the right, opposing the rest of Custer's brigade and Devin. Merritt and Custer attempted several times to take Lomax and Clingman by storm. The 1st New York Dragoons dashed into the field across from the Confederates, only to be slammed back by brutal volleys at close range. "It has always seemed a marvel how any of us escaped alive," a New Yorker reminisced, "for the shower of lead was simply terrific." A battalion from the 1st Michigan ventured a mounted charge and had no better success. "No sooner had they come within range," a witness related, "than the rebels poured volley after volley into them, and unable to withstand it, they broke." Ensconced on high ground, the Confederates "had decidedly the advantage," a Union man conceded, "and could shoot us down like turkeys in a pen, while our shots were ineffective." Merritt concluded that it was impossible to overrun Lomax and Clingman "without great loss, if at all." Devin, who was supposed to turn the southern end of the rebel line, faced a similar predicament in front of Wickham's barricades.[57]

Determined to capture Cold Harbor, Torbert came up with a new plan. While most of his troopers kept the rebels pinned in place, he would send a force around the northern end of the Confederate line and turn the enemy position. When the rebels started falling back, the main Union body would attack. Torbert selected Merritt to lead the flanking force, consisting of his 1st and 2nd United States Cavalry and Custer's 5th Michigan. Merritt's and

Custer's remaining regiments on Cold Harbor Road—the 1st New York Dragoons, 6th Pennsylvania Cavalry, and 1st, 6th, and 7th Michigan—were to put up a strong show of force to hold the Confederates in place.[58]

The ploy was a resounding success. When Merritt's flankers slipped past Clingman's left, McKethan's 51st North Carolina, thrust well in front of the main Confederate line, found itself in a dangerous spot. Cavalry to the left of the 51st regiment gave way, and bullets tore into the Tar Heels' left flank. Clingman dispatched two companies to fend off the enemy, but the captain in charge "acted badly," Clingman later wrote, and "kept his men lying down." When Lomax's line started to falter—rebel troopers streamed rearward by squads, "alleging that their ammunition had given out"—Clingman pulled back McKethan and tried to re-form his brigade along a fence. "As I was retiring to point out the several positions each regiment was to occupy, a portion of a shell took away the front of my hat and slightly wounded my forehead," Clingman wrote. "Though somewhat stunned for an instant, I was not disabled at all, but observed that all the cavalry in reserve on my right had likewise retired." Once Merritt's flanking movement was well under way, Major Melvin Brewer, commanding a battalion in the 6th Michigan, ordered a charge with drawn sabers. "This charge produced the desired effect," Custer reported. "The enemy, without waiting to receive it, threw down their arms and fled, leaving their dead and wounded on the field." A New Yorker saw "many hand to hand struggles" as Union soldiers vaulted over Lomax's works and into the thinning line of rebel defenders.[59]

The unraveling of Clingman's and Lomax's line across Cold Harbor Road dangerously exposed Wickham's left flank. Taking advantage of the confusion, Devin renewed his attack, leaving Wickham no choice but to fall back with the rest of the Confederates. The next rallying point was high ground about a mile west of Cold Harbor. Clingman and Fitzhugh Lee retired to this low ridge and began forming a new line running generally north to south across Cold Harbor Road. Torbert's Federals cut off several of Clingman's troops and, according to Clingman, captured about a hundred of them. Lee lost some eighty troopers, including dashing Major Thomas Flournoy of the 6th Virginia Cavalry, who was killed.[60]

As night came on, Torbert called off the pursuit and set his men to consolidating their position at Cold Harbor. Weary Union troopers occupied works recently evacuated by the rebels and began "reversing" them to face west. A mile west, Clingman's and Lee's soldiers were digging as well, hurriedly fortifying their shallow ridge. To their relief, more of Hoke's brigade arrived from Mechanicsville and helped extend their line. Near dark, Clingman's 61st North Carolina marched up, as did Colquitt's brigade of Georgians, and filed

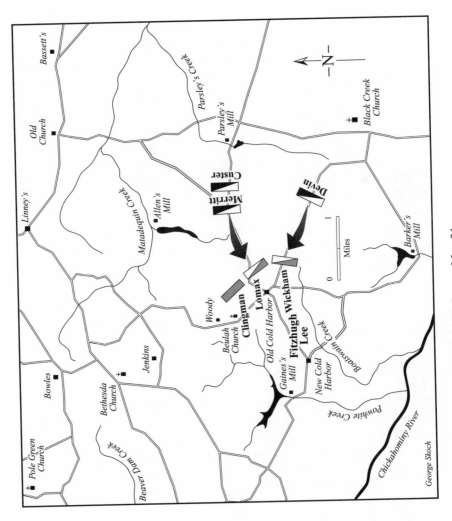

Sheridan's capture of Old Cold Harbor on May 31

George Skoch

into place on Clingman's right. Fitz Lee wanted to launch a counterattack before Torbert had a chance to consolidate his hold on Cold Harbor, but nightfall ruled out further fighting. Lee's horsemen, smarting from yet another defeat, bivouacked south of Cold Harbor Road, off the right end of the new Confederate line.[61]

Sheridan's men had added another victory to their impressive list of triumphs. And Cold Harbor was now firmly in Union hands.

"I do not feel able to hold this place."

General Lee had received his nephew's warning that Federals were advancing on Cold Harbor sometime around 4:00 P.M. According to Fitzhugh Lee, his pickets had spotted only cavalry, but it was possible that Smith's 18th Corps was following behind. It seemed to General Lee that Grant was acting precisely as he had predicted and was aiming to take Cold Harbor. Lee had already sent Hoke and Fitzhugh Lee to guard the critical intersection, but if Grant really meant to throw in Smith, more Confederate infantry would be needed. At this juncture, the day's flurry of enemy attacks along Totopotomoy Creek seemed spent, and Lee felt comfortable pulling troops from his main line and forwarding them to Cold Harbor. He issued orders to Anderson to withdraw from Totopotomoy Creek, shift behind Early, and march southeast to join Hoke.

Lee's purpose in sending Anderson to Cold Harbor was to deflect the Union threat to his right flank. Several years after the war, the 1st Corps's artillery commander, Porter Alexander, suggested a second purpose. Lee, Alexander wrote, had planned for Anderson to join Hoke and then sweep northeast behind Warren, "taking him in flank, while Hill and [Early] pressed them in front." Alexander provided more details in an informal manuscript he prepared for his family. Lee's plan, he explained, "was that our corps should move by night to the vicinity of Cold Harbor, where it was to unite with Hoke's division, and first crush Sheridan's cavalry. Then it was to wheel around to the left, and come down on the flank and rear of Grant's fortified line. Once fairly started, success might mean the driving of Grant back to the Pamunkey." Building on Alexander's narrative, the eminent biographer Douglas Southall Freeman claimed that Lee "saw an opportunity for striking the blow he had so long wished to deliver. If he could attack the enemy at Cold Harbor, before the Federal left was in position, he might double it up." The image of Lee boldly advancing to Cold Harbor to take the offensive has become a standard fixture in Confederate lore.[62]

No contemporaneous evidence, however, supports the notion that Lee planned a flanking movement at Cold Harbor. Lee ordered Anderson to the crossroads in response to Fitzhugh Lee's alarm that Federals were advancing on the intersection. Lee said nothing to Anderson about attacking, and surviving official records, as well as Lee's correspondence and Anderson's official report, breathe not a word about a flanking operation or anything resembling one. Nor is there any record of Lee's directing Early or Hill to support a turning movement. The sole source for the flank-attack story is Alexander's postwar jottings. These are slim reeds indeed, as Alexander's narratives are rife with errors about Lee's whereabouts and intentions on May 30 and 31. For example, Alexander asserts that Lee "did not even yet suspect the presence of Smith's troops" and hence entertained "high hopes of a great victory." Lee's correspondence, however, refutes that premise. Lee summoned Hoke in the first place because he knew Smith had reached White House and feared he might march on Cold Harbor. Lee's choice of Anderson rather than Early for the mission further confirms that Lee's purpose was defensive, not offensive. Early was Lee's most aggressive corps head and was posted considerably nearer Cold Harbor than was Anderson, the army's least experienced lieutenant. In sum, not only did Lee issue no written orders contemplating a flank attack, he did not send the man he would have used had he intended to go on the offensive.[63]

Anderson started to pull his troops out of line—they held entrenchments stretching from Breckinridge's right, near Atlee Station Road, over to Early's left, near Hundley's Corner, a distance of approximately two miles—shortly after 4:00 P.M. Kershaw left first and started south, passing behind Early's earthworks. Pickett followed, then Field. To fill the gap created by Anderson's departure, Breckinridge extended to the right and Early to the left. Hill contributed Heth's division, which marched south behind Breckinridge and slipped into the works formerly occupied by Pickett near Pole Green Church. Lee rode in his carriage to Shady Grove Church to be nearer the next day's action. "I am directed by General Lee to say that he wishes you to get every available man in the ranks by tomorrow," Lee's aide Taylor informed Anderson. "Gather in all stragglers and men absent without proper authority. Send to the field hospitals and have every man capable of performing the duties of a soldier returned to his command. Send back your inspectors with instructions to see that the wishes of the general commanding are carried out. Let every man fit for duty be present." Anderson was on an important mission, and Lee wanted to ensure that he succeeded.[64]

Anderson reported his progress at 7:00 P.M. Hoke's division, he wrote, now extended across Cold Harbor Road and reached half a mile north. Skirmishing continued in Hoke's front, he added, but the enemy appeared to be only cavalry. His scouts informed him of a farm road that ran from Albert Allison's farm, behind Hoke, to Beulah Church, about a mile north of Cold Harbor. Anderson proposed that in the morning, when his men were in place, he and Hoke should launch a two-pronged reconnaissance-in-force, exploring northeast out Mr. Allison's road and Cold Harbor Road to "find out positively what is before me."[65]

On the heels of Anderson's letter, Lee received further word from his nephew. A Union force, Fitzhugh Lee reported, had driven his cavalry and Clingman's infantry from Cold Harbor. He was persuaded that he now faced infantry. He was wrong—his opponents were only Torbert's cavalrymen, fighting dismounted like infantry—but General Lee had no reason to question the accuracy of the intelligence. Baldy Smith, he concluded, must have arrived at Cold Harbor, a development that magnified the importance of Anderson's mission. Together, Anderson and Hoke marshaled about 21,000 soldiers, and Lee promptly took steps to ensure their joint action. "General Hoke will, whilst occupying his present relative position to you, be under your control," Lee's headquarters instructed Anderson. "[Hoke] was directed to see you and arrange for cooperation tomorrow."[66]

Three weeks earlier, Anderson had inaugurated his tenure as corps commander with a spectacular march that saved Spotsylvania Court House for the Confederates by blocking Grant's movement south. Stench from fires and corpses in the Wilderness had dictated the timing of Anderson's march, and fate rather than military acumen had brought him to the right place at the right moment. Now Lee was entrusting him with another blocking maneuver every bit as important as his assignment at Spotsylvania Court House. Lee could only hope that the combination of luck and skill that had brought Anderson success on the first venture would help the soft-spoken general again.

A fateful cascade of events had brought Cold Harbor to the forefront of Grant's and Lee's attention. Federal commanders initially had no intention of using the place in their offensive operations. They considered the road junction significant only because Confederates might exploit it as a staging area to harass Union supply lines and thwart Smith's arrival. Lee, however, had interpreted Smith's appearance at White House as presaging a Union push along roads below his right flank. To find out more, he had sent Butler's cavalry through Cold Harbor on May 30. The exploratory foray had escalated into the heated engagement at Matadequin Creek, a fight that Lee had read as confirming Union interest in the sector. He increased the stakes by sending Fitzhugh Lee and Hoke to Cold Harbor to prevent the Federals from taking the junction. Sheridan, fearing that the Confederates intended to attack him, went on the offensive on May 31 and ratcheted the stakes higher still. Now Lee, concerned that Sheridan was in the vanguard of Smith's corps, reacted by shifting Anderson's entire corps there. Paradoxically, each side was hurrying troops toward the star-shaped intersection out of erroneous beliefs about its opponents' intentions. Perhaps the greatest irony was that Lee's concentration toward Cold Harbor was the factor that finally sparked Grant's and Meade's interest in the place.

Cold Harbor loomed larger in each side's thinking as the evening of May 31 progressed. Late in the day, Warren's pickets detected Anderson's troops marching south behind Early's fortifications. "My officers at Bethesda Church distinctly heard the enemy moving artillery in that vicinity toward our left," the 5th Corps's commander alerted headquarters, "in the direction of Cold Harbor." After dark, Sheridan sent word that he had taken Cold Harbor but was uncertain what to do next. His troopers, he pointed out, had captured more than sixty of Clingman's men. That meant that he was fighting not only cavalry, but infantry as well. His scouts also reported a second infantry brigade—Colquitt's—entrenching alongside Clingman. "I do not feel able to hold this place, and have directed General Torbert to resume his position of this morning," Sheridan wrote headquarters. "Lee's line of battle is in front of Mechanicsville, and, with the heavy odds against me here, I do not think it prudent to hold on." Confederates, he added, were extending south to cover the bridges across the Chickahominy.[67]

Warren's and Sheridan's dispatches landed like bombshells at Union headquarters. Warren's report indicated that Lee was now shifting part of the Army of Northern Virginia toward Cold Harbor. And Sheridan's intelligence confirmed that Beauregard was reinforcing Lee. At least two Confederate brigades had already arrived from Bermuda Hundred and were deploying a short distance west of Cold Harbor. There was no telling how much more of Beauregard's force was on the way. Unless the Federals moved quickly, a formidable Confederate force would congregate below Warren's lower flank. The consequences, to paraphrase Lee's frantic message to Davis the night before, could be disastrous.

Jarred from its lethargy, the Union high command sprang to action. Meade scrawled out a dispatch directing Sheridan to hold Cold Harbor at all hazards, and a courier sped off with the message. Infantry, Grant and Meade decided, must also be sent to Cold Harbor, and quickly. At first blush, Smith's 18th Corps, camped only nine miles away, seemed the logical choice. Smith, however, was an uncertain quantity. Most of his troops had scant experience fighting big battles, and his supply trains had not yet arrived. Better, Grant and Meade decided, to give the assignment to one of the Potomac Army's combat-hardened outfits.[68]

Meade had toyed all day with withdrawing Wright from Totopotomoy Creek and shifting him behind Warren to act as a reserve. Sending the 6th Corps to Cold Harbor was but a logical extension of this thinking. The only sticking point was the distance that Wright would have to march. Cross-country, the Overton plantation was only about nine miles from Cold Harbor. Troops, however, had to follow roads, and the best route—from the Overton Plantation to Polly Hundley Corner, through Haw's Shop to Linney's Corner and Old Church, then down Bottoms Bridge Road and back along Cold Harbor Road—ran fully fifteen miles. Shortcuts were possible but risky. The road from Haw's Shop through Mrs. Via's farm to Shady Grove Road shaved off a mile or so, but Wright's marching column would have to pass through Warren's wagons, hospitals, and headquarters accouterments, losing valuable time. Similarly, the wagon road from the Whitlock place to Shady Grove Road threading behind Burnside's line saved distance but would bring Wright's column through Burnside's and Warren's rear units. Meade finally settled on the longer route but left Wright latitude to take a shorter one if he could find it. "You will immediately withdraw your corps from its present position and move to Cold Harbor about two and a half miles east of Bethesda Church," Meade instructed Wright at 9:45, getting the compass point wrong but the distance about right. "Our cavalry now have possession of Cold Harbor, having this afternoon driven from it the enemy's cavalry and infantry," Meade added. "The cavalry are directed to hold on until your arrival, and it is of the utmost importance you should reach the point as soon after daylight as possible."[69]

Reflecting further, Grant saw that Baldy Smith might still play an important role. When Wright reached Cold Harbor, almost three miles would separate him from Warren's left flank near Bethesda Church. This critical gap would provide the Confederates an inviting opportunity to slice between Warren and Wright and turn the flanks of both Union corps. It occurred to Grant that Smith's corps at Bassett's was the logical choice for filling the interval. Marching to Cold Harbor, Smith could form on Wright's right flank and reach north to Warren.

Since Smith was still operating under Grant's command, Grant directed his aide Orville Babcock to write Smith instructing him to leave Bassett's farm in the morning, march to Cold Harbor, and form on Wright's northern flank. Until now, Grant's messages to Smith had directed him to take the 18th Corps to New Castle Ferry, a destination that fit when the Potomac army was initially crossing the Pamunkey. For a reason that has never been explained—

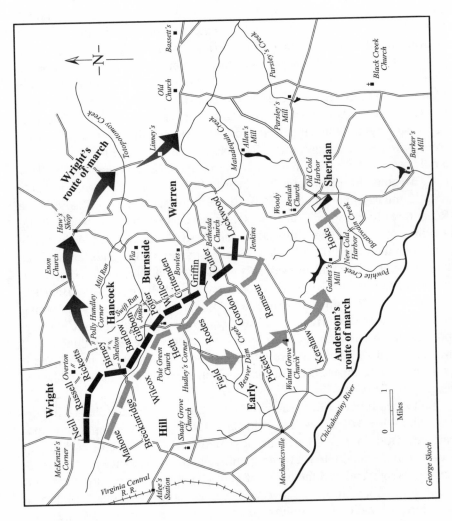

McKenzie's
Corner

Neill

Russell   Overton

Ricketts

Wright

Enon
Church

"Polly Hundley"
Corner   Mill Run

Shelton

Birney   Swift Run

Barlow   Jones

Gibbon

Hancock

Via

Burnside

Wilcox   Bowles

Potter

Crittenden

Griffin

Cutler

Bethesda
Church

Lockwood

Jenkins

Warren

Linney's

Old
Church

Bassett's

Parsley's Creek

Allen's
Mill

Matadequin Creek

Parsley's
Mill

Black Creek
Church

**Wright's
route of march**

Totopotomoy Creek

Haw's
Shop

Mahone

Breckinridge

Wilcox

Pole Green
Church

Field

Rodes

Heth

Shady Grove
Church

Hadley's Corner

Hill

Gordon

Beaver Dam Creek

Ramseur

Pickett

Walnut Grove
Church

Kershaw

Early

Woody

Beulah
Church

Old Cold
Harbor

Sheridan

New Cold
Harbor Creek

Hoke

Boatswain Creek

Gaines's
Mill

Barker's
Mill

Powhite Creek

**Anderson's
route of march**

Chickahominy River

Mechanicsville

Virginia Central
R. R.

Atlee's
Station

0   1
Miles

George Skoch

Anderson's and Wright's shifts on night of May 31–June 1

perhaps exhaustion was to blame, or maybe simple inattention to detail—Babcock inadvertently substituted New Castle Ferry for Cold Harbor in his new directive to Smith. The general, wrote Babcock, was to "move your command to New Castle and take a position on the right of [Wright] who moved to this position since last night. You will place yourself between Genl Wright and Gen Warren." The order, of course, ran counter to the high command's overall plan. The 5th and 6th Corps were not at New Castle Ferry, and marching there would only take Smith away from the 6th Corps's destination at Cold Harbor. Babcock's error represented yet another mistake attributable in part to the divided nature of the Union command.[70]

While a courier rushed Babcock's mistaken order to Smith, Wright prepared to march. "I am ordered to move at once to Cold Harbor," he notified Hancock at 10:30 P.M., "and shall withdraw Ricketts's division on your left first, and Neill's which covers my right last, and my skirmishers will be withdrawn an hour after Neill moves." Wright's soldiers were not happy about the assignment. They had torn up railroad near the North Anna River on May 26, marched without sleep all that night and the next day, continued to Crump's Creek on May 28, pushed out to Hanover Court House on May 29, marched twelve hours on May 30 to Totopotomoy Creek, and skirmished all day on the 31st. Now they were being asked to make a fifteen-mile, all-night march to Cold Harbor. "We are going to have another of those killing night marches as soon as we can start out of a country worse than the wilderness if possible," the aide Holmes grumbled. "Our night and day marching, when not on a fixed fight," a 6th Corps soldier observed, "had completely worn us out and [we] were so reduced in strength and mental perception that it was a matter of dispute whether we were living or dead."[71]

Wright's discontents shuffled onto the road around midnight. "Another nasty night," Holmes scrawled in his diary. "Dust horrible."[72]

Sheridan, it developed, was also on the move. He had heard nothing from his superiors since alerting them that evening to the Confederate infantry buildup to his west, and he had no idea that headquarters had suddenly attached importance to Cold Harbor. He saw no point pitting Torbert against an enemy infantry force of unknown strength to protect an intersection that headquarters, so far as Sheridan could tell, seemed determined to ignore. Under cover of darkness—it was now probably 10:00 P.M.—Torbert's troopers slipped quietly from their entrenchments at Cold Harbor, mounted, and rode east toward their previous night's camps.

The last blue-clad rider had scarcely departed when Sheridan received Meade's latest dispatch instructing him to hold Cold Harbor "at all hazards." Sheridan immediately ordered Torbert to turn back. During the early morning hours of June 1, the same Union troopers who had left Cold Harbor a few hours before rode back, filed silently into Fitzhugh Lee's former works, and continued "reversing" the entrenchments to face west. "It was done so quietly," Torbert later boasted, "that I do not believe the enemy knew that I had, for a time, withdrawn from their front." Sheridan supervised the dispositions. "The troops, without reserves, were then placed behind our cover dismounted, boxes of ammunition distributed along the line, and the order passed along that the place *must* be held," the cavalry commander wrote. "All this was done in the darkness, and while we were working away at our cover the enemy could be distinctly heard from our skirmish line giving commands and making preparations to attack."[73]

The battles at Cold Harbor were about to begin.

VII

JUNE 1

Grant and Lee Jockey for Position

"Like a knight of old."

THE TRAMP OF SOLDIERS marching toward Old Cold Harbor filled the early morning hours of Wednesday, June 1. Torbert's cavalry was rushing back to the crossroads and taking up strong positions in anticipation of a spirited fight at first light. Devin's brigade, backed by parts of Davies's brigade of Gregg's division, held the road junction itself. Custer's brigade reached north along the road to Beulah Church, and Merritt's brigade completed the line to the church and the home of David Woody, soon to become important landmarks. The Union cavalrymen resumed their task of adapting Fitzhugh Lee's abandoned works to face west and threw up new entrenchments along Beulah Church Road—"made of a dismantled rail fence and a few inches of earth," a Federal related. When the works were completed, the troopers filed into them, forming a line a single man deep. "By the side of each man," a soldier remembered, "was a pile of cartridges that he might load and fire with great rapidity." Some cavalrymen—Custer's Michigan regiments and the 1st New York Dragoons of Merritt's brigade—carried seven-shot repeating carbines. Williston's consolidated battery, twelve pieces strong, rolled to the front. "I do not remember any other engagement in which so many pieces of artillery were posted directly on a skirmish line with no line of battle behind it and no reserves," remembered Kidd of the 6th Michigan. "It was an expedient born of a desperate emergency."[1]

A mile west, Hoke arranged his division along a gentle ridge perpendicular to Cold Harbor Road. Clingman's Tar Heels, on Hoke's left, reached north to a tributary flowing west into Gaines's Mill Pond a short distance in their rear. Colquitt's Georgians brought Hoke's line south from Clingman's left to Cold Harbor Road. During the night, Martin's North Carolina brigade had arrived and continued the line south of the road, the 17th North Carolina on the brigade's left, the 42nd North Carolina in the center, and the 66th North Carolina on the right, "all digging for dear life," an officer recalled, "and by next morning completing a fair line of entrenchments." Hagood's South Carolinians came up near 3:00 A.M. and formed in reserve.[2]

North of Cold Harbor Road and a quarter of a mile behind the burgeoning Confederate line stood Albert Allison's home. A road originated at the Allison place, slanted northeast to Beulah Church and continued across the headwaters of Matadequin Creek to the farm of a Mrs. Allen. This was the road that Anderson had mentioned in his 7:00 P.M. dispatch to Lee as one of the two routes—along with Cold Harbor Road—that he and Hoke intended to explore in the morning.[3]

Kershaw's division, in the van of Anderson's corps, reached Mr. Allison's road shortly before daybreak. After a brief rest, the soldiers started northeast along the route to initiate the 1st Corps's phase of the reconnaissance. Anderson expected Hoke to advance in tandem on Cold Harbor Road, Hoke and Kershaw supporting each other. Communication between Anderson and Hoke, however, left much to be desired. While Kershaw fed his division east along Mr. Allison's farm road, Hoke's men remained behind their earthworks. Whether Hoke's failure to move out stemmed from imprecision on Anderson's part or intransigence on Hoke's is not clear. Hagood, commanding a brigade under Hoke, later claimed that Hoke told him that "Kershaw's division was to lead the attack, and when Kershaw sent Hoke word that he had reached a certain point (Beulah Church) on the road, Hoke was to advance Hagood's brigade . . . to cooperate in the attack." Hoke's version as relayed to Hagood was flatly contrary to Anderson's and Kershaw's intent, which envisioned a simultaneous advance. As neither Anderson nor Hoke evidenced much skill in cooperative operations on other occasions, it is impossible to determine the source of the confusion.[4]

Meade was acutely aware of Hoke's deployment along Cold Harbor Road and of Anderson's movement to join him. To counter this dangerous buildup of Confederates off Warren's left flank, he had withdrawn Wright from the army's right flank and sent him on a fifteen-mile march to Cold Harbor, stressing that he must reach the junction as near to dawn as possible. Extricating the 6th Corps from the toils of Totopotomoy Creek, however, took considerably longer than Meade had expected. Ricketts's division was not on the road until after midnight. Russell's division followed soon afterward, but the rear elements of Neill's division could not get off until 4:30 A.M. Meade's frustration grew as Wright fell increasingly behind his timetable. Clearly the 6th Corps could not reach Cold Harbor anywhere near first light. Sheridan, who could hear Kershaw's Confederates filing into line west of him, was also anxious and bombarded Wright with messages urging haste. The 6th Corps, exhausted from weeks of marching and combat, labored along roads ankle-deep in dust. "The night was sultry and oppressive," Wright's aide Lieutenant Colonel Martin T. McMahon remembered. "Many of our horses and mules were dying of thirst, yet they had to be forced through streams without halting to drink."[5]

The other source of reinforcements for Sheridan's beleaguered division at Cold Harbor was Smith's 18th Corps, camped at Mr. Bassett's place near Old Church. The previous evening, Smith had requested clarification of earlier orders directing him to New Castle Ferry. He received Grant's response, penned by Babcock, at sunrise on June 1. The dispatch unequivocally directed him to proceed "to New Castle and take a position on the right of [Wright] who moved to this position since last night." Once at New Castle, Smith was to "place yourself between Genl Wright and Gen Warren." Smith, of course, had no way of knowing that Babcock really intended him to go to Cold Harbor and had inadvertently substituted "New Castle" for the proper destination. From the urgent tone of Babcock's dispatch, Smith "deemed minutes to be of importance" and set his troops on the road to New Castle Ferry without breakfast. The march was short—New Castle Ferry was two miles from the Bassett farm—and on arriving at his destination, Smith discovered that he was alone. He could find no sign of the 5th or 6th Corps. Posting most of his troops on hills near the river, Smith set a party to constructing a bridge across the Pamunkey and sent Captain Francis U. Farquhar to find Grant and determine whether his instructions were mistaken. Riding into Old Church around 8:00 A.M., Farquhar met the bedraggled head of Wright's column, which was just then huffing up. Farquhar showed Wright Babcock's instructions directing the 18th Corps to deploy next to the 6th Corps at New Castle. Wright recognized that something was amiss and fired off a note to Smith. "General Wright thinks there must be some misapprehension," the aide McMahon wrote Smith at 8:10 A.M., "as he has been ordered to Cold Harbor, and is now on his way there."[6]

The 6th Corps was at least an hour's march from Cold Harbor. The 18th Corps had even farther to go and had to take the same road as the 6th Corps, an infallible recipe for a traffic jam. Meade's efforts to reinforce Sheridan at Cold Harbor by daylight had fallen victim to the vicissitudes of night marches and a misplaced word in a dispatch. Unwittingly, Union commanders had afforded the Confederates a rare opportunity to attack an isolated cavalry division with an overwhelming infantry force. What, indeed, was the fate of

Torbert's troopers as they waited in vain for reinforcements Meade had promised to send?

Kershaw's division had started northeast along Mr. Allison's road shortly after sunrise, marching toward Beulah Church and the Woody house. Leading was a brigade of South Carolina troops formerly under Kershaw. When Kershaw was elevated to division head the previous winter, Colonel John Henagan, the brigade's senior colonel, had assumed temporary command. On May 31, the brigade had met its new and likely permanent leader, Colonel Lawrence M. Keitt.

An ardent secessionist and champion of Negro slavery, Keitt had achieved national notoriety following the passage of the Kansas-Nebraska Act of 1854. Senator Charles Sumner of Massachusetts had excoriated South Carolina's Senator Andrew P. Butler for proslavery views in a blistering speech on the Senate floor. Butler's cousin, Congressman Preston Brooks, beat the aged Sumner with a cane in the Senate chamber for insulting his kinsman and his state. Keitt, a congressman at the time, accompanied Brooks and egged him on. Following an attempt by the House of Representatives to censure Brooks and Keitt, the two men resigned and were both overwhelmingly reelected. In December 1860, when South Carolina seceded, Keitt again resigned his seat in Congress. No sunshine patriot, he raised the 20th South Carolina, participated in Charleston's defense against the Union naval blockade, and saw brutal combat defending Battery Wagner.

The thirty-nine-year-old Keitt and his regiment arrived in Richmond on May 29. Like the South Carolina regiments Matthew Butler had recently brought to Virginia, the 20th South Carolina was large, numbering perhaps nine hundred men. Many of Keitt's soldiers had seen combat on the South Carolina coast, but they had no experience in field operations, especially as these had evolved in Virginia in 1864. Paying a visit to President Davis on May 30, Keitt asked for assignment to Kershaw's Brigade. The outfit, after all, hailed from South Carolina, and the month's fighting had left it badly depleted. Keitt's regiment was bigger than the rest of the brigade's regiments combined, and its addition would bring the force up to strength. "We called it the 20th Army Corps," a veteran remembered. Davis, doubtless aware that Lee was looking for a permanent replacement to lead the brigade, gave Keitt the nod. This made Keitt the brigade's senior officer and, according to protocol, its de facto head. Lee acquiesced in the arrangement, suggesting that Keitt "had better exercise the command some time before any appointment is made for the brigade."[7]

The men of Kershaw's old brigade welcomed the reinforcements. The sol-

diers were well acquainted with Keitt, at least by reputation. His fiery de-
meanor had served him splendidly as an orator. Whether his temperament
suited him for the task at hand remained to be seen. Keitt, for his part, felt
self-assured. "I wish you could see the confidence of our troops," he wrote
his wife on May 31 after joining the army on Totopotomoy Creek. "They feel
as led by the hand of providence."[8]

As Keitt's column neared Beulah Church, his skirmishers ran into Torbert's pickets and began exchanging "desultory fire." Keitt, riding at the head
of his new command on a horse loaned to him by Kershaw, called a halt and
formed his troops along Allison's Road in preparation to charge. The remainder of the division stopped and waited, expecting the column to start up again
soon. "Colonel Keitt had never before handled such a body of troops in open
field, and his pressing orders to find the enemy only added perplexity to his
other difficulties," the brigade's historian later observed. "Every man in
ranks knew that he was being led by one of the most gifted and gallant men
in the South, but every old soldier felt and saw at a glance his inexperience
and want of self-control. Colonel Keitt showed no want of aggressiveness and
boldness, but he was preparing for battle like in the days of Alva or Turenne,
and to cut his way through like a storm center."[9]

Judging from Union accounts, Keitt formed his brigade in a compact mass,
company front, his own 20th South Carolina leading. Brigadier General
Goode Bryan's Georgia brigade, coming behind Keitt, double-quicked
toward the firing. "As we advanced on the run the sharpshooters of the enemy
were pouring hot fire into our ranks and killing and wounding a great many
of our men," recollected Captain A. J. McBride of the 10th Georgia. Jumping
onto a breastwork remaining from the 1862 campaign, McBride was wounded
by shrapnel.[10]

Mr. Allison's road entered a dense stand of woods a short distance before
reaching Beulah Church. Keitt decided not to venture a frontal attack into the
woods. An open field, however, angled southeast toward Old Cold Harbor,
and Keitt oriented his brigade to march across the clearing. Kershaw's veterans were appalled. On the far side of the open ground stood a dense oak
thicket swarming with Federals. "The order of advance was given with never
so much as a skirmish line in front," an officer recalled. "Keitt led his men
like a knight of old—mounted upon his superb iron-gray, and looked the em-
bodiment of the true chevalier that he was."[11]

Keitt's brigade moved out, the 20th South Carolina in front, sharpshooters
stationed on the left to protect the brigade's flank. As Keitt angled toward
Beulah Church Road, Union pickets redoubled their fire. Torbert's troopers
along Beulah Church Road waited quietly. "'Hold your fire until they are

close upon us,' was the order passed along the Union line," according to an officer in the 1st New York Dragoons. Pressing on, the 20th South Carolina let out a resounding rebel yell. "When they came within point blank range of the Union works, there was a crash of musketry, and the redoubt was hidden in yellow smoke," a Federal remembered. "A sheet of flame came from the cavalry line," Captain Theophilus F. Rodenbough of the 2nd United States Regulars observed, "and for three or four minutes the din was deafening." Custer's troopers, on Merritt's left, also opened fire, and bullets sang into Keitt's men from front and flank. Union horse artillery pitched in, increasing the carnage. Keitt, riding proudly at the head of his troops, was shot from his saddle. "Thereupon the regiment went to pieces and threatened to overwhelm the rest of the brigade," the 1st Corps's artillerist Robert Stiles reported, adding derisively: "I have never seen any body of troops in such a condition of utter demoralization. They actually groveled upon the ground and attempted to burrow under each other in holes and depressions." Major James M. Goggin tried to rally the soldiers, but to no avail. "We actually spurred our horses upon them," recollected Stiles, exaggerating perhaps to make his point, "and seemed to hear their very bones crack, but it did no good; if compelled to wriggle out of one hole they wriggled into another." A second charge was cobbled together but failed as miserably as the first. Union casualties were slight. The 1st Michigan Cavalry, adjoining Merritt's left, came under fire. Captain William M. Brevoot, eulogized by Major Kidd as "one of the bravest and best officers in the brigade," was killed by a bullet through his head, and Captain William M. Heazlett fell wounded.[12]

Union bands provided a rousing backdrop to the slaughter. "We at once struck up 'Yankee Doodle,'" wrote Sergeant Walter H. Jackson of the 1st New York Dragoons' brass band. "After their first repulse, and when they had fallen back to reform, we gave them 'Dixie;' and when they advanced them the second time, gave them 'Hail Columbia' on the horns, while the boys put in the variations with their carbines, smashing their ranks worse than before." Union artillery scoured a portion of Keitt's line that extended east into the woods. "To add to the horror of the scene," stated the 1st New York Dragoons' Lieutenant Joseph N. Flint, "the woods took fire from exploding shells from Williston's battery, and the shrieks of the rebel wounded were first heightened, then stifled, by the flames."[13]

Kershaw called off the assault. "I am on the hill in front of Beulah," he informed Anderson at 8:45 A.M. "I attacked them with two brigades. Got very near their works and then stopped." Federals, he noted, held Beulah Church and prevented him from advancing farther. "Colonel Keitt is killed or wounded," he added. "I am trying to get his body."[14]

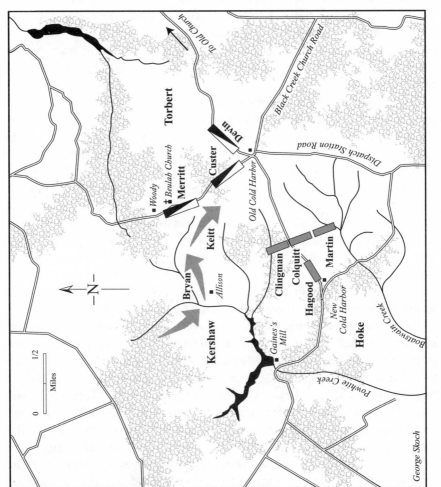

Keitt's attack against Torbert on morning of June 1

George Skoch

Keitt's losses were surprisingly light. The highest estimate came from Corporal W. C. Hall of Company E, who counted 77 men killed, wounded, and missing from the 20th South Carolina. A recent tally reveals 80 casualties for the regiment. Since the regiment led the attack and received the brunt of Torbert's firepower, the brigade's total loss could not have exceeded 150 men. Jesse Gradick, proclaimed by one of his compatriots "the laziest man in our county and the loudest," was the only sharpshooter wounded from the brigade. Bryan's Georgians were not major players and presumably lost even fewer men.[15]

While Keitt's soldiers scrambled for safety, the rest of Kershaw's division, stringing back toward Mr. Allison's house, reflexively started building earthworks, using the road as a guide. "Without any general instructions," the artillerist Alexander recounted, "men here and there began to dig dirt with their bayonets and pile it with their tin cups to get a little cover." Soon everyone was heaving earth to construct knee-deep trenches with mounds in front. "As the country was generally flat," Alexander continued, "orders were given to close up the column and adapt its line as the line of battle, distributing our guns upon it at suitable points." Alexander remembered seeing a man suddenly drop to his hands and knees and gasp in great gulps of breath. "A hole in the back of his soiled, gray shirt showed where a stray bullet had gone in his lungs," Alexander wrote. "I had never before realized exactly what knocking the breath out of one means, and it made an impression on me."[16]

After a few adjustments, Kershaw's division stood behind earthworks facing generally east, arrayed in the order in which it had marched. Keitt's brigade—reverting because of Keitt's mortal wound to Colonel Henagan—held the brigade's left. Brigadier General Benjamin G. Humphreys's Mississippi brigade came next, then Bryan's brigade. Brigadier General William T. Wofford's Georgia brigade formed the division's right, his own right resting on a thickly wooded ravine cut by the small branch that ran back to Gaines's Mill Pond. Hoke's division picked up on the ravine's south side, with Clingman's brigade immediately below the ravine and Colquitt's and Martin's brigades continuing the line southeast across Cold Harbor Road. Clingman, concerned about a 75-yard gap created by the ravine, wanted Wofford's southernmost regiment to reach across the swale and connect with his left. When the regiment's commander refused, Clingman considered extending his own troops across the branch. Hoke, however plugged the interval by shifting Hagood's brigade about 150 yards in front of the ravine, overlapping the adjacent ends of his own and Kershaw's lines.[17]

The position selected by Hoke and Kershaw formed the backbone of the Confederate line facing Cold Harbor. Unlike Lee's carefully drawn fortress along Totopotomoy Creek, no one had planned the new position. Clingman and Fitzhugh Lee had entrenched there because it had seemed the most convenient place to rally when Torbert drove them from Cold Harbor the night before. And Kershaw had formed on Clingman's left because Keitt's little battle with Torbert forced him to halt there. The position was accidental, but it had natural strengths. Kershaw's and Hoke's wings each thrust slightly forward, forming a broad funnel, its mouth facing toward the Federals. This reentrant angle, to use a military term, vastly magnified the line's defensive capacity, since troops marching into it would receive deadly crossfire. The position's weakness was the wooded ravine between Hoke and Kershaw. If Federals breached the gap, they could enfilade both Confederate wings.

The new line had much in common with the position held by many of these same Confederates in front of Spotsylvania Court House. Three weeks earlier, Fitzhugh Lee had fallen back on a wooded ridge named Laurel Hill. Kershaw had occupied high ground there, and Laurel Hill had become the keystone for the Confederate defense at Spotsylvania Court House. By coincidence, Fitzhugh Lee and Kershaw had been instrumental in selecting the line fronting Cold Harbor. The Spotsylvania line had contained a critical weakness in the Mule Shoe salient, built to accommodate the vagaries of terrain. The burgeoning line at Cold Harbor had comparable weakness in the little ravine between Kershaw and Hoke. Time would tell whether the Federals would exploit the ravine with the same effectiveness they had brought against the Mule Shoe.

In an unbroken string of battles since Yellow Tavern, Union cavalry had consistently bested its rebel counterparts. Now Sheridan could rightfully boast that he had beaten Confederate infantry as well. The artillerist Alexander attributed Keitt's repulse to Sheridan's "magazine guns," which dramatically magnified Sheridan's numbers. The fight bolstered the Union army's perception of its own invincibility—and conversely, of the precarious state of affairs on the rebel side.[18]

Critics ridiculed Keitt for his improvident attack. The criticisms, however, were unfair. Responsibility lay with Kershaw, who was well aware of Keitt's inexperience and should never have placed him in the forefront of a major reconnaissance against an enemy of unknown strength. And he should never have permitted Keitt to press on alone. A concerted movement by Kershaw's entire division—or, as Lee had envisioned, by Anderson and Hoke in combination—might have overrun Sheridan's stronghold at Cold Harbor. Anderson's artillery chief Alexander thought that "perhaps more vigor might have been put into our offensive." Keitt's lone assault was doomed to fail, denying the Confederates a superb opportunity to overrun the isolated pocket of cavalry holding Cold Harbor.[19]

The impulsive assault also spoke poorly of Anderson, who was supposed to coordinate with Hoke. During Keitt's attack, Hoke's soldiers remained in their entrenchments, listening to the sound of distant firing. "Afterwards," reported Hoke's brigadier Hagood, "a courier to General Hoke announced that the attack was foregone," and Hoke stayed in place. Kershaw, however, had expected Hoke's assistance and complained bitterly about Hoke's failure to participate. "I have no cooperation from General Hoke," he wrote shortly after Keitt's repulse, "and the brunt of the enemy's strength is in that direction." The paucity of evidence makes it impossible to determine precisely where the breakdown in coordination occurred. Ultimate responsibility, however, lay with Anderson, whom Lee had charged with supervising the movement. In retrospect, Anderson had been a poor choice for a maneuver of such importance.[20]

Near 9:00 A.M., Wright's aide Thomas Hyde rode into Old Cold Harbor to alert Sheridan that the 6th Corps was approaching. Hyde found the cavalry commander near the front—Hyde thought him "the most nervy, wiry incarnation of business, and business only, I had yet met"—delivered his message, borrowed a carbine from a wounded trooper, and joined Torbert's firing line. "We had a belief in the infantry that those carbines would not hit anything, and I confirmed the belief so far as I was concerned," Hyde reminisced. "To be sure there was nothing but smoke to fire at as a general thing, and though in dead earnest then, I am happy in the conviction that I did not hurt anybody."[21]

The fighting over, Sheridan scrawled a dispatch to Meade's aide Humphreys. "In obedience to your instructions I am holding Cold Harbor," he announced. "The enemy assaulted the right of my lines this morning, but were handsomely repulsed. I have been very apprehensive," he admitted with candor, "but General Wright is now coming up." Sheridan informed Wright that they faced at least a division of infantry and expressed concern that more Confederates might be on the way. Wright judged that he could safely hold the intersection with his corps unless the rebels launched a major offensive, a move that seemed unlikely in the aftermath of Keitt's repulse. "I shall cover the road intersections at Cold Harbor, and refuse my left somewhat," he wrote Humphreys, "but as I can't connect with Warren, I could wish that Smith, who I understand is to fill the gap, could come up."[22]

Soon Ricketts's division, at the head of the 6th Corps, marched into Cold Harbor. Custer's band greeted the weary troops with blasts of "Hail Columbia" as they occupied the trenches formerly held by Torbert. "Never were reinforcements more cordially welcomed," Kidd reminisced. "In solid array and with quick step [the 6th Corps] marched out of the woods in rear of the line, and took our place. The tension was relaxed and for the first time since midnight the cavalrymen drew a long breath."[23]

Headquarters in the meantime corrected its orders to Smith. Learning from Captain Farquhar that Smith was at New Castle Ferry, Grant dispatched Babcock to direct him to proceed immediately to Cold Harbor. Smith retraced his morning's route and pushed on to Old Church, where Wright's 6th Corps blocked the way. Through the long and hot morning, his troops marked time while Wright's men passed by. Headquarters accepted responsibility for the delay. "Smith must be close upon Wright's column," Dana wrote at 10:00 A.M., "though a mistake in the terms of his order, in which the words New Castle were inserted instead of Cold Harbor, delayed his starting this morning." While Smith waited for Wright's troops to move on, Grant tidied up his command relationships—at least on paper—by formally placing the 18th Corps under Meade. At noon Meade reaffirmed that Smith was to start for Cold Harbor as soon as Wright had passed. "Take position on his right," Meade instructed, "endeavoring to hold the road from Cold Harbor to [Beulah] Church."[24]

After the war, Smith criticized Grant's and Meade's failure to get infantry support to Sheridan more quickly. "When the concentration upon Cold Harbor was determined upon," he wrote years later, "had the Eighteenth Corps been ordered to join Sheridan it would have reached him on the night of the 31st, with about the same length of march it did make, and would have been fresh for battle early on the morning of the 1st." Grant's logistics, Smith complained, had been "terrible."[25]

Headquarters clearly muffed its handling of the 18th Corps by directing the troops to New Castle Ferry when it really wanted them to go to Cold Harbor. But the decision to rush Wright rather than Smith to Sheridan's relief was not as unreasonable as Smith later made it out to be. Smith's men had been traveling for three days; their baggage and excess ammunition had not yet arrived; and they were unaccustomed to hard marching. Most important, Smith's ability to mesh with the Potomac Army was unknown, and most of his troops were relatively inexperienced in fighting the likes of Lee. While Smith had little more than half as far to march as Wright, there were serious questions about how quickly he could cover the ground, and no one knew how his novices would stack up against Lee's veterans. As events unfolded, Wright's and Smith's failure to reach Cold Harbor before Keitt's attack had no adverse consequences. Sheridan did perfectly fine without reinforcements, repelling Keitt and holding his own until Wright arrived. He lacked the

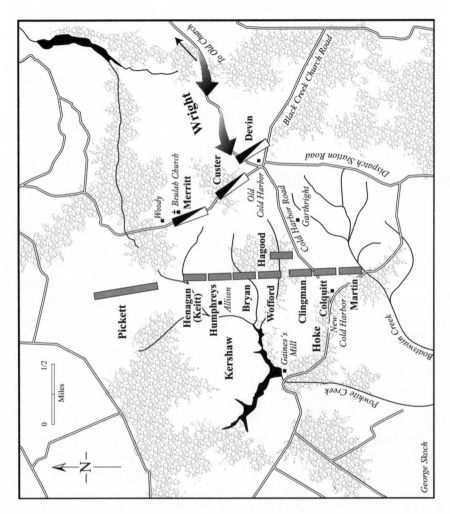

Union and Confederate movements to Old Cold Harbor on morning of June 1

strength to mount a counteroffensive, but at this juncture Union headquarters was not contemplating one.

"How would you feel to see your father lying in a ditch?"

Until now, Grant and Meade had considered the concentration at Cold Harbor a defensive ploy. By midmorning, however, they began to see the movement in a different light. Soon two infantry corps—two-fifths of the Army of the Potomac—would be massed at Cold Harbor. Opposing them were Hoke's division and elements from Anderson's 1st Corps. Most of these Confederates had only recently arrived and had not had time to entrench. Here, perhaps, was the weak spot in Lee's defense. If Wright and Smith attacked quickly enough, they might be able to roll up the Confederate right flank and get into Lee's rear.

Meade advised Smith at noon of headquarters's offensive mindset: "General Wright is ordered to attack the enemy as soon as his troops are up, and I desire you should cooperate with him and join in the attack." Time was of the essence, and Meade took pains to explain why. "The enemy have not long been in position about Cold Harbor," he stressed, "and it is quite important to dislodge, and, if possible, rout him before he can entrench himself."[26]

With Wright and Smith in motion, the task of holding the main Union line along Totopotomoy Creek fell to Hancock, Burnside, and Warren, arrayed north to south in that order. Their job was to keep Hill, Breckinridge, and Early occupied and exploit any offensive opportunities that arose. For most of the Potomac army, June 1 was another sweltering day of heat, snipers, and insects. "Considerable fuddling around and firing along the picket line," a Pennsylvanian wrote in his diary.[27]

Wright's departure had made Hancock's 2nd Corps the Union army's northern element. Hancock's disgruntled soldiers expected more pointless charges and maneuvers. Tempers were short, and troops who hoped to go home soon kept their heads low. A drummer in the 4th Maine—the regiment had two weeks of service remaining—almost got killed when he put on a Confederate uniform in jest. Edgy soldiers mistook him for a real rebel and shot at him, and everyone reached for weapons. "It was a decidedly serious joke," a Maine man recounted, "one that nearly cost him his life and undoubtedly taught that sheepskin pounder a lesson he will not soon forget."[28]

Shortly after Wright's corps pulled out, Hancock withdrew Birney from his advanced position on the Confederate side of Totopotomoy Creek, leaving only skirmishers in the captured pits. Mott's brigade eased into the works formerly held by Wright near the Overton house and sent pickets out the road leading to McKenzie's Corner. The pickets spotted Confederates entering neighboring sections of Wright's abandoned line. Presuming that the rebels intended to turn the 2nd Corps's flank, they reported the development to Mott. Soldiers from the 1st United States Sharpshooters investigated but found only unarmed Confederates looking for butchered beef that Wright's men had left behind. The Sharpshooters slipped west along Wright's vacated works and traded pot shots with Mahone's Confederates. The rest of the 2nd Corps remained in its previous day's entrenchments, in places only a few hundred yards from the rebel earthworks.[29]

At 6:45 A.M., Meade urged Hancock to "press the enemy with your skirmishers, and endeavor to develop his line of battle and line of works." Birney could do little, having pulled back to the Federal side of the creek. Barlow, in Hancock's center, tried advancing his flanks to see if Confederates were still there and was not surprised to discover that they were. Miles, on Barlow's right, captured outlying rebel posts and scooped up prisoners but could make no significant progress. Colonel Richard Byrnes's brigade, on Barlow's left, overran some entrenchments and hunkered down to watch Sleeper's battery "do good execution" against Confederates posted in his front. Gibbon, on Hancock's far left, remained stymied in front of formidable Confederate works guarding Pole Green Church Road.[30]

Hancock polled his division heads and received discouraging news. "The enemy's works are just reported as well filled with men since our sharpshooters have been pushing forward" Gibbon advised, adding that the ground in his front was "well swept by infantry and artillery." Barlow was also at a standstill. "There is no doubt that the works in front of my skirmish line are fully manned by a line of battle," he noted, and proffered advice: "I do not believe that these assaults upon entrenched lines through thick woods, where we do not know the ground, are likely to be successful where the enemy hold their line in force"—stating what had been painfully obvious to the army's foot soldiers for weeks. He recommended against attacking but promised to "cheerfully try it if ordered." Hancock alerted headquarters that his division commanders considered the prospects for offensive action "quite unfavorable, the enemy's position being one of great natural strength, and his works fully manned."[31]

Burnside, on Hancock's left, was also unable to make appreciable headway. Potter shifted north of Totopotomoy Creek to fill the gap created when Hancock stretched right to cover Wright's vacated works. Willcox held the 9th Corps's line to Shady Grove Road, where he connected with Crittenden, who anchored his right flank on the roadway and refused his left east, running a line of troops more or less parallel with Shady Grove Road and facing south. "We have been feeling the enemy this morning, and find no noticeable change," Burnside notified headquarters. His scouts had heard sounds behind the Confederate line during the night—"as if artillery and wagons were moving to the [south]"—but otherwise things seemed quiet.[32]

Warren, massed south of Burnside, faced Early's entrenchments. Brigadier General Bartlett, whose brigade held the right of Warren's line, abutting Crittenden, could see Confederates marching south in heavy columns "at double quick" behind Early's earthworks. Cutler's skirmishers along Old Church Road also spotted marching rebels—they belonged to Pickett's and Field's divisions of Anderson's corps, hurrying to join Kershaw—but could not tell whether they were anything other than skirmishers. Similar intelligence came from Lockwood, on Warren's southern flank. Confederates passed "so near that we could hear their voices," an officer recollected, "and their tramping shook the earth where we lay." The 5th Corps aide Roebling watched Anderson's rebels drift across Warren's front toward Cold Harbor, flankers passing "directly in front of our skirmish line." Roebling forwarded his observations to Meade, who ordered Warren to attack "at once." Warren advanced skirmishers to feel for weak points in Early's fortifications, but the country was marshy and cut with streams, and Early's artillery had the range down perfectly. "Our skirmish line everywhere comes in sight of entrenchments," Warren reported at 11:30 A.M. He was powerless to break through to Anderson's southbound column.[33]

Meade also wanted Warren to reach south and connect with the troops congregating at Cold Harbor. The assignment was difficult, as no roads led directly from Warren's flank to the settlement, and the 5th Corps would have to traverse marshy terrain around the headwaters of Matadequin Creek. "Got more or less bogged in a swamp," a colonel who explored the country related, "and arrived at no place in particular." And since Cold Harbor was nearly five miles from Warren's northern flank, lengthening the 5th Corps to cover the entire distance would leave Warren an exceedingly thin line. If Warren stretched his corps across the entire interval, he would lack the troops necessary to break through Early's works and attack Anderson's column. Headquarters had given Warren inconsistent objectives. "I do not propose to connect with [Cold Harbor] by more than a skirmish line at first," the flustered general advised headquarters. Meade, Warren wrote his wife Emily, "is very nervous and disagreeable lately and one would think from his tone we were doing nothing." The day was hot, and nothing seemed to be going right.[34]

*   *   *

Around noon, Grant and Meade moved their headquarters to Mrs. Via's house to be closer to the evolving battlefront. Their aides milled about in the yard, anxiously awaiting news from Wright and Smith. Lyman picked cherries from a tree in front of the house and chatted with Mr. and Mrs. Currie, whose nearby farm had seen Warren's repulse of Willis on May 30. Union soldiers had gutted Mrs. Currie's home, and she was hopping mad. "A week ago I had no sympathy with the South against the North," she ranted, "but now I wish the ground would open and swallow both me and the Yankee army!" Her husband seemed resigned to his fate and tried to control her. "There, there, hold your tongue," he admonished. "Don't mind her, gentlemen," he urged the Union officers. "It's only her way, she's in a flurry."[35]

Meade remained hopeful that Warren would either attack the Confederates shifting across his front or link with the forces gathering at Cold Harbor. Warren's aide Roebling gamely took a detachment of Maryland troops on a zigzagging route along a patchwork of roads that finally came out at Mr. Woody's house, near Beulah Church. Anderson's Confederates, he reported, had only recently departed and were withdrawing west. "I have extended my line now so that it is nearly all taken up a single line of battle," Warren informed headquarters at 1:30 P.M., adding that the "enemy is strongly entrenched along my whole front." With the 5th Corps extended, Warren saw no possibility of attacking unless he pulled troops out of formation to create an assault column. "I believe that nothing but a strong attack can carry the enemy's position," he concluded, "and I must have a strong force on hand to hold on with, which I have not."[36]

While Warren looked helplessly on, Anderson's Confederates completed their movement south. Grant already entertained a low opinion of the 5th Corps's commander and blamed him for letting the Confederates pass. "Warren fired his artillery at the enemy," Grant later wrote, "but lost so much time in making ready that the enemy got by, and at three o'clock he reported the enemy so strongly entrenched in his front, and besides his lines were so long that he had no mass of troops to move with." Grant was unimpressed by Warren's excuses. "He seemed to have forgotten that lines in rear of an army hold themselves," Grant observed, "while their defenders are fighting in their front."[37]

As the afternoon passed, Grant and Meade considered how to concentrate reinforcements for Wright's and Smith's impending attack. Warren was obviously not capable of contributing in any meaningful way. What about Hancock? Grant had generally relied on the Union 2nd Corps for his offensive thrusts, but the troops were now occupied in useless forays along Totopotomoy Creek. Instead of leaving them there, headquarters reasoned, would it not make better to sense to shift them south, where battle seemed imminent? The late hour and the marching distances made it impossible for Hancock to participate in Wright's and Smith's attack scheduled for the afternoon. But certainly Hancock could move closer to the action. "You will make your arrangements and withdraw your corps tonight and move, via Haw's Shop, to the rear of Bethesda Church," Meade instructed Hancock at 3:30 P.M. "Your corps will be massed somewhere in the vicinity of these headquarters, at Via's house," he added. "You will begin to withdraw as soon as it is dark. Notify Burnside when the last of your troops move and you withdraw your pickets."[38]

Meade's order had not yet gone out—Wright and Smith were still shuffling into Cold Harbor, and Warren was watching Anderson's rebels stream south—when Confederate activity intensified on Hancock's front. Hill sent his Florida brigade against the Union works along Atlee Station Road, along with Brigadier General Gabriel C. Wharton's brigade of Breckinridge's command, attempting to drive Birney's men out of pits the Federals had captured the previous day. To help Birney, Tidball's artillery opened near the Shelton place, enfilading the sector. "Firing sharp and continuous," Hancock's aide Mitchell noted. Then intelligence arrived from Gibbon that rebels were marching to the right, "apparently in great haste." Gibbon's information and the attacks against Birney seemed to augur a Confederate movement to turn Hancock's right, near the Overton house. "I am not well placed for a fight on that side," Hancock informed headquarters, "as I am hugging the enemy close on the other side, and the backs of two of my divisions [Barlow's and Gibbon's] are in that direction."[39]

To determine whether Confederates were in fact leaving Gibbon's front and shifting to attack Birney, Hancock directed Gibbon to make an "active demonstration, supported by a line of battle." At 4:30, Gibbon sent troops toward Hundley's Corner, McKeen's brigade on the right, Owen's brigade on the left, and Smyth's brigade in reserve. Opposing them were Cooke's and Kirkland's brigades of Heth's division, supported by Captain Willis J. Dance's, Captain Benjamin H. Smith's, and Captain Charles B. Griffin's batteries of Lieutenant Colonel Robert A. Hardaway's 2nd Corps battalion.[40]

McKeen's soldiers marched toward the entrenched rebel line at an angle, making the 36th Wisconsin, near McKeen's right, the first regiment to enter the field fronting the enemy works. A few hundred yards ahead loomed the rebel entrenchments, bristling with artillery. The Wisconsin troops—four novice companies—advanced to double quick. When they were fifty yards from the works, a cannon boomed, and two brigades of rebel muskets fired into the clearing. "The enemy opened upon the advancing line with grape, and very severe musketry from the front with oblique fire from right and left, making it almost impossible for a man to live on the field," a Federal wrote. McKeen's veteran regiments returned a volley and dropped back, but the Wisconsin men continued ahead. "The works we charged were about [180 yards] across a cleared field," twenty-year-old Lieutenant Willie H. Lamberton of the 36th Wisconsin wrote home. "We made about half the distance when they opened on us with grape and canister—and Oh horror! I never wish to see another charge if they prove as fatal as this." Some soldiers reached the rebel earthworks and clambered over, only to be captured. Raked by immense firepower, the remainder lay down in front of the works and hid behind a slight rise that sheltered them from the leaden storm. Confederates worked into the field and captured several soldiers. Other Federals lay quiet until dark and crawled back to safety.[41]

David Coon of the 36th Wisconsin wrote his daughter Emma about the ordeal. "How would you feel," he asked, "to see your father lying in a ditch behind a bank of earth all day, with rebel bullets flying over his head, so that his life was in danger if he should raise to his feet, without a chance to get anything to eat, and about four o'clock P.M., starting with several hundred others running across an open field toward a rebel battery with rebel bullets, grape and canister, flying like hail, and men falling killed and wounded all about him, and finally all hands ordered to fall on our faces so that the storm could pass over us, and then be obliged to lie in that position until covered by the darkness of night so that we could get away?"[42]

The 36th Wisconsin sustained brutal casualties. Of 240 soldiers participating in the charge, 140 were killed, wounded, or captured. The pattern would soon become the norm. "In this charge, the [36th Wisconsin] confirmed a conviction received from our own experience, that new troops frequently assault with more vigor than those that have been longer in the service," an officer observed. "The latter are always more self-possessed under fire, far easier maneuvered in battle, and quickly recover from defeat; but the former are frequently filled with such enthusiasm as gives a powerful impetus to an assault." In ensuing assaults, casualties would be concentrated in new regiments, and they would be severe.[43]

Hancock had instructed Brooke, on Barlow's left, to support the right of Gibbon's advance. Gibbon, however, did not advance his division's right wing and sent no orders to Brooke to move out. As with most charges made that bloody day, it is doubtful that more troops would have improved the chance of success. Lee's entrenchments were simply too strong to break. "Gibbon made quite a demonstration of assault on their works this P.M.," Hancock reported of the one-sided affair, "but the ground was so swept by artillery that it was not thought best to order an absolute assault, but our skirmish line was held by a brigade, and entrenched against them within 200 steps of them."[44]

Dana summed up feelings at headquarters. The day had witnessed a succession of lost opportunities, he observed. Meade had expected Wright to arrive at Cold Harbor by daylight and attack the rebels congregating in front of Sheridan. Instead, the 6th Corps commander had "reconnoitered, skirmished, and delayed," Dana claimed. Had Wright reached Cold Harbor on schedule, Dana thought, he could have routed the force that later attacked Sheridan, "and an advantage might easily have been gained which, followed up by Sheridan's two divisions of cavalry, might have led to the dispersal of Lee's army." As Dana saw it, "Wright blundered in the execution of his order to march to Cold Harbor."[45]

Dana also criticized Warren. "Warren was ordered to attack a column of the rebel infantry which was passing toward Old Cold Harbor," he noted, "but instead of falling on it in force he opened with artillery, and at 3:00 P.M. reported that the intrenchments of the enemy were exceedingly strong, and that his own lines were so long that he had no mass of troops to attack with." Grant and Meade, Dana wrote, "are intensely disgusted with these failures of Wright and Warren." Meade, Dana went on, "says that a radical change must be made, no matter how unpleasant it may be to make it; but I doubt whether he will really attempt to apply so extreme a remedy."[46]

Unknown to Dana, the time for maneuvering and jockeying for position was over. By 5:00 P.M., Wright and Smith were finally at Cold Harbor, girding to advance west against Hoke and Kershaw. Meade had hoped to attack before the rebels had time to dig in, but fate had worked against him. Hoke's men had been in place since the previous night, and Kershaw's troops had been given several hours to entrench, pitch up earthworks, clear fields of fire, and spread obstacles in front of their line. Pickett's and Field's divisions were now ensconced on Kershaw's left, linking the rebels in front of Cold Harbor with the rest of the Confederate line. "The pickets" a newspaperman recalled, "were hard at work digging rifle pits and felling trees, in a narrow strip of wood half a mile from the Union troops, who could see the axes and shovels gleaming in the descending sun." The killing was about to resume.[47]

"We had a hot time at Ashland."

While Union infantrymen skirmished and maneuvered, Wilson's cavalry set out from Hanover Court House to destroy the two railroad bridges across the

South Anna River. Wilson decided to split his division for the operation. Chapman was to take the 18th Pennsylvania Cavalry and 2nd New York Cavalry northwest along Hanover River Road; this force would do the actual wrecking of the bridges. But Chapman's route would leave him vulnerable to attack, since large numbers of Confederate cavalrymen—both of Rooney Lee's brigades, and Wright's as well—had evacuated Hanover Court House in the direction of Ashland, a small town seven miles west. As soon as the Confederates learned that Chapman was burning railroad trestles, they would inevitably rush north to stop him. Wilson's solution was to dispatch a second force, under McIntosh, west along the Ashland Road to screen Chapman's left flank, fending off Rooney Lee and any other rebel cavalry units lurking in the vicinity. For his screening operation, McIntosh was to take the 5th New York Cavalry, the 2nd Ohio Cavalry, and the 1st Connecticut Cavalry. The rest of Wilson's division—the 1st Vermont, 3rd Indiana, 3rd New Jersey, and 8th New York Cavalry—was to remain at Hanover Court House, ready to join either of the two expeditions as needed.[48]

Wilson's two forces started off at about the same time. Chapman had fairly easy going. Camped along Hanover River Road in his path were Ridgely Brown's 1st Maryland Cavalry and the Baltimore Light Artillery, both still commanded by Bradley Johnson and together numbering no more than 150 men. Johnson put up a brave front, falling back slowly as Chapman approached. Severely outnumbered, he petitioned Rooney Lee for help. But Lee's two brigades were on the Ashland Road and already confronting McIntosh, and Lee did not see how he could spare troops to assist Johnson. He sent a courier alerting Johnson that his hands were full and that he was being driven back as well. He promised to watch the Marylanders' southern flank and urged Johnson to make at least a "little fight for the bridges." Miffed, Johnson replied that his 150 men "couldn't do [what Lee's] division of cavalry couldn't" and that he "was going back, too."[49]

Concerned that Chapman might become isolated, Wilson sent him the 1st Vermont and 3rd Indiana Cavalry. A squadron under Captain Oliver T. Cushman of the 1st Vermont turned north at Wickham's Station and destroyed the Virginia Central Railroad bridge over the South Anna River while Chapman's main body pushed Johnson's Marylanders back to Ellett's Crossing and the Richmond, Fredericksburg, and Potomac Railroad. "We fought the enemy from point to point," a Marylander recollected, "in hopes that reinforcements would be sent us, and thus save the bridges." Reinforcements, however, were not forthcoming. Hoping to redeem what was fast becoming an impossible situation, Johnson deployed his small force at Ellett's Crossing, fully aware that the stand had little chance of success. Leaving Colonel

Brown in charge there, Johnson rode west to locate a place for the troops to fall back on.[50]

Chapman's column reached Ellett's Crossing around 2:00 P.M. Confronted by an overwhelming force, Brown decided to do the unexpected and attack. Ordering a mounted charge, he rode to the front of his small band and led them in a forlorn assault against Chapman's four regiments. Brown made an irresistible target, and a Union trooper shot him through the right eye, the bullet passing out the back of his head. Brown tumbled from his mount, mortally wounded. Demoralized, the Marylanders retreated, bringing his body with them.[51]

Johnson heard the ruckus and galloped back to Ellett's Crossing. By the time he arrived, Chapman was preparing to launch a charge of his own. As Johnson pondered the situation—Chapman was "making disposition for an advance which it was apparent we could not withstand with our small command," Brown's adjutant George Booth remembered of those tense moments—reinforcements in the form of the 3rd North Carolina Cavalry arrived from Rooney Lee. Johnson was distraught over Brown's death and refused the help. "I don't want your squadron," he told Lee's aide Captain Theodore S. Garnett, leading the regiment. "Colonel Brown has just been killed. I cannot stop the enemy here." Calling in his men, Johnson retreated south along the Richmond, Fredericksburg, and Potomac Railroad toward Ashland. His way now clear, Chapman seized Ellett's Crossing and dispatched Captain Cushman to the nearby railway bridge, which he wrecked as thoroughly as he had the first span. "Both of these bridges were most effectually destroyed by fire, including trestle work as well as superstructure," Chapman later reported, "as also the water tanks, and the road was further damaged by the destruction of small bridges and cattle guards at different points."[52]

Ashland was a quaint Virginia town fifteen miles north of Richmond. It owed its existence to the Richmond, Fredericksburg, and Potomac Railroad. Initially named "Slash Cottage" after the nearby "Slashes of Hanover," birthplace of Henry Clay, the town hosted an elaborate resort replete with a spa, hotel, and guest cottages. By 1860, horseraces and casinos had attracted visitors from Richmond, many of whom built summer homes and commuted by train. "In one short decade," a local historian noted, Ashland "had come a long way from a large stand of trees in the middle of a slash where pigeons came to roost, to a thriving mineral springs resort that attracted picnickers for the day or families for the week."[53]

War was not new to Ashland. The place was close to Richmond, it lay on the rail line, and Telegraph Road, the major north-south wagon route from

Richmond to Washington, passed less than half a mile east of town. Ashland had been a popular target for Union raiders, and its location drew the war to it again. Two and a half miles north at Ellett's Crossing, Johnson's Marylanders were trying to fend off Chapman's Federals. And a few miles east, on the road to Hanover Court House, McIntosh's three regiments were driving Rooney Lee west toward the town.

Lee was hard pressed. Nearing Ashland, he left a token force on Ashland Road to retard McIntosh's progress, led the rest of his division south along farm roads, and turned west to Telegraph Road. This placed him southeast of town, where he began setting up a defensive line to bar McIntosh's direct route to Richmond. Colonel John Hammond's 5th New York Cavalry, in the fore of McIntosh's column, easily pushed aside the small force of Confederates remaining on Ashland Road, crossed Telegraph Road, and rode victoriously to the railway station in the center of town. Colonel Purington's Ohio troopers came close behind and joined Hammond's men tearing up tracks and destroying the train station.

Hammond's and Purington's rapid advance had left McIntosh's rearmost regiment—the 1st Connecticut—several miles back on the Ashland Road. Around noon, Wade Hampton, who was camped a few miles away at Atlee's Station on the Virginia Central Railroad, received alarms from Rooney Lee alerting him to McIntosh's progress. Hampton immediately started north with his brigade commander Thomas Rosser and three Virginia regiments, intending to enter Ashland Road behind McIntosh and attack him from the rear.[54]

Hampton and Rosser reached Ashland Road shortly after the tail of McIntosh's force had passed. "The road was narrow and obstructed by a thick, bushy forest," Rosser recounted, "and while the enemy was not in sight, so recently had the rear of his column passed that the water from a branch was still running into the tracks made by his horses in the mud on its bank, not having had time to fill." Leaving Rosser to harass McIntosh's rear, Hampton galloped off to coordinate with Rooney Lee. Rosser and his three regiments rode west along Ashland Road and discovered to their delight that elements from the 1st Connecticut Cavalry had strayed onto a side road, leaving McIntosh's supply wagons unprotected. "Our regiment was marching quietly in the rear with our pack train and headquarters dog Cash," a man in the 1st Connecticut recollected. The New Englanders had no inkling that rebels were about to attack.[55]

At Rosser's signal, Colonel Thomas Massie's 12th Virginia Cavalry pitched into the 1st Connecticut—"came down upon them like lice in Egypt," a Federal said of the unexpected assault. "The servants, who were riding and leading the pack animals, of course were terribly scared and dashed right down the road through the center of our regiment, throwing it, for the time being, into some confusion," a Connecticut man remembered. While New Englanders scattered, Rosser's Virginians loaded up on delicacies from Union wagons and captured McIntosh's spare mounts accompanying the rear guard. A trail of beans proved especially intriguing and led to an overturned mulecart. "Don't kill me," bawled the driver, who was relieved to discover the Confederates more interested in his cargo than in him. "The effect of this rear attack was to scatter the enemy in every direction through the woods, breaking up his organization," Rosser reported, "but in doing so I encumbered my men with prisoners, horses, and wagons." Colonel Blakeslee, commanding the 1st Connecticut, ordered his soldiers to open ranks and let the panicked packhorses run through. While Rosser's troopers collected booty, Blakeslee rallied his men along both sides of Ashland Road in hopes of making a stand.[56]

Rosser's lead squadron, under Lieutenant George Baylor, drove Blakeslee back in vicious hand-to-hand fighting. "The woods were very thick, so that I could get but few men in action at a time," Blakeslee related, "and the woods were filled with rebels, so that a saber charge in the road was impracticable." Blakeslee estimated that he re-formed seven times during his heated rearguard fight. Disabled by a severe hand wound, he relinquished command to Major George O. Marcy. Colonel Purington, whose Ohio troopers were ripping up track at Ashland, heard the firing and sent Squadron D, under Lieutenant Melancthon C. Cowdery, to help Blakeslee. The additional Federals caught Rosser by surprise. "I had kept only two squadrons in the saddle unencumbered," Rosser wrote. The balance of the command was guarding the prisoners and captured property and was scattered along the road for over a mile. Cowdery's squadron charged into Baylor's troopers, and men fought at close quarters, firing pistols and slashing with sabers. "Everything was about to break," Rosser recounted, "when Private [Holmes] Conrad, who was at my side, rushed to [the 11th Virginia] and seized its colors and called to his old comrades to save their flag that had waved triumphantly upon so many glorious fields, and rushed with it into the ranks of the enemy." The Virginians piled into the Federals and regained the initiative. "Following up his success," Hampton later put it, "Rosser pressed the enemy vigorously and in a series of brilliant charges—some of which were over dismounted men—he drove [the last of McIntosh's troopers] into Ashland." Federals posted in houses finally stopped Rosser's progress with a "galling fire," a Virginian reported.[57]

While Rosser mauled the tail of McIntosh's column, Rooney Lee arrayed his two brigades—Pierce Young's North Carolinians and John Chambliss's

Virginians—in line across Telegraph Road and the railroad, blocking the routes south of Ashland. Hampton, now actively coordinating the Confederate defense, saw an excellent opportunity to capture McIntosh's entire force. He had three brigades—Rosser's, Young's, and Chambliss's—concentrated against McIntosh's three regiments. Rosser held Ashland Road, blocking McIntosh's way back to Hanover Court House. Young and Chambliss, south of town, closed off McIntosh's route toward Richmond. Telegraph Road and the Richmond, Fredericksburg, and Potomac Railroad led north from town, toward Ellett's crossing, but Johnson's Maryland troopers, reinforced by elements from Gilbert Wright's brigade, stood across those routes. The closest Union reinforcements to Ashland—Chapman's troopers—were still at Ellett's Crossing, pulling up tracks and oblivious to McIntosh's predicament. With rebels hemming him in on three sides, McIntosh's only way out was to flee west. This, Hampton reasoned, would take him away from the Union army and only temporarily postpone his inevitable capture.

While Hampton completed his preparations to snag McIntosh, a battery of Confederate horse artillery under Major James F. Hart rolled up. McIntosh was now bottled up in Ashland, surrounded by a Confederate force outnumbering him better than three to one. "Attack at once," Hampton ordered, determined to exploit his advantage and capture the isolated Union brigade.[58]

McIntosh girded to repulse the impending onslaught. He stationed his horse artillery in town and posted his men in houses along the rail embankment and behind breastworks hastily erected across neighboring woods and fields. McIntosh's line formed a semicircle, the arc's center facing east, on Ashland Road, and its ends resting on the railroad north and south of Ashland. The 2nd Ohio, under Purington, faced north, controlling the railroad and Telegraph Road in the direction of Johnson's Marylanders. The 1st Connecticut, now under Major Marcy, faced east across the Ashland Road, confronting Rosser. And Colonel Hammond's 5th New York looked south, toward Rooney Lee's two brigades under Young and Chambliss.

Hampton began his attack by sending Young's Tar Heels in a headlong charge to break McIntosh's line between Telegraph Road and Ashland Road. Elements from Hammond's and Marcy's regiments deadlocked Young in bitter fighting. Young—"an exceedingly handsome, gallant, and enterprising officer," Wilson later described him—fell wounded when a ball passed through his left breast and exited near his left shoulder. Command of his brigade devolved once again on Colonel Baker of the 3rd North Carolina Cavalry. When the North Carolinians ran low on ammunition, they "fought the enemy with stones and brick-bats," a Confederate recalled. Hammond's Federals, armed with seven-shot carbines, held firm, killing and wounding more than seventy

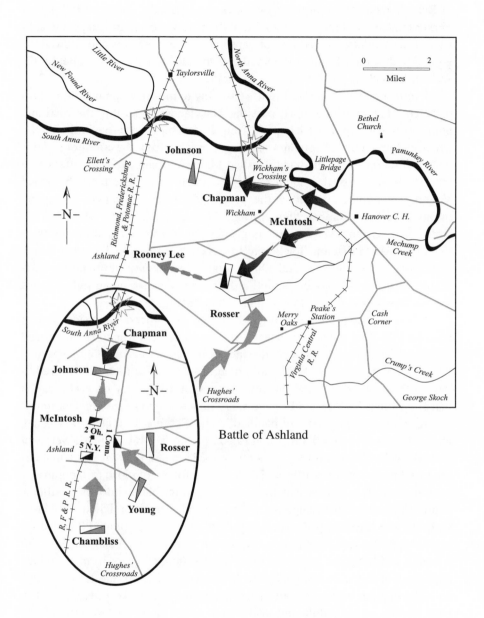

Battle of Ashland

of Baker's men. "Several times our boys were partially surrounded," a New York related, "but the ceaseless fire of their carbines and the grape and canister of the artillery mowed fearful gaps in the enemy's lines, and strewed the ground with slain." Hammond joined the wounded when a rebel bullet hit his scabbard, cracking the bone above his ankle.[59]

McIntosh sent a courier to Ellett's Crossing to inform Chapman of his predicament. The courier slipped past the Marylanders guarding the road and pounded into Chapman's camp. Wilson, it developed, was visiting Ellett's Crossing to see how Chapman was doing. Learning from the courier of McIntosh's situation, he immediately rushed Major William Wells's battalion of the 1st Vermont Cavalry south along Telegraph Road. The battle-hardened Vermonters numbered among the best of Sheridan's troopers. Punching through the Marylanders, they stormed into Ashland, where McIntosh directed them east to assist the 1st Connecticut against Rosser near the intersection of Ashland Road and Telegraph Road. North of town on Telegraph Road, a portion of Purington's 2nd Ohio—eight dismounted companies under Major Nettleton—deployed behind a ditch and waged a fierce fight against the Marylanders and the 5th North Carolina Cavalry.[60]

Sounds of combat rattled through the streets of Ashland. Both sides fought dismounted, often at close quarters. "It was strange but true to see rebel and Union soldiers firing from opposite sides of the same tree," an Ohioan wrote. "The rebels were so thick that we could scarcely miss them if we fired at random," he claimed, "and but few shots went astray." A Federal recalled that for a time, McIntosh's brigade was "in serious confusion and in imminent danger of being roughly handled." The Confederates also took heavy losses. North of town on Telegraph Road, the 5th North Carolina's Sergeant James Wyche Tillett led twelve men in a sortie to shoot down gunners manning McIntosh's horse artillery. Tillett's little force got close to the guns by creeping through bushes and fired a volley point-blank into the artillery. Union skirmishers in Purington's ditch rose and shot all of Tillett's soldiers. Only the sergeant escaped. "In the space of forty feet I counted 22 dead rebels, and there was a large number wounded," an Ohio man claimed. The 9th Virginia of Chambliss's brigade drove Connecticut troopers from a wooded area south of town, shooting Captain Addison G. Warner of the 1st Connecticut. The captain was wounded in the thigh, and when two officers tried to prop him up in his saddle and lead him to safety, a bullet tore through his head, killing him. A Union minié ball split a Confederate's mouth. "The contact of the ball with his teeth sounded to me very much as if it had struck and shattered a china plate or cup," a witness remembered.[61]

McIntosh asked Major Wells of the 1st Vermont to have a message taken back to Wilson. "[McIntosh's] whole brigade was on the skirmish line," Wells told Captain Horace K. Ide, who was to carry the message to Wilson, "and if he should withdraw, the enemy might make a rush and capture his artillery, but if General Wilson could attack with his other brigade, he thought they could drive the rebels." Wilson, it developed, had already ordered the rest of the 1st Vermont to Ashland. In the nick of time the Vermont troopers, commanded by Lieutenant Colonel Addison W. Preston, thundered down the rail line, drove the Marylanders aside, and opened an escape route north. The infusion of fresh soldiers bought McIntosh the breathing spell that he needed. His fought-out cavalrymen quickly withdrew along the tracks— "We got away the best we could," a Connecticut man admitted—toward Ellett's Crossing and the main body of Chapman's brigade, leaving behind most of their dead and wounded. Confederates wounded the 2nd Ohio's Captain Albert Barnitz in the right thigh during the withdrawal and shot his horse from under him. A few Connecticut soldiers lingered at the depot long enough to bury the popular Warner in a neighboring yard. Confederates seemed on the verge of overwhelming Preston's 1st Vermont when the 5th New York, armed with Spencer repeating carbines, arrived from below town and laid down a carpet of fire. "As our men were between them and the advancing tide of the enemy," a Vermonter recalled, "they did about as much damage to us as to the rebels, except perhaps the noise of the volleys convinced the rebels that there was a reserve." The New Yorkers served as rear guard for the retreat up the rail line, Confederates nipping at their heels. "In getting [McIntosh] out of the scrape we got into one and had to leave on the double quick," a Vermont man conceded. Recollected another: "Soon the road was filled with the debris of several regiments drifting to the rear, which tide General Wilson and his staff vainly endeavored to check."[62]

McIntosh's brigade joined Chapman at Ellett's Crossing near nightfall. Fagged-out horsemen rode back to Hanover Court House and slipped into their camps of the previous evening. "Command all extricated after much hard fighting," Wilson wrote of the affair. "That night we returned to Hanover Court House, after marching fifteen miles to make eight, not being able to return the way we came," an Ohioan grumbled. "As we drank our coffee that night our souls were full of bitterness, and we fully expressed our sentiments as our conversation turned on the good men who had fallen and the good men who will fall."[63]

The Battles of Hanover Court House and Ashland, as the cavalry fights came to be called, yielded mixed results. Wilson's assignment was to protect the interval between the Union army and the Pamunkey and to destroy the railroad bridges, and he achieved both objectives. His plan to divide his force and send both prongs into unfamiliar territory, however, almost cost him McIntosh's brigade. Wilson never intended to fight at Ashland and was surprised by the vehemence of the Confederate onslaught. He paid a steep price, losing 183 men. McIntosh accounted for 145 of these casualties, as his troops did most of the fighting. The highest losses were in the 1st Connecticut, with 33 casualties; the 5th New York, with 24; the 2nd Ohio, with 65; and the 1st Vermont of Chapman's brigade, with 33. Confederate laborers repaired the bridges in days, underscoring the venture's futility. In the larger picture, Wilson's expedition had no discernible impact on the campaign. It also did nothing to further Wilson's standing with his superiors or with his men. "We had a hot time at Ashland, where we ran up against a heavy force and got rather the worst of it," an Ohio trooper candidly admitted. "Our division and brigade commanders I think did not handle their commands very well," was a Vermont soldier's assessment.[64]

The verdict on the Confederate side was also mixed. The rebels lost about the same number of men as the Federals. A recent tabulation documents about a hundred losses for Young, 50 for Chambliss, 20 for Rosser, and 20 for the Maryland troops, bringing total rebel losses for the two days of combat to approximately 190 men. Young's wounding and Colonel Brown's death cut deeply. Southerners also complained that Hampton had fumbled an excellent chance to capture McIntosh's isolated cavalry brigade. "The whole affair was badly managed on our part," Rooney Lee's aide Garnett carped, "and what should have been a great victory for us must be numbered among the 'lost opportunities.'" Other southerners, however, were impressed with Hampton's performance. "In the cavalry fight yesterday, Rosser pitched into Wilson's rear whilst Rooney Lee was amusing him in front," one of Gilbert Wright's officers wrote. "The Yankees were badly stampeded."[65]

The Confederates did gain something important from the fight: Hampton was maturing as a leader. He had improvised a plan on the spur of the moment that contained Wilson's threat and came close to destroying part of the Union force. The Federals had managed to get away, but not through any dereliction on Hampton's part. In an inspiring counter to the string of Union cavalry victories during the past month, he had shown that the Army of Northern Virginia's mounted arm remained a formidable force. And Hampton's subordinates—particularly Rosser—had performed admirably. After the battle, Hampton received a note from General Lee expressing "gratification at the handsome defeat of the enemy." Also important to the Confederates were the provisions and horses—between 300 and 500 fresh mounts, according to estimates—that Rosser had captured.[66]

The battle at Ashland, like most Civil War cavalry engagements, was stirring to participants but represented little more than a sideshow. While Wilson's troopers burned bridges and battled in the streets of the little resort town, foot soldiers in blue and gray skirmished along Totopotomoy Creek and girded for battle near a crossroads named Old Cold Harbor. Infantry, not cavalry, would determine the fate of the campaign.

VIII

June 1

Grant Attacks at Cold Harbor

"You will get all the fighting you want before night."

ROADS AND TERRAIN figured prominently as Union and Confederate forces deployed for battle on the afternoon of June 1. Federal troops and wagons laden with supplies passed through Old Church, continued south along Bottoms Bridge Road to Spottswood Liggan's place, and turned west to Old Cold Harbor. The dilapidated tavern at the crossroads served as the Union nerve center. Officers directed most of the soldiers north along Beulah Church Road toward David Woody's farm. Woods shaded the western side of the road. Weary, dust-caked men formed in the trees, lining up along a north-south axis and facing west toward the rebels. Other soldiers turned south at Old Cold Harbor onto Dispatch Station Road and staked out the southern leg of the Union line.

The farmland between the armies was typical of the gently undulating countryside northeast of Richmond. Nature had designed the checkerboard of fields, forests, and ravines to favor the defense. A short distance west of the Union line, Confederate skirmishers waited in rifle pits large enough to hold two or three men. Dirt heaped in front, the excavations looked like animal burrows, inspiring soldiers to dub them "gopher holes." Half a mile beyond came an advance set of entrenchments, then a cleared field of fire, then obstacles, and finally the main Confederate line, sited on commanding ground and bristling with muskets and artillery.

The Confederate earthworks ran generally north to south through woods, although in places—most notably next to Cold Harbor Road—they crossed open fields. Boatswain Creek's headwaters drained the fields south of the road, creating a marshy, wooded depression below the lower end of the rebel line. North of the road, three small streams pierced the Confederate line and emptied into Gaines's Mill Pond well behind the rebel works. The lower stream, later called "Bloody Run," passed through the wooded ravine between Hoke and Kershaw about a quarter mile north of the roadway. A second ravine entered the rebel position three-eighths of a mile farther north, along the modern battlefield park boundary. Another half mile north, a third ravine defined Kershaw's left flank, due west of Mr. Woody's house. Whether these ravines would help the Confederates or their foes depended on how each army's field commanders used them.

Ricketts's division in the 6th Corps's advance had reached Cold Harbor around 10:00 A.M. The soldiers had been on the road for eleven hours, leaving a few men so tired "as to frequently actually unconsciously march into scrub trees by the wayside or anything else in the line of march before awaking," an officer recalled. "It was simply impossible to keep awake as overtaxed nature had reached its limit." Some soldiers thought they were going to White House Landing to guard the army's supply base. Others speculated they were on their way to reinforce Butler in an operation to capture Richmond from the south. "Now, boys, you are all mistaken," a veteran insisted. "This is one of Grant's flank movements, and you will get all the fighting you want before night."[1]

From Cold Harbor, Ricketts shuttled his troops north along Beulah Church Road. Colonel Benjamin F. Smith's brigade stopped halfway to Mr. Woody's house and piled into woods west of the road. Colonel William S. Truex's brigade deployed on Smith's left, reaching south toward the Cold Harbor intersection. The dusty men were grateful for shade but disturbed to find corpses from Keitt's and Torbert's fight earlier that morning. The woods had burned in places, and charred bodies dotted patches of smoldering ashes where fires had raged. "It was a sad sight for anyone," reflected Major Lemuel A. Abbott of the 10th Vermont. Ricketts threw out a picket line under Lieutenant Colonel Otho H. Binkley of the 110th Ohio. Taking 250 men from his own regiment and 150 more from the 87th Pennsylvania, Binkley advanced west into the fields. Rebel skirmishers opened from their gopher holes, Binkley's troops took whatever cover they could find, and a swelling patter of musketry provided a backdrop for Ricketts's slumbering soldiers.[2]

Near noon, Russell's division reached Cold Harbor and moved into place straddling Cold Harbor Road, two brigades north of the roadway and two south. Emory Upton's brigade marched a short distance north on Beulah Church Road and settled into woods on Ricketts's left. A grove of mulberry trees grew nearby, a Connecticut soldier noted, "well laden with delicious fruit, and it did not take long for several of the boys to get into these trees and load up with mulberries." Upton's troops dug rudimentary rifle pits, and a detail buried dead rebels from the morning fight. Upton sent the 121st New York out as pickets, replacing a detachment of Torbert's cavalrymen that had been patrolling toward the rebel lines. Colonel Clinton Beckwith arrayed the New Yorkers in close skirmish order and fanned west into the field, hoping to take the Confederates by surprise and drive them from their pits. "They broke as soon as they saw us begin to charge," Beckwith reported, "and we kept them on a dead run until they reached their [advance line of] works." Unable to continue farther, the New Yorkers lay down in the field, concealed from the rebels by scrubby pine and broom sedge. Some of Beckwith's men crossed Cold Harbor Road and drove Confederate skirmishers from a house and outbuildings—most likely the home of Miles Garthright and his wife, Margaret—a quarter of a mile in front of the developing Union line. Stacking barrels and farm implements into barricades, the New Yorkers fortified the house and held it against a series of spirited rebel forays to take it back.[3]

The rest of Russell's division spread out south of Upton. Brigadier General Henry L. Eustis covered the interval from Upton's left to Cold Harbor Road, posting his troops in open fields north of the road. Colonel William H. Penrose's brigade of six New Jersey regiments settled into an orchard in the southwest quadrant of the Cold Harbor intersection, behind the Garthright house, their right adjoining Eustis's left. Colonel Nelson Cross's New York and Pennsylvania brigade trudged south along Dispatch Station Road behind Penrose and formed below the New Jersey troops.

It was during these deployments—all of the 6th Corps was up except Neill's division—that Wright received Meade's noontime order to attack as soon as possible. "The last division of the corps is moving in," Wright wrote back, "and as soon as in position I shall press my skirmish line forward, to develop strength and position of enemy." Around 2:30, Neill's division trudged up and deployed on Cross's left. The troops were exhausted, having left Totopotomoy Creek ten hours before. "First the sun was hot enough to bake meat," a Massachusetts man reminisced. "Then the roads and fields by the passage of troops was ground to a powder which filled the air, and got into the noses, mouths, eyes, and ears and in addition the pine woods were blazing in fierce flame on both sides of the road and the thick black smoke almost choked us." A tired warrior remembered soldiers "resting in all shapes beside the road in the shade of the trees."[4]

Neill's lead elements marched into fields west of Dispatch Station Road and drove back pickets from Fitzhugh Lee's cavalry. Leaving Wheaton's brigade east of Cold Harbor to guard wagons, Neill arrayed the rest of his division into a tight formation facing west. In front was Colonel Lewis A. Grant's crack Vermont brigade. Grant's front line consisted of Lieutenant Colonel Samuel E. Pingree's 2nd Vermont and Lieutenant Colonel Reuben C. Benton's 1st Vermont Heavy Artillery, a large novice regiment that had joined the Potomac army during the Spotsylvania campaign. The rest of Grant's brigade—the 1st, 4th, 5th and 6th Vermont—formed a second line, and the 3rd Vermont spread out as skirmishers. Colonel Oliver Edwards's brigade of Massachusetts and Rhode Island regiments stood behind Grant and was backed in turn by Colonel Daniel D. Bidwell's mixed brigade from Maine, New York, and Pennsylvania.[5]

The troops of Baldy Smith's 18th Corps showed up close to 3:00 P.M., fuming over the mistaken order that had sent them to New Castle Ferry earlier that morning. The error had increased their marching distance by several miles and put them on the road during noontime heat. "The memory of that day's march will exist so long as any man who was in it continues to live," a New Hampshire soldier predicted. "The temperature, even in the shade, must have been close up to, if not above, blood heat, and following much of the time, as the troops had to, directly in the rear of the baggage train of the 6th Corps, the dust was worse, if possible, than the heat." A coating of nondescript brown covered everything and everyone. "The men were almost suffocated before the next halt was reached, and could hardly be recognized," another soldier wrote. "Added to this there had been a cavalry fight in the region a few days before, and the effluvia of dead animals tainted the air." Wright's troops had a low opinion of Smith's men. "Hallo, parlor soldiers," veterans called to the bedraggled forms stumbling past.[6]

Smith was under instructions both to join Wright in the afternoon's assault and to reach north to Bethesda Church and link with Warren. On arriving at Cold Harbor, he discovered that he could not do both. "My scant force would not have filled the space between the 5th and 6th Corps, and, making that connection, I should have had no lines with which to make an attack," Smith later wrote. "As I could not obey both requirements of the order, I determined to aid in the attack, and began formation of my lines immediately." Rather than stretch his force thin, he decided to deploy in strength north of Wright, extending the Union line to Woody's farm. Thus massed, he hoped to throw the 18th Corps's entire weight into the assault.[7]

Smith's foremost division, under Charles Devens, appeared first. Passing through Cold Harbor, Devens rode near Edwards's brigade of Neill's division. Devens had formerly commanded the brigade, and soldiers cheered him as he passed. The general was ill, an Indiana man noticed, and was "compelled to rest frequently on a chair which was carried for him, and when he rode had to be lifted on his horse." Marching north along Beulah Church Road, Devens's troops massed on Ricketts's right in a skirt of woods. An Indiana, Maine, and New York brigade, under Colonel Jeremiah Drake, deployed first, its left touching Ricketts. Colonel William B. Barton's brigade arrived next, passed behind Drake, and formed on his right. A man in the 115th New York recollected that much of Devens's division was "badly used up, and a large number of the men lay along the dusty road and under the burning rays of the southern sun, utterly unable to move." Devens placed soldiers too fatigued to fight in his rear as a reserve.[8]

It was now 4:00 P.M. Wright's artillery opened to soften the distant Confederate line for the impending attack. Smith's guns, under Captain Elder, rolled into place along Beulah Church Road and joined in. Confederate pieces responded—Cabell's battalion, assigned to Kershaw, and Major J. P. W. Read's battalion, accompanying Hoke—and hurled shells into the Federal line. "There was a furious artillery duel for some time," a man in the 10th Massachusetts wrote, "which, as was often the case, was more noisy than harmful." A projectile tore through the orchard south of Cold Harbor and stuck William Oliver of the 15th New Jersey on the head, killing him and catapulting his body into the air. Farther north, soldiers in the 9th New York Heavy Artillery, many of them under fire for the first time, decided they valued their lives more than their unsoiled clothing. "No consideration of our apparel prevented the closest embraces of Mother Earth," a man remembered. Three batteries posted in support of Upton kept up a "furious cannonading," a Pennsylvanian recalled. A Union shell fell short, blowing off the right arm of the 96th Pennsylvania's adjutant and shattering another man's foot. "For a long time the solid shot flew back and forth between [Union and Confederate batteries], right above our heads, lopping off twigs, limbs, and even large branches, which came crashing down among the ranks," a Connecticut man related. "Our boys were so weary with the march and previous day's work that they went sound asleep while the shells were screeching over us."[9]

Five o'clock came. Smith's next division, under William Brooks, arrived and marched into place north of Devens, extending the Union line past Beulah Church—or what remained of the church, as someone had set fire to the building, burning it to the ground. Colonel Guy V. Henry posted his brigade in woods above Devens and threw out the 92nd New York as skirmishers. Brigadier General Hiram Burnham placed the 118th New York and 8th Connecticut behind Henry and moved the rest of his brigade—the 13th and 10th New Hampshire—onto Henry's right, anchoring the right end of the Union line on Mr. Allison's road in front of the Woody house. Seeking a better jumping-off point for his attack, Brooks advanced portions of Henry's and Burnham's brigades west toward the Confederates. The 13th New Hampshire descended into a swampy depression, clambered up the far side of a forty-foot bluff, and spread out along the edge of a field. The 40th Massachusetts pushed forward on the left and found shelter behind a rail fence. Soldiers lay under grueling fire from Confederate earthworks half a mile away, waiting for the order to charge. "We have been within range of the enemy's shot and shell for a long time, but now we are near his infantry lines, and hundreds of his bullets whistle and whack among the trees about us" a New Hampshire man wrote. "Rebel shells burst over our heads, and the pieces come down among us, or else rip and tear through the trees, favoring us with the falling branches." Brooks posted his final brigade, under Brigadier General Gilman Marston, in reserve on Beulah Church Road. "Everything in this vicinity gave evidence of a hard cavalry fight of recent occurrence," a soldier noted. "Dead horses, broken sabers and carbines together with little mounds of earth here and there told more plainly than words of the desperate nature of the conflict that had occurred here."[10]

John Martindale's division arrived around 5:30 P.M. Smith was concerned about the two-mile gap between the northern end of his line and Warren's southern flank. Rather than add Martindale to his battle line, he arrayed the division perpendicular to the rest of his troops, facing north toward the gap to prevent rebels from turning his flank. Brigadier George J. Stannard's brigade held the left of Martindale's line, abutting Burnham, and Colonel Griffin A. Stedman Jr.'s brigade moved into place on the division's right.

The yawning gap separating the Union army's two wings also troubled Meade. Earlier in the day, at Meade's urging, Warren had sent his aide Roebling to explore the road network south of Bethesda Church. Wending along farm roads, Roebling reached Woody's farm just as Smith's lead elements arrived. Concluding that he could do nothing to help Smith—Roebling had only a detachment of Maryland troops—the aide sent a courier to report the situation to Warren and started back. Meade, however, kept trying to goad Warren into doing something. "Generals Wright and Smith will attack this evening," he wrote the 5th Corps commander. "It is very desirable you should join in this attack, unless in your judgment it is impracticable."[11]

Warren faced a dilemma. It was manifestly impossible for him to hold an extended line and simultaneously mass enough troops to attack. To appease Meade, Warren decided to dispatch Lockwood's division to bolster Wright and Smith. Around 5:00 P.M., he rode to Lockwood's headquarters, only to find that the general had left to inspect his skirmish line. The day had been filled with frustrations for Warren, and he unleashed a tirade against Lockwood in front of the absent general's astonished staff. He became "very impatient and very angry," an aide reported, and used "very harsh language." Unwilling to wait, Warren left a note for Lockwood. "Wright is engaging the enemy on your left up the Cold Harbor Road," the message said. "Advance your entire command along this road, and take part in the action if opportunity offers. A division will support you." Then he rode back to his own headquarters.[12]

Lockwood returned at 6:00 P.M., and an aide briefed him on Warren's stormy visit. After reading Warren's note, Lockwood ordered his division to start toward Cold Harbor right away. Neither Warren nor Lockwood, however, knew what Roebling had learned—that no road ran directly from Bethesda Church to Cold Harbor. Walnut Church Road, leading south from Bethesda Church, appeared to go in the right direction but soon veered southwest, heading away from Old Cold Harbor and into the lower sector of Early's fortifications. The only way for Lockwood to reach Wright's and Smith's burgeoning line was to weave through a labyrinth of farm roads. Roebling, however, had not returned, and Lockwood knew nothing about the road system. Shortly after 6:00 P.M., he set off on an impossible mission.

Meade was also worried about the stretch of undefended country extending from Wright's southern flank to the Chickahominy River, a distance of about a mile and a half. Fitzhugh Lee's cavalry, stationed below Hoke's line, controlled this sector, and some of his Confederates held the lower reaches of Dispatch Station Road, near the river. Meade reasoned that keeping rebel horsemen away from the southern Union flank and opening the direct route across the Chickahominy would be an ideal assignment for Sheridan, and he directed the cavalry commander to scout in that direction. Sheridan, however, had already settled his troopers into camps well east of Cold Harbor. It would be "impossible," he wrote Meade at 6:00 P.M., "to get the command together to make the reconnaissance before dark." Men and horses were exhausted, he added, promising to "make the reconnaissance early tomorrow morning."[13]

While Lockwood wandered along obscure byways and Sheridan rested his soldiers and their mounts, Wright and Smith were left to wage their battle with the troops already at hand.

The Confederates, well aware of the apparently endless column of Union soldiers streaming into Cold Harbor, busily strengthened their line in anticipation of attack. Hoke's division held the Confederate right, with Martin's

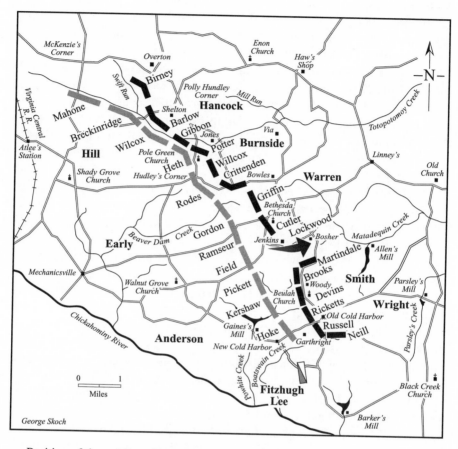

Position of the armies, afternoon of June 1

North Carolinians south of Cold Harbor Road, facing Cross. Colquitt's Georgians straddled the road, facing Penrose and Eustis, and Clingman's North Carolinians continued the line north to the ravine cut by Bloody Run, facing Upton and Truex. Hoke's remaining brigade—Hagood's South Carolinians—stood in advance of Clingman and slightly to his left, facing Colonel Smith's Union brigade and covering the gap in the Confederate formation cut by Bloody Run. Kershaw's line consisted of Wofford's Georgians on the right, facing Drake; Bryan's Georgians, facing Barton; Humphreys's Mississippians, facing Henry; and Henagan's South Carolinians, opposing Burnham. During the afternoon Pickett arrived and formed his division on Kershaw's left. Field's division filled the space between Pickett's left and the right of Early's corps.[14]

As Neill's troops marched up and extended the Union line well south of Cold Harbor, Hoke became anxious. Martin's Tar Heels already held works south of the road, but Neill's appearance lengthened the Federal line beyond Martin's southern flank, raising the specter that Union troops might advance past the end of Martin's works and turn the rebel position. Fitzhugh Lee's cavalry, patrolling south of Martin, lacked the strength to repulse a determined infantry attack. To keep his entrenchments abreast of Neill, Hoke decided to extend the lower end of his line with Hagood's South Carolina brigade. Hagood was guarding the bushy ravine between Clingman and Kershaw, but as Hoke saw it, Neill's threat took priority. He ordered Hagood to withdraw, march south behind the Confederate line, and take up a new position on Martin's right, facing Neill. He neglected, however, to notify Kershaw or Clingman that Hagood was leaving. As Hagood withdrew, he left the ravine an undefended pathway into the Confederate line.[15]

Hagood's South Carolina soldiers rushed south in column of four behind Clingman and Colquitt, crossed Cold Harbor Road, and continued behind Martin, lengthening Hoke's line another quarter mile south to Boatswain Creek, a steep-banked stream that provided a firm natural anchor for the southern end of the Confederate position. Skirmishers from the 3rd Vermont were driving in pickets from Fitzhugh Lee's cavalry just as Hagood arrived. Hagood immediately sent Captain James F. Izlar of the Edisto Rifles, 25th South Carolina, to repulse the Yankees, which he did. "The line of battle followed under a sharp fire of shells," Hagood recounted, "and, prolonging the general line, proceeded rapidly to entrench."[16]

Colquitt, Martin, and Hagood held strong terrain south of Cold Harbor Road, much of it concealed by a wooded fringe. "In front, the ground fell off abruptly into a lower plateau," Hagood wrote, "and on its right and right rear were the low grounds of the Chickahominy and one of its tributaries."

Penrose's brigade, Cross's brigade, and all of Neill's division were half a mile away, across open fields. The Confederates set to strengthening their imposing position. "A windrow of rails from the adjacent fences was laid; such spades and mattocks as they had were wielded by willing hands; and bayonets, tin cups, plates, and even the unaided hands lent assistance in digging a trench inside the rails and raising a parapet upon them," Hagood recounted. "The rapidity with which this was done was laughable," he added, "and would have been incredible to anyone who had not seen soldiers who knew the value of earthworks, however slight, work under similar circumstances." Noted a man in the 25th South Carolina: "It is indeed surprising what a large amount of work can be accomplished in a short space of time with no better implements than tin cups and bayonets under such circumstances, especially if the Yankee sharpshooters are getting in their work in good style."[17]

While Hagood's troops dug, Captain Izlar reconnoitered the lower end of Neill's line. Supporting him was a battery—in all likelihood horse artillery attached to Fitzhugh Lee—which began enfilading the Federals. Izlar's foray and the eruption of cannon fire from the south put a scare into Neill, who had no idea of the size of the rebel force materializing below him. To protect his exposed left flank, he bent the lower end of his line east to Dispatch Station Road. When he had completed his dispositions, Edwards's brigade, Bidwell's brigade, and most of Lewis Grant's brigade faced south. Neill's reorientation of his division left only two regiments—Pingree's 2nd Vermont and Charles K. Fleming's battalion of the 1st Vermont Heavy Artillery, led by Lieutenant Colonel Benton—facing west and available to participate in the assault.[18]

Neill dispatched the 3rd Vermont to drive off Izlar and his artillery support. "We advanced under terrific fire from artillery and musketry until within five hundred yards of their works," a Federal recollected, "and finding it impossible to advance farther we halted and began to dig pits with our bayonets." Neill also directed Edwards to press south, and the brigade set off at "double quick to oppose this demonstration," a Massachusetts man reported. "The rebels saw us coming and made a break for the cover of the woods, and gave us a very severe artillery fire," another Federal related. Rather than pursue, Edwards's veterans "went to work with tin plates, tin cups, or anything, and scooped up a pile of sand in front of us and took shelter behind it."[19]

Meade's orders placed Wright in charge of the offensive. This was heady responsibility for Wright and his first experience leading a major operation. To complicate matters, Smith held higher rank than Wright, a relationship that was bound to cause friction, and the two men had never worked together. The situation cried out for the presence of Grant, Meade, or someone designated by them to oversee the attack. But while Wright and Smith girded for a major offensive, Grant and Meade remained with their aides at Mrs. Via's farm, several miles distant by road. Throughout the campaign, the two top Union commanders had seldom visited the front, leaving corps heads to manage the details of the battles. The absence of a guiding hand had cost the Federals several opportunities, most notably in the Wilderness on May 5–6, at Laurel Hill on May 8, and at the Mule Shoe on May 12. Seemingly indifferent to the offensive at Cold Harbor on June 1, Grant and Meade squandered another excellent chance.

Union battle lines were complete by 6:00 P.M. Eight hours had passed since midmorning, when Wright's lead elements had reached Cold Harbor. Only two hours of daylight remained. Wright and Smith had to assault now or wait until morning. Well aware that this was the last opportunity to attack before the Confederates were fully entrenched, Wright ordered the charge. Artillery quieted. Soldiers slipped off their knapsacks and made ready.

The Federals held an impressive edge in manpower. Wright and Smith had assembled the better part of six divisions, numbering approximately 30,000 troops. Opposing them across a front of a mile and a half were Hoke's and Kershaw's two divisions, totaling slightly over 10,000 soldiers. Two of the available Union divisions, however, would not participate in the attack. Martindale's division faced north in anticipation that Confederates might come streaming through the gap between Smith and Warren. And most of Neill's division looked south to guard against a rebel attack from that direction. All told, only four Union divisions, numbering perhaps 20,000 soldiers, would take part in the offensive. The battle line, from north to south, consisted of the divisions of Brooks, Devens, Ricketts, and Russell, with Neill contributing two Vermont regiments. But even with two divisions tied up protecting their flanks, the Federals held a two-to-one advantage over the Confederates. Whether they could overcome the defensive power of field fortifications remained to be seen.

"It was no holiday work."

South of Cold Harbor Road, Penrose's brigade, Cross's brigade, and two regiments from Grant's brigade, oriented along a north-south axis, prepared to march across half a mile of open field toward Colquitt's, Martin's and Hagood's entrenched line. Prospects for success were remote.

Penrose's New Jersey troops waited anxiously in the orchard southwest of Cold Harbor, their right resting on the road. At Spotsylvania Court House these veterans had experienced firsthand the tremendous advantage that earthworks gave the defense. Looking across the field toward the distant tree line, they knew what to expect. Penrose ordered the advance, and the 4th New Jersey started forward as skirmishers, followed by the 1st and 3rd New Jersey. Moving out of the orchard, they marched past the Garthright house and the 121st New York's skirmish line and emerged fully into the open plain. Artillery and musketry redoubled from the distant ridge. "They raked us terribly with canister," remembered Penrose's adjutant Captain Charles R. Paul. "The ground was, within a brief space of time, strewn with the fallen," a soldier reported. The 1st and 3rd New Jersey pressed through the leaden storm to within a few hundred yards of Colquitt's works. Unable to continue, the 3rd New Jersey took shelter behind a knoll in the field. The 1st New Jersey broke and streamed back along Cold Harbor Road toward the relative safety of the orchard.[20]

Penrose had kept the 15th and 10th New Jersey in the orchard as a reserve. Gambling that more troops might tip the balance, he ordered them into the fight. "We were able to see but little," the 15th New Jersey's adjutant Edmund D. Halsey recalled. "Directly an officer appeared from the trees, beckoning us to come." Leading the way, the 15th New Jersey passed through the apple trees and into the clearing. "The line which had charged ahead of us had disappeared obliquely to the right," Halsey related. "The First New Jersey regiment was coming back by the road." As the 15th New Jersey advanced, its right sweeping below Cold Harbor Road, a rebel battery opened from front and left. The regiment's Lieutenant Colonel Edward L. Campbell halted the troops, ordered a half wheel to the left, and marched his command "rapidly forward through a storm of canister and musketry to a small knoll, about a hundred and fifty feet from the battery," a soldier wrote. Halting again, Campbell's men fired toward the guns and silenced them. A little to their right and front, on top of another knoll, the 3rd New Jersey's Captain Charles A. Wahl conspicuously waved his saber to set an example for his soldiers.[21]

Buffeted by fire from Georgians in front and North Carolinians to the left, Campbell and Wahl pulled a short distance back. The 10th New Jersey formed in support of the 15th New Jersey, and men began scooping out trenches. Their position was precarious. They were well in advance of the main Union line, their left was unprotected, and rebels were firing into them from earthworks no more than fifty yards away. A Union battery in their rear compounded their difficulty by dropping shells into them. "Ogden Whitesell ran back, by the Colonel's orders, to have it cease firing," the 15th New Jersey's historian recorded, "but the stupid or frightened Captain insisted upon his fratricidal work until another message was sent him, that if he did not stop, we should fire into him." The New Jersey troops tenaciously held on to their advanced position, firing so rapidly that their muskets became too hot to hold.[22]

Cross tried to advance his brigade to protect the lower end of Penrose's line, selecting the 23rd Pennsylvania—a colorfully attired Zouave regiment with little combat experience—to lead the attack, supported by the equally inexperienced 82nd Pennsylvania. Stepping out, the two novice regiments from the Keystone State drove rebel skirmishers through a narrow strip of woods. Confederates set the trees on fire as a delaying tactic, but the Pennsylvanians pressed into the clearing. There they re-formed, with the 95th Pennsylvania moving up to the right of Cross's line and the 122nd New York onto the left of the line. At Cross's command, the four regiments started forward at a run.[23]

The results were predictable. "As we emerged from the woods the rebels opened fire and our men commenced dropping," Major T. L. Poole of the 122nd New York wrote in his diary. Canister chewed into Cross's line, slowing the veteran regiments, but the greenhorns kept on. "In a few moments the ground was covered with their dead and wounded," a Tar Heel coolly observed. The 23rd Pennsylvania reached Martin's works, fought bitterly, and retired, lacking the strength to exploit its temporary gain. Retreating several hundred yards to the shelter of a small ravine, the Pennsylvanians followed the example of the New Jersey men on their right and started digging. The charge had cost them 8 officers and 181 soldiers killed and wounded.[24]

Lewis Grant advanced Pingree's 2nd Vermont and Fleming's battalion of the 1st Vermont Heavy Artillery in tandem with Cross's brigade on his right, pushing west toward Hagood's entrenchments. "It was no holiday work," a Vermonter recollected. "The enemy was well posted, his lines covered and concealed by woods, while the attacking troops moved over open ground." Companies H and E of the battalion drifted right and became entangled with the 122nd New York of Cross's brigade. Vermont and New York troops veered northwest along Cross's front toward Penrose's New Jersey brigade. They tried to persuade soldiers from Cross's 23rd and 82nd Pennsylvania to get out of their ravine and join them in a renewed assault, but the terrified novices refused to budge. "Don't go a step," their officers warned them. "It is useless." While the Pennsylvanians stayed down, hordes of New Yorkers and Vermonters moved out of the ravine and marched gamely ahead, reaching within 150 yards of the rebel works. They could go no farther. "We were ordered to lie down and soon to fall back over the brow of the hill, which was done in good order, bringing in the wounded," recollected a soldier in Company E of the Vermont battalion. The 122nd New York, which had fielded 140 men for the charge, lost 75 of them.[25]

The rest of Fleming's battalion and the 2nd Vermont pursued a more westerly course. When artillery and musketry picked up from the far woods, veterans of the 2nd Vermont lay down and gouged pits in the sandy soil. Novices of the 1st Vermont Heavy Artillery marched to within three hundred yards of the rebel works only to discover that they were alone, their left and right flanks exposed. Taking a cue from the veterans, regimental commander Benton ordered his men to lie flat, and they hugged the earth, securing "partial shelter from the bullets which whistled over and around them," a Vermonter recollected. They remained pinned in the field until nightfall, losing 13 men killed and 107 wounded. Pingree, whose soldiers of the 2nd Vermont were old hands at this sort of thing and knew exactly what to do, counted only 9 casualties.[26]

North of Cold Harbor Road, on Penrose's right, Eustis's brigade of four regiments from Maine, Wisconsin, and Pennsylvania girded to attack. Eustis was unquestionably brilliant—the native Bostonian had graduated first in his West Point class and had taught engineering at Harvard—but he suffered from poor health, reputedly ate opium, and seemed ill-suited to the pressure of combat. He had temporarily relinquished command of his brigade in the Wilderness and was absent again on June 1, leaving Lieutenant Colonel Gideon Clark of the 119th Pennsylvania in charge. The brigade contained mostly veterans—it had been Russell's command until he was elevated to head the division—and the absence of firm leadership was demoralizing. Almost a mile away, across a swath of open field, ran Confederate earthworks held by the left wing of Colquitt's brigade and the right wing of Clingman's. "This was the most exposed position of General Hoke's line," a southerner noted, "the entrenchments running through a large open field, not a tree in front or rear for several hundred yards." As Eustis's men would discover, it was also the most exposed Union sector north of Cold Harbor Road. Charging across cleared ground into the teeth of Colquitt's and Clingman's earthworks was little better than suicide, and Eustis's veterans knew it.[27]

Upton's brigade, on Eustis's right, faced Clingman's North Carolinians. Recently promoted to brigadier general for his innovative assault against the

Confederate Mule Shoe on May 10, Upton epitomized the aggressive field commander. He hailed from upstate New York and was a staunch abolitionist who waged war against Confederates with fervor driven by religious zeal. Fighting under Upton carried a high price. The core of his brigade—the 5th Maine, 121st New York, and 95th and 96th Pennsylvania—were veterans. By the end of the Spotsylvania campaign, the four regiments totaled less than 1,100 men.

On May 21, the 2nd Connecticut Heavy Artillery, freshly plucked from forts around Washington, reached the Army of the Potomac and was assigned to Upton. The regiment contained 1,500 soldiers and more than doubled the size of Upton's brigade, making his numbers "very respectable," an aide remarked. Virtually none of the newcomers, however, had battle experience. Heading them was Colonel Elisha S. Kellogg. The forty-year-old New Englander had led a colorful life, part of it as a sailor, and flaunted a "certain brusque roughness," an admirer noted. "I am but a rough man," Kellogg reputedly said of himself. Big-hearted and motivated by a strong sense of honor, he also possessed a "quick, ardent temperament," spiced his speech with expletives, and was not "careful of consequences when aroused." Unlike his soldiers, Kellogg was no stranger to warfare, having performed conspicuously commanding artillery during McClellan's Peninsula campaign.[28]

Dwight Kilbourn of the 2nd Connecticut Heavy Artillery noted his surroundings. "We are lying behind the rifle pits and shells from both sides are flying over our heads and skirmishers are firing on our right," he wrote. "Beyond us is an open field 50 rods wide and the Johnnies are in rifle pits in the pines beyond." Lieutenant Francis W. Morse, one of Upton's aides, had been through this several times before and rendered an even more negative assessment. "The situation was as dubious a one as I ever saw," he concluded. "To charge across a plain exposed to the fire of twenty thousand rifles, and any number of batteries, seemed almost madness."[29]

Upton formed his brigade in four lines, each containing some five hundred men. Eager to prove his regiment's worth, Kellogg volunteered his troops for the first three lines. The final line contained the 5th Maine, 95th and 96th Pennsylvania, and the portion of the 121st New York not on skirmish duty. These veterans, after all, had seen their share of combat, and they considered it only fair that newcomers led the way this time.[30]

The 2nd Connecticut Heavy Artillery lined up in a shallow depression, protected from rebel artillery by the remains of earthworks erected during McClellan's time. Upton conferred with Kellogg, making certain that he understood the part his novices were to play. At Spotsylvania Court House,

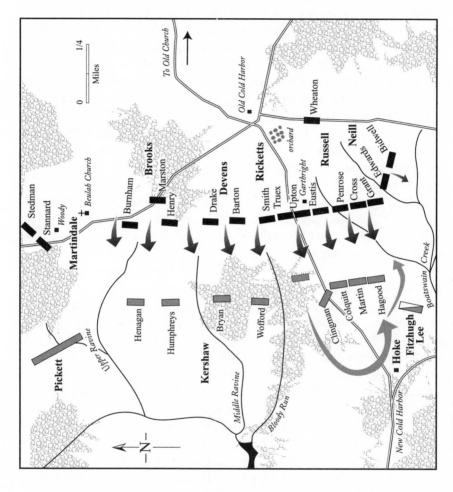

Cold Harbor attack on evening of June 1

Upton had discovered that troops improved their odds against earthworks by charging quickly without stopping to shoot. He advised Kellogg to follow that practice. The blustery colonel was "fully impressed with a sense of what was before us," an aide noted as he watched Kellogg draw the shape of the rebel line on the ground and instruct his officers how to conduct the attack. Major James Hubbard's 1st Battalion, four companies strong, formed Kellogg's front line. Behind came the four companies of Major James Q. Rice's 2nd Battalion. The third line was the 3rd Battalion's four companies under Major William B. Ells. Kellogg reminded his subordinates that veterans had jeered at the Connecticut men, derisively calling them band-box soldiers. "Now we are called on to show what we can do at fighting," the colonel stressed. "He felt confident," an aide remembered, "we would in this, our first fight, establish, and ever afterward maintain a glorious reputation, as a *fighting* regiment."[31]

At Kellogg's instructions, the Heavies discarded their knapsacks in the protected hollow and climbed over the old earthworks. They listened attentively while Kellogg addressed them. "Now, men, when you have the order to move on, go in steady, keep cool, keep still until I give you the order to charge, and then go arms a-port, with a yell," he directed. No one, he stressed, was to "fire a shot until you are within the enemy's breastworks." With a final word of assurance—"I will be with you," he reminded his soldiers—he placed himself at the head of the formation. "Forward! Guide center! March," Kellogg shouted, and his regiment started forward. Upton, who rode near the front line, observed that the regiment seemed "anxious to prove its courage and [moved] to the assault in perfect order."[32]

Ricketts's division, on Upton's right, started off at about the same time as Upton. Eustis's brigade, however, remained stationary, leaving Upton's left flank unprotected as his brigade advanced. Russell had directed Upton to guide left, but Eustis's failure to make a timely start rendered it impossible to comply. Russell decided that Upton should continue ahead in any event and sent the corps's assistant adjutant, Lieutenant Colonel McMahon, with instructions for Upton to advance without regard to a guide.[33]

Kellogg's first line, colors in the center, crossed a stretch of open field and entered a pine thicket. The second battalion followed fifty yards behind. "I glanced at the lines," Captain James Deane of Company L wrote, "and they were as straight as if we were parading in a review." Edward S. Roberts of Company E recalled the air "full of screeching shot and shell, and blue with bullets; men [were] falling on all sides. With all of this terrible rattle and noise the boys seemed to be as cool and calm as on a battalion drill; orders could be very distinctly heard."[34]

The 121st New York's skirmishers had done their work well, and the Connecticut men marched over the first line of abandoned rebel rifle pits without a hitch. They went down a gentle declivity, then started up a slight ascent on the far side, breaking into a small clearing freshly cut from the forest. Seventy yards ahead lay newly felled trees, branches intertwined. Behind the obstacles were fresh heaps of dirt. Headlogs lined the top, and sunshine glinted from musket barrels. It took Kellogg and his lead battalion a moment to comprehend their situation. They had reached the main rebel line. Some Heavies broke and ran "pell mell through our regiment toward the rear," a Connecticut man related. Captain Deane saw a sergeant dart back, "begging us not to go in." Deane whacked him on the back with his saber, and he shut up.[35]

Upton had emerged in front of the 51st North Carolina of Clingman's brigade. Confederates began systematically firing volleys, the rear rank shooting first, then the front rank. "A sheet of flame, sudden as lightning, red as blood, and so near that it seemed to singe the men's faces, burst along the rebel breastwork," a Federal remembered. "The ground and trees close behind our line were ploughed and riddled with a thousand balls that just missed the heads of the men." The 1st Battalion dropped flat on the ground just as a second volley whizzed overhead. The Confederate line slanted southeast toward Cold Harbor Road, giving Clingman's troops stationed on the right of the 51st North Carolina unobstructed shots at the left of Upton's line. Musketry and artillery fire tore into huddled blue-clad forms. "It was the work of almost a minute," a Federal noted. "The air was filled with sulphurous smoke, and the shrieks and howls of more than two hundred and fifty mangled men rose above the yells of triumphant rebels and the roar of their musketry." A soldier in Kellogg's first line wrote home that the "musketry was terrible but not so awful as the cries of the wounded."[36]

Beckwith's New Yorkers watched from the safety of the woods. "As soon as the heavies began to charge, the Rebel works were bordered with a fringe of smoke from the muskets and the men began to fall very fast, and many wounded began going to the rear," Beckwith wrote. "A little in front of the works there was a hollow and, as the column went into this, it seemed to pause and the rear lines closed up. The rebel fire was very effective and it seemed to us from where we stood that our poor fellows would all get shot. The ground over which they had passed was covered with men. We could see them fall in all shapes. Some would fall forward as if they had caught their feet and tripped and fell. Others would throw up their arms and fall backward. Others would stagger about a few paces before they dropped."[37]

Kellogg halted to re-form, then attempted to storm the Confederate line as Upton had instructed. In most places, obstacles prevented anyone from getting close. The Confederates had left two paths through the tangle of felled trees, wide enough for four men to march abreast, and Kellogg funneled troops into these openings. A few soldiers on his right made it to the rebel works and held them briefly before falling back. But for most of the attackers, the avenues became deathtraps where the North Carolinians concentrated their fire.

Kellogg led the charge into the slashings. An aide caught a glimpse of him, blood from a wound smearing his cheek. Clingman, who had posted himself with the 51st North Carolina, later wrote of seeing "a tall and uncommonly fine looking officer in the front rank of the enemy's column," waving his hat over his head and cheering his men on. The officer—Clingman remembered that the attacking troops wore new blue uniforms and were reputedly fresh from garrison duty—was putting his hat back on when the Tar Heels fired a volley. Federals with Kellogg claimed that the colonel was ordering a retreat when two bullets hit him above the ear. More balls tore into his arm and his face, and his lifeless form crumpled on top of tangled trees and branches. A few Heavies tried to force their way through "but were swept away by a converging fire," a witness related. "Wild and blind with wounds, bruises, noise, smoke and conflicting orders, the men staggered in every direction, some of them falling upon the very top of the rebel rampart, where they were completely riddled with bullets."[38]

Upton had ridden to the front on his large bay. His horse was shot, but the general was uninjured. "Lie down," he screamed. "Don't return the fire!"

Upton's second line, fifty yards behind the first, was oblivious to the danger. "Lie down! Lie down!" Upton cried, and men dropped to the ground. The 3rd line came up next—Major Ells fell wounded in the leg—and also lay down at Upton's directions. Bullets tore into prone forms. One ball struck Captain Deane in the forehead and knocked him over. "My head bled profusely," Deane wrote, "but when I got the blood out of my eyes, I saw the men of the third line were just up to me, and begging an old handkerchief from one of them tied my head, took a swig of cold coffee from the good fellow's canteen, got on my feet, and took my place by my own men."[39]

Infuriated at the failure of Eustis's brigade to advance on Upton's left, Russell took command of the outfit and started it across the field toward Colquitt's Georgians. A shallow ravine angled across this part of the field, starting six hundred yards in front of Colquitt's left, slicing southwest, and crossing Colquitt's line near the road. Under Russell's direction, Eustis's troops marched into the swale and massed there, screened from Confederate fire. With a yell, they dashed into the open. "Our cannon sent charge after charge of canister into their ranks," William Smith of the 23rd Georgia noted, "and the infantry made their Enfields crack again." A Georgian remembered the "heavy fire of musketry, and canister and grape mowing through their line." The Federal formation "was shattered, broken into fragments and flying in confusion," he added. Russell was wounded in the arm. Eustis's and Upton's attacks had failed as completely as Penrose's, Cross,' and Grant's forays to the south.[40]

Ricketts did not know it, but fate had placed his division directly across from the ravine cut by Bloody Run that separated Clingman and Kershaw. Truex's brigade formed the southern wing of Ricketts's battle formation, its left abutting Upton's right. The 14th New Jersey, formerly commanded by Truex, made up Truex's front line, the 87th Pennsylvania and the 151st New York the second line, and the 10th Vermont the third line. The 106th New York waited in reserve with instructions to bring up stragglers and take charge of prisoners. Truex planned for the 14th New Jersey to charge the rebel works, fire a volley, and fall to the ground. Troops coming behind were then to pass over the New Jersey regiment and press home the attack.[41]

Colonel Smith's brigade formed north of Truex. The 6th Maryland and 138th Pennsylvania made up Smith's first line, and the 9th New York Heavy Artillery—another large novice regiment that had arrived as the army was leaving Spotsylvania Court House—filled his second and third lines. A reserve line contained the 122nd Ohio, the 126th Ohio, and the portion of the 110th Ohio not on picket duty with Lieutenant Colonel Binkley. "There was just enough air in motion to open the folds of our colors and the flags danced in the breeze as if eager for the forward movement," a Buckeye remembered.[42]

Accidents of ground and uncoordinated advances by elements on both sides of Ricketts's line disrupted the division's movement. Truex was under orders to guide left on Upton, maintaining the division's contact with the rest of the 6th Corps. Smith was to guide right, keeping touch with Devens's division of the 18th Corps. Hurrying to keep abreast of Upton, Truex outpaced Smith. Then the right portion of Truex's brigade entered Bloody Run's swampy and heavily timbered reaches. Encountering the advance line of Confederate works, the 14th New Jersey fired its volley and dropped as instructed. The second and third lines dashed up to press the attack. "Double quick, march!" officers exhorted. Charging ahead, a mix of Pennsylvania, New York, and Vermont soldiers broke over the advance rebel earthworks. Occupied only a short time before by Hagood's South Carolinians, the works were now virtually empty.[43]

Truex kept going, his right wing slogging deeper into the muddy ravine while his left crossed more open ground to the south. Bullets fired by Wofford's Georgians sang into the brigade's exposed right flank. "I was with no support on my right whatever," Major Abbott of the 10th Vermont wrote, "which, owing to an enfilading fire from the enemy in that direction, greatly handicapped the right of the line." A soldier in the 151st New York found it "laughable, although in the midst of death, to see men in the mud and water waist deep, under a galling fire." Truex did not realize it right away, but his brigade had penetrated between Clingman and Kershaw.[44]

Smith's brigade advanced independently on Truex's right, lagging behind to keep contact with Devens. "On either hand could be seen the long, sinuous line, from which men were constantly dropping as they were hit by the enemy's bullets, but the line heeded not," a soldier in the 9th New York Heavy Artillery recalled. Crossing the field under "galling fire from the enemy's sharpshooters," Smith's men also poured into the wooded ravine. "We had scarcely penetrated the woods when the enemy opened with musketry and artillery," a soldier in the 138th Pennsylvania recounted. "The shot and shell came upon us like a hailstorm. The whiz-zoo-oo of the bullets, the rattle of the grape, and the roar of shells—tearing up the earth and wrenching large limbs from trees, hurling them in all directions—added to the awful grandeur of the scene, and was well calculated to test the courage of the stoutest heart." Overrunning the northern segment of the advance works recently abandoned by Hagood, Smith's brigade plunged into the thick of the marsh. "The mud was knee deep," George R. Imler of the 138th Pennsylvania noted in his diary. Disoriented in the swampy ravine, portions of Smith's brigade angled left, mingling with Truex's men. Other of his troops drifted right, into the exposed southern end of Wofford's formation. Chance had given the Federals the advantage they needed to break the rebel line.[45]

Clingman's northernmost regiment, Lieutenant Colonel John Murchison's 8th North Carolina, had entrenched immediately south of Bloody Run, its left refused and resting in the woods. The balance of the brigade strung south, with the 51st North Carolina next to the 8th, then the 31st, with the 61st North Carolina holding the right end of Clingman's line next to Colquitt. When word first reached Clingman that soldiers were advancing through the ravine to his left, he presumed they were Hagood's men—he still had no idea that Hoke had withdrawn Hagood and sent him to the southern end of his line— and he ordered his troops not to fire.[46]

Discovering that the approaching figures were Federals, Murchison's Confederates fired a few volleys into the ravine. The Yankees disappeared into the trees, and Clingman directed his soldiers to let the gunsmoke clear so that he could see. Captain Fred R. Blake of Clingman's staff craned for a look. "Here they are, as thick as they can be!" he cried. Rising on his toes and peering into the ravine, Clingman saw a column heading his way, thirty men in front and massed compactly. "Our pickets came running in," recollected an officer in the 8th North Carolina. "Immediately the line was formed behind the works and for a few moments silence reigned along the entire line."[47]

Judging from accounts filed after the battle, Federals attacking the 8th North Carolina belonged to the 106th New York. The regiment had started off in Truex's last line, but the confused advance into the ravine ended any semblance of order. Regiments stumbled into disconnected fights, frequently without support and oblivious to the part played by companion regiments. Some units funneled up the ravine and came out in Murchison's rear. By chance, the 106th New York was adjacent to Murchison's flank when Truex figured out what had happened and rushed to exploit his windfall. The brigade's adjutant spurred his horse to Colonel Charles Townsend, commanding the regiment. "Colonel Townsend, your front is clear," he announced. "The orders are for you to charge your regiment."[48]

The New Yorkers felt confident, having survived the charge across the field with few casualties. "Men of the 106th, you are ordered to make another charge," Townsend told them. "Move forward, shoulder to shoulder, arms aport. Forward, march!" Townsend at their head, the New Yorkers angled leftward out of the ravine and into the 8th North Carolina's refused flank. "Charge bayonets!" Townsend shouted as his regiment piled onto the works, scooping up prisoners and chasing Tar Heels. Murchison rallied some of his troops and launched a determined counterattack, cutting off portions of Townsend's command. "Truly we had marched into the jaws of death and the mouth of hell," it seemed to one New Yorker. Surrounded by Confederates, Townsend refused to surrender and was shot in the head.[49]

As the 106th New York battled for survival, more elements from Truex's brigade pitched in. Accounts are fragmentary, and units became mixed, making it impossible to reconstruct with certainty the sequence of attacks or even the relative position of regiments. Most of Truex's soldiers, joined perhaps by elements from Smith's brigade, filtered through the ravine and turned south to enfilade Clingman's line and stream into the Confederate rear. More Federals—the portion of Truex's brigade south of the ravine, next to Upton— struck the Confederate front at the same time. "The Eighth Regiment was attacked in front, flank, and rear," was how it appeared to the 8th North Carolina's historian. "I see the scamps! I see them," shouted Lieutenant Charles G. Newton of the 10th Vermont as his soldiers emerged from the ravine. A minié ball sliced through Newton's throat, killing him, but his men charged on. "Here it appeared to me [the 8th North Carolina] made a bold stand," remembered Alonzo Ansden of the 10th Vermont. "Our brigade in good line (and order) were marched up in close proximity with them, each line face to face, standing (falling) about three rods apart, and the leaden hail flying thick and fast, among and around each line, thinning and felling many brave soldiers." Soldiers from the 87th Pennsylvania, bayonets slashing the air, leapt over a set of low works and drove back more of Murchison's men. "Charge on! Go ahead," Union officers cried. Truex was wounded in the hand, and Lieutenant Colonel Caldwell K. Hall of the 14th New Jersey, the brigade's senior officer, took charge. Colonel John W. Schall, heading the 87th Pennsylvania, was wounded in the right arm but remained with his regiment.[50]

As Murchison's defenses collapsed, the next Confederate regiment in line to the south—Colonel Hector McKethan's 51st North Carolina, confronting Upton—found its left exposed. Clingman directed Murchison to pull his survivors back and throw up a new line perpendicular to his old works, extending west from the 51st North Carolina. "The order to retire was not understood by part of our men, and they were cut off," a Confederate recalled. An isolated fragment of the 51st North Carolina, together with part of the 8th North Carolina, "continued the fight until nearly surrounded, not only with live, but also dead Yankees." Murchison fell mortally wounded, shot in the head.[51]

Truex's charge through the 8th and 51st North Carolina fragmented the Union brigade. The experience of the 14th New Jersey's Captain John C. Patterson was typical. Finding himself isolated with portions of three companies, Patterson worked left and located the rest of the regiment fighting for its life. Leading a body of fourteen volunteers, Patterson charged the Confederates. Many rebels threw down their weapons. When some began shooting, Patterson stepped to Major James R. McDonald of the 51st North Carolina, put a pistol to his head, and told him to order his soldiers to stop firing. The major complied. "In about ten to fifteen minutes," Patterson recounted, "I secured and turned over to the Provost Marshal one hundred and sixty-six men, including one major, three captains, and three lieutenants."[52]

Clingman's aide Captain William H. S. Burgwyn scrambled to salvage the collapsing rebel line. Conferring with Clingman, he ordered the regiment immediately to the south—the 31st North Carolina, under Lieutenant Colonel Charles Knight—out of its earthworks, intending for it to join the remains of the 51st North Carolina in a countercharge. But before Burgwyn could shift

Knight's troops into place, a fresh wave of Federals slammed into McKe-than's regiment. Truex's flanking force had opened the way for the Union soldiers pinned in the field to join the attack. As the 51st North Carolina col-lapsed, the left portion of Truex's line charged over the works. Upton also shuttled some of Kellogg's men to the right, piled them into the fortifications, then charged south along the rebel line, capturing the sector of entrenchments where Kellogg had been killed. Now the 31st North Carolina stood unpro-tected, and Burgwyn ordered that regiment to fall back as well. Of Cling-man's four regiments, only Colonel James D. Radcliff's 61st North Carolina, on the right of the brigade, held. "I rallied the [31st North Carolina] some-what about one hundred yards in rear and about the center of the 61st [North Carolina] which regiment still kept in the trenches," Burgwyn wrote. Troops dropping back from other Tar Heel regiments splayed west from the 61st in a makeshift line, attempting to contain Truex's and Upton's breakthrough.[53]

Devens had arrayed his division north of Ricketts and parallel to Beulah Church Road, Drake's brigade abutting the 6th Corps, and Barton's brigade, which came up just as the attack began, on the division's right. A Harvard graduate and outspoken Massachusetts politician, Devens had fought in the Army of the Potomac's early campaigns and had commanded a brigade in Oliver O. Howard's 11th Corps, sharing in Howard's rout at Chancellorsville. "Historians cannot explain the rewards of this celebrated piece of military ineptitude," a student of the Union high command once opined, "in which the corps commander was promoted to commander of the Army of the Ten-nessee under W. T. Sherman and Devens was advanced to brevet major gen-eral 'for highly meritorious service.'" Devens remained popular with the Army of the Potomac, but he was quite ill.[54]

"Put your brigade in immediately," Devens ordered, and Drake's soldiers stepped from the oak forest fringing Beulah Church Road into the field, half a mile across and cut by ravines. "On the other side was a ridge thickly wooded, in front and under cover of which was the enemy's line of gopher holes and on the ridge a perfect line of rifle pits strongly manned," a New Yorker noted. "At a distance on the right front were the enemy's batteries, in such a position as to enfilade the line advancing across the open field." An Indiana man thought that "the rebel works on the opposite side of the field, in the edge of the timber, were of very irregular form, which gave the enemy great advantage over us."[55]

Wofford's Georgians opened from the distant ridge—"volleys of musketry from the front and grape, canister, and shrapnel from the artillery on the right," a New Yorker recollected. Men fell, but survivors closed ranks and pressed steadily on. The 13th Indiana's color sergeant, Charley Truax, was shot and looked "to the right and to the left, as though he wanted someone to save the flag," a Hoosier remembered. Another man took the colors from Truax, and Drake's soldiers continued across the field and into the woods fronting the advance Confederate line. Drake directed his men to fix bayonets and led the charge. Leaping onto the rebel entrenchments, he waved his sword and "fairly danced with exultation," a witness recollected. "There boys, see those devils run," Drake shouted. "Did I not tell you you would drive them out?"[56]

As Drake's brigade battered its way to the main line of works, Wofford's Confederates focused their fire on the 112th New York, inflicting severe casualties and mortally wounding Drake. "I was busy as a bee loading guns and giving out the cartridges to the men in front so that they might fire rapidly," wrote Captain Charles Sanders of Company A, Cobb's Georgia Legion. "During the intervals of the fight the men were laughing [at] how many they had killed." Unable to maintain their precarious lodgment, Drake's soldiers retired to the eastern edge of the woods and began digging in, awaiting reinforcements. Help came in the form of Barton's brigade, which had just reached its jumping-off point on Beulah Church Road. Barton hurriedly ordered his men into the field without waiting for them to remove their knapsacks or fix their bayonets. They charged along a trajectory slightly north of Drake, the 48th New York on the left of the line, the 115th New York in the center, and the 76th Pennsylvania on the right. "On reaching the clearing, every man seemed to comprehend at a glance the desperate work before us and with a wild cheer we struck a double-quick," a New Yorker maintained. "Some ran faster than others and soon our line was going forward in a broken and irregular manner." A soldier wounded early in the charge watched his companions run across the clearing. "I expected every moment to see the colors stop and the regiment reform, but, well for them all perhaps, they could not be constrained," he wrote. "Had they halted to reform I doubt whether they would have gained the works."[57]

Barton's men hit the edge of the woods immediately north of Drake's brigade, the lower portion of their line overlapping Drake's troops. Together the two brigades charged toward Wofford's main line. "We struck into the woods over logs and brush and so great was the excitement that I never saw the enemy earthworks until we come within ten feet of them," John W. Reardon of the 115th New York wrote his sister the next day. Color sergeant William Porch of the 48th New York had been unfairly accused of cowardice at Drewry's Bluff, where he had taken the colors to the rear under orders, and he was anxious to redeem his reputation. "Now, Billy, show them that you are no coward," a friend called out. Porch leaped onto Wofford's works and was slammed by a score of bullets. Throwing his arms around the flag, he toppled with it into the rebel entrenchments. Losing a flag to the enemy was considered disgraceful, and regiments that lost their colors were generally barred from carrying them for three months. Higher-ups, however, deemed Porch's conduct so valorous that they issued an order permitting the 48th to carry its colors without the customary penalty.[58]

Expecting stubborn resistance, Drake's and Barton's soldiers were surprised to find Wofford's troops giving way. "The enemy had now stopped firing and were running," a soldier in the 115th New York wrote home. "Some were shot down. Others more wise threw down their arms and surrendered. Some jumped over the works and cried out, 'Give the rebels hell boys. I'm glad to get out of this!'" Barton's men, who had not had time to fix their bayonets before they charged, surmised that the Confederates were running because they thought their attackers were armed with seven-shot carbines. When the captives discovered that Barton's soldiers carried only ordinary muskets, a Federal gloated, "they showed unmistakable signs of the greatest anger and chagrin."[59]

More instrumental in Wofford's collapse than imagined seven-shooters was the appearance of Ricketts's division on the Georgians' flank and rear. "We were flanked and had to fall back in a hurry," one of Wofford's officers related. It is impossible to determine precisely which of Ricketts's units penetrated north, although most were probably from Colonel Smith's brigade. It is also impossible to gauge the relative impact of Ricketts's flanking elements and of Devens's frontal attack. Doubtless both contributed to Wofford's collapse. The next day, Baldy Smith claimed that Devens had taken the rebel works and 250 prisoners. "The division of General Ricketts," he added, "coming up on the left, aided General Devens in holding the pits so gallantly taken." Dana, likely drawing on Smith's communication, noted that the 18th Corps had broken the enemy line, rendering "easier the subsequent capture of another part of the same works by General Ricketts." In truth, Ricketts's fortuitous turning movement facilitated Devens's breakthrough.[60]

The dual assault against Wofford's front and flank was wildly successful. Wofford's entire brigade—the 16th, 18th, and 24th Georgia, the 3rd Georgia Battalion Sharpshooters, Cobb's Legion, and Phillips Legion—fled from their earthworks. "We were fighting away, when all at once a perfect shower of bullets came from behind—for the Yankees advancing in as from the rear, and a line was also advancing from the front," Captain Sanders of Cobb's Legion recollected. "We all saw that we had to get out of that place, and that quick, too." Few rebels stood on ceremony. A soldier in the 18th Georgia remembered sprinting away "at breakneck speed." Sanders agreed, admitting: "I didn't know until then how fast I could run." Part of Goode Bryan's brigade on Wofford's left broke as well. Bryan's rightmost regiment, the 53rd Georgia, fell back as Wofford's adjoining men retreated, exposing its flank. "We discovered [Wofford's collapse] in time to save ourselves," Arthur B. Simms of the regiment wrote his sister a few days later. "We ran off in very great disorder and never rallied in an hour or two." The 51st Georgia, next in line on the north, also fell back. The rout stopped at the 10th Georgia, which held its ground. The regiment was probably posted along the central of the three ravines, and the remainder of Bryan's brigade simply "curled back," as Kershaw later related, forming a defensive line along that strong natural feature. "Our regiment got credit for standing under such circumstances," Eugene A. Thompson of the 10th Georgia proudly claimed.[61]

A half-mile interval now yawned between the 61st North Carolina on Clingman's right and the 10th Georgia on the northern end of Bryan's line. Jubilant men in blue sent captured rebels to the rear in a steady stream. "They came back without anyone guarding them on the run to get out of the way of the Rebs' bullets," a Union man recalled. "We told them to make for the rear." A soldier in the 9th Maine thought the prisoners appeared "well pleased." A Union victory seemed in the making.[62]

William Brooks had posted his division on Devens's right, his own right flank tracking along Mr. Allison's Road. Like Devens, Brooks had served earlier in the war with the Army of the Potomac and had commanded a division at Chancellorsville. "He is rather a rough old fellow," an associate noted, "and no starch about him."[63]

Guy Henry's brigade of five regiments drawn from Connecticut, Massachusetts, New York, and Pennsylvania constituted the left of Brooks's formation, abutting Devens. The brigade of Hiram Burnham—who like Devens and Brooks was a former Potomac army man—made up Brooks's right wing. Two of Burnham's regiments—the 118th New York and 8th Connecticut—supported Henry, and his remaining two regiments deployed to the right, the 13th New Hampshire in front and the 10th New Hampshire behind. Brooks's remaining brigade, under Gilman Marston—a New Hampshire lawyer and politician who had also seen service in the Army of the Potomac—stood in reserve.[64]

Brooks's brigades under Henry and Burnham stepped off in tandem with Devens's division. Many of the soldiers looked forward to the fight, which would be their first. "Our forced all-night, hot and dusty march from White House rather unfitted us," a man in the 118th New York remembered, "yet we felt anxious to prove ourselves to the veterans under Grant and Meade." Henry, on the division's left, sent out the 92nd New York as skirmishers and advanced the rest of his brigade from its wooded cover along Beulah Church Road into the open plain. "They were badly raked by an enfilading battery, and many of the troops, being for the first time under such a galling fire, were somewhat shaken," a Connecticut man recalled. Lieutenant Colonel Hiram Anderson Jr., heading the 92nd New York, was killed during the advance, but his skirmishers managed to get across the plain, descend into a thickly wooded ravine, and charge up the far bluff to the first line of rebel rifle pits. Facing Henry's troops was Humphreys's Mississippi brigade, a rugged set of adversaries who had proved their mettle at Laurel Hill on May 8 by stalling the Union army's advance toward Spotsylvania Court House. Ensconced behind multiple lines of pits and entrenchments, the Mississippians were virtually invincible.[65]

Burnham's attack, to the north of Henry, was bloody but mercifully brief. "Our part of this work is done in less than five minutes—reliable persons have said, in less than three minutes," Captain James M. Durell of the 13th New Hampshire related. The New Hampshire men dashed three hundred yards across open ground to a little ridge. Confederate skirmishers—probably some of Henagan's South Carolinians—abandoned their rifle pits, retired to a backup line, and began shooting at the Federals in their front. Fire also poured into the New Hampshire men from the left. The 118th Pennsylvania of Henry's brigade, it developed, had formed a battle line perpendicular to Burnham and was shooting into its sister brigade. "Friendly fire" killed several soldiers and ceased only after Colonel Aaron F. Stevens, commanding the New Hampshire regiment, reported the situation to Henry.[66]

The 13th New Hampshire was pinned in the field, protected only by the low ridge. A soldier recalled "lying down on our faces, with guns to the front and bayonets fixed, ready to repel a charge if the enemy attempted one, and receiving the fire of a strong line of his men behind another ridge and in other rifle pits, in the field, still farther to our right and front." Burnham's attack had stalled under "sheets of bullets flying over our bodies," a man in the 13th New Hampshire admitted. Burnham brought up his 10th New Hampshire, and Marston added troops from his brigade, but the fresh soldiers could make no progress. "They are much exposed also," a Federal who watched the slaughter recalled grimly, "and as they lie upon the ground we can see the frequent sudden start, shudder, and struggle, of a man here and there among them, indicating wounds and death."[67]

Henry—an "intrepid young West Pointer of magnetic presence and merciless discipline," a soldier said of him—refused to concede defeat. First he tried to goad Colonel Stevens into charging with his 13th New Hampshire. An officer protested that advancing "two rods into that field meant certain annihilation for the 13th," and Stevens agreed. Henry then directed Lieutenant Colonel George E. Marshall, commanding the 40th Massachusetts, to try his hand. Marshall's regiment moved onto the 13th New Hampshire's left, and the Confederates who had pinned Stevens's troops shifted their fire, killing and wounding several of Marshall's soldiers. Some of the Massachusetts men sought cover behind an apple tree, only to become inviting targets. When the regiment's color bearer was shot, Marshall galloped over, picked up the banner on the point of his sword, then tumbled to the ground as a bullet hit his horse and set it plunging wildly.[68]

Henry labored to rally the fragments of his brigade. A soldier in the 21st Connecticut recalled him "reckless of himself, [riding] back and forth, crowding on his men." Inspired by Henry's example, the 40th Massachusetts ran forward and captured the next set of Confederate rifle pits. "With a smile of cool defiance," a witness claimed, Henry "leaped his horse over the enemy's works, and as the dying steed lay struggling on the parapet, its rider coolly standing in its stirrups, emptied his revolver in the very faces of the awestruck foe." Marshall died in the attack, but Henry survived—he later received the Medal of Honor—and in short order the Stars and Stripes fluttered from the captured breastworks. Henry could see the main Confederate entrenchments a few hundred yards farther on and concluded that they were unassailable. Retiring to a stand of woods on the 13th New Hampshire's left, Henry re-formed his battered regiments and began throwing up defensive fortifications.[69]

Concerned about a gap between his own left and Devens's right, Brooks shifted part of Marston's brigade south. Colonel Edgar M. Cullen of the 96th New York stayed behind, pleading illness. "He was not a coward," concluded Captain William Kreutzer of the 98th New York. "The fault was his nervous constitution." The 139th New York tried to bridge the interval by latching onto Devens's northern flank, and the 98th New York formed twenty paces back, supporting the 139th. Marston's soldiers took the first line of rebel works with little difficulty, but their movement put them slightly in advance of Henry's brigade and exposed their right to rebel musketry and cannon fire. Devens's entire division was now pinned down and taking severe losses.[70]

While combat flared in front of Brooks and Devens, Martindale finished aligning his division facing north, toward Bethesda Church, and dug in. Stedman's brigade, on Martindale's left, received annoying fire from Cabell's guns a mile away that enfiladed his line. "Twenty solid shot or shells, by actual count, passed between the 12th [New Hampshire] and the 148th New

York, beside many others that passed over or fell short," a soldier recalled, "yet no one of either regiment, so far as known, was injured." A wag conjectured that rebel gunners were "practicing to see how near [they] could come and not hit anybody."[71]

"Men of Connecticut, stand by me!"

At 7:30 P.M.—the offensive had been grinding on for well over an hour—Wright sent a dispatch to Meade. "Everything is going well up to this time," he advised. "We have gained upon the enemy on the right, and hold our own on the left. We have taken many prisoners." Wright was concerned, however, about reports from captives that Lee was bringing up reinforcements. "I think that you should send me reinforcements tonight, if possible," Wright pleaded. "The result is not yet decided."[72]

The battle was indeed far from over. Colquitt, Martin, and Hagood had immobilized the Federals south of Cold Harbor Road. North of the road, Eustis lay pinned in front of Colquitt. And on the far upper end of the line, Brooks was stalemated in front of Henagan and Humphreys. Prospects for Union success lay in the battlefield's center. The lower ravine—Bloody Run—had afforded Ricketts a fortuitous opportunity to pierce the rebel line between Clingman and Wofford and to send troops storming into the exposed flanks of the two Confederate brigades. With the rest of the Union army several miles away by road, however, Federal reinforcements could not possibly arrive before dark. Meanwhile, Confederate commanders, were rushing troops to each end of the breach. Brandishing a fence rail, Clingman labored to construct a new defensive line anchored on the 61st North Carolina. To the north, elements from Bryan's brigade held on by the middle ravine, waiting for Kershaw to send fresh troops to their assistance.[73]

At first, Colquitt was oblivious to Clingman's plight. "The enemy had been so easily repulsed in Colquitt's front that we were perfectly amazed to [see] Clingman's men running and the enemy pouring over our breastworks," a Georgian reported. "This exposed the whole of Colquitt's line to an enfilading fire." A strikingly handsome lawyer and politician, Colquitt had served in the Mexican War and had participated in some of the Army of Northern Virginia's toughest battles. Recognizing the severity of the crisis, he pulled the 28th Georgia, five companies from the 27th Georgia, and at least one company from the 23rd Georgia out of line and sent them running to Clingman. His remaining three regiments—the 6th, 19th, and 23rd Georgia—extended to fill the vacancies. Colquitt's adjutant, Captain George G.

Gratton, galloped ahead, waving his hat and cheering the men on. "Along the crest of a hill, for a half mile, and under a terrific fire of canister and shrapnel, rushed these gallant men to the rescue of our troops," a southern correspondent informed his readers.[74]

North Carolinians and Georgians charged together, slamming into Upton and Truex. It was almost night. Federal units were hopelessly entangled, and the ferocious counterattack caught them by surprise. Colquitt's men, a Georgian wrote, piled into Clingman's abandoned works, now swarming with Federals, "before they knew it, and the Yankees ordered them to surrender; but they would not." Both sides fought tenaciously in darkening woods, individual units often battling alone with no discernible coordination. Upton tried to keep the 2nd Connecticut together by posting soldiers on the eastern face of the captured earthworks. "Thousands and thousands of bullets 'zipped' back and forth over the bodies of the slain—now striking the trees, high up, with a 'spud,' and now piercing the ground under foot," a Federal wrote. Standing behind a tree, Upton would shoot, hand his musket back to soldiers behind him, and receive a loaded one in return, repeating the process as rapidly as he could fire. "Men of Connecticut, stand by me!" the general shouted when some men gave way. "We must hold this line!" Lieutenant Edward Hubbard sent word that his Company F might be overrun, but Upton was insistent. "You must hold it," Upton ordered. "If they come there, catch them on your bayonets, and pitch them over your heads." In the confusion, Hubbard's company was cut off, and Hubbard guided it into a ravine, looking for a way back. "Halt, who comes here," a voice challenged in the darkness. "Company F, 2nd Connecticut," Hubbard answered. "For a moment all was quiet except a low voice passing along the line, and then a flash, and a terrific volley went over our heads," one of Hubbard's men recounted. Realizing they had stumbled into rebel lines, Hubbard's Federals darted back along their ravine before the Confederates could reload. To their relief, they emerged near their regiment.[75]

While Colquitt hurried to Clingman's assistance, Kershaw forwarded troops to regain ground lost by Wofford's and Bryan's collapse. Humphreys's Mississippi brigade, next to Bryan, was heavily engaged fending off Henry's onslaught. Henagan's South Carolinians, however, had pinned Burnham's men securely behind their shallow ridge and had troops to spare. Kershaw summoned Major William Wallace, commanding the 2nd South Carolina on Henagan's northern flank. "I found the General in a good deal of excitement," Wallace wrote of the meeting. "He informed me that our lines had been broken on the right of his division, and directed me to hasten there, and if I found a regiment of the enemy flanking his regiment, to charge them."[76]

Wallace marched the 2nd South Carolina's 127 men toward the breach. Accompanying him was Captain B. M. Whitener's 3rd South Carolina Battalion, containing at most another 175 men, and a napoleon from Callaway's battery, under Lieutenant Robert Falligant. Occupying the captured works immediately in front of Bryan's 10th Georgia were the 112th New York and 48th New York of Devens's division. "It was a dreadful place to hold," the 48th New York's historian attested, "with the rebels massed just at the foot of the hill, on the right, and pouring in upon us a deadly flanking fire." The New Yorkers felt abandoned. They had broken the Confederate line, but their superiors were nowhere to be found, and they badly needed support. The commander of the 48th New York tried to get the 47th New York, on his left, to assist in a charge, but communication was impossible. "We were compelled to wait and suffer," he remembered, "hoping that some general officer would become interested to find our whereabouts, and organize some new movement, by which we would be relieved."[77]

Boldly leading his small force, Wallace charged into the Federals occupying the captured works. Falligant advanced his gun with Wallace's infantry, "coming into battery and fighting fiercely whenever the enemy seemed to be holding the brigade in check, and limbering up and moving forward with it while it was advancing." Wallace's momentum overwhelmed the New Yorkers. "At this point the carnage was terrible," the 112th New York's historian reported. "The enemy was fairly upon us," remembered John Nichols of the 48th, "and before we could gather ourselves to repel the attack, someone, without authority, had called out to retreat." Private John Pickett of the 2nd South Carolina captured the 48th New York's colors, and the dispirited Federals retired east through the woods, furious at their superiors for deserting them. "After securing a victory," Nichols wrote years later, his anger undiminished, "we had been left alone and unsupported, to be shot down like sheep."[78]

Elements from the 9th New York Heavy Artillery received a brutal baptism of fire. Kershaw's aide Goggin had rushed three pieces from the 1st Company Richmond Howitzers toward the breach to assist Falligant. "We ran the guns into the line of battle, along a slight work Kershaw's men had hurriedly thrown up, just to the left of the part of the line which the Federals had taken, and were still holding," a gunner related. "We pushed up until we got an enfilade fire upon their lines." Part of Colonel Smith's force that had flanked Wofford out of his works, the New Yorkers made easy marks for the rebel artillerists. "It seemed as though all of the artillery of the enemy were massed at that particular spot," a Federal recollected, "for had hell been turned up sideways, to our inexperienced eyes, the sight could not have been more fiery." Another man suggested that if one fancied "omnipotence shaking the whole region, like an enormous corn popper over Inferno itself, some idea of the way firing began and culminated might be gained." A Confederate gunner described it more matter-of-factly: "A few case-shots screaming down their line sent them flying."[79]

Rallying at the edge of the woods, the broken New York regiments found Devens reclining under a tree "in a state of complete helplessness and demoralization," according to Nichols. The ailing general insisted that the troops turn and renew the attack, but no one took him seriously. Recognizing that Devens was not thinking clearly, they ignored him and began digging. The Union assault was spent.[80]

While combat sparked along Wright's and Smith's wing of the Union army, the Federal force's northern wing—Hancock's, Burnside's, and Warren's corps, covering five miles from Mr. Overton's home to Bethesda Church—pressed tightly against Hill's, Breckinridge's, and Early's Confederates. Heavy skirmishing erupted around 7:00 P.M. on the interface between the 5th and 9th Corps. Crittenden's line, on the 9th Corps's southern end, extended across Shady Grove Road and bent sharply east, running parallel to the road and facing south toward Beaver Dam Creek. The brigades of Brigadier General James H. Ledlie and Colonel Joseph M. Sudsburg held this refused stretch of line, which skewed awkwardly at a right angle to the works across Shady Grove Road. A soldier termed Crittenden's dog-legged line an "odd piece of engineering never explained to us."[81]

Griffin's 5th Corps division picked up the Union line south of Beaver Dam Creek. Between Crittenden and Griffin ran a marshy, heavily wooded tongue of land that Federals dubbed Magnolia Swamp. Griffin had posted Bartlett's brigade on the marsh's southern fringe, partly refused and facing north to mirror the refused segment of Crittenden's line on the other side of the swamp. Ayres's brigade stood near Griffin's left, reaching toward Old Church Road, and Sweitzer's brigade waited in reserve.

The wooded swath between Crittenden and Griffin provided a hidden avenue of attack for Early's Confederates similar to the path that Bloody Run had afforded Ricketts. Late in the day, Early had decided to use Beaver Dam Creek and its wooded banks to probe the Federals in his front. Gordon, in the center of Early's line, dispatched elements from his division along the ravine, and Rodes, on Early's northern flank, initiated a companion attack along Shady Grove Road. The timing of Early's assault—Wright's and Smith's attacks to the south had reached fever pitch—suggests that its purpose was to pin down Union troops and divert Grant's and Meade's attention from their offensive at Cold Harbor.[82]

Crittenden's division was cursed with perhaps the most inept leaders in the Army of the Potomac. The commander himself had arrived only a few weeks earlier, replacing the highly respected Brigadier General Thomas G. Stevenson, who had been killed on May 9. Demoted from corps command after a dismal performance at Chickamauga, Crittenden seemed resentful and distracted. Ledlie, commanding Crittenden's largest brigade, was a recent political appointment with little combat experience. A heavy drinker, he had nearly wrecked his brigade by ordering a hopeless and unnecessary assault against Confederate works at Ox Ford on the North Anna River. Sudsburg, heading a small brigade of three regiments, had performed little better. And the division's final component, Elisha Marshall's Provisional Brigade, contained mostly novice troops in heavy artillery regiments. "Our division is in a terrible state of discipline and organization," one of Crittenden's aides wrote home.[83]

Rodes selected a North Carolina brigade for his attack against Crittenden. Led by Colonel Risden T. Bennett of the 14th North Carolina, the brigade contained six veteran regiments drawn from Ramseur's former command and from Brigadier General George H. Steuart's brigade, disbanded after its mauling at the Bloody Angle. The Tar Heels attacked east along Shady Grove Road, slamming into two of Marshall's heavy artillery regiments and the 59th Massachusetts of Ledlie's brigade. More rebels—Brigadier General Clement A. Evans's brigade of Georgians, of Gordon's division—emerged from the swamp to the south. Confederates seemed to be popping up everywhere. "The enemy charged first on our left, then on our front, then on our right, then on the right of the Fifth Corps," a Pennsylvanian noted. "Four charges, one just after the other."[84]

Relatively inexperienced Union troops on Shady Grove Road broke without returning fire and ran "pell mell," according to a witness, disrupting the rest of Crittenden's division. Some veteran units held, however, and Orlando Willcox, whose division occupied earthworks on Crittenden's right, acted decisively, firing artillery into the rebels and sending his 60th Ohio and 51st Pennsylvania to help seal the breach. Bullets pierced Willcox's hat and coat, but the general was not hit. By now, Bennett's Confederates had enfiladed the refused portion of Crittenden's line south of the road, driving out Ledlie's troops and occupying sections of his works. Colonel Sudsburg was nowhere to be seen. Finally the 100th Pennsylvania's adjutant, Lieutenant Samuel G. Leasure, found the brigade head and requested orders. "He did not tell me or give any directions at all," Leasure wrote. Exasperated, the 3rd Maryland's

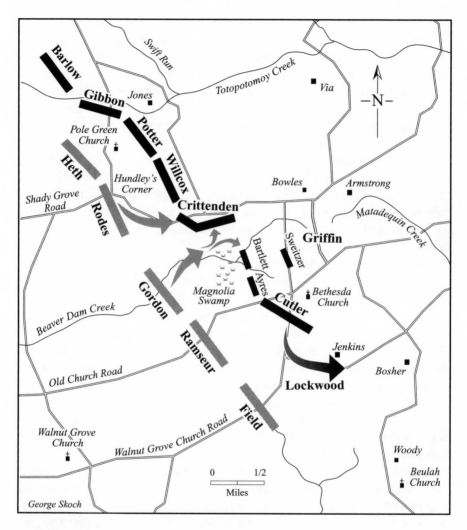

Bethesda Church attack on evening of June 1

Lieutenant Colonel Gilbert P. Robinson took charge of the brigade and rushed Sudsburg's troops to the endangered point. It was almost dark, and Robinson's men fired at flashes from Bennett's muskets. "Our aim was sure and the volley effective," a soldier in the 21st Massachusetts noted, "for they immediately fell back out of sight." The scare over, Crittenden's skirmishers returned to their former posts.[85]

Leasure was disgusted over the division's bad showing. "I was sick at heart for a few minutes," he wrote the next day. "Nobody gave any orders, General Crittenden apparently not caring what was done." As Leasure saw it, "if [Sudsburg's] men had not been veterans and used to such things, there would have been a perfect Bull Run on a small scale." Bennett later remarked that "but for the fall of darkness we might have scored a great success."[86]

At the same time Bennett attacked north of Magnolia Swamp, Evans hit Griffin's division south of the swamp. Led by sharpshooters from the 60th Georgia, the 38th and 26th Georgia worked their way along the marshy finger to a point close to the northern end of Griffin's line. Bartlett's troops were building earthworks on high ground south of the swamp when they heard bursts of musketry and saw pickets from the inexperienced 29th Massachusetts tumbling back. Running to investigate, veterans from the 83rd Pennsylvania discovered that Confederates had formed in the marsh, driven back the Massachusetts pickets, and were advancing on the ridge. Bartlett waited until the rebels crested the rise, then ordered his soldiers to fire. Caught by surprise, the Confederates retreated back to the swamp.[87]

Evans's men traded shots with Bartlett's soldiers well into the night. "The amount of firing on this occasion was, for a small affair, perfectly tremendous," a man in the 83rd Pennsylvania recorded. "Along the line of the whole brigade there was, for the space of half an hour, a vivid sheet of flame; and so continuous was the rattle of musketry that it sounded at a distance as if a terrible battle was in progress." For all the noise, there were few casualties. The 29th Massachusetts lost fifteen men, but none of Bartlett's other regiments suffered appreciable loss. Gordon's losses were also minor. "We found that it was much more to our advantage to have them charge upon our lines than it was for us to charge upon theirs," a Union veteran reflected. Elements from Sweitzer's brigade came up toward the end of the action but did not become engaged. Cutler also sent Colonel J. William Hofmann's brigade, but Griffin concluded that he did not need them and sent them back.[88]

While Griffin waged his little fight at Magnolia Swamp—Warren described Gordon's attack as a "strong feeler"—Lockwood's division wandered off on a trajectory that took it steadily away from the front. The general had set out from Bethesda Church around 7:00 A.M. intending to traverse the two-mile stretch of farmland separating the 5th Corps's southern flank from the northern end of Smith's line at David Woody's farm. The initial stages of his route took him near Early's entrenchments, where Confederate skirmishers harassed his column. Half a mile south of Bethesda Church, a road branched east, winding past the home of a Mrs. Jenkins and the farm of a Mr. Bosher. Another road veered south at the Bosher farm, then doubled back southwest and came out at the Woody farm. The route provided tolerable passage through the swampy upper reaches of Matadequin Creek, and Lockwood decided to follow it.

Turning left toward Mrs. Jenkins's place, Lockwood started east. Night was falling, the general was unfamiliar with the maze of farm roads, and Warren had neglected to furnish a guide. Roebling, who was returning from the Woody farm with his detachment of Maryland troops, rode into Mrs. Jenkins's yard just as the tail of Lockwood's column passed through. "They were lost," Roebling wrote, "and had no definite idea where they were going, except in the direction of the firing." Rather than leave Lockwood to grope in the dark, Roebling directed him to camp on Mr. Bosher's farm, where he would at least be out of harm's way.[89]

As Lockwood's troops bivouacked, Roebling rode back to Bethesda Church. It was uncommonly dark—an orderly strayed off the road and his horse drowned in a swamp—but Roebling finally reached 5th Corps headquarters and reported to Warren. The way to Cold Harbor was not yet open, he explained, and he described Lockwood's misadventures. Warren was still in a ferocious mood, doubtless aggravated by Grant's and Meade's constant complaints about his failure to carry out assignments. The artillerist Wainwright, who had run afoul of Warren earlier that day over artillery placements, found him as "ugly and cross-grained as he could be." The corps commander even berated his staff officers, "cursing them up and down as no man has a right to do," reported Wainwright. It was the end of a dismal day, and Lockwood, who had done his best to comply with Warren's orders, became a convenient target for the high-strung New Yorker's anger.[90]

Warren fired off a note to Meade. "In some unaccountable way [Lockwood] took his whole division, without my knowing it, away from the left of the line of battle, and turned up at dark 2 miles in my rear, and I have not yet got him back," he railed. "All this time the firing should have guided him at least. He is too incompetent, and too high rank leaves us no subordinate place for him. I earnestly beg that he may at once be relieved of duty with this army." Meade wrote back promising to relieve Lockwood. Crawford, who had been without a division since the Pennsylvania Reserves left, was to take Lockwood's place. In an ironic twist of fate, an irate Phil Sheridan would relieve Warren ten months hence for imagined transgressions remarkably similar to those that Warren attributed to Lockwood.[91]

"We are pegging away here."

Grant and Meade spent an anxious afternoon and evening at Mrs. Via's farm. The front at Cold Harbor was three miles away by direct line and considerably farther by road, leaving the generals to speculate about developments from the sounds of the fighting. Engineers had run telegraph lines connecting the Via place to Burnside's, Warren's, and Wright's headquarters, and Hancock had a line across to Burnside, allowing him to relay information to headquarters as well. The corps commanders, however, were far too busy to dictate telegraphs.

Around 6:00 P.M., waiting for news of Wright's and Smith's offensive, Meade penned a letter to his wife, Margaretta. "While I am writing the cannon and musketry are rattling all along our lines—but we have become so accustomed to these sounds that we barely notice them," he told her. The Confederates, he explained, had once again extended their line, forcing the Federals to try and slip around their flank in search of a weak point. "We are pegging away here and gradually getting nearer and nearer to Richmond, although its capture is still far off," he added. "Then will begin the tedious process of a quasi-siege like that of Sebastopol, which will last as long unless we can get hold of their rail roads and cut off their supplies; then they must come out to fight." He closed with what was really on his mind. "The papers are giving Grant all the credit of what they call success," he wrote. "I hope they will remember this if anything goes wrong. I wish I could go home and be quiet." Meade's son, George G. Meade Jr., also wrote Margaretta that evening. "Papa is quite well and in very good spirits," he reported in an assuring tone, trying to put a happy face on a bad situation, "and I think Grant thoroughly appreciates him and it will be all right in the end."[92]

Grant, Meade, and their staffs spent a fretful hour listening to the swell of combat, first to the south and then closer by, as Early attacked along Magnolia Swamp and Shady Grove Road. Then good news started to arrive. At 7:30 P.M., Wright telegraphed that he had taken the first line of enemy works and was bringing in prisoners from Hoke's and Anderson's commands. Half an hour later, Wright reported that fighting on his front was quieting. Word arrived from Burnside not long afterward that the assaults against his left and Warren's right had been repulsed.[93]

But all was not favorable. Confederates, Wright warned, were fortifying on Dispatch Station Road, between his left flank and the Chickahominy. Perhaps they were planning a major turning movement. It was critical, Meade concluded, to reinforce Wright as quickly as possible. Earlier that afternoon, headquarters had decided to pull Hancock from the northern end of the Union line and move him behind Warren and Burnside. Wright's latest dispatch persuaded Meade to shift Hancock all the way to the southern end of the Union line, where he could support Wright and extend the Federal formation to the Chickahominy. "You must withdraw as soon as possible as we want you to move to the left," he told Hancock shortly after 8:00. Hancock expressed concern that his extrication would take time, but Meade would countenance no delay. "You must make every exertion to move promptly and reach Cold Harbor as soon as possible," he ordered. "At that point you will take position to reinforce Wright on his left, which it is desired to extend to the Chickahominy."[94]

Another note from Wright underscored the urgency of Hancock's movement. "Prisoners say that all of [Anderson's] corps is here, and that the rest of the army is moving down against us in very large force," the 6th Corps commander wrote at 9:30. "My position is not secure." Grant read the note and endorsed across the bottom: "General Hancock had better be advised to get one division of his corps through to Wright before daylight, and the whole corps as soon as possible."[95]

Grant and Meade considered their next move. Meade now expected Hancock to reach Cold Harbor around six o'clock the next morning and recommended that he join the assault. Grant concurred. "The attack should be renewed tomorrow morning by all means, but not till Hancock is within supporting distance of Smith," he directed. "Warren should attack in conjunction with Smith and Wright, and Burnside should be held in readiness to support Warren."[96]

Wright's recent march to Cold Harbor had demonstrated the difficulties of transferring an entire corps from one flank of the army to the other. Judging from Wright's experience, Hancock's chances of reaching the place at an early hour and in any condition to fight were small. The two-mile gap between Warren's left and Smith's right remained another troubling piece of unfinished business, as it dangerously divided the Union army and inhibited coordination between the two wings. "What news?" Meade telegraphed Warren. "Is the road from Bethesda Church to Cold Harbor open?" Receiving no response, Meade's aide Humphreys sent another telegraph. "Do you connect with General Smith?" he inquired. "If not, do you know how far apart his left and your right are? Is the road open from Bethesda Church and

Woody's?" Warren's reply was disappointing. He had heard nothing from Smith since the fighting began, and the road south was not open.[97]

Meade had not heard from Baldy Smith all evening either, and he was beside himself with agitation. Near midnight, Smith's aide Farquhar arrived with a message. In it, Smith reported that he held a tenuous line from Woody's place across Beulah Church Road and south along captured rifle pits, making a "very obtuse V." Martindale was thinly spread without reserves; Brooks, in the center, had a partial second line; and Marston's brigade formed a second line for Devens, on the left. Smith closed on a grim note. He would "leave it for the general commanding to determine as to how long I can hold this line if vigorously attacked, one division being almost entirely out of ammunition, and one brigade of General Brooks having but a small supply on hand," he wrote. "I am entirely without forage," he added. "I have to request that medical stores be sent to my wounded, as I had left before mine had been sent to me."[98]

Meade had been in a bad mood all evening. "First he blamed Warren for pushing out without orders," the aide Lyman recollected. "Then he said each corps ought to act for itself and not always be leaning on him. Then he called Wright slow." Now Meade listened incredulously as Farquhar confirmed that Smith had brought little ammunition or transportation and that he "considered his position precarious." Exasperated, Meade roared at the aide: "Then why in hell did he come at all for?"[99]

At 11:00 P.M., Meade issued orders for the next morning's assault. As soon as Hancock reached Cold Harbor, he was to "take position on the left of the 6th Corps and at once attack the enemy, endeavoring to turn his right flank and interpose between him and the Chickahominy." If circumstances required, Hancock could support Wright instead of attacking, but in either case he must bring his force "to bear against the enemy as promptly and vigorously as possible." Wright and Smith also were to attack as "vigorously as possible," as was Warren, with Burnside standing ready to reinforce him. "If we can strike a concerted and vigorous blow tomorrow," Meade emphasized, "it may most materially affect our position."[100]

Smith received Meade's order shortly after midnight. He was incensed, as Meade knew he was out of ammunition. In the heat of anger, he dashed off a response. "I have endeavored to represent to you my condition," he wrote. "In the present condition of my line an attack by me would be simply preposterous; not only that, but an attack on the part of the enemy of any vigor would probably carry my lines more than half their length." He had asked Wright for a hundred thousand rounds of ammunition, he added, and closed on a somber note. "Deserters report the enemy massing on my right for an attack early in the morning." Grant's and Meade's prospect for an early offensive appeared increasingly remote.[101]

While Union brass plotted and quarreled, firefights sparked along opposing lines west of Old Cold Harbor. Wright and Smith held rifle pits and entrenchments recently vacated by the enemy. Combat on Upton's front was especially vicious as Clingman and Colquitt battled to recover lost ground. Upton summoned his veteran regiments to the front, where they joined the fought-out Connecticut soldiers. "The rebels held the same entrenchments the 2nd [Connecticut Heavy Artillery] were in on either side, and at intervals during the night would rise and pour a volley of musketry into our boys," a Federal remembered. Wounded men lay stranded between the lines, "some cursing, some praying, some calling for water, while others cried for help, all mingled in one continued howl," a soldier recalled.[102]

Commanders on Baldy Smith's front groped blindly to plug gaps in their lines. Brooks, fearing a night attack, dispatched Colonel Frederick F. Wead's 98th New York, sent earlier to him from Marston's brigade, to occupy vacant rebel earthworks nearby. A staff officer guided Wead's men along a narrow trail that was almost invisible in the dark. When a volley tore into the New Yorkers, the aide announced that he was going back for instructions and disappeared. Wead had his men lie down as bullets splattered into them. "Our ignorance of the place, the darkness, the wood, the uncertainty whether the firing is from friend or foe increase the horrors of that night's battle," a New Yorker wrote. Wead was wounded and relinquished command to Captain Kreutzer, who managed to lead the regiment to safety. Wead and other wounded men crawled back later that night. The pointless exercise cost the regiment forty-two men killed and wounded.[103]

The Confederates labored to seal off the breach around the middle and lower ravines. During the night, Anderson decided to construct a new segment of line linking Kershaw with Hoke and brought troops over from the northern end of his formation to man it. From Field he took the brigades of Brigadier Generals Evander McIver Law, George T. "Tige" Anderson, and John Gregg, forwarding them to Kershaw. Pickett contributed Brigadier General Eppa Hunton's brigade, which marched south behind the Confederate works to reinforce Clingman. Anderson concluded that the works Wallace had reoccupied along the northern bank of the middle ravine were sound. Wofford, however, had taken up a temporary line behind his former works that seemed poorly sited and incapable of fending off a determined attack. As a stopgap, Field supervised the layout of a new line running from Falligant's position across to Hoke. The line resembled a horseshoe, looping west to form a pocket encompassing the lower and middle ravines and the ground between them. If the Federals attacked, they would meet massive frontal fire and crossfire from both sides of the pocket.[104]

Clingman, with Colquitt's assistance, had regained parts of the works captured from him and was busy building new works a short distance back. Upton's and Truex's men dug new fortifications no more than fifty yards away. Hoke sent an aide directing Clingman to evacuate the northern portion of his line to make way for Hunton's reinforcements, but Clingman wanted to keep his men in place until Hunton arrived, fearing that Federals would discover the empty works and seize them. The aide insisted that Clingman withdraw at once, "as [Hunton's] brigade was approaching and confusion might be produced." Clingman dutifully ordered his soldiers to vacate a hundred and fifty yards of line. When they pulled out, Federals took over most of the abandoned works as Clingman had predicted. Hunton's lead regiment, the 28th Virginia, soon appeared and waged a disoriented fight in the dark to reclaim the entrenchments. The regiment's Private Cornelius Debo was impressed by an "old man with half of his hat brim shot off" who encouraged the Virginians "as if they were his own children." Near morning, when the fighting abated, Debo shared a piece of "moldy corn dogger" with the old man. The figure removed his raincoat, and Debo starred in disbelief at the stars on his collar. Recognizing Clingman, Debo and his companions felt newfound respect for the general and his Tar Heels.[105]

Hoke reshuffled his brigades. Clingman was completely fought out and retired to the rear as a reserve. Hagood vacated his position on Hoke's right and marched north, slipping into Clingman's vacated entrenchments. When the shuffling was finished, Martin formed Hoke's right, south of Cold Harbor Road; Colquitt formed the division's center, with most of his brigade south of Cold Harbor Road; and Hagood held the division's left, occupying Clingman's former position. Hunton's Virginians linked Hagood's left and "Tige" Anderson's right. From there, the new line ran in a concave sweep to Kershaw's right flank.[106]

All night, wounded Federals made their way to field hospitals in the rear. The 6th Corps's hospital, near the orchard south of Cold Harbor Road, was well provisioned. The 18th Corps, however, had arrived without medical provisions, and its wounded congregated on a hillside near the Kelly house, half a mile east on Cold Harbor Road, drawing on the 6th Corps's medical supplies. Field hospitals took in 952 men from the 6th Corps and some 800 from the 18th Corps. Confederate artillery shells winged into the 6th Corps's hospital, showering everyone with dirt. Under cover of darkness, surgeons ventured out to recover the more severe cases from the field. "We were in considerable danger on the open plain, but as soon as we reached the regiment were somewhat more secure," wrote the 15th New Jersey's adjutant. "Our men had instinctively begun scraping the earth together in front of them, and making a ditch in which they might lie out of sight, without waiting for orders. With a view of preventing their digging rifle pits the enemy fired volley after volley as close as possible to our heads, and making the dirt fly over us. We could only escape by clinging close to mother earth."[107]

Captain Deane of the 2nd Connecticut Heavy Artillery walked back to tend to his head wound. Reaching the hollow where the regiment had formed for its initial charge, he found a straggler rifling through the men's knapsacks. He kicked the thief, who scurried off, and continued to the 6th Corps's hospital. Surgeons placed him next to his friend Major Ells. The bullet had gone in below Deane's hairline, plowed a three-inch furrow, and lodged in his skull above the right ear. A Philadelphia surgeon named Henry cut Deane's scalp and pulled the bullet out with forceps, "which slipped off at the first attempt," Deane recounted, "but by pinching the bullet hard he brought it out the second trial."[108]

Richmond was only seven miles away, and wounded Confederates who could bear the journey went there. Soldiers had carried Colonel Keitt to a nearby house, where Dr. Alexander S. Salley tended him. The South Carolinian had been shot through the liver and was in severe pain. After giving him whiskey and morphine, Dr. Salley took him to another house out of range of Union artillery. Keitt slept that night. The next morning, however, he was bleeding internally and clearly failing. Informed of his fate, he gave the doctor clothes from his carpetbag and asked to be buried near his father at Tabernacle Church in Charleston. "I then asked him if he had any message to leave me," Dr. Salley wrote a few days later. "He remained silent for a moment," Salley explained, "and then said, with a tear, 'My two children and my wife.' I do not think that he spoke after these words."[109]

The battle had been intense but short. Casualties were surprisingly light, probably because nightfall brought an end to organized fighting. Union casualties totaled about 2,200, made up of 1,200 in the 6th Corps and 1,000 in the 18th Corps. This was far fewer men than the Army of the Potomac had lost each day in the Wilderness or in any of its big assaults at Spotsylvania Court House. And unlike many of those earlier attacks, this one had produced concrete results. The Confederate line had almost broken, and Federal forces were pressed cheek-by-jowl against the rebel fortifications, pinning the Confederates in place in anticipation of a renewed offensive in the morning. "As severe as it was," Captain Charles H. Porter of the 39th Massachusetts later observed of the attack, "it was well worth the cost."[110]

The brigades of Truex, Smith, and Upton had borne the brunt of the fight for the 6th Corps, and their casualties showed it. Close to half of Wright's subtractions—545 men—came from Ricketts's division, Truex losing 340 and Colonel Smith 205. Most of the remaining casualties came from Russell's division, with Upton's brigade, which lost 324 men, accounting for over half. Attrition in officers was high. Truex, for example, lost seven officers killed, ten wounded, and four captured. Truex himself was wounded, as was his replacement, Colonel Schall of the 87th Pennsylvania. Colonel William W. Henry of the 10th Vermont was wounded in the hand. Lieutenant Colonel Townsend, leading the 106th New York, was killed.[111]

The 18th Corps's casualties were distributed fairly evenly over the four brigades most heavily engaged. In Devens's division, Barton's brigade suffered 224 casualties, and Drake's brigade 320. From Drake's command, the 112th New York lost 153; the 169th New York, 94; the 9th Maine, 62; and the 13th Indiana, 11. Most of the remaining 18th Corps losses—about 450— were in Henry's and Burnham's brigades of Brooks's division. Drake was mortally wounded, and by the time the fight was over, a major commanded his brigade. Chief among the fatalities after Drake was Colonel John McConihe of the 169th New York.[112]

Regimental losses confirmed a trend. The large new regiments, eager to prove themselves and untutored in field warfare, sustained severe losses. Soldiers in the leaner, experienced regiments knew when to fight and when to dig and consequently stood better chances of surviving. Upton's brigade was a case in point. Brigade Inspector Fred Sanborn counted 1,505 men in the 2nd Connecticut Heavy Artillery on May 31. A head count shortly after June 1 showed 313 men killed, wounded, and missing from the regiment, including Colonel Kellogg. The battle had cost the new outfit fully 20 percent of its numbers. By contrast, in the same charge, the brigade's veteran regiments— the 95th and 96th Pennsylvania, 5th Maine, and 121st New York—lost a total of 11 men. A similar pattern governed losses in Colonel Smith's brigade, where one green regiment—the 9th New York Heavy Artillery, which went into battle with less than half its strength—lost 125 men. The remaining six regiments in Smith's brigade sustained 80 casualties altogether. In Neill's sector, only the veteran 2nd Vermont and the novice 1st Vermont Heavy Artillery were engaged. The 2nd Vermont lost about 10 men; the 1st Vermont Heavy Artillery, 120.[113]

Some veteran regiments—such as the 10th Vermont with 80 casualties and the 14th New Jersey with slightly over 100—were badly hurt. By and large, however, casualties on June 1 showed that veterans of the Wilderness, Spotsylvania Court House, and North Anna battles had developed healthy respect for defensive earthworks. Writers later alluded to a "Cold Harbor syndrome," claiming that the carnage Union soldiers witnessed in the fighting there persuaded them to shy away from assaulting entrenched positions. In fact, by the time the Army of the Potomac reached Cold Harbor, veterans had already learned that valuable lesson. Cold Harbor is where newcomers discovered what old-timers already knew.[114]

Confederate losses totaled about 1,800 men, only slightly lower than Union losses. Kershaw's division lost about 500 men, half of them in Wofford's brigade, a quarter in Bryan's brigade, and the remainder evenly spread across Humphreys's and Henagan's brigades. Hoke's division lost well over a thousand men, well over half of them—around 600—from Clingman's brigade. The only appreciable loss in Pickett's division came from Hunton's brigade, which lost about 180 soldiers in its night fight to recapture Clingman's entrenchments. The force that Anderson assembled to recapture Kershaw's broken sector—Law's, Gregg's, and Tige Anderson's brigades from Field's division, and Wallace's South Carolina contingent—lost a little over 200 men. Confederate casualties showed a pattern comparable to that on the Union side. When Wofford's veterans were flanked they knew to run, and so incurred comparatively light losses, a large portion being men who surrendered. Clingman's relatively inexperienced soldiers stood and fought, sustaining almost three times Wofford's casualties.[115]

Generalship in both armies was mixed. Lee was not present for the fight. Dispatches place him at Shady Grove as late as 4:00 P.M. Whether he left Shady Grove later in the evening is unclear, but the distances involved and the general's poor health make it likely that he was nowhere near the battlefront until well after dark. Local commanders managed the fight. Mistakes there were—most notably Hoke's withdrawal of Hagood's brigade without alerting Clingman and Kershaw. But once Ricketts had penetrated into the ravine formed by Bloody Run, the response was all that Lee could have desired. Clingman put up a determined resistance, and Colquitt quickly dispatched the troops necessary to retake Clingman's shattered line. Anderson, too, rose to the occasion, sealing the breach on Kershaw's front and forwarding Hunton's brigade to assist Clingman. Wallace received special commendation. Kershaw was so impressed with the South Carolina major's performance that he recommended him for immediate promotion to brigadier general. "There is not a more gallant or efficient officer in the brigade," he informed Anderson later that night.[116]

June 1 represented a missed opportunity for the Federals. Grant and Meade knew the importance of striking before Anderson and Hoke entrenched. Every passing minute reduced the chances for Union success, but no one at the top seemed willing to take charge and move things along. Consequently Wright's and Smith's marches to Cold Harbor were wretched, uncoordinated affairs involving wrong roads and interminable waits. And when they finally arrived, no one was present to provide overall purpose and guidance to their attacks. Cooperation between Wright and Smith—as between Hoke and Anderson—was haphazard, and the two corps commanders never conferred during the fight. Nor did they achieve meaningful coordination within their own corps. Ricketts, Russell, and Neill fought independent battles, cooperating only fortuitously, and Wright kept no troops in reserve to exploit local gains. Smith, for his part, failed to follow up Devens's capture of Wofford's and Bryan's entrenchments. Brigade commanders such as Drake and Henry proved capable in combat, but their accomplishments went for naught. Broader issues of strategy were simply never addressed. Only two regiments from Neill's division, for example, became seriously engaged. The rest of the division was perfectly situated to turn the lower end of the Confederate line. No one, however, had an eye on the larger picture, and the opportunity for a flanking maneuver seems never to have been considered. "The enemy failed to reap any material advantage from our confusion," Simms of the 53rd Georgia wrote home in a letter that aptly summarized the situation. "I think they must not have known it. If Grant had known what he might have done by following up the small advantage on our line, I think he could have inflicted quite a heavy loss upon us."[117]

But despite shortcomings at higher levels, the fight of June 1 gave Union morale a needed boost. The 18th Corps had fought shoulder to shoulder with the 6th Corps and proved itself a worthy addition to the Army of the Potomac. Colonel Grant praised Benton and his 1st Vermont Heavy Artillery for their "gallant conduct." Kellogg and the 2nd Connecticut Heavy Artillery also received high praise. A soldier noted that "many think Colonel K was very rash in rushing with his men right into and through 2 lines of rebel rifle pits," but condemnation of the dead colonel was rare. "His men owe the preservation of their lives to the high state of discipline in which he had his regiment," said Upton. "Nobly did our regiment sustain its good name, and prove that the 'band box regiment' was a fighting regiment—that two years of 'rusting' in the defenses of Washington had not rusted out our fighting qualities," a Connecticut man boasted. Ricketts's showing was also heartening, as his division had done poorly earlier in the campaign. "Please give my thanks to Brig. Gen. Ricketts and his gallant command for the very handsome manner in which they conducted themselves today," Meade telegraphed Wright.

"The success attained by them is of great importance, and if promptly followed up will materially advance our operations." Wright forwarded the dispatch to Ricketts, endorsing it "with great pleasure."[118]

Could the Union commanders "promptly" follow up their success of June 1? Thus far in the campaign the army had rarely achieved the coordination necessary for rapid deployment. The answer this time would come as no surprise, and it would be written large in blood.

Grant's supply depot at White House Landing on the Pamunkey.
Library of Congress

Twin pontoon bridges at the Nelson's Bridge crossing on the Pamunkey.
Library of Congress

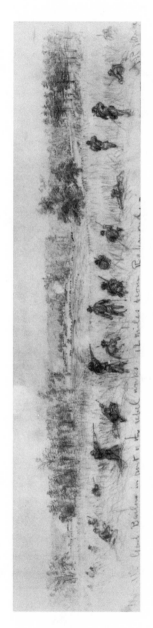

Barlow's Union troops skirmishing with Breckinridge's Confederates on Totopotomoy Creek near the Shelton house on May 30.
Library of Congress

The Pennsylvania Reserves in their last fight at Bethesda Church on May 30.
Library of Congress

Baldy Smith's 18th Corps disembarking at White House on the Pamunkey.
Library of Congress

Union line near the Garthright house at Cold Harbor on June 2.
Library of Congress

Geathwrights House. Battle Field of. Cold Harbor. Va (front view)

A Union soldier's sketch of the Garthright house and outbuildings.
Fredericksburg and Spotsylvania National Military Park Library

The 7th New York Heavy Artillery breaching the Confederate line at Edgar's salient on June 3.

Library of Congress

Colonel James P. McMahon of the 164th New York mounting Martin's Confederate works at Cold Harbor on June 3.

Library of Congress

Workers collecting Union dead at Cold Harbor after the war.
Library of Congress

Massachusetts veterans visiting Burnett's Tavern at Old Cold Harbor in 1887.
Richmond National Battlefield Park

IX

JUNE 2

Grant Misses an Opportunity

"A slow and wearisome march toward the right."

HANCOCK'S 2ND CORPS began leaving its Totopotomoy Creek defenses shortly after dark on June 1, intending to join Wright and Smith at Cold Harbor in time to renew the offensive early on the morning of June 2. Gibbon pulled out first, followed by Barlow and Birney. Breckinridge's pickets discovered the movement and aggressively probed Hancock's entrenchments to determine if the entire corps was involved. The Union commander left a skeleton force to cover his withdrawal, but Confederate skirmishers captured many rearguard troops, including a sizable contingent from the 86th and 124th New York under Lieutenant Charles Stewart. "The withdrawal will take some time," Hancock cautioned Meade, "as our line is very complicated and close to the enemy." Eleven o'clock saw Barlow and Gibbon tramping east along Atlee Station Road, not yet to Haw's Shop. Birney was not under way until near midnight.[1]

The 2nd Corps's march became a grueling ordeal reminiscent of Wright's trek the previous day. Surviving records do not clarify Hancock's intended route, but apparently he was to proceed east along Atlee Station Road, turn south at Haw's Shop, cross to Shady Grove Road by way of Mrs. Via's farm, continue to Old Church Road behind Bethesda Church, then cut over to Cold Harbor Road on a farm trace passing by Allen's Mill Pond, shaving three miles from the route that Wright had taken the previous day. Meade sent his topographical engineer, Captain William H. Paine, to guide Hancock and expedite his progress. A self-taught engineer and surveyor, the thirty-eight-year-old New Hampshire native numbered among the army's most capable scouts, mapmakers, and guides. He had led Meade to Gettysburg the night of

July 1, 1863, and more recently, at Spotsylvania, had ushered the 5th Corps on its night march to Lee's right flank on May 13–14.[2]

The 2nd Corps turned south, crossed Totopotomoy Creek at Mrs. Via's farm, and continued across Shady Grove Road to Old Church Road. Somewhere along the way, Paine led one of Hancock's divisions—probably Birney's—down a path that he presumed would shorten the march. This time the capable guide's talents failed him. His diary indicates that he was sick, which might explain his mistake. The road narrowed, guns became wedged between trees, and Paine finally had to turn the troops around and double back. "In the darkness much confusion arose throughout the column, and the troops became mixed to a degree which made it difficult to straighten them out again," recollected Hancock's aide Francis Walker. "The night had been intensely hot and breathless, and the march through roads deep with dust, which rose in suffocating clouds as it was stirred by thousands of feet of men and horses and by the wheels of the artillery, had been exceedingly trying."[3]

Hancock's lead division, under Barlow, reached Cold Harbor at 6:00 A.M. The rest of the corps trailed back for several miles and would need "some time" to arrive, Hancock concluded. "There was a good deal of straggling," he reported to Meade, "owing to extreme fatigue of the men and the dusty roads." The aide Lyman was not surprised. "It was badly managed, or rather it was difficult to manage, like all those infernal night marches, and so part of the troops went fifteen miles instead of nine and there was any amount of straggling and exhaustion," he wrote home. "I consider fifteen miles by night equal to twenty-five by day, and you will remember our men have no longer the bodily strength they had a month before; indeed, why they are alive, I don't see."[4]

Grant had hoped to renew the offensive at Cold Harbor shortly after daylight. The schedule was manifestly impossible. Not only was Hancock in no condition to attack, but Smith was still complaining about deficiencies in manpower and ammunition. "I think my line perfectly indefensible without more troops," was Smith's bottom line. Meade had instructed Wright to give Smith ammunition, and until that happened, he felt obliged to direct Hancock to hold a division at Cold Harbor to assist the 18th Corps if necessary. "The attack ordered for this morning shall take place at 5:00 o'clock this afternoon," Meade notified his corps commanders, bowing to the inevitable. "Such examinations and arrangements as are necessary will be made immediately."[5]

With only two of his three divisions available to take part in an assault, Hancock conferred with Wright about where best to put them. The 6th Corps commander recommended that Hancock string his troops south from Cold

Harbor along Dispatch Station Road to Turkey Hill, where high ground over-looked the approaches from the Chickahominy. "I shall admit no unneces-sary delay," Hancock informed headquarters, "but it will be several hours before my command is ready to attack."[6]

Hancock's departure left the 9th Corps holding the northern end of the Union line. Meade had sent a message notifying Burnside that Hancock would be moving, but the note apparently failed to reach the 9th Corps commander, who was caught by surprise when Gibbon's division next to him suddenly disappeared, leaving his northern flank unprotected. "Am I to understand that Hancock is to withdraw entirely, leaving me on the right flank of the army," the puzzled general wrote headquarters, "or is he only withdrawing to his old position in rear of his present one?" On learning that Hancock was indeed departing, Burnside scrambled to take up a more defensible line. "I shall withdraw into my old line [of May 30], which is the only way I can protect my right flank," he advised headquarters. "I have ordered all my artillery, trains, and hospitals on the south side of [Totopotomoy Creek]." Meade's relations with Burnside were strained, and the army commander was not about to ignore his subordinate's insinuation that no one had warned him of Hancock's departure. "You were advised this afternoon, per Captain [John C.] Bates, aide-de-camp, that Hancock was ordered to withdraw at dark, and you were directed to make the necessary disposition to cover your right flank," Meade wrote back. "I do not see, therefore, why you should be surprised at the withdrawal of Gibbon, though I must admit Hancock should have with-drawn him last." Meade approved Burnside's request to refuse the right end of his line but insisted that he keep the left end in contact with Warren's right. "You should endeavor to get a reserve of moveable troops to meet any at-tempt to turn your right flank," Meade suggested, adding: "The Totopotomoy ought to be a strong line to rest your flank on."[7]

Burnside's soldiers shifted all night, moving east almost half a mile into entrenchments they had dug two days before. By morning on June 2, the en-tire corps was south of Totopotomoy Creek. Potter's division anchored the 9th Corps's right on the creek near the Whitlock house, and part of his divi-sion extended east along the creek to guard against a flank attack. Willcox's division continued the 9th Corps's line south, and Crittenden's division held the sector along Shady Grove Road, its left still angling east along the upper reaches of Magnolia Swamp. Confederate skirmishers harassed Burnside's soldiers as they fell back. By morning, however, the 9th Corps was firmly ensconced in its former works.

Warren, immediately south of Burnside, also labored to rectify his line.

Griffin held the 5th Corps's right, reaching from Magnolia Swamp south to Bethesda Church; Cutler continued the line south across Walnut Church Road to Matadequin Creek's marshy headwaters; and Lockwood, on Mrs. Jenkins's farm, formed the corps's lower wing. A quarter-mile gap of wetland separated Lockwood from Cutler, but Roebling, who had stationed Lockwood at Mrs. Jenkins's place the night before, felt Lockwood's position was strong and commended the general on his deployment. "I remarked that I was sorry to inform him that General Warren differed from us as to its merits," Lockwood later wrote of his conversation with Roebling; "that one of my staff missing me passed a portion of the night at General Warren's headquarters; that the general denounced the movement as not contemplated by his orders, declared we would be captured or cut to pieces and bring on a general engagement; and further, that he had made use of very harsh and damning language respecting me personally." Not unexpectedly, orders soon arrived removing Lockwood and replacing him with Crawford, who immediately went to work connecting the division with the rest of Warren's line. He extended Kitching's brigade across the marsh, linking his right with Cutler; placed Bates's brigade across Mrs. Jenkins's fields; and continued the line south with Lyle's brigade and the Maryland Brigade. Wainwright liberally buttressed Crawford's wing with artillery, placing Captain James H. Cooper's, Captain Albert S. Sheldon's, and Bigelow's batteries near the Jenkins house and shoring up the left flank with Breck's battery. As Union pieces rolled into place, Confederate 1st Corps guns began firing across the fields at them. "After a pretty hot artillery duel," Breck noted, "both sides seemed to suspend firing as if by mutual consent, although we gave the last shot."[8]

Warren reported his situation to Meade at 5:00 A.M. His line ran nearly five miles from Magnolia Swamp on the north to a point about a mile west of David Woody's farm, he explained, exaggerating the distance by over a mile. His engineers had to incorporate swamps into the line, Warren continued, reducing the number of troops needed to hold the position, but he was still stretched thin and lacked reserves. He had not yet connected with Smith, he added, and did not believe he could do so without dangerously thinning his line. "With our entrenchments and artillery I believe we can hold against any probable efforts of the enemy," Warren concluded, "but it is too weak to attack."[9]

Warren's report sat poorly with headquarters. Grant and Meade wanted the entire army to participate in the day's assault, something Burnside and Warren could not do with their attenuated lines. Burnside, headquarters decided, ought to withdraw from Totopotomoy Creek and mass behind Warren's right, near Bethesda Church. This, Meade reasoned, would enable Warren to slide south, connect with Smith, and still have troops to spare. "Warren is ordered to close the interval between himself and General Smith, about 1 mile, and also to contract his line so as to hold one half of his force available," was how Humphreys explained the plan to Burnside. "The commanding general directs that you move simultaneously with General Warren so as to keep massed in rear of his right, prepared to support General Warren and meet any attempt to turn his right flank, or for any other contingency." The two corps, Humphreys stressed, would be responsible for defending the army's right flank, and headquarters expected "mutual cooperation."[10]

Warren set about "contracting" his line as Meade had directed by moving Griffin southeast to Bethesda Church, leaving behind a strong force of pickets to disguise the departure. At the same time Burnside, on Warren's right, started withdrawing the 9th Corps in phases, aiming to mass it near Bethesda Church, behind Warren's right flank. While Crittenden kept his division in place across Shady Grove Road to screen the movement, Potter and Willcox pivoted south, crossed Shady Grove Road east of Crittenden, and regrouped at Bethesda Church. Potter was under way by 10:00 A.M., just as Confederates from Heth's division advanced into the vacuum north of Totopotomoy Creek created by Hancock's departure. "They are seemingly now lying in the woods in the rear of Washington Jones's house," Potter reported of the rebels, "feeling about with their skirmishers and scouts, apparently to ascertain the disposition of our force." But aside from minor skirmishing, Potter and Willcox got cleanly away. Prospects that Warren and Burnside would be in place to participate in the major assault now set for 5:00 P.M. seemed promising.[11]

Lee had kept close watch on Grant's movements. He had anticipated that Grant might shift troops from the northern end of his line to the south and had hoped to counter by mirroring the Federal movement. As soon as he received word that Hancock was withdrawing, Lee intended to pull Breckinridge and elements from Hill from the northern end of the Confederate formation and send them south. As early as the morning of June 1, Lee had considered transferring Breckinridge from the Atlee Station Road sector to buttress Hoke, but pressure from Hancock's troops had prevented Breckinridge from leaving.

Lee learned of Hancock's withdrawal the night of June 1 almost as soon as it happened. Its purpose was obvious: Grant meant to reinforce Wright and Smith and renew his offensive at Cold Harbor. Unless Lee could reinforce Hoke and extend the Confederate line south to match Grant's new deployment, the Army of Northern Virginia would face a serious crisis. To counter three Federal corps, Hoke and Kershaw needed a massive infusion of troops.

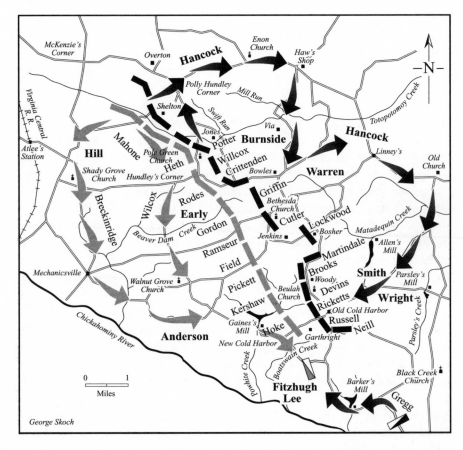

Grant's and Lee's reinforcement of the Cold Harbor sector on June 2

Time was critical, as reinforcements had to reach the southern wing of the Confederate army before Grant could bring Hancock into play. The Union commander's penchant for early morning attacks was now familiar to Lee. Quite simply, Breckinridge had to reach the Cold Harbor sector by dawn. The fate of the battle—and probably of the war—depended on it.

Lee selected Major Henry B. McClellan to guide Breckinridge on his night march. Lee had used McClellan during the Wilderness campaign as a courier and guide, and the young Virginian's resourcefulness had impressed him. McClellan, however, was not as familiar with the road network as Lee had supposed, and he did not have a map. By following farm roads behind the Confederate line, Breckinridge could reach his destination in about six miles. But McClellan was unsure of the way. Rather than risk becoming lost, he decided to lead Breckinridge southwest along main roads to Mechanicsville, then double back southeast through Gaines's Mill and on to the Cold Harbor Road. McClellan did not know it, but his roundabout course added at least six miles to Breckinridge's distance. The night of June 1–2 befuddled guides from both armies.

Around midnight, Breckinridge's men began a "slow and wearisome march toward the right," heading toward Mechanicsville. Not only was McClellan ignorant of shortcuts, he also apparently had no idea of the necessity for haste. Recognizing that the soldiers were tired from three days and nights of front-line duty, McClellan let them rest every half hour, although a veteran still thought the trek "entailed upon us great physical suffering and exhaustion." Near daylight on June 2, McClellan reached Mechanicsville after a seven-mile march and stopped for Breckinridge's men to eat breakfast. They were still five miles from their destination.[12]

As the early morning hours passed, Lee, who had set up headquarters near Gaines's Mill, became increasingly concerned. The sun rose, and still McClellan had not arrived. Then reports came in that Hancock's lead elements were appearing at Cold Harbor. Where was McClellan with Breckinridge's soldiers? Unless they came soon to support Hoke and extend the Confederate line south, the army's right flank would be dangerously vulnerable. Recovered from his dysentery, Lee mounted Traveler and rode toward Mechanicsville in search of the missing reinforcements. He reached the village around 10:00 A.M. The major, still oblivious to the necessity for haste, was there with Breckinridge and his troops. Lee immediately ordered them to hurry toward Cold Harbor.[13]

By midmorning, probably while still at Mechanicsville, Lee had decided to shift even more troops to his southern wing. With Hancock gone from the northern end of the Union line and Burnside pulling back, Mahone's and Wilcox's divisions of Hill's 3rd Corps were now virtually unopposed. Hancock's appearance at Cold Harbor had erased any doubt from Lee's mind about Grant's intentions. To further counter the Union buildup, Lee ordered Mahone and Wilcox to start south right away, taking care to specify that they were to follow the shorter route behind Early, Anderson, and Hoke. They were under way by noon, making what one Virginia soldier described as a "forced march." Lee was meeting unit for unit Grant's shift of troops from the upper end of the battle line to the south. The critical question was whether Grant would strike before Confederate reinforcements could arrive.[14]

Lee also interpreted Hancock's withdrawal as affording an opportunity to take the offensive. By Lee's reckoning, Burnside—Meade's least talented commander—now held the northern end of the Union line. Opposing him was Jubal Early, Lee's most aggressive corps head, with his own 2nd Corps and Heth's division of the 3rd Corps. Looking to exploit Burnside's retrograde movement, Lee ordered Early to attack. "Endeavor to get upon the enemy's right flank and drive [him] down in front of our line," were Lee's instructions, and Early set about arranging his troops to launch an assault very similar to the attack he had made the previous evening. Once again, Gordon was to form the southern wing of the Confederate battle line, charging east and exploiting Magnolia Swamp to drive a wedge between the 5th and 9th Corps. At the same time, Rodes, on Gordon's left, was to attack east along Shady Grove Road, slamming into Crittenden, driving back the 9th Corps, and widening the interval between the 9th Corps's left and the 5th Corps's right. The new wrinkle in Early's plan was Heth, whose division was to serve as Early's maneuverable element. While Gordon and Rodes pushed east, Heth, on the northern end of the Confederate line, was to plunge into the void created by Potter's and Willcox's withdrawal, then loop south across Shady Grove Road and into Warren's and Burnside's rear. "The plan of attack was that my division should form on the left of General Early's force," Heth later explained, "and that I should begin the attack which was to be taken up successively by the troops on my right." If Grant expected Lee to let him maneuver unopposed, he was badly mistaken.[15]

"Unless the enemy attack us, the time will be devoted to rest."

The Union high command did not recognize it, but all morning and well into the afternoon, the Army of Northern Virginia's southern flank was ripe for attack. Part of Hoke's division extended south of Cold Harbor Road for about half a mile. Colquitt's Georgians manned the entrenchments to Boatswain

Creek, and Martin's three North Carolina regiments carried the works onto the northern extension of Turkey Hill. Here the rebel fortifications ended. The Chickahominy River passed about a mile and a half to the south, and the only Confederates defending the interval between the army and the river were Fitzhugh Lee's cavalrymen, 2,000 strong at best. General Lee, of course, was extremely concerned about his southern flank. Until reinforcements arrived from the northern end of his line—Breckinridge still had five miles to cover from Mechanicsville, and Wilcox and Mahone faced a comparable march behind Early's, Anderson's, and Hoke's entrenchments—the fate of the Confederate right flank rested in his nephew's hands. The Federals, it seemed, had stolen a march on Lee. If they recognized their advantage soon, the Confederates would be in serious trouble.

Neither Grant nor Meade, however, was sure where the Confederate line ended or how strongly its southern flank was defended. Neither commander had visited the front, and none of their subordinate generals seemed eager to take a look, either. Penrose, Cross, and the two Vermont regiments involved in the June 1 attack could attest that the rebels facing them were well dug in. None of the Federal field commanders, however, knew what the rebel line looked like south of Boatswain Creek and along Turkey Hill, although they certainly had sufficient troops on hand to find out. Neill's division, on the southern end of Wright's line, contained at least 7,000 soldiers, most of whom had been spared the previous day's fighting. With a little enterprise, the 6th Corps elements could have brushed aside Fitzhugh Lee's horsemen, turned Martin's flank, and undermined the integrity of the entire Confederate position. Enterprising Union commanders, however, were not in evidence on this part of the field. Perhaps taking a cue from their superiors, neither Wright nor Neill showed a spark of initiative.

The possibilities for turning Lee's flank did not end with Wright and Neill. Hancock's 2nd Corps, close to 25,000 strong, poured into Cold Harbor all morning. Tired as these troops were, with a short march they could have deployed south of Neill, wrested Turkey Hill from Lee's cavalrymen, and enfiladed the rebel entrenchments. But as the 2nd Corps soldiers arrived, Hancock sent them into fields around Cold Harbor to rest. Headquarters, after all, had postponed the attack until 5:00 P.M., and Hancock was in no mood to push his men harder than necessary. Besides, Baldy Smith was still calling for ammunition, and until he received supplies, headquarters wanted Hancock to hold a division in readiness to support him. Grant and Meade had fixed their minds on an army-wide attack toward the end of the day, and the idea of a turning movement occurred neither to them nor to Hancock.

The day before, Meade had ordered Sheridan to reconnoiter between the rebel line and the Chickahominy, and Sheridan had promised to start early on June 2. Since returning from his Richmond raid, however, the army's cavalry head had studiously ignored Meade's instructions, and he showed no inclination to change his ways now. He left Wilson's division at Hanover Court House to recover from its scrape with Hampton at Ashland and watch the roads north of the army. Torbert's division he sent south along Bottoms Bridge Road to investigate the whereabouts of Matthew Butler's fought-out cavalrymen. That left only David Gregg's division available to carry out Meade's assignment. Around 5:30 A.M., Gregg started from his camp near Parsley's Mill and rode southeast to Sumner's Upper Bridge on the Chickahominy. While Henry Davies remained near the river with most of his brigade, Colonel Irvin Gregg took his own brigade and a regiment or two from Davies and turned north along Dispatch Station Road. Sheridan's subtractions had reduced the reconnaissance-in-force envisioned by Meade to an exploratory mission involving little more than a brigade.

Around midmorning, the 1st Maine Cavalry, leading Gregg's mounted column, reached Barker's Mill, a mile and a quarter south of Old Cold Harbor and adjacent to the eastern side of Turkey Hill. Fitzhugh Lee's troopers spied them coming and opened fire, precipitating a lively exchange. Colonel Charles H. Smith, heading the 1st Maine Cavalry, dismounted his troopers and marched through woods toward the Confederates. Driving rebel skirmishers from a low ridge, Smith discovered the main rebel line on a second ridge farther back. Fitzhugh Lee ordered up horse artillery—Johnston's battery and a section of Shoemaker's battery under Lieutenant Edmund H. Moorman, both commanded by Major James Breathed—and the Maine troopers dropped behind the roll of their ridge for cover. A solid shot hit the regiment's chaplain, George Bartlett, cutting him in half. Guided by the army's chief engineer, Martin Smith, rebel cavalrymen threw up breastworks and settled in to defend their high ground. Many of them must have remembered that day three weeks earlier when they had fought a similar delaying action behind fence-rail barricades on critical high ground at Laurel Hill.[16]

Gregg dismounted the 2nd and 13th Pennsylvania Cavalry and sent them to reinforce the Maine troopers. Another look at Lee's position persuaded him not to press the issue, and his command spent the rest of the morning and most of the afternoon hiding behind the ridge. "Cavalry could not do anything," a Pennsylvanian grumped in his journal. Ricocheting cannon balls kept the horsemen alert, and the Maine men whiled away the time auctioning off their dead chaplain's horse and effects. Aside from the chaplain, the regiment's only casualties were an officer and an enlisted man killed and five men wounded. "The position of the regiment, just below the brow of a hill, accounts for the comparatively small loss," a Federal reflected, "for there was ammunition enough thrown at it to have given each man his weight, almost." Fitzhugh Lee's losses apparently did not exceed twenty men. His cavalrymen considered the fight nothing more than a routine skirmish.[17]

By half past seven in the morning, Meade and his staff had set off from Mrs. Via's farm toward Cold Harbor. Traveling partly by road and cutting cross-country at places, they came out near the Kelly house, site of Wright's head-quarters and a 6th Corps field hospital. "Of all the wastes I have seen, this first sight of Cool Arbor"—a term many Federals used for Cold Harbor—"was the most dreary," Lyman recorded. "Fancy a baking sun to begin with; then a foreground of breastworks; on the left, Kelly's wretched house; in the front, an open plain, trampled fetlock deep into fine, white dust and dotted with caissons, regiments of many soldiers, and dead horses killed in the previous cavalry fight. On the sides and in the distance were pine woods, some red with fires which had passed through them, some grey with the clouds of dust that rose high in the air. It was a Sahara intensified, and was called here Cool Arbor!"[18]

Gibbon, following behind Barlow, reached Cold Harbor at about the same time as Meade. Holding Barlow east of the intersection to support Baldy Smith, Hancock directed Gibbon to advance a short distance west on Cold Harbor Road and form a line reaching diagonally southeast to Dispatch Station Road. In the process, Gibbon was to relieve Neill's division, which in turn was to withdraw back to Cold Harbor. When Birney showed up—he was expected in the next hour or so—Barlow was to march onto Gibbon's left and extend his own division toward high ground at Turkey Hill. Birney was to remain at Cold Harbor and serve as Smith's reserve until Neill had completed his withdrawal. Neill would then shift north to support Smith, and Birney would move south to support Gibbon and Barlow. All of this shifting, marching, and countermarching had a purpose. By 5:00 P.M.—the time set for the big assault—Meade wanted Hancock's corps united in a line running south of Cold Harbor Road, with Neill's 6th Corps division north of the road, supporting Smith's and Wright's offensives.

Penrose's and Cross's 6th Corps brigades were still holding advanced positions west of Dispatch Station Road they had gained the previous day. The 15th New Jersey huddled behind its little knoll close to Colquitt's fortifications. "The firing in front was almost continuous," a New Jersey man remembered, "and hit almost every man who exposed himself." Crossing the half mile of cleared ground back to Dispatch Station Road meant certain death. Unable to get food or water, the New Jersey soldiers hunkered low behind their dirt piles. Colonel Campbell made his headquarters in a hole and stretched a piece of tent overhead for protection from the sun. Union artillery occasionally fired over the troops, and errant shells landed in their works.[19]

Gibbon arrayed his division a short distance west of Cold Harbor, his right touching Cold Harbor Road near the Garthright house and his left angling slightly southeast to brush Dispatch Station Road about half a mile away. Tyler's brigade made up the right of Gibbon's front line, Smyth's brigade the left. Behind Tyler, in the apple orchard that had served as Penrose's starting point the previous day, was McKeen's brigade, and behind Smyth was Owen. The main Confederate works—manned by Colquitt's and Martin's brigades, of Hoke's division—were about half a mile away, and rebel skirmishers were scattered across the intervening field in rifle pits and behind embankments. The northern portion of Tyler's brigade—held by the 8th New York Heavy Artillery, another large novice regiment—was about a quarter of a mile behind Penrose's and Cross's entrenchments. Artillery fire from the distant rebel line kept winging in, and snipers in pits fired at anyone who showed himself. A soldier was watching two of his companions in arms talking not twenty feet away when he "heard a 'cluck,'" he wrote, "and saw one of the men's heads lay over on his shoulder with a little spot showing on his forehead where the bullet went in—a rebel bullet had found its mark." Taking a cue from veteran troops on their left, the New Yorkers hastily began digging.[20]

As Smyth's brigade came up on Tyler's left, Neill's division retired, relinquishing their earthworks under severe fire. "This was a rather of a ticklish place for a timid person to be in," wrote Wilbur Fisk of the 2nd Vermont. "When the 2nd Corps came to relieve they came along with their heads up as if nothing was the matter. But when the bullets began to 'zip' 'zip' amongst them pretty lively they curled down and got up to the works in their respective places as quickly as was possible."[21]

Birney reached Cold Harbor late in the morning, freeing Barlow to march south, spread out on Gibbon's left, and establish a line east of Dispatch Station Road. Barlow started moving into place around noon, posting Brooke's brigade on his right, next to Smyth, and Miles's brigade on his left. Colonel Clinton D. MacDougall's brigade of six New York regiments formed in reserve behind Brooke, and Byrnes edged behind Miles. Barlow considered stretching Miles's troops south to the Chickahominy, but Hancock told him to stay put. Gregg's cavalry, still huddled behind its ridge, already controlled the road to the river. Better that Barlow leave that job to cavalry, Hancock admonished, than for him to stretch his line too thin.[22]

It was now 2:00 P.M. The day was hot, and Hancock expressed concern that his troops were too weary to attack. Grant, who had a poor understanding of the Cold Harbor sector and the growing strength of the Confederate position, decided to cancel the assault once again, citing the "want of preparation for an attack this evening, and the heat and want of energy among the men from moving during the night last night." Lyman noted that the offensive was postponed "by reason of the exhausted state of the 2nd Corps." Rescheduling the operation for June 3, Grant directed Meade that "all changes of position already ordered should be completed today and a good night's rest given the men preparatory to an assault at, say, 4:30 in the morning." The Army of the Potomac would get a rest, and the Confederates would get twelve more hours to perfect their earthworks. The delay would prove fatal to Union fortunes on the Cold Harbor front.[23]

News that the attack was off for the evening slowed Union deployments to a crawl. Around 3:00, Neill marched north behind Hancock's line and took up a new position on Ricketts's left. Birney at the same time meandered south from Cold Harbor, placing his division in reserve between Gibbon and Barlow. Soldiers from Byrnes's brigade of Barlow's division stole away to the apple orchard. "When the men had an opportunity they would pull down the green apples and eat them, from the effects of which it is feared that some of them suffered more than from the bullets of the enemy," a Pennsylvanian noted. "Unless the enemy attack us, the time will be devoted to rest," Hancock's aide Walker advised the 2nd Corps's division heads. "Meanwhile commanders should have their lines in a defensible condition and sufficiently close to the enemy. Division commanders will examine the ground well and have the proper points of attack selected. It is very probable that the assault will be ordered at the earliest hour tomorrow."[24]

Despite their commander's insistence on haste—for all Lee knew, Hancock might attack at any moment—Confederate reinforcements seemed to move in slow motion. Breckinridge's troops did not start from Mechanicsville until almost noon. As they marched past Gaines's Mill and Lee's headquarters, soldiers cheered them as the "heroes of New Market." About a mile behind Hoke's line, they reached a road junction designated on maps as New Cold Harbor and turned right, traversing the battlefields of 1862. Decaying knapsacks, canteens, and shell fragments lay scattered everywhere. "In the heads of ravines or sinks were mounds with arms, legs, and skulls protruding, where bugs and dogs had been rooting and scratching for their contents," a man recalled. Hoke's soldiers were delighted to see Breckinridge's reinforcements. The new arrivals, many of them from Virginia's mountainous west, looked rough and homespun, but their recent victory over Sigel at New Market entitled them to respect. First to appear was Brigadier General Gabriel C. Wharton's brigade, containing the 30th Virginia Battalion, the 51st Virginia, and the 62nd Virginia. Behind came Brigadier General John Echols's brigade with the 22nd Virginia, the 23rd Virginia Battalion, and the 26th Virginia Battalion. Echols was ill and had temporarily relinquished command to his senior officer, the 22nd Virginia's Colonel George S. Patton, whose grandson would achieve fame in later wars. Captain J. Parran Crane's 2nd Maryland and Captain William F. Dement's 1st Maryland Battery brought up the rear.[25]

By most accounts, Breckinridge reached Fitzhugh Lee's line on Turkey Hill between 3:00 and 4:00 P.M. Barlow's division was settling into place half a mile east, behind Dispatch Station Road. Barlow had sent skirmishers and sharpshooters to probe Turkey Hill, and they prowled the interval between the developing battle lines, shooting anyone who showed himself. Relieving Fitz Lee's cavalrymen "under a galling fire from concealed riflemen," Breckinridge's men began strengthening the light works the troopers had built. Patton's brigade dug in on Martin's right, Wharton formed on Patton's right, and the Marylanders, who arrived last, threw up a reserve line a few hundred yards behind Patton. "No sooner had we settled ourselves in our position than our men, who were handy with dirt—being most of them farmers and laboring men—set themselves to strengthening our breastworks," recollected Captain Morton of the 26th Virginia Battalion. "It was not long before they presented a pretty fair protection against the constant fire from the enemy's pickets and sharpshooters, who were strongly posted in a piece of wood land immediately in our front." Maryland troops tore shingles from the abandoned McGehee family home between their position and Patton's main line and used them as shovels.[26]

Colonel Edgar, commanding the 26th Virginia Battalion, ordered two companies under Captain Edward S. Read to drive off Barlow's skirmishers. Marylander John Hatton remembered Read's men "creeping upon the enemy as upon wild game, but more cautiously because human life was at stake." After advancing a short distance, the Virginians threw themselves "flat upon the ground and behind logs and stumps to escape annihilation." One by one they came back, leaving several dead and wounded soldiers behind in the no-man's land. His effort to clear his front of enemy skirmishers having failed, Edgar concentrated on strengthening his entrenchments.[27]

Fitzhugh Lee's line, now occupied by Breckinridge, was flawed. Near Breckinridge's left, where it joined Martin's North Carolinians, the Confederate works bulged forward in a sharp salient, each of its two faces about two hundred yards long. Edgar's 26th Virginia Battalion of Patton's brigade and the Kanawha Company from the 22nd Virginia occupied the V-shaped formation, along with two or three guns from Captain William H. Caskie's Virginia Battery, of Hoke's division. These soldiers—Edgar had about four hundred men, and the Kanawha Company another fifty—stood spaced some three feet apart. Protruding toward the Federals, the salient drew more fire than all the rest of Breckinridge's line. A short distance in front of its apex, the ground dropped off sharply, affording enemy troops a place to mass out of sight. As the 1st Corps artillery chief, Alexander, later noted, the salient "was a piece of bad location of our line, allowing a dead space in front to come up to within forty to eighty yards." At this juncture, however, Edgar's men could do little to change the layout of their works. "We had to make the most of it," Captain Edgar decided, "and stand or fall where we were." At Edgar's urging, Patton sent a lieutenant to find Breckinridge and alert him to the "exposed and weak condition of our line." He was unable to find the general, however, and gave up the search, much to Edgar's distress.[28]

By now, Confederates were streaming onto Turkey Hill. No sooner was Breckinridge in place than Wilcox's 3rd Corps division arrived from Totopotomoy Creek. Lane's North Carolina brigade formed behind Wharton, advanced obliquely to the south, drove off a few stray Union cavalrymen and skirmishers, and secured the ground on Breckinridge's right. Wilcox's remaining brigades, under Scales, Thomas, and McGowan, pounded up and extended the line south. McGowan's South Carolinians occupied the army's lower flank, in front of the home of the Martin family, half a mile north of the Chickahominy. "We were on the extreme right of the army," a Carolinian recounted, "holding the last shoulder of the ridge that rises from the swamp of the Chickahominy, and erecting our works along McClellan's military road." Wilcox's attack was a relatively bloodless affair. The division lost only three or four men wounded, but one of them was Lane, shot in the thigh by a Union sharpshooter. Command of Lane's brigade devolved on the senior colonel, John D. Barry.[29]

Mahone's division arrived next and deployed in support of Colquitt and Martin. A brigade of Floridians on Mahone's right entrenched a short distance behind Crane's Marylanders and to their left. The 2nd, 5th, and 8th Florida had been with Lee throughout the campaign and were terribly decimated, numbering perhaps 275 soldiers. On May 28, 1,100 men from the 9th, 10th, and 11th Florida had joined them. The commander of these fresh troops, Brigadier General Joseph Finegan, was still basking in glory from his victory at Olustee, Florida. The new men, many of them overweight and sickly, were a "hard-looking lot of soldiers," a veteran recalled. "They were all smoked from the lightwood knots and had not washed or worn it off yet; and being so far down south, they had not received many clothes—only what their mothers or wives had spun or woven for them, and to see their little homespun jackets and the most of them with bed quilts instead of blankets." Along with the Maryland troops, Finegan's soldiers provided additional support for Colonel Edgar's salient. "We found out there was trouble ahead of us," recollected Private George H. Dorman, one of Finegan's newcomers. "So we went to work with our bayonets digging up the old Virginia soil, soon striking into red clay."[30]

Confederate infantry now strongly occupied high ground that the Federals might have captured with ease only two hours before. Grant's opportunity to flank Lee was gone. The Union commander had been contemplating a head-on assault. His failure to take advantage of the opening available to him until late on June 2 now left him few other courses of action.

Barlow reported the situation on his front at 5:00 P.M. He had arranged his two largest brigades—those under Brooke and Miles—in battle lines east of Dispatch Station Road, with Miles's left swung somewhat forward. Confederate infantry—Breckinridge's troops—occupied Turkey Hill in front of him. "Their position is on a crest nearly parallel with the road and [west] of the road, and higher and more commanding than ours," Barlow observed. "They command our position with artillery, while we have no good position for guns, and they have been throwing canister over our lines." The rebels, he reported, "have their usual line of works and a line of battle." A Union sharpshooter noted "the same old view" west of Dispatch Station Road. "In every direction across [the Confederate] front were seen the brownish red furrows which told of rifle pits," he wrote, "while at every commanding point in the rebel line rose stronger and higher works, above which peered the dark muzzles of hostile artillery."[31]

Determined to test the strength of the rebel position, Barlow ordered Miles to advance his brigade, positioned on the southern end of the Union line. The brigade commander and future Indian fighter formed a skirmish line consisting of the 26th Michigan, the 140th Pennsylvania, and two companies from the 2nd New York Heavy Artillery, recently assigned to the brigade. Marching across a field, Miles's troops reached Dispatch Station Road under heavy fire from Breckinridge's fortifications. Soldiers from the 2nd New York Heavy Artillery sought cover in the road cut, a Pennsylvanian claimed, and refused to continue on, but the 26th Michigan and 140th Pennsylvania double-quicked ahead and apparently reached the sheltered dip below Edgar's salient. "We lay close to the works and were protected from the fire of the enemy," a Pennsylvanian wrote. Miles decided against advancing farther and ordered his men back. A captain in the 140th Pennsylvania asserted that he and his troops made "the best time for fast running then on record." The venture cost the 26th Michigan twenty soldiers.[32]

Barlow relayed his findings to headquarters. "The enemy's skirmish line is quite active, and at times presses ours," he noted. "We have no ground in front but what is commanded by the enemy's guns." Most disturbing was the identity of the opposing rebels. Prisoners captured during Miles's foray reported that both of Breckinridge's brigades were there. When Barlow had left Totopotomoy Creek the night before, Breckinridge had been in front of him. Having made a forced march to the other end of the army, he found Breckinridge confronting him again! The shift of the 2nd Corps from the right flank of the army to the left flank had, in the end, achieved little, as Lee had successfully countered Grant's maneuver with corresponding movements of his own. Once again, the Confederates faced the Union army from a strong natural position.[33]

"Shooting and bayoneting them without mercy."

The sector where Wright's and Smith's corps had fought on June 1 remained relatively quiet on June 2. Dead and wounded men covered the fields between Cold Harbor Road and the road from Mr. Allison's to the Woody place. Corpses lay "in every conceivable position," wrote S. Millet Thompson of the 13th New Hampshire. "Many bodies are bent backwards, as if the spine were trying to touch ends that way," he observed. "One body is thus arched up, and is resting upon the shoulders and heels. The coat capes are turned up over many faces, other faces are bare, others hidden, the bodies lying face down; but the most lie as they fell, and are badly torn—it is a walk of sickening and unutterable horrors." Grant and Meade visited the sector in the afternoon, as did Baldy Smith. Smith asked for a musket and was about to fire at the nearby Confederate works when Lieutenant George H. Taggard of the 13th New Hampshire requested him to put down the gun. The men, Taggard explained, were under strict orders not to shoot unless attacked. Smith dutifully returned the weapon, "a major general obeying a lieutenant's request, and possibly one of his own orders," Thompson reflected.[34]

Burnside, following Meade's directive to mass behind Warren's right, spent the afternoon completing his movement of Potter and Willcox to Bethesda Church. Crittenden, on Shady Grove Road, served as the pivot for their withdrawal and covered the 5th Corps's northern flank. Warren concentrated Griffin's division at Bethesda Church, posting pickets from Bartlett's brigade in advanced works running south from Magnolia Swamp. Ayres's brigade stood across Old Church Road, Cutler covered the road toward Walnut Church, and Crawford continued the 5th Corps line south to a point west of Mr. Woody's farm. Most of the soldiers spent the day resting, writing letters, and feeling sorry for themselves. "I never knew before what campaigning was," an officer wrote home. "Our men are pretty well used up by this campaign." A soldier groused that he was "dirty and ragged not having had a change of clothing for a month." Another man detailed his condition in a letter to his sister. "My pants I cut off just below the knees as they were filled with mud and weighed too much so I must look very much like an overgrown turkey," he reported. "My lovely hat (I bought one you know for four dollars and a half) is filled with holes and covered with a compound of mud and grease. Perhaps it would look better if I did not use it for a holder to my coffee pot." Sharpshooters on both sides fired constantly. One particularly troublesome rebel marksman holed up in a chimney and, according to a Wisconsin man, "shot at everyone that exposed their person in the least."[35]

When Potter and Wilcox were safely encamped at Bethesda Church, Burnside sent word to Crittenden to retire east along Shady Grove Road and join them. Burnside and Warren were on bad terms, however, and apparently Burnside failed to notify the 5th Corps commander that he was pulling Crittenden east. As Crittenden withdrew, the northern end of Griffin's entrenched picket line, manned by Bartlett, was left exposed. A summer storm—"the hardest shower I ever saw," Lieutenant Colonel George P. Hawkes of the 21st Massachusetts proclaimed—erupted around 4:00 P.M., just as Crittenden's troops started off. The rain helped conceal their departure not only from the rebels, but from Bartlett's unsuspecting pickets as well.[36]

Confederate skirmishers soon discovered that Crittenden was leaving and reported the movement to Early. All afternoon, the Confederate 2nd Corps commander, pursuant to Lee's instructions, had been searching for a chink in Burnside's and Warren's defenses. Crittenden's retirement gave him his opportunity. Seizing the moment, Early ordered a massive offensive. Gordon's division, on Early's southern wing, was to move east against Griffin on a front extending from Magnolia Swamp to Old Church Road. Rodes's division, on Gordon's left, was to charge along Shady Grove Road and hit Crittenden's column in the rear. And Heth, whose division stood posted north of Shady Grove Road, was to slice east cross-country, veer south, and descend in the Union rear.

Crittenden's troops had left their earthworks and marched about a mile east on Shady Grove Road when Rodes's Confederates caught up with them. Unexpectedly, rebels began firing into Sudsburg's brigade, bringing up the division's rear. "It was a regular case of surprise," a Union aide admitted,

"and things looked very nasty for a little while." Ordering his rearguard skirmishers to try and "hold the enemy in check as long as possible," Sudsburg
hurried east with the rest of Crittenden's division while the 21st Massachusetts fought a desperate delaying action. "The retreat down to Bethesda
Church, a distance of some three or four miles, was most exciting, the Johnnies following us up pretty closely," a Bay Stater recalled. "Once in a while
we would make a stand. Then they would bring up their artillery, and lines
of infantry would swing into place. Then we would quietly drop back again."
The Massachusetts regiment lost forty-seven men, but the time that it bought
enabled the rest of the division to escape.[37]

Nearing the Bowles farm, Crittenden deployed his troops in a line south
of Shady Grove Road, facing north. Sudsburg's brigade formed Crittenden's
left, Marshall's Provisional Brigade his right, and Ledlie's brigade remained
in reserve. Rodes's troops marched into woods along the north side of Shady
Grove Road and formed parallel to the road, facing south. In an ironic twist
of fate, Crittenden faced north in a line almost identical to that held by Ramseur's Confederates when they attacked Warren on May 30. And the Confederates—Rodes's division—stood approximately in Warren's former position,
looking south.

Combat quieted as Rodes established his battle lines and waited for Heth,
who was working through woods to the north in an effort to reach the Via
farm and deploy on Rodes's left. Private Porter C. Burns, on picket duty in
front of Marshall's brigade, loved watches and had cobbled a repair kit from
items scavenged from abandoned blacksmith shops. His pockets were stuffed
with timepieces comrades had given him to fix. Jumping at the opportunity
to play at his hobby, Burns spread a rubber blanket, removed a watch, and
began taking it apart. Suddenly a bugle sounded and Rodes's men stormed
from the far woods. "It was laughable, amidst all the excitement, to see Comrade Burns, in a nervous state, trying to get the corners of the blanket together
to save the watch," a fellow soldier remembered. "As he ran the pieces could
be heard jingling and being strewn along the ground." Marshall's pickets fell
back on their brigade, and one man was almost run over by the colonel of the
24th New York Cavalry (dismounted), whose horse became uncontrollable.[38]

Burnside did not like to miss meals. He had set up camp near Bethesda
Church and was resting under a tree with his staff in anticipation of dinner
when musketry erupted to the north, in the direction of Shady Grove Road.
Ending his repast, Burnside sprang into his saddle and rode to investigate.
Troops and animals were darting in all directions. "A panic seized the team-
sters," a Federal recollected, "who waited not for orders, but crowded into

the roads, lashing their mules furiously and turning the air blue with their oaths."[39]

Approaching Shady Grove Road from the south, Burnside found Crittenden's division embroiled in a nasty fight. Marshall, on Crittenden's right, was moving his brigade forward to occupy a set of rifle pits built during the fight of May 30. His pickets came streaming back, pursued by Risden Bennett's North Carolina brigade of Rodes's division. Realizing the importance of seizing the old works before the Confederates got into them, Marshall rushed his 24th New York Cavalry, 14th New York Artillery, and 2nd New York Rifles forward at a double quick. Marshall won the race, and his winded troops piled into the earthworks. Halting Bennett's advance, Marshall linked his left with Sudsburg and placed the 2nd Pennsylvania Heavy Artillery on his right, slightly refused to protect the brigade's flank.[40]

At the sound of musketry, Willcox rushed the 20th Michigan of Benjamin Christ's brigade north from its camp at Bethesda Church. The Michiganders reached Shady Grove Road in time to wage a vigorous defense of the intersection at the Bowles farm, to the right of Marshall's brigade. Forming on the reverse side of Warren's old works, Major George G. Barnes deployed the 20th in a thin line reaching over to Marshall. Rodes's Confederates advanced into a field in front of the Michigan troops and tried several times to break Barnes's line. The Michiganders held, although their ammunition ran low and they lost some thirty-three men.[41]

Sudsburg, on Marshall's left, ventured a charge in an attempt to drive back Rodes's Confederates. "As we advanced, a withering fire met us from our right front, while a long line of graybacks were seen hurrying around toward our left with evident intention to flank our brigade," a soldier in the 21st Massachusetts noted. Halting in a field, Sudsburg's Federals lay down and fired into Rodes's Confederates in front of them. Rebels kept edging around Sudsburg's left, and more slipped between Sudsburg and Marshall, threatening to envelop both Union brigades. Not surprisingly, Sudsburg was nowhere to be found. "Our brigade now receiving the concentrated fire from three directions, and although we had given as good as we had received, the knowledge that we were virtually without a leader served to weaken the unity of spirit," remembered Private George A. Hitchcock of the 21st Massachusetts. "Men were being mowed down like grass, and having no protection from the deadly fire, it is not strange that our line melted away." The 48th Pennsylvania retreated south toward Bethesda Church, followed by the 21st Massachusetts. Colonel Hawkes of the 21st tried to stem the collapse by gathering men around the colors, but his troops kept darting rearward, seeking cover behind trees and in gullies. Private Hitchcock ended up in a rifle pit shaped omi-

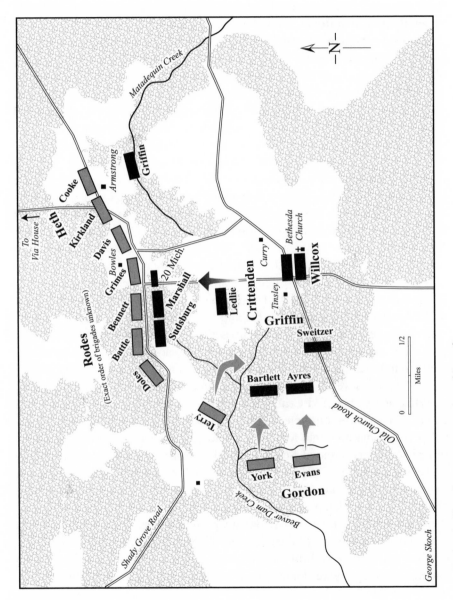

Bethesda Church sector on evening of June 2

nously like a grave and half filled with water from the recent shower. Complicating matters, Sudsburg's retreat uncovered Marshall's left, forcing Marshall to swing his leftmost two regiments at right angles to his front to protect his flank. Marshall lost close to 440 men, some 335 of them as prisoners. Badly battered, the Union troops formed a new line facing north and held on.[42]

Both sides brought up artillery, and Sudsburg's troops hugged the ground as shells whizzed over from front and rear. "A pretty sharp time of it for about two hours," a Pennsylvanian recollected. Sudsburg's losses, like those of Marshall's brigade on his right, were severe. The 100th Pennsylvania lost 80 men, the 21st Massachusetts 47, and the 3rd Maryland 10. "We are all worn down to 'Fighting Weight,'" joked adjutant Leasure, "but must not give up on the present state of affairs." Ledlie's brigade, supporting Captain Albert F. Thomas's 2nd Battery (B), Maine Light Artillery, apparently suffered more from misdirected Union artillery fire than from Confederate bullets. "The battery was on slightly rising ground, but the shells stripped as they were fired from the guns, and as the firing was unusually bad, it was most destructive to [the 56th Massachusetts] as the strips of the shells and shot flew around us right and left," wrote Colonel Weld. "It was bad enough to be killed by the rebels, but to have our own men shoot us was worse."[43]

Weld would have been pleased to learn that the shelling also bothered the Confederates. Bennett's chief-of-staff considered the cannonading the worst he had experienced, save at Gettysburg. "Solid shot, shell, grape, canister, spherical case—every conceivable projectile of death that can be hurled from the satanic throats of the monstrous engines of war—were mercilessly showered around us," he wrote. A shell exploded among Bennett's aides, killing two, wounding several, and spraying the survivors with brains and blood.[44]

While Rodes battered Crittenden, Heth's lead elements—Kirkland's and Davis's brigades—completed their cross-country tramp to get into Burnside's rear. Emerging into Mrs. Via's fields, Heth's men cut telegraph wires, turned south, and crossed Shady Grove Road onto the Armstrong property. Potter's right-hand brigade, under Simon Griffin, camped in the Armstrong fields, discovered the Confederates bearing down "like a hawk upon a chicken," a New Hampshire man related. "We were not prepared to receive them, as we were in the field without any particular formation, but the officers in command were equal to the occasion. They gave their orders in rapid succession, and a more skillful movement of troops was never executed." Two batteries accompanying Potter rolled into place and began firing into Heth's advancing line.[45]

Heth's and Potter's battle was brief but furious. During his advance, Heth had become separated from Rodes's division on his right. Davis's mixed Mis-

sissippi and North Carolina brigade charged into the Armstrong field, repulsed Potter's lead elements, but became embroiled in a deadly stand-up
fight against some of Potter's soldiers ensconced in a wooded finger of Matadequin Creek. Kirkland's brigade managed to cover the left of Davis's advance, but Davis's right received severe enfilading fire, compelling him to
retire north of Shady Grove Road. Cooke's brigade came up on Kirkland's
left toward the end of the fight but blundered into a swamp, where it flailed
about in semidarkness "over fallen timbers and through mud and water." Realizing that he could make no headway against Potter, Heth gave up the attack, pulled the rest of his division north of Shady Grove Road, and began
entrenching on Rodes's left. He reported his loss "heavy considering the
numbers engaged." Kirkland was seriously wounded, and command of his
brigade devolved on Colonel George H. Faribault of the 47th North Carolina.
A bullet also shattered the left arm of Colonel Alfred Horatio Belo, commanding the 55th North Carolina in Davis's brigade.[46]

While Potter fought Heth, Burnside advanced Curtin's brigade from
Bethesda Church to assist Crittenden against Rodes. Marching across open
ground and apparently led by Burnside himself, the troops presented a
"splendid spectacle," an onlooker remembered, calling the movement "a review under fire." By the time Curtin reached the front, however, the steam
had gone out of Rodes's attack. Pulling his men north of Shady Grove Road,
Rodes, like Heth on his left, began digging in. He, too, had taken severe
losses. Colonel Bennett was seriously wounded and Brigadier General
George P. Doles, the thirty-four-year-old commander of a Georgia brigade,
was killed. A bullet struck Doles in the left breast near the nipple, passed
through his heart, and exited under his right arm, shattering it. Colonel William R. Cox of the 2nd North Carolina replaced Bennett, and Colonel Philip
Cook of the 4th Georgia assumed command of Doles's brigade.[47]

At the same time that Rodes and Heth were fighting Burnside along the east-
west axis defined by Shady Grove Road, Gordon was assailing Griffin along
a north-south front running from Magnolia Swamp to Old Church Road. Crittenden's withdrawal east along Shady Grove Road had uncovered the northern end of Griffin's picket line. Part of Gordon's division—most likely
William Terry's Virginia brigade—poured through Magnolia Swamp and
turned south, enfilading the pickets of Bartlett's brigade and swarming into
their rear. The rest of Gordon's division—a Louisiana brigade under Colonel
Zebulon York, and Clement Evans's Georgians—attacked straight ahead
from the west. It was an "ugly situation," Major Ellis Spear of the 20th Maine
recorded. "The sweep was so sudden and in such force there was little resis-

tance," another Federal remembered. Enfilading south along Bartlett's picket line, Terry's Confederates captured about four hundred prisoners from the Union brigade. Portions of the 118th Pennsylvania managed to change front and face north toward the approaching Confederates but were powerless to arrest their progress. In short order, Terry's flanking force had overrun Bartlett's entire picket line and was emerging on the right flank of Ayres's brigade, immediately south of Bartlett.[48]

Warren quickly rearranged the remainder of his corps to deflect the attack. Cutler extended somewhat to the right, reaching north toward Old Church Road. Griffin, whose division was massed in front of Bethesda Church, turned to face northwest. Ayres remained on Old Church Road; Bartlett formed the rest of his brigade on Ayres's right, extending northeast toward Crittenden's left; and Sweitzer waited near Bethesda Church, in reserve. "The enemy have followed up Burnside quite fast, and their skirmishers have got around to the Via house and cut the telegraph line," Warren alerted headquarters at 4:30 P.M. "We are having now quite a brisk fight," he added. "I think we will have no trouble to hold on here," he assured Meade, "but I think we should not leave without restoring our control of the Via house and getting back our telegraph wire." As usual, Warren could not resist criticizing his superiors. "I think your instructions to me about taking up position for attack were conflicting," he chided Humphreys, not without justification. "For me to close in to General Smith's right, keep half my troops in reserve, and let Burnside mass on my right would bring him to Cold Harbor and have retired my line from the enemy. This movement of the enemy stops our march for the present."[49]

Warren's and Gordon's fight was a bloody affair. Ayres's brigade, holding the 5th Corps's advance line of works on Old Church Road, contained five Regular United States regiments and four volunteer regiments. The Regulars were disdainful of the volunteers, and particularly so of the brigade's 140th and 146th New York, which were outfitted in colorful Zouave uniforms. On June 1 another Zouave regiment—the 5th New York, a reorganized version of the old Duryea's Zouaves, once commanded by Warren—had joined Ayres's brigade. Consolidated with it was the 12th New York, a merger that gave the latter regiment's veterans deep concern. "A present source of annoyance lies in the fact that the 5th is a Zouave regiment," Robert Tilney of the 12th wrote home, "and we fear we may be compelled to adopt its uniform, which consists of crimson zouave pants, buff leather gaiters, light blue jacket with scarlet braids sprawling fantastically over it, a variegated waistband wound round half a dozen times, and, horror on horrors, a crimson skull cap with a yellow tassel, or else a crimson or white turban." Complained Tilney: "I suppose I would be permitted to continue the detailed duty uniform, but one cannot tell; one thing is certain, I will not wear the other without a fight."[50]

Marching toward Ayres were Evans's Georgians, most of them veterans. But Evans, like Ayres, had also just received a new regiment, the 12th Georgia Battalion. Commanded by Lieutenant Colonel Henry D. Capers, the battalion had waged a stubborn defense of Fort Sumter in 1863. In late May, carrying a colorful silk battle flag inscribed with "Fort Sumter" on one side and "Battery Wagner" on the other, Capers's men had joined Evans's brigade. June 2 would be their introduction to warfare Virginia style. "They were also fixed up in better garb than we were," a veteran in the 61st Georgia observed, "and some of our boys said that some of their officers looked too proud and dudeish for soldiers, and they were afraid they would give way and the enemy would flank us."[51]

Capers's battalion and two companies from the 61st Georgia fanned out in front of Evans's battle line. Facing them was the 146th New York. "We strung out in skirmish order and advanced as rapidly as possible with our bodies bent to the ground to avoid the musket balls that whizzed over our heads," the New York regiment's historian recorded. "Keeping our knapsacks up close to our heads, we crawled along, stopping occasionally just long enough to aim and fire."[52]

Ayres's men, facing west toward Evans, had no inkling that Terry's Virginians had torn through Bartlett's line to their north and were about to emerge on their flank. Soldiers in the 155th Pennsylvania realized something was horribly wrong when bullets began singing in from their right and rear. Evacuating their works, they ran "as fast as our legs and the thick underbrush would let us," a Pennsylvanian remembered, "and with all our haste we were not a minute too soon." The 146th New York's first intimation of Gordon's turning movement came "when the bullets commenced pinging at us from behind and our brigade commander came hurrying up shouting that the 'Rebs' were in our rear and every man was ordered to look out for himself," the regiment's historian wrote. "The first thought of each man was to escape from the trap in which we had been so neatly caught. We took to our heels and most of our regiment succeeded in breaking through and reaching the main line in the rear, but a large number of the brigade were captured."[53]

Sensing Ayres's confusion, Capers ordered his men to charge. Leaping onto the advanced works, they dove into the disordered body of Federals, "shooting and bayoneting them without mercy," according to a Georgian. As the 146th New York fell back, the 5th New York received the brunt of the attack. "These were Zouaves, fancy rigged gentlemen in red pants and caps," a southerner noted, "which made a fine mark for our rifle men." The 5th New

York's commander, Colonel Cleveland Winslow, was shot in the arm. Capers also fell wounded, but his soldiers pressed on, driving Zouaves before them. "They turned and fought us all the way back to their line of battle," a Georgian recollected of the 5th New York, "but they were poor marksmen, for they seldom hurt one of our boys." Tilney of the 5th New York did not disagree. "At the first fire the 5th broke and ran and could not be rallied," he admitted.[54]

Lieutenant William Fowler tried in vain to rally part of the 146th New York and make a stand. "We hastily formed line, and took possession of some works near, but were completely enfiladed and compelled to fly," Fowler wrote. "We rallied the men once, but it was a mere sacrifice of life, and the order to fall back was given, followed by the 'tallest running' on record." Ayres's Regulars held only a bit longer. "We were busily preparing to repel the imminent assault on our front," John C. White of the 15th United States related, "when we heard a rush upon our right, and saw to our demoralization a massed column rapidly advancing with fixed bayonets, while over the parapet of the abandoned works in our rear, was double-quicking, as if on parade, a perfectly dressed line of Confederates at an 'arms port!'" The Regulars sprinted left, hoping to escape the trap. "Resistance was, of course, out of the question," wrote White, "since we were surrounded upon three sides, and as their field batteries had been run up, the slaughter was heavy." White managed to find an empty rifle pit extending rearward and escaped down it, running so fast that he thought he "resembled the 'governor' of a steam engine, as my haversack on one side and my canteen on the other each were flying out at an angle of thirty degrees."[55]

Retreating to the 5th Corps's works immediately west of Bethesda Church, Ayres's men waged a desperate hand-to-hand fight with Evans's rebels, who seemed determined to break through. "Some said our new soldiers never stopped in their charge until they went on to Washington," a soldier in the 31st Georgia later remarked of Capers's men, many of whom were last seen vaulting over the Federal works. When Sergeant Henry S. Hopps, carrying the 12th Georgia Battalion's flag, fell seriously wounded, Adjutant Frank W. Baker seized the colors only to fall mortally wounded himself. Major George M. Hanvey, who had succeeded the wounded Capers in command, was severely wounded. "The enemy were mixed in with us," remembered Fowler of the 146th New York, "and I saw one of their color bearers shot dead scarcely thirty feet away from me." A Confederate account put Capers's losses at 112. Colonel Winslow of the 5th New York, although seriously wounded, remained in the saddle until Warren arrived and ordered him to the hospital. He died a few days later.[56]

Gordon's attack had pushed Griffin back to Tinsley's farm, where Grimes's men had overrun the Pennsylvania Reserves on May 30. Ayres's brigade stood across Old Church Road, facing Evans, and Bartlett's brigade stretched north across the Tinsley fields, covering the road to the Bowles place and fending off York and Terry. Rittenhouse's and Captain Patrick Hart's batteries fired west from the Tinsley yard, and Lieutenant James Stewart's battery aimed north, toward Shady Grove Road. Wainwright placed Captain Charles A. Phillips's and Richardson's batteries east of the road to the Bowles house so that they could shoot both north toward Rodes and west toward Gordon. "It must have been a very hot place in that corner around the Tinsley house," Wainwright surmised, "for our line made a perfect right angle there with the enemy close up on both sides."[57]

Night was fast approaching. Unable to drive Ayres and Bartlett from their main line of works, Gordon pulled back a short distance and entrenched, like Rodes and Heth on his left. The Union 5th and 9th Corps also dug in, Burnside facing north, his left touching Warren's right. "The enemy now have the breastworks we built when we had our fight night before last," Warren reported, "and we hold their position." Before dark, Roebling visited Potter to find out how far east the rebel line extended. From the Armstrong farm, he could see Heth's flank brushing Shady Grove Road. "There was a chance here for Potter's division to have got into the rear of the rebel line which might have resulted in the capture of [the Confederates] before night," Roebling later wrote. "I took one of Potter's staff officers to the spot who agreed with me; I reported the circumstances to Generals Potter and Burnside but they took no notice of it." Early's Confederates had quieted, and none of the 9th Corps' generals wanted to stir them up again.[58]

The June 2 fight at Bethesda Church was short but fierce. Historians have largely ignored the battle, sandwiched between the big attack on the evening of June 1 and the even bigger assault on June 3. Burnside lost a little under a thousand men and Warren well over five hundred. The Confederates claimed to have captured five hundred prisoners—Roebling put the number at four hundred—including the heads of the 12th and 14th Regulars, whose regiments were decimated, the 12th Regulars alone losing ninety-six men. "These officers seemed to care nothing about themselves," a Richmond correspondent noted, "their great anxiety being to learn something about the fate of their colors."[59]

Early's orders had been to attack Grant's right flank and pound it south. Hammer he had, but the Federals had not budged appreciably beyond Shady Grove Road. "In this movement there was some heavy fighting and several hundred prisoners were taken by us," was all Early ever said about the battle. Lee mentioned the assault approvingly in his evening report to Richmond, noting that Early "drove the enemy from his entrenchments, following him until dark." Early commended Terry for his fine performance, and Capers's battalion won approbation. "We never had any doubts about the fighting qualities of the officers and men of the 12th Georgia Battalion again," a veteran remembered.[60]

Low Confederate casualties attested to the fighting skill of the veteran Confederate 2nd Corps. Early had launched vigorous attacks on June 1 and 2. Rodes's division, however, had lost only some 270 soldiers in both actions; Gordon's division, about 300, a disproportionate number of them in Capers' battalion; and Ramseur perhaps 50. Heth, who joined Early for the June 2 offensive, lost in the range of 400 men. The campaign had drastically diminished the 2nd Corps, but the outfit retained its ability to hit hard.[61]

Warren's men had nothing good to say about the battle. "The enemy came upon us from our right and rear," an officer in the 11th Regulars admitted. "I did not stop to inquire what the rebels thought about it, but we were very much surprised indeed." An officer in the 14th Regulars complained more bluntly: "No precaution seemed to have been taken to protect [Griffin's] flank, nor did the general staff of the army see that movements were so coordinated as to guard against such surprises. We lost thousands of prisoners and many valuable lives from this method of issuing orders and then trusting to luck that they would be properly and successfully carried out." Lieutenant Fowler of the 146th New York declared his regiment's rout "a repetition of the affair of May 5 [in the Wilderness], and, considering our numbers, almost as serious."[62]

Burnside received scathing criticism. Mills of Crittenden's staff thought that the 9th Corps's withdrawal "should have been prompt and speedy, and the pickets not drawn in until we were well started." Leasure of Sudsburg's brigade expressed disgust over the absence of leadership. "The only general I saw at the front was General Griffin, 5th Corps, who gave some orders which I obeyed," he wrote, "or I suppose the brigade would never have received any orders." The 9th Corps's generals, Wainwright tartly observed, "do not seem to have covered themselves with glory."[63]

Grant viewed Burnside's and Warren's feeble counterattacks as fumbled opportunities to catch part of Lee's army outside of its works. "We ought to be able to eat them up," he remarked when he heard the details. "Generally I am not in favor of night attacks, but I think one might be justified in such a case as the present." In his memoirs, Grant commented that "the [Confederate] attacks were repulsed, but not followed up as they should have been. I was so annoyed at this that I directed Meade to give orders to his corps commanders that they should seize all such opportunities when they occurred, and not wait for orders, all of our maneuvers being made for the very purpose of getting the enemy out of his cover." Lyman summarized the perception at headquarters. "The enemy in force swung around Via's house and gobbled up several miles of our telegraph wire, besides several hundred prisoners," he wrote home. "We ought to have just eaten them up; but as it was, we only drove them back into some rifle pits we had formerly abandoned, and then the line was formed as originally ordered, with Burnside swung round to cover our right flank from Bethesda Church toward Linney's house, while the enemy held Via's house and a line parallel to our own."[64]

"If we could smash them up, the Chickahominy lay behind them."

Nightfall saw the two armies locked closely together in a sprawling formation resembling an upside-down L. Opposing lines meandered six miles from the Armstrong farm to the Chickahominy River. Darkness ended active fighting, although musketry crackled along picket lines and in the narrow no-man's land between the armies where skirmishers clashed.

Lee's position was as strong as any he had held since the Wilderness. By the morning of June 3, the central portion of the Confederate defense—Anderson's corps and Hoke's division—had been in place for over forty-eight hours. The southern end of the Confederate line—Breckinridge's, Wilcox's, and Mahone's divisions—had enjoyed more than twelve hours to entrench, as had the northern end, held by Early and Heth. "It is a rule that, when the rebels halt, the first day gives them a good rifle pit; the second, a regular infantry parapet with artillery in position; and the third a parapet with abattis in front and entrenched batteries behind," Lyman noted. Sometimes, the aide thought, rebels could "put this three days' work in the first twenty-four hours." Lyman's calculations had a measure of accuracy, but the staffer still underestimated the industry of Lee's men. At this stage of the campaign, twelve hours was more than adequate for southern soldiers to construct impregnable defenses.[65]

The Army of Northern Virginia's line had evolved in response to Union moves. No one had planned it or laid it out in advance. The final product, however, masterfully exploited the terrain. Wilcox's division held the southern Confederate flank on Turkey Hill, overlooking the Chickahominy lowlands on the right and Dispatch Station Road in front. Breckinridge's division picked up on Wilcox's left, with Wharton's brigade ensconced on high ground north of Wilcox and Patton's brigade holding the adjacent stretch of line. Hoke's division started on Breckinridge's left, Martin's brigade carrying the Confederate line north along high ground to Boatswain Creek and Colquitt's brigade continuing the formation to Cold Harbor Road. An entire division—Mahone's of the 3rd Corps—waited in reserve behind Hoke. A few Union 6th Corps elements remained south of the road, but Hancock's corps was the predominant Federal presence in the sector. Gibbon's division faced Martin and Colquitt across open ground strewn with corpses from Penrose's, Cross's, and Grant's charges the afternoon of June 1. Barlow's division extended Hancock's line south of Gibbon, facing Breckinridge, and Birney's division remained in reserve.

The Confederates had greatly strengthened their defenses north of Cold Harbor Road, where Wright and Baldy Smith had made inroads the previous evening. Hagood's brigade now reached from Cold Harbor Road north toward Bloody Run. Clingman supported Hagood, and Hunton carried the formation north across the forested lower ravine. Kershaw's division, reinforced by brigades from Field's division, continued the line in an inverted-horseshoe-shaped formation to the middle ravine's northern bank. Late on June 2, Law, whose Alabama brigade had entrenched above the middle ravine, bent his line sharply west to eliminate a salient in the works near Falligant's gun. "That no mistake should be made in the location of the works, I procured a hatchet," Law later wrote, "and accompanied by two members of my staff, each with an armful of stakes, went out after dark, located the line, and drove every stake upon it." Law's new line overlooked the central ravine's marshy low ground and afforded a superb defensive position. Bryan's troops formed in reserve behind Law, "Tige" Anderson's Georgians continued the line south of the ravine, and Gregg linked Anderson with Hunton. Wofford remained in reserve behind the horseshoe's pocket. "The parapet was five feet high," a Confederate who spent the night digging with his bayonet recollected, "with a ditch four feet deep in front and a wide shallow ditch on the inside, and a banquette for the men to stand on while firing." When Law's men finished their new works, they leveled much of the abandoned entrenchments. "A better horseshoe connection around the gap between Kershaw and Hoke was built to replace the temporary one of the night before," the artillerist Alexander explained, "and our entrenchments everywhere got all the work we were able to put upon them." If Union troops tried to break through, they would find themselves in a trap, enfiladed from both sides.[66]

The Union line immediately north of Cold Harbor Road looked much as it had when fighting stopped on June 1. Eustis and Upton held the sector between Cold Harbor Road and Bloody Run, with Upton's troops in places

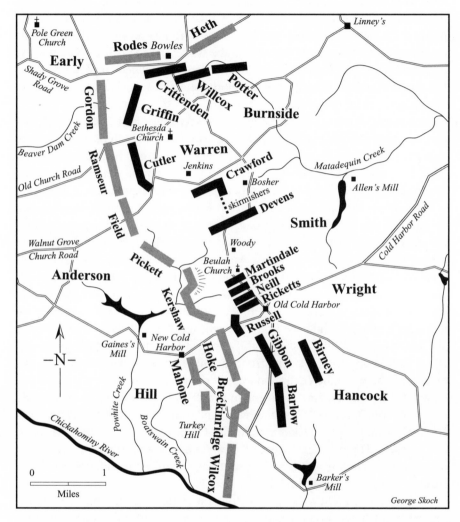

Situation at nightfall on June 2

occupying works they had taken from Clingman and reversed to face west. "We fixed head logs on the works and built sheltered outlooks with ammunition boxes filled with dirt, rigged decoys for the rebels to fire at and would fire at their puffs of smoke," one of Upton's officers recalled. Musketry was incessant, and anyone who peered over the works risked his life. "Great many dead laying on the field unburied of the 2nd Connecticut of our brigade," Lieutenant Lewis Luckenbill of the 96th Pennsylvania wrote in his diary. "All black. Awful bad smell."[67]

Meade had made several changes in the sector north of Upton. Ricketts's division was still on Upton's right, ensconced in entrenchments facing the lower ravine. Devens's division, on Ricketts's right, had been badly hurt on June 1. Convinced that Devens could only "act on the defensive," Baldy Smith had pulled him out of line and into Martindale's entrenchments, facing north into the interval between the 18th Corps and Warren. After Hancock deployed south of Cold Harbor Road, Wright withdrew Neill's division from the lower end of the Union line, shifted it north through Cold Harbor, and posted it on Ricketts's right flank, where Devens had been. Neill's replacement of Devens precipitated a lively bout of skirmishing—the 139th Pennsylvania, forming Neill's advanced skirmish line, lost its commander, Lieutenant Colonel William H. Moody, shot in the abdomen, and several soldiers were killed or wounded while the regiment relieved the 48th New York. Brooks slid his division south, pressing tightly against Ricketts's northern flank, and Martindale's division took up a front roughly similar to that held by Brooks on June 1, between the central and upper ravines. When these changes were complete, Devens held the north end of Smith's line, facing north; Martindale held a line on Devens's left, facing west; and trailing south of Martindale was Brooks's 18th Corps division and the 6th Corps divisions of Neill, Ricketts, and Russell. The practical effect of these changes was to remove Devens's battle-torn division from the active front and to replace it with two relatively fresh divisions under Martindale and Neill.[68]

Pickett's and Field's 1st Corps divisions extended the rebel line north toward Old Church Road. Opposing them were Crawford's 5th Corps division and a thin line of pickets stringing south from the lower end of Crawford's works. Early's corps picked up near Old Church Road, facing Warren's main body. Ramseur's division formed Early's right, opposite Cutler; Gordon's division continued Early's line north across Old Church Road and bent sharply northeast, angling toward Shady Grove Road and facing Griffin; and Rodes's division, on Early's left, completed the 2nd Corps's line to Shady Grove Road, confronting Griffin and Crittenden. Heth's division picked up there and occupied earthworks along Shady Grove Road looking south, its right near the Bowles farm and its left near Mrs. Via's farm road. Facing north toward Heth was the extreme right of the Federal line, under Potter.

Rain picked up again after dark. Trenches filled with water, and cooking fires sputtered out. Soldiers of both armies spent a miserable night trying to keep dry. "Every indication pointed to an early attack," the Alabamian Evander Law remembered, and his soldiers labored all night putting finishing touches on their earthworks. Still smarting from the loss of Colonel Keitt, the 20th South Carolina erected an impressive set of works. Trained in building coastal fortifications, they constructed a bulwark eight feet high and six to seven feet thick in places. "How much higher, and thicker they would have got it, if the enemy had not interrupted them, gracious only knows!" an artillerist remarked. "Of course they couldn't begin to shoot over it, except at the sky; perhaps they thought anything blue would do to shoot at and the sky was blue. But it was a fact, that when the enemy advanced next morning, this big regiment was positively 'Hors du combat.'" In the battlefield's southern sector, Colonel Edgar asked his brigade commander, Patton, to send him reinforcements or let him change his line so that he no longer had ground hidden from view in front of his salient. "Unable to accomplish either," Edgar later wrote, "I worked my men nearly all night, in the drizzling rain, to strengthen my defenses, leaving but an hour before daylight to lie down and rest, I alone keeping watch." He was depressed, he recollected, "with a sense of impending catastrophe."[69]

General Lee had two pieces of unfinished business. First was his evening dispatch to Richmond. "This morning the enemy's movement to our right continuing, corresponding changes were made in our line, Breckinridge's command and two divisions of General Hill being placed on the right," Lee wrote. "General Early, with Ewell's corps and Heth's division, occupied our left, and was directed to endeavor to get upon the enemy's right flank and drive him down in front of our line. General Early made the movement in the afternoon and drove the enemy from his entrenchments, following him until dark. While this attack was progressing General Hill reinforced Breckinridge with two brigades of Wilcox's division and dislodged the enemy from Turkey Hill, in front of our extreme right."[70]

Lee also had business with his aide McClellan, whom he summoned to his tent. The general was sitting on a camp stool when McClellan entered. A map lay open on his knee. Tracing a road with his index finger, Lee looked at McClellan. "Major," he said, "this is the road to Cold Harbor."

"Yes, General," McClellan answered. "I know."

"Not another word was spoken," McClellan later wrote, "but that quiet reproof sunk deeper and cut more keenly than words of violent vituperation would have done."[71]

The army-wide assault set for 4:30 the next morning was vintage Grant. Hancock, Wright, and Smith were to charge straight ahead "in the hope of driving [Lee] from his position," Grant later explained. Burnside and Warren, facing north, were also to attack "at all hazards," swinging left to help Smith if possible. The corps commanders were enjoined to cooperate, although headquarters provided no mechanism to ensure joint action. Grant and Meade had no patience for mediating squabbles among subordinates.[72]

Meade had instructed his generals to keep the time of the attack secret. Union soldiers, however, could tell as well as their Confederate counterparts that an assault was imminent. Writing more than thirty years later, Grant's aide Porter left a vivid account of Federal troops at Cold Harbor "calmly writing their names and home addresses on slips of paper, and pinning them on the backs of their coats, so that their dead bodies might be recognized upon the field, and their fate made known to their families at home." The scene painted by Porter has become a standard fixture in accounts of the battle. His dramatic scenario is suspect, however, as nothing in letters, diaries, or contemporaneous newspaper accounts corroborates it. Union soldiers did resort to name tags in November 1863, when they thought they would be called to attack an imposing rebel position at Mine Run. But no one who was at Cold Harbor—at least until Porter's narrative appeared—mentioned similar happenings there, raising the likelihood that this is no more than another of the sensational inventions that frequent his memoir. Judging from surviving letter and diaries, Union soldiers were no more concerned about the assault scheduled for the morning of June 3 than they had been before the campaign's other major attacks. "We were acting very much unlike the stern and silent soldiers we read of," a man in the 8th New York Heavy Artillery recalled, "for we were laughing and chatting, speculating upon the prospect before us as if it were a mere holiday or some bore of a parade." The artillerist Frank Wilkeson, visiting another regiment, found "some of the men were sad, some indifferent; some so tired of the strain on their nerves that they wished they were dead and their troubles over."[73]

Grant's plan for June 3 mirrored his assaults on May 10 and May 12 at Spotsylvania Court House, when he had hurled his entire army at Lee's entrenched line, hoping to find a weak spot and break through. The technique had achieved limited success—Upton breached the rebel line on May 10, and Hancock overran the head of the Mule Shoe on May 12—but Union commanders had failed to exploit their gains. Several things had gone wrong.

Sometimes reinforcements had not materialized. Other times, reinforcements had been too plentiful, cramming too many troops into too narrow a front. During both of the big Spotsylvania assaults, field commanders had neglected to coordinate their movements, and no general had been present at the front with overall responsibility for the operation. The big attacks had been disjointed, badly managed affairs, launched in ignorance of Confederate dispositions and trusting to blind luck that troops would stumble upon weak points in the rebel fortifications.

Grant's scheme for June 3 repeated the mistakes made at Spotsylvania. Once again, Lee held formidable earthworks running along strong ground. The Federals had no idea whether Lee had a weak point or where it might be. Yet Grant was about to launch the Army of the Potomac on a general attack with no more cogent plan than the off chance that the Confederate line might collapse somewhere along its length. Had he learned nothing from the previous month's battles?

Grant was aware that grand assaults against entrenched positions had a dismal track record. His last attempt to overrun Lee's line en masse had come on May 18, when Confederate artillery shredded a charge by the Union 2nd and 6th Corps in minutes. Since then, he had eschewed frontal attacks, deciding not to assail Lee's inverted V below the North Anna River and resisting a major attack against Lee's Totopotomoy Creek line. Why now, after more than two weeks of maneuvering and jockeying for position, did he find the time ripe for another major offensive?

Grant's change of mind arose from several practical considerations. High on the list was his assessment of Confederate morale. In the past two weeks, Lee had missed several excellent opportunities. During the maneuvers from Spotsylvania Court House, Grant's army had spread across twenty miles of countryside, leaving several units unsupported and vulnerable to attack. Rather than exploit his windfall, Lee had retreated behind the North Anna. Grant had followed, and again the normally aggressive Lee had held back, permitting Grant to cross part of his army at Jericho Mills before launching a failed attempt to drive him back. Grant had then unwittingly impaled his army across the apex of Lee's inverted V, but Lee had once more neglected to exploit his advantage. "Lee's army is really whipped," Grant had written while on the North Anna, and he believed it. "I may be mistaken, but I feel that our success over Lee's army is already insured," he promised Washington.

Recent events strengthened Grant in his opinion that the Army of Northern Virginia was on its last legs. The Union army executed a risky withdrawal across the North Anna, but Lee did not attack. Then Lee failed to oppose

Grant's crossing of the Pamunkey, permitting the Union force to sidle several miles closer to Richmond without a fight. Lee, it was true, had drawn a strong line along Totopotomoy Creek, but his attempts at offensive action were feeble affairs. Sheridan had driven Hampton back at Haw's Shop; Warren had wrecked Early's foray at Bethesda Church; Sheridan had mauled Butler at Matadequin Creek and repulsed Fitzhugh Lee from Cold Harbor; and wonder of wonders, a handful of Sheridan's regiments had rebuffed Anderson's 1st Corps at Cold Harbor. Wright's and Smith's assaults on the evening of June 1 also offered heartening promise. After all, Federals had broken the Confederate line and rolled up a fair part of it, taking an impressive haul of prisoners. Only nightfall and the absence of reinforcements had prevented a greater victory. But now Hancock was up, Smith was supplied with ammunition, and the attack could be renewed at first light, giving the Union forces a full day to exploit their gains. Viewed from this perspective, now was the time to strike.

In many ways, Lee's deployment at Cold Harbor invited assault. The Chickahominy was in the Confederate rear. If Lee's lines broke, the rebel army would have to funnel across only a few bridges. The confusion would work to Grant's advantage, enabling him to cut off and capture much of the Confederate force. Of equal importance, Grant saw few alternatives other than attacking. Lee's left was anchored on the Totopotomoy swamps and would be difficult to turn. And now that Breckinridge, Wilcox, and Mahone had shifted to Lee's right, that flank was almost impossible to turn as well. Simply put, aside from attacking, Grant's options were to stay where he was and acquiesce in another deadlock or to undertake another broad maneuver south, crossing the Chickahominy downriver from Lee and swinging west toward Richmond below the river. "A serious problem now presented itself to General Grant's mind," the aide Porter later wrote—"whether to attempt to crush Lee's army on the north side of the James, with the prospect in case of success of driving him into Richmond, capturing the city perhaps without a siege, and putting the Confederate government to flight; or to move the Union army south of the James without giving battle, and transfer the field of operations to the vicinity of Petersburg."[74]

Stalemate was not in Grant's program. By remaining in front of Lee at Cold Harbor, Grant would forfeit the initiative, giving the rebels time to regroup and undertake their own offensives, perhaps in combination with Beauregard. Impasse was also politically unacceptable. The Republican convention was opening in Baltimore and would soon nominate its presidential candidate. Lincoln could not have his nation's premier army sitting idly on its haunches, apparently outgeneraled. "The expense of the war had reached nearly four million dollars a day," the aide Porter noted. "Many of the people in the North were becoming discouraged at the prolongation of the contest."

Grant was mindful that maneuvering south and slicing below the Chickahominy avoided stalemate but raised new problems, as the Union army would have to cross a river while engaging the enemy. Grant had managed that feat brilliantly at the North Anna, but Lee might not let him off so easily again. Halleck strongly opposed shifting the battlefront south of the Chickahominy. "It is a most serious obstacle to be passed by a large army or by its supplies," he warned. "Moreover, in the summer months, it is exceedingly unhealthy, as is the James River below Richmond." Even if Grant successfully crossed the Chickahominy, there was no guarantee that he would confront Lee on terms any better than those that he now had. Political considerations kept nagging. "If the army were transferred south of the James without fighting a battle on the north side," Porter recalled of discussions at headquarters, "people would be impatient at the prospect of an apparently indefinite continuation of operations."[75]

Grant also was privy to intelligence that Lee was ill. Warren had alerted Humphreys on May 30 that a deserter reported Lee sick. The next day, Hancock informed headquarters of an escaped slave's account that Lee "went to Richmond sick three days ago." On June 1 a Delaware soldier repeated a deserter's statement that "Lee is ill in Richmond and Ewell in command of the rebels." A southern correspondent on June 2 reported that "yesterday General Lee was brought to the city, too seriously indisposed to longer continue in the field." The ailment—"a derangement of the bowels," he called it—required Lee to rest a few days to regain his health. It is not known whether Grant credited these persistent reports of Lee's illness, but the chance to fight the Army of Northern Virginia when its commander was sick or absent presented an opportunity he would certainly have wanted to exploit.[76]

The decision probably came down to a few points. Dallying at Cold Harbor was politically and militarily unacceptable. "Delays are usually dangerous," the aide Porter noted, "and there was at present too much at stake to admit of further loss of time in ending the war, if it could be avoided." Maneuvering around Lee's northern flank was not feasible, and shifting south entailed crossing the Chickahominy, a risky proposition in light of Lee's proximity. Maneuvering south was also of doubtful utility in light of supply difficulties, the increased likelihood of disease, and uncertainty over whether the move would bring any military advantage. "The front was the assailable part," Humphreys later noted, "though it had not been reported that it was practicable to carry it by assault; and the question was whether to take the chances of an assault there, which, if successful, would give the opportunity of inflicting severe loss upon Lee when falling back over the Chickahominy, as that must necessarily be attended with some disorder of his troops." Grant gained nothing by waiting. He expected no new reinforcements, and delay simply gave Lee more time to dig in.[77]

Different generals might have reached different conclusions based on the same facts. But certainly Grant's decision to attack at Cold Harbor was reasonable given the information at hand and the alternatives. "It was a nice question of judgment," Porter later noted. "After discussing the question thoroughly with his principal officers, and weighing all the chances, he decided to attack Lee's army in its present position. He had succeeded in breaking the enemy's line at Chattanooga, Spotsylvania, and other places under circumstances which were not more favorable, and the results to be obtained now would be so great in case of success that it seemed wise to make the attempt."[78]

While attacking Lee at Cold Harbor made eminent sense, the nature of the assault—an army-wide charge against Lee's entire entrenched line—provoked legitimate criticism. Hancock's aide Walker put his finger on the fallacy of Grant's style of warfare. "The characteristic fault of the campaign," he opined, "was attacking at too many points." As Walker saw it—and it is difficult to disagree with him—Grant's responsibility as commander was to "discover that weak point; to make careful and serious preparation for that attack, and to mass behind the assaulting column a force that shall be irresistible, if only once the line be pierced." Instead, Grant's attacks had been "weak affairs in almost every case, unsupported; and mere shoving forward of a brigade or two now here now there, like a chess player shoving out his pieces and then drawing them right back." Wainwright roundly criticized Grant's penchant for massive attacks across Lee's entire formation. "There may have been some plan in it," he wrote, "but in my ignorance I cannot help but think that one big, sustained attack at one point would have been much more likely to succeed."[79]

Lyman was skeptical from the outset. "I can't say I heard with any great hope the order, given last night, for a general assault at 4:30 the next morning!" he wrote. "But I had no more hope of it, after Spotsylvania, than I had of taking Richmond in two days." An officer in Hancock's corps later noted that "direct assaults on well intrenched lines rarely proved successful during the war." Upton's attack on May 10 and the 2nd Corps's assault against the Mule Shoe on May 12 had almost succeeded, the officer thought, because "in both those instances there was a heavy massing of troops and the assault was against one point only of the enemy's entrenchments." Weighed against that history, the broad attack ordered for the morning of June 3 struck many as tragic. "Now the order was to charge along the whole length of the line, some seven miles or more in length," a critic lamented, "hit or miss."[80]

Warren peppered Meade with grievances all evening. Crittenden had left without warning, he alleged, breaking the connection with the 5th Corps's pickets and enabling Gordon's rebels to exploit the gap between his and Burnside's corps. Burnside's attempt to flank the Confederates with Potter, Warren asserted, "accomplished nothing, and his troops holding them in front did nothing either." The rebels, Warren went on, could not be expected to remain where they were until morning. "I hardly know what you would like to have us to do under the circumstances," he complained. "I will do the best I can when morning comes. If the enemy is where he was this evening, I shall have to fight him here, for I cannot well withdraw to another position. If he has retired I will close in at once with General Smith. My connection with him now is quite complete."[81]

Around 11:00 P.M., Roebling visited Meade's headquarters near Cold Harbor to explain the state of affairs and to deliver a note from Warren. Upset by Warren's and Burnside's inability to cooperate, Roebling asked Meade to come to Bethesda Church in the morning and take command himself. "This he refused at once," Roebling recalled, "saying that at 3 A.M. he had ordered his coffee, at 4 he was going to mount with his staff, and at 6 he would smash the rebel army at Cold Harbor." Meade seemed receptive to the idea of putting either Burnside or Warren in charge at Bethesda Church but directed Roebling to speak with Grant about it. "The Lieutenant General did not have much to say one way or the other," noted Roebling, although Grant did express reservations about putting Warren over Burnside, who was considerably senior. Meade finally dictated a note for Roebling to take back to Warren. Roebling facetiously described it as directing the two generals to be "good boys and not quarrel, that they should attack the enemy at precisely 1800 seconds after 4 o'clock, and if the enemy gave way at all we should at once follow him closing to the left and south." Observed Roebling: "Inasmuch as the enemy was due north of us this latter injunction was a manifest impossibility." Leaving his frustrating interview, Roebling discovered that someone had stolen his horse. He returned to Warren at 2:00 A.M. on a borrowed mount.[82]

Roebling's interview with the army's high command boded poorly for the impending offensive. Neither Grant nor Meade had visited the front. They had no understanding of the terrain, failed to grasp the disposition of either their own force or the enemy's, and evidenced no interest in coordinating their corps. The assault would be a blind charge, trusting to luck. Unfortunately for the soldiers making the attack, luck on the Union side had run out.

X

June 3, 4:30–5:30 a.m.

Hancock, Wright, and Smith Attack at Cold Harbor

"A simple brute rush in open day on strong works."

RAIN FELL SHORTLY before daylight on June 3, "refreshingly us exceedingly," a Federal recalled. Mist hugged close to the ground, obscuring objects more than a few yards ahead. Moisture dripped from trees, and fog seemed unusually dense. The scene was chillingly familiar to the Union 2nd Corps's veterans. Three weeks before, on a foggy, rain-drenched morning very much like this one, they had lined up for a 4:30 a.m. charge against Lee's Mule Shoe at Spotsylvania Court House. Now their superiors wanted them to repeat that performance. "I must confess that order was not received with much hilarity," a corporal in the 19th Maine recalled. "There was some hooting at the brigade commanders by the soldiers, but when it was ascertained that these officers themselves were going to lead the men, there was no further hesitation."[1]

A signal gun was to announce the attack, sending Hancock's, Wright's, and Smith's corps lunging toward the Confederate entrenchments. To the north, Warren and Burnside were to attack as well, pinning down Confederate troops there and swinging south, if possible, rolling up the Confederate line and taking pressure off Smith's northern flank.

Grant had ordered the offensive. Meade, however, was responsible for deploying his corps, coordinating their movements, and posting reserves to exploit any gains. "I had immediate and entire command of the field all day," Meade wrote his wife. The Pennsylvanian still smarted from the humiliation of his subordinate position and thoroughly disapproved of Grant's hard-hitting, army-wide assaults. Facing a disagreeable assignment, he dealt with it by doing little. The record reveals no steps to reconnoiter the ground, coordinate the army's elements, or tend to the things that diligent generals ordinarily do before sending soldiers against fortified enemy lines. During the finger-pointing following the botched assaults at Spotsylvania, Grant's aides had decried Meade's inability to translate Grant's plans into action. "The result of Grant's having a middleman was to make the whole organization wooden," Lieutenant Colonel Adam Badeau had observed. "Meade severed the nerve between the commander in chief and the army. He was a non-conductor." Grant was well aware that Meade was ill-suited to his aggressive style of fighting but felt he had to keep him on. Someone, after all, had to manage the tactical minutiae of running the army. June 3 would underscore the consequences of leaving operational details of a major offensive to a general with no heart for the assignment.[2]

Meade announced the time for the attack and left his corps commanders to cooperate. Baldy Smith, his 18th Corps divisions in place immediately to the north of Wright's formation, asked Wright about his plan of attack and offered to subordinate his charge to the 6th Corps's assault. "His reply was that he was going to assault in his front," Smith later wrote. "I was, therefore, forced to make mine independently, yet keeping up the communication with the 6th Corps." Nothing suggests that Wright and Hancock attempted to coordinate their offensives. And on the army's northern wing, relations between Warren and Burnside, true to Roebling's prediction, had deteriorated so badly that the two generals ceased communicating. As events developed, Warren and Burnside would not start their attacks until nearly three hours after the appointed time, leaving Hancock, Wright, and Smith to make the great attack at Cold Harbor unaided. The Army of the Potomac was a dysfunctional family, and the man charged with bringing harmony to it had no patience for the task.[3]

Hancock's plan was a model of simplicity. Barlow and Gibbon were to "attack at such points on the front of their respective divisions as the commanders may select at 4:30 A.M.," he instructed, while Birney remained in reserve, "ready to support either." Hancock's soldiers had shifted into position late on June 2, and no one, including division heads, had a clear idea of the terrain they would cross or the precise layout of the enemy line. "The division commanders only knew that they were to push forward until they struck the enemy's works," an officer recorded. "The attack was a simple brute rush in open day on strong works."[4]

Barlow's division held the southern end of the attack formation. Nelson Miles's brigade stood as Barlow's left wing, with the 26th Michigan arrayed as skirmishers and supported by the 140th Pennsylvania to protect the division's southern flank. Miles's battle line, from south to north, consisted of the 81st Pennsylvania, 61st New York, 183rd Pennsylvania, and 5th New Hampshire. Colonel Joseph N. C. Whistler's 2nd New York Heavy Artillery—a novice regiment containing some 1,700 soldiers that had joined the army at the end of the Spotsylvania campaign—held the right of Miles's formation. Waiting in reserve behind Miles was Colonel Richard Byrnes's famed Irish Brigade, containing the 69th, 88th, and 63rd New York, the 28th Massachusetts, and the 116th Pennsylvania. Barlow's right wing consisted of Colonel John R. Brooke's brigade posted in two lines. The first line contained Colonel Lewis Morris's 7th New York Heavy Artillery, a large, newly arrived regiment with more men than the rest of Brooke's regiments combined. After joining up with the army on May 18, Morris's soldiers had fought their first serious engagement at Totopotomoy Creek five days before. The 148th Pennsylvania, 53rd Pennsylvania, 145th Pennsylvania, 2nd Delaware, and the 64th and 66th New York made up Brooke's second line. In reserve behind Brooke waited MacDougall's brigade of New Yorkers.[5]

Roused from slumber at 3:30 A.M., Barlow's troops formed in woods several hundred yards east of Dispatch Station Road. Half of the 148th Pennsylvania, under Major Robert H. Forster, spread out in front as skirmishers. Their assignment was to drive rebel pickets back to the main works and then drop to the ground while the rest of the brigade passed over them. Shortly before 4:30, Forster's skirmishers disappeared into the mist toward Dispatch Station Road. Spattering gunfire announced they had engaged rebel pickets. Artillery opened from the distant rebel line, and the 11th New York Independent Battery in Brooke's rear replied. After a few minutes, an aide rode through the powder smoke and ordered the guns to stop firing. The infantry was about to charge.[6]

At 4:30 A.M., the 10th Massachusetts Light fired a shot signaling the attack. "Then was there indeed a veritable tempest," Private John D. Billings of the battery recalled. "At once it was responded to by the entire line, and by the rebels as well, who seemed to have been anticipating it. It had the fury of the Wilderness musketry, with the thunders of the Gettysburg artillery superadded." Reminisced Billings: "It was simply terrific."[7]

Barlow's two front brigades stepped off, Brooke on the right and Miles on the left. Brooke rode with the 7th New York Heavy Artillery as it passed out of the woods and into a field, tramping through "damp, tall, wet grass and clinging bushes." Reaching the field's western edge, soldiers descended into the trace of Dispatch Station Road, worn a few feet below the ground by years of traffic. A small field extended to the west. Beyond, the ground rose to the Confederate works.[8]

On the far ridge stood the salient in Breckinridge's line, held by Colonel

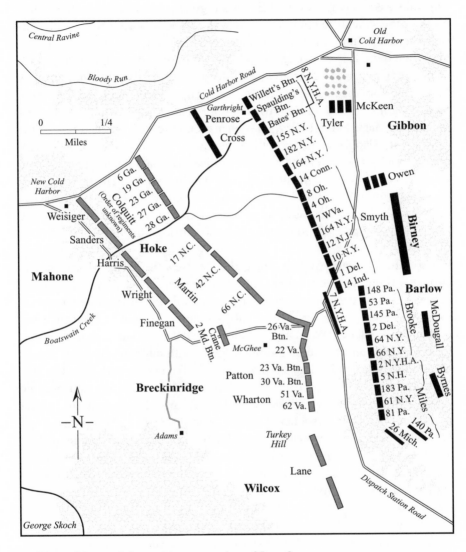

Hancock's attack formation on morning of June 3

Edgar's 26th Virginia Battalion, the 22nd Virginia's Kanawha Company, and Captain Caskie's guns. More of Edgar's regiment manned the stretch of line north of the salient, joining on its left with the 66th North Carolina of Martin's brigade. South of the salient waited the 22nd Virginia and the 23rd Virginia Battalion. Edgar's trenches had flooded during the night, driving some of his soldiers back to drier ground to sleep. Spotting Barlow's lines as they "emerged from the mist in our front," Edgar hurried his troops into position. Caskie's guns opened on the advancing blue-clad forms, as did Captain Dement's 1st Maryland Artillery, on higher ground to the right and rear of the salient, "its Napoleons firing nothing but canister." Retreating Confederate pickets briefly obstructed the artillery until a Maryland gunner jumped onto the works and waved them out of the way with his swab. "The fire ran down our lines from left to right like the keys of a piano," remembered a man in the 66th North Carolina, "and to the sharp crack of our rifles was added the roar of artillery as it joined them in the wild music of the hour—the carnival of death."[9]

Crossing Dispatch Station Road, the 7th New York Heavy Artillery in Brooke's front line came under brutal fire. The color bearer was shot, and a volunteer seized the colors. Two more bearers fell, and twice more volunteers took their places. "The air seemed buoyant and we were flying," recollected Lieutenant Frederick W. Mather of the regiment. "Cannon belched forth a torrent of canister, the works glowed brightly with musketry, a storm of lead and iron struck the blue line, cutting gaps in it," a gunner with the 11th New York Light saw from the rear. "Still they pushed on, and on, and on," he wrote. "But, how many of them fell!" Officers urged men on at the double quick, and the mass of soldiers scrambled up the incline. "The ground was blue with the dead and wounded who fell under the deadly fire of our artillery and infantry at close range," Colonel Edgar recollected, "far more than the writer ever saw fall on an equal area on any other battlefield." Reaching the sheltered hollow in front of the salient, the New Yorkers regrouped. "The grape and canister went over our heads with a 'swish,'" Mather wrote, "much as a charge of fine shot goes among a flock of blackbirds."[10]

Re-forming his regiment, Colonel Morris ordered them ahead. Bayonets flashing, soldiers of the 7th New York Heavy Artillery poured over the salient's walls and into the defenders. Virginians met them at the parapets, shooting and stabbing. Crammed tightly together, men waged brutal, individual fights with bayonets and muskets wielded like clubs. "Here was enacted one of those awful scenes so seldom known in war," recollected Lieutenant W. W. George of Edgar's battalion. "The fighting was at close range, and hand to hand." A Federal shot George in the neck and rammed a bayonet into his left side, only to be brained by a Confederate bashing him over the head with a gun butt. "Clubbed muskets, bayonets, and swords got in their deadly work," confirmed Augustus Du Bois of the 7th New York. "As I reached the top of the works a brave fellow confronted us," he remembered. "Standing below he thrust the bayonet into the comrade by my side and was about to give me the same dose, but a charge from my gun changed his mind."[11]

Combat swirled around Sergeant George Allen Woodrum, the 26th Virginia Battalion's illiterate, twenty-year-old color bearer who had fearlessly led his company in the attack on Sigel's lines at New Market. The night before, Woodrum had found a brass bar shaped like a spear. Polishing it, he had fastened it on the end of his flagstaff and shown it to Captain Morton, who remarked that it looked pretty. "It is not only pretty," Woodrum responded, "but if anybody tries to get these colors, I'll run this through him." Captain Morton thought it unlikely that the enemy would get close enough for Woodrum to use his spear, but the young man was insistent. "We are going to have a graveyard fight tomorrow," he predicted, "and are mighty apt to get mixed up."[12]

Woodrum, Colonel Edgar, and the battalion's adjutant, Brown Craig, stood in the middle of the salient, surrounded by the swirling melee. Spotting the flag, a Union officer and two men elbowed through the mob to Woodrum and demanded that he surrender the banner. "This is the way I surrender, damn you," Woodrum shouted and ran the spear through the officer's body. The men accompanying the officer shot Woodrum, who fell tightly gripping the staff. More Yankees rushed for the flag, but rebels drove them back. According to Captain Morton, Woodrum opened his eyes, "saw that his precious flag was still safe, and with one last superhuman effort pulled himself forward and, reaching over, tore the colors from the staff, threw them behind [the enemy], and fell back a corpse." Christopher B. Humphreys of the regiment clasped the flag until four Federals wrested it from him and passed it back out of sight. Corporal Terrence Begley of the 7th New York Heavy Artillery was credited with capturing the flag. Killed a few months later at Reams Station, he posthumously received the Medal of Honor for his feat. Federals bayoneted Edgar in the shoulder, captured him, and killed his adjutant Craig. Resistance was futile, and Edgar's Virginians began surrendering. One enraged Confederate fired into the 7th New York's color guard, then threw down his musket and hollered, "I surrender." The regiment's color sergeant jammed his flagstaff's steel point into the rebel's mouth. "You spoke too late!" he roared. Herding captives into low ground immediately behind the salient, Federals made them bow low and mark time to the tune of "Yankee Doodle."[13]

Patton's officers later emphatically denied that their troops had broken and run. Witnesses from nearby units saw things differently. Edgar's battalion, an officer in the 66th North Carolina asserted, "gave way and yielded with scarcely more than a show of resistance." A Marylander in the reserve line thought the Virginians ran "at a rate of speed that would have distanced any modern sprinter that I have seen and ruled him out of the race."[14]

Miles's brigade—all of it except the 26th Michigan and 140th Pennsylvania, picketing the army's flank—stepped off on the left of the 7th New York Heavy Artillery. The ridge across from Miles rose less sharply than in Brooke's front. Miles had no sheltered places, leaving his troops exposed during most of their advance. Wharton's Virginians tore into them with heavy fire. The 2nd New York Heavy Artillery, on the right of Miles's line, took severe casualties—over ninety by one count—and dove for cover in the depression carved by Dispatch Station Road. The three veteran Pennsylvania and New York regiments on Miles's left also halted, probably huddling in the road cut as well. Only one of Miles's regiments—the 5th New Hampshire—kept advancing.

Commanded by Colonel Charles E. Hapgood, the 5th New Hampshire boasted a venerable history. It had fought in most of the Potomac army's big battles and had seen bloody combat in the Wheatfield at Gettysburg. The regiment's survivors had returned to New Hampshire in August of 1863 and then spent the winter and spring guarding prisoners at Point Lookout, Maryland. Numbering 550 men, many of them new recruits, the regiment rejoined the Army of the Potomac on June 1 in time to participate in Hancock's all-night march to the army's southern flank. This was their first combat operation since Gettysburg, and they were anxious to show they still had their fighting edge.[15]

A sergeant alerted Hapgood that regiments on both sides of the 5th New Hampshire had halted in the roadbed, but the colonel insisted that his troops press on. Up the ridge to the right, Morris's New Yorkers were overrunning the Confederate line. Enemy fire seemed lighter there, so Hapgood directed his troops to execute a right half-wheel and march toward the south face of the salient, some four hundred yards away. "In making the right wheel on the double quick," a New Hampshire sergeant recollected, "the left wing of the regiment was somewhat confused owing to the men taking the short cut, as we used to call it, so our line was more than a single line when we struck the works." Moving quickly without pausing to fire, Hapgood's regiment broke into the southern edge of Edgar's salient next to the 7th New York Heavy Artillery and began scooping up prisoners.[16]

Colonel Patton and Captain John K. Thompson, heading the 22nd Virginia, watched the New Hampshire soldiers storming over the works on their left. Estimating that Hapgood's trajectory would take him through the main Confederate line, Patton ordered Thompson to keep his men in place and dispatched his adjutant to alert the Maryland and Florida troops in the rear.[17]

Punching into the salient, Hapgood spotted the Confederate reserve line occupied by Captain Crane's 2nd Maryland three hundred yards west. A rise sheltered Crane's men from direct fire, and buildings—the McGehee family dwelling—obscured their view. A few hundred yards behind the Marylanders and somewhat to their left were entrenchments manned by Finegan's Floridians. Hapgood decided to press his attack before the southerners had time to react.

Continuing beyond the salient, the 5th New Hampshire advanced toward McGehee's house. A few Maryland troops spotted them approaching but assumed they were Confederates. Their true identity became clear as they gathered around the house and outbuildings and began firing into Crane's men, killing a few soldiers still wrapped in blankets. Private Charles H. Weems of the 2nd Maryland squinted through the fog at the flag waving by the McGehee house. "I see the gridiron, boys," Weems called. At the same moment Captain John W. Torsch cried out, "Let's charge 'em! It is the enemy—charge!" Crane's men—there were about four hundred of them—needed no urging. "Descrying the stars and stripes within our lines, they made what I can only describe as a spontaneous charge," a Maryland soldier recollected, "every man seemingly inspired with the idea that upon him depended the fate of the day."[18]

Finegan's Floridians also recognized the crisis. "The Yanks didn't stop, but kept right on," recalled Private Dorman of the brigade. "By this time it was getting light so we could see them coming. They were about seventy-five to eighty yards from us." Captain Council Bryan of the 5th Florida watched panic-stricken Virginians running back, "hatless, leaving their guns and anything that impeded their flight." The Floridians waited until the stampeding Virginians were out of the way, then charged east, seeking to batter back Hapgood's Federals. "Our boys rose with a yell," Captain Bryan recollected, "poured two volleys into the advancing droves of Yankees then jumped the breastworks and charged them." Mounting the works his troops had built during the night, Colonel David Lang of the 8th Florida waved his men on. "Charge, boys, charge!" he shouted. "We all rose," remembered Dorman, "and with a yell fired our muskets toward them and moved forward quick time."[19]

Marylanders and Floridians each later claimed to have spearheaded the Confederate counterattack, relegating their rivals to a supporting role. Perhaps J. William Thomas, a Maryland soldier, got it right in his diary. "Yanks break our line a little to our left and front," he wrote. "The line in rear of us [Finegan's Floridians] charge. No order given us, but a majority of the [Maryland] battalion cannot be restrained and rush in with them."[20]

Running furiously on Finegan's right, Crane's troops charged into the McGehee house and outbuildings. The New Hampshire soldiers fought stubbornly, some crawling under the house and shooting from behind brick piers supporting the structure. The Confederate onslaught was irresistible and forced Hapgood's regiment back into the salient. The 66th North Carolina, north of the breach, bent back its right and, according to Martin's adjutant, Captain Charles G. Elliott, "fired hotly upon the enemy on the front and on the right."[21]

Crane's and Finegan's momentum carried the two brigades into the salient's base, where Morris's New Yorkers were locked in furious combat with the remnants of Edgar's Virginians, corralling prisoners and squelching stubborn pockets of resistance. "Looking off in a field beyond, what was our dismay in seeing a long line of gray approaching on the run," Du Bois of the 7th New York recollected. "We had lost all semblance of organization," he admitted. "Green soldiers though we were, our short experience had taught us to know just when to run, and run we did, I assure you." Colonel Morris kept his head. Gathering several New Yorkers around him, he had them load two of Caskie's captured guns with powder and canister and turn them on the Confederates. The pieces were ready to fire, but Morris could not find the friction primers necessary to discharge them.[22]

Marylanders and Floridians slammed into the "veritable mob," as a participant termed the mass of soldiers from New York, New Hampshire, and Virginia packed inside the salient. At the same time, Captain Thompson's Confederates from the 22nd Virginia, south of the salient, pinched across the base of the V, and fire from the 66th North Carolina slanted in from the north. "The conflict was brief but terrible," a Marylander reported. "It was hand to hand; the artillery was wrested from the Federals, and they were driven out of the salient at the point of the bayonet." Some of Crane's troops had drilled in artillery during the previous winter, and Lieutenant Charles B. Wise of the regiment solicited volunteers to man Caskie's guns. Turning the pieces on the Federals—and apparently finding the missing friction primers—they sprayed canister into the enemy at close range. Lieutenant Samuel T. McCullough of the 2nd Maryland, shot within ten yards of the salient's tip, wrote that he "had the satisfaction of seeing the bluebellies lying in heaps in front of me."[23]

The 5th New Hampshire was in a terrible predicament. "The other regiments of [Miles's] brigade had not carried the enemy's works," Hapgood recognized, "and that part of [Brooke's] brigade, which went over on our right, was obliged to retire." The 5th New Hampshire, the regiment's Major James E. Larkin admitted, was "unavoidably in some disorder from charging so great a distance, fired upon from front and both flanks, and failing of any support." The Granite State men's only hope was to escape through the tangle of troops, and Hapgood gave the order to retreat. "Back we went," a New Englander remembered, "being assisted by the battery on the left, which had been manned again." Their rearward trajectory angled them across the 23rd Virginia Battalion. "We saw the enemy flying in great disorder back to their own lines, from the salient angle and the line thereof nearest to our front, moving across our front in much plainer view than when they charged a few minutes before," Lieutenant Colonel Clarence Derrick of the 23rd Virginia Battalion recalled. "We poured volleys into the flying crowd."[24]

Brooke's second line, containing his veteran regiments, had advanced to Dispatch Station Road, and MacDougall's brigade, charged with supporting Brooke, stood ready east of the road, where the 7th New York Heavy Artillery's advance had begun. Birney's entire division, some 8,000 strong, waited in reserve, listening to the roar of combat and waiting for the signal to join in. The signal never came. "There in our front lay, sat, and stood the second line, the supports," the artillerist Wilkeson later noted. "Why did they not go forward and make good the victory?"[25]

The answer to Wilkeson's query is not altogether clear. Brooke, it seems, had ridden forward with the 7th New York Heavy Artillery, witnessed the regiment's breakthrough, and ridden back to adjust his second line's direction of march to ensure that it hit the salient squarely. He had just directed Colonel James A. Beaver, commanding the second line, to wheel his troops to the right when canister knocked him unconscious. "Tell Colonel Beaver he is in command and to push into the works," Brooke instructed when he regained his senses. An aide conveyed the order to Beaver, who started the second line up the hill. According to the 148th Pennsylvania's adjutant, Lieutenant Joseph W. Muffly, the delay occasioned by Brooke's wounding proved fatal. "The enemy's supports crowded into the works which had just been carried," he wrote, "the assaulting troops began to stream back, [and the supporting line] was checked at the rail fence half way up the slope, not thirty yards from the enemy's position." Recognizing the salient as a "death trap," most of Beaver's men began entrenching, all the while under plunging fire from rebels in the salient and along the adjoining stretch of works. A few soldiers reached the crest and helped retard the Confederates so that Federal troops in the salient could escape. Casualties were severe and included Colonel Orlando H. Morris, leading the 66th New York. "We dropped under the hill," Beaver related, "pushed up gradually and got a little dirt thrown up which soon grew into a rifle pit." Adjutant Muffly recorded that "plates and bayonets, bare hands and rails from the fence, extended the work, deepened and established it, until it gave a precarious shelter." Concluding that the attack was a failure, Barlow decided against sending MacDougall into the fray.[26]

Byrnes's Irish Brigade, supporting Miles, contributed little to the assault. Jettisoning several men unfit for duty "between fatigue and green apples," the brigade advanced behind Miles and came under grueling fire from Wharton's Virginians. "I never had balls whistle so thick apast me nor ever want them to whistle half so thick again," a Pennsylvanian wrote home. Most of Byrnes's troops stopped at Dispatch Station Road and hid in the cut, vying for space with elements from Miles's brigade seeking shelter in the same depression. There they came under direct fire from Wharton and enfilading fire from Lieutenant Colonel William J. Pegram's Confederate 3rd Corps batteries farther south on the ridge. "So long as the men could hug the ground the loss was not great," a Federal recounted, "as the pieces could not be depressed sufficiently to strike the line." Retreating across the clearing behind them proved to be a different matter. "As the men were absolutely without shelter," a soldier related, "they fell in great numbers." A minié ball passed through the arm and back of Captain James D. Brady of the 63rd New York and struck Colonel Byrnes, commanding the brigade, mortally wounding him.[27]

Abandoned and without support, Morris did his best to extricate his 7th New York Heavy Artillery from Confederates closing in from three sides. The artillerist Wilkeson looked on from high ground east of Dispatch Station Road. "The powder smoke curled lowly in thin clouds above the captured works," he observed. "Then the firing became more and more thunderous. The tops of many battle flags could be seen indistinctly, and then there was a heavy and fierce yell, and the thrilling battle-cry of the Confederate infantry floated to us." Suddenly the New Yorkers who had entered the works a few minutes before came tumbling back, heading for the relative safety of Beaver's makeshift works and the swale. "All organization was lost," Wilkeson saw. "The Confederate infantry appeared behind their works and nimbly climbed over, as though intent on following up their success, and their fire was as the fury of hell."[28]

Regrouping his shattered regiment behind Beaver's fortifications, Morris attempted a counterattack up the hill to recover the salient. "They were repulsed by our men with heavy loss," a Floridian observed. "The ground in front was covered with dead and wounded Yankees, and they were glad to retire." Carnage was also evident inside the salient. "The land was almost covered with dead and dying men," noted Private Dorman, "from one breast-works to the other." Bending low behind their entrenchments, soldiers of the 7th Heavy Artillery "pressed their bodies into the earth, like moles," a student of the regiment noted. "Fought like hell and got licked like damnation," was the New Yorker Mather's verdict on the assault.[29]

The fight at Edgar's salient had been brief. Men who were there estimated that it lasted between ten and twenty minutes. "The whole thing seemed to pass like a skyrocket," Lieutenant Colonel Derrick of the 23rd Virginia Battalion remembered. Confederate losses were relatively small. Edgar's battalion, which absorbed the shock of the attack, lost 219 men, and the Kanawha Company lost about 25. Crane's Marylanders got off relatively lightly, losing 6 killed and 32 wounded, and the Florida brigade lost about 30. Many captured Confederates managed to escape when the Union troops fled. When Colonel Edgar heard the Floridians and Marylanders charging, he fell to the ground and refused to go on, pointing to the bayonet wound in his shoulder. His captors fled, leaving him between hostile lines. "I lay flat on my belly until Finegan's brigade drove the penetrating column over our works," Edgar reminisced, "and then crawled in." Edgar's men enjoyed tormenting their prisoners, some of whom were their former captors. "Bow to your betters, Yanks," they instructed, mimicking the humiliating routine the Federals had recently put them through. "Sing Dixie with all your might and holler for Jeff Davis!"[30]

By a recent count, the 7th New York Heavy Artillery suffered 422 casualties during the brief fight, with 84 killed, 261 wounded, and 77 captured. The 5th New Hampshire, which went into the fight with only 550 men, lost 202, well over a third of its strength.[31]

"It was simply a butchery."

Gibbon's division held the northern wing of Hancock's formation, reaching across open fields from the right end of Barlow's line on Dispatch Station Road north to Cold Harbor Road, a distance of about a mile. The Corcoran Legion was on the north of Gibbon's line, its right anchored on Cold Harbor Road, near the Garthright house. Raised in New York in 1862 by Brigadier General Michael Corcoran, a popular figure in the Irish community, the brigade had initially consisted of the 155th, 164th, 182nd, and 170th New York. Its assignments had been humdrum affairs, including outpost duties at Newport News and Suffolk and guard duty along the Orange and Alexandria Railroad. The colorful Corcoran had died in December 1863, and in mid-May war had caught up with his Legion, which joined the Army of the Potomac in time to participate in Grant's final attack at Spotsylvania Court House.

After crossing the Pamunkey, Meade had brought the Legion up to fighting strength by adding the 8th New York Heavy Artillery. The Legion also received a new commander, Brigadier General Robert O. Tyler. A West Point graduate versed in artillery, Tyler was no stranger to combat, having fought in McClellan's Peninsula campaign as well as at Fredericksburg, Chancellorsville, and Gettysburg, where he had headed the artillery reserve. He had returned to the army on May 18 commanding a division of heavy artillery regiments. The 8th New York Heavy Artillery more than doubled the size of the Corcoran Legion—the fat regiment contained over 1,600 soldiers—but added nothing by way of experience. Like other heavy artillery regiments sent to Virginia in May 1864, it had spent the war in garrison duties. Recruited in western New York, it was led by Colonel Peter A. Porter, a Harvard graduate and son of a former secretary of war and hero of the War of 1812. Ironically, Porter's cousin was John Breckinridge, heading the Confederate division posted a short distance to his south, and his wife Mary was also a Breckinridge.

Tyler arrayed the Corcoran Legion in a single line of two ranks nearly half a mile long. On the brigade's right, nearest Cold Harbor Road, was Colonel Porter's 8th New York Heavy Artillery. Major James Willett's 1st Battalion held the right of the regiment, next to the road; Major Erastus M. Spaulding's 2nd Battalion stood on Willett's left; and Lieutenant Colonel Willard W. Bates's 3rd Battalion formed the regiment's left flank. The rest of the Legion extended south, with the 155th New York adjoining the 8th New York Heavy Artillery, then the 182nd New York, and finally the 164th New York on the left end of the brigade. The 170th New York, which had taken severe casualties at the North Anna, remained in reserve to protect Gibbon's artillery.[32]

The terrain that the Legion had to cross was formidable. Willett and Spaulding faced Colquitt's Georgians across the same half mile of cleared ground that had cost Penrose, Cross, and the Vermont troops so dearly on June 1. Penrose and Cross, still holding advanced positions secured during their earlier attack, could attest to the tremendous firepower that Colquitt had concentrated on the clearing. "There was little passing between the regiment and the rear," a man in Penrose's outfit remembered. "It was foolhardiness to run any unnecessary risk. There was a constant fire from the rebel sharpshooters, that hit almost every man that exposed himself."[33]

Boatswain Creek's headwaters originated south of Spaulding's battalion to form a swampy, heavily wooded tract a quarter mile across. When the 8th New York Heavy Artillery advanced, its southernmost battalion, under Bates, along with the 155th New York and 182nd New York on Bates's left, would head directly into the swamp. The 164th New York, on the southern end of the Legion's line, could avoid the worst of the marshy ground by veering around its southern edge. That maneuver, however, would detach the regiment from the rest of the brigade and bring it against a segment of rebel works held by Martin's Tar Heels. Although headquarters had ordered reconnaissances, Hancock and Gibbon were apparently ignorant of Boatswain Creek and the disruption it would cause their charge. The failure of Union planners to take the swamp into account was especially puzzling because the creek had been an integral part of the Federal defensive line during the Battle of Gaines's Mill in June 1862.

Smyth's brigade stretched south from Tyler's left, reaching toward Barlow's northern flank. Extending in double lines from north to south were the 14th Connecticut, 8th and 4th Ohio, 7th West Virginia, 12th New Jersey, 10th New York, 1st Delaware, and 14th Indiana, facing Martin's entrenched North Carolinians. Unlike Tyler's less experienced soldiers, Smyth's troops were seasoned veterans, having fought with the Army of the Potomac since Antietam. Gibbon's remaining two brigades waited in reserve, McKeen behind Tyler and Owen behind Smyth. Gibbon directed them to form in "close column of regiments," each brigade's regiments stacked in successive lines, one behind the other, giving the brigades relatively narrow fronts but considerable depth. They were to wait until Tyler's and Smyth's extended lines found weak points. Then, as Gibbon later explained, they were to "push rapidly forward and over the front line in column and effect a lodgment, if possible, on the enemy's works, and not to deploy till they got there."[34]

Colonel Peter Porter had spent an anxious night. The impending attack across half a mile of open ground was bound to cost his 8th New York Heavy Artillery dearly. Major Willett, commanding the 1st Battalion, on the right of Porter's line, sought shelter from the drizzle under a tree near the Garthright house. Before daylight, Porter, who had been up all night, visited Willett. Sitting together on a log, they drank coffee and discussed the charge they were to make at dawn. A few bullets smacked nearby—sharpshooters, Willett thought—and the colonel stood to leave. "With a smile and in a cheerful tone, he spoke a few kind words," Willett reminisced, "and was leaving me when he turned about, reached out his hand, and with a shake of anxiety and sorrow on his face said, 'Goodby Major,' and was gone."[35]

The 8th New York Heavy Artillery's deployment into a line of two ranks worried some soldiers. "When a charge is usually made it is done by massing four or five lines so as to make it a positive victory," Lieutenant Eli Nichols of the regiment wrote a few days later. "We had no support, not even a single line. Everyone knew that it must be death to move." Lieutenant Nichols was mistaken about the absence of support—McKeen's brigade was waiting to exploit a breakthrough should one materialize—but he faithfully captured the men's mood. They were about to embark on their first major attack, and they were nervous. "A light rain was falling," Private Nelson Armstrong remembered, "and through the dim light we could see the gray uniforms, the rows of shining bayonets, and the enemy serenely waiting and watching our movements behind strong fortifications."[36]

Colquitt's Georgians squinted back through the fog toward the distant Union line. Troops seemed to be massing, presaging an attack. "This morning early the enemy began to show symptoms of making another assault," William Smith of the 23rd Georgia wrote in his diary. Safe behind their entrenchments, Colquitt's men relished a Union attack. "This campaign is the first in which our troops have had the privilege of fighting behind protection of any kind, and it is fun for them," a Georgian explained. "They lounge about with their accoutrements on and gun close at hand, laughing and talking until someone passes it up or down the line, 'look out boys, here they come.' Every man springs to his place, and waits until the enemy gets close up, when the rear rank fires by volleys, then the front rank, after which each one fires soon as he can load. Some load for others to shoot—each working rapidly, but calmly, until the enemy are repulsed." The Georgians were ready for the New Yorkers.[37]

At the signal gun's discharge, Major Willett ordered his men over their protective works. "Standing upon the parapet I looked anxiously to the left about a minute," Willett recollected, "when I saw Colonel Porter suddenly appear upon the top of the breastworks near the extreme left of the regiment." Porter drew his sword, jumped onto the works by the colors, and with a flourish of his blade ordered the men ahead. "It was but the work of a moment to form our line," recollected Captain James Maginnis, temporarily commanding Spaulding's battalion, "and on we went, guns at a trail, arms and bayonets fixed."[38]

Penrose's men, still in their advanced entrenchments, were under orders to join the attack when Tyler's line reached them. Looking back, they watched the 8th New York Heavy Artillery start across the clearing. "When we first saw them the enemy did also, and opened fire on them," a man in the 15th New Jersey recalled. "They had to cross the same wide field we had passed on the first, every inch of it swept by the enemy."[39]

Musketry and cannon fire picked up from the far works. The clearing afforded no cover, and men began falling. "The rebels instantly opened on us a perfect storm of musketry, all along the lines, also grape and canister, and the air was full of messengers of death," Captain Maginnis recalled. "The lead and iron filled the air as the snow flakes in an angry driving storm." Major Willett's brother Joseph remembered that the "work of death" began right away. "Shells screamed through the air bursting over our heads while the rattle of musketry was terrible," he wrote. Closer the 8th New York Heavy Artillery drew to Colquitt's line, and men fell faster, survivors closing gaps in the ranks. Soldiers crowded together, instinctively seeking comfort from the press of others around them. They advanced more rapidly, first at a double-quick, then some broke into a run. It seemed to Lieutenant Nichols that "few men fell until we reached within [eighty yards] of the enemy's first line, when they opened upon us with canister [and] grape hurling it into our faces and mowing down our lines as wheat falls before the reaper." He found it "terrible to see our brave boys falling so rapidly and without a chance of success," as he put it in a letter home a few days later. "God grant that I may never see the like again."[40]

Willett's and Maginnis's battalions jammed into the interval between Boatswain Swamp and the road. The third battalion, under Bates, peeled left, slipping south of the swamp. Slammed by relentless fire, Willett broke connection with Maginnis. Sixth Corps troops on Willett's right—Eustis's brigade of Russell's division—had not advanced, baring Willett's right flank to angling fire from Hagood's South Carolinians north of Cold Harbor Road. Willett continued over entrenchments thrown up by the New Jersey troops— "the 8th New York charged over us and on toward the enemy," a man in the 10th New Jersey noted—and emerged into horrendous fire. "Major Willett attempted to close the ranks, drew his revolver and was about to give the command to fire when a ball struck him in the shoulder passing out I believe above the lung just grazing the jugular vein," Willett's brother recorded. "On, still unfaltering, the Battalion passed until within [twenty yards] of the rebel breastworks—when a terrible enfilading fire of grape and canister swept along the line." Troops, he noted, "fell as grass before the Reaper—only swifter." The charge's momentum stalled, "stopped from sheer exhaustion within a stone's throw of the enemy's works." Continuing on was impossible, and retreating across the open field spelt certain death. "After halting in our charge," Lieutenant Henry R. Swan wrote home the next day, "we could neither advance nor retire." A Georgian remembered that he and his companions "had a cross fire on them that it was almost impossible for a man to live under." Washington L. Dunn of the 27th Georgia noted in his diary that the Federals "did not come closer than our rifle pits."[41]

Attrition in command was tremendous. Early in the charge a cannonball shattered Tyler's ankle. Colonel Porter, now commanding the brigade, pressed on at the head of the 8th New York, almost to Colquitt's works. There a bullet tore through his neck, knocking him to the ground. According to one account, he stood partway up, fell to his knees, and cried, "Dress upon the colors!" Riddled by as many as six bullets, he toppled lifeless in front of the Confederate line. Command devolved on Colonel James P. McIvor of the 170th New York. McIvor, however, was in the rear with his regiment, guarding the artillery, and powerless to influence developments at the front.[42]

Porter's leftmost battalion, under Bates, slanted south into a stand of thick timber and undergrowth. Rebel works, hidden in brush on the other side of Boatswain Creek, came alive with fire. "The air seemed completely filled with screaming, exploding shell and shot of all descriptions, and our soldiers were falling fast," a Heavy recollected. "We were located where we could not advance, neither could we retreat without exposing the company or ascending a rise of ground which would expose us to the enemy." Like their compatriots to the north, they bent low and scrambled for cover. "Lying close to the ground, some of us loading and firing, while others passed rails from an old fence which chanced to be a few rods in the rear, we placed the rails in line in front of us," a Union man recalled, "then, with bayonet, knife, or any other implement to be had, dug a trench, throwing the earth onto the rails as a protection against the enemy's musketry."[43]

Colquitt had stopped the 8th New York Heavy Artillery cold. "It could not be called a battle," wrote W. I. Hallock of the regiment. "It was simply a butchery, lasting only ten minutes." Lieutenant Swan agreed. "It was horrible," he wrote home. "It is a wonder that a single man escaped the hail storm of bullets and shell." A New Jersey soldier who watched the carnage likened it to the biblical destruction of the host of Sennacherib. "It was the most sickening sight of this arena of horrors," he remembered, "and the appearance of these bodies, strewed over the ground for a quarter of a mile, and in our view for days, can never fade from our recollections." A Georgian concurred. "The open field in front of Colquitt is blue with Yankees," he wrote. "I have never seen as many dead in one place. In front of two companies of the 28th Georgia regiment several [men] counted seventy-five dead Yankees, and the slaughter in front of the other regiments was equally great." A man in the 6th Georgia noted that his own regiment lost only two men, making the fight "the most fortunate battle we had ever been in, if we take into consideration the magnitude of the battle and the great disparity of numbers."[44]

The charge was over for the 8th New York Heavy Artillery. The ordeal for the regiment's survivors, however, was just beginning. For the next sixteen hours, they would lie pinned in front of Colquitt's entrenchments, digging and fighting for their lives.

Tyler's remaining regiments had advanced simultaneously with the 8th New York Heavy Artillery. The 155th and 182nd New York, next to Bates's battalion, ended up in the same morass as the Heavies to their right. Captain Michael Doran, commanding the 155th New York, dressed the regiment behind the protective cover of a ridge and sent it forward. Cresting a small rise, the New Yorkers came into sight of the main rebel line about 150 yards away. "Balls commenced literally to mow us down," the 155th's adjutant, 1st Lieutenant John Russell Winterbotham, wrote home the next day. Doran's soldiers found themselves under devastating fire in front of a muddy ravine carved by a feeder to Boatswain Creek. "There was a marsh in front of our regiment," a man in the 155th reported, "and I doubt if we could have reached the enemy works even if they had not been there to oppose us." Soldiers attempted to return fire, reported Winterbotham, but "they were no match for the entrenched rebels, and the supports failed to come up but they would not fly but stood like heroes." The 155th took devastating casualties— some 130 men, about half the soldiers who made the charge—but was unable to advance. Realizing the hopelessness of his situation, after thirty minutes of fruitlessly trading fire with the Confederates from a distance of only 50 yards, Captain Doran pulled his regiment's remnants back behind a slight ridge 150 yards from the rebel line, where the troops began digging. The 182nd New York, on Doran's left, also dropped behind the ridge, losing 94 soldiers in the process. "We felt it was murder, not war," Private Newell Smith of the 155th New York reported, "or that at best a very serious mistake had been made." Adjutant Winterbotham concluded likewise: "The idea of our charging the enemy's line with the number we had was preposterous."[45]

On the Corcoran Legion's left, Colonel James P. McMahon edged the 164th New York south of Boatswain Creek's lower tributary, separating his regiment from the rest of the brigade. Ahead was the northernmost regiment of Martin's Confederate brigade, the 17th North Carolina, waiting behind earthworks on ascending ground running from Boatswain Creek onto Turkey Hill's northern shoulder. Decked out in gaudy blue-and-red Zouave uniforms, McMahon's men made inviting targets. They advanced through a hail of musketry—many Carolinians fired "buck and ball," a deadly combination of three buckshot and a ball—overran an advanced line of works, captured an officer and forty-five soldiers, and continued on. Attacking a second line of entrenchments—perhaps another advance line, or maybe the main works themselves—McMahon's New Yorkers waged a fierce face-to-face fight with the North Carolinians. Unable to maintain their hold, they dropped back and began digging in. The charge cost McMahon 11 officers and 143 men killed, wounded, and captured. Chief among the casualties was McMahon himself. Several versions of his death circulated, although none was penned by anyone there to see it. His brother, the 6th Corps aide Martin McMahon, described a hero's death astride rebel earthworks, flag in hand. Winterbotham, whose regiment fought near to the 164th New York and who was a close friend of the fallen colonel's, told a different but equally poignant tale. "When all his men had been shot down around him," the adjutant wrote home a week later, "and he had so few about him that the rebels said they thought they were coming in to give themselves up instead of to assault his works, [they] called upon him to surrender, but he would not do it and they shot him down." Two Confederates from the 17th North Carolina captured the New York regiment's flag, Lieutenant Wilson G. Lamb of the 17th later claimed. Dead Yankees, Lamb reported, lay strewn in front of the regiment's works so thickly "that one could have walked on their bodies its whole extent."[46]

At the discharge of the signal gun, Smyth's soldiers had stepped off in tandem with and just to the south of Tyler's men. Advancing at first through woods, they engaged Confederate pickets but missed the killing volleys of musketry devastating the Corcoran Legion. They emerged from the forest a few hundred yards from Martin's Confederates, who were arrayed on high ground. As Smyth's troops started up the gentle slope, concentrated musketry and artillery fire rocked them back on their heels.

Smyth was an Irishman, but the similarity between his brigade and Corcoran's Irish Legion ended there. Smyth's men were veterans well versed in the killing power of entrenchments—they had helped repel Pickett's charge at Gettysburg—and they quickly recognized the current venture as a forlorn exercise. Regiments on the northern end of Smyth's line, opposing the 42nd North Carolina of Martin's brigade, grasped the situation soon enough to avoid serious losses. The 14th Connecticut entered into "some sharp skirmishing but no general engagement," according to the regiment's historian, and had the good sense to entrench "in front of the enemy's works and remain quiet." The 4th Ohio, on the 14th Connecticut's left, saw somewhat more action. "We were at once met by shot, shell and canister," an Ohio soldier remembered. "Nothing daunted, most of the men hurried forward, drove in the skirmishers and sharpshooters of the enemy, captured their rifle pits, came within a few rods of the Confederate earthworks, but being without support, fell back a few rods, formed a new line in the edge of a wood in the first line of captured rifle pits, threw up breastworks of timber and whatever came first to hand and could be made available." Judging from the 4th Ohio's losses—three killed and seventeen wounded—the regiment's retreat to the woods was more precipitous than the soldier's account implied.[47]

Losses mounted on the southern portion of Smyth's line, where terrain was more open and where the Confederate position—held by Martin's 42nd and 66th North Carolina—swung forward, giving gunners of Major Charles R. Grandy's battery, Norfolk Light Artillery Blues, clear fire into the flank of the advancing Federals. Skirmishers from the 12th New Jersey took a loaf of corn bread from a dead rebel near the edge of the woods—carefully cutting off the blood-soaked portion before eating the rest—and stepped into the field facing rising ground. Trees had disordered the regiment's line, and the troops re-formed on the western edge of the clearing. Captain James McComb, commanding the 12th New Jersey, had just arranged his troops when a shell whizzed lengthwise along the line "about two feet from the ground," a soldier recollected, "and so close that it seemed to knock down almost every man in the regiment, just by the force of its wind." The shell hit McComb, who was a pace in front of the regiment, and horribly mangled his leg. While their commander lay bleeding on the ground—he would die a month later from the injury—the regiment started across the field. "Our flank was in air, and the rebel batteries began to rake our line endways with grape and canister," Private William P. Haines remembered. "As the rebels very pointedly refused to vacate, we hurriedly fell back, gathering up the wounded as we ran, and sought shelter in the edge of the woods, and back of the same tree from which we had rolled the dead rebel a few minutes before." Sergeant George A. Bowen of the regiment recorded in his diary: "Advanced to within a few yards of their main line, but we were overpowered and outnumbered and we fell back behind a small rise of the ground." Casualties numbered about fifty, highest for any regiment in Smyth's brigade.[48]

The 10th New York Battalion, known as the National Zouaves, pressed forward on the 12th New Jersey's left. Emerging from the woods, the soldiers saw before them "an open space completely swept by cannon and musketry," according to a New Yorker. "The fire was murderous," he recalled, "and it would have been a sheer impossibility to have crossed the open ground which intervened and captured the intenchments with our thin and straggling line." A few men made the attempt and were killed or wounded. The rest of the regiment began digging behind a slight rise 150 yards from the rebel works.[49]

Smyth's charge was over. "We advanced to the enemy's guns and earthworks but not being supported we had to fall back a short distance where we erected a line of works," Smyth noted in his diary. His report was blunt. "When the command arrived at from 60 to 100 yards from the enemy's works the ranks had become so thinned and the fire from the enemy's artillery and musketry was so destructive that the men were compelled to halt and seek such shelter as presented itself." Captain Elliott of Martin's brigade watched the repulse with satisfaction. "My position in the center and on a ridge gave me a splendid view of the grand encounter, and I could see the battle far down to the left, " he recalled. "Never will the inspiring sight be effaced from my memory."[50]

While Tyler and Smyth charged into the teeth of Colquitt's and Martin's fortifications, McKeen and Owen waited in reserve. "The two supporting brigades," an officer explained, "were ordered to push rapidly forward and over the front line in column and effect a lodgment in the enemy's works, and not to deploy until they got over."[51]

McKeen's brigade, behind Tyler on the right of Gibbon's formation, started across the stretch of field bounded by Cold Harbor Road on the north and Boatswain Swamp to the south. Corpses from the 8th New York Heavy Artillery dotted the way, and injured New Yorkers were dribbling back. "The ground presented a most pitiful sight with its dead and wounded," an officer recollected. As McKeen's men advanced, minié balls and shells from Colquitt's line slammed into their tightly packed column. Squinting through the fog, the Federals could discern red clay marking the rebel entrenchments, but no figures were visible. Lieutenant J. E. Hodgkins of the 19th Massachusetts remembered the "terrible fire of grape and canister from the enemy batteries while the musketry rolled terribly."[52]

McKeen's depleted veteran regiments formed the front of the advancing brigade. Behind came the 36th Wisconsin, a novice regiment that had lost heavily on June 1. As the situation became clear—another suicidal charge against impenetrable rebel defenses— the veterans slowed their march, many of them taking cover behind Penrose's works. "Its men seemed to catch the position at once," a New Jersey soldier later remarked, "and neither went back, nor forward to destruction, like the new regiment." The 36th Wisconsin found itself in the fore of the advancing column.[53]

McKeen was killed during the advance. The scholarly looking twenty-nine-year-old Princeton graduate had seen distinguished service with the 2nd Corps from the battlefields at Fair Oaks, the Sunken Road at Antietam, Marye's Heights at Fredericksburg, and the Wheatfield at Gettysburg and was "the idol of his men and the admiration of his superiors," according to Hancock's aide Walker. Command devolved on Colonel Frank A. Haskell of the 36th Wisconsin, the brigade's senior colonel. Conspicuous at Gettysburg, Haskell had so impressed Gibbon that the division commander intended to recommend his promotion to brigadier general. Haskell halted behind a low roll of ground seventy-five yards from Colquitt's entrenchments, re-formed the brigade, and ordered a charge. "The men rose to obey but were met by a shower of bullets," a soldier in the 36th Wisconsin related. Realizing that he could never take the works by storm, Haskell directed his troops to lie down. Within seconds, he was shot in the head and killed. "Taking advantage of a little rise in the land in our front," a man in the 19th Maine wrote, the brigade "fell upon the ground, and, in an incredibly short space of time, with bayonets, tin plates, or whatever they could lay their hands upon, threw up a slight earthwork in front, sufficient to protect them from the enemy's bullets." Lieutenant Hodgkins of the 19th Massachusetts took a party of six men back across the field to get picks and spades. "We started on our perilous journey, as the rebel sharpshooters were firing at any stray soldiers moving across the field," he recalled. "We moved on the double quick from one work to another arriving in safety, and returned all right with the implements of labor when the work went on in good earnest."[54]

As McKeen's brigade swung to the right, Joshua Owen's brigade shifted left. Born in Wales, Owen had pursued varied prewar careers as a teacher, lawyer, and legislator in Pennsylvania. Commanding the Philadelphia Brigade—the 152nd New York and five regiments from Pennsylvania, including the recently arrived 184th Pennsylvania—he had aroused Gibbon's ire at Spotsylvania Court House by retreating after Gibbon had directed him to attack. He also got off to a bad start on June 3. "I was up before daylight and riding to the front to see that the troops were all in position ready for the assault, at the hour named, in accordance with the orders issued the night before," Gibbon wrote. "I found one whole brigade including its commander [Owen] sound asleep." Awakening Owen and his men, Gibbon sent them to the front.[55]

An unrepentant Owen continued to ignore his superior's instructions. Gibbon wanted the Philadelphia Brigade to attack in column, and he made that point explicit: Owen was to "assault the enemy's works with his brigade in column in rear of the right of Colonel Smyth's brigade, and not to deploy his column [in line] until the head of it reached the enemy's intrenchments." Owen started out as directed, massing his brigade in eight lines and pushing ahead behind Smyth's right flank, the 184th Pennsylvania leading. When he reached the swampy terrain on Smyth's right, however, he decided on another tack. Instead of advancing as ordered, he inclined sharply southwest through woods, emerging in line on Smyth's left flank.[56]

Confederate works loomed only 150 yards away, on high ground. The Philadelphia Brigade, by accident rather than design, had come out northeast of Edgar's salient, facing the 66th North Carolina. The Marylanders and Flo-

ridians had launched their counterattack, and Barlow's troops—the 7th New
York Heavy Artillery and the 5th New Hampshire—were streaming back
down the slope. Accounts later claimed that portions of Owen's brigade
broke into Edgar's salient and captured prisoners—a deed of dubious validity
attributed variously to the 184th Pennsylvania and the 152nd New York.
There can be no doubt, however, that Owen's troops came under severe fire
and entrenched on Smyth's left, forming a junction with the 7th New York
Heavy Artillery on their left. The 152nd New York dug in less than a hundred
yards from the salient's northern face, probably in the sheltered hollow. "The
side hill below the line in front was filled with men who were engaged in
loading and passing the muskets to those in front," a New Yorker recalled,
"who were keeping up an incessant fire." One of Barlow's guns fired over
the Philadelphia Brigade in an attempt to knock down the McGehee house.
"For the purpose of getting the exact range," a soldier recorded, "the cannon
was depressed to such a degree that the solid shot and shell fell short and
buried in the side hill, exploding among the men, causing great consternation,
as there was no remedy but to lay still and receive the death dealing missiles."[57]

Gibbon was furious. "General Owen, instead of pushing forward in column through Smyth's line, deployed on his left as soon as the latter became
fully engaged," he wrote, "and thus lost the opportunity of having his brigade well in hand and supporting the lodgment made by Smyth and McMahon." Gibbon preferred charges against Owen, who was mustered out of
service in mid-July. In truth, Owen's decision to shift left of Smyth had been
an opportune move. Contrary to Gibbon's assertion, Smyth and McMahon
had made no lodgment, and throwing Owen's brigade into the Boatswain
Creek sector would only have increased Union casualties. Difficult terrain
and the strength of Martin's works—Mahone's entire division was waiting in
reserve behind this very point—guaranteed a Union failure. By moving left,
Owen unintentionally brought his troops to the only place where the 2nd
Corps had broken the Confederate line. He arrived too late to assist, but that
was not his fault.[58]

Martin's three North Carolina regiments had done yeomen's work, fending off portions of the Corcoran Legion, Smyth's brigade, and Owen's brigade. Martin, a forty-five-year-old professional soldier who had lost his right
arm in the Mexican War, reveled in the fight. "General Martin cheered his
men, and their enthusiasm was great," the adjutant Elliott remembered.
"Mostly armed with smooth-bore muskets, they poured an incessant fusillade
of buck and ball into the brave lines that charged and recharged, and fell,

many of them, on our works." Martin's losses were light, although among them was Colonel A. Duncan Moore, commanding the 66th North Carolina.[59]

Hancock had located his headquarters immediately behind Burnett's Tavern at Cold Harbor. A shell fragment shattered the leg of a staffer standing next to him, and another staff officer—Major John Garrett—fell seriously wounded. The engineer Major Brainerd had been assigned to the 2nd Corps and watched in horror as a rebel shell hit an artillery caisson filled with powder some hundred yards away and exploded it with a terrific noise. "Looking around in that direction we saw a column of white smoke ascending toward the clouds," recollected Brainerd, "expanding as it ascended, until it disappeared far above, while scattered around on the ground nearby lay the blackened and charred remains of six artillerymen." Soon four men stumbled in carrying a bloody litter with Tyler lying on it, followed by a "stream of bleeding men" seeking aid.[60]

"We kept our heads low while digging."

Unlike Hancock's troops, who first saw the Cold Harbor front the previous afternoon, Wright's soldiers had held the same ground for more than two days and understood exactly what they faced. The day before, Upton's aide Morse had been aghast to learn that an attack was planned for later that afternoon. Riding to division headquarters, Morse asked Russell if he knew the situation on his front. Russell replied that he was aware of the strength of the Confederate position and intended to discuss the attack with Wright. "By great urging the corps commander was induced to come to the front long enough to see the ground," Morse wrote, "and when he saw eighty dead, black, bloated bodies of the 2nd Connecticut lying about he concluded to defer the assault until 4:00 A.M. the next day." In truth it was Grant, not Wright, who postponed the attack, but Wright doubtless agreed with the decision. Morse considered the overnight delay no improvement at all. "It certainly seemed pleasanter to be killed in a delightful afternoon," he fumed, "than on a dark morning before breakfast."[61]

Russell was aggressive but not reckless. He had commanded Eustis's brigade on June 1 and knew firsthand the folly of charging across open ground into the teeth of the Confederate line. Around 4:00 A.M., Wright, Russell, and a coterie of staff and engineer officers rode along Russell's sector, attracting considerable attention from Confederate sharpshooters in adjacent fields. They agreed that it would be suicidal for Upton and Eustis to attack, and word quickly spread that Wright had countermanded the assault order. "This was very welcome news to us, because had we charged a majority of us must inevitably have been shot," an officer in the 121st New York recounted. "Every inch of that ground in front of us was commanded by sharpshooters, and our works being farther advanced than those on either flank we would have received a partially enfilading fire."[62]

Russell rode across Cold Harbor Road and inspected Penrose's and Cross's positions. The two brigades had entrenched across Gibbon's line of attack. They were too weak to assault by themselves, but Russell decided they might stand a chance if they joined Gibbon's charge. Taking his cue from Russell, Colonel Campbell, commanding the 15th New Jersey, instructed his soldiers to stay put until Gibbon's battle line reached them. "General Russell," a New Jersey officer claimed, "seeing the fate of [the 8th New York Heavy Artillery], withdrew his order for us to advance, for it would certainly have resulted in our destruction, and losing the hold we had."[63]

When Gibbon attacked south of Cold Harbor Road, Eustis's brigade, still under Lieutenant Colonel Clark, advanced cautiously "under a heavy storm of lead from the enemy," a Pennsylvanian recorded, "and halted under the crest of a small hill." Having sweltered through June 2 on this very ground— "our rifle pits kept the balls off, but not the sun," a man recalled—Clark knew all about Hagood's earthworks and the South Carolina sharpshooters who killed anyone venturing into the open. Understanding that it was death to send his men over the rise, he set them to constructing breastworks from brush and fallen timber. When Russell suggested Clark at least try to advance, Clark had the 49th Pennsylvania prepare the way. "Half of the men standing under arms, two men from each company, with spade and gun, were sent [eighty feet] to the front to commence digging, then directly two more were sent out," a soldier from the Keystone State related of the tedious trenching operation. David A. Stohl of the 49th Pennsylvania meanwhile discovered that some of Hagood's works were closer than anyone had realized, and Russell ordered the 49th Pennsylvania to complete its advanced line as quickly as possible. When the new works were finished, the rest of the regiment leapfrogged into them, and the 119th Pennsylvania darted into the 49th Pennsylvania's former works. Hagood's Confederates maintained a constant fire, but Russell's policy of keeping his troops entrenched held casualties to a minimum. "Our regiment not actively engaged," a man in the 5th Wisconsin candidly wrote home, accurately summing up Eustis's contribution to the attack.[64]

Upton's troops, on Eustis's right, did not even pretend to attack. "Another assault was ordered," Upton explained, "but, being deemed impracticable along our front, was not made." The 95th and 96th Pennsylvania held works they had taken from Clingman on June 1 and had reversed to face a new Confederate line no more than thirty yards away in places. Rebel sharpshooters "tried hard to 'pink' Yankee heads all day but we kept our heads low while digging," a Pennsylvanian remembered. "Some of our boys paid them back in their own coin." The 121st New York lay near Upton's rear works, recuperating from its harrowing two-day stint on picket duty. "We all feel very much worn out and foot sore and feel like so many old men almost helpless," a New Yorker recalled. Upton also kept the 2nd Connecticut Heavy Artillery in the rear, near the hollow where the regiment had formed for its assault on June 1. As fighting intensified, he shifted some Connecticut men toward Cold Harbor Road, where they suffered a few casualties from long-range fire. "This, I presume, was our part of the movement of June 3, which the larger histories regard as *the* battle of Cold Harbor," Adjutant Theodore F. Vaill of the 2nd Connecticut Heavy Artillery later wrote. For the survivors of Colonel Kellogg's bloody attack, June 1 would always be *the* battle of Cold Harbor.[65]

Eustis's and Upton's offensives were so tentative that Hagood's Confederates never realized that an attack had occurred. "It may sound incredible," Hagood reminisced, "but it is nevertheless strictly true, that the writer of these Memoirs, situated near the center of the line along which this murderous repulse was given, and awake and vigilant of the progress of events, was not aware at the time of any serious assault having been given." Upton's brigade, which had been severely mauled on June 1, lost an aggregate of twenty-one men on June 3. Eustis's casualties were of the same order.[66]

Ricketts's division faced into Bloody Run, toward Hunton's Virginians, and showed no more enthusiasm for attacking than did Russell's division on its left. Colonel Truex had been wounded on June 1, and the 87th Pennsylvania's Colonel Schall, although himself wounded that same day and with his arm in a sling, now commanded Truex's brigade. Smith's brigade, on Schall's right, also had a new head. Smith was ill, and Colonel John W. Horn of the 6th Maryland substituted for him at the last minute. "I received order to assume command of the brigade," Horn related, "at the same time I received orders that the enemy's works were to be charged at once."[67]

Schall's soldiers, on the division's left, were under orders not to fire until they reached the Confederate works. The brigade's lead elements slogged into the swampy ravine, but none of them ever got close to their objective. During the night, the 28th Virginia had dug advance works across Bloody Run, and Hunton had reinforced the stronghold with units from the 19th and 56th Virginia, plugging the ravine. "We advanced under a murderous fire in

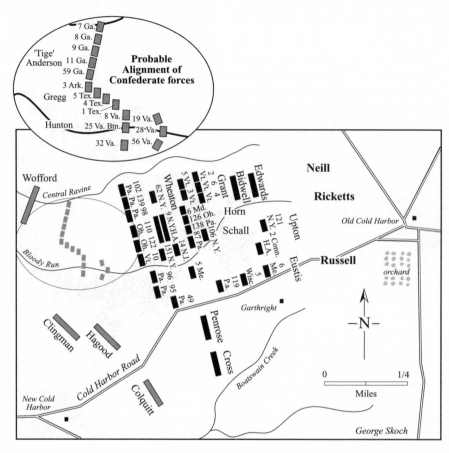

Wright's attack formation on morning of June 3

our front from the enemy's artillery, sharpshooters and when in range of its main line of battle were simply slaughtered," wrote Major Abbott of the 10th Vermont, evidently mistaking Hunton's advance line for the main Confederate fortifications. Adding to their discomfort, Schall's men pushed past the northern end of Upton's brigade, exposing their left to enfilading fire from Hagood's South Carolinians. Captain John C. Schoen of the 151st New York took three companies to shore up the southern end of the line, charged, and fell shot through the heart.[68]

Unable to make headway, Schall's soldiers started digging in "under a severe artillery fire of the enemy," a Federal recalled. Schall was shot in the arm again, and command of the brigade devolved on Lieutenant Colonel Hall of the 14th New Jersey. "Our loss was again very heavy, especially in officers," Truex reported. The 10th Vermont posted sixty-two casualties in the futile movement, including three captains. "It was designed to attack along our whole line at once," Major Peter Vredenburgh of the 14th New Jersey wrote home of the assault, "but it fizzled in some part of it, and that upset the design."[69]

Horn meanwhile scrambled to deploy his brigade on Schall's right, placing the 110th and 122nd Ohio in the first line, the 9th New York Heavy Artillery in the second and third lines, and the 6th Maryland, 126th Ohio, and 138th Pennsylvania in a fourth line. His men stood ready to advance, bayonets fixed. But troops of Neill's division, on their immediate right, did not move, and Horn had been instructed to guide on Neill. So when Schall's brigade stepped out, Horn remained stationary, uncovering Schall's right flank. After a brief wait, Horn ordered his first line forward, but Confederate fire slammed into the exposed right flank where Neill was supposed to be. "Finding a farther advance would be hazardous, I gave the order to halt," Colonel Binkley of the 110th Ohio reported. His men lay down and quickly constructed a "rude line of fence rails," according to an Ohioan, "exposed to a severe cross fire from artillery and musketry." The 122nd Ohio lost seventy men, among them Lieutenant James J. Hartley, killed when a cannonball tore off the back of his head. Apparently Horn's first line was the only portion of the brigade engaged. The 9th New York Heavy Artillery moved up "within plain sight of the enemy's works, which seem formidable," a man in the 9th New York Heavy Artillery remembered, "but luckily for us we [were] not ordered to assault them."[70]

Neill's division had shifted onto the 6th Corps's right flank late on June 2, relieving Devens's division of the 18th Corps. The position Neill's men had left was unpleasant, but the new front seemed even worse. A soldier "got it nearly right," thought Wilbur Fisk of the 2nd Vermont, "when he said we were to be taken out from one nasty hole to be put into another nastier one." Jammed between Ricketts on his left and Brooks's 18th Corps division on his right, Neill shoehorned his troops into a narrow column, brigades stacked one behind another. In front came Frank Wheaton's brigade, a predominantly Pennsylvania outfit that had missed the worst of the June 1 fighting on a rear-guard assignment protecting wagons. Behind Wheaton were the brigades of Lewis Grant, Daniel Bidwell, and Oliver Edwards, the latter containing many troops whose terms of service were almost finished.[71]

Wheaton arranged his regiments with the 102nd Pennsylvania on the right and the 139th and 98th Pennsylvania extending south. As the front was too narrow for his entire brigade, he posted the 62nd New York in reserve. "The troops advanced with spirit," he reported, "carrying the first and imperfect line of rifle pits of the rebels running diagonally with our front." Continuing through woods, Wheaton's men reached the edge of a clearing. The main Confederate line—Gregg's Texas and Arkansas regiments off Wheaton's left, and Tige Anderson's Georgians in his front—was plainly visible two hundred yards away. Marching into the field, Wheaton's soldiers received devastating volleys from the Georgians and Texans. "[The enemy] came forward in four lines, about fifty yards apart, and thus presented the fairest of targets for Texas and Arkansas marksmanship," recollected J. B. Polley of the 4th Texas. "Men could not live in the fire poured on them from front and flanks, and although in the first rush a few came within seventy yards of our lines, they halted, about faced, and fled as fast as legs could carry them." D. H. Hamilton of the 1st Texas agreed that the "slaughter was fearful to look at." Remembered J. H. Cosgrove of the 4th Texas: "The artillery also played havoc with a heavy crossfire at close range."[72]

Raked by converging musketry and artillery fire, Wheaton's shattered brigade fell back to the first line of works it had crossed during its advance. The 102nd and 139th Pennsylvania "reversed" the entrenchments and huddled low to avoid annihilation. There was no room for the 98th Pennsylvania, whose soldiers loaded and fired in the open, "suffering all the while great losses," according to Wheaton. The 62nd New York marched up and helped the 139th Pennsylvania repel Confederates occupying part of the same works and enfilading the brigade. Ricketts, however, had not moved far enough to cover Wheaton's left flank, and Brooks's division, on Wheaton's right, had fallen back, uncovering the 102nd Pennsylvania on the brigade's northern flank. Unprotected, the 102nd Pennsylvania lost nearly fifty men, including Lieutenant Colonel William McIlwaine, mortally wounded, and Major Thomas McLaughlin, seriously wounded. "The fight is awful," a soldier jotted in his diary. Its leadership in shambles, the 102nd Pennsylvania retired to more sheltered ground. Wheaton managed to rally some troops, but with fire slanting in from front and both flanks, his hold on the works remained tenuous.[73]

Lewis Grant's Vermont soldiers had lined up close behind Wheaton, the 3rd and 5th Vermont in front, followed by the 4th, 6th, and 2nd Vermont, with the 1st Vermont Heavy Artillery in reserve. At Neill's direction, Colonel Thomas O. Seaver's 3rd Vermont relieved the 139th Pennsylvania, and the 5th Vermont, under Captain Friend H. Barney, relieved the rest of Wheaton's line. The remaining Vermont regiments moved up and prepared to attack. "Everything indicated that a regular engagement was going to take place," recollected the Vermonter Fisk. "Colonel Pingree came around and told the company commanders to instruct the men to keep closed up and maintain as straight a line as possible in going through the woods." Fisk and his compatriots understood that the odds were against them. "Well we could make another charge and do it bravely but after so much hard fighting we did not feel that enthusiasm we did at first," he reminisced. "I dreaded the contest. If there had been an honorable way for me to get out of it I should have done so. But duty said go forward and trust in God and so I was determined to do."[74]

The 3rd and 5th Vermont now held Neill's front. Leaving the protection of the captured entrenchments and moving up to the tree line, they came under blistering fire from the main Confederate works. "They had no protection except the trees at the edge of the woods," Colonel Grant later wrote. "I asked for authority to withdraw these regiments, leaving only a skirmish line to hold the edge of the woods. This authority was refused. Being, however, satisfied that men were needlessly exposed, and that a skirmish line would hold the position as well as a line of battle and with less loss of life, and having obtained the direction of the assistant adjutant general of the division in the matter, I withdrew those regiments, leaving a skirmish line from each."[75]

Neill's advance had ended. The Confederate position "was most too strong to take with the bayonet, and so we substituted spades and picks, with which we have dug them out of the strip of woods," one Federal reflected. Mused another: "Singular as it may seem, the rebs in our front are fortified in an open field and we are in pits in the woods." Skirmishers from the 3rd and 5th Vermont remained sharply engaged, lying on the ground at the edge of the trees. "The enemy's main lines were in full view from the skirmish line," a Vermonter recalled, "his intrenchments evidently strong and amply defended, and artillery and musketry were in full and eager play on both sides." The

Vermont Brigade lost about 100 men on June 3, most of them from the 3rd and 5th Vermont. The 1st Vermont Heavy Artillery, in the brigade's rear, lost a single man. Wheaton's losses approximated 180, almost a third of them in the 139th Pennsylvania. Bidwell's and Edwards's brigades were not engaged and sustained only minor losses.[76]

Nowhere did the 6th Corps reach the main Confederate line. Along most of the corps's front, no advance of consequence was even attempted. The Confederates were simply too well fortified, and Wright and his field commanders knew it.

"More like a volcanic blast than a battle."

Baldy Smith's 18th Corps, north of Wright, faced into the concave horseshoe that Anderson and Kershaw had constructed the day before. Thick woods concealed the contours of the rebel position. Smith expected the Confederates to fortify the ravines, but he had no idea that they had turned them into killing grounds. When his soldiers advanced, they would march deep into the declivity formed by Kershaw's recessed line and receive fire from three directions. "In front of my right was an open plain, swept by the fire of the enemy, both direct and from our right," Smith later wrote. "On my left the open space was narrower, but equally covered by the artillery of the enemy." Near the center of his line, however, was a wooded swale—the middle ravine, fully covered by Law's, Bryan's, Wofford's, and Tige Anderson's brigades of the Confederate 1st Corps. The swale, Smith decided, would shelter his troops from the fire that made the field between his line and the Confederates so deadly to traverse. "Through this ravine," he wrote, "I determined that the main assault should be made." Unknown to Smith, he was sending his soldiers into the jaws of Kershaw's trap.[77]

Smith gave detailed instructions to Martindale and Brooks, whose divisions were to make the attack. Martindale was to form his troops into a compact column, "closed en masse, preceded by a heavy skirmish line and flankers on right flank." Advancing down the middle ravine, he was to capture the troublesome rebel battery—Falligant's gun, buttressed by the Richmond Howitzers—and press ahead "till some strong commanding position is gained." If Martindale could not penetrate the ravine, he was to shift right, form along the ravine's northern bank, and attack there. Brooks was to charge in column a short distance south of the middle ravine. If he found himself jammed too tightly against the 6th Corps, he was to move to the right and cooperate with Martindale north of the ravine. Smith later summarized the plan as follows: "General Martindale with his division was ordered to move down the ravine, while General Brooks with his division was to advance on the left, taking care to keep up the connection between Martindale and the 6th Corps, and if, in the advance, these two commanders should join, he (General Brooks) was ordered to throw his command behind General Martindale, ready to operate on the right flank, if necessary."[78]

Sending the 148th New York forward as skirmishers, Martindale arranged his division as Smith had prescribed. Orders called for him to move in "column of division," an exceedingly narrow formation the width of two companies in double lines. Thus arrayed, a full-strength regiment would form a mass of troops eighty-two men wide and ten men deep. Stedman's brigade, some 1,800 strong, headed Martindale's column, with the 12th New Hampshire leading, followed by the 11th Connecticut, 8th Maine, and 2nd New Hampshire. Stannard's brigade of some 600 soldiers formed the next column, with the 27th Massachusetts, 25th Massachusetts, 23rd Massachusetts, and 55th Pennsylvania massed from front to back in that order. Brooks posted his division on Martindale's left, most of it also in column of division. Behind a screen of skirmishers from the 10th New Hampshire came Marston's brigade, with the 98th New York leading, followed by the 81st, 96th, and 139th New York. Henry's brigade was next in line, and Burnham's brigade brought up the rear.[79]

Smith would make his offensive with troops who had seen little action on June 1. Leading Brooks's attack was Marston's brigade, which had been spared the main assault two days before. And this would be the first time Martindale's two brigades, under Stedman and Stannard, had encountered the Army of Northern Virginia. "I made a study of the faces around me," remembered George E. Place of the 12th New Hampshire. "Every face was more or less pale, but all had a determined look, except a New York recruit by the name of Hayes. He was trembling, and his face was pale as death."[80]

Confederates had been fortifying the middle ravine all night. Law's Alabamians, reinforced by Bryan's Georgians, held waist-high entrenchments on high ground overlooking the northern bank. They had leveled a segment of their works that had formed a sharp angle on the north side of the ravine and constructed new works sloping back more gradually, eliminating the salient. The 15th Alabama, commanded by Colonel William C. Oates, held the left of Law's line, with the regiment's left resting on the abandoned works. The 4th, 44th, 47th, and 48th Alabama extended to the right along the new line. Law posted a Parrott gun on his left where Oates's regiment adjoined the 13th Mississippi of Humphreys's brigade, another on the right of his brigade to enfilade approaching troops, and a third gun in his center. The Confederates

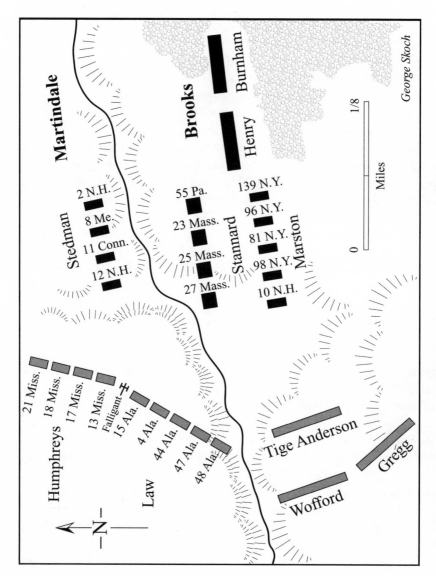

Smith's attack formation on morning of June 3

George Skoch

waited in two lines behind their fortifications, and pickets under Major George W. Cary of the 4th Alabama patrolled well to the front.[81]

Promptly at 4:30 A.M., Brooks's lead brigade, under Marston, started off in column of division a short distance south of the middle ravine. A native of New Hampshire, Marston was a graduate of Harvard Law School. He had served in Congress during the first two years of the war, although he spent much of his term on the battlefield rather than in Washington, and he knew how to handle troops. He sent the 10th New Hampshire, on loan from Burnham's brigade, skirmishing ahead to the first line of Confederate rifle pits. Behind came the main assault column, Colonel Wead's 98th New York leading. Unlike Martindale's troops to their north, Wead's men had fought here on June 1 and were intimately familiar with the ground.[82]

Cary's Alabama pickets offered token resistance and ran back to the main line of Confederate works to sound the alarm. "Look out, they are coming," the pickets shouted as they climbed back over the entrenchments. "Get over, boys, get over," soldiers behind the works cried. "I did not get over very gracefully, but fell over," recollected William C. Jordan of the 15th Alabama. Unbuckling his cartridge belt, Jordan, like other men around him, poured his cartridges onto the ground to facilitate loading.[83]

Marston unwittingly led his brigade into the open maw of the Confederate horseshoe. Tige Anderson's Georgians stood directly in front, and Law's Alabamians angled toward the Federals to their north. "A heavy line of blue was seen emerging from the timber on our right opposite Anderson's Georgians," Adjutant Robert T. Coles of the 4th Alabama remembered. "On they came within musket range of General Anderson's front, when a murderous fire was opened by his entire brigade," Coles continued. "Then our brigade and the artillery joined in with a right flank fire, causing the front column to hesitate, thus throwing the rear lines forward in a confused mass." Colonel Oates of the 15th Alabama observed that Confederate artillery, loaded with double charges of canister, "made frightful gaps through the dense mass of men."[84]

Terrific fire slammed into Marston's Federals from in front and from the right. With a cheer, the four New York regiments charged a short distance ahead, overrunning Confederate rifle pits remaining from Wofford's former line. Soldiers in the 98th New York recognized bodies of their comrades killed two days earlier, already turned black. Now the brigade was irrevocably inside the rebel horseshoe. "They then charged the second line, which was so arranged that they were exposed to a front and two cross fires," a man in the 81st New York remembered. "The fire of the rebels concealed in another line of rifle pits in front and from the enclosed works on the right was too murderous for any troops long to sustain," Marston reported. "The ground was swept with canister and rifle bullets until it was literally covered with slain." Colonel Wead, commanding the 98th New York, leaped onto the works and was shot through the neck, dying shortly afterward. Lieutenant Colonel Edgar Perry, heading the 139th New York, was also killed. His column shattered, Marston pulled his troops back to regroup.[85]

Stedman's brigade of Martindale's division, on Marston's right, also stepped off at 4:30. The twenty-six-year-old Stedman rode gallantly in front, brandishing a ramrod like a sword. Expecting to take the rebel works by storm, he had ordered his troops to remove their percussion caps and to charge with their bayonets fixed. Passing through a stretch of woods, the head of Stedman's column reached the open field shortly after Marston had launched his assault. Skirmishers from the 148th New York stopped, giving the rest of the brigade time to gather inside the tree line. The Confederate works were hazily visible four hundred yards ahead, across cleared ground. Captain Thomas E. Barker, commanding the 12th New Hampshire, was aghast at the prospect of sending his tightly massed troops against the rebel entrenchments. "I tried my best to get Colonel Stedman, commanding the column, to deploy [the soldiers in line]," Barker wrote the next day. "He would not allow it but said, 'Go as you are!'"[86]

Baldy Smith was at the front to supervise the attack. The situation troubled him. The 6th Corps on Brooks's left had scarcely advanced, leaving Marston's southern flank unprotected, and killing fire from Law's Confederates was pelting Marston's right flank as well. Feeding Martindale's two brigades into the maw of Kershaw's horseshoe had nothing to recommend it. "It is simply an order to slaughter my best troops," a man in the 27th Massachusetts claimed to have heard Smith say. "I have no discretion left me."[87]

To save Marston and salvage what he could from the attack, Smith decided to split Martindale's division. Stedman's brigade was to advance along the right side of the middle ravine, "faced to the right to protect the right flank of the moving column." While Stedman angled northwest to quell Law's and Humphreys's fire, Stannard's brigade was to advance along the ravine's southern margin, moving in tandem with Brooks's brigades on his left. Most important, Smith later explained, "General Martindale was ordered to keep his front covered as much as possible, and to move only when General Brooks moved." After making his instructions clear to Martindale, Smith rode off to inspect Brooks's line.[88]

Martindale waited at the edge of the woods, listening for the sound of firing to the south that was to signal that Brooks was sending the rest of his division forward. Suddenly musketry erupted to the south. Assuming that

Brooks was renewing his attack—an erroneous conjecture, it developed, as the firing came from Neill's feeble advance—Martindale gave orders to move out. Stedman's brigade passed through the skirmishers and into the open field, veering northwest as Smith had instructed. Stannard, coming behind, marched along the southern margin of the middle ravine, expecting Brooks to keep pace on his left.[89]

As they emerged into the field, the soldiers of Stedman's lead regiment, the 12th New Hampshire, tried to discern the contours of the rebel position. "A line of breastworks runs zig-zag; one in front, the other on our left," a New Hampshire soldier noted. "We cannot see a man in these works, for a dense cloud of battle smoke rests all along the line." Law's Alabamians, however, could see the approaching Federals clearly. "Only a few minutes elapsed [after the repulse of Marston] when a second and more determined assault was made on our immediate front," Coles of the 4th Alabama related.[90]

The Alabama line erupted in fire—"to those exposed to the full force and fury of that dreadful storm of lead and iron that met the charging column, it seemed more like a volcanic blast than a battle, and was about as destructive," Captain Asa W. Bartlett of the 12th New Hampshire recalled. "We were now so near the breastworks that I could see the flash of their musketry quivering through the bank of smoke that lay above them," recounted George Place of the same regiment. "Men bent down as they went forward, as if trying, as they were, to breast a tempest," remembered Sergeant Enoch C. Piper. "The files of men went down like rows of blocks or bricks pushed over by striking against each other." Assuming that the soldiers around him were dropping to the ground because of orders that he had missed, Sergeant Jacob B. Tuttle of Company K hit the dirt too. He did not realize that he was lying among dead men until he saw living members of the regiment continuing on. Captain Barker, commanding the 12th New Hampshire, also thought that soldiers were lying down to avoid enemy fire and ordered Captain Edwin E. Bedee to get them going again. "I soon found," Bedee afterward told Barker, "that nothing but the judgment trump of the Almighty would ever bring those men upon their feet again." Noted the Alabamian Coles: "Our artillery, giving double shotted canister at not exceeding one hundred yards, did most effective work, while our infantry poured repeated and destructive volleys into the apparently solid mass of blue."[91]

Cursing the generals who had ordered him into this trap, Captain Barker vented his spleen on the brigade's adjutant, Stephen R. Reynolds. Napoleon, Reynolds countered, had considered charging in column the most effectual way. "The most effectual way of murdering men, I agree, and there is the evidence of it," Barker replied, pointing to the field thick with dead and wounded troops. A bullet hit Reynolds in the shoulder the next moment, as though punctuating Barker's point. Captain Bartlett remembered that Barker was "so wrought up by his anger and the excitement of the occasion, that he declared with an oath that he would not take his regiment into another such charge, if Jesus Christ himself should order it."[92]

The 12th New Hampshire's offensive was finished. Half the regiment lay spread across the field in front of the Confederate works. Live soldiers sprawled among dead and wounded comrades, hoping rebels would mistake them for corpses. "Many of the wounded left on the field and unable to get under cover were deliberately shot dead by the inhuman rebel wretches," Captain Bartlett claimed, "and this was done so long after the charge and its excitement were over that every such shot made the one who aimed it little better than a cold-blooded murderer." Bartlett asserted that the Confederates "not only shot at those who showed any signs of life, but amused themselves by making targets of the bodies of those that were dead." Stedman's remaining regiments had watched as the 12th New Hampshire was "thrown back by the pitiless hail," a Federal recalled. Hoping to avoid the fate of the New Hampshire men, they retired to the woods and began digging pits along the tree line.[93]

While Stedman attacked north of the middle ravine in a forlorn attempt to squelch Law's flanking fire, Stannard descended into the ravine, apparently hugging the south edge as Martindale had instructed. Stannard's "Star Brigade" had figured prominently in Butler's ill-fated attack on Drewry's Bluff, where it sustained severe casualties. The men of the Star Brigade "felt that they had been sacrificed rather than defeated," a soldier in the 27th Massachusetts claimed. They were looking for an opportunity to "wipe out this seeming disgrace."[94]

At Stannard's command, the 27th Massachusetts fanned out as skirmishers, advanced into the open field, and drove rebel skirmishers from a line of rifle pits. The 25th Massachusetts came immediately behind, followed by the 23rd Massachusetts, all marching in a compact column of division. Through the fog—it was "a dark, gloomy morning," a soldier recalled—Stannard's men could see the profile of the main rebel works. "We calculated the chances, and we felt that they were terribly against us," a Bay Sate soldier remembered. "But to 'obey orders' is a soldier's duty. 'Wait for a time to die!'"[95]

As the Massachusetts troops pressed on, rebel artillery opened, enfilading their advance. "Double-shotted rebel guns hurled grape, canister, and shrapnel, and the earth quivered under the mighty shock of battle," a New England er remembered. Then the troops reached musket range. "To the howl and groan of heavy ordnance was added the hum of 'minies' and the t-zip of bullets," a soldier recalled the sounds of battle. "Then came the dreadful 'Whitworths,' which made the air instinct with warning or quickened it with vivid alarm—long wails that fatefully bemoaned the deaths they wrought, fluttering screams that filled the space with horror, and cries that ran the diapason of terror and despair." Still the Star Brigade advanced, crossing the ravine where the stream made a short jog to the south, and found themselves in a second line of pits—the portion of line abandoned by Law during June 2. There they stood face-to-face with the main rebel works lining the brow of a low hill rising some fifteen feet above them. "Great ugly gaps rent in the line were quickly closed by the comrades of the fallen," remembered a man in the 27th Massachusetts.[96]

The 27th and 25th Massachusetts had separated during the advance, and they now faced different sectors of Law's works. Colonel Josiah Pickett, leading the 25th, waved his sword overhead. "Come on, boys," he shouted. "Forward, double-quick! Charge!" Adjutant Coles of the 4th Alabama watched the approach: "A Federal regiment, entirely alone and unsupported, very suddenly emerged from a ravine on the right front of the position occupied by the 4th Alabama. Their colors flying, the Colonel in command waving his sword and urging his men forward, they advanced directly on the 4th Alabama." Coles and his companions admired the courage of these troops— "it appeared to be downright murder to kill men in the performance of an act so courageous," he later reflected. But Colonel Pinckney D. Bowles, commanding the 4th Alabama, did not hesitate. "When the advancing line reached within seventy yards," he later wrote, "I ordered my line to fire."[97]

Bryan's Georgians busily loaded muskets and handed them to the Alabamians. "The charging column," Colonel Oates of the 15th Alabama wrote, "received the most destructive fire I ever saw. They were subjected to a front and flank fire from infantry, at short range, while my piece of artillery poured double charges of canister into them. I could see the dust fog out of a man's clothing in two or three places at once where as many balls would strike him at the same moment." Samuel H. Putnam of the 25th Massachusetts remembered smoke and flame enveloping the rebel works. "Volley after volley of musketry sent bullets through our ranks like hail," Putnam related. "At the same moment we received an enfilading fire of artillery on both right and left flanks." Colonel Pickett recalled "a storm of bullets, shot, and shell that no human power could withstand." A Confederate gunner described the effect of his double shots of canister. "[The Union column] resolved itself into a

formless crowd, that stood stubbornly there, but could not get one step farther," he related. "And then, for three or four minutes, at short pistol range,
the infantry and our Napoleons tore them to pieces. It was deadly and bloody
work! They were a helpless mob now; a swarming multitude of confused
men." It seemed to him that the Federals were "simply melting away under
the fury of our fire."[98]

Colonel Pickett of the 25th Massachusetts went down, shot through the
hip. Soldiers frantically clawed at the ground, seeking to throw up a measure
of protection. Others flattened themselves behind the abandoned rebel rifle
pits. A sergeant carrying the flag noted by Coles—a blue silk banner with the
state arms on one side, presented to the regiment by ladies in Worcester—fell
wounded, and Corporal John E. Lewis caught the colors from his hands and
marched on, men falling around him. Now far in advance of the disintegrating
line, he, too, was shot. Mortally wounded, he plunged the flagstaff into the
ground and collapsed, still clasping the banner. Private David Casey ran forward, tore the flag from the dead corporal's hand, and darted back with it to
his regiment. Casey's heroism won him the Medal of Honor.[99]

The 27th Massachusetts, under Major William A. Walker, pressed its attack with no better success. "Forward, struggling like maddened billows
against breakers, mown down by scores," a man in the 27th Massachusetts
described the charge, "but onward, till the second line of rifle pits are
reached." Passing over the portion of line abandoned by Law during June 2,
they, too, came face-to-face with Law's main line. "It was a position trying
the stoutest hearts," recollected William P. Derby of the 27th. "Before us, on
a commanding eminence, were the enemy's works, with salients near our
right and left, and with center well refused." In a desperate but futile act,
the Massachusetts men pressed ahead. "Conceive the fierce onslaught, midst
deafening volleys of musketry, thunderings of artillery, and the wild, mad
yell of battle," a participant wrote. "See the ranks mowed down as they contend for every inch they advance, until the lines crumble and break before the
iron tempest." Farther advance was impossible. "We couldn't retreat without
being killed," recalled a man in the 23rd Massachusetts, which had arrived
in time to join the slaughter, "and to stand where we were meant death." To
Private Amos Stillman of the 23rd, his jacket perforated by bulletholes, the
answer was simple. "Drop, boys," he shouted, and soldiers threw themselves
down, seeking shelter in contours of the land; others ran the short distance
back to the last rifle pits they had crossed. "Midway, between the fire of contending hosts, we crouched behind the captured rifle pits, the air rent with an
unearthly contest," a Bay Stater recalled. Law's losses were minor, the main

casualty being Law himself, who received a severe but not fatal wound just above his eyebrow.[100]

Stannard's charge was over in minutes. "It became at once evident, in view of the converging fire of musketry and the direct fire of artillery which was cutting down each successive [line] as it rose from the knoll, that it would be impossible for a sufficient number of men to reach the works to produce any effect upon the enemy," wrote Stannard, who accompanied his brigade. "As no concert of action on the part of other commands was apparent, I ordered the remnant of my command to retire to the rifle pits."[101]

The 23rd, 25th, and 27th Massachusetts lay sprawled across the field and huddled against the east side of reversed rebel works. "It was almost impossible to move and live, the lifting of a head or hand being a signal for volleys of musketry," recollected Derby of the 27th Massachusetts. Men worked their bodies into the ground to gain shelter and stacked corpses as barriers against plunging fire. Looking back, Derby noticed that the "surface of the field seemed like a boiling cauldron, from the incessant pattering and plowing of shot, which raised the dirt in geysers and spitting sands." During a truce a few days later, a rebel major told Major Fish of the 27th Massachusetts, "It was one of the bravest and most useless charges I ever witnessed." Other Confederates thought so as well. "I had seen the dreadful carnage in front of Marye's Hill at Fredericksburg, and on the 'old railroad cut' which Jackson's men held at Second Manassas; but I had seen nothing to exceed this," Law reflected. "It was not war; it was murder."[102]

Brooks's division, south of Stannard, was also finished for the day. Riding over from Martindale's front, Smith was appalled at the fire raking Marston's brigade and ordered Brooks "not to move his men farther, but keep them sheltered till the cross-fire was over." Marston pulled his brigade back. Some men took shelter in works crisscrossing the field, and others retired into woods where they had started. "Our force now commenced throwing up entrenchments within about 100 yards of the enemy's lines and exposed the while to a galling fire," 1st Lieutenant Richard W. L'Hommedieu of the 139th New York noted in his journal.[103]

Some of Marston's retreating soldiers streamed rearward through Guy Henry's brigade, slated to charge next. Discouraged by Marston's traumatic reverse, Henry cautiously advanced three regiments to the first line of captured rebel works and directed the rest of his brigade to lie down. On reaching the front, Major Hiram B. Crosby of the 21st Connecticut found himself "exposed to a sharp fire of shot and shell, both direct and enfilading, from the enemy's works, which were barely two hundred yards distant." Pressed against the ground, the Connecticut men were somewhat protected from the Confederate firepower and took "comparatively light" losses. Henry's sharpshooters fired steadily to keep rebel artillerists from working their guns. "The Union soldiers were lying flat on their faces, hugging their mother earth with ardent affection," a Connecticut man remembered. "Many and many a gallant fellow was shot thus as he lay, hit squarely in the top of the head by a missile whose projectile force would almost carry it lengthwise through his body. Solid shot from an enfilading battery far to the right came crashing through the trees, showering broken limbs and iron fragments upon us." It seemed to one man hunkering low in a captured pit that "all the powers of earth and of hell [were] concentrated in the endeavor to sweep away every vestige of the Federal army."[104]

Burnham's brigade remained in reserve and did not charge. The rear was safer than the front, but Confederate fire came in regularly, forcing Burnham's troops to take cover. Corpses still abounded from the fighting on June 1, and soldiers from the 118th New York stacked the bodies and covered them with earth for protection. "The dirt would sometimes sift down and expose a hand or foot, or the blackened face of the dead," a New Yorker related.[105]

As far as Smith was concerned, his attack had reached impasse. "General Martindale got into so hot a place that he was forced to assault the works without the assistance of the column of General Brooks," he wrote Meade. "While I was on the front of General Brooks the enfilading fire of the enemy was so heavy as to force me to give the order to General Brooks not to attempt to advance his column of attack until this fire was slackened. This fire being entirely on my right, I have had nothing but artillery to use against it, and have therefore been unable to silence it." He added: "My troops are very much cut up, and I have no hopes of being able to carry the works in my front unless a movement of the 6th Corps on my left may relieve at least one of my flanks from this galling fire."[106]

While Smith was writing Meade, Kershaw was forwarding a vastly different message to Anderson. "We are sustaining little loss," the South Carolinian reported. "Damaging the enemy seriously." His line was holding, and his guns were doing good service. "If they keep up this game long," he concluded, "we will have them."[107]

"Shamed a cadet at his first year at West Point."

The big assault of June 3 at Cold Harbor lasted less than an hour. Grant had envisioned a coordinated offensive by the entire army, but only the 2nd, 6th, and 18th Corps had participated. Even that attack was piecemeal, and well over half the troops available for the assault were never seriously engaged. Only seven of Hancock's twelve brigades advanced, and in Wright's corps, only one brigade—Wheaton's—attempted anything remotely resembling an attack. Wright's remaining nine brigades either stayed where they were or pressed forward a few hundred yards and began digging. Baldy Smith's participation was limited to three brigades out of seven. Stories of fields littered with blue-clad corpses convey distorted pictures of what really happened. A few sectors saw tremendous slaughter, but along much of the battle line Union losses were minor, and many Confederates had no idea that an offensive had even been attempted. The popular image of a massive Union onslaught at Cold Harbor belongs more to the dustbin of Civil War mythology than to real history.

Union casualties have been grossly exaggerated and probably did not exceed 3,500. Commentators have suggested numbers ranging from 7,500 to well above 12,000, all supposedly incurred during a few terrible minutes after dawn. (In reality the assault sputtered on for about an hour, not the eight minutes some writers have claimed.) The 12,000 estimate in fact reflects the official tally of *all* casualties for the entire Cold Harbor campaign—12,788, to be exact—embracing the cavalry battles of May 31 and June 1, the 6th and 18th Corps attacks at Cold Harbor on June 1, the 5th and 9th Corps fights around Bethesda Church from June 1 forward, and casualties in all Union corps for the remainder of their stay at Cold Harbor and during their movement across the Chickahominy and James Rivers toward Petersburg. The oft-quoted 7,500 figure derives from attempts by early postwar writers to estimate all Union losses for June 3, a day that included a great deal more fighting than just the grand assault.[108]

Precise casualty figures for the June 3 assault are elusive. Some regiments reported losses for the entire day or aggregated figures for several days running. Different computations often appear for a regiment in the official tally, in the regiment's published history, and in handwritten returns at the National Archives. By culling these sources and adjusting to reconcile reports covering multiple days of fighting, it is possible to arrive at a figure closer to reality than the inflated numbers that have marred histories of the battle almost since the shooting stopped.

The 6th Corps's losses were minor. Russell's division reported fewer than a hundred casualties; Neill's approximated 280; and Ricketts's staff recorded 219. All told, the 6th Corps lost perhaps 600 troops on June 3. The three 18th Corps brigades that charged into Kershaw's horseshoe, however, were terribly mauled. Martindale reported that his two brigades under Stedman and Stannard entered the fight with some 3,400 soldiers. He counted 1,043 casualties—nearly a third of the men engaged—made up of 98 men killed, 634 wounded, and 311 missing, the latter presumably captured or killed. Stannard's brigade was wrecked, losing by Stannard's reckoning 31 commissioned officers, including his entire staff, and 462 enlisted men, for total subtractions of 493. "As the assaulting column moved up I lost the commanding officer of nearly every regiment of my command," the general wrote. "In the 27th Massachusetts, Major [William A.] Walker being killed, the command devolved upon Captain [Adin W.] Caswell; the 25th, Colonel [Josiah] Picket and Major [Cornelius G.] Atwood both being wounded, and Lieutenant Colonel [Orson] Moulton being captured by the enemy, the command devolved upon Captain [James] Tucker. In the 55th, Captain [John C.] Shearer and [James S.] Nesbit, both being wounded within a few moments of each other, the command devolved upon Captain George H. Hill. Major [Ethan A. P.] Brewster, Twenty-third Massachusetts, was also wounded at this time, leaving Colonel [Andrew] Elwell, of that regiment, my only field officer." The 27th Massachusetts, serving as Stannard's skirmishers, sustained about 85 casualties; the 23rd Massachusetts, about 55; and the 55th Pennsylvania, another 55. The 25th Massachusetts, in the fore of Stannard's assault column, counted 202 losses out of 300 men engaged. Stedman's brigade lost about 550 troops. The 12th New Hampshire, spearheading his assault, counted about 150 subtractions, and the remaining 400 casualties were distributed fairly evenly among his other regiments. Marston's brigade, the only portion of Brooks's division seriously engaged, lost about 500 soldiers. The 81st New York lost 15 of its 24 commissioned officers and 166 of its 290 men—more than half its complement—and its color guard was "completely annihilated." The 98th New York, which lost 61 men, came back with fifty-two bulletholes in its flag. Colonel Wead of the 98th New York and Lieutenant Colonel Edgar Perry of the 139th New York were both killed.[109]

The 2nd Corps staffer Mitchell estimated that Hancock's loss for June 3 exceeded 3,000 soldiers and included "its bravest and best, both of officers and men." The Official Return of Casualties, however, shows that Mitchell's number refers to losses in Barlow's and Gibbon's divisions from June 2 through June 15, a period that included a lot of fighting in addition to the June 3 attack. Meade's staffer Humphreys analyzed Hancock's June 3 losses after the war and put them in the range of 2,200 officers and men, a figure that might be low but is probably closer to the truth than Mitchell's 3,000. Attrition in leadership was severe and included five brigade heads. Tyler, commanding a brigade in Gibbon's division, was wounded and succeeded by Porter of the 8th New York Heavy Artillery, who was killed. McKeen, also leading one of Gibbon's brigades, was killed, and his successor, Haskell of the 36th Wisconsin, was killed immediately afterward. In Barlow's division, Byrnes was killed, Brooke was severely wounded, and Brooke's successor, Morris of the 66th New York, was killed. Regimental heads were cut down at a daunting rate, chief among them McMahon of the 164th New York.[110]

Second Corps casualties reflected the campaign's prevailing pattern. New regiments lost heavily while veteran regiments, knowledgeable of risks entailed in attacking entrenched positions, generally took only light casualties. The experience of Barlow's division is a case in point. Brooke's brigade spearheaded the attack, and Brooke's first line—made up solely of the 7th New York Heavy Artillery—lost 422 officers and men. Brooke's six veteran regiments, all in his second line, lost a total of 150 to 200 men. In Miles's brigade, the 5th New Hampshire—recently filled with new recruits—led with 202 losses, followed by the novice 2nd New York Heavy Artillery with 91. MacDougall's brigade, in reserve, sustained hardly any casualties, reporting only 35 losses altogether from June 2 through June 15. Byrnes's five veteran regiments lost about 150 men. Total losses for Barlow were probably slightly above a thousand, with over half of that total—624—coming from only two regiments.[111]

Gibbon initially placed his casualties in the June 3 assault at 65 officers and 1,032 men killed and wounded, very close to Barlow's subtractions. Later, in his memoirs, Gibbon raised the number to 1,628, purportedly adding missing men he had neglected to count. On close scrutiny, his original estimate seems more accurate. Heading the list, of course, was the 8th New York Heavy Artillery with 475 casualties, the highest rate for any regiment in the battle and possibly the highest regimental loss in a single engagement during the entire war. The rest of the Corcoran Legion, which was fairly new to the Potomac army and largely inexperienced in assaulting earthworks, also paid in blood, with the 155th New York reporting over 130 casualties, the 182nd New York 94, and the 164th New York 154. In contrast, Smyth's veteran brigade reported only 227 casualties for the entire June 2–15 period. And McKeen's losses were concentrated in the greenhorn 36th Wisconsin, which counted some 78 men killed, wounded, and captured, well over half the brigade's subtractions for June 3. Judging from campaign returns, casualties in Owen's veteran brigade could not have exceeded a hundred men.[112]

The contrast in casualties between Smyth's veterans and the Corcoran Legion's newcomers on their right was striking. The Legion's 164th New York lost some 154 men in a stirring charge led by Colonel McMahon. Smyth's veteran 14th Connecticut on the 164th New York's immediate left— battle-wise warriors who had been through Antietam, Fredericksburg,

Chancellorsville, Gettysburg, the Wilderness, and Spotsylvania Court House—charged across comparable ground, quickly grasped the hopelessness of the endeavor, and after "sharp skirmishing" began throwing up earthworks. The 164th New York's pluck earned it an inspirational drawing by the battlefield artist Alfred Waud depicting McMahon, one hand grasping the regimental flag and the other holding his sword high, meeting a hero's death. Waud did not bother to draw the 14th Connecticut digging holes nearby to protect itself from Confederate fire. These veterans, however, received more rewarding compensation, reporting losses of under 10 men. They did what most veteran regiments did when facing entrenched earthworks at this stage of the war, advancing as far as practical, then entrenching to hold the ground.[113]

Hancock's total losses on June 3 were approximately 2,500. But more than a third of that number—almost 900—came from two regiments, the 7th and 8th New York Heavy Artillery. And those two regiments and just three more—the 155th and 164th New York, and the 5th New Hampshire—accounted for over half of Hancock's losses. The total loss in the Corcoran Legion was about 900 men, the worst beating sustained by any brigade that day. Slaughter was confined to discrete sectors, but for the units finding themselves in those places, June 3 was devastating.

Losses for the day thus amounted to some 1,500 for the 18th Corps, at most 2,500 for the 2nd Corps, and probably 600 for the 6th Corps, yielding approximately 4,500 men officers and men dead, wounded, and missing. Many casualties, however, occurred after the initial charge had ended. Anecdotal accounts suggest that attrition from sharpshooters, artillery fire, and Confederate attacks toward evening may have inflicted up to a quarter of the day's casualties. All things considered, the grand charge at Cold Harbor on June 3 produced about 3,500 Union casualties. Confederate casualties were disproportionately smaller. The only appreciable losses were at the salient, where Patton's brigade lost close to 275 men—some 190 of them from the 26th Virginia Battalion—Crane's 2nd Maryland lost 42, and Finegan's Floridians lost somewhere around 100. Hoke's and Kershaw's divisions lost at most 300 soldiers, bringing total Confederate subtractions during the attack to slightly over 700 men.[114]

In retrospect, Grant's June 3 offensive had little chance of succeeding. The Confederate line was simply too strong and the assault too disjointed. Writing more than forty years later, the Confederacy's postmaster general, John H. Reagan, described a conversation with Lee on the Cold Harbor battlefield on June 3. Lee, Reagan claimed, told him that Grant was hurling columns six to ten men deep against his position. "General, if he breaks your line, what reserves have you?" Reagan inquired. "Not a regiment," Lee replied. "And that has been my condition since the fighting commenced on the Rappahannock. If I shorten my lines to provide a reserve, he will break them."[115]

Lee's alleged remarks to Reagan bore no relation to the actual condition of the Confederate line and were likely aimed at persuading Richmond to send more men.. The Army of Northern Virginia was awash with reserves. Four brigades from Pickett's and Field's divisions had shifted south to backstop Hoke's and Kershaw's line across the lower and middle ravines. Far from being hard pressed when Baldy Smith attacked, Law's Alabama troops were "in fine spirits, laughing and talking as they fired," according to Law. Bryan's brigade supported Law, handing the Alabamians loaded muskets; Wofford's and Gregg's brigades supported Tige Anderson; and Clingman's brigade acted as a reserve for Hunton and Hagood. South of Cold Harbor Road, Mahone's entire 3rd Corps division, four brigades strong, waited behind Colquitt and Martin, and Crane's Marylanders stood in reserve behind Edgar's salient. On the Confederate right, adjoining Breckinridge, Wilcox's entire 3rd Corps division was never even engaged. Except for Finegan's brigade of Mahone's division, the two 3rd Corps divisions south of Cold Harbor Road fired scarcely a shot.[116]

Union commanders did nothing to enhance their prospects, slim as those might have been. Meade made no pretense at leadership, and his corps and division heads floundered. Presented with tightly massed targets, the Confederates slaughtered Baldy Smith's soldiers as they came into range, shredding Stedman's, Stannard's, and Marston's narrow columns from front to back much as a sharpener grinds a pencil. Wright never ventured anything resembling an assault. Russell's division stayed put; Ricketts tested the waters with tentative probes, then dug in; and Neill pushed his lead brigade under Wheaton a short distance toward the rebel works and stopped. Hancock, reputedly Meade's best field commander, put in a dismal performance. He could not see Barlow's front from his headquarters near Cold Harbor and relied on couriers for information. Although he had posted Birney in reserve to exploit a breakthrough, he did nothing when the 7th New York Heavy Artillery breached Edgar's salient. "We might have held on in Barlow's front had Birney's division moved promptly to its support, which was not done," Hancock's aide Mitchell wrote, blaming "great delay occurring on Birney's part or that of his subordinates" for the lapse. Birney, however, could not move until Hancock directed him to do so, and Hancock did not learn of the break in time to send him in. Hancock had performed poorly in the Wilderness and at Spotsylvania Court House, and Cold Harbor represented his worst day yet. Even the normally aggressive Barlow was in bad form. When

Brooke's attack stalled, Barlow not only failed to order up MacDougall's reserve brigade but also sent his other reserve brigade, under Byrnes, too far south to assist Brooke. "Our movement was not commanded right and we gained nothing but lost severely," was the verdict of Daniel Chisholm of the 116th Pennsylvania. "I guess we should have acted as a support for [Miles] but some mistake was made through some of the officers."[117]

Over the years, Union participants to a man condemned the spasmodic cluster of disconnected charges early on June 3 that passed for a grand offensive. Tactical problems inherent in coordinating an assault across a seven-mile front probably doomed the venture from the outset. The operation, Wright's aide Hyde asserted, "would have shamed a cadet at his first year at West Point." Smith later opined that Grant's plan of attack—an attack along the whole line—"is denounced by the standard writers on the art of war, and belongs to the first period in history after man had ceased to fight in unorganized masses." Grant agreed that the offensive had been botched. "I have always regretted that the last assault at Cold Harbor was ever made," he wrote from his deathbed. Carefully employing the passive voice, Grant's *mea culpa* left future generations to speculate whether the general's regrets were over his decision to attack on June 3 or, more pointedly, over Meade's bungled management of the affair. About the bottom line, however, Grant never equivocated. "No advantage whatever was gained to compensate for the heavy loss we sustained," he wrote.[118]

XI

JUNE 3

Lee Stalemates Grant Again

"Like hogs in a pen."

HALF PAST FOUR on the morning of June 3 found Meade and his staff at the Kelly house. Wright, who had made the Kelly place his headquarters, had gone to the front. Meade could hear muffled sounds of battle but could see nothing of the conflict. "There has been no fight of which I have seen so little as this," noted Lyman. "The woods were so placed that the sound, even, of the musketry was kept away, and the fighting, though near us, was completely shut from view."[1]

Meade eagerly awaited news from the front. As combat heated, Confederate shells dropped into the Kelly yard, one passing directly over the telegraph tent and cutting off a mule's hind legs. At 5:15 word arrived from Hancock that Barlow had broken into Breckinridge's works, capturing colors and guns. Meade and his aides were excited and considered the breakthrough "a gleam of hope for our success," Lyman recalled. Fifteen minutes later, prospects darkened. Barlow could not hold the works that he had carried—Edgar's salient—and had retired a short distance. At 6:00 A.M., more details came in from Hancock. Gibbon and Barlow had pressed close to the enemy but were unable to carry the line. Birney had advanced to Gibbon's and Barlow's jumping-off point, but Hancock doubted whether pushing more troops into the fray would help. "I shall await your orders," Hancock wrote Meade, "but express the opinion that if the first dash in an assault fails,"—clearly the case here—"other attempts are not apt to succeed better." Meade, however, was not about to quit. Grant had left him in charge of the offensive, and he was determined to make an aggressive showing. "You will make the attack and support it well, so that in the event of being successful, the advantage gained can be held," Meade directed Hancock. "If unsuccessful report at once."[2]

Dispatches from Hancock painted an increasingly dismal picture. Rather than renewing its attack, the 2nd Corps was digging in. "General Gibbon is making temporary entrenchments to try and hold his advance position, but expresses the opinion that it is not tenable," Hancock informed headquarters at 6:45. "The enemy's line was carried in one or two points, but not held." A report also arrived from Wright: the 6th Corps had taken rifle pits in the Confederate skirmish line and was attempting to push on. Wright added that Smith had briefly occupied a comparable line on his right but seemed to be retiring. Seeking guidance, Meade at 7:00 wrote Grant for his "views as to the continuance of these attacks, if unsuccessful." Grant's response left Meade considerable latitude. "The moment it becomes certain an assault cannot succeed, suspend the offensive" he instructed, "but when one does succeed push it vigorously, and if necessary pile in troops at the successful point from wherever they can be taken." There could be no doubt that deciding whether to continue or suspend the attacks rested solely in Meade's hands. Apprehensive about how Grant would judge his actions and wanting more information, Meade decided to persist. "I desire every effort be made to carry the enemy's works," he wrote Hancock. "Of course, if this is deemed impractical, after trial, the attack should be suspended, but the responsibility for this must be on your own judgment." After this transparent attempt to pass the decision on to Hancock, he closed: "I cannot give more decided orders. Report promptly." Grant's aide Adam Badeau later explained the thinking at headquarters. "The fact that Hancock had penetrated the rebel lines, although afterwards he was thrust out, and that all the other corps commanders had carried rifle pits—all seemed to show that more might be done."[3]

Meade's bellicose language was at sharp odds with reality. The army's southern wing was in no condition to renew the offensive. Hancock's, Wright's, and Smith's corps lay pinned under severe fire from the entrenched Confederate line, in places less than a hundred yards away. Dead and wounded men filled the no-man's land between opposing works. One of Kershaw's soldiers recalled corpses lying "in places like hogs in a pen—some side by side, across each other, some two deep, while others with their legs lying across the head and body of their dead comrades." Living men mimicked the dead in hope of staying alive until night, when they could crawl back to their lines under cover of darkness.[4]

Farther south, soldiers from the 8th New York Heavy Artillery huddled so close to Colquitt's entrenchments they could hear rebels talking. Blue-clad forms covered the field from where the regiment had begun its charge almost to Colquitt's line. The biggest heaps lay near the Confederate works. "We remained in the hot sun, crouched down in the little works we had constructed, so close to the enemy as to be unable to get to the rear for water or any necessaries of life without a volley of musketry after us," Private Nelson Armstrong remembered. "Sharp skirmishing was a frequent occurrence on any part of the line, and no man could stand erect one single moment without forming a target for the enemy's guns." Recollected another New Yorker: "Every stump and tree and molehill is a shelter and every man is working himself into the ground; so near the rebel works that some of our men creep in and have their wounds dressed in response to the invitation of the enemy; so near that one actually brings away a piece of corn bread thrown to him by a 'Johnny.'"[5]

In Gibbon's southern sector, Smyth's and Owen's Federals dug in opposite Martin's Tar Heels. "The lines, now but a few rods apart, held each other as in a vise," a soldier wrote. "Neither Confederate nor Unionist dared show his head above the parapets lest he be 'peeled,' nor was it safe for either to attempt to leave the works, nor for anyone to go to them." Remaining low behind mounds constructed from dirt and limbs, soldiers passed loaded muskets to the front line, where men kept up incessant fire. A soldier in the 152nd New York elevated a fence rail to help Union batteries in the rear better gauge the range. Men in the 4th Ohio raised hats on ramrods to draw enemy fire while their companions shot back at flashes from rebel muskets. "The works themselves were nearly bullet proof, and there was no danger save when one gave way to the provocation induced by the everlasting shooting, raised his head to see where the nonsense came from, determined on vengeance, and was himself pecked," a Buckeye reported. "There was more disposition to fun than seriousness," he claimed, "as some of the nervous ones juked and dodged when the balls had passed and danger was over; then there was such a scatterment made among the Johnnies, when the howitzers dropped an occasional round shot among them, and furnished us a good opportunity for rifle practice as their heads went bobbing, back into the trenches." George Bowen of the 12th New Jersey anguished at cries of wounded men between the lines, groaning and calling for water. "We can do nothing," he wrote in his diary. "It is as if there was an impassable gulf between us." Recollected a Mississippian in Mahone's division: "We mowed them down in good numbers. We felt sorry for them and wished that they had had sense enough to stay at home."[6]

Perhaps nowhere were the blue and gray pressed closer than around Edgar's salient. Finegan's Floridians occupied the works, and elements from Brooke's and Owen's brigades crammed the protected hollow immediately in front of the salient or hunkered behind piles of dirt less than fifty yards away. Musketry was incessant, and Federal artillery west of Dispatch Station

Road kept up unrelenting fire. The salient, protruding toward ground swarming with Federals, received fire from three sides. "In the bloody angle or
death trap it was almost as much as a man's life to show his head even for a
moment," remembered Captain James F. Tucker of the 9th Florida. "The fire
was galling, and came so thick and fast that our colors were riddled, and the
flagstaff perforated in a number of places. The feeling was that by holding up
an open hand Minie balls could be caught as if hailstones." No one could
come or go from the salient, and communication with the rear was almost
impossible. "Orders from and reports to headquarters," Tucker related, "had
to be transmitted by word of mouth or though the medium of a cap box passed
hand to hand, and ammunition was replenished the same way." Another Floridian wrote home: "If you raise your head in a minute you have a hole in
your head."[7]

As morning advanced, cries for water from wounded men lying between
the lines became insistent. Finally Lieutenant Joah D. O'Hern of the 2nd Florida could stand it no more and began gathering canteens. "What are you
going to do, Joah?" a companion asked. "I'm going to get some water for
the boys," he replied. "Man, you can't do it," his friend warned. "A rat
couldn't pass over that field unhurt." Undaunted, O'Hern slung the canteens
over his shoulder and started running across an open space toward a small
stream. "For the first hundred yards the balls from the Federals fell so thickly
around him that it seemed he must fall every second," a witness recalled.
Then the northerners sensed the purpose of O'Hern's mission and stopped
shooting. Reaching the water, O'Hern filled the canteens and started back
across the field. As he neared the Confederate lines, the Federals gave him a
cheer. Good will, however, was short-lived, and the combatants returned to
killing with a vengeance.[8]

The southern wing of the Union army had been fought to a standstill. Meade,
however, still hoped that the northern wing might accomplish something.
Burnside and Warren occupied the line they had established after their fight
against Early and Heth the previous evening. The 9th Corps—Willcox on the
left, Potter on the right, and Crittenden in reserve—spread east from Bethesda
Church along Old Church Road, facing north toward Heth's Confederates.
The 5th Corps picked up west of Bethesda Church, Griffin adjoining Willcox,
Cutler carrying the line south across Walnut Church Road, and Crawford ex-
tending to a point immediately west of David Woody's farm. Griffin faced
Rodes and Gordon, Cutler faced Ramseur, and Crawford opposed Field's and
Pickett's divisions of the Confederate 1st Corps.

Meade had expected Burnside and Warren to attack at 4:30 A.M. in support of the main assault, but neither commander was ready in time. "We could plainly hear the roar of guns upon the left in the early morning," a 9th Corps soldier noticed as the main attack exploded to the south. Half an hour later—Hancock's Wright's, and Smith's offensive was in full swing—one of Warren's troops complained of being "awakened by picket firing, the balls dropping among us as we ate breakfast." Warren justified his inaction by reminding headquarters that he was stretched thin. "In spite of all my efforts, I am unable to shorten my line yet so as to get any reserve beside the single line of battle," he wrote Meade at 6:00. "I cannot well advance unless those on my right or left succeed in doing so." Burnside, on Warren's right, busied himself shifting troops. "There was of course no attack made at 4:30 A.M. by the 9th Corps," Warren's aide Roebling noted derisively, admitting, however, that the 5th Corps had not budged either. "Our own corps was strung out in such a thin line that we would do well if we would hold our own," he added, parroting Warren. Finally, sometime between 6:00 and 6:30—Hancock, Wright, and Smith had finished their attacks, failed, and begun entrenching—Burnside's front started heating up.[9]

Potter's division, on Burnside's right, faced north toward a marshy finger of Matadequin Creek. Opposing Potter was Cooke's brigade, on the left end of Heth's line. Cooke had deployed some of his North Carolinians as skirmishers in the swamp, placed others in Mr. Armstrong's farmhouse and outbuildings, and posted the remainder in entrenchments immediately north of Shady Grove Road. Anticipating that Potter would attack his flank—"we could hear distinctly the orders given by their officers," one of Cooke's men recalled—Heth summoned Lieutenant Colonel William T. Poague and directed him to post artillery east of Cooke. Poague protested that the position was too exposed, but Heth insisted that he needed guns to protect his flank. Bringing up Captain William Wyatt's Albemarle Artillery and Lieutenant Thomas J. Richards's Madison Light Artillery, Poague sent them to the point designated by Heth, unhitched the horses, and dove for cover. "The two batteries came into position in handsome style, and just as the guns were unlimbered the enemy's infantry opened on us, not a scattering fire of skirmishers, but with a prefect hail of bullets from their line of battle, just as I had feared," Poague recounted. "In less time than I can write it, both batteries were disabled. Not an officer escaped. Two were mortally struck and the rest more or less badly wounded." With his adjutant's help, Poague ran two of Richards's guns to an embankment closer to Cooke where they could enfilade the field in front of Heth's line.[10]

Around 7:00 A.M.— two and a half hours late—Burnside began his offensive. Potter led with Curtin's brigade, holding Simon Griffin's brigade in reserve. "Forward was the word from Colonel Curtin," recalled William P. Hopkins of the 7th Rhode Island, "and forward we went through an underbrush swamp so dense it was impossible to maintain line formation." Another New Englander noticed soldiers "going to the knees in mud nearly ever step and under a heavy fire, men falling on every hand, the dead sinking into the mud and the wounded dragged back by comrades."[11]

Driving back Heth's skirmishers, Curtin's troops emerged onto solid ground north of Matadequin Creek, captured Cooke's advanced rifle pits, and drove rebels from the farm buildings. Continuing into a clearing, they came under blistering fire from Cooke's main line on high ground north of Shady Grove Road. "The right of the brigade encountered a strong line of works in open ground, covered by artillery in position, which could not be overcome," a Massachusetts man related of his experience with Poague's guns. "We on the left were exposed to the fire from the enemy entrenched line, not [160 feet] distant, and our flank was entirely exposed to a heavy crossfire." The field south of Shady Grove Road became a slaughter pen. "We were ordered not to give an inch of ground," one of Curtin's men recounted. "The ammunition was soon exhausted, and the cartridge boxes of the killed and wounded comrades were emptied for a fresh supply." A Tar Heel remembered the attack as especially hard-fought: "One line [of Federals] would fire and fall down, another step over, fire and fall down, each line getting nearer us, until they got within sixty or seventy-five yards of some portions of our line, but finding themselves cut to pieces so badly, they fell back in a little disorder." Curtin's men began digging. "By the aid of bayonets (to loosen the earth) and tin dippers we were enabled to throw up a slight line of earth works, which protected us in a small degree from the storm of bullets which the enemy were firing at us," a Federal reported.[12]

Davis's and Kirkland's brigades occupied entrenchments west of Cooke. "We were in 'apple pie' order behind our new line of breastworks," a soldier in the 55th North Carolina wrote, "which had been captured from the enemy the evening previous and which with very little labor during the night had been turned and rendered an admirable breastworks to stop Yankee balls." Noted another Confederate: "We did not wait long until the lines of blue coats were seen advancing in splendid order."[13]

The Federals moving up on Curtin's left belonged to Hartranft's brigade of Willcox's division. Brushing aside Heth's skirmishers, Hartranft's first line—the 8th Michigan, 27th Michigan, and 109th New York, under Colonel Dorus M. Fox—pressed north toward the Bowles farm. A second line, under Colonel William Humphrey and comprising the 51st Pennsylvania and 2nd Michigan, came close behind. Pushing to the front, the 51st Pennsylvania advanced at the double-quick, bayonets fixed, while Heth's men "poured volley after volley into the regiment," a Federal recalled. A ball tore through Lieutenant Isaac Fizone's head, killing him instantly, and continued through Colonel Edwin Shall's neck, killing Shall as well. The Pennsylvania regiment managed to capture an advance line of rifle pits at the price of 87 men killed and wounded but could go no farther. The 27th Michigan—"subjected to a perfect shower of bullets from the enemy in front," a Michigan man related— piled in next to the Pennsylvanians, and soon Hartranft's entire brigade was up.[14]

From Hartranft's position, Kirkland's and Davis's works were visible about two hundred yards across a clearing opening into the Bowles farm. Slightly concave, the rebel line formed a re-entrant angle, with four guns— also from Poague's battalion—posted at the apex. "The enemy fired but few shots from these guns," Hartranft reported, "as my sharpshooters watched the gunners closely, but his infantry, in his lines stretching off to my left, enfiladed my line, which had no cover from the left, and being little from the front, the troops made temporary cover by using their bayonets, tin cups, plates, etc." To counter Poague's pieces, Willcox ordered up two guns each from Captain Jacob Roemer's and Captain Adelbert B. Twitchell's batteries. Poague's fire, however, remained too "close and sharp" for Union artillery to be employed effectively. Concerned about the situation, Burnside asked Willcox whether he could carry the Confederate works. "I consulted with Major J. St. Claire Morton, chief engineer of the corps, and my two brigade commanders, Hartranft and Christ," Willcox wrote, "and decided I could succeed, provided my artillery could be first got into position." But for the time, Heth had stymied Burnside's offensive. "It soon became apparent that the enemy only intended advancing to the line of breastworks occupied by our sharpshooters about three hundred yards distant," one of Davis's southerners observed, "and they were suffered to proceed with the admonition, 'thus far, and no farther shalt thou come.'"[15]

Griffin's 5th Corps division posted on Hartranft's left also pitched in. Ordered to maintain connection with the 9th Corps, Griffin directed his rightmost brigade, under Sweitzer, to advance in lockstep with Hartranft. Colonel Tilton, commanding the 22nd Massachusetts and eighty men from the 4th Michigan, led the way. Behind came the 9th and 32nd Massachusetts, the 62nd Pennsylvania, and the 21st Pennsylvania, a new dismounted cavalry regiment recently assigned to the brigade and armed with Spencer carbines. Tilton's troops had scarcely left their breastworks when volleys from Rodes's Confederates slammed into them. "Moving forward at a run, we charged across the open field to the woods on our front, about six hundred yards, driving everything before us, and halting only when we had lost one-fourth of the regiment, and got within one hundred and fifty yards of the enemy's breast-works," John L. Parker of the 22nd Massachusetts recalled. "Never shall I forget the storm of bullets, grape and canister that was rained upon us," swore the 32nd Massachusetts's Henry B. James. "My comrades fell on my right and left till I thought there would be none left to tell the tale." When James bent to tie his shoe, his comrades thought he had been hit and ran over to help him. "I was up in an instant, and on with the rest," he related.[16]

Unable to budge Rodes from Shady Grove Road, Sweitzer's men followed the example of Hartranft's and Curtin's soldiers on their right and began dig-ging. Their line bowed forward, enabling Confederates on each flank to fire into the opposite Federal flank's rear. "We sheltered ourselves as best we could," a Massachusetts man reported, but casualties were high. The 22nd Massachusetts lost twenty-six men, including Captain Joseph Baxter, shot through the bowels; Corporal Edward M. Walton, shot through the chin; and Private George A. Steele, returned the day before from furlough, shot through the heart. The 32nd Massachusetts counted fifty-two casualties, "most of them by grape and canister while crossing the field." When Confederate sharpshooters ensconced in the upper story of a barn began picking off Sweitzer's men, Sweitzer brought up Captain Phillips's 5th Massachusetts Battery. Firing at the barn from behind Sweitzer's line, Phillips started by shooting high, then gradually lowered the trajectory. His third shot "struck fairly making the splinters fly in a shower," a Federal recalled, noting that "the Confederates vacated and did not return."[17]

Burnside's and Warren's attacks had advanced the 9th and 5th Corps's line only a few hundred yards, narrowing the gap between them and the Confeder-ate works but nowhere reaching the Confederate position. "The whole move was a gradual swing around to our right," Wainwright noted, "Bartlett's bri-gade finally coming round at right angles to [Old Church Road] on a line with that of Ayres, and the 9th Corps stretching from there northeast to the Armstrong house, with their skirmishers across the Shady Grove Road." The rest of the 5th Corps remained in line extending to the south and was not seriously engaged. By 7:30, Burnside and Warren—like Hancock, Wright, and Smith to their south—were deadlocked in front of impenetrable Confed-erate fortifications.[18]

His offensive at a standstill, Burnside hit upon conducting a joint operation with Wilson's cavalry division. Wilson's troopers had spent June 2 around Hanover Court House recovering from their close call at Ashland and patrol-ling the interval between the Union army and the Pamunkey. Late in the day, Colonel Louis P. DiCesnola arrived from Port Royal with 4,000 infantry and

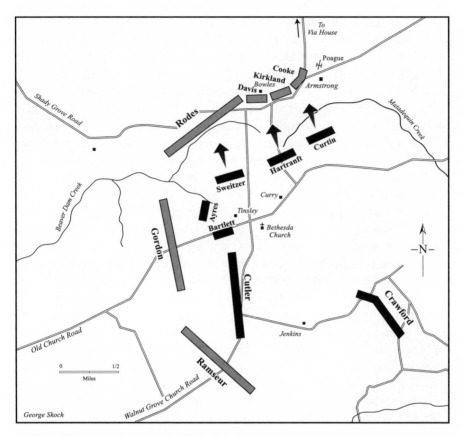

Burnside's and Warren's attacks on morning of June 3

cavalry. Temporarily assigned to Wilson, DiCesnola's force "was composed of motley detachments on the way to the army," Wilson described it, "and added but little to our strength and nothing to our mobility."[19]

Isolated at Hanover Court House, Wilson decided to shift southeast to re-establish contact with the Union army. He set off around 7:00 P.M. on June 2, leading his troopers and DiCesnola's recent arrivals on a miserable night march. "The clattering of horses feet over lost canteens, sabers, etc., twice men and horses under our feet—hats knocked off by overhanging branches—roads leading through swamps—over corduroys—up and down hill—a darkness so intense that at times I could see no part of my horse," a New Jersey man recalled. It was still dark when Wilson's horsemen reached Old Church and bivouacked. "My men were so tired that they could hardly sit their jaded and half-famished horses," Wilson wrote.[20]

Shortly after sunrise on June 3, Wilson deployed his troopers along the two-mile stretch of road running from Old Church to Burnside's right. DiCesnola's troops, now thoroughly worn out, marched through Old Church and massed behind the 9th Corps. At 5:45 A.M., Humphreys, acting under the erroneous belief that Wilson had camped somewhere around Crump's Creek, directed him to hold Haw's Shop and Hanovertown and to attack Heth's Confederates in the rear. The message caught up with Wilson at Old Church two hours later—Burnside's attack was already over—and the cavalryman fired off a note asking for clarification. Burnside, he explained, had contacted him, expressed concern that Confederates might turn the 9th Corps's right flank, and asked him to help protect the right end of the infantry line. "To go now by Haw's would require a circuit of 7 miles," Wilson reminded Humphreys. "Shall I go, or perfect the arrangement"—watching Burnside's flank—"indicated in the first part of this communication?"[21]

After consulting with Burnside, headquarters decided that Wilson should leave DiCesnola with the 9th Corps, take his mounted force back to Haw's Shop, and attack Heth's Confederates from behind. If all went as planned, Wilson would plow into Heth's rear around 1:00 P.M., the same time that Burnside was to attack Heth from in front. The dual offensive, Burnside wrote headquarters, "I hope will be productive of good results."[22]

Various corps heads advised Meade of their status between 7:30 and 8:00. "We have carried the first line of the enemy's works, and are now reforming the line, with a view to assaulting the main line," Burnside wrote, trying to put a positive spin on the fact that Heth had stopped him cold. Warren reported also, stressing that his line was still too extended to accomplish anything. Wright's analysis of why the 6th Corps could not move was especially intriguing. "I am in advance of everything else," he wrote. "If I advance my right farther, without a corresponding advance by the Eighteenth Corps, I am, from the form of the enemy's lines, taken in flank and reverse. My left [next to Gibbon] cannot well be advanced for the same reason." In short, Wright suspected he could carry the works in his center but was afraid to try because his flanks could not safely move. "My losses will show that there has been no hanging back on the part of the Sixth Corps, which has so far moved very satisfactorily," he assured Meade, ignoring the fact that only one of his brigades had done anything remotely resembling an attack. "I may be pardoned for suggesting that the important attack for our success is by the Eighteenth Corps," he concluded. Baldy Smith, however, saw things differently and complained that he could not assault until the 6th Corps moved.[23]

With Wright and Smith blaming each other for their own inaction, Meade threw all pretense of coordination to the winds. "General Wright has been ordered to assault at once and to conduct his attack without reference to your advance," Humphreys wrote Smith at 8:00, "and the commanding general directs that your assault be continued without reference to General Wright's." Colonel Wainwright was astounded when he heard about the directive. "After the failure [of the initial attacks], there was still a more absurd order issued, for each commander to attack without reference to its neighbors, as they saw fit," he wrote, "an order which looked as if the commander, whoever he is, had either lost his head entirely, or wanted to shift responsibility off his own shoulders."[24]

Smith wrote back complaining of shortages in ammunition but otherwise promised to do his best. "I will do whatever can be done, and attempt whatever may be ordered," he assured Meade. "I have ordered all my troops available for the new column." More bad news dribbled in from Hancock. Gibbon and Barlow were willing to renew their assaults, he explained, but enfilading artillery fire prevented them from moving. Their troops held advanced ground, Hancock assured Meade, and were "only awaiting the decision of the question whether any additional assaults are wise." The 2nd Corps commander was not optimistic. "I consider that the assault failed long since," he informed Meade, "but I volunteered the statement that we would cling to the advanced positions gained, so that, if any success were gained by other corps on our right, we would feel ready to try it again, as we would feel that additional chances had arisen." Unless he could silence the rebel batteries, he did not consider further attacks possible.[25]

Meade remained insistent. Wright, he wrote Hancock, believed he could make progress if the 2nd and 18th Corps also attacked. "It is of the greatest importance no effort should be spared to succeed," Meade stressed, doubtless anxious to leave a paper trail sufficiently belligerent to satisfy Grant that he had done his best. "Wright and Smith are both going to try again, and unless you consider it hopeless I would like you do the same." Hancock remained pessimistic. "An assault can be promptly repeated if desired, but division commanders do not speak encouragingly of the prospect of success since the original attacks failed," he wrote back. "Unless success has been gained in other points, I do not advise persistence here."[26]

The reporter William Swinton claimed in 1866 that Meade's directive to his corps commanders to try to renew their assaults incited mutiny in the ranks. "The order was issued through these officers to their subordinate commanders, and from them descended through the wonted channels," Swinton wrote in his *Campaigns of the Army of the Potomac,* "but no man stirred, and the immobile lines pronounced a verdict, silent, yet emphatic, against further slaughter." Swinton's story of soldiers refusing en masse to obey suicidal orders makes engaging reading and appears in most histories of the battle, but it is highly suspect. The evening after the battle, Swinton wrote a detailed account of the day's events and mentioned nothing about troops refusing to charge. With the exception of a single narrative from the 12th New Jersey, no letters, diaries, or any other contemporaneous narratives document refusals of soldiers to obey orders to renew the attack. None of the corps commanders favored resuming the offensive, and none of them ordered their soldiers back into the killing ground between the opposing works. On the 6th Corps front, officers and soldiers alike recognized that advancing was "a simple and absolute impossibility," Wright's aide McMahon noted, "and the order was obeyed simply by renewing the fire from the men as they lay in position." Necessity compelled soldiers elsewhere to do as Wright's men did, inching ahead where possible to throw up new works, or simply firing in place. But being unable to advance was not the same as refusing to advance. Grant banned Swinton from headquarters after discovering him monitoring private conversations and evicted him from the army early in July 1864. Perhaps the reporter's treatment by Grant and Meade led him to pen his sensational account of an army sullenly refusing to budge.[27]

Swinton's postwar version provoked vociferous denials. Grant insisted that he "never gave an order to any army that I commanded during the rebellion to make an attack where it was disobeyed." Hancock's aide Walker dismissed Swinton's claim as "erroneous," and another officer fumed that "never was a baser libel or a more unfounded and gratuitous slander uttered." Swinton's statement "has been squarely denied by Grant and indignantly repelled by many soldiers," wrote George G. Benedict in his history of the Vermont units. "Certainly there was never a time when the 6th Corps or the Vermont

Brigade refused to attack when ordered." Noted another veteran: "That the commanding general should issue a distinct order, and that the soldiers of his army should utterly refuse to take the first step toward its obedience, is not to be believed for a moment."[28]

A midmorning attack did take place, but it was made by the Confederates, not by the Federals. Around 10:00 A.M., in a desperate gambit to drive the Yankees back and gain breathing room, Finegan directed Major Pickens Bird of the 9th Florida to take a skirmish line over Edgar's salient. Bird and his men recognized that the order was, as a student of the venture noted, "at best, irresponsible, and, at worst, criminal." Bird instructed company commanders to detail every fifth man for the assignment. A soldier to the core, Bird called above the din, "Attention, skirmishers. Forward, march." Lieutenant Henry W. Long of the regiment remembered that many troops considered the order "foolhardy" and refused to comply. When Captain Robert D. Harrison's company balked, Harrison jumped onto the breastworks, waved his sword in encouragement, and was immediately shot. Major Bird made it over the works and some thirty yards toward the Federals before he, too, was cut down. Seeing Bird fall, Captain Tucker leapt over the works, ran to the major, lifted him in his arms, and fell severely wounded. Lieutenant Benjamin Lane ran to the wounded officers, picked up Bird, and began carrying him back when a Yankee bullet took him down, mortally wounding him. The ill-advised attack was over within minutes, and survivors of the 9th Florida tried to rescue their wounded officers lying in a shallow trench in front of the salient. When firing abated, Sergeant Peter N. Bryan crawled out to Tucker and dragged the paralyzed captain back into the works. Floridians also pulled Bird to safety, and the two men lay wedged with other wounded soldiers between traverses—"like so many sardines in a box," Tucker recalled— for the rest of the day. Tucker had three bulletholes through his hat from the charge and received a fourth when enfilade fire cut a furrow in his scalp and clipped off a lock of hair. Bird died four days later, but Tucker survived and sent his fiancée the tuft of hair shot from his head.[29]

Despite Meade's prodding, none of his corps commanders showed any inclination to resume the offensive. Bridling at Meade's insinuation that he was dilatory, Warren protested that he was "not waiting for anybody, but putting in whenever I can judiciously." His corps was stretched only one soldier deep, he reminded Meade, adding: "I cannot maintain the battle all day this way without reinforcements." The solution, Warren suggested, was to retract his left. Meade, however, wanted him to extend his left and was aghast at this proposal. "It will not do to draw in your left," he fired back. "Smith, who is attacking, is seriously checked by an enfilade from his right, which would be relieved by an advance of your left." At all cost, Meade stressed, Warren must make contact with the 18th Corps. "There are no reinforcements to send you," he added, "all of the corps here being fully engaged endeavoring to break through the enemy's line, as yet without success, but not without hope of ultimate success." Ultimate success, however, looked increasingly remote. "As yet I do not get much encouragement from commanders to hope for a successful issue to an attack," read the latest dispatch from Hancock, pretty well summarizing the state of affairs along the entire line. Tacitly admitting that he expected no more action from the 2nd Corps, Meade withdrew Birney's division and shifted it north between Warren and Smith. Warren was grateful for the reinforcements but did not think he could accomplish anything with them.[30]

Writing some thirty years afterward, Baldy Smith claimed that Meade visited his lines and gave him a "verbal" order to make another assault. "That order I refused to obey," Smith asserted. According to Smith's account, Comstock of Grant's staff came by an hour later, examined his lines with Smith's aide Captain Farquhar, and left "thoroughly satisfied" to explain the situation to Grant. "What Colonel Comstock reported I never knew," Smith wrote, "but I heard nothing more from headquarters on the subject." Smith's description of his strident refusal to comply with Meade's oral instruction probably represents nothing more than wishful thinking on his part. He mentioned no such incident in his official report, and his account did not appear until after Meade's death. Meade never wrote of the incident, nor did Comstock, Grant, or anyone other than Smith. It is impossible to imagine Meade, who had exhausted his patience with Smith, tolerating open insubordination and never saying or doing anything about it. Smith's story is also at odds with his written assurances to Meade, penned at the time of his purported refusal to comply with Meade's orders, that he would "do whatever can be done, and attempt whatever may be ordered." Like many tales surrounding the fight of June 3, Smith's postwar boast belongs more to the realm of fantasy than to fact.[31]

Grant visited the front around 11:00 A.M. His purpose, he later explained, was to "see for myself the different positions gained and to get [the corps heads'] opinion of the practicality of doing anything more in their respective fronts." They repeated what they had been saying all morning. "Hancock gave the opinion that in his front the enemy was too strong to make any further assault promise success," Grant wrote. "Wright thought he could gain the lines of the enemy, but it would require the cooperation of Hancock's and Smith's corps. Smith thought a lodgment possible, but was not sanguine;

Burnside thought something could be done on his front, but Warren differed."[32]

Shortly after noon, Grant issued orders ending the attack. "The opinion of corps commanders not being sanguine of success in case an assault is ordered, you may direct a suspension of farther advance for the present," read the commander's missive. "Hold our most advanced positions, and strengthen them. Whilst on the defensive, our line may be contracted from the right, if practicable. Reconnaissances should be made in front of every corps, and advances made to advantageous positions by regular approaches." The Union offensive at Cold Harbor was over.[33]

"A standup fight in an open field against an intrenched foe."

While Grant was formally terminating the offensive that had actually died several hours earlier, fighting flared up again on Burnside's front. Around 10:00 A.M., Wilson's division had left Old Church, crossed Totopotomoy Creek, and continued northwest toward Haw's Shop, where the cavalryman intended to turn south and slice into Heth's rear. Coincidentally, in a fortuitous replication of events on May 28, Wade Hampton was riding with some of Rooney Lee's horsemen east from Atlee's Station on a reconnaissance toward Haw's Shop, on a collision course with Wilson. In front of Lee's column were troopers from the 2nd and 5th North Carolina Cavalry of Baker's brigade. Near Haw's Shop, the Tar Heels encountered the 8th New York Cavalry in Wilson's advance and launched an impetuous charge replete with "deafening yells." The second battle of Haw's Shop was on.[34]

Surprise favored the Confederates. Major William P. Roberts, leading the two North Carolina regiments, routed the New Yorkers and drove them back on the rest of Chapman's brigade. Now facing a large body of Union horsemen, Roberts retreated into a stand of woods southwest of Haw's Shop. There his men dismounted and threw up breastworks three lines deep, inviting the Federals to charge.[35]

Near 1:00 P.M., Wilson accepted Roberts's challenge. Accompanied by horse artillery, the 1st Vermont Cavalry and the 5th and 8th New York Cavalry dismounted and charged into the woods toward the Confederates. According to Wilson, his troopers marched steadily forward in open order, "their rapid-fire carbines pouring out volley after volley, capturing prisoners and clearing up the country as they went along." Fighting was severe and in "Indian style," a Vermont man wrote. During the advance, a Confederate shot Lieutenant Colonel Preston, commanding the 1st Vermont, through the back, the bullet passing near his heart. After several attempts, Preston's soldiers managed to drag his body to safety. They threw water in his face to revive him, but he soon died.[36]

Wilson's battle line overlapped Major Roberts's position, rendering the Confederate line untenable. As elements from the 1st Vermont began slipping around Roberts's left flank, Rooney Lee directed the Tar Heels to retire. Federals pressed from their right and front. "The cross fire of artillery and musketry just mowed down the rebels," a Union man remarked. Falling back to Enon Church, the North Carolinians relinquished Haw's Shop to Wilson. "Gordon's old brigade made but poor fight," Wilson wrote of the affair in his diary. Rooney Lee, however, thought that Roberts's two regiments had done all that could be expected and congratulated them "for their gallant conduct on the occasion."[37]

Wilson's and Roberts's engagement lasted a few hours but generated surprisingly few casualties on either side. Besides Preston, Captain Oliver T. Cushman of the 1st Vermont was killed, and Colonel William H. Benjamin of the 8th New York was shot in the leg. Altogether, however, Wilson's casualties did not exceed twenty officers and men. On the Confederate side, Roberts, commanding the two North Carolina regiments, was wounded, and about twenty of his men were captured, wounded, or killed.

While Wilson fought his heated action against the Tar Heels, Burnside, who had not yet learned that Grant had canceled the offensive, prepared to attack Heth. Ninth Corps infantry details labored beside artillerists, digging positions for guns to support the assault. "The workmen were shot down every moment," Willcox wrote of the hazardous undertaking. Finally Willcox sent in Indian marksmen from the 1st Michigan Sharpshooters, who hid behind pine trees and methodically picked off Confederates, gaining breathing room for the northern troops. In preparation for the attack, Willcox shifted Hartranft somewhat left, giving his brigade a shorter stretch of field to cross to reach Heth's line.[38]

Potter also accelerated his preparations on Burnside's right, moving Captain Edward W. Rogers's 19th New York Battery near the front in support of Curtin's and Simon Griffin's brigades. The 17th Vermont, on the east end of Griffin's line, wheeled into a field and formed at right angles to the rest of the brigade. Subjected to ferocious enfilading fire from Heth's men across Shady Grove Road, Lieutenant Colonel Charles Cummings, commanding the regiment, shifted two companies to the right to support his skirmishers. They managed to silence the enfilading fire and discovered a masked Confederate battery waiting for the brigade to advance. Concluding that his position was untenable, Griffin withdrew from the clearing. The unequal bout of combat—

"a standup fight in an open field against an intrenched foe," Cummings later described it—cost the regiment sixteen men.[39]

The 6th New Hampshire and 32nd Maine of Griffin's brigade took cover in a sunken farm road, safe from Confederate fire. The 31st Maine, however, extended into the field and came under heavy musketry. "We held our position perhaps five hundred feet from the rebel earthworks which blazed and smoked and cracked like a great bunch of fire crackers, and the air around us hissed with flying minnies and buckshot," Sergeant Major L. O. Merriam of the 31st related. "Firing wildly at the smoking woods in our front was simply throwing bullets away, so shutting my teeth tight to keep my nerves in working order, I aimed each shot with all the care I could at the puffs of smoke in our front." After the regiment had lost some seventy-five men and gained not an inch of ground, Griffin sent orders to fall back. "I never repeated the order of the commanding officer more vigorously than that," remembered Merriam.[40]

At 3:00 P.M., Burnside instructed Potter and Willcox to attack. Gazing across the field at Heth's entrenchments, the 9th Corps's soldiers rightly judged the venture suicidal. Just as Colonel Fox stepped off leading Hartranft's first line, a note reach Burnside alerting him that Grant had canceled the offensive. Breathing a sigh of relief, Burnside countermanded his order to assault. His troops, equally relieved, settled down behind their earthworks. The 5th Corps staffer Roebling, who never had anything good to say about the 9th Corps, speculated tongue-in-cheek that Burnside had called off his attack "perhaps because there was a prospect of success." In fact, there was no prospect of success, and the cancellation was Grant's doing, not Burnside's.[41]

Wilson, who was winding up his fight at Haw's Shop, had no way of knowing that Burnside had aborted his assault. Still assuming that he was to attack Heth's rear in cooperation with the 9th Corps, Wilson started Chapman south with some four hundred troopers from the 2nd New York Cavalry and 3rd Indiana Cavalry, along with Captain Dunbar R. Ransom's 3rd United States Artillery, Battery C. Fording Totopotomoy Creek, Chapman's force came into Mrs. Via's clearing, picketed by soldiers from the 22nd Virginia Battalion of Brigadier General Birkett D. Fry's brigade. Attacking, Chapman pried the Virginians from their stronghold at the Via place, held the farm for about an hour, then left. Fry's men claimed that they "drove them back with ease," but the Federals insisted they had departed of their own volition. "Failing to establish communication with the infantry on my left," Wilson wrote, "I withdrew to the [north] side of the Totopotomoy." McIntosh camped near Haw's Shop, with Ransom's battery. Chapman, with Lieutenant Frank S.

French's battery, covered the road from Hanovertown to Old Church, posting a regiment at Hanovertown.[42]

The day's fighting on the battlefield's northern sector was over. The offensive had cost Warren about 400 soldiers and Burnside double that number, for a total of 1,200 casualties on the 5th and 9th Corps fronts. As Early and Heth had held firm, neither Warren nor Burnside had anything to show for their losses. Their sole contribution was to increase the Army of the Potomac's tally of men killed, wounded, and captured for the day on all fronts to slightly over 6,000.[43]

Confederate casualties in the northern sector are difficult to calculate, as losses were generally reported for the period June 1–3. Heth's division, which bore the brunt of the offensives on June 2 and 3, lost 560 men those two days, 170 of them from Davis's brigade, 133 from Cooke's, 175 from Kirkland's, and about 85 from Fry's. Perhaps a third of Heth's losses occurred on June 3, when he acted on the defense. Rodes's division, which was not heavily engaged on June 3, lost perhaps a hundred men that day, bringing total rebel losses in the sector for June 3 to about 300. Historians have estimated the Army of Northern Virginia's total losses for June 3 as falling between 1,000 and 1,500 soldiers, an approximation that modern counts confirm.[44]

Toward evening, Finegan decided to attempt once again to drive the Federals back from the salient. This time he gave the assignment to Captain Charles Seton Fleming's veteran 2nd Florida, augmented by elements from other veteran Florida regiments. The 2nd Florida had been gutted at Seven Pines, Gettysburg, and the Wilderness and numbered only about forty-five men. Fleming was a handsome scion of a prominent Florida family—his brother Francis P. Fleming later became the state's governor—and the troops liked him. Finegan's order to repeat the attack that Major Bird had already proved impossible took Fleming aback. Fully aware that the assignment was futile, he asked for confirmation of the order and learned to his astonishment that he had heard it correctly. "I have been told that the order was all a mistake and was not so intended," wrote Captain Tucker, who witnessed Fleming's reaction and was inclined to give Finegan the benefit of the doubt. "Probably a verbal order was passed down the line from mouth to mouth," Tucker surmised, "and some qualifying or optional directions were dropped in its transmission."[45]

Leaning against the interior wall of the breastworks, Fleming took off his watch and handed it to a man next to him. He gave his pocket-book and papers to Dr. Richard P. Daniel, the 8th Florida's surgeon and a close friend.

Then he addressed his soldiers, telling them that he had been ordered to go, that he wanted them to follow, and that he expected this to be the last order he would ever give them. He exposed himself on the works while he talked, and a soldier warned him to be careful. "He remarked that it did not matter," a witness recounted, "'twas only the difference of a few moments." Fleming cast several glances toward Tucker, lying in agony between the traverses, but said nothing to him. "The occasion was too serious," Tucker recalled. "The crucial moment had come." At the signal, Fleming and his men vaulted over the works. "There was no touch of the elbow to give confidence and encouragement, no wild and exultant 'Rebel yell,' as with a massed brigade or division making a charge, to stimulate," Tucker observed. "There was neither impulsiveness nor excitement to dull the sense of peril. Their one and only consolation was consciousness of duty performed, however dire the consequences might be to themselves." Tucker summed up his impressions: "To my mind their behavior was superlatively heroic, and I much doubt if it has ever been surpassed."[46]

Bravery was no shield from bullets. With a shout of "Good-by, boys," Fleming dashed forward and was immediately shot. Bullets cut his men down almost as soon as they emerged on the Union side of the works. A few days later, during a truce to collect wounded soldiers from between the lines, Alabamians found Fleming's body within thirty yards of the salient. Not a man who charged with him survived.[47]

Around 8:00 P.M., Martin's North Carolinians girded to attack Smyth's and Owen's brigades of Gibbon's division in their front. Who gave the order and why is not apparent from existing records, although its objective might have been to help Finegan drive the Federals back in his front. Commotion behind Martin's lines alerted Smyth's and Owen's soldiers, who reserved their fire and made sure that extra cartridges lay close at hand. The sun had dipped below the horizon when artillery behind Martin opened, raking the Union position. Most of the projectiles, an Ohio man remembered, passed high. "Soon the commands of their officers were heard, then the well known yell, then the rush for the line," the Philadelphia Brigade's historian wrote. Soldiers in blue peered into the darkness, where they could see forms charging across the no-man's land toward them. "The men rose in their places and poured in heavy volleys of musketry," a Union soldier recalled, "and for a few moments there was a struggle as severe as in the morning." One of Smyth's troops recounted that the rebels "received a volley from our first line, then immediately from our second, whilst the first loaded and again fired, took the guns of the second, and with a keen outlook, kept up an accurate firing at the objects on their front, whilst others continued to load as rapidly as possible, and handed over the loaded pieces and in return received and reloaded the empty guns." The technique proved effective, inflicting about a hundred casualties, breaking the attack, and driving the Confederates back to their own works. A Federal noted cheerfully that "this was the first time we had an opportunity to repel a charge whilst occupying breastworks."[48]

The evening counterattacks gained the Confederates nothing. The day's fighting had cost Finegan some 275 casualties. His prompt repulse of Barlow's troops at Edgar's salient elicited praise, but his forlorn attacks afterward reflected bad judgment or, according to some accounts, an undue fondness for alcohol. The Florida soldiers, however, won the approbation of Lee's veterans. "If they did have on bed quilts and homespun jackets, they made a reputation that morning that proved they were as good as the best we had in our army," a soldier averred. Toward midnight, veteran Confederates on each side of the Florida men took up the cry, "Three cheers for Finegan's brigade!" Writing years later, a Floridian reminisced: "I need not say that we felt good over it, and I am not ashamed to say we deserved it."[49]

"I see no end to this matter."

Finegan's and Martin's assaults closed active fighting at Cold Harbor. "Tonight all the trenching tools were ordered up and the lines were strengthened, and saps run out, so as to bring them still closer to the opposing ones," Lyman reported in a letter home. "And there the two armies slept, almost within an easy stone-throw of each other; and the separating space ploughed by cannon-shot and clotted with the dead bodies that neither side dared to bury!" Reflected Lyman: "I think nothing can give a greater idea of deathless tenacity of purpose, than the picture of these two hosts, after a bloody and nearly continuous struggle of thirty days, thus lying down to sleep, with their heads almost on each other's throats! Possibly it has no parallel in history."[50]

The maneuvers that Grant initiated with his withdrawal from the North Anna River over a week before had reached impasse. Cold Harbor would follow the Wilderness, Spotsylvania Court House, and the North Anna as fourth on Grant's list of failed offensives. The armies would remain locked together nine more days. Men would die, generals would bicker over truces, and Grant would devise a new plan of maneuver designed to steal a march on Lee, cross the James River, and slice Richmond's critical rail connections at Petersburg. But the offensive phase of the Cold Harbor operation was over. "We gained nothing save a knowledge of their position and the proof of the unflinching bravery of our soldiers," was Lyman's verdict.[51]

Grant advised Halleck of the state of affairs. "We assaulted at 4:30 o'clock this morning, driving the enemy within his entrenchments at all points, but without gaining any decisive advantage," he reported. "Our troops now occupy a position close to the enemy, some places within 50 yards, and are intrenching. Our loss was not severe," he added, minimizing his casualties, "nor do I suppose the enemy to have lost heavily." Dana also penned a note to War Secretary Stanton. "At noon we had fully developed the rebel lines, and could see what was necessary to get through them," he reported, adding that Grant had suspended the attack after querying the corps commanders. "We hold all the positions gained, except that temporarily occupied by Barlow," Dana wrote. "Of our losses no returns have yet been made. General Grant estimates the number of killed and wounded at about 3,000."[52]

Early the next morning, Dana discussed the question of casualties with Meade's staff and updated his report. "Adjutant General [Seth] Williams reports to me that our entire losses in killed, wounded, and missing during the three days' operations around Cold Harbor will not exceed 7,500," he wrote, referring to the combined operations from June 1 through June 3. Williams's statement to Dana fairly represented headquarters's assessment of casualties—in a letter home Meade figured the day's losses at "roughly" 7,500, and his aide Biddle wrote home that losses for June 3 "will amount to about 5,000 in all." In the absence of complete casualty returns, estimates were all that headquarters could do, and the approximations fell in the same general range quoted by Dana. A century later, conspiracy theory devotees claimed that Grant conspired to put a lid on his true casualties at Cold Harbor until the Republican convention, scheduled to convene on June 7, had nominated Lincoln. Nothing about the timing or accuracy of reports on Cold Harbor, however, differs significantly from the timing or accuracy of battle reporting throughout the campaign. On Monday, June 6, the *New York Herald* published a front-page report parroting Dana's latest dispatch that losses for the previous three days' fighting around Cold Harbor "will not exceed, according to the Adjutant General's report, seven thousand five hundred." The next day—June 7—the *New York Times* ran a headline reporting "heavy losses on our side" at Cold Harbor, in a battle that produced "no decisive result." The accompanying article estimated casualties at 5,000 to 6,000 and candidly described the failure of the attack. That same day, the Republican convention opened in Baltimore. The following day, delegates nominated Lincoln for president, fully cognizant of the bloodshed at Cold Harbor and of Grant's failure to achieve success there.[53]

When viewed in the war's larger context, the June 3 attack falls short of its popular reputation for slaughter. Grant lost more men each day in the Wilderness and on two different days at Spotsylvania Court House than he did on June 3, making his main effort at Cold Harbor only the fifth bloodiest day for the Federals since crossing the Rapidan. The two years preceding Cold Harbor had seen a host of days in which Union and Confederate armies each sustained far more casualties than Grant suffered on June 3. Lee's casualties in three days fighting at Gettysburg, for example, exceeded 22,000, with Confederate losses on the last day of the battle topping 8,000. Pickett's famous charge at Gettysburg—a frontal attack that lasted about as long as Grant's main morning attack at Cold Harbor—cost the Confederates between 5,300 and 5,700 men, a number well in excess of the 3,500–4,000 that Grant lost during his main June 3 attack. And while cumulative casualties in Grant's successive battles against Lee were high, no single day of Grant's pounding saw the magnitude of Union casualties that McClellan incurred in one day at Antietam, and no three consecutive days of Grant's warring proved as costly to the Union as Meade's three days at Gettysburg. In the Overland campaign, Grant waged several consecutive battles, one after the other. Unlike his predecessors, who disengaged after their battles and left Lee to repair his losses, Grant followed up his fights with a vengeance. In the end, he had something to show for his efforts.[54]

The month of relentless combat and brutal assaults culminating in the June 3 offensive took a profound toll on Union officers and men. "It has been fight, fight, fight," a surgeon wrote home on June 4. "Every day there is a fight, and every day the hospital is again filled." He was "heartsick over it all," he continued. "If the Confederates lost in each fight the same number as we, there would be more chance for us; but their loss is about one man to our five, from the fact that they never leave their earthworks, whereas our men are obliged to charge even when there is not the slightest chance of taking them."[55]

Lyman noted that Warren seemed especially careworn. "For thirty days now, it had been one funeral procession past me, and it has been too much," Warren told the aide. "Today I saw a man burying a comrade, and, within half an hour, he himself was brought in and buried beside him. The men need some rest." Meade's staffer Biddle voiced similar concern. "This had been an unparalleled campaign," he wrote home on June 4. "The army has been fighting continuously for a month without any intermission." Lyman, who had a knack for cutting to the heart of things, described the cumulative effect of the Wilderness, Spotsylvania, North Anna, and Cold Harbor operations: "The best officers and men are liable, by their greater gallantry, to be first disabled; and, of those who are left, the best become demoralized by the failures, and the loss of good leaders; so that, very soon, the men will no longer charge entrenchments and will only go forward when driven by their officers." Adjutant John R. Higgenbotham of the 155th New York echoed Lyman's observation. "This charging on earthworks and the terrible losses sustained truly has dispirited many of the Old Army of the Potomac regiments, and they do not go in half as our [new] men," he wrote home.[56]

Although Grant and his subordinates were frustrated at their inability to pierce Lee's line at Cold Harbor, they did not consider the reverse any more serious than Lee's previous rebuffs. Reviewing the week's operations, Grant and Meade thought they had done rather well, having turned Lee out of his North Anna line, maneuvered him nearly twenty miles closer to the Confederate capital, and cornered him against Richmond. The attempt to punch through Lee's works at Cold Harbor had failed, but the campaign still held fair prospects for ultimate success. "The battle ended without any decided results, we repulsing all attacks of the enemy and they doing the same," Meade wrote home the next morning. "The enemy, as usual, were strongly fortified, and we have pretty well entrenched ourselves. How long this game is to be played it is impossible to tell," he conceded, "but in the long run, we ought to succeed, because it is in our power more promptly to fill the gaps in men and material which this constant fighting produces." Meade's aide Biddle was more pessimistic than his boss. "The accounts in the papers are preposterous," he wrote home. "They represent Lee's army as demoralized and in full retreat for Richmond. I only wish I could form the same opinion. I feel sanguine of our ultimate success, but it can only be accomplished by time and by hard fighting. The rebel army fight desperately and have contested heroically every inch of ground. They have fallen back because they have been outflanked, but in no case has it been a disorderly retreat with our army on their heels."[57]

Some Union soldiers also believed that the Confederacy's end was near, although how near remained a matter of debate. "We have faith to believe that we will enter Richmond soon," wrote a private in Company E, 2nd Connecticut Heavy Artillery, on June 4. "The entire army have unlimited confidence in Gen. Grant, and do not doubt the triumphant result of the campaign." The army was "within eight miles of Richmond now and in the best of spirits," another Federal observed. "We all think if we are successful in this campaign that the war is over but we are all in hopes that the stars and stripes will wave over Libby Prison and Bell Island and the Confederate capital the 4th of July." Others took a more jaded view. "For thirty days we have slept in the open air and rain, no shelter, no change of diet; up four nights out of five, and engaged every day," Major Vredenburgh of the 14th New Jersey wrote home. "The rebels are strong yet, in front of us, and I see no end to this matter without other combinations, or perhaps an exhaustion of supplies at Richmond. All this stuff you see in the papers about our brilliant victories, immense losses of the enemy and their full retreat for Richmond, are absurd. We have killed a great many of them as they have of us, but as we moved to the left and south so did they, until now they are between us and Richmond, as they have ever been. If we should move to the left again so would they likewise move enough to keep us at bay, but the papers would call it, I suppose, another rebel retreat."[58]

Grant's strengths during the operations from the North Anna River to Cold Harbor were the same qualities that had sustained him in the campaign's earlier operations—persistence, refusal to treat reverses as defeats, and reliance on maneuver to break Lee's deadlocks. Foiled at the North Anna, Grant again turned to maneuver. Cleverly disguising his intentions with a cavalry demonstration, he evacuated his entrenchments under cover of darkness, crossed the river, and headed east. Lee had no idea where Grant had gone until the Union army appeared some thirty miles downstream. Seldom mentioned by historians, Grant's virtually bloodless withdrawal from the North Anna and his shift to Hanovertown ranks among the war's most successful maneuvers.

Grant, however, had a disconcerting habit of launching operations without planning what to do if they succeeded. His plan to breach Lee's Mule Shoe at Spotsylvania had been masterfully conceived but failed because he neglected to consider in advance the steps to take when Lee's line broke. The same failing marred his movements after crossing the Pamunkey. Grant tarried, losing the advantage maneuver had gained him. Uncertain of Lee's whereabouts, he used infantry to make reconnaissances more appropriately undertaken by cavalry. Discovering Confederates at Totopotomoy Creek barring the way to Richmond, he slid left, feeling for openings, and Lee countered, provoking heated engagements. The road network immediately south offered excellent opportunities to turn Lee's flank and get into the rebel army's rear, but the Union commander seemed blind to the possibilities. More by circumstance than by planning, each army shuttled troops toward Cold Harbor. Determined to maintain the initiative, Grant launched an attack late on June 1 with two army corps. The Confederate line collapsed across a broad front, but nightfall prevented the Federals from exploiting their gains. The next day—June 2—afforded Grant a superb chance to hurt Lee, but again he missed an opportunity. Poor cavalry work was partly to blame, as was Grant's apparent disbelief that Lee would leave his line exposed. Of all Grant's mistakes in the Cold Harbor campaign, his failure to exploit the gap between Lee's southern flank and the Chickahominy looms largest.

Grant has been roundly criticized for assailing Lee's line the morning of June 3. Viewed in the campaign's larger context, the decision made sense. Recently reinforced by the 18th Corps, the Army of the Potomac was stronger than ever. Grant believed that the Confederates were on their last legs, and everything that had happened since crossing the Pamunkey, from Early's botched assault at Bethesda Church to Wright's and Smith's breakthrough on June 1, supported him in that conclusion. Lee now stood a mere seven miles from Richmond, his back to a river. Delay, Grant determined, would serve no purpose, and further maneuvering would be difficult and uncertain in outcome. A successful assault at this juncture stood to wreck the Confederate army, capture Richmond, and bring the war to a speedy conclusion. What better gift could Grant offer President Lincoln on the eve of the Republican convention? Aggressive by nature and accustomed to taking risks, Grant seized the moment. If the offensive worked, the rewards would be tremendous. If it failed, he would simply treat the reverse as he had his earlier disappointments at the Wilderness, Spotsylvania Court House, and the North Anna River and try another tack. In short, the consequences of not assaulting, thereby forfeiting the chance for quick victory and extending the war, seemed worse than those of attacking and failing. "Could we succeed by a general assault in breaking [Lee's] lines, the annihilation of his army was certain, as he would be driven back into the Chickahominy, whence escape was impossible," was how a Union engineer put the case for attacking. "The hazard was great but General Grant concluded to take the chance." In many respects, Grant's reasoning underlying his decision to attack on June 3 at Cold Harbor paralleled the reasons that led Lee to launch his ill-fated assault on July 3 at Gettysburg. Both attacks were gambles, but in both instances, the payoff in the event of success promised to be large.[59]

The piecemeal assaults at Cold Harbor reflected problems inherent in the Union army's leadership. Grant ordered the offensive, but Meade managed it, eager for an opportunity to prove himself. "I had immediate and entire command on the field all day," Meade had assured his wife Margaretta, "the Lieutenant General honoring the field with his presence only about one hour in the middle of the day." Meade, however, did virtually nothing to reconnoiter the ground, coordinate the assault columns, or bring up reserves. His abdication of responsibility reflected the underlying tension between him and Grant. Meade disagreed with Grant's penchant for army-wide offensives but lacked the backbone to air his dissatisfaction forcefully. Although his corps commanders made it clear by 7:00 A.M. that the assault could not succeed, Meade was loath to cancel the offensive and risk Grant's disapproval. He sought Grant's opinion, doubtless hoping that Grant would assume responsibility. Instead he received Grant's common-sense advice to persist if he thought he could succeed and to stop if he did not. Meade waffled for several hours, attempting to goad his subordinates into action. Grant finally interviewed the corps commanders, interceded, and ended the offensive. Far from behaving like an uncaring "butcher," Grant intervened to save lives when Meade, seemingly paralyzed by indecision, appeared incapable of acting.[60]

None of the subordinate Union commanders distinguished himself in the Cold Harbor operations. Hancock's attack on June 3 was an uncoordinated affair bereft of intelligent generalship. Warren had a good day on May 30, when he repulsed Early at Bethesda Church, but his subsequent operations in tandem with Burnside were acrimonious, disjointed measures that fell short of their potential. Wright on June 1 achieved the unusual feat of breaching the Confederate line, but his breakthrough was the consequence of accident rather than planning, and his contribution to the June 3 offensive was negligible. Of all the corps commanders, Baldy Smith held most promise. Unlike many of the Potomac army's generals, he actively supervised troops on the field and pushed offensives with energy and spirit. Troubling, however, was his sour relation with Meade and his failure to work in harmony with his fellow corps heads. Even more troubling was Sheridan. His troopers continued to do well against their Confederate counterparts—the Ashland debacle excepted—but relations between Sheridan and Meade had deteriorated so badly that the Union mounted arm operated almost independently from the infantry force, a state of affairs that contributed mightily to the Potomac army's woes.

Wracked by command difficulties, the Federal force at Cold Harbor seemed adrift, a rudderless ship. Grant should have more clearly demarcated responsibility between himself and Meade, either insisting that Meade take charge of tactical details, or taking charge himself. Writing on June 4, Colonel Wainwright reflected the army's uncertainty over who was really in command. "I would give a great deal to know if this mode of attacking works is Grant's or Meade's idea," Wainwright wondered. "The orders come to us from Meade, but I cannot think it is his, having the opinion I have of his ability as a general." Emory Upton wrote his sister that he was "disgusted" with the army's generalship. "Our men have, in many instances, been foolishly and wantonly sacrificed," he explained. "Assault after assault has been ordered upon the enemy's entrenchments, when they knew nothing about the strength or position of the enemy. Thousands of lives might have been spared by the exercise of a little skill; but, as it is, the courage of the poor men is expected to obviate all difficulties." Complained Upton: "I must confess that, so long as I see such incompetency, there is no grade in the army to which I do not aspire."[61]

Grant stumbled at Cold Harbor, although not as badly as his detractors have claimed. True to form, he remained undaunted by the reverse and immediately began planning his next move. His challenge in the coming stage of operations was to find a way to harmonize his style of command with that of the Potomac army and its generals.

Confederates considered June 3 an unambiguous victory. "So far every attack of the enemy has been repulsed," Lee wrote President Davis at 1:00 P.M. on June 3. "The only impression made on our line was at a salient of General Breckinridge's position, where the enemy broke through and captured part of a battalion. He was immediately driven out with severe loss by General Finegan's brigade and the Maryland Battalion, and the line restored." That evening, Lee updated War Secretary Seddon on the eventful day. "Our loss today has been small," he wrote, "and our success, under the blessing of God, all that we could expect."[62]

Lee's generalship, like Grant's, had been mixed. Locked into place south of the North Anna River, Lee had forfeited the initiative to his opponent. Several times before—most notably at the Mule Shoe on May 12—Lee had misunderstood Grant's plans and nearly come to grief, and he misread Grant's intentions again, mistaking Grant's feint with Wilson as presaging a Union move around his left flank. Grant's slowness on May 28 and 29, however, enabled Lee to shift to Totopotomoy Creek and block the Union advance. Lee's progressive countermoves as the Union army worked south of Totopotomoy Creek underscored both the general's continued aggressiveness and the slippage in his command structure. His plan on May 30 for Anderson to strike Warren on Shady Grove Road while Early attacked from the south was well conceived but badly executed. Early needlessly sacrificed Colonel Willis's brigade by sending it unsupported against Warren's entrenched line at the Bowles farm, and Early's and Anderson's failure to coordinate doomed the offensive. During the night of May 31–June 1, Lee tried to regain the initiative by sending Anderson to the Cold Harbor sector, where he was to act in conjunction with Hoke. The two generals, however, had different ideas about their joint operation, which ended disastrously in an unsupported attack by Colonel Keitt reminiscent of Willis's foray two days before. Anderson's and Hoke's continuing failure to communicate—exacerbated by Hoke's neglect to apprise even his own brigade commanders of important movements—almost produced another disaster on the evening of June 1, when Federals exploited the undefended gap at Bloody Run. Lee's difficulties achieving coordination among his subordinates were every bit as serious as the command problems bedeviling Grant.

Critics have rightly faulted Grant for neglecting to exploit the interval between the southern end of Lee's line and the Chickahominy River. Equally lax, however, was Lee's failure to close the gap sooner. During most of June 2, Lee was unable to shift troops rapidly enough to counter Grant's deployments, leaving the Confederate force in serious peril. By midmorning, Grant had enough men in place to turn the Confederate flank, but Lee did not plug the interval until midafternoon. As happened frequently in the campaign, the failure of Union commanders to exploit opportunities Lee left open to them saved the Army of Northern Virginia.

Almost everything, however, went right for Lee on June 3. His line was well sited along strong ground, and reinforcements buttressed potential weak points at Edgar's salient and Kershaw's horseshoe. Cooperation among Confederate subordinate commanders was all that Lee could have wished. So far as the record indicates, Lee had very little to do with the conduct of the defense. His generals simply held their lines and shot down approaching Union troops. Finegan's and Crane's reserves spontaneously closed the single Federal breach at Edgar's salient in minutes. During the running fights from May 26 through June 2, Lee and Grant had each lost about 5,000 soldiers. June 3 changed the tally from parity to almost a two-to-one advantage for the Confederates, 6,000 southern losses since leaving the North Anna compared with 11,000 northern losses in the same period.

Success buoyed Lee's soldiers. Grant, it was true, had maneuvered from the Rapidan River to the gates of Richmond, but his offensive seemed to be losing steam. "The Yankees came up to the butchery splendidly, and our men like shooting them so well, that they say as long as they can get ammunition and something to eat, they will stand in breastworks and let Grant bring up the whole Yankee nation," a Georgian boasted. "Our troops are in excellent spirits and perfectly confident," another Confederate wrote from the trenches. "They want no easier task than to whip the Yankees when they have works to fight behind. Grant I think has displayed but very poor generalship thus far. He will never take Richmond with his force and if he continues to fight like he has been fighting, it will not take General Lee's army thirty days to destroy his whole force." An officer crowed that Grant's initials "U. S." stood for "Unfortunate Strategist," and that the campaign had rendered him "the worst used up Yankee commander that we have ever combated. He is the very man for us and will end the war in our favor, I [trust]—sooner than any other man in Yahooland." Colonel Taylor of Lee's staff reflected the mood at headquarters. "Old U. S. Grant is pretty tired of it—at least appears so," he

wrote his fiancée. "We are in excellent trim—even in fine spirits—and ready
for a renewal of the fight whenever the signal is given." Several years later,
Lee's aide Lieutenant Colonel Charles S. Venable still regarded the June 3
victory as "perhaps the easiest ever granted to Confederate arms by the folly
of the Federal commanders."[63]

Lee had earned high marks as a defensive fighter, deadlocking an army
nearly double the size of his own force, and Cold Harbor added to his laurels.
But impressive as Lee's victories were, the pattern of the campaign remained
troubling. Each time Lee fought Grant to stalemate, the Union general shifted
to new ground closer to Richmond, maintaining an intense regimen of maneuver and attack that prevented Lee from taking the initiative and steadily
curtailed his ability to countermaneuver. "We must destroy this army of
Grant's before he gets to the James River," Lee reputedly told Jubal Early.
"If he gets there it will become a siege, and then, it will be a mere question
of time." The Federals were also winning the numbers game. While Grant
would ultimately lose about 55,000 soldiers from the Rapidan to the James,
Lee would lose about 33,000 in the same period. Grant's subtractions were
numerically greater than Lee's, but his percentage of loss was smaller, Grant
losing about 45 percent of the force he took across the Rapidan, Lee losing
over 50 percent. And Grant could draw on a deep manpower pool for reinforcements, while Lee's prospects for fresh troops were limited. Despite set-
backs such as Cold Harbor, Grant was losing soldiers at a lower overall rate
than his adversary and could better replace his vacancies. Simple arithmetic
dictated that Grant must ultimately prevail.[64]

Southerners not blinded by Lee's Cold Harbor victory saw that attrition in
Confederate ranks augured poorly for the Army of Northern Virginia. Confederate losses from May 5 to June 3 approximated fully half the number of
men who had accompanied Lee into the Wilderness. Totopotomoy Creek and
Cold Harbor alone had cost Lee about 6,000 soldiers, slightly less than 10
percent of his army. Of the four corps commanders who began the campaign
with Lee—Longstreet, Ewell, Hill, and Stuart—only Hill remained, and his
precarious health was troublesome. The shifting continued on June 4, with
Colonel Bryan Grimes taking over Junius Daniel's brigade (Daniel was killed
on May 12), Brigadier General James Conner taking over Samuel McGowan's brigade (McGowan having been wounded on May 12, and his successor Colonel Joseph N. Brown captured on May 23), and Brigadier General
Rufus Barringer assuming command of the North Carolina cavalry brigade
previously commanded by James Gordon (mortally wounded on May 11),
John Baker, and Pierce Young (wounded on June 1). Colonel Philip Cook
took over Doles's Georgia brigade, Doles having been killed on June 2. Also

formalized were temporary appointments of Anderson to lead Longstreet's corps, Early to head Ewell's corps, Mahone to command Anderson's old division, Ramseur to command Early's old division, Cox to head Ramseur's old brigade, Brigadier General Thomas F. Toon to led Brigadier General Robert D. Johnston's brigade, and Brigadier General Zebulon York to head the army's two Louisiana brigades, each of which had lost their regular commanders. Totopotomoy Creek and Cold Harbor might have been Confederate victories, but their net effect was to accelerate the Army of Northern Virginia's demise. Lee could ill afford many more successes like these.[65]

Soldiers of both armies settled in for a harrowing night. LeGrand James Wilson, the 42nd Mississippi's surgeon, visited Heth's front after dark, congratulating his friends who were still awake. "It was the first time I had ever been on the lines in the night, and it was a strange and novel scene," he wrote. "About two thirds of the men were fast asleep, lying in every conceivable position, propped up or leaning against the breastworks, or lying in the ditch, with a cartridge box or blanket for a pillow." Even dozing men clasped their rifles, and soldiers who were awake kept close watch on Potter's works two hundred yards away, shooting at anything that moved. There was no moonlight, but Wilson could see the level space between the opposing earthworks thickly strewn with bodies.

Reaching the 42nd Mississippi, Wilson satisfied himself that his friends were unharmed. "I am thankful we have all escaped," Captain A. M. Nelson of the regiment told him, nodding toward the dark expanse between the lines. "The ground out there is nearly covered with their dead and wounded, and it is really distressing to hear those poor fellows out there crying for water and help." A wail rose from the battlefield "that chilled our blood, and caused our hearts to stand still," Wilson later wrote. Three soldiers insisted on going into the no-man's land to rescue the sufferer. While they slipped over the entrenchments, Wilson and Captain Nelson went along the line, warning soldiers not to shoot. After an anxious interval, the three men returned and lifted a wounded Federal over the works. Severely injured and parched from thirst, he thanked them for saving his life. "After supplying his wants," Wilson recollected, "I had him carried out to the hospital, dressed his wounds, and next morning sent him in to Richmond, to the city hospital."[66]

While dramatic incidents played all night across Cold Harbor's bloody fields, Grant pondered his options. "I now find, after more than thirty days of trial, that the enemy deems it of the first importance to run no risks with the armies they now have," he later wrote Halleck. "They act purely on the defensive, behind breastworks, or feebly on the offensive immediately in front of them." Continuing the offensive here held no more appeal than it had at the North Anna. "Without a greater sacrifice of human life than I am willing to make," he explained, "all cannot be accomplished that I have designed outside of the city." Laying his plans, Grant contemplated sending cavalry west toward Charlottesville to cut the Virginia Central Railroad, then shifting the Army of the Potomac south and west, cutting off the rest of Lee's supplies and isolating Richmond. If the plan succeeded—if Grant could steal another march on Lee, and rapidly follow it up—the campaign would become a siege, an eventuality that Grant and Lee both understood spelt the Confederacy's doom.[67]

Fifteen miles south of the armies, under a moonless sky, the James River followed a winding course east. Here, Grant perceived, was the key to his next move.

Appendix 1
The Union Order of Battle

ARMY OF THE POTOMAC
Major General George G. Meade

PROVOST GUARD
Brigadier General Marsena R. Patrick
1st Massachusetts Cavalry, Companies C and D
80th New York
3rd Pennsylvania Cavalry
68th Pennsylvania
114th Pennsylvania

ARTILLERY
Brigadier General Henry J. Hunt

VOLUNTEER ENGINEER BRIGADE
Brigadier General Henry W. Benham

50TH NEW YORK ENGINEERS
Lieutenant Colonel Ira Spaulding

BATTALION U.S. ENGINEERS
Captain George H. Mendell

2ND ARMY CORPS

Major General Winfield S. Hancock
1st Vermont Cavalry, Company M

1ST DIVISION
Brigadier General Francis C. Barlow

1st Brigade
Colonel Nelson A. Miles
26th Michigan
5th New Hampshire[a]
2nd New York Heavy Artillery
61st New York
81st Pennsylvania
140th Pennsylvania
183rd Pennsylvania

2nd Brigade
Colonel Richard Byrnes[b]
28th Massachusetts
63rd New York
69th New York
88th New York
116th Pennsylvania

3rd Brigade
Colonel Clinton D. MacDougall
39th New York
52nd New York
57th New York
111th New York
125th New York
126th New York

2ND DIVISION
Brigadier General John Gibbon

1st Brigade
Colonel H. Boyd McKeen[d]
19th Maine
1st Company Sharpshooters
15th Massachusetts
19th Massachusetts
20th Massachusetts
7th Michigan
42nd New York
59th New York
82nd New York (2nd Militia)
184th Pennsylvania
36th Wisconsin

2nd Brigade
Brigadier General Joshua T. Owen
152nd New York
69th Pennsylvania
71st Pennsylvania
72nd Pennsylvania
106th Pennsylvania

3rd Brigade
Colonel Thomas A. Smyth
14th Connecticut
1st Delaware
14th Indiana
12th New Jersey
10th New York Battalion

3RD DIVISION
Major General David B. Birney

1st Brigade
Colonel Thomas W. Egan
20th Indiana
3rd Maine
40th New York
86th New York
124th New York
99th Pennsylvania
110th Pennsylvania
141st Pennsylvania
2nd U.S. Sharpshooters

2nd Brigade
Colonel Thomas R. Tannatt
4th Maine
17th Maine
3rd Michigan
5th Michigan
93rd New York
57th Pennsylvania
63rd Pennsylvania
105th Pennsylvania
1st U.S. Sharpshooters

3rd Brigade
Brigadier General Gershom Mott
1st Maine Heavy Artillery
16th Massachusetts
5th New Jersey

4th Brigade
Colonel John R. Brooke[c]
2nd Delaware
7th New York Heavy Artillery
64th New York
53rd Pennsylvania
145th Pennsylvania
148th Pennsylvania

108th New York
4th Ohio
8th Ohio
7th West Virginia

4th Brigade
Brigadier General Robert O. Tyler[e]
8th New York Heavy Artillery
155th New York
164th New York
170th New York
182nd New York

6th New Jersey
7th New Jersey
8th New Jersey
11th New Jersey
26th Pennsylvania
115th Pennsylvania

4th Brigade
Colonel William R. Brewster
11th Massachusetts
70th New York
71st New York
73rd New York
74th New York
120th New York
84th Pennsylvania

Artillery Brigade
Colonel John C. Tidball
Maine Light, 6th Battery (F)
Massachusetts Light, 10th Battery
New Hampshire Light, 1st Battery
1st New Jersey Light, Battery B
1st New York Light, Battery G
4th New York Heavy, 3rd Battalion
New York Light, 11th Battery
New York Light, 12th Battery
1st Pennsylvania Light, Battery F
1st Rhode Island Light, Battery A
1st Rhode Island Light, Battery B
4th United States, Battery K
5th United States, Batteries C and I

---

[a]Arrived June 1.
[b]Killed June 3, replaced by Colonel Patrick Kelly.
[c]Wounded June 3, replaced by Colonel Orlando H. Morris, who was killed on June 3 and replaced by Colonel Lewis O. Morris.
[d]Killed June 3, replaced by Colonel Frank A. Haskell, who was killed on June 3.
[e]Wounded June 3, replaced by Colonel James P. McIvor.

5TH ARMY CORPS

Major General Gouverneur K. Warren

12th New York Battalion

1ST DIVISION
Brigadier General Charles Griffin

1st Brigade
Brigadier General Romeyn B. Ayres
5th New York[a]
140th New York
146th New York
21st Pennsylvania Dismounted Cavalry[b]
91st Pennsylvania
155th Pennsylvania
2nd U.S., Companies B, C, F, H, I, and K
11th U.S., Companies B, C, D, F, and G, 1st Battalion
12th U.S., Companies A, B, C, D, and G
12th U.S., A, C, D, F, and H, 2nd Battalion
14th U.S., 1st Battalion
17th U.S., Companies A, C, D, G, and H, 1st Battalion
17th U.S., Companies A, B, and C, 2nd Battalion

2nd Brigade
Colonel Jacob B. Sweitzer
9th Massachusetts
22nd Massachusetts
32nd Massachusetts
4th Michigan
62nd Pennsylvania

2ND DIVISION
Brigadier General Henry H. Lockwood[c]

1st Brigade
Colonel Peter Lyle
16th Maine
13th Massachusetts
39th Massachusetts
104th New York
90th Pennsylvania
107th Pennsylvania

2nd Brigade
Colonel James L. Bates
12th Massachusetts
83rd New York
97th New York
11th Pennsylvania
88th Pennsylvania

3rd Brigade
Colonel Nathan D. Dushane
1st Maryland
4th Maryland
7th Maryland
8th Maryland
Purnell (Maryland) Legion

3RD DIVISION
Brigadier General Samuel W. Crawford

1st Brigade
Colonel Martin D. Hardin
1st Pennsylvania Reserves
2nd Pennsylvania Reserves
6th Pennsylvania Reserves
7th Pennsylvania Reserves
11th Pennsylvania Reserves
13th Pennsylvania Reserves

3rd Brigade
Colonel Joseph W. Fisher
5th Pennsylvania Reserves
10th Pennsylvania Reserves
12th Pennsylvania Reserves

Independent Brigade
Colonel G. Howard Kitching
6th New York Heavy Artillery
15th New York Heavy Artillery

4TH DIVISION
Brigadier General Lysander Cutler

1st Brigade
Colonel William W. Robinson
7th Indiana
19th Indiana
24th Michigan
1st Battalion, New York Sharpshooters
2nd Wisconsin
6th Wisconsin
7th Wisconsin

2nd Brigade
Colonel J. William Hofmann
3rd Delaware
4th Delaware[d]
46th New York
76th New York
95th New York
147th New York
56th Pennsylvania
157th Pennsylvania[e]

3rd Brigade
Colonel Edward S. Bragg
121st Pennsylvania
142nd Pennsylvania
143rd Pennsylvania
149th Pennsylvania
150th Pennsylvania

3rd Brigade
Brigadier General Joseph J. Bartlett
20th Maine
18th Massachusetts
1st Michigan
16th Michigan
44th New York
83rd Pennsylvania
118th Pennsylvania

Artillery Brigade
Colonel Charles S. Wainwright
Massachusetts Light, 3rd Battery (C)
Massachusetts Light, 5th Battery (E)
Massachusetts Light, 9th Battery
1st New York Light, Battery B
1st New York Light, Battery C
1st New York Light, Battery D
1st New York Light, Batteries E and L
1st New York Light, Battery H
New York Light, 5th Battery
New York Light, 15th Battery
1st Pennsylvania Light, Battery B
4th United States, Battery B
5th United States, Battery D

[a] Arrived June 1.
[b] Arrived June 1.
[c] Removed June 2, replaced by Brigadier General Samuel W. Crawford.
[d] Arrived June 1.
[e] Arrived June 1.

6TH ARMY CORPS

Major General Horatio G. Wright
8th Pennsylvania Cavalry, Company A

1ST DIVISION
Brigadier General David A. Russell

1st Brigade
Colonel William H. Penrose
1st New Jersey
2nd New Jersey
3rd New Jersey
4th New Jersey
10th New Jersey
15th New Jersey

2nd Brigade
Brigadier General Emory Upton
5th Maine
121st New York
95th Pennsylvania
96th Pennsylvania
2nd Connecticut Heavy Artillery

3rd Brigade
Brigadier General Henry L. Eustis
6th Maine
49th Pennsylvania
119th Pennsylvania
5th Wisconsin

2ND DIVISION
Brigadier General Thomas H. Neill

1st Brigade
Brigadier General Frank Wheaton
62nd New York
93rd Pennsylvania
98th Pennsylvania
102nd Pennsylvania
139th Pennsylvania

2nd Brigade
Brigadier General Lewis A. Grant
1st Vermont Heavy Artillery[a]
2nd Vermont
3rd Vermont
4th Vermont
5th Vermont
6th Vermont

3rd Brigade
Colonel Daniel D. Bidwell
7th Maine
43rd New York
49th New York
77th New York
61st Pennsylvania

3RD DIVISION
Brigadier General James B. Ricketts

1st Brigade
Colonel William S. Truex[b]
14th New Jersey
106th New York
151st New York
87th Pennsylvania
10th Vermont

2nd Brigade
Colonel Benjamin F. Smith
6th Maryland
9th New York Heavy Artillery
110th Ohio
122nd Ohio
126th Ohio
67th Pennsylvania
138th Pennsylvania

Artillery Brigade
Colonel Charles H. Tompkins
Maine Light, 4th Battery (D)
Maine Light, 5th Battery (E)
Massachusetts Light, 1st Battery (A)
1st New Jersey Light, Battery A

4th Brigade
Colonel Nelson Cross
65th New York
67th New York
122nd New York
23rd Pennsylvania
82nd Pennsylvania

4th Brigade
Colonel Oliver Edwards
7th Massachusetts
10th Massachusetts
37th Massachusetts
2nd Rhode Island

New York Light, 1st Battery
New York Light, 3rd Battery
4th New York Heavy (1st Battalion)
1st Ohio Light, Battery H
1st Rhode Island Light, Battery C
1st Rhode Island Light, Battery E
1st Rhode Island Light, Battery G
5th United States, Battery E
5th United States, Battery M

---

[a]Also known as the 11th Vermont.
[b]Wounded June 1, replaced by Colonel John W. Schall, who was wounded on June 1 and June 3.

9th Army Corps
Major General Ambrose E. Burnside

8th U.S.

1st Division
Major General Thomas L. Crittenden

1st Brigade
Brigadier General James H. Ledlie
35th Massachusetts
56th Massachusetts
57th Massachusetts
59th Massachusetts
4th U.S.
10th U.S.

2nd Brigade
Colonel Joseph M. Sudsburg
3rd Maryland
21st Massachusetts
100th Pennsylvania

Provisional Brigade
Colonel Elisha G. Marshall
2nd New York Mounted Rifles (Dismounted)
14th New York Heavy Artillery
24th New York Cavalry (Dismounted)
2nd Pennsylvania Provisional Heavy Artillery

Artillery
2nd Maine Light Battery (B)
14th Massachusetts Battery

2nd Division
Brigadier General Robert B. Potter

1st Brigade
Colonel John I. Curtin
36th Massachusetts
58th Massachusetts
51st New York
45th Pennsylvania
48th Pennsylvania
7th Rhode Island

2nd Brigade
Colonel Simon G. Griffin
31st Maine
32nd Maine
6th New Hampshire
9th New Hampshire
11th New Hampshire
17th Vermont

Artillery
11th Massachusetts Battery
19th New York Battery

3rd Division
Brigadier General Orlando B. Willcox

1st Brigade
Colonel John F. Hartranft
2nd Michigan
8th Michigan
17th Michigan
27th Michigan
109th New York
51st Pennsylvania

2nd Brigade
Colonel William Humphrey
1st Michigan Sharpshooters
20th Michigan
60th Ohio
50th Pennsylvania

Artillery
7th Maine, Battery G
34th New York Battery

4th Division
Brigadier General Edward Ferrero

1st Brigade
Colonel Joshua K. Sigfried
27th U.S. Colored Troops
30th U.S. Colored Troops
39th U.S. Colored Troops
43rd U.S. Colored Troops

2nd Brigade
Colonel Henry G. Thomas
19th U.S. Colored Troops
23rd U.S. Colored Troops
31st U.S. Colored Troops

Artillery
Pennsylvania Independent Battery D
3rd Vermont Battery

CAVALRY CORPS
Major General Philip H. Sheridan

1st Division
Brigadier General Alfred T. A. Torbert

1st Brigade
Brigadier General George A. Custer
1st Michigan
5th Michigan
6th Michigan
7th Michigan

2nd Brigade
Colonel Thomas C. Devin
4th New York
6th New York
9th New York
17th Pennsylvania

Reserve Brigade
Brigadier General Wesley Merritt
19th New York (1st Dragoons)
6th Pennsylvania
1st U.S.
2nd U.S.
5th U.S.

2nd Division
Brigadier General David McM. Gregg

1st Brigade
Brigadier General Henry E. Davies Jr.
1st Massachusetts
1st New Jersey
10th New York
6th Ohio
1st Pennsylvania

2nd Brigade
Colonel J. Irvin Gregg
1st Maine
2nd Pennsylvania
4th Pennsylvania
8th Pennsylvania
13th Pennsylvania
16th Pennsylvania

3rd Division
Brigadier General James H. Wilson

1st Brigade
Colonel John B. McIntosh
1st Connecticut
3rd New Jersey
2nd New York
5th New York
2nd Ohio
18th Pennsylvania

2nd Brigade
Colonel George H. Chapman
3rd Indiana
8th New York
1st Vermont

Horse Artillery

1st Brigade Horse Artillery
Captain James M. Robertson
6th New York Battery
2nd U.S., Batteries B and L
2nd U.S., Battery D
2nd U.S., Battery M
4th U.S., Battery A
4th U.S., Batteries C and E

2nd Brigade Horse Artillery
Captain Dunbar R. Ransom
1st U.S., Batteries E and G
1st U.S., Batteries H and I
1st U.S., Battery K
2nd U.S., Battery A

18th Army Corps
Major General William F. Smith

1st Division
Brigadier General William T. H. Brooks

1st Brigade
Brigadier General Gilman Marston
81st New York
96th New York
98th New York
139th New York

2nd Brigade
Brigadier General Hiram Burnham
8th Connecticut
10th New Hampshire
13th New Hampshire
118th New York

3rd Brigade
Colonel Guy V. Henry
21st Connecticut
40th Massachusetts
92nd New York
58th Pennsylvania
188th Pennsylvania

Artillery Brigade
Captain Samuel S. Elder
1st United States, Battery B
4th United States, Battery L
5th United States, Battery A

2nd Division
Brigadier General John H. Martindale

1st Brigade
Brigadier General George J. Stannard
23rd Massachusetts
25th Massachusetts
27th Massachusetts
9th New Jersey
55th Pennsylvania

2nd Brigade
Colonel Griffin A. Stedman Jr.
11th Connecticut
8th Maine
2nd New Hampshire
12th New Hampshire
148th New York

3rd Division
Brigadier General Charles Devens Jr.

1st Brigade
Colonel William B. Barton
47th New York
48th New York
115th New York
76th Pennsylvania

2nd Brigade
Colonel Jeremiah C. Drake[a]
13th Indiana
9th Maine
112th New York
169th New York

3rd Brigade
Brigadier General Adelbert Ames
4th New Hampshire
3rd New York
117th New York
142nd New York
97th Pennsylvania

Appendix 2
The Confederate Order of Battle

ARMY OF NORTHERN VIRGINIA

General Robert E. Lee

1ST ARMY CORPS

Major General Richard H. Anderson

KERSHAW'S DIVISION
Brigadier General Joseph B. Kershaw

Kershaw's Brigade
Colonel John W. Henagan[a]
2nd South Carolina
3rd South Carolina
7th South Carolina
8th South Carolina
15th South Carolina
20th South Carolina
3rd South Carolina Battalion

Humphreys's Brigade
Brigadier General Benjamin G. Humphreys
13th Mississippi
17th Mississippi
18th Mississippi
21st Mississippi

Wofford's Brigade
Brigadier General William T. Wofford
16th Georgia
18th Georgia
24th Georgia

FIELD'S DIVISION
Major General Charles W. Field

Jenkins's Brigade
Colonel John Bratton
1st South Carolina
2nd South Carolina
5th South Carolina
6th South Carolina
Palmetto Sharpshooters

Gregg's Brigade
Brigadier General John Gregg
3rd Arkansas
1st Texas
4th Texas
5th Texas

Law's Brigade
Brigadier General Evander McIver Law
4th Alabama
15th Alabama
44th Alabama
47th Alabama
48th Alabama

PICKETT'S DIVISION
Major General George E. Pickett

Kemper's Brigade
Brigadier General William R. Terry
1st Virginia
3rd Virginia
7th Virginia
11th Virginia
24th Virginia

Hunton's Brigade
Brigadier General Eppa Hunton
8th Virginia
19th Virginia
25th Virginia Battalion (City Battalion)
32nd Virginia
56th Virginia
42nd Virginia Cavalry battalion

Barton's Brigade
Brigadier General Seth M. Barton
9th Virginia
14th Virginia
38th Virginia
53rd Virginia
57th Virginia

ARTILLERY
Brigadier General E. Porter Alexander

Haskell's Battalion
Major John C. Haskell
Flanner's (North Carolina) Battery
Garden's (South Carolina) Battery
Lamkin's (Virginia) Battery
Ramsay's (North Carolina) Battery

Huger's Battalion
Lieutenant Colonel Frank Huger
Fickling's (South Carolina) Battery
Moody's (Louisiana) Battery
Parker's (Virginia) Battery
Smith's (Virginia) Battery
Taylor's (Virginia) Battery
Woolfolk's (Virginia) Battery

Cabell's Battalion
Colonel Henry C. Cabell
Callaway's (Georgia) Battery
Carlton's (Georgia) Battery
McCarthy's (Virginia) Battery
Manly's (North Carolina) Battery

Cobb's (Georgia) Legion
Phillips (Georgia) Legion
3rd Georgia Battalion Sharpshooters

Bryan's Brigade
Brigadier General Goode Bryan
10th Georgia
50th Georgia
51st Georgia
53rd Georgia

Anderson's Brigade
Brigadier General George T. Anderson
7th Georgia
8th Georgia
9th Georgia
11th Georgia
59th Georgia

Benning's Brigade
Colonel Dudley M. DuBose
2nd Georgia
15th Georgia
17th Georgia
20th Georgia

Corse's Brigade
Brigadier General Montgomery D. Corse
15th Virginia
17th Virginia
18th Virginia
29th Virginia
30th Virginia

Hoke's Brigade
Lieutenant Colonel William G. Lewis
6th North Carolina
21st North Carolina
54th North Carolina
57th North Carolina
1st North Carolina Battalion

[a]Replaced by Colonel Lawrence M. Keitt May 31–June 1.

2ND ARMY CORPS
Lieutenant General Richard S. Ewell[a]

RAMSEUR'S DIVISION
Major General Stephen D. Ramseur

Pegram's Brigade
Colonel Edward Willis[b]
13th Virginia
31st Virginia
49th Virginia
52nd Virginia
58th Virginia

Johnston's Brigade
Colonel Thomas F. Toon
5th North Carolina
12th North Carolina
20th North Carolina
23rd North Carolina

GORDON'S DIVISION
Major General John B. Gordon

Evans's Brigade
Brigadier General Clement A. Evans
13th Georgia
26th Georgia
31st Georgia
38th Georgia
60th Georgia
61st Georgia
12th Georgia Battalion

Louisiana Brigade
Colonel Zebulon York
1st Louisiana
2nd Louisiana
5th Louisiana
6th Louisiana
7th Louisiana
8th Louisiana
9th Louisiana
10th Louisiana
14th Louisiana
15th Louisiana

RODES'S DIVISION
Major General Robert E. Rodes

Daniel's Brigade
Brigadier General Bryan Grimes
32nd North Carolina
43rd North Carolina
45th North Carolina
53rd North Carolina
2nd North Carolina Battalion

Ramseur's Brigade
Colonel Risden T. Bennett
1st North Carolina
2nd North Carolina
3rd North Carolina
4th North Carolina
14th North Carolina
30th North Carolina

Battle's Brigade
Brigadier General Cullen A. Battle
3rd Alabama
5th Alabama
6th Alabama
12th Alabama
26th Alabama
61st Alabama

ARTILLERY
Brigadier General Armistead L. Long

Braxton's Battalion
Lieutenant Colonel Carter M. Braxton
Carpenter's (Virginia) Battery
Cooper's (Virginia) Battery
Hardwicke's (Virginia) Battery

Nelson's Battalion
Lieutenant Colonel William Nelson
Kirkpatrick's (Virginia) Battery
Massie's (Virginia) Battery
Milledge's (Georgia) Battery

Page's Battalion
Major Richard C. M. Page
W. P. Carter's (Virginia) Battery
Fry's (Virginia) Battery
Page's (Virginia) Battery
Reese's (Alabama) Battery

Cutshaw's Battalion
Major Wilfred E. Cutshaw
Carrington's (Virginia) Battery
W. Garber's (Virginia) Battery
Tanner's (Virginia) Battery

Terry's Brigade
Brigadier General William Terry
2nd Virginia
4th Virginia
5th Virginia
10th Virginia
21st Virginia
23rd Virginia
25th Virginia
27th Virginia
33rd Virginia
37th Virginia
42nd Virginia
44th Virginia
48th Virginia
50th Virginia

Doles's Brigade
Brigadier General George Doles[c]
4th Georgia
12th Georgia
44th Georgia

Hardaway's Battalion
Lieutenant Colonel Robert A. Hardaway
Dance's (Virginia) Battery
Graham's (Virginia) Battery
B. Griffin's (Virginia) Battery
Jones's (Virginia) Battery
B. H. Smith's (Virginia) Battery

---

[a]Replaced by Major General Jubal A. Early on May 27.
[b]Mortally wounded May 30, replaced by Colonel John S. Hoffman
[c]Killed June 2, replaced by Colonel Philip Cooke.

3RD ARMY CORPS
Lieutenant General Ambrose P. Hill

HETH'S DIVISION
Major General Henry Heth

Davis's Brigade
Brigadier General Joseph R. Davis
2nd Mississippi
11th Mississippi
26th Mississippi
42nd Mississippi
55th North Carolina

Cooke's Brigade
Brigadier General John R. Cooke
15th North Carolina
27th North Carolina
46th North Carolina
48th North Carolina

Walker's Brigade
Brigadier General Birkett D. Fry
40th Virginia
47th Virginia
55th Virginia
22nd Virginia battalion
13th Alabama
1st Tennessee (Provisional)
7th Tennessee
14th Tennessee

WILCOX'S DIVISION
Major General Cadmus M. Wilcox

Lane's Brigade
Brigadier General James H. Lane[b]
7th North Carolina
18th North Carolina
28th North Carolina
33rd North Carolina
37th North Carolina

McGowan's Brigade
Lieutenant Colonel J. F. Hunt
1st South Carolina (Provisional)
12th South Carolina
13th South Carolina
14th South Carolina
1st South Carolina (Orr's Rifles)

Scales's Brigade
Brigadier General Alfred M. Scales[c]
13th North Carolina
16th North Carolina
22nd North Carolina
34th North Carolina
38th North Carolina

MAHONE'S DIVISION
Brigadier General William Mahone

Sanders's Brigade
Colonel John C. C. Sanders
8th Alabama
9th Alabama
10th Alabama
11th Alabama
14th Alabama

Mahone's Brigade
Colonel David A. Weisiger
6th Virginia
12th Virginia
16th Virginia
41st Virginia
61st Virginia

Harris's Brigade
Brigadier General Nathaniel H. Harris
12th Mississippi
16th Mississippi
19th Mississippi
48th Mississippi

Finegan's Brigade
Brigadier General Joseph Finegan
2nd Florida
5th Florida

ARTILLERY
Colonel R. Lindsay Walker

Poague's Battalion
Lieutenant Colonel William T. Poague
Richard's (Mississippi) Battery
Utterback's (Virginia) Battery
Williams's (North Carolina) Battery
Wyatt's (Virginia) Battery

Pegram's Battalion
Lieutenant Colonel William J. Pegram
Brander's (Virginia) Battery
Cayce's (Virginia) Battery
Ellett's (Virginia) Battery
Marye's (Virginia) Battery
Zimmerman's (South Carolina) Battery

McIntosh's Battalion
Lieutenant Colonel David G. McIntosh
Clutter's (Virginia) Battery
Donald's (Virginia) Battery
Hurt's (Alabama) Battery
Price's (Virginia) Battery

Richardson's Battalion
Lieutenant Colonel Charles Richardson
Grandy's (Virginia) Battery
Landry's (Louisiana) Battery
Moore's (Virginia) Battery
Penick's (Virginia) Battery

8th Florida
9th Florida
10th Florida
11th Florida

Wright's Brigade
Brigadier General Ambrose R. Wright
3rd Georgia
22nd Georgia
48th Georgia
2nd Georgia Battalion
10th Georgia Battalion

Kirkland's Brigade
Brigadier General William W. Kirkland[a]
11th North Carolina
26th North Carolina
44th North Carolina
47th North Carolina
52nd North Carolina

Thomas's Brigade
Brigadier General Edward L. Thomas
14th Georgia
35th Georgia
45th Georgia
49th Georgia

Cutts's Battalion
Colonel Allen S. Cutts
Patterson's (Georgia) Battery
Ross's (Georgia) Battery
Wingfield's (Georgia) Battery

[a]Wounded June 2, replaced by Colonel George H. Faribault.
[b]Wounded June 2, replaced by Colonel John D. Barry.
[c]Ill during much of the campaign, brigade frequently led by Colonel William L. Lowrance.

CAVALRY CORPS
Major General Wade Hampton[a]

HAMPTON'S DIVISION
Major General Wade Hampton

Young's Brigade
Colonel Gilbert J. Wright
7th Georgia
Cobb's (Georgia) Legion
Phillips (Georgia) Legion
Jeff Davis (Mississippi) Legion
20th Georgia Battalion

Rosser's Brigade
Brigadier General Thomas L. Rosser
7th Virginia
11th Virginia
12th Virginia
35th Virginia Battalion

Butler's Brigade
Brigadier General Matthew C. Butler
4th South Carolina
5th South Carolina
6th South Carolina
7th South Carolina[b]

FITZHUGH LEE'S DIVISION
Major General Fitzhugh Lee

Lomax's Brigade
Brigadier General Lunsford L. Lomax
5th Virginia
6th Virginia
15th Virginia

Wickham's Brigade
Brigadier General Williams C. Wickham
1st Virginia
2nd Virginia
3rd Virginia
4th Virginia

WILLIAM H. F. LEE'S DIVISION
Major General William H. F. Lee

Chambliss's Brigade
Brigadier General John R. Chambliss
9th Virginia
10th Virginia
13th Virginia

Gordon's Brigade
Colonel John A. Baker[c]
1st North Carolina
2nd North Carolina
3rd North Carolina
5th North Carolina

HORSE ARTILLERY
Major R. Preston Chew

Breathed's Battalion
Major James Breathed
Hart's (South Carolina) Battery
Johnston's (Virginia) Battery
McGregor's (Virginia) Battery
Shoemaker's (Virginia) Battery
Thomson's (Virginia) Battery

[a]Following James Ewell Brown Stuart's death on May 12, General Lee left the top position in his cavalry corps unfilled. Wade Hampton, as senior division commander, acted as corps commander.
[b]On May 29, Brigadier General Martin W. Gary arrived with the 7th South Carolina. During the actions in this book, the 7th South Carolina operated under Butler, although Gary was ostensibly exercising independent command.
[c]Colonel Baker commanded the brigade during most of the actions in this book, although Brigadier General Pierce M. B. Young was in command during the actions at Hanover Court House and Ashland.

BRECKINRIDGE'S DIVISION
Major General John C. Breckinridge

Echols's Brigade
Brigadier General John Echols[a]
22nd Virginia
23rd Virginia Battalion
26th Virginia Battalion

Wharton's Brigade
Brigadier General Gabriel C. Wharton
30th Virginia Battalion
51st Virginia
62nd Virginia (Mounted)

McLaughlin's Artillery Battalion
Major William McLaughlin
Chapman's (Virginia) Battery
Jackson's (Virginia) Battery

Maryland Line[b]
Colonel Bradley T. Johnson
2nd Maryland
1st Maryland Cavalry
1st Maryland Battery
2nd Maryland Battery
4th Maryland Battery

---

[a]Temporarily replaced by Colonel George S. Patton on May 30.
[b]The Maryland infantry units were placed under Breckinridge, and the Maryland cavalry units joined Lomax's cavalry brigade.

HOKE'S DIVISION
Major General Robert F. Hoke

Martin's Brigade
Brigadier General James G. Martin
17th North Carolina
42nd North Carolina
66th North Carolina

Clingman's Brigade
Brigadier General Thomas L. Clingman
8th North Carolina
21st North Carolina
51st North Carolina
61st North Carolina

Hagood's Brigade
Brigadier General Johnson Hagood
11th South Carolina
21st South Carolina
25th South Carolina
27th South Carolina

Colquitt's Brigade
Brigadier General Alfred H. Colquitt
6th Georgia
19th Georgia
23rd Georgia
27th Georgia
28th Georgia

ARTILLERY

Read's 38th Virginia Battalion Artillery
Major John P. W. Read
Blount's (Virginia) Battery
Caskie's (Virginia) Battery
Macon's (Virginia) Battery
Marshall's (Virginia) Battery

Notes

PREFACE

1. Henry C. Baird Papers, in E. C. Gardiner Collection, HSP; William Swinton, *Campaigns of the Army of the Potomac* (New York, 1866), 440n; Edward A. Pollard, *The Lost Cause* (New York, 1867), 510; John C. Ropes, "Grant's Campaign in Virginia in 1864," in *PMHSM* 4, 495; E. B. Long, "Ulysses S. Grant for Today," in *Ulysses S. Grant: Essays and Documents,* ed. David L. Wilson and John Y. Simon (Carbondale, Ill., 1981), 22.

2. Walter H. Taylor, *General Lee: His Campaigns in Virginia, 1861–1865, with Personal Reminiscences* (Norfolk, Va., 1906), 238; Peter W. Alexander dispatch, May 18, 1864, *Columbia (S.C.) Daily South Carolinian,* May 29, 1864.

3. Clifford Dowdey, *Lee's Last Campaign: The Story of Lee and His Men Against Grant, 1864* (New York, 1960), 297; Jay Winik, "A Narrative of Hell," *New York Times Book Review,* September 16, 2001, p. 23.

I   MAY 25, 1864 *Lee Deadlocks Grant on the North Anna*

1. Details of Grant's plan of campaign against Lee are described in Gordon C. Rhea, *The Battle of the Wilderness, May 5–7, 1864* (Baton Rouge, 1994), 46–59.

2. For details of the Spotsylvania campaign, see Gordon C. Rhea, *The Battles for Spotsylvania Court House and the Road to Yellow Tavern, May 7–12, 1864* (Baton Rouge, 1997).

3. Adam Badeau, *Military History of General Ulysses S. Grant, from April, 1861, to April, 1865* (3 vols.; New York, 1881), 2, p. 235; Wesley Brainerd, *Memoir of the 50th New York Volunteer Engineers,* ed. Ed Malles (Knoxville, Tenn., 1997), 226–7. Details of the North Anna operation are in Gordon C. Rhea, *To the North Anna River: Grant and Lee, May 13–25, 1864* (Baton Rouge, 2000).

4. Charles S. Venable, "The Campaign from the Wilderness to Petersburg," *SHSP* 14, p. 535.

5. Morris Schaff, *The Battle of the Wilderness* (Boston, 1910), 201; Tyler Dennett, ed., *Lincoln and the Civil War in the Diaries and Letters of John Hay* (New York, 1939), 67; Horace Porter, *Campaigning with Grant* (New York, 1897), 70. For a more thorough discussion of the

reasons behind the Potomac army's defensive mindset, see Gordon C. Rhea, Richard Rollins, Stephen Sears, and John Y. Simon, "What Was Wrong with the Army of the Potomac," *North and South* 4 (2001), 12–8.

6. George G. Meade to wife, April 4, 13, 1864, in George Meade, ed., *Life and Letters of George Gordon Meade* (2 vols.; New York, 1913), 2, pp. 187, 189; Henry H. Humphreys, *Andrew Atkinson Humphreys: A Biography* (Philadelphia, 1924), 219.

7. Allan Nevins, ed., *Diary of Battle: The Personal Journals of Colonel Charles S. Wainwright, 1861–1865* (New York, 1962), 338; Abbott Spear, ed., *Civil War Recollections of General Ellis Spear* (Orono, Me., 1997), 113; Ulysses S. Grant, "Preparing for the Campaign of '64," in *B&L* 4, p. 97 n.

8. Francis B. Carpenter, *Six Months at the White House with Abraham Lincoln* (New York, 1866), 283.

9. Meade to wife, May 19, 23, 1864, in Meade, *Life and Letters* 2, pp. 197–8; Grant, "Preparing for the Campaign of '64," 98.

10. David S. Sparks, ed., *Inside Lincoln's Army: The Diary of Marsena Rudolph Patrick, Provost Marshal General, Army of the Potomac* (New York, 1964), 377; William B. Rawle, *History of the Third Pennsylvania Cavalry, Sixtieth Regiment Pennsylvania Volunteers, in the American Civil War* (Philadelphia, 1905), 430.

11. James C. Biddle to wife, May 4, 5, 1864, in George G. Meade Collection, HSP; Horace Porter, *Campaigning with Grant,* 115; Badeau, *General Ulysses S. Grant,* 2, pp. 186–7; Theodore Lyman's journal, in Theodore Lyman Collection, MHS; George R. Agassiz, ed., *Meade's Headquarters, 1863–1865: Letters of Colonel Theodore Lyman from the Wilderness to Appomattox* (Boston, 1922), 126; Andrew A. Humphreys, *The Virginia Campaign of '64 and '65* (New York, 1883), 83 n. 1.

12. George B. Sanford *Fighting Rebels and Redskins: Experiences in Army Life of Colonel George B. Sanford, 1861–1892,* ed. E. R. Hagemann (Norman, Okla., 1969), 223–4; Thomas W. Hyde, *Following the Greek Cross; or, Memories of the Sixth Army Corps* (Boston, 1894), 208.

13. Nevins, ed., *Diary of Battle,* 405; Ulysses S. Grant, *Personal Memoirs of U. S. Grant* (2 vols.; New York, 1886), 2, pp. 214–5; George G. Meade to John Rawlins, June 21, 1864, in Meade Collection, HSP; Badeau, *Ulysses S. Grant,* 2, p. 184.

14. John Gibbon, *Personal Recollections of the Civil War* (New York, 1928), 227–30.

15. Return of Casualties, in *OR*, Vol. 36, Pt. 1, pp. 119–65. The number of soldiers mustered out from each regiment averaged between 150 and 250. With 37 regiments leaving during May and June, Grant stood to loose between 5,000 and 9,000 veterans by expiration of terms of enlistment.

16. "List of troops sent to front," ibid., Pt. 3, pp. 738–9.

17. Ulysses S. Grant to Henry W. Halleck, May 21, 1864, ibid., 45; Halleck to Montgomery C. Meigs and John G. Barnard, May 21, 1864, ibid., 68–9; Grant to Halleck, May 22, 1864, ibid., 77; Meigs and Barnard to Halleck, May 23, 1864, ibid., 140–1; Grant to Halleck, May 25, 1864, ibid., 183; Grant, *Personal Memoirs,* 2, pp. 151–2.

18. Gibbon, *Personal Recollections,* 229; Robert S. Robertson to parents, May 25, 1864, in FSNMP; James L. Rea to wife, May 26, 1864, in Thomas Clemens Collection, USAMHI.

19. Wayne C. Temple, ed., "A Signal Officer with Grant: Letters of Captain Charles L. Davis," in *Civil War History* 7 (1961), 434.

20. William A. Miller to sister, May 26, 1864, in FSNMP; Harry H. Hall, *A Johnny Reb Band from Salem: The Pride of Tarheelia* (Raleigh, 1963), 90; R. Lockwood Tower, ed., *Lee's*

Adjutant: The Wartime Letters of Colonel Walter Heron Taylor, 1862–1865 (Columbia, S.C., 1995), 162.

21. James S. Wingard to brother, May 25, 1864, in Simon P. Wingard Papers, DU; Tower, *Lee's Adjutant,* 162; Lewis Warlick to Corrie, May 19, 1864, in Cornelia McGimsey Collection, SHC; L. Calhoun Cooper to mother, May 25, 1864, in Book 129, FSNMP; Dispatch, May 27, 1864, *Columbia (S.C.) Daily South Carolinian,* June 3, 1864.

22. I am grateful to Alfred C. Young III for assistance in evaluating Lee's strength. Mr. Young's tabulations, in summary form, appear in his "Numbers and Losses in the Army of Northern Virginia," *North and South* 3 (March 2000), 15–29.

23. Jedediah Hotchkiss to Henry Alexander White, January 12, 1897, in Jedediah Hotchkiss Collection, LC.

24. Special Orders 126, May 14, 1864, in *OR,* Vol. 36, Pt. 2, p. 1001.

25. Robert E. Lee to Jefferson Davis, April 15, 1864, in *OR,* Vol. 33, pp. 1282–83.

26. Isaac Hall, *History of the Ninety-Seventh Regimental New York Volunteers (Conkling Rifles) in the War for the Union* (Utica, New York, 1890), 190; Argus, "From the Army of the Potomac, May 28, 1864," *New York Daily News,* June 2, 1864; Washington A. Roebling's report, in Gouverneur K. Warren Collection, NYSLA; Grant, *Personal Memoirs,* 2, p. 250; Grant to Halleck, May 26, 1864, in *OR,* Vol. 36, Pt. 3, pp. 206–7.

27. Grant to Halleck, noon, May 25, 1864, in *OR,* Vol. 36, Pt. 3, p. 183.

28. Grant to Halleck, May 26, 1864, ibid., 206–7. The council of war is described in Nevins, ed., *Diary of Battle,* 388, and in Merlin E. Sumner, ed., *The Diary of Cyrus B. Comstock* (Dayton, Ohio, 1987), 269–70.

29. Brainerd, *Bridge Building in Wartime,* 227.

30. Orders, May 26, 1864, 10:00 A.M., in *OR,* Vol. 36, Pt. 3, p. 211.

31. Nevins, ed., *Diary of Battle,* 388.

II MAY 26–27 *Grant Shifts to the Pamunkey*

1. Grant to Halleck, May 26, 1864, in *OR,* Vol. 36, Pt. 3, p. 207; Meade to Grant, 10:00 A.M., May 26, 1864, ibid., 207; Rufus Ingalls to Meigs, 2:00 P.M., May 26, 1864, ibid., 208; Special Orders No. 145, ibid., 209–10.

2. Rufus R. Dawes to wife, May 26, 1864, in Rufus R. Dawes, *Service with the Sixth Wisconsin Volunteers* (Marietta, Ohio, 1890), 277–8; Robert Tilney to family, May 29, 1864, in Robert Tilney, *My Life in the Army: Three Years and a Half with the Fifth Army Corps, Army of the Potomac, 1862–1865* (Philadelphia, 1912), 77–8; Frank Wilkeson, *Recollections of a Private Soldier in the Army of the Potomac* (New York, 1887), 120–1.

3. Gordon C. Rhea, "Union Cavalry in the Wilderness: The Education of Philip H. Sheridan and James H. Wilson," in *The Wilderness Campaign,* ed. Gary W. Gallagher (Chapel Hill, 1997), 108–9; Edward G. Longacre, *From Union Stars to Top Hat* (Harrisburg, Pa., 1972), 14.

4. James H. Wilson's report, in *OR,* Vol. 36, Pt. 1, p. 880; James H. Wilson diary, in James H. Wilson Collection, LC; Louis N. Boudrye, *Historic Records of the Fifth New York Cavalry, First Ira Harris Guard* (Albany, N.Y., 1874),134.

5. Henry R. Dalton's report, in *OR,* Vol. 36, Pt. 1, p. 662; Emory Upton's report, ibid., 671; Alanson A. Haines, *History of the Fifteenth Regiment New Jersey Volunteers* (New York, 1883), 195–6; Ezra K. Parker, *From the Rapidan to the James Under Grant* (Providence, R.I., 1909), 21; Walter H. Farwell manuscript, Palmer Regimental Collection, WRHS.

6. Martin L. Smith diary, May 25–27, 1864, in Charles E. Phelps Collection, Maryland Historical Society, Baltimore.

7. Walter H. Taylor to Ewell, 10:45 A.M., May 26, 1864, in *OR,* Vol. 51, Pt. 2, p. 960; Lyman Jackman and Amos Hadley, eds., *History of the Sixth New Hampshire Regiment in the War for the Union* (Concord, N.H., 1891), 269; William P. Hopkins, *The Seventh Regiment Rhode Island Volunteers in the Civil War* (Providence, R.I., 1903), 179; J. N. Jones diary, May 26, 1864, in *Civil War Times Illustrated* Collection, USAMHI.

8. Charles Marshall to Richard H. Anderson, May 26, 1864, in *OR,* Vol. 36, Pt. 3, p. 834.

9. George Q. Peyton, *A Civil War Record for 1864–1865,* ed. Robert A. Hodge (Fredericksburg, Va., 1981), 36; Buckner McGill Randolph diary, May 26, 1864, VHS; J. A. Lineback diary, May 26, 1864, in *Winston-Salem Daily Sentinel,* January 9, 1915.

10. Arabella M. Wilson, *Disaster, Struggle, Triumph: The Adventures of 1,000 "Boys in Blue"* (Albany, N.Y., 1870), 252; Charles D. Page, *History of the Fourteenth Regiment Connecticut Volunteer Infantry* (Meriden, Conn., 1906), 283; William P. Haines, *The Men of Company F, with Description of the Marches and Battles of the 12th New Jersey Volunteers* (Mickleton, N.J., 1897), 64; Joseph R. C. Ward, *History of the One Hundred and Sixth Regiment Pennsylvania Volunteers* (Philadelphia, 1883), 259; Benjamin Y. Draper diary, May 26, 1864, in FSNMP; Thomas A. Smyth's report, in *OR,* Vol. 36, Pt. 1, p. 451.

11. Robert E. Lee to James A. Seddon, May 26, 1864, in *OR,* Vol. 36, Pt. 3, p. 834.

12. R. H. McBride dispatch, May 30, 1864, in *Washington, D.C., Daily Morning Chronicle,* June 2, 1864.

13. John J. Woodall diary, May 26, 1864, in RNBP.

14. Farwell memorandum, in Palmer Regimental Collection, WRHS; Alanson A. Haines, *Fifteenth Regiment New Jersey Volunteers,* 196; Henry R. Dalton's report, in *OR,* Vol. 36, Pt. 1, p. 662; Upton's report, in *OR,* Vol. 36, Pt. 1, p. 671; Edward G. Longacre, "From the Wilderness to Cold Harbor in the Union Artillery," *Manuscripts* 35 (1983), 211.

15. Tilney to family, May 29, 1864, in Tilney, *My Life in the Army,* 77–8.

16. Grant, *Personal Memoirs,* 2, p. 254; General Orders, May 26, 1864, in *OR,* Vol. 36, Pt. 3, p. 223.

17. Itinerary of Ayres's Brigade, in *OR,* Vol. 36, Pt. 1, p. 554; Cunningham's report, ibid., 570; Orders, May 26, 1864, ibid., Pt. 3, p. 226; Gouverneur K. Warren's journal, May 26, 1864, ibid., Pt. 1, p. 543; John Bancroft diary, May 26, 1864, in BL.

18. Otho H. Binkley's report, in *OR,* Vol. 36, Pt. 1, p. 743; John Chester White journal, 76, in LC; John C. White, "A Review of the Services of the Regular Army During the Civil War," in *Journal of the Military Service Institution of the United States* (December 1912), 64–5; George G. Hopper manuscript, Michigan MOLLUS Collection, BL; George A. Bowen diary, May 26, 1864, in FSNMP; Robert S. Robertson, *Personal Recollections of the War* (Milwaukee, 1895), 115; Tilney to family, May 29, 1864, in Tilney, *My Life in the Army,* 77–8; Robert C. Carter, comp., *Four Brothers in Blue; or, Sunshine and Shadows of the War of the Rebellion* (Austin, Tex., 1978), 409.

19. Ira Spaulding's report, in *OR,* Vol. 36, Pt. 1, p. 311; Brainerd, *Road Building in Wartime,* 227–9; Winfield S. Hancock to Meade, 9:15 A.M., May 26, 1864, in *OR,* Vol. 36, Pt. 3, pp. 212–3; Meade to Hancock, 10:00 A.M., May 26, 1864, ibid., 213.

20. Wilkeson, *Recollections of a Private Soldier,* 123; William R. Driver memorandum, 7:00 P.M., May 26, 1864, in *OR,* Vol. 36, Pt. 3, pp. 215–6; .2nd Corps Circular, 8:30 P.M., May 26, 1864, in *OR,* Vol. 36, Pt. 3, p. 216.

21. Circular, May 26, 1864, in *OR,* Vol. 36, Pt. 3, pp. 228–9; Committee of the Regiment, *History of the Thirty-Fifth Regiment Massachusetts Volunteers* (Boston, 1884), 242.

22. George A. Bowen diary, May 26, 1864, in FSNMP; John B. Gordon to A. S. Pendleton, 2:30 A.M., May 27, 1864, in *OR,* Vol. 51, Pt. 2, p. 964; Robert E. Rodes to Pendleton, May 27, 1864, in *OR,* Vol. 51, Pt. 2, p. 962.

23. Robert Keating, *Carnival of Blood: The Civil War Ordeal of the Seventh New York Heavy Artillery* (Baltimore, 1998), 87–8; Henry C. Houston, *The Thirty-Second Maine Regiment of Infantry Volunteers* (Portland, Me., 1903), 191–2.

24. Houston, *Thirty-Second Maine Regiment,* 189; Robert B. Potter's report, in *OR,* Vol. 36, Pt. 1, pp. 929–30; Heinz K. Meier, ed., *Memoirs of a Swiss Officer in the American Civil War* (Bern, 1972), 164; Benjamin F. Powelson, *History of Company K of the 140th Regiment Pennsylvania Volunteers* (Steubenville, Ohio, 1906), 37–8; C. A. Stevens, *Berdan's United States Sharpshooters in the Army of the Potomac, 1861–1865* (St. Paul, Minn., 1892), 440–1; Thomas F. Galwey, *The Valiant Hours: An Irishman in the Civil War* (Harrisburg, Pa., 1961), 227; Richard F. Miller and Robert F. Mooney, *The Civil War: The Nantucket Experience, Including the Memoirs of Joseph Fitch Murphey* (Nantucket, Mass., 1994), 105.

25. Hyland C. Kirk, *Heavy Guns and Light: A History of the 4th New York Heavy Artillery* (New York, 1890), 247–8; R.W.B. to editor, June 7, 1864, *Springfield (Mass.) Daily Republican,* June 22, 1864; *History of the Fourth Maine Battery Light Artillery in the Civil War, 1861–1865* (Augusta, Me., 1905), 77–8; Osceola Lewis, *History of the One Hundred and Thirty Eighth Regiment Pennsylvania Volunteer Infantry* (Norristown, Pa., 1866), 100–1.

26. Seth Williams to Ambrose E. Burnside, 4:00 A.M., May 27, 1864, in *OR,* Vol. 36, Pt. 3, p. 256; Burnside to Williams, 5:00 A.M., May 27, 1864, ibid., 256–7; Lyman's journal, May 27, 1864, in MHS.

27. Lyman's journal, May 27, 1864, in MHS; Lyman to family, May 27, 1864, in Agassiz, ed., *Meade's Headquarters,* 128.

28. Charles H. Crawford, "Flying Pontoons with Grant's Army," in Book 7, RNBP.

29. Agassiz, ed., *Meade's Headquarters,* 17; Sanford, *Fighting Rebels and Redskins,* 225. Gregory J. W. Urwin paints a vivid picture of Custer in his *Custer Victorious: The Civil War Battles of General George Armstrong Custer* (Rutherford, N.J., 1983), 57–9.

30. McBride dispatch, May 30, 1864, *Washington, D.C., Daily Morning Chronicle,* June 2, 1864; Deloss S. Burton to friends, May 30, 1864, in *Civil War Times* 22 (1983), 26–7.

31. Spaulding's report, in *OR,* Vol. 36. Pt. 1, p. 312; Alford T. A. Torbert's report, ibid., 804; Dexter McComber diary, May 27, 1864, in Clarke Historical Library, Central Michigan University, Mount Pleasant, Mich.; George Perkins diary, May 27, 1864, in Michael T. Russert Private Collection; McBride dispatch, May 30, 1864, *Washington, D.C., Daily Morning Chronicle,* June 2, 1864.

32. Founded in 1672, Hanovertown was the upriver landing on the Pamunkey and site of two tobacco warehouses. Silting in the Pamunkey led to the establishment of new warehouses downriver at New Castle. The structures at Hanovertown fell into disuse, although British prisoners were quartered there during the Revolutionary War. See Malcolm H. Harris, "The Port Towns of the Pamunkey," *William and Mary Quarterly* 23 (October 1943), 510–6. One of Custer's men passing through on May 27, 1864, noted that Hanovertown contained "not a single dwelling": "The Michigan Cavalry Brigade," *Detroit (Mich.) Free Press,* June 15, 1864.

33. Joseph R. Haw, "Haw's Shop Community, of Virginia," *Confederate Veteran* 33 (1925), 340; Torbert's report, in *OR,* 36, Pt. 1, p. 804. Colonel Russell A. Alger, who commanded the 5th Michigan Cavalry during the Richmond raid, had gone to Washington on sick leave, leaving Major Magoffin in field command.

34. Marshall to Lee, May 27, 1864, and indorsements, in *OR,* Vol. 36, Pt. 3, pp. 836–7.

35. Lee to Seddon, 6:45 A.M., May 27, 1864, ibid., 836.

36. Peyton, *Civil War Record,* 36; "H. W. Wingfield Diary," *Bulletin of the Virginia State Library* 16 (1927), 40.

37. G. Moxley Sorrel to John C. Breckinridge, May 27, 1864, in *OR,* Vol. 36, Pt. 3, p. 839; G. Moxley Sorrel's journal, May 27, 1864, in MC; Michael West, *30th Battalion Virginia Sharpshooters* (Lynchburg, Va., 1995), 92; Louis H. Manarin, ed., "The Civil War Diary of Rufus J. Woolwine," *Virginia Magazine of History and Biography* 71 (1963), 436–7; Edward P. Alexander, *Military Memoirs of a Confederate* (New York, 1907), 534; J. A. Lineback diary, May 26, 1864, *Winston-Salem Daily Sentinel,* January 9, 1915; Kenneth Rayner Jones diary, May 27, 1864, in SHC; Cadmus M. Wilcox's report, in VSL; Franklin Gardner Walter Civil War Diary, May 27, 1864, in FSNMP.

38. Nevins, ed., *Diary of Battle,* 388.

39. William T. Schoyer, ed., *The Road to Cold Harbor: Field Diary, January 1–June 12, 1864, of Samuel L. Schoyer, Captain, Company G, 139th Pennsylvania Volunteer Regiment* (Pittsburgh, 1986), 91–2.

40. Lyman's journal, May 27, 1864, in Lyman Collection, MHS.

41. Reuben C. Benton's report, in *OR,* 36, Pt. 1, p. 718; Jessica H. DeMay, ed., *The Civil War Diary of Berea M. Willsey* (Bowie, Md., 1995), 151; R.W.B. to editor, June 7, 1864, *Springfield (Mass.) Daily Republican,* June 22, 1864; Alfred S. Roe, *The Tenth Regiment Massachusetts Volunteer Infantry, 1861–1864* (Springfield, Mass., 1909), 281; Milton H. Myers diary, May 27, 1864, in Book 153, FSNMP; Donald Chipman, ed., "An Essex County Soldier in the Civil War: The Diary of Cyrille Fountain," *New York History* 66 (1985), 293.

42. Roebling's report, May 27, 1864, in Warren Collection, NYSLA; William S. Tilton's report, in *OR,* Vol. 36, Pt. 1, p. 564; Alfred S. Roe, *The Thirty-Ninth Regiment Massachusetts Volunteers, 1862–1865* (Worcester, Mass., 1914), 207; Nevins, ed., *Diary of Battle,* 389.

43. John L. Parker, *History of the Twenty-Second Massachusetts Infantry, the Second Company Sharpshooters, and the Third Light Battery, in the War of the Rebellion* (Boston, 1887), 451; George W. Mason to editor, July 5, 1864, *Litchfield (Conn.) Enquirer,* July 7, 1864.

44. Carter, comp., *Four Brothers in Blue,* 410; Theodore F. Vaill, *History of the Second Connecticut Volunteer Heavy Artillery, Originally the Nineteenth Volunteers* (Winsted, Conn., 1868), 54; J. L. Smith, *History of the Corn Exchange Regiment: 118th Pennsylvania Volunteers, from Their First Engagement at Antietam to Appomattox* (Philadelphia, 1888), 447; John L. Parker, *Twenty-Second Massachusetts Infantry,* 451.

45. George Breck, "In the Field near Hanovertown, Va., May 30, 1864," *Rochester Union and Observer,* June 21, 1864; Lemuel A. Abbott, *Personal Recollections and Civil War Diary, 1864* (Burlington, Vt., 1908), 67; John L. Parker, *Twenty-Second Massachusetts Infantry* 451–2.

46. Ruth L. Silliker, ed., *The Rebel Yell and the Yankee Hurrah: The Civil War Journal of a Maine Volunteer, Private John W. Haley, 17th Maine Regiment* (Camden, Me., 1985), 163; Galwey, *Valiant Hours,* 227; Gibbon, *Personal Recollections,* 225–6; James E. Irwin diary, May 27, 1864, in BL; J. N. Jones memoir, May 27, 1864, in *Civil War Times Illustrated* Collection, USAMHI.

47. John B. McIntosh's report, in *OR,* Vol. 36, Pt. 1, p. 888; *Annual Report of the Adjutant General of the State of Connecticut for the Year Ending March 31, 1865* (New Haven, 1865), 413; J. B. V. Gilpin diary, May 27, 1864, in E. N. Gilpin Papers, LC.

48. Philip H. Sheridan to Andrew A. Humphreys, 9:00 A.M., May 27, 1864, in *OR,* Vol. 36, Pt. 3, p. 257.

49. Paul B. Means, "Sixty-Third Regiment," in *Histories of the Several Regiments and Battalions from North Carolina in the Great War, 1861–65,* ed. Walter Clark (5 vols.; Goldsboro, N.C., 1901), 3, p. 608.

50. "The Recent Cavalry Operations," *Atlanta Daily Intelligencer,* June 14, 1864; James H. Kidd, *Personal Recollections of a Cavalryman with Custer's Michigan Cavalry Brigade in the Civil War* (Ionia, Mich., 1908), 319.

51. Kidd, *Personal Recollections,* 319.

52. Torbert's report, in *OR,* Vol. 36, Pt. 1, p. 804.

53. William W. Goldsborough, *The Maryland Line in the Confederate States Army* (Baltimore, 1900), 198; Samuel H. Miller, ed., "The Civil War Memoirs of the First Maryland Cavalry, C.S.A., by Henry Clay Mettam," *Maryland Historical Magazine* 58 (1963), 153. Bradley Johnson commanded the Maryland Line, made up of infantry and cavalry from Maryland. During the last week of May, the Maryland line was divided, its infantry going to Breckinridge's division and its cavalry remaining under Johnson and going to Fitzhugh Lee's division.

54. Thomas C. Devin's report, in *OR,* Vol. 36, Pt. 1, p. 837; Henry P. Moyer, *History of the Seventeenth Regiment Pennsylvania Volunteer Cavalry* (Lebanon, Pa., 1911), 271.

55. George W. Booth, *Personal Reminiscences of a Maryland Soldier in the War Between the States, 1861–1865* (Baltimore, 1898), 114. A recent recounting of the action at Pollard's farm is in Robert J. Driver Jr., *First and Second Maryland Cavalry C.S.A.* (Charlottesville, Va., 1999), 76–9.

56. Booth, *Personal Reminiscences,* 114; George A. Custer's report, in *OR,* Vol. 36, Pt. 1, pp. 820–1.

57. Harry T. Pollard, "Some War Events in Hanover County," *Hanover County Historical Society Bulletin* 52 (1995), 2.

58. Booth, *Personal Reminiscences,* 115; Samuel H. Miller, ed., "Civil War Memoirs of the First Maryland Cavalry," 153; Goldsborough, *Maryland Line,* 198–9; Bradley T. Johnson to wife, June 2, 1864, in Bradley T. Johnson Papers, DU.

59. Custer's Report, in *OR,* Vol. 36, Pt. 1, pp. 820–1; Alexander Walker's report, ibid., 832; Asa B. Isham, *An Historical Sketch of the Seventh Regiment Michigan Volunteer Cavalry* (New York, 1893), 52. "We had a race of several miles, in which several men were lost on weak horses," Johnson wrote a few days later. "I have a report of one killed, 16 wounded, 28 missing, but many of the latter men wounded, but we don't know which they were" (Johnson to wife, June 2, 1864, in Johnson Papers, DU).

60. Kidd, *Personal Recollections,* 320. Kidd qualified his account by admitting that he was "not positive that these were the particular tunes the bands played."

61. William P. Roberts, "Additional Sketch Nineteenth Regiment," *Histories of the Several Regiments,* ed. Walter Clark, 2, p. 101; Rufus Barringer to V. C. Barringer, January 27, 1866, in Rufus Barringer Papers, SHC. Some Confederate accounts reported the North Carolina cavalry's withdrawal as orderly. See, e.g., Omega to editor, June 22, 1864, *Wilmington (N.C.) Daily Journal,* July 4, 1864.

62. Devin's Report, in *OR,* Vol. 36, Pt. 1, pp. 836–7. A Union account credits 1st Lieutenant John T. Rutherford of Troop L, 9th New York, with leading the charge across Crump's Creek. According to this account, Rutherford and his compatriots forded the creek, drove the rebels back on their reserves, and demanded the surrender of Baker's entire brigade. When a rebel officer called Rutherford's bluff, the brazen Federal shot the officer's horse, then whipped him in hand-to-hand combat. Concluding that his command was too small to guard the entire rebel brigade, Rutherford selected 100 as prisoners and led them back. F. F. Beyer and O. F.

Keydel, *Deeds of Valor: How America's Civil War Heroes Won the Congressional Medal of Honor* (Stamford, Conn., 1992), 329–31. An account from Baker's brigade, however, claims that Captain C. W. McClammy's company of the 3rd North Carolina Cavalry acting as Baker's rear guard repulsed the Union assault and captured several Yankees and horses; Omega to editor, June 22, 1864, *Wilmington (N.C.) Daily Journal,* July 4, 1864.

63. Booth, 115–6; *Richmond Examiner,* May 30, 1864. Alfred Young's figures show 45 North Carolina casualties and 46 Maryland casualties.

64. Booth, *Personal Reminiscences,* 115–6; Bradley T. Johnson to wife, June 2, 1864, in Johnson Papers, DU.

65. David A. Russell to Martin T. McMahon, 11:00 A.M., May 27, 1864, in *OR,* Vol. 36, Pt. 3, pp. 254–5; Robert S. Westbrook, *History of the 49th Pennsylvania Volunteers* (Altoona, Pa., 1898), 203; George Lewis, *The History of Battery E, First Regiment Rhode Island Light Artillery* (Providence, R.I., 1892), 305–6.

66. Sheridan to Humphreys, 5:20 P.M., May 27, 1864, in *OR,* Vol. 36, Pt. 3, pp. 258–9; Charles A. Dana to Edwin W. Stanton, 7:00 A.M., May 28, 1864, ibid., Pt. 1, p. 80.

67. Pollard, "Some War Events in Hanover County," 2–3.

68. Richard E. Beaudry, ed., *War Journal of Louis N. Beaudry, Fifth New York Cavalry* (Jefferson, N.C., 1996), 123.

69. Lyman's journal, May 27, 1864, in Lyman Collection, MHS; Sparks, ed., *Inside Lincoln's Army,* 378.

70. Committee of the Regiment, *History of the Thirty-Sixth Regiment Massachusetts Volunteers* (Boston, 1884), 184. See Dorothy F. Atkinson, *King William County in the Civil War: Along Mangohick Byways* (Lynchburg, Va., 1990), 163–70, for a superb discussion of routes of the various Union army corps and of their camp sites.

71. Dana to Stanton, May 27, 1864, 5:00 P.M., in *OR,* Vol. 36, Pt. 1, p. 80; "Details of the Great Movement," *Philadelphia Inquirer,* June 6, 1864.

72. Francis A. Walker, *History of the Second Army Corps in the Army of the Potomac* (New York, 1887), 498; Galwey, *Valiant Hours,* 227; Silliker, ed., *Rebel Yell,* 163; Roe, *Tenth Regiment Massachusetts,* 281; Theodore Gerrish, *Army Life: A Private's Reminiscences of the Civil War* (Portland, Me., 1882), 192; Amos M. Judson, *History of the Eighty-Third Regiment Pennsylvania Volunteers* (Erie, Pa., 1865), 212–3; O. R. Howard Thomson and William H. Rauch, *History of the Bucktails: Kane Rifle Regiment of the Pennsylvania Reserve Corps* (Philadelphia, 1906), 317; Warren to Humphreys, 7:10 P.M., May 27, 1864, in *OR,* Vol. 36, Pt. 3, p. 253; John L. Parker, *Twenty-Second Massachusetts Infantry,* 451; Beaudry, ed., *War Journal,* 123.

73. Peyton, *Civil War Record,* 36; William M. Dame, *From the Rapidan to Richmond and the Spotsylvania Campaign* (Baltimore, 1920), 190–1.

74. Fitzhugh Lee to Robert E. Lee, 9:00 P.M., May 27, 1864, in *OR,* Vol. 51, Pt. 2, p. 963.

75. Fitzhugh Lee to Robert E. Lee, 12 P.M., May 27, 1864, ibid., 963–4; Fitz Lee to Robert E. Lee, May 27, 1864, ibid., 962.

76. Fitzhugh Lee to Robert E. Lee, 9:00 P.M., May 27, 1864, in *OR,* Vol. 51, Pt. 2, p. 963; Taylor to Anderson, 7:30 P.M., May 27, 1864, ibid., Vol. 36, Pt. 3, p. 838.

77. Richard S. Ewell's report, ibid., Pt. 1, p. 1074; Stephen D. Ramseur's report, ibid., 1082. Command of Ramseur's brigade devolved on Colonel William R. Cox. Details of Ewell's departure are in Donald Pfanz, *Richard S. Ewell: A Soldier's Life* (Chapel Hill, 1998), 396–403.

III MAY 28 *Sheridan and Hampton Meet at Haw's Shop*

1. Brainerd, *Bridge Building in Wartime,* 231; Dana to Stanton, 7:00 A.M., May 28, 1864, in *OR,* Vol. 36, Pt. 1, p. 80.

2. Wilbur Fisk diary, May 28, 1864, in Wilbur Fisk Papers, LC; Lyman's journal, May 27, 1864, in Lyman Collection, MHS.

3. Wright to Humphreys, 7:30 A.M., May 28, 1864, in *OR,* Vol. 36, Pt. 3, p. 270; Wright to Humphreys, 8:20 A.M., ibid., 270–1; Spaulding's report, ibid., Pt. 1, p. 312.

4. Roebling's report, in Warren Collection, NYSLA; 5th Corps Circular, May 28, 1864, in *OR,* Vol. 36, Pt. 3, p. 270: Lyman's journal, May 28, 1864, in MHS.

5. Sheridan's report, in *OR,* Vol. 36, Pt. 1, p. 793.

6. Ibid.; David McGregg's report, ibid., 854; James W. Forsyth to Gregg, May 28, 1864, ibid., Pt. 3, p. 273. See also Philip H. Sheridan, *Personal Memoirs of P. H. Sheridan* (2 vols.; New York, 1888), 1, p. 398.

7. Joseph P. Brinton's report, in *OR,* Vol. 36, Pt. 1, p. 865; Itinerary of the 8th Pennsylvania Cavalry, ibid., 868; Itinerary of the Sixteenth Pennsylvania Cavalry, ibid., 870. Remaining behind were the 2nd, 8th, and 16th Pennsylvania Cavalry. A careful analysis of Union numbers appears in Bryce A. Suderow, "May 28, 1864: Haw's Shop, Virginia," in RNBP.

8. Lee to Davis, May 28, 1864, in Clifford Dowdey, ed., *Wartime Papers of Robert E. Lee* (New York, 1961), 753–4.

9. Lee to Breckinridge, 5:00 P.M., May 28, 1864, in *OR,* Vol. 36, Pt. 3, p. 844; Edward P. Alexander to father, May 28, 1864, in Edward P. Alexander Collection, SHC; Sorrel's Journal, May 28, 1864, in MC; Henry Heth's report, in MC; Cadmus M. Wilcox's report, in VSL.

10. Means, "Additional Sketch, Sixty-Third Regiment," in *Histories of the Several Battalions,* ed. Walter Clark, 3, p. 604. A correspondent reported that "since Fitz Lee's failure to capture the Negro troops in Charles County after breaking down his cavalry in a hard ride, he is censured bitterly": Gamma letter of May 26, 1864, *Mobile Daily Advertiser and Register,* June 2, 1864.

11. Fitzhugh Lee's report, in MC; Fitzhugh Lee to Walter H. Taylor, 7:30 A.M., May 28, 1864, in *OR,* Vol. 51, Pt. 2, p. 966.

12. Edward L. Wells, *A Sketch of the Charleston Light Dragoons* (Charleston, S.C., 1888), 34–5; C. M. Calhoun, *Liberty Dethroned* (N.p., n.d.), 122; Orlando, "Butler's Cavalry," *Charleston Daily Courier,* September 21, 1864.

13. Wells, *Charleston Light Dragoons,* 38.

14. Charles P. Hansell, "History of the 20th Georgia Battalion of Cavalry," 6, in GDAH. Rosser asserted that "Colonel Rutledge, commanding the brigade, was directed to report to me" (Thomas L. Rosser, "Annals of the War: Rosser and His Men," *Philadelphia Weekly Times,* April 19, 1884). During the battle, however, Fitzhugh Lee issued orders to Rutledge's regimental commanders.

15. Thomas L. Pinckney diary, 5, in South Carolina Historical Society, Charleston; Horation Nelson diary, May 18, 1864, in Harold E. Howard, ed., *"If I Am Killed on This Trip, I Want My Horse Kept for My Brothers"* (Manassas, Va., 1980), 14.

16. Haw, "Haw's Shop Community," 340–1.

17. Noble D. Preston, *History of the Tenth Regiment of Cavalry, New York State Volunteers* (New York, 1892), 188; Noble D. Preston, "Hawes's Shop," *National Tribune,* April 21, 1887.

18. St. George Tucker Brooke autobiography, 46, in VSL.

19. Preston, *Tenth Regiment of Cavalry,* 189; Brooke autobiography, 46.

20. Brooke autobiography, 46.

21. Ibid.; Preston, "Hawes's Shop"; William P. Lloyd, *History of the First Regiment Pennsylvania Reserve Cavalry* (Philadelphia, 1864), 95.

22. Lloyd, *First Regiment Pennsylvania Reserve Cavalry,* 95.

23. Preston, *Tenth Regiment of Cavalry,* 189; Lloyd, *First Regiment Pennsylvania Reserve Cavalry,* 95.

24. Frank M. Myers, *The Comanches: A History of White's Battalion, Virginia Cavalry, Laurel Brigade, Hampton Division, A.N.V., C.S.A.* (Baltimore, 1871), 290; George Baylor, *Bull Run to Bull Run: Four Years in the Army of Northern Virginia* (Richmond, 1900), 212; R. Preston Chew's report, in Lewis Leigh Collection, USAMHI; John J. Shoemaker's report, in William Black diary, Virginia Military Institute Library; James Breathed's report, in SHC.

25. Gilbert Thompson memoirs, May 31, 1864, in LC.

26. Joseph R. Haw, "The Battle of Haw's Shop," *Confederate Veteran* 33 (1925), 374; Myers, *The Comanches,* 290.

27. N. Davidson's Dispatch, *New York Herald,* June 2, 1864; Perkins memoir, in Michael Russert Collection; Edward P. Tobie, *History of the First Maine Cavalry* (Boston, 1887), 276; Benjamin W. Crowninshield, *A History of the First Regiment of Massachusetts Cavalry Volunteers* (Boston, 1891), 218.

28. Preston, *Tenth Regiment of Cavalry,* 189-90; Lloyd, *First Regiment Pennsylvania Reserve Cavalry,* 95.

29. Well A. Bushnell memoir, in Palmer Regimental Papers, WRHS; J. N. Roberts to C. F. Wolcott, September 28, 1905, in *Fortieth Annual Reunion of the Sixth Ohio Volunteer Veteran Cavalry* (N.p., 1905).

30. Pinckney diary, 6; Rosser, "Annals of the War."

31. Myers, *The Comanches,* 290; Baylor, *Bull Run to Bull Run,* 212; Crowninshield, *First Regiment of Massachusetts Cavalry,* 218; Tobie, *First Maine Cavalry,* 276-7; Perkins memoir, in Michael Russert Collection.

32. Brooke autobiography, 50-1.

33. Preston, *Tenth Regiment of Cavalry,* 207.

34. Wells, *Charleston Light Dragoons,* 40; Hansell, "20th Georgia Battalion of Cavalry," 7.

35. Wade Hampton Connected Narrative, 38, in SCL; Wells, *Charleston Light Dragoons,* 41-2; Hansell, "20th Georgia Battalion of Cavalry," 7.

36. Orlando, "Butler's Cavalry," *Charleston Daily Courier,* September 21, 1864; Pinckney diary, 6; Hansell, "20th Georgia Battalion of Cavalry," 7.

37. Edwin M. Haynes, *A History of the Tenth Regiment, Vermont Volunteers, with Biographical Sketches of the Officers Who Fell in Battle* (Lewiston, Me., 1870), 131.

38. Wright to Humphreys, 11:50 A.M., May 28, 1864, in *OR,* Vol. 36, Pt. 3, p. 271; Frank Wheaton's report, ibid., Pt. 1, p. 688; William H. Moody memorandum, in Book 115, FSNMP; Robert Hunt Rhodes, ed., *All for the Union: The Civil War Diary and Letters of Elisha Hunt Rhodes* (New York, 1991), 155; Edwin M. Haynes, *Tenth Regiment, Vermont Volunteers,* 131; Binkley's report, in *OR,* Vol. 36, Pt. 1, p. 743; William McVey diary, May 28, 1864, in Ohio Historical Society, Columbus; Francis Cordrey manuscript, 51, in Scott C. Patchen Private Collection; Joseph K. Newell, *Ours: Annals of 10th Regiment, Massachusetts Volunteers in the Rebellion* (Springfield, Mass., 1875), 275; Special Orders, May 27, 1864, in *OR,* Vol. 36, Pt. 3, pp. 253-4; Lyman's journal, May 28, 1864; Carter, comp., *Four Brothers in Blue,* 410; Westbrook, *49th Pennsylvania Volunteers,* 203.

39. Gouverneur K. Warren's journal, May 28, 1864, in *OR,* Vol. 36, Pt. 1, p. 543; Charles S. Wainwright's report, ibid., 646.

40. Theophilus F. Rodenbough, "Sheridan's Richmond Raid," in *B&L* 4, p. 193; "The Battle of Hawes's Shop," *Philadelphia Inquirer,* June 3, 1864.

41. J. L. Smith, *Corn Exchange Regiment,* 448–9.

42. John W. Kester's report, in *OR,* Vol. 36, Pt. 1, p. 861.

43. Preston, "Hawes's Shop."

44. Walter R. Robbins, *War Record and Personal Experiences* (N.p., n.d.), 86–7; Henry R. Pyne, *Ride to War: The History of the First New Jersey Cavalry* (Brunswick, N.J., 1861), 210.

45. William Stokes to family, May 29, 1864, in Lloyd Halliburton, *Saddle Soldiers: The Civil War Correspondence of General William Stokes of the 4th South Carolina Cavalry* (Orangeburg, S.C., 1993), 140; Pinckney diary, 6; Benjamin H. Rutledge memorandum, 308, in South Carolina Historical Society, Charleston.

46. Wells, *Charleston Light Dragoons,* 42–3; Orlando, "Butler's Cavalry," *Charleston Daily Courier,* September 21, 1864.

47. Wells, *Charleston Light Dragoons,* 42; Orlando, *Columbia Daily South Carolinian,* September 25, 1864; Preston, "Hawes's Shop."

48. Pyne, *Ride to War,* 210–2; Warren C. Hursh, "Battle of Hawes's Shop," *National Tribune,* November 11, 1886. Hursh, who witnessed the shot that wounded Robbins, claimed that he and the aggrieved private "had a hearty laugh at seeing the Captain dancing from the pain of the shot."

49. Pyne, *Ride to War,* 211; Orlando, "Butler's Cavalry," *Charleston Daily Courier,* September 21, 1864; Hansell, "20th Georgia Battalion of Cavalry," 7.

50. N. Davidson's dispatch, May 29, 1864, in *New York Herald,* June 2, 1864; "Gen. John Irvin Gregg," *National Tribune,* January 26, 1892; "From the Army of Northern Virginia," *Richmond Enquirer,* May 31, 1864.

51. Preston, "Hawes's Shop."

52. Wilkeson, *Recollections of a Private Soldier,* 124.

53. Rawle, *Third Pennsylvania Cavalry,* 431; William J. Dailey diary, May 28, 1864, in USAMHI; Pollard, "Some War Events," 3.

54. Jubal A. Early, *Autobiographical Sketch and Narrative of the War Between the States* (Bloomington, Ind., 1960), 361.

55. Hampton Connected Narrative, 39.

56. Samuel Cormany diary, May 28, 1864, in FSNMP; Theophilus F. Rodenbough, comp., *From Everglade to Cañon with the Second Dragoons* (New York, 1875), 309; Devin's report, in *OR,* Vol. 36, Pt. 1, p. 837. For the time of Custer's departure from Crump's Creek, see Dexter Macomber diary, May 28, 1864, in Clarke Historical Library, Central Michigan University.

57. Samuel L. Gracey, *Annals of the Sixth Pennsylvania Cavalry* (Philadelphia, 1878) 251; G. W. Beale, *A Lieutenant of Cavalry in Lee's Army* (Boston, 1918), 158; Wesley Merritt's report, in *OR,* Vol. 36, Pt. 1, p. 848; Hampton Connected Narrative, 38.

58. "The Battle of Hawes's Shop," *Philadelphia Inquirer,* June 3, 1864; Sanford, *Fighting Rebels and Redskins,* 225–6. The 5th and 6th Michigan each had about 150 men in the fight (Eric J. Wittenberg, ed., *One of Custer's Wolverines: The Civil War Letters of Brevet Brigadier General James H. Kidd, 6th Michigan Cavalry* [Kent, Ohio, 2000], 88).

59. Pyne, *Ride to War,* 212–3; Karla Jean Husby, comp, and Eric J. Wittenberg, ed., *Under Custer's Command: The Civil War Journal of James Henry Avery* (Washington, D.C., 2000), 79.

60. Kidd, *Personal Recollections,* 324–5; Pyne, *Ride to War,* 212–3.

61. Kidd, *Personal Recollections,* 326; "General Custer," *Washington, D.C., Daily Morning Chronicle,* June 7, 1864; "The Battle of Hawes's Shop," *Philadelphia Inquirer,* June 3, 1864; Brooke autobiography, 38.

62. Orlando, "Butler's Cavalry," *Charleston Daily Courier,* September 21, 1864; Wells, *Charleston Light Dragoons,* 44–5; Ulysses R. Brooks, *Butler and His Cavalry* (Columbia, S.C., 1909), 209.

63. Hansell, "20th Georgia Battalion of Cavalry," 7; Allen Edens to family, May 29, 1864, in Walbrook D. Swank, ed., *Confederate Letters and Diaries, 1861–1865* (Mineral, Va., 1988), 146.

64. Joseph Fred Waring diary, May 29, 1864, in SHC; Hansell, "20th Georgia Battalion of Cavalry," 7; John Gill, *Reminiscences of Four Years as a Private Soldier in the Confederate Army, 1861–1865* (Baltimore, 1904), 99–100; Kidd, *Personal Recollections* 327; Isham, *Historical Sketch,* 53; Hampton Connected Narrative, 39; Edward L. Wells, *Hampton and His Cavalry in '64* (Richmond, 1899), 160. Hampton reputedly told Rosser after the war, "We had a strong position and could have held it until now, but Rooney Lee reported that the infantry was coming up on his flank and he could not hold his position longer, and the whole line was, therefore, ordered to withdraw" (Haw, "Battle of Haw's Shop," 375).

65. Charles F. Wolcott, "Army Story," in *Report of the Proceedings of the Sixth Ohio Cavalry* (1911), 40–1.

66. Pyne, *Ride to War,* 213; Wells, *Charleston Light Dragoons,* 44; Woodall diary, May 28, 1864; Russell Alger's report, in *OR,* Vol. 36, Pt. 1, p. 830; Hansell, "20th Georgia Battalion of Cavalry," 8.

67. Pinckney diary, 6. Pinckney claimed that he wrote to Ingersoll after the war asking for the sword. Failing to receive a satisfactory reply, he applied through a friend in the Senate. Ingersoll refused to return the blade, noting that it was his by right of capture, but that he might sell it back. Pinckney refused on the grounds that Ingersoll should "not have the satisfaction of getting money from me for it."

68. Robert E. Lee to Breckinridge, 5:00 P.M., May 28, 1864, in *OR,* Vol. 36, Pt. 3, p. 844; T. C. Morton, "Incidents of the Skirmish at Totopotomoy Creek, Hanover County, Virginia, May 30, 1864," in *SHSP* 16, p. 47.

69. William Stokes to family, May 29, 1864, in Halliburton, *Saddle Soldiers,* 140; Gracey, *Annals of the Sixth Pennsylvania Cavalry,* 251; Beale, *Lieutenant of Cavalry,* 158; Wilkeson, *Recollections of a Private Soldier,* 125–6.

70. *New York Tribune,* June 4, 1864; Sheridan's report, in *OR,* Vol. 36, Pt. 1, p. 821; T. A. Jeffords letter, May 29, 1864, *Charleston Daily Courier,* June 3, 1864; Orlando, "Butler's Cavalry," *Charleston Daily Courier,* September 21, 1864; Wells, *Charleston Light Dragoons,* 45–6; Stokes to family, May 29, 1864, in Halliburton, *Saddle Soldiers,* 140; "From the Army of Northern Virginia," *Richmond Enquirer,* May 31, 1864; Hansell, "20th Georgia Battalion of Cavalry," 8; *Philadelphia Inquirer,* June 3, 1864; Custer's report, in *OR,* Vol. 36, Pt. 1, p. 821. I am grateful to Allred Young for helping me sort through Confederate losses.

71. Henry E. Davies, *General Sheridan* (New York, 1895), 117; Sheridan's report, in *OR,* Vol. 36, Pt. 1, p. 793; Orlando, "Butler's Cavalry," *Charleston Daily Courier,* September 21, 1864; Hursh, "Battle of Hawes's Shop"; Wells, *Charleston Light Dragoons,* 46–7.

72. *Philadelphia Inquirer,* June 3, 1864; Wells, *Charleston Light Dragoons,* 46–7.

73. Sheridan, *Personal Memoirs,* 1, pp. 401–2.

74. J. M. Reynolds to William J. Dickey, June 1, 1864, in Dickey Family Papers, GDAH; Martin L. Smith to wife, May 29, 1864, in James S. Schoff Collection, CL.

75. J. D. Ferguson, "Memoranda of the Itinerary and Operations of Major General Fitzhugh Lee's Cavalry Division," 4–5, in DU; Haw, "Battle of Haw's Shop," 375; Hampton Connected Narrative, 38.

76. Myers, *The Comanches,* 291.

77. One Hundred and Fifty-Fifth Pennsylvania Association, *Under the Maltese Cross: Antietam to Appomattox, the Loyal Uprising in Western Pennsylvania, 1861–1865, Campaigns 155th Regiment* (Pittsburgh, 1910), 282; Alexander B. Pattison diary, May 28, 1864, in Book 68, FSNMP.

78. Robert S. Robertson, *Personal Recollections of the War,* 116; Nelson Miles's report, in *OR,* Vol. 36, Pt. 1, p. 371.

79. Nathaniel Michler, "Table of distances between the separate camps [and that] of the major-general commanding during the campaign from May 4 to July 12, 1864," in *OR,* Vol. 36, Pt. 1, p. 303; Sumner, ed., *Diary of Cyrus B. Comstock,* 270; Lyman's journal, May 28, 1864; Judith White [Brockenbrough] McGuire, *Diary of a Southern Refugee, During the War* (New York, 1867); Abraham Harshberger memoir, in *Civil War Times Illustrated* Collection, USAMHI; Robert Tilney to family, May 29, 1864, in Tilney, *My Life in the Army,* 80–1.

80. Beta dispatch, May 30, 1864, in *New York Daily Tribune,* June 3, 1864.

81. Tilney, *My Life in the Army,* 79–80; Dawes to family, May 29, 1864, in Dawes, *Service with the Sixth Wisconsin,* 278–9; Charles H. Brewster to family, May 28, 1864, in David W. Blight, ed., *When This Cruel War Is Over: The Civil War Letters of Charles Harvey Brewster* (Amherst, Mass., 1992), 309; George Breck to editor, May 30, 1864, *Rochester Union and Advertiser,* June 21, 1864.

82. Charles J. Calrow, "Cold Harbor: A Study of the Operations of the Army of Northern Virginia and the Army of the Potomac from May 26 to June 13, 1864," 30–1, typescript in RNBP.

83. Lee to Seddon, 6:00 P.M., May 28, 1864, in *OR,* Vol. 36, Pt. 3, p. 843.

IV MAY 29 *Grant Searches for Lee*

1. George M. Gilchrist to mother, May 30, 1864, in George M. Gilchrist Collection, LC; James J. Hartley to wife, May 29, 1864, in Garber A. Davidson, ed., *The Civil War Letters of the Late 1st Lieut. James J. Hartley, 122 Ohio Infantry Regiment* (Jefferson, N.C., n.d.), 89; Washington A. Roebling to Emily Warren, May 29, 1864, in Earl Schenck Miers, ed., *Wash Roebling's War* (Newark, 1961), 25; "The Richmond Campaign," *Boston Daily Advertiser,* June 2, 1864.

2. Dana to Stanton, 8:00 A.M., May 29, 1864, in *OR,* Vol. 36, Pt. 1, p. 81.

3. Mark De Wolfe Howe, ed., *Touched with Fire: Civil War Letters and Diary of Oliver Wendell Holmes, Jr., 1861–1864* (New York, 1969), 133; Miers, ed., *Wash Roebling's War,* 25; Abbott, *Personal Recollections,* 67; Chipman, "Diary of Cyrille Fountain," 293.

4. Lewis H. Steiner diary, May 29, 1864, in Maryland Historical Society; John W. Horn's report, in *OR,* Vol. 36, Pt. 1, p. 739; Pollard, "Some Events in Hanover County," 3; Cordrey manuscript, in Scott C. Patchen Private Collection, 51.

5. Charles C. Coffin, *Redeeming the Republic: The Third Period of the Rebellion in the Year 1864* (New York, 1890), 168; Sparks, ed., *Inside Lincoln's Army,* 379.

6. Warren to Humphreys, 8:30 A.M., May 29, 1864, in *OR,* Vol. 36, Pt. 3, p. 300; Burnside

to Meade, May 29, 1864, ibid., 309; Humphreys to Warren, 10:30 A.M., May 29, 1864, ibid., 301.

7. Humphreys to Burnside, 9:45 A.M. and 10:45 A.M., May 29, 1864, ibid., 310; Burnside's report, ibid., Pt. 1, p. 913; Roebling report, in Warren Collection, NYSLA; J. L. Smith, *Corn Exchange Regiment,* 448.

8. Dana to Stanton, 2:00 P.M., May 29, 1864, in *OR,* Vol. 36, Pt. 1, p. 81; Sumner, ed., *Diary of Cyrus B. Comstock,* 270; Grant to Halleck, May 29, 1864, in *OR,* Vol. 36, Pt. 3, p. 289; Meade, *Life and Letters,* 2, p. 199.

9. Torbert's report, in *OR,* Vol. 36, Pt. 1, p. 805; Custer's report, ibid., 822; Wilson diary, May 29, 1864, in Wilson Collection, LC; Wilson to James W. Forsyth, 12:30 P.M., May 29, 1864, in *OR,* Vol. 36, Pt. 3, p. 311; Robert G. Athearn, ed., "The Civil War Diary of John Wilson Phillips," *Virginia Magazine of History and Biography* 62 (1954), 104; Isaac Gause, *Four Years with Five Armies* (New York, 1908), 248–9.

10. Humphreys to Hancock, 8:45 A.M., May 29, 1864, in *OR,* Vol. 36, Pt. 3, pp. 293–4; Humphreys, *Virginia Campaign,* 166.

11. James I. Robertson Jr., ed., *The Civil War Letters of General Robert McAllister* (New Brunswick, N.J., 1965), 430.

12. Joseph B. Kershaw to G. Moxley Sorrel, May 29, 1864, and attached sketch, in *OR,* Vol. 36, Pt. 3, p. 845; Rutledge memorandum, 312, in South Carolina Historical Society, Charleston.

13. Lee to Breckinridge, 6:45 A.M., May 29, 1864, ibid., 848.

14. Nathaniel Michler's report, ibid., Pt. 1, p. 290; Charles W. White's report, ibid., 760; Henry R. Dalton's report, ibid., 662; Ann H. Britton and Thomas J. Reed, eds., *To My Beloved Wife and Boy at Home: The Letters and Diaries of Orderly Sergeant John F. L. Hartwell* (Madison, N.J., 1997), 233; Alanson A. Haines, *Fifteenth Regiment New Jersey Volunteers,* 197; Edmund D. Halsey report, in USAMHI; Vaill, *Second Connecticut,* 55–6. For the identity of the Confederate cavalrymen opposing Russell, see Henry F. Jones to Martha T. Jones, June 1, 1864, in Civil War Miscellaneous Papers, GDAH; Noah J. Brooks diary, May 29, 1864, in SHC; and Waring diary, May 29, 1864, in SHC. The terms of the 1st and 3rd New Jersey were due to expire June 1. The 2nd New Jersey had already been ordered home, and 138 soldiers from the regiment who elected to remain were assigned to the 15th New Jersey.

15. "2nd Corps memoranda," in *OR,* Vol. 36, Pt. 1, p. 364; Robert S. Robertson, *Personal Recollections of the War,* 116–7; St. Clair A. Mulholland, *The Story of the 116th Regiment Pennsylvania Volunteers in the War of the Rebellion: The Record of a Gallant Command* (Philadelphia, 1899), 231; Frederick M. Edgell's report, in *OR,* Vol. 36, Pt. 1, p. 521; Keating, *Carnival of Blood,* 92.

16. "2nd Corps memoranda," in *OR,* Vol. 36, Pt. 1, p. 365; Nathan Church's report, ibid., 374; John R. Brooke's report, ibid., 412–3; Ezra D. Simons, *A Regimental History of the One Hundred and Twenty-Fifth New York State Volunteers* (New York, 1888), 215; Meade to Grant, 3:30 P.M., May 29, 1864, in *OR,* Vol. 36, Pt. 3, p. 290; W. P. Wilson to Hancock, 2:50 P.M., May 29, 1864, ibid., 295.

17. William S. Tilton's report, in *OR,* Vol. 36, Pt. 1, p. 564; Nevins, ed., *Diary of Battle,* 392–3; J. L. Smith, *Corn Exchange Regiment,* 449; Glenn Brasher, "'Hell's Half Acre': The Battles Around Bethesda Church, May–June 1864," in RNBP. According to Brasher (3 n. 8), the Via house was torn down in the mid-1980s. A man who helped dismantle the home recalled bloodstains on the doors and other signs that Union surgeons had removed them and used them as operating tables.

18. Warren to Humphreys, 3:30 P.M., May 29, 1864, in *OR,* Vol. 36, Pt. 3, p. 302; White

journal, 77–8, in LC; White, "Review of the Services of the Regular Army During the Civil War," 65.

19. Taylor to Anderson, 3:30 P.M., May 29, 1864, in *OR,* Vol. 36, Pt. 3, p. 846; Lee to wife, May 29, 1864, in Dowdey, *Wartime Papers,* 756.

20. Walter H. Taylor to Anderson, addendum, 3:30 P.M., May 29, 1864, in *OR,* Vol. 36, Pt. 3, p. 846; Taylor to Anderson, 5:30 P.M., May 29, 1864, ibid.

21. Fitzhugh Lee to R. E. Lee, 5:00 P.M., May 29, 1864, and Fitzhugh Lee to Wade Hampton, May 29, 1864, both ibid., Vol. 51, Pt. 2, pp. 967–8.

22. Grant to Meade, 4:00 P.M., May 29, 1864, ibid., Vol. 36, Pt. 3, p. 290.

23. Meade to Grant, 5:15 P.M., May 29, 1864, ibid., 290.

24. Michler's report, ibid., Pt. 1, p. 290; Henry Keiser diary, May 29, 1864, in Harrisburg Civil War Roundtable Collection, USAMHI.

25. Howe, ed., *Touched with Fire,* 134–7, 142.

26. Newell, *Annals of 10th Regiment, Massachusetts Volunteers,* 276; Roe, *Tenth Regiment Massachusetts,* 281; Wheaton's report, in *OR,* Vol. 36, Pt. 1, p. 688; Edward Lewis Hoon diary, May 29, 1864, in Francis A. Lord, ed., "Diary of a Soldier—1864," *North South Trader* 4 (1976), 13; DeMay, ed., *Civil War Diary of Berea M. Willsey,* 152.

27. Vignettes about the Shelton home and its history are in William H. Shelton, "A Mansion Rich in Virginia's History," *New York Times,* August 19, 1928; Hanover County Historical Society, *Old Homes of Hanover County, Virginia* (Hanover, Va., 1983), 45–6.

28. Robert S. Robertson, *Personal Recollections of the War,* 117; Robert S. Robertson, "From Spotsylvania Onward," in *War Papers Read Before the Indiana Commandery Military Order of the Loyal Legion of the United States* (Indianapolis, 1898), 350–2; Shelton, "A Mansion Rich in Virginia's History," *New York Times,* August 19, 1928.

29. Robert S. Robertson, "Diary of the War," ed. Charles N. and Rosemary Walker, in *Ft. Wayne (Ind.) Old Fort News* 28 (1965), 198.

30. 2nd Corps addenda, in *OR,* Vol. 36, Pt. 1, p. 365; Nelson Penfield's report, ibid., 405; Thomas C. Godfrey's report, ibid., 497; "Itinerary of the 4th Brigade, 3rd Division, 2nd Army Corps," ibid., 503; John E. Burton's report, ibid., 529; Carter, comp., *Four Brothers in Blue,* 415; Chase diary, May 29, 1864, in *Civil War Times Illustrated* Collection, USAMHI; Silliker, ed., *Rebel Yell,* 64.

31. Robert S. Robertson, "Diary of the War," 198; Hancock to Williams, 9:00 P.M., May 29, 1864, in *OR,* Vol. 36, Pt. 3, p. 297.

32. Wainwright's report, in *OR,* Vol. 36, Pt. 1, p. 646; Edwin C. Bennett, *Musket and Sword; or, The Camp, March, and Firing Line in the Army of the Potomac* (Boston, 1900), 248–9; "H. W. Wingfield Diary," 40; Peyton, *Civil War Record,* 37.

33. Roebling's report, in Warren Collection, NYSLA; Carter, comp., *Four Brothers in Blue,* 413–4; Meade to Warren, 6:00 P.M., May 29, 1864, in *OR,* Vol. 36, Pt. 3, p. 302; Harold A. Small, ed., *The Road to Richmond: The Civil War Memoirs of Major Abner R. Small of the 16th Maine Vols.; With His Diary as a Prisoner of War* (Berkeley, Calif., 1957), 147.

34. Warren to Meade, 8:00 P.M., May 29, 1864, in *OR,* Vol. 36, Pt. 3, p. 303.

35. Ronald G. Watson, *From Ashby to Andersonville: The Civil War Diary and Reminiscences of George A. Hitchcock* (N.p., 1997), 206; Lestor Hildreth diary, May 29, 1864, in Book 153, FSNMP; Mulholland, *116th Regiment Pennsylvania Volunteers,* 231–2; James L. Bowen, *History of the Thirty-Seventh Regiment Massachusetts Volunteers in the Civil War of 1861–1865* (Holyoke, Mass., 1884), 325; Alanson A. Haines, *Fifteenth Regiment New Jersey Volunteers,* 197; James M. Greiner et al., eds., *A Surgeon's Civil War: The Letters and Diary of*

Daniel M. Holt, M.D. (Kent, Ohio, 1994), 194; Westbrook, *49th Pennsylvania,* 203–4; White journal, in LC; John L. Parker, *Twenty-Second Massachusetts Infantry,* 455.

36. Lyman's journal, May 29, 1864, in MHS.

37. Ibid.; Luther A. Rose diary, May 29, 1864, in Luther A. Rose Papers, LC.

38. Robert S. Robertson, *Personal Recollections of the War,* 117–8.

39. Horace Porter, *Campaigning with Grant,* 156.

40. Humphreys, *Virginia Campaign,* 167; Meade to Warren, 7:00 P.M., May 29, 1864, in *OR,* Vol. 36, Pt. 3, p. 303; Meade to Wright, 7:00 P.M., May 29, 1864, ibid., 307; Meade to Burnside, 7:00 P.M., May 29, 1864, ibid., 310.

41. Taylor to Anderson, 6:30 P.M., May 29, 1864, in *OR,* Vol. 36, Pt. 3, p. 847; Pendleton's report, ibid., Pt. 1, p. 1048; Richard H. Anderson's report, in DU.

42. Smith to wife, May 29, 1864, in Schoff Collection, CL.

43. Halleck to Butler, 10:00 A.M., May 26, 1864, in *OR,* Vol. 36, Pt. 3, p. 234; Halleck to Grant, 8:20 P.M., May 24, 1864, ibid., 145.

44. Grant, *Personal Memoirs,* 2, p. 133; Grant to Halleck, 7:00 A.M., May 21, 1864, in *OR,* Vol. 36, Pt. 3, p. 43; George B. McClellan manuscript, in McClellan Papers, Vol. D-9, reel 71, frame 730ff., LC; Agassiz, ed., *Meade's Headquarters,* 140. I am indebted to John Hennessy for leading me to material on Smith and sharing with me his impressions of that intriguing figure.

45. Sparks, ed., *Inside Lincoln's Army,* 330; Nevins, ed., *Diary of Battle,* 330;

46. Butler to Halleck, 1:00 P.M., May 27, 1864, in *OR,* Vol. 36, Pt. 3, p. 261; Asa W. Bartlett, *History of the Twelfth Regiment, New Hampshire Volunteers, in the War of the Rebellion* (Concord, N.H., 1897), 198; Smith to Grant, 10:30 P.M., May 28, 1864, in *OR,* Vol. 36, Pt. 3, p. 285.

47. Millett S. Thompson, *Thirteenth Regiment of New Hampshire Volunteer Infantry in the War of the Rebellion, 1861–1865* (Boston, 1888), 335.

48. Ibid., 336.

49. Lee to Davis, May 28, 1864, in Dowdey, *Wartime Papers,* 754.

50. Davis to Lee, May 28, 1864, in *OR,* Vol. 51, Pt. 2, pp. 965–6.

51. Beauregard to Davis, May 29, 1864, ibid., Vol. 36, Pt. 3, p. 849.

52. Lee to Davis, 9:00 P.M., May 29, 1864, in Dowdey, *Wartime Papers,* 756.

53. Lee to Davis, May 30, 1864, ibid., 757.

V	MAY 30	*The Armies Clash at Bethesda Church and Matadequin Creek*

1. Hancock's report, in *OR,* Vol. 36, Pt. 1, p. 343; Smyth's report, ibid., 451; J. Henry Sleeper's report, ibid., 518; Thomas Smyth's diary, May 30, 1864, in Delaware Public Archives, Dover; William Kepler, *History of the Fourth Regiment Ohio Volunteer Infantry* (Cleveland, 1886), 178; Neill W. Ray, *Sketch of the 6th Regiment N.C. State Troops* (N.p., n.d.), 31.

2. Robert S. Robertson, *Personal Recollections of the War,* 119; Robert S. Robertson, "Diary of the War," 198; "General Grant's Great Campaign," *Harper's Weekly,* June 25, 1864.

3. Hancock's report, in *OR,* Vol. 36, Pt. 1, p. 343; "2nd Corps Daily Memoranda," ibid., 365; John C. Tidball's report, ibid., 511–2; John B. Vande Wiele's report, ibid., 526.

4. Shelton, "A Mansion Rich in Virginia's History," *New York Times,* August 19, 1928.

5. J. E. Holland to Hancock, 8:15 A.M., May 30, 1864, in *OR,* Vol. 36, Pt. 3, p. 325; Hancock to Williams, 9:25 A.M. and 9:40 A.M., May 30, 1864, ibid., 326; Miles's report, ibid., Pt. 1, p. 371.

6. Charles H. Weygant, *History of the One Hundred and Twenty-Fourth Regiment New York State Volunteers* (Newburgh, N.Y., 1877), 345–6; David Craft, *History of the One Hundred Forty-First Regiment Pennsylvania Volunteers, 1862–1865* (Towanda, N.Y., 1885), 207–8.

7. Warren to Burnside, May 30, 1864, in *OR,* Vol. 36, Pt. 3, p. 335.

8. Ibid.

9. A. S. Marvin Jr. to Griffin, 7:00 A.M., May 30, 1864, ibid., 348; Tilton's report, ibid., Pt. 1, p. 564; Edwin C. Bennett, *Musket and Sword,* 249–51; John L. Parker, *Twenty-Second Massachusetts Infantry,* 455; Carter, comp., *Four Brothers in Blue,* 417.

10. Francis J. Parker, *The Story of the Thirty-Second Regiment Massachusetts Infantry* (Boston, 1880), 218–9.

11. Warren to Humphreys, 8:00 A.M., May 30, 1864, in *OR,* Vol. 36, Pt. 3, p. 337.

12. Warren to Humphreys, 11:12 A.M., May 30, 1864, ibid., 339

13. Meade to Wright, 7:00 P.M., May 29, 1864, ibid., 307.

14. R.W.B. to editor, June 7, 1864, *Springfield (Mass.) Daily Republican,* June 22, 1864; Maurus Oestreich diary, May 30, 1864, in Harrisburg Civil War Roundtable Collection, USAMHI.

15. Oliver Edwards's report, in *OR,* Vol. 36, Pt. 1, p. 674; Wheaton's report, ibid., 681; DeMay, ed., *Civil War Diary of Berea M. Willsey,* 152; H. F. Jones to sister, June 1, 1864, in GDAH.

16. During May and June 1862, many of McClellan's soldiers had marched through Peake's Station and were well aware of the Mechanicsville Road. Ricketts and Russell were not involved in the earlier events there and, according to their reports, did not learn about the road until Russell's scouts rediscovered it.

17. Lewis Luckenbill diary, May 30, 1864, in Historical Society of Schuylkill County, Pottsville, Pa. Henry Keiser of the 96th Pennsylvania, thought they had reached the rebel picket line (Keiser diary, May 30, 1864, in Harrisburg Civil War Roundtable Collection, USAMHI).

18. Wright to Humphreys, 10:00 A.M., May 30, 1864, in *OR,* Vol. 36, Pt. 3, p. 353. Cash Corner is now called Cross's Corner.

19. A. P. Hill to Charles S. Venable, 8:45 A.M., May 30, 1864, ibid., Vol. 51, Pt. 2, p. 969.

20. Bradley T. Johnson to Taylor, 10:00 A.M., May 30, 1864, ibid., 970; Johnson to Taylor, May 30, 1864, ibid., 971; Marshall to Butler, 8:00 A.M., May 30, 1864, in Brooks, *Butler and His Cavalry,* 224.

21. S. Franklin [Stringfellow] to Lee, 10:00 A.M., May 30, 1864, in *OR,* Vol. 36, Pt. 3, pp. 850–1.

22. Lee to Anderson, 11:00 A.M., May 30, 1864, ibid., 851.

23. Early to Lee, noon, May 30, 1864, ibid., 854.

24. Lee to Anderson, 2:00 P.M., May 30, 1864, ibid., 851.

25. Dana to Stanton, 1:00 P.M., May 30, 1864, ibid., Pt. 1, p. 82.

26. William N. Pendleton's report, ibid., 1048; Robert S. Robertson, "Diary of the War," 198–9.

27. Edwin B. Houghton, *Campaigns of the Seventeenth Maine* (Portland, Me., 1866), 193; Gilbert Adams Hays, comp., *Under the Red Patch: Story of the Sixty-Third Regiment Pennsylvania Volunteers, 1861–1864* (Pittsburgh, 1908), 248; John W. Roder's report, in *OR,* Vol. 36, Pt. 1, p. 536; Tidball's report, in *OR,* Vol. 36, Pt. 1, pp. 511–2.

28. George M. Edgar, "When Grant Advanced Against a Wall," 1, in George M. Edgar Collection, SHC.

29. Morton, "Skirmish at Totopotomoy Creek," 48–50.

30. Shelton, "A Mansion Rich in Virginia's History," *New York Times,* August 19, 1928; Robert S. Robertson, "Diary of the War," 198–9. An account of the Shelton family's refusal to leave appears also in Walker, *Second Army Corps,* 501–2.

31. Walker, *Second Army Corps,* 500–1; "2nd Corps addenda," in *OR,* Vol. 36, Pt. 1, p. 365; Kirk, *Heavy Guns and Light,* 250–2; Shelton, "A Mansion Rich in Virginia's History," *New York Times,* August 19, 1928.

32. Holland to Hancock, transmitted in Hancock to Humphreys, 3:30 P.M., May 30, 1864, in *OR,* Vol. 36, Pt. 3, p. 327; Nelson Ames, *History of Battery G* (Marshalltown, Iowa, 1900), 110.

33. Wright to Humphreys, 1:30 P.M., May 30, 1864, in *OR,* Vol. 36, Pt. 3, p. 353.

34. Wright to Humphreys, 4:20 P.M., May 30, 1864, ibid., 353–4; Wright to Humphreys, 1:30 P.M., May 30, 1864, ibid., 353; Hancock to Seth Williams, 6:00 P.M., May 30, 1864, ibid., 328; Humphreys, *Virginia Campaign,* 167.

35. James L. Bowen, *Thirty-Seventh Regiment Massachusetts Volunteers,* 325; Brewster to mother, June 2, 1864, in Blight, ed., *When This Cruel War Is Over,* 311; Rhodes, ed., *All for the Union,* 155–6.

36. Meade to Wright, 5:30 P.M., May 30, 1864, in *OR,* Vol. 36, Pt. 3, p. 354; Charles H. Tompkins's report, ibid., Pt. 1, p. 757.

37. Warren to Humphreys, 2:10 P.M., May 30, 1864, ibid., Pt. 3, pp. 339–40.

38. "The Pennsylvania Reserves," *Philadelphia Inquirer,* June 6, 1864. The Bowles house, torn down in 1995, had reputedly been occupied by descendants of Patrick Henry (Brasher, "'Hell's Half Acre,'" 4 n. 14, in RNBP).

39. Burnside to Humphreys, May 30, 1864, in *OR,* Vol. 36, Pt. 3, p. 356.

40. Lyman's journal, May 30, 1864, in MHS; Lyman to family, May 30, 1864, in Agassiz, ed., *Meade's Headquarters,* 134; Meade to Warren, 2:40 P.M., May 30, 1864, in *OR,* Vol. 36, Pt. 3, p. 340.

41. Guy Fuller's report, in *OR,* Vol. 36, Pt. 1, pp. 585–6; Judson, *Eighty-Third Regiment Pennsylvania Volunteers,* 213; Roebling's report, in Warren Collection, NYSLA; Henry B. James, *Memories of the Civil War* (New Milford, Conn., 1898), 71.

42. Warren to Meade, 3:00 P.M., May 30, 1864, in *OR,* Vol. 36, Pt. 3, p. 341.

43. Sheridan's report, ibid., Pt. 1, p. 794. The history of Old Church is related in Hanover County Historical Society, *Old Homes of Hanover County Virginia,* 39–40.

44. Devin's report, in *OR,* Vol. 36, Pt. 1, p. 837; Moyer, *Seventeenth Regiment Pennsylvania Volunteer Cavalry,* 272.

45. Joseph Ioor Waring, "The Diary of William G. Hinson During the War of Secession," in *South Carolina Historical Magazine* 75 (1974), 17. Butler's other regiment—the 6th South Carolina—had arrived from the south, but apparently did not join the expedition.

46. Moyer, *Seventeenth Regiment Pennsylvania Volunteer Cavalry,* 272; Devin's report, in *OR,* Vol. 36, Pt. 1, p. 838.

47. Devin's report, in *OR,* Vol. 36, Pt. 1, p. 838; Moyer, *Seventeenth Regiment Pennsylvania Volunteer Cavalry,* 272.

48. Devin's report, in *OR,* Vol. 36, Pt. 1, p. 838; Merritt's report, ibid., 848; James R. Bowen, *History of the First New York Dragoons During Three Years of Active Service in the Great Civil War* (Lyons, Mich., 1900), 173; Wells, *Charleston Light Dragoons,* 50.

49. Merritt's report, in *OR,* Vol. 36, Pt. 1, p. 848; Gracey, *Annals of the Sixth Pennsylvania Cavalry,* 254.

50. Custer's report, in *OR,* Vol. 36, Pt. 1, p. 822; Husby, comp., and Wittenberg, ed., *Under*

Custer's Command, 81; Albert Rhett Elmore, "Incidents of Service with the Charleston Light Dragoons," *Confederate Veteran* 24 (1916), 541. Alger had reassumed command of the 5th after returning from sick leave.

51. Wells, *Charleston Light Dragoons,* 50–2; Orlando, "Butler's Cavalry," *Charleston Daily Courier,* September 21, 1864. The location of the Charleston Light Dragoons in the Liggan family fields is documented in voluminous correspondence in the Middleton Family Papers, South Carolina Historical Society, Charleston.

52. Kidd, *Personal Recollections,* 330; Gracey, *Annals of the Sixth Pennsylvania Cavalry,* 254; John N. Cumming to wife, May 31, 1864, in John Cumming Collection, DU; Orlando, "Butler's Cavalry," *Charleston Daily Courier,* September 21, 1864.

53. Waring, "Diary of William G. Hinson," 18; Gabriel E. Manigault manuscript, in SCL; Hansell, "20th Georgia Battalion of Cavalry," 9.

54. Sheridan's report, in *OR,* Vol. 36, Pt. 1, p. 794; Torbert's report, ibid., 809; Custer's report, ibid., 822; Husby, comp., and Wittenberg, ed., *Under Custer's Command,* 81; Gray Nelson Taylor, *Saddle and Saber: Civil War Letters of Corporal Nelson Taylor* (N.p., n.d.), 152 .

55. Butler to Lee, May 30, 1864, in Brooks, *Butler and His Cavalry,* 225; Orlando, "Butler's Cavalry," *Charleston Daily Courier,* September 21, 1864; Manigault manuscript, in SCL; William Stokes to wife, June 2, 1864, in Halliburton, *Saddle Soldiers,* 143. Alfred Young helped me tabulate Confederate losses.

56. Early to Lee, 11:00 P.M., May 30, 1864, in *OR,* Vol. 51, Pt. 1, pp. 244–5; Early, *Autobiographical Sketch,* 362; Terry L. Jones, ed., *The Civil War Memoirs of Captain William J. Seymour: Reminiscences of a Louisiana Tiger* (Baton Rouge, 1991), 131.

57. H. N. Minnigh, *History of Company K, 1st Infantry, Pennsylvania Reserves* (Duncansville, Pa., 1891), 36–7. Bethesda Church is described in the *Boston Evening Journal,* June 6, 1864, and Nevins, ed., *Diary of Battle,* 396. Built in 1831, it originally housed a Baptist congregation, and later a new group known as the Disciples of Christ. Ironically, Bethesda in Hebrew means "house of mercy." The building burned in 1868. See Brasher, "'Hell's Half Acre,'" 1–2, in RNBP.

58. Thomson and Rauch, *Bucktails,* 318–9; James B. Thompson memoir, Civil War Miscellaneous Collection, USAMHI.

59. Thompson memoir, Civil War Miscellaneous Collection, USAMHI.

60. Evan M. Woodward, *Our Campaigns: The Second Regiment Pennsylvania Reserve Volunteers* (Philadelphia, 1865), 317; Charles H. Minnemeyer diary, May 30, 1864, in Save the Flags Collection, USAMHI; Minnigh, *History of Company K,* 37; Martin D. Hardin, *Twelfth Pennsylvania Reserves* (New York, 1891), 189; Pulaski Cowper, comp., *Extracts of Letters of Major General Bryan Grimes to His Wife* (Raleigh, N.C.,1884), 54. I relied upon Alfred Young's calculations for Grimes's losses.

61. Nevins, ed., *Diary of Battle,* 393.

62. "Letter from Nelson's Battalion, Ewell's Corps," Richmond Daily Chronicle, July 24, 1864; "Extracts from the Diary of an Officer of General Lee's Army," in Robert A. Hardaway Papers, MC.

63. J. Howard Kitching to wife, May 31, 1864, in Theodore Irving, *"More Than Conqueror"; or, Memorials of Col. J. Howard Kitching* (New York, 1873), 134–5; Nevins, ed., *Diary of Battle,* 393; Journal of 6th New York Heavy Artillery, in Paul Lounsbury manuscript, Civil War Miscellaneous Collection, USAMHI.

64. Warren to Meade, 4:00 P.M., in *OR,* Vol. 36, Pt. 3, p. 341; Humphreys to Warren, 4:15 P.M., ibid., 341; Humphreys to Warren, 4:45 P.M., ibid., 342.

65. Wainwright's report, ibid., Pt. 1, p. 646; Lester I. Richardson's report, ibid., 652–3; James S. Thorpe, *Reminiscences of Army Life During the Civil War* (N.p., n.d.), 48.

66. Small, ed., *Road to Richmond,* 147; Charles E. Davis, *Three Years in the Army: The Story of the Thirteenth Massachusetts Volunteers from July 16, 1861, to August 1, 1863* (Boston, 1894), 353. Lockwood's division contained most of the units formerly under Brigadier General John C. Robinson, whose division was disbanded after his wounding on May 8. Warren had assigned two of Robinson's brigades to other divisions and directed its third brigade of Maryland regiments to report directly to him. On May 26, as the army prepared to leave the North Anna, Lockwood arrived, bringing with him several new regiments. Lockwood's reconstituted division contained the brigades of Colonels Peter Lyle, James L. Bates, and Nathan T. Dushane. During the morning of May 30, Warren brought Lyle's division back from Linney's Corner and reunited it with the division.

67. Hardin, *Twelfth Pennsylvania Reserves,* 190.

68. Woodward, *Second Pennsylvania Reserves,* 253; Carlton's dispatch, May 31, 1864, *Boston Evening Journal,* June 7, 1864. The precise location of Hardin's brigade remains unclear. Several wartime accounts place Hardin's entrenchments near the Bowles garden and slave huts, implying that they were north of Shady Grove Road. Union accounts also discuss rebel bodies in the Bowles family's garden, supporting the conclusion that Hardin posted his men north of the road. The postwar map prepared by Nathaniel Michler, however, shows Union earthworks immediately south of the road, although those works may have been thrown up a few days later, when the Federal line faced north rather than south.

69. J. R. Sypher, *History of the Pennsylvania Reserve Corps* (Lancaster, Pa., 1865), 545; Minnemeyer diary, May 30, 1864, Hardin, *Twelfth Pennsylvania Reserves,* 190; William Fowler to family, May 31, 1864, in *Memorials of William Fowler* (New York, 1875), 84–5.

70. Alexander, *Military Memoirs,* 534; G. Moxley Sorrel, *Recollections of a Confederate Staff Officer* (New York, 1917), 260; Tyrone Powers to Editor, June 2, 1864, *Atlanta (Ga.) Daily Constitutionalist,* June 5, 1864.

71. Charles B. Christian, "The Battle at Bethesda Church," *SHSP* 33, p. 59.

72. Nevins, ed., *Diary of Battle,* 393; Richardson's report, in *OR,* Vol. 36, Pt. 1, p. 653; Woodward, *Second Pennsylvania Reserves,* 253; "Extracts from the Diary of an Officer of General Lee's Army," in Hardaway Papers, MC; R. E. McBride, *In the Ranks: From the Wilderness to Appomattox Court House* (Cincinnati, 1881), 68.

73. Richardson's report, in *OR,* Vol. 36, Pt. 1, p. 653; D. A. Hendrick's dispatch, May 30, 1864, in *New York Herald,* June 3, 1864.

74. Christian, "Battle at Bethesda Church," 59.

75. David F. Ritchie, *Four Years in the First New York Light Artillery,* ed. Norman L. Ritchie (New York, 1997), 164.

76. Minnigh, *History of Company K,* 38; Thomson and Rauch, *Bucktails,* 320.

77. Carlton's dispatch, May 31, 1864, *Boston Evening Journal,* June 7, 1864; Christian, "Battle at Bethesda Church," 59.

78. Wainwright's report, in *OR,* Vol. 36, Pt. 1, p. 646; Charles E. Mink's report, ibid., 656; Charles L. Anderson's report, ibid., 658; Richardson's report, ibid., 653; George Breck letter, *Rochester Union and Advertiser,* June 21, 1864; Ritchie, *Four Years in the First New York Light Artillery,* 165.

79. Ritchie, *Four Years in the First New York Light Artillery,* 164–5; Archie P. McDonald, ed., *Make Me a Map of the Valley: The Civil War Journals of Stonewall Jackson's Topographer* (Dallas, 1973), 208; Breck letter, *Rochester Union and Advertiser,* June 21, 1864; McBride, *In*

the Ranks, 69; "The Pennsylvania Reserves," *Philadelphia Inquirer,* June 6, 1864; Woodward, *Second Pennsylvania Reserves,* 254; "Our Army Correspondence," *Mobile Daily Advertiser and Register,* June 7, 1864; Christian, "Battle at Bethesda Church," 59–60; Peyton, *Civil War Record,* 38.

80. "The Pennsylvania Reserves," *Philadelphia Inquirer,* June 6, 1864; Christian, "Battle at Bethesda Church," 60–1.

81. Arthur A. Kent, ed. *Three Years with Company K: Sergt. Austin C. Stearns, Company K, 13th Massachusetts Infantry* (Rutherford, N.J., 1976), 275; Breck letter, *Rochester Daily Union and Advertiser,* June 21, 1864; McBride, *In the Ranks,* 69; Carlton's dispatch, May 31, 1864, *Boston Evening Journal,* June 7, 1864; Christian, "Battle at Bethesda Church," 61.

82. Frank H. Elvidge diary, May 31, 1864, in Thomas Chamberlin, *History of the One Hundred and Fiftieth Regiment Pennsylvania Volunteers, Second Regiment, Bucktail Brigade* (Philadelphia, 1905), 255.

83. Warren to Humphreys, 6:30 P.M., May 30, 1864, and Meade indorsement, in *OR,* Vol. 36, Pt. 3, p. 343; Meade to Wright, 7:00 P.M., May 30, 1864, ibid., 354; Humphreys to Hancock, 6:50 P.M., May 30, 1864, ibid., 328; Humphreys to Burnside, 6:50 P.M., May 30, ibid., 358.

84. Larry B. Maier, *Rough and Regular: A History of Philadelphia's 119th Regiment of Pennsylvania Volunteer Infantry, The Gray Reserves* (N.p., 1997), 218–9; Abbott, *Personal Recollections,* 67–8; Wright to Humphreys, 7:00 P.M., May 30, 1864, in *OR,* Vol. 36, Pt. 3, p. 354.

85. Burnside to Humphreys, May 30, 1864, in *OR,* Vol. 36, Pt. 3, p. 358; Burnside to Humphreys, May 30, 1864, ibid., 359.

86. Humphreys to Hancock, 6:50 P.M., May 30, 1864, ibid., 328; Hancock to Humphreys, 7:20 P.M., May 30, 1864, ibid., 329; Birney to Walker, 9:00 P.M., May 30, 1864, ibid., 334; Mott to Birney, ibid., 335; Gibbon to Hancock, 8:45 P.M., May 30, 1864, ibid., 333; Kepler, *Fourth Regiment Ohio Volunteer Infantry,* 178; John D. Smith, *The History of the Nineteenth Regiment of Maine Volunteer Infantry, 1862–1865* (Minneapolis, 1909), 184; John D. Billings, *The History of the Tenth Massachusetts Battery of Light Artillery in the War of the Rebellion* (Boston, 1881), 193.

87. Barlow to Walker, 9:00 P.M., May 30, 1864, in *OR,* Vol. 36, Pt. 3, pp. 332–3; John R. Brooke's report, ibid., Pt. 1, p. 413; Fred Mather memoirs, quoted in Keating, *Carnival of Blood,* 97.

88. Hancock's report, in *OR,* Vol. 36, Pt. 1, p. 343; Breckinridge to Taylor, 10:00 P.M., May 30, 1864, ibid., Pt. 3, p. 855.

89. William S. R. Brockenbrough to Harriett Middleton, September 16, 1864; Henry W. Richardson to O. H. Middleton, December 19, 1864; and M. E. L. to Mrs. Middleton, August 1, 1864, all in Middleton Family Papers, South Carolina Historical Society, Charleston.

90. Lyman's journal, May 30, 1864, in MHS; Lyman to family, May 30, 1864, in Agassiz, ed., *Meade's Headquarters,* 132–3.

91. Hopkins, *Seventh Regiment Rhode Island Volunteers,* 180–1; Watson, *From Ashby to Andersonville,* 208; James M. Stone, *Personal Recollections of the Civil War, by One Who Took Part in It as a Private Soldier in the 21st Volunteer Regiment of Infantry from Massachusetts* (Boston, 1918), 169; Weygant, *One Hundred and Twenty-Fourth Regiment,* 346–7; Craft, *One Hundred Forty-First Regiment,* 208; J. D. Bloodgood, *Personal Reminiscences of the War* (Cincinnati, 1893), 275

92. Warren to Meade, 9:00 P.M., May 30, 1864, in *OR,* Vol. 36, Pt. 3, pp. 345–6; Ritchie, *Four Years in the First New York Light Artillery,* 165; Rose diary, May 30, 1864, in Rose Papers, LC; Rufus Dawes to wife, May 31, 1864, in Dawes, *Service with the Sixth Wisconsin Volunteers,* 279.

93. Warren to Humphreys, 1:00 P.M., May 31, 1864, in *OR,* Vol. 36, Pt. 3, p. 391; Crawford to A. S. Marvin Jr., May 31, 1864, ibid., 397; Hendrick's dispatch, in *New York Herald,* June 3, 1864; Nevins, ed., *Diary of Battle,* 393–4.

94. Sheridan to Humphreys, 7:00 P.M., May 30, 1864, in *OR,* Vol. 36, Pt. 3, p. 361.

95. Richard W. L'Hommedieu journal, May 29–30, 1864, in RNBP, Book 56; William L. Hyde, *History of the One Hundred and Twelfth Regiment N.Y. Volunteers* (Fredonia, N.Y., 1866), 80.

96. Thompson, *Thirteenth Regiment of New Hampshire Volunteer Infantry,* 336; James A. Emmerton, *Record of the Twenty-Third Regiment Massachusetts Volunteer Infantry in the War of the Rebellion, 1861–1865* (Boston, 1886), 202; John L. Cunningham, *Three Years with the Adirondack Regiment: 118th New York Volunteers Infantry* (Norwood, Mass., 1920), 126–7; William P. Derby, *Bearing Arms in the Twenty-Seventh Massachusetts Regiment of Volunteer Infantry During the Civil War* (Boston, 1883), 295; Bartlett, *Twelfth Regiment, New Hampshire,* 199; Martin A. Haynes, *History of the Second Regiment, New Hampshire Volunteers* (Manchester, N.H., 1865), 231.

97. Thompson, *Thirteenth Regiment of New Hampshire Volunteer Infantry,* 337.

98. Hermann Everts, *A Complete and Comprehensive History of the Ninth Regiment New Jersey Volunteers Infantry* (Newark, N.J., 1865), 119; Thompson, *Thirteenth Regiment of New Hampshire Volunteer Infantry,* 337.

99. Grant to Smith, 7:30 P.M., May 30, 1864, in *OR,* Vol. 36, Pt. 3, p. 371.

100. Grant to Meade, 6:40 P.M., May 30, 1864, ibid., 323; Meade to Warren, 10:30 P.M., May 30, 1864, ibid., 346.

101. Brooks, *Butler and His Cavalry,* 227–9; Hansell, "20th Georgia Battalion of Cavalry," 10; Wells, *Charleston Light Dragoons,* 45–55.

102. Brooks, *Butler and His Cavalry,* 227–9; Hansell, "20th Georgia Battalion of Cavalry," 10; J. M. Reynolds to William J. Dickey, June 1, 1864, in GDAH; Rutledge memorandum, 313, in South Carolina Historical Society.

103. Ivanhoe dispatch, May 31, 1864, *Richmond Daily Examiner,* June 1, 1864; Soldat dispatch, *Richmond Sentinel,* June 1, 1864. In addition to Pegram's 270 casualties and Grimes's 118, Alfred Young documents losses in Cox's brigade of 81, Doles's brigade of 17, and Battle's brigade of 57.

104. Sorrel, *Recollections of a Confederate Staff Officer,* 260.

105. Early to Lee, 11:00 P.M., May 30, 1864, in *OR,* Vol. 51, Pt. 1, p. 245; Early to Lee, 4:30 A.M., May 31, 1864, ibid., Pt. 2, p. 974; Anderson to Early, 8:00 P.M., May 30, 1864, ibid., Vol. 36, Pt. 3, p. 854; "Diary of the First Army Corps," May 30, 1864, ibid., Pt. 1, p. 1058; Early to Anderson, June 1, 1864, in "Spicy Correspondence between Generals Early and Anderson," *Cincinnati Daily Commercial,* March 31, 1865.

106. Anderson to Early, June 3, 1864, in "Spicy Correspondence between Generals Early and Anderson," *Cincinnati Daily Commercial,* March 31, 1865.

107. Christian, "Battle at Bethesda Church," 59; Peyton, *Civil War Record,* 38; Buckner McGill Randolph diary, May 30, 1864, in VHS; Terry L. Jones, ed., *Civil War Memoirs of Captain William J. Seymour,* 132.

108. Susan Leigh Blackford, comp., *Letters from Lee's Army; or, Memories of Life In and Out of the Army in Virginia During the War Between the States* (New York, 1947), 249.

109. Lee to Bragg, May 30, 1864, in Dowdey, *Lee's Dispatches,* 207.

110. Beauregard to Bragg, 10:35 A.M., May 30, 1864, in *OR,* Vol. 51, Pt. 2, pp. 971–2; Beauregard to Bragg, 5:00 P.M., May 30, 1864, ibid., 972; Robert Ransom Jr. to David Urquhart, May 30, 1864, ibid., 971.

111. Lee to Davis, 7:30 P.M., May 30, 1864, in Dowdey, *Wartime Papers,* 758–9.

112. Bragg to Beauregard, 10:30 P.M., May 30, 1864, in *OR,* Vol. 36, Pt. 3, p. 857.

VI MAY 31 *The Armies Drift toward Cold Harbor*

1. Dana to Stanton, 6:00 A.M., May 31, 1864, in *OR,* Vol. 36, Pt. 1, p. 83.

2. Early to Lee, 4:30 A.M., May 31, 1864, ibid., Vol. 51, Pt. 2, p. 974.

3. Thomas L. Clingman, "Second Cold Harbor," in *Histories of the Several Regiments,* ed. Walter Clark, 5, p. 197. An abstract from field returns dated May 21, 1864, lists Clingman's aggregate present for duty at 1,596, including the 61st North Carolina, left behind to guard his line at Bermuda Hundred. See *OR,* Vol. 36, Pt. 3, p. 817. Alfred Young's count puts Hoke's division at about 6,800 men.

4. Clingman, "Second Cold Harbor," 197; Johnson Hagood, *Memoirs of the War of Secession* (Columbia, S.C., 1910), 254–5.

5. Wells, *Charleston Light Dragoons,* 56; J. D. Ferguson memoranda, May 31, 1864, in DU; Fitzhugh Lee's report, in MC; Orlando, "Butler's Cavalry," *Charleston Daily Courier,* September 21, 1864.

6. Daniel Godkin to wife, May 31, 1864, in Lewis Leigh Collection, USAMHI.

7. Circular, 7:30 A.M., May 31, 1864, in *OR,* Vol. 36, Pt. 3, p. 376.

8. Wright to Humphreys, 9:05 A.M., and Wright to Humphreys, received 9:30 A.M., May 30, 1864, both in *OR,* Vol. 36, Pt. 3, p. 399; Ricketts to McMahon, May 31, 1864, ibid., 400; Charles J. House, "How the First Maine Heavy Artillery Lost 1,179 Men in 30 Days," *Maine Bugle* 2 (1895), 92; George H. Coffin, *Three Years in the Army* (N.p., 1925), 12; McAllister's report, in *OR,* Vol. 36, Pt. 1, p. 496; Cornelius Van Santvoord, *The One Hundred and Twentieth Regiment New York State Volunteers* (Roundout, N.Y., 1894), 130–1.

9. Russell C. White, ed., *The Civil War Diary of Wyman S. White, First Sergeant of Company F, 2nd United States Sharpshooter Regiment, 1861–1865* (Baltimore, 1991), 252; Bloodgood, *Personal Reminiscences,* 275.

10. Kate M. Scott, *History of the One Hundred and Fifth Regiment of Pennsylvania Volunteers* (Philadelphia, 1877), 108; Silliker, ed., *Rebel Yell,* 164–5; Tidball's report, in *OR,* Vol. 36, Pt. 1, p. 512; McKnight's report, ibid., 531; Roder's report, ibid., 536; Stevens, *Berdan's United States Sharpshooters,* 441–2.

11. Morton, "Skirmish at Totopotomoy Creek," 51.

12. Robert S. Robertson, *Personal Recollections of the War,* 121; Morton, "Skirmish at Totopotomoy Creek," 52–3.

13. Delavan S. Miller, *Drum Taps in Dixie: Memories of a Drummer Boy, 1861–1865* (Watertown, N.Y., 1905), 99–100. Robertson related his experiences on Totopotomoy Creek in *Personal Recollections of the War,* 121–3; "From Spotsylvania Onward," in *War Papers Read Before the Indiana Commandery Military Order of the Loyal Legion of the United States* (Indianapolis, 1898), 356–7; and "Diary of the War," 202–4.

14. Robert L. Stewart, *History of the One Hundred Fortieth Regiment Pennsylvania Volunteers* (Philadelphia, 1912), 205–6; Hildreth diary, May 31, 1864, in FSNMP; Mulholland, *Story of the 116th Regiment Pennsylvania,* 232; Daniel Chisholm to father, May 31, 1864, in W. Springer Menge and J. August Shimrak, eds., *The Civil War Notebook of Daniel Chisholm* (New York, 1989), 116; Brooke's report in *OR,* Vol. 36, Pt. 1, p. 413.

15. Ernest L. Waitt, *History of the Nineteenth Regiment Massachusetts Volunteer Infantry*

(Salem, Mass., 1906), 317; Kenneth C. Turino, *The Civil War Diary of Lieut. J. E. Hodgkins, 19th Massachusetts Volunteers* (Camden, Me., 1994), 90; John G. B. Adams, *Reminiscences of the Nineteenth Massachusetts Regiment* (Boston, 1899), 97–8; Charles A. Storke to James M. Aubery, in James M. Aubery, *The Thirty-Sixth Wisconsin Volunteer Infantry* (Milwaukee, 1900), 58–9.

16. Charles H. Banes, *History of the Philadelphia Brigade* (Philadelphia, 1876), 264–5; Anthony W. McDermott, *A Brief History of the 69th Regiment Pennsylvania Veteran Volunteers* (Philadelphia, 1889), 42–3; Ward, *One Hundred and Sixth Regiment*, 261. The church was ignited by shells from the Third Richmond Howitzers on June 1 (William S. White, "A Diary of the War, or What I Saw of It," in *Contributions to a History of the Richmond Howitzer Battalion*, 2 [1883], 261).

17. Meade to Hancock, 10:20 A.M., May 31, 1864, in *OR,* Vol. 36, Pt. 3, p. 379; Humphreys to Wright, 10:20 A.M., May 31, 1864, ibid., 400.

18. Wright to Humphreys, 11:20 A.M., and 12:00 M., May 31, 1864, ibid., 401; Edward E. Russell diary, May 31, 1864, in Niagara County Historical Society, Lockport, N.Y.; Abbott, *Personal Recollections,* 69; Myers diary, May 31, 1864, in RNBP; Alanson A. Haines, *Fifteenth Regiment New Jersey Volunteers,* 198; *The National Tribune Scrap Book* (Washington, D.C., n.d.), 82; E. S. Roberts, "Soldiers Hustled from Mulberry Trees," *Canaan Connecticut Western News,* August 24, 1911; Dwight Kilbourn diary, May 31, 1864, in Civil War Diaries and Journals Collection, Rutgers University Library.

19. Wright to Humphreys, 1:15 P.M., May 31, 1864, in *OR,* Vol. 36, Pt. 3, p. 401; Wright to Humphreys, 2:10 P.M., May 31, 1864, ibid., 402; Wright to Hancock, 3:00, May 31, 1864, ibid., 382.

20. Circular, May 31, 1864, ibid., 409.

21. Watson, *From Ashby to Andersonville,* 208; Massachusetts Historical Society, *War Diary and Letters of Stephen Minot Weld, 1861–1865* (Boston, 1979), 299–300; Warren Wilkinson, *Mother, May You Never See the Sights I Have Seen: The Fifty-Seventh Massachusetts Veteran Volunteers in the Last Year of the Civil War* (New York, 1990), 149; Samuel George Leasure to mother, May 31, 1864, in M. Gyla McDowell Collection, Pennsylvania State University Library.

22. John E. Irwin diary, May 31, 1864, in BL; Byron M. Cutcheon, comp., *The Story of the Twentieth Michigan Infantry* (Lansing, Mich., 1904), 128; Potter to Burnside, 1:45 P.M., May 31, 1864, in *OR,* Vol. 36, Pt. 1, p. 409; Potter's report, ibid., 930; Joseph Gould, *The Story of the Forty-Eighth, a Record of the Campaigns of the Forty-Eighth Regiment Pennsylvania Veteran Volunteer Infantry* (Philadelphia, 1908), 187–8; Oliver C. Bobbyshell, *The 48th in the War, Being a Narrative of the 48th Regiment, Infantry, Pennsylvania Veteran Volunteers, During the War of the Rebellion* (Philadelphia, 1895), 152–3.

23. Potter to Burnside, 5:00 P.M., May 31, 1864, in *OR,* Vol. 36, Pt. 3, pp. 409–10; Committee of the Regiment, *Thirty-Fifth Regiment Massachusetts,* 244.

24. John D. Vautier, *History of the 88th Pennsylvania Volunteers in the War for the Union, 1861–1865* (Philadelphia, 1894), 186.

25. Barbara M. Croner, *A Sergeant's Story: Civil War Diary of Jacob J. Zorn 1862–1865* (Apollo, Pa., 1999), 118; Avery Harris memoir, May 31, 1864, in USAMHI; Sypher, *Pennsylvania Reserve Corps,* 546–7.

26. Dawes, *Service with the Sixth Wisconsin,* 280; Mary Warner Thomas and Richard A. Sauers, eds., *"I Never Want to Witness Such Sights": The Civil War Letters of First Lieutenant James B. Thomas, Adjutant, 107th Pennsylvania Volunteers* (Baltimore, 1995), 186.

27. Medical Director's report, in *OR,* Vol. 36, Pt. 1, p. 243; Humphreys, *Virginia Campaign,* 170–1.

28. Sheridan to Humphreys, 12:20 P.M., May 30, 1864, in *OR,* Vol. 36, Pt. 3, p. 361; Wilson's report, ibid., Pt. 1, p. 880.

29. Wilson to Humphreys, 10:30 P.M., May 31, 1864, ibid., 872; Wilson to Humphreys, 11:00 P.M., May 31, 1864, ibid., 872–3.

30. Wilson diary, May 30, 1864, in LC; Robert K. Krick, *Lee's Colonels* (Dayton, Ohio, 1992), 409; Gilpin diary, May 30, 1864, in LC.

31. Wilson diary, May 30, 1864, in LC; Wilson to Humphreys, 9:00 P.M., May 30, 1864, in *OR,* Vol. 36, Pt. 3, p. 363.

32. George A. Purington's report, in *OR,* Vol. 36, Pt. 1, p. 894; Albert Barnitz's Field Notes, June 2, 1864, in Brinecke Barnitz Papers, Yale University Library.

33. Gause, *Four Years with Five Armies,* 250–1.

34. Waring diary, May 31, 1864, in SHC; W. W. Abercrombie to wife, June 1, 1864, in GDAH; Chew's report, USAMHI; "The First Connecticut Cavalry," *New Haven Daily Palladium,* June 21, 1864.

35. Beaudry, ed., *War Journal,* 124–5; Wilson's report, in *OR,* Vol. 36, Pt. 1, p. 880.

36. Wilson to Humphreys, 1:30 P.M., May 31, 1864, in *OR,* Vol. 36, Pt. 3, p. 413.

37. Wilson diary, May 31, 1864, in LC; Wilson to Humphreys, 11:00 P.M., May 31, 1864, in *OR,* Vol. 36, Pt. 3, p. 414; Wilson's report, ibid., Pt. 1, p. 881; James H. Wilson, *Under the Old Flag* (2 vols.; New York, 1912), 1, p. 429.

38. Old Po'Keepsie to editor, May 12, 1864, in *Painesville (Ohio) Telegraph,* June 23, 1864.

39. McIntosh's report, in *OR,* Vol. 36, Pt. 1, p. 888; Purington's report, ibid., 894; Wilson's report, ibid., 881.

40. Waring diary, May 31, 1864, in SHC; "Recent Cavalry Operations," *Atlanta Daily Intelligencer,* June 14, 1864; "Barringer's North Carolina Brigade of Cavalry," *Raleigh (N.C.) Daily Confederate,* February 22, 1865.

41. Old Po'Keepsie to editor, June 12, 1864, *Painesville (Ohio) Telegraph,* June 23, 1864.

42. Wilson's report, in *OR,* Vol. 36, Pt.1, p. 881; "The First Connecticut Cavalry," *New Haven Daily Palladium,* June 21, 1864.

43. Old Po'Keepsie to editor, May 12, 1864, *Painesville (Ohio) Telegraph,* June 23, 1864; Purington's report, in *OR,* Vol. 36, Pt. 1, p. 894; Gause, *Four Years in Five Armies,* 253; Luman Harris Tenney, *War Diary, 1861–1865* (Cleveland, 1914), 117.

44. Gause, *Four Years in Five Armies,* 254.

45. "First Regiment Cavalry," in *Annual Report of the Adjutant-General of the State of Connecticut,* 412–3; Athearn, ed., "Civil War Diary of John Wilson Phillips," 104; "Recent Cavalry Operations," *Atlanta Daily Intelligencer,* June 14, 1864; Publication Committee of the Regiment, *History of the Eighteenth Pennsylvania Cavalry* (New York, 1909), 24.

46. John W. Chowning diary, May 31, 1864, in Mary Ball Washington Library, Lancaster, Va.; R. L. T. Beale, *History of the Ninth Virginia Cavalry in the War Between the States* (Richmond, 1899), 126; David Cardwell, "When the Gallant Lieutenant Ford Was Killed," *Confederate Veteran* 26 (1918), 207–8; Gause, *Four Years with Five Armies,* 251; "The First Connecticut Cavalry," *New Haven Daily Palladium,* June 21, 1864.

47. Wilson to Humphreys, 11:00 P.M., May 31, 1864, in *OR,* Vol. 31, Pt. 3, p. 414; Alberta R. Adamson et al., eds., *Recollections of the War of the Rebellion: A Story of the Second Ohio Volunteer Cavalry* (Wheaton, Ill., 1996), 81; Wilson diary, May 31, 1864, in LC. Alfred Young helped me calculate Confederate losses.

48. William F. Smith, "The Eighteenth Corps at Cold Harbor," in *B&L* 4, p. 222; Rawlins to Smith, 1:00 P.M., May 28, 1864, in *OR,* Vol. 36, Pt. 3, p. 285; Emmerton, *Record of the Twenty-Third Regiment Massachusetts,* 202–3.

49. William F. Smith, "Eighteenth Corps at Cold Harbor," 222; Rawlins to Smith, 1:00 P.M., May 28, 1864, in *OR,* Vol. 36, Pt. 3, p. 285.

50. Ella Moore Bassett Washington diary, May 31, 1864, in VHS.

51. Smith to Grant, May 31, 1864, in *OR,* Vol. 36, Pt. 3, p. 410 [9:00 P.M. message erroneously listed in *OR* as 9:00 A.M.].

52. Torbert's report, in *OR,* Vol. 36, Pt. 1, p. 805; Sheridan's report, ibid., 794; Sheridan, *Personal Memoirs,* 1, p. 405; Gracey, *Annals of the Sixth Pennsylvania Cavalry,* 255.

53. Fitzhugh Lee to General Lee, 3:15 P.M., May 31, 1864, in *OR,* Vol. 36, Pt. 3, p. 858.

54. Torbert's report, ibid., Pt. 1, p. 805; James R. Bowen, *First New York Dragoons,* 174–7; "Custer's Cavalry Brigade," *Detroit Advertiser and Tribune,* June 16, 1864.

55. Devin's report, in *OR,* Vol. 36, Pt. 1, p. 839; Moyer, *Seventeenth Regiment Pennsylvania Volunteer Cavalry,* 341. Devin reported that he met pickets from the 5th Michigan, but he was in error, as the pickets were from the 6th Michigan. See Kidd, *Personal Recollections,* 331.

56. Clingman, "Second Cold Harbor," 197–8.

57. Merritt's report, in *OR,* Vol. 36, Pt. 1, p. 848; James R. Bowen, *First New York Dragoons,* 176–7.

58. Merritt's report, in *OR,* Vol. 36, Pt. 1, pp. 848–9; Custer's report, ibid., 822; Torbert's report, ibid., 805.

59. Clingman, "Second Cold Harbor," 198; Merritt's report, in *OR,* Vol. 36, Pt. 1, pp. 848–9; Torbert's report, ibid., 805; Custer's report, ibid., 822; "Custer's Cavalry Brigade," *Detroit Advertiser and Tribune,* June 16, 1864; "The Michigan Cavalry Brigade," *Detroit Free Press,* June 15, 1864; James R. Bowen, *First New York Dragoons,* 177. Clingman's mangled hat is on display at the North Carolina History Museum in Raleigh.

60. Clingman, "Second Cold Harbor," 198–9.

61. Fitzhugh Lee's report, MC; Ferguson memoranda, DU; Clingman, "Second Cold Harbor," 198–9. Alfred Young helped me calculate Fitzhugh Lee's losses.

62. Alexander, *Military Memoirs,* 535; Gary W. Gallagher, ed., *Fighting for the Confederacy: The Personal Recollections of General Edward Porter Alexander* (Chapel Hill, 1989), 398; Douglas Southall Freeman, *R. E. Lee* (4 vols.; New York, 1934–35), 2, p. 375.

63. Alexander claims, for example, that on May 30, a brigade of Union infantry appeared on Old Church Road, and that Lee, whom Alexander implies was with him, ordered Early to send a brigade to attack. Early, Alexander says, selected Pegram's Brigade. Official correspondence, however, makes it clear that Lee was miles away at Atlee's Station on May 30 and that Early's foray out Old Church Road had nothing to do with the appearance of a Union brigade. Alexander also attributes the failed Confederate attack on June 1 in part to Lee's failure to put Hoke's division under Anderson. In fact, Lee did put Hoke under Anderson, and the note from Lee notifying Anderson of that fact appears in the official records. See Taylor to Anderson, May 31, 1864, in *OR,* Vol. 36, Pt. 3, p. 858.

64. 1st Corps memorandum, May 31, 1864, ibid., Pt. 1, p. 1058; Taylor to Anderson, May 31, 1864, ibid., Pt. 3, p. 858; Heth's report, in MC.

65. Anderson to Lee, 7:00 P.M., May 31, 1864, in *OR,* Vol. 51, Pt. 2, p. 974.

66. Taylor to Anderson, May 31, 1864, ibid., Pt. 3, p. 858.

67. Warren to Humphreys, May 31, 1864, ibid., 393; Sheridan to Humphreys, May 31, 1864, ibid., 411.

68. Smith to Grant, 9:00 P.M., May 31, 1864, ibid., 410 [erroneously printed as 9:00 A.M., rather than P.M.].

69. Howe, ed., *Touched with Fire,* 136, 138; Wright to Humphreys, 4:30 P.M., May 31, 1864, in *OR,* Vol. 36, Pt. 3, p. 403; Humphreys to Wright, 5:15 P.M., May 31, 1864, ibid; Meade to Wright, 9:30 P.M., May 31, 1864, ibid., 404.

70. Babcock to Smith, June 1, 1864, in John Y. Simon, ed., *The Papers of Ulysses S. Grant* (20 vols; Carbondale, Ill., 1967–1999), 10, p. 499; William F. Smith, "Eighteenth Corps at Cold Harbor," 222.

71. Wright to Hancock, 10:30 P.M., May 31, 1864, in *OR,* Vol. 36, Pt. 3, p. 383; Howe, ed., *Touched with Fire,* 136; Francis Cordrey, "Life and Comments of a Common Soldier," 51, in Scott C. Patchen Collection.

72. Howe, ed., *Touched with Fire,* 138.

73. Sheridan's report, in *OR,* Vol. 36, Pt. 1, p. 794; Torbert's report, ibid., 806; Sheridan, *Personal Memoirs,* 1, pp. 407–8.

VII JUNE 1 *Grant and Lee Jockey for Position*

1. James R. Bowen, *First New York Dragoons,* 180; Rodenbough, comp., *From Everglade to Cañon with the Second Dragoons,* 310.

2. Clingman, "Second Cold Harbor,"199; Charles G. Elliott, "Martin's Brigade, of Hoke's Division," in *SHSP,* 23, p. 192; William V. Izlar, *A Sketch of the War Record of the Edisto Rifles, 1861–1865* (Columbia, S.C., 1914), 61.

3. The road past Mr. Allison's is described in Calrow, "Cold Harbor," 90. It does not appear on postwar maps because it was destroyed during the Cold Harbor operations. A good map of part of the road appears in Thompson, *Thirteenth Regiment New Hampshire Volunteer Infantry,* 353.

4. Hagood, *Memoirs,* 255.

5. William S. Truex's report, in *OR,* Vol. 36, Pt. 1, p. 726; Upton's report, ibid., 671; Wheaton's report, ibid., 688; Martin T. McMahon, "Cold Harbor," in *B&L* 4, pp. 214–5.

6. Smith's report, in *OR,* Vol. 36, Pt. 1, p. 999; McMahon to Smith, 8:10 A.M., ibid., Pt. 3, p. 467; William F. Smith, "Eighteenth Corps at Cold Harbor," 222–3. Grant's order of June 1 referred to by Smith does not appear in the official records but is mentioned in Smith's official report. Clearly the headquarters aide got Smith's destination wrong. Had "Old Cold Harbor" been substituted for "New Castle," the order would have made sense. Wright was on his way to Old Cold Harbor. When he got there and went into line, Warren would be on his right, separated from Wright by a gap of well over a mile.

7. Lawrence M. Keitt to wife, May 30 and 31, 1864, Keitt Papers, DU; Lee to Davia, May 31, 1864, in R. E. Lee Papers, DU. On May 30, Lee had urged Anderson to "consult General Kershaw at once, so that a good commander may be recommended for [Kershaw's] brigade as soon as practicable" (*OR,* Vol. 36, Pt. 3, p. 851).

8. James A. Milling "Recollections," *Confederate Veteran* 6 (1997), 9; Keitt to wife, May 31, 1864, in Keitt Collection, DU.

9. D. Augustus Dickert, *History of Kershaw's Brigade* (Newberry, S.C., 1899), 369; Alexander, *Military Memoir,* 536.

10. A. J. McBride, "Some War Experiences," in Book 20, RNBP; John W. Lynch, ed., *The Dorman-Marshbourne Letters* (Senoia, Ga., 1995), 71.

11. Dickert, *Kershaw's Brigade,* 369; Milling "Memoir," 9.

12. Rodenbough, "Sheridan's Richmond Raid," in *B&L* 4, p. 193; Robert Stiles, *Four Years Under Marse Roberts* (New York, 1903), 274; Gallagher, ed., *Fighting for the Confederacy,* 399; "Custer's Cavalry Brigade," *Detroit (Mich.) Advertiser and Tribune,* June 16, 1864; Kidd, *Personal Recollections,* 33–4.

13. James R. Bowen, *First New York Dragoons,* 181–2.

14. Kershaw to Sorrel, 8:45 A.M., June 1, 1864, in Edward P. Alexander Collection, SHC.

15. W. C. Hall diary, June 1, 1864, in RNBP, Book 47; Milling, "Memoir," 9. Alfred Young documents 80 casualties in the 20th South Carolina, although some of those losses may have occurred later in the day.

16. Alexander, *Military Memoirs,* 536; Gallagher, ed., *Fighting for the Confederacy,* 399.

17. Clingman, "Second Cold Harbor," 199; Calrow, "Cold Harbor," 92½.

18. Alexander, *Military Memoirs,* 536.

19. Gallagher, ed., *Fighting for the Confederacy,* 399.

20. Hagood, *Memoirs,* 257; Kershaw to Sorrel, June 1, 1864, in Alexander Collection, SHC.

21. Thomas W. Hyde, *Following the Greek Cross,* 208.

22. Sheridan to Humphreys, 9:00 A.M., June 1, 1864, in *OR,* Vol. 36, Pt. 3, p. 470; Wright to Humphreys, 9:00 A.M., June 1, 1864, ibid., 454.

23. Edwin M. Haynes, *Tenth Regiment, Vermont,* 134; Kidd, *Personal Recollections,* 335.

24. Smith's report, in *OR,* Vol. 36, Pt. 1, p. 999; Special Orders No. 25½, ibid., Pt. 3, p. 466; Dana to Stanton, 10:00 A.M., June 1, 1864, ibid., Pt. 1, p. 84; Meade to Smith, ibid., 999.

25. William F. Smith, "18th Corps at Cold Harbor," 230.

26. Meade to Smith, 12 M., June 1, 1864, in *OR,* Vol. 36, Pt. 3, p. 466.

27. William A. Hunter, ed., "The Civil War Diaries of Leonard C. Ferguson," in *Pennsylvania History* 14 (1947), 209.

28. Peter P. Dalton, *With Our Faces to the Foe: A History of the 4th Maine Infantry in the War of the Rebellion* (Union, Me., 1998), 332; Silliker, ed., *Rebel Yell,* 165.

29. Hancock's report, in *OR,* Vol. 36, Pt. 1, p. 344; McAllister's report, ibid., 496; 2nd Corps Circular, 12:30 A.M., June 1, 1864, ibid., Pt. 3, p. 442; Stevens, *Berdan's United States Sharpshooters,* 442–3.

30. Miles's report, in *OR,* Vol. 36, Pt. 1, p. 371; James Fleming's report, ibid., 390.

31. Gibbon to Hancock, June 1, 1864, ibid., Pt. 3, p. 438; Barlow to Hancock, in Hancock to Humphreys, June 1, 1864, ibid., 438; Barlow to Walker, 11:40 A.M., June 1, 1864, ibid., 437; Hancock's report, ibid., Pt. 1, p. 344.

32. Burnside to Seth Williams, 7:20 A.M., June 1, 1864, ibid., Pt. 3, p. 459; Burnside's report, ibid., Pt. 1, p. 913.

33. Charles Ricketts to Warren, 10:15 A.M., June 1, 1864, ibid., Pt. 3, p. 447; Warren to Meade, 10:30 A.M., June 1, 1864, ibid; Warren to Meade, 11:30 A.M., June 1, 1864, ibid.; Roebling's report, in Warren Papers, NYSLA; Roe, *Thirty-Ninth Regiment Massachusetts Volunteers,* 210–1.

34. Warren to Meade, 8:30 A.M., June 1, 1864, in *OR,* Vol. 36, Pt. 3, p. 446; Warren to wife, May 31, 1864, in Warren Collection, NYSLA.

35. Meade to Smith, June 1, 1864, in *OR,* Vol. 36, Pt. 3, p. 466; Lyman's journal, June 1, 1864, in Lyman Collection, MHS.

36. Meade to Warren, *OR,* Vol. 36, Pt. 3, p. 449; Roebling to Warren, 1:30 P.M., June 1, 1864, ibid.; Warren to Meade, 1:30 P.M., June 1, 1864, ibid., 448; Small, ed., *Road to Richmond,* 148; Roebling's report, in Warren Collection, NYSLA. Accompanying Roebling were the 8th

Maryland and six companies of the 1st Maryland; Charles Camper and J. W. Kirkley, *Historical Record of the First Regiment Maryland Infantry* (Washington, D.C., 1871), 153–4.

37. Grant, *Personal Memoirs,* 2, pp. 265–6.

38. Meade to Hancock, 3:30 P.M., June 1, 1864, in *OR,* Vol. 36, Pt. 3, p. 440.

39. "2nd Corps Addendum," ibid., Pt. 1, p. 366; Hancock to Williams, 3:30 P.M., June 1, 1864, ibid., 439–40; "General Lee's Army," *Daily Richmond Enquirer,* June 2, 1864.

40. Hancock to Williams, 3:30 P.M., June 1, 1864, in *OR,* Vol. 36, Pt. 3, pp. 439–40; Smyth diary, June 1, 1864, in Delaware Public Archives, Dover; Heth's report, in MC; Robert A. Hardaway's report, in *OR,* Vol. 36, Pt. 1, p. 1090.

41. Aubery, *Thirty-Sixth Wisconsin Volunteer Infantry,* 60–1; "The Late Lieut. Lamberton, Thirty-Sixth Regiment," *Milwaukee Daily Sentinel,* June 21, 1864; Ward, *One Hundred and Sixth Regiment Pennsylvania Volunteers,* 261; John H. Thorp, "Forty-Seventh Regiment," in *Histories of the Several Regiments,* ed. Walter Clark, 3, p. 95; Lee to Seddon, June 1, 1864, in *OR,* Vol. 51, Pt. 2, p. 977; *Richmond Dispatch,* June 3, 1864. Lieutenant Lamberton was killed charging Confederate earthworks on June 3.

42. David Coon to Emma, June 5, 1864, in LC.

43. Banes, *Philadelphia Brigade,* 266; Aubery, *Thirty-Sixth Wisconsin Volunteer Infantry,* 61.

44. Brooke's report, in *OR,* Vol. 36, Pt. 1, p. 413; Barlow to Walker, 7:45 P.M., June 1, 1864, ibid., Pt. 3, p. 444; Hancock to Williams, 8:30 P.M., ibid., 439.

45. Dana to Stanton, 5:00 P.M., June 1, 1864, ibid., Pt. 1, p. 85.

46. Ibid. Dana's criticism of Warren was unfair. As one of Warren's subordinates noted after the war, in order to reach Anderson's column, Warren had to "smash Early and then get to Anderson, always supposing that you had got over Early" (Charles H. Porter to Warren, November 28, 1881, in Warren Collection, NYSLA). With respect to the day's operations, Warren later wrote that he was "very seldom favored with an idea of what was expected during Grant's command, so I do not think I had any instruction whatever in regard to Anderson's movement" (Warren to Porter, November 29, 1881, in Warren Collection, NYSLA). See also David M. Jordan, *"Happiness Is Not My Companion": The Life of General G. K. Warren* (Bloomington, Ind., 2001), 157–8.

47. Charles C. Coffin, *Redeeming the Republic,* 182.

48. Wilson's report, in *OR,* Vol. 36, Pt. 1, p. 881; McIntosh's report, ibid., 888; Charles C. Suydam's report, ibid., 890; Wilson diary, June 1, 1864, in LC.

49. Bradley T. Johnson to wife, June 2, 1864, in DU.

50. Ibid.; Goldsborough, *Maryland Line,* 200; Samuel H. Miller, ed., "Civil War Memoirs of the First Maryland Cavalry," 154; Chapman's report, in *OR,* Vol. 36, Pt. 1, p. 900

51. Booth, *Personal Reminiscences,* 117–8; Samuel H. Miller, ed., "Civil War Memoirs of the First Maryland Cavalry," 54; George S. Woolley manuscript, quoted in Driver, *First and Second Maryland Cavalry C.S.A.,* 81. Goldsborough claimed that Brown "was killed by a stray bullet when all was comparatively calm, and no fighting going on."

52. Chapman's report, in *OR,* Vol. 36, Pt. 1, p. 900; Booth, *Personal Reminiscences,* 117; Robert J. Trout, ed., *Riding with Stuart: Reminiscences of an Aide-de-Camp, by Captain Theodore S. Garnett* (Shippensburg, Pa., 1994), 77.

53. Rosanne Groat Shalf, "Macmurdo House Paper—1994," unpublished manuscript.

54. Wilson's report, in *OR,* Vol. 36, Pt. 1, p. 881; Chowning diary, June 1, 1864, in Mary Ball Washington Library, Fredericksburg.

55. Thomas L. Rosser, "Promotion for Extraordinary Skill," in *Lost Cause* 1 (1898), 1; "First Regiment Cavalry," in *Annual Report of the Adjutant General,* 413; "The 1st Conn.

Cavalry," *New Haven Daily Palladium,* June 21, 1864. Rosser gives a slightly different rendition of the same events in "Annals of the War: Rosser and His Men," *Philadelphia Weekly Times,* April 19, 1884.

56. Purington's report, in *OR,* Vol. 36, Pt. 1, p. 895; Baylor, *Bull Run to Bull Run,* 214; Rosser, "Promotion for Extraordinary Skill," 1; "The Recent Cavalry Operations," *Atlanta Daily Intelligencer,* June 14, 1864; "The 1st Conn. Cavalry," *New Haven Daily Palladium,* June 21, 1864.

57. Rosser, "Promotion for Extraordinary Skill," 1; "First Regiment Cavalry," in *Annual Report of the Adjutant General,* 413–4; "The 1st Conn. Cavalry," *New Haven Daily Palladium,* June 21, 1864; Hampton Connected Narrative, 40; William P. McDonald, *Laurel Brigade,* 245–8. Rosser was so impressed with Conrad's bravery that he told Hampton about him that day and later formally recommended him for promotion; Rosser letter, January 2, 1865, in Holmes Conrad Combined Service Record, Roll 61, NA.

58. Hampton Connected Narrative, 40; Chew's report, in USAMHI.

59. D. B. R. "Barringer's North Carolina Brigade of Cavalry," *Raleigh (N.C.) Daily Confederate,* February 22, 1865; James H. Wilson, *Under the Old Flag,* 1, p. 430; Rufus Barringer to V. C. Barringer, January 27, 1866, in Rufus Barringer Papers, SHC; Waring diary, June 3, 1864, in SHC; Boudrye, *Historic Records of the Fifth New York Cavalry,* 137.

60. Hampton Connected Narrative, 40; "Army Correspondence," *Painesville (Ohio) Telegraph,* June 23, 1864; George G. Benedict, *Vermont in the Civil War: A History of the Part Taken by the Vermont Soldiers and Sailors in the War for the Union* (2 vols.; Burlington, Vt., 1888), 2, pp. 642–3; Horace K. Ide, *History of the First Vermont Cavalry Volunteers in the War of the Great Rebellion* (Baltimore, 2000), 173; Trout, ed., *Riding with Stuart,* 78; Barnitz field notes, June 1, 1864, in Barnitz Papers, Yale University Library.

61. "Army Correspondence," *Painesville (Ohio) Telegraph,* June 23, 1864; Benedict, *Vermont in the War,* 2, pp. 643; Trout, ed., *Riding with Stuart,* 78; A. McDonald to Mrs. Addison G. Warner, June 2, 1864, *Windham County (Conn.) Transcript,* June 16, 1864; Beale, *Lieutenant of Cavalry in Lee's Army,* 153.

62. Ide, *1st Vermont Cavalry,* 174–5; Benedict, *Vermont in the War,* 2, p. 643; "The First Connecticut Cavalry," *New Haven Daily Palladium,* June 21, 1864; Barnitz field notes, June 1, 1864; J. L. Sperry to sister, June 5, 1864, in DU; Adamson, *Recollections of the War,* 81; Eri Davidson Woodbury to family, June 5, 1864, in Dartmouth University Library.

63. Wilson diary, June 1, 1864, in LC; "Army Correspondence," *Painesville (Ohio) Telegraph,* June 23, 1864.

64. Robert W. Hatton, ed., "Just a Little Bit of the Civil War, as Seen by W. J. Smith, Company M, 2nd O V. Cavalry," in *Ohio History* 84 (1975), 115; William Wells to family, June 4, 1864, in William Wells Collection, University of Vermont Special Collections.

65. Trout, ed., *Riding with Stuart,* 78–9; Waring diary, June 3, 1864, in SHC.

66. *Richmond Daily Dispatch,* June 3, 1864; *Richmond Examiner,* June 3, 1864; "Progress of the Campaign in Virginia," *Charleston Mercury,* June 4, 1864; Baylor, *Bull Run to Bull Run,* 214; Theo. S. Barker to Wade Hampton, June 2, 1864, in Hampton Connected Narrative, 41. The recent tabulation was made by Alfred Young.

VIII   JUNE 1   *Grant Attacks at Cold Harbor*

1. P. Robertson, "A Reminiscence of Cold Harbor," *National Tribune,* March 30, 1884; Abbott, *Personal Recollections,* 70–1.

2. "Itinerary of Third Division, Sixth Army Corps," in *OR,* Vol. 36, Pt. 1, p. 721; George R. Prowell, *History of the Eighty-Seventh Regiment, Pennsylvania Volunteers* (York, Pa., 1901), 147; Abbott, *Personal Recollections,* 69–70; J. Warren Keifer's report, in *OR,* Vol. 36, Pt. 1, p. 734; Binkley's report, ibid., 748; "Notes from the Battlefield—No. 4," *Xenia (Ohio) Torchlight,* June 19, 1864.

3. Isaac O. Best, *History of the 121st New York State Infantry* (Chicago, 1921), 154–5; Britton and Reed, eds., *To My Beloved Wife and Boy at Home,* 235.

4. Wright to Humphreys, 2:10 P.M., June 1, 1864, in *OR,* Vol. 36, Pt. 3, p. 455; Roe, *Tenth Regiment Massachusetts,* 284; Rhodes, ed., *All for the Union,* 156; Nelson V. Hutchinson, *History of the Seventh Massachusetts Volunteer Infantry in the War of the Rebellion* (Taunton, Mass., 1890), 195.

5. Benedict, *Vermont in the War,* 1, p. 462; Benton's report, in *OR,* Vol. 36, Pt. 1, p. 717. Neill's brigade under Frank Wheaton was posted in reserve near Cold Harbor, guarding wagons. The 10th and 37th Massachusetts formed Edwards's first line, the 7th Massachusetts and 7th Rhode Island his second line.

6. Bartlett, *Twelfth Regiment, New Hampshire,* 200; Derby, *Bearing Arms,* 296; William L. Hyde, *One Hundred and Twelfth Regiment N.Y. Volunteers,* 81.

7. Derby, *Bearing Arms,* 297; Smith's report, in *OR,* Vol. 36, Pt. 1, p. 999.

8. James H. Clark, *The Iron Hearted Regiment* (Albany, N.Y., 1865), 125–6; Catherine Merrill, *The Soldiers of Indiana in the War for the Union* (Indianapolis, 1869), 635. Devens's third brigade, under Adelbert Ames, remained behind to help guard White House Landing.

9. Pendleton's report, in *OR,* Vol. 36, Pt. 1, p. 1049; William L. Haskin, *The History of the First Regiment of Artillery* (Portland, Me., 1879), 202–3; Alanson A. Haines, *Fifteenth Regiment New Jersey Volunteers,* 201–2; Alfred S. Roe, *The Ninth New York Heavy Artillery* (Worcester, Mass., 1899), 98; Keiser diary, June 1, 1864, in USAMHI; Vaill, *Second Connecticut,* 60; Captain James Deane memoir, June 1, 1864, in Connecticut Historical Society.

10. Thompson, *Thirteenth Regiment of New Hampshire,* 343–4; L'Hommedieu journal, June 1, 1864, in Book 56, RNBP.

11. Roebling to Warren, 2:45 P.M., June 1, 1864, in *OR,* Vol. 36, Pt. 3, p. 449; Meade to Warren, 4:00 P.M., June 1, 1864, ibid.; Roebling's report, in Warren Papers, NYSLA.

12. Henry H. Lockwood to Williams, June 10, 1864, in *OR,* Vol. 36, Pt. 3, p. 726.

13. Sheridan to Humphreys, 6:00 P.M., June 1, 1864, ibid., 470.

14. Surviving accounts make it possible to plot the sequence in which brigades were posted and the forces opposing them. Once fighting started, however, units shifted and became intermingled.

15. Clingman claimed that he received no notice of Hagood's withdrawal, but that Hagood later told him that he had notified Kershaw. Kershaw, however, said that neither he nor Wofford had been told about the withdrawal. Clingman, "Second Cold Harbor," 199–200; Kershaw to Alexander, July 9, 1868, Kershaw to Sorrel, June 1, 1864, both in Alexander Collection, SHC.

16. Hagood, *Memoirs,* 257.

17. Ibid., 258; Izlar, *War Record of the Edisto Rifles,* 61.

18. Lewis Grant's report, in *OR,* Vol. 36, Pt. 1, p. 707; Benedict, *Vermont in the War,* 1, p. 462. Neill also dispatched the 5th Vermont to guard an artillery piece brought up to help buttress the endangered flank. For the attack, Benton commanded Major Fleming's battalion, consisting of Companies F, L, K, H, and temporarily, E.

19. Houghton, "Ordeal of Civil War," 37–8; Brewster to mother, June 2, 1864, in Blight, ed., *When This Cruel War Is Over,* 312; Rhodes, ed., *All for the Union,* 156–7; Hutchinson,

Seventh Massachusetts, 195; "From the Tenth Regiment," *Springfield (Mass.) Daily Republican,* June 22, 1864; Lewis C. White reminiscences, 13, in Save the Flags Collection, USAMHI.

20. Charles R. Paul diary, in Murray J. Smith Collection, USAMHI; Alanson A. Haines, *Fifteenth Regiment New Jersey Volunteers,* 202.

21. Alanson A. Haines, *Fifteenth Regiment New Jersey Volunteers,* 202.

22. Ibid.

23. Survivors Association, *Twenty-Third Pennsylvania Volunteers* (Philadelphia, 1882), 114–5.

24. Ibid., 115; W. W. Clayton, *History of Onondaga County New York* (Syracuse, 1878), 115; George M. Rose, "Sixty-Sixth Regiment," in *Histories of the Several Regiments,* ed. Walter Clark, 3, p. 688.

25. C. Porter, "Did Soldiers Refuse to Charge!" *National Tribune,* March 7, 1889; Benton's report, in *OR,* Vol. 36, Pt. 1, p. 718.

26. Benton's report, in *OR,* Vol. 36, Pt. 1, p. 718; Benedict, *Vermont in the War,* 1, p. 463.

27. "Fight of the 1st and 3rd—Colquitt's Brigade," *Macon Daily Telegraph,* June 14, 1864.

28. Francis W. Morse, *Personal Experiences in the War of the Great Rebellion, from December, 1862, to July, 1865* (Albany, N.Y., 1866), 98; "Col. Elisha S. Kellogg," *Connecticut War Record* 2 (September 1864), 263. Different sources give different figures for Upton's regiments. I rely on Upton's returns for May 31, 1864, by brigade inspector Fred Sanborn (Fred Sanborn memoirs, in LC).

29. Kilbourn diary, June 1, 1864, in Civil War Diaries and Journals Collection, Rutgers University Library; Morse, *Personal Experiences,* 101.

30. Kilbourn diary, June 1, 1864, in Rutgers University Library.

31. "Col. Elisha S. Kellogg," 262–3; Theodore F. Vaill to Enquirer, June 9, 1864, *Litchfield (Conn.) Enquirer,* June 23, 1864; Vaill, *Second Connecticut,* 61.

32. Vaill, *Second Connecticut,* 62.

33. Upton's report, in *OR,* Vol. 36, Pt. 1, p. 671.

34. Ibid.; Deane memoir, June 1, 1864, in Connecticut Historical Society; Edward S. Roberts, "War Reminiscences," *Canaan Connecticut Western News,* August 24, 1911.

35. Upton's report, in *OR,* Vol. 36, Pt. 1, p. 671; Vaill, *Second Connecticut,* 64, 65n, 62; Deane memoir, June 1, 1864, in Connecticut Historical Society.

36. Vaill, *Second Connecticut,* 62–3; Lewis Bissell to father, June 2, 1864, in Mark Olcott, comp., *The Civil War Letters of Lewis Bissell* (Washington, D.C., 1981), 245.

37. Best, *121st New York,* 155.

38. "Col. Elisha S. Kellogg," 263; Kilbourn diary, June 1, 1864, in Rutgers University Library; Clingman, "Second Cold Harbor," 201; Vaill, *Second Connecticut,* 63. Clingman's claim that he saw Kellogg shot in front of him is suspect. He told this tale ten years after the fact, and it does not appear in his initial accounts of the battle.

39. Vaill, *Second Connecticut,* 63; Theodore F. Vaill to Enquirer, June 9, 1864, in *Litchfield (Conn.) Enquirer,* June 23, 1864; George H. Bates to family, June 2, 1864, in Schoff Collection, CL; Captain James Deane memoir, June 1, 1864, in Connecticut Historical Society.

40. "Fight of the 1st and 3rd—Colquitt's Brigade," *Macon Daily Telegraph,* June 14, 1864; "The Battle of Cold Harbor," *New York Daily Tribune,* June 8, 1864; William Smith diary, June 1, 1864, in Zack C. Waters Private Collection, Rome, Georgia.

41. Prowell, *Eighty-Seventh Regiment Pennsylvania,* 148.

42. Keifer's report, in *OR,* Vol. 36, Pt. 1, p. 734; Binkley's report, ibid., 748; "Notes from the Battlefield—No. 4," *Xenia (Ohio) Torchlight,* June 19, 1864; Cordrey manuscript, 53, in Scott Patchen Collection.

43. Edwin M. Haynes, *Tenth Regiment, Vermont,* 135–6; Prowell, *Eighty-Seventh Regiment Pennsylvania,* 148–9.

44. Abbott, *Personal Recollections,* 71; James McManus, *Batavia (N.Y.) Spirit of the Times,* June 25, 1864, quoted in Paul S. Beaudry, *The Forgotten Regiment: History of the 151st New York Volunteer Infantry Regiment* (N.p., 1995), 123.

45. Roe, *Ninth New York Heavy Artillery,* 99; Osceola Lewis, *One Hundred and Thirty-Eighth Regiment Pennsylvania,* 104–5; John Harrold, *Libby, Andersonville, Florence: The Capture, Imprisonment, Escape, and Rescue of John Harrold* (Philadelphia 1870), 21; Richard A. Gray Jr., ed., *1864 Pocket Diary of Pvt. George R. Imler, Co. E, 138th Regiment Pennsylvania Volunteers* (N.p., 1963), 49.

46. Clingman, "Second Cold Harbor," 200.

47. Ibid., 200–1; John E. Dugger to Mrs. Henderson, June 10, 1864, in John S. Henderson Papers, SHC.

48. P. Robertson, "Reminiscence of Cold Harbor," *National Tribune,* March 30, 1884.

49. Ibid.; H. T. J. Ludwig, "Eighth Regiment," in *Histories of the Several Regiments,* ed. Walter Clark, 1, p. 404.

50. Edwin M. Haynes, *Tenth Regiment, Vermont,* 140; William S. Truex's report, in *OR,* Vol. 36, Pt. 1, p. 726; Michael I. Himan, "The Charge at Cold Harbor," *National Tribune,* April 24, 1884; Alonzo Ansden manuscript, in William O. Bourne Papers, LC.

51. Ludwig, "Eighth Regiment," 404; A. A. McKethan, "Fifty-First Regiment," in Walter Clark, ed., *Histories of the Several Regiments,* ed. Walter Clark, 3, pp. 211–2; Herbert M. Schiller, ed., *A Captain's War: The Letters and Diaries of William H. S. Burgwyn, 1861–1865* (Shippensburg, Pa., 1994), 148.

52. John C. Patterson account, in Bernard A. Olsen, ed., *Upon the Tented Field* (Red Bank, N.J., 1993), 240.

53. Schiller, *Captain's War,* 148.

54. Ezra J. Warner, *Generals in Blue: Lives of the Union Commanders* (Baton Rouge, 1964), 122–3; William L. Hyde, *One Hundred and Twelfth Regiment N.Y. Volunteers,* 82.

55. William L. Hyde, *One Hundred and Twelfth Regiment N.Y. Volunteers,* 82; Alonzo Alden, "169th New York: A Brilliant Record," in USAMHI; George E. Lowry, "Cold Harbor: The Story of the Slaughter as Told by an Indiana Veteran," *National Tribune,* November 25, 1886.

56. Lowry, "Cold Harbor" *National Tribune,* November 25, 1886; Alonzo Alden, "169th New York: A Brilliant Record"; William L. Hyde, *One Hundred and Twelfth Regiment N.Y. Volunteers,* 82.

57. William L. Hyde, *One Hundred and Twelfth Regiment N.Y. Volunteers,* 82–3; E. Barber, "The Gallant Part Taken in the Fight by Drake's Brigade," *National Tribune,* April 8, 1886; Charles Sanders to Sister, June 8, 1864, in GDAH; A. A. McLauchlin, "The 115th New York," *National Tribune,* December 13, 1886.

58. Abraham J. Palmer, *The History of the Forty-Eighth Regiment, New York State Volunteers* (Brooklyn, N.Y., 1885), 151–2; J. W. Reardon to sister, June 2, 1864, in RNBP.

59. Reardon to sister, June 2, 1864, in RNBP; James H. Clark, *Iron Hearted Regiment,* 125–6; Charles W. Scharff, "The Battle of Cold Harbor," *National Tribune,* May 20, 1886.

60. Sanders to Sister, June 8, 1864, in GDAH; W. F. Smith to Meade, June 2, 1864, in *OR,* Vol. 36, Pt. 3, p. 507; Dana to Stanton, June 2, 1864, 4:00 P.M., ibid., Pt. 1, p. 87. Smith amended his report a few days later. "In a verbal report to me, I understood General Devens . . . positively to say that his first line preceded the first line of Sixth Corps on his left in the assault in

the woods and capture of the rifle-pits," he wrote on June 4. "In a further conversation with him this morning, he says this was not so, and that he was preceded by the first line of the Sixth Corps. I regret exceedingly the injustice done the Sixth Corps, and beg that my dispatch be corrected to this extent" (Smith to Meade, June 4, 1864, in *OR,* Vol. 36, Pt. 3, p. 589).

61. A. J. Cone, "A Close Call," *Confederate Veteran* 27 (1919), 372; Charles Sanders to sister, June 8, 1864, in Mills Lane, ed., *Dear Mother, Don't Grieve About Me, If I Get Killed, I'll Only Be Dead: Letters from Georgia Soldiers in the Civil War* (Savannah, 1977), 296–8; Arthur B. Simms to sister, June 4, 1864, in Jane B. Peacock, ed, "A Georgian's View of the War in Virginia: The Civil War Letters of A. B. Simms," in *Atlanta Historical Journal* 23 (1979), 107; Kershaw to Alexander, July 9, 1868, in Alexander Papers, SHC; Eugene A. Thompson to parents, June 4, 1864, in RNBP.

62. John R. Rhoades to Sarah, June 2, 1864, in Rutherford B. Hayes Presidential Center, Fremont, Ohio; Orlando P. Sawtelle to parents, June 6, 1864, in Civil War Miscellaneous Collection, USAMHI.

63. Chester K. Leach to unknown, July 20, 1862, in Chester K. Leach Collection, University of Vermont.

64. Guy V. Henry's report, in *OR,* Vol. 36, Pt. 1, p. 1012; Burnham's report, ibid., 1008.

65. Cunningham, *Three Years with the Adirondack Regiment,* 127.

66. Aaron F. Stevens's report, in *OR,* Vol. 36, Pt. 1, p. 1011; Thompson, *Thirteenth Regiment of New Hampshire Volunteer Infantry,* 344–5.

67. Thompson, *Thirteenth Regiment of New Hampshire Volunteer Infantry,* 344–7.

68. Ibid., 347–8.

69. Members of the Regiment, *The Story of the Twenty-First Regiment, Connecticut Volunteer Infantry* (Middletown, Conn., 1900), 232–3; Henry's report, in *OR,* Vol. 36, Pt. 1, p. 1012.

70. Gilman Marston's report, in *OR,* Vol. 36, Pt. 1, p. 1005; William Kreutzer, *Notes and Observations Made During Four Years of Service with the Ninety-Eighth New York Volunteers, in the War of 1861* (Philadelphia, 1878), 198–9.

71. Bartlett, *Twelfth Regiment, New Hampshire,* 201.

72. Wright to Humphreys, 7:30 P.M., June 1, 1864, in *OR,* Vol. 36, Pt. 3, p. 455.

73. Clingman, "Second Cold Harbor," 202.

74. "Fight of the 1st and 3rd—Colquitt's Brigade," *Macon Daily Telegraph,* June 14, 1864; William Smith diary, June 1, 1864, in Zack C. Waters Private Collection.

75. Schiller, *Captain's War,* 148; Washington L. Dunn diary, June 1, 1864, in Book 23, RNBP; Vaill, *Second Connecticut,* 65–6; Upton's report, in *OR,* Vol. 36, Pt. 1, p. 671; Edward S. Roberts, "War Reminiscences," *Canaan Connecticut Western News,* August 24, 1911.

76. William Wallace's report, in Dickert, *Kershaw's Brigade,* 370.

77. Ibid.; "Letter from McLaw's Old Division," *Augusta (Ga.) Constitutionalist,* June 16, 1864; James M. Nichols, *Perry's Saints; or, The Fighting Parson's Regiment in the War of the Rebellion* (Boston, 1886), 226–8; William L. Hyde, *One Hundred and Twelfth Regiment N.Y. Volunteers,* 83.

78. Stiles, *Marse Robert,* 276–7; *Savannah Morning News,* June 13, 1898; James M. Nichols, *Perry's Saints,* 229–31; William L. Hyde, *One Hundred and Twelfth Regiment N.Y. Volunteers,* 83; Wallace's report, in Dickert, *Kershaw's Brigade,* 370; Mac Wyckoff, *A History of the 2nd South Carolina Infantry: 1861–1865* (Fredericksburg, Va., 1994), 127–8; Kershaw to Alexander, July 9, 1868, in Alexander Collection, SHC.

79. Roe, *Ninth New York Heavy Artillery,* 99; Dame, *From the Rapidan to Richmond,* 197–8.

80. James M. Nichols, *Perry's Saints,* 230–1.

81. Committee of the Regiment, *Thirty-Fifth Regiment Massachusetts Volunteers,* 245 n; Samuel G. Leasure letter, June 2, 1864, reproduced in William G. Gavin, *Campaigning with the Roundheads: The History of the Hundredth Pennsylvania Veteran Volunteer Infantry Regiment in the American Civil War, 1861–1865* (Dayton, Ohio, 1989), 447.

82. Risden T. Bennett, whose brigade of Tar Heels made the attack on Shady Grove Road, later wrote that the purpose of the offensive was "to draw the attention of the foe, then concentrating on his great blow to be delivered the next day on our right." Risden T. Bennett, "Fourteenth Regiment," in *Histories of the Several Regiments,* ed. Walter Clark, 1, p. 727.

83. Committee of the Regiment, *Thirty-Fifth Regiment Massachusetts Volunteers,* 245 n; Leasure letter, June 2, 1864, in Gavin, *Campaigning with the Roundheads,* 447.

84. Risden T. Bennett, "Fourteenth Regiment," 727; "From Our Army in Virginia," *Savannah Morning News,* July 20, 1864; Hamilton Dunlap diary, quoted in Gavin, *Campaigning with the Roundheads,* 448.

85. Willcox's report, in *OR,* Vol. 36, Pt. 1, p. 942; Gavin, *Campaigning with the Roundheads,* 444; Watson, *From Ashby to Andersonville,* 209; George P. Hawkes's Morning Report Book, June 1, 1864, in Coco Collection, USAMHI; Committee of the Regiment, *Thirty-Fifth Regiment Massachusetts Volunteers,* 245.

86. Leasure letter, June 2, 1864, in Gavin, *Campaigning with the Roundheads,* 447–8; Risden T. Bennett, "Fourteenth Regiment," 727.

87. "From Our Army in Virginia," *Savannah Morning News,* July 20, 1864; Judson, *Eighty-Third Regiment Pennsylvania,* 102; William H. Osborne, *The History of the Twenty-Ninth Regiment of Massachusetts Volunteer Infantry, in the Late War of the Rebellion* (Boston, 1877), 298–9.

88. Osborne, *Twenty-Ninth Regiment of Massachusetts Volunteer Infantry,* 299–300; Gerrish, *Army Life,* 193; Tilton's report, in *OR,* Vol. 36, Pt. 1, p. 565; Lysander Cutler's report, ibid., 613.

89. Warren to Meade, June 1, 1864, ibid., Pt. 3, p. 451; Lockwood to Williams, June 10, 1864, ibid., 727; Roebling's report, in Warren Papers, NYSLA.

90. Roebling's report, in Warren Papers, NYSLA; Nevins, ed., *Diary of Battle,* 396.

91. Warren to Meade, June 1, 1864, in *OR,* Vol. 36, Pt. 3, pp. 451–2; Meade to Warren, 11:00 P.M., June 1, 1864, ibid., 452. Lockwood's defense appears in Lockwood to Williams, June 10, 1864, ibid., 726–8.

92. Meade to wife, June 1, 1864, in Meade Collection, HSP; George G. Meade Jr. to mother, June 1, 1864, in Meade Collection, HSP.

93. Charles E. Cadwallader to Humphreys, in *OR,* Vol. 36, Pt. 3, p. 456; Wright to Humphreys, ibid.

94. Meade to Hancock, 8:10 P.M., June 1, 1864, ibid., 440; Hancock to Williams, 8:30 P.M., June 1, 1864, ibid.; Meade to Hancock, 9:00 P.M., June 1, 1864, ibid., 441.

95. Wright to Meade, 9:30 P.M., June 1, 1864, and Grant's indorsement, ibid., 457.

96. Comstock to Meade, 10:40 P.M., June 1, 1864, ibid., 433.

97. Meade to Warren, 8:30 P.M., June 1, 1864, ibid., 451; Humphreys to Warren, 9:50 P.M., June 1, 1864, ibid.; Warren to Humphreys, 11:00 P.M., June 1, 1864, ibid.

98. Smith to Humphreys, 10:30 P.M., June 1, 1864, ibid., 468.

99. Lyman's journal, June 1, 1864, in Lyman papers, MHS. Smith gives his version of Meade's exchange with Farquhar in his report, *OR,* Vol. 36, Pt. 1, p. 1000.

100. Meade to Hancock, 11:00 P.M., June 1, 1864, in *OR,* Vol. 36, Pt. 3, pp. 441–2; Meade

to Wright, 10:15 P.M., June 1, 1864, ibid., 463; Meade to Warren, 11:00 P.M., June 1, 1864, ibid., 452; Meade to Smith, 10:05, June 1, 1864, ibid., Pt., 1, p. 1001.

101. Smith's report, ibid., 1001.

102. Best, *121st New York,* 156–7; Luckenbill diary, June 1, 1864, in Historical Society of Schuylkill County; *Winsted (Conn.) Herald,* June 10, 1864; Vaill, *Second Connecticut,* 66; "2nd Connecticut Heavy Artillery," *New Haven Daily Morning Journal,* June 27, 1864.

103. Kreutzer, *Notes and Observations,* 199–200.

104. Dickert, *Kershaw's Brigade,* 371; Charles W. Field, "Campaign of 1864 and 1865," in *SHSP* 14, pp. 548–9; Evander McI. Law, "From the Wilderness to Cold Harbor," in *B&L* 4, pp. 138–9; J. Gary Laine and Morris M. Penny, *Law's Alabama Brigade in the War Between the Union and the Confederacy* (Shippensburg, Pa., 1996), 269; Map in Kershaw to Alexander, July 9, 1868, in Alexander Papers, SHC. Law claimed to have supervised the layout of the line. Field, however, makes it clear that he was in charge. "Leaving two of my brigades in my thin lines to hold them," he wrote, "with the three others (Law's Alabamians, Anderson's Georgians, and Gregg's Texans) I went to [Kershaw's] assistance, and relieving two of his brigades, I laid out and made a new breastwork in rear of the old one taken from Kershaw or some one, and connected it with the old one" (Field, "Campaign of 1864 and 1865," 548–9).

105. Clingman, "Second Cold Harbor," 204; Cornelius Debo manuscript, in Frank E. Fields Jr., *28th Virginia Infantry* (Lynchburg, Va., 1985), 32–3.

106. Hagood, *Memoirs,* 259.

107. Thomas A. McParlin's report, in *OR,* Vol. 36, Pt. 1, pp. 343–4; Adjutant Edmund D. Halsey's account, in Alanson A. Haines, *Fifteenth Regiment New Jersey Volunteers,* 203–4; Edmund D. Halsey diary, in USAMHI.

108. Deane memoir, June 1, 1864, in Connecticut Historical Society.

109. A. S. Salley to Alex, June 8, 1864, and John to Mrs. Keitt, June 8, 1864, both in Keitt Papers, DU.

110. Humphreys, *Virginia Campaign,* 176; Charles H. Porter, "The Battle of Cold Harbor," in *PMHSM* 4, p. 330.

111. Ricketts's casualties are reported in James Read, "Diary of Movements of the 3rd Division 6th Army Corps," 49, in James B. Ricketts Papers, Manassas National Battlefield Park. For Upton's casualties, I have relied on the return prepared by Fred Sanborn, Upton's brigade inspector, on June 4, 1864, in LC.

112. William B. Barton's report, in *OR,* Vol. 36, Pt. 1, pp. 1018–9; William L. Hyde, *One Hundred and Twelfth Regiment N.Y. Volunteers,* 82–3.

113. Sanborn memoirs, in LC; Roe, *Ninth New York Heavy Artillery,* 100; Return of Casualties, in *OR,* Vol. 36, Pt. 1, p. 173; Benton's report, ibid., 718.

114. Edwin M. Haynes, *Tenth Regiment, Vermont,* 135. The official history of the 14th New Jersey reported a doubtful 240 casualties, but Peter Vredenburgh of the regiment wrote home on June 4 that the regiment lost "a little more than a hundred." J. Newton Terrill, *Campaign of the Fourteenth Regiment New Jersey Volunteers* (New Brunswick, N.J., 1884), 64; Olsen, *Upon the Tented Field,* 239.

115. I am indebted to Alfred Young for documenting Confederate losses on June 1. The numbers can be only approximate, as most Confederate units reported losses for the full time that they were at Cold Harbor, making it difficult to extrapolate those specifically of June 1 with precision. Of Wofford's 260 losses, fully 160 were prisoners.

116. Kershaw to Sorrel, June 1, 1864, in Alexander Papers, SHC.

117. Simms to sister, June 4, 1864, in Peacock, "Georgian's View of the War in Virginia," 107.

118. Josiah Corban to wife, June 7, 1864, in Connecticut Historical Society; "Col. Elisha S. Kellogg," 263; *Winsted (Conn.) Herald,* June 10, 1864; Osceola Lewis, *One Hundred and Thirty-Eighth Regiment Pennsylvania,* 105–6.

IX JUNE 2 *Grant Misses an Opportunity*

1. J. F. J. Caldwell, *The History of a Brigade of South Carolinians, First Known as Gregg's, and Subsequently as McGowan's Brigade* (Philadelphia, 1866), 157; Hancock to Williams, 8:30 P.M., June 1, 1864, in *OR,* Vol. 36, Pt. 1, p. 440; Hancock to Williams, 10:50 P.M., June 1, 1864, ibid., 441; Thomas D. Marbaker, *History of the Eleventh New Jersey Volunteers* (Trenton, N.J., 1898), 187; Weygant, *One Hundred and Twenty-Fourth Regiment New York,* 347.

2. Meade to Hancock, 9:00 P.M., June 1, 1864, in *OR,* Vol. 36, Pt. 3, p. 441; Earl B. McElfresh, *Maps and Mapmakers of the Civil War* (New York, 1999), 248.

3. Walker, *Second Army Corps,* 506; William H. Paine's diary, June 2–4, 1864, in New York Historical Society. I am indebted to Elizabeth McCall for alerting me to Paine's diary and for transcribing part of it. Hancock's precise route is a matter for conjecture. Several accounts speak of his marching through Old Church, but Thomas A. McParlin, the Potomac army's medical director, says he passed by way of Allen's Mill Pond (McParlin's report, in *OR,* Vol. 36, Pt. 1, p. 244.)

4. Walker, *Second Army Corps,* 506; Hancock to Humphreys, June 2, 1864, in *OR,* Vol. 36, Pt. 3, p. 481; Agassiz, ed., *Meade's Headquarters,* 139.

5. Hancock to Williams, 8:30 P.M., June 1, 1864, in *OR,* Vol. 36, Pt. 3, p. 440; Smith's report, ibid., Pt. 1, p. 1002. Humphreys's order to Hancock is reported as 1:30 P.M., although it most certainly was 1:30 A.M. (*OR,* Vol. 36, Pt. 3, p. 482).

6. Smith to Meade, June 2, 1864, ibid., 505; Meade to Hancock, 7:20 A.M., June 2, 1864, ibid., 481; Hancock to Humphreys, June 2, 1864, ibid.

7. Burnside to Humphreys, June 1, 1864, ibid., 461; Williams to Burnside, 8:00 P.M., June 1, 1864, ibid., 462; Burnside to Humphreys, 9:25 P.M., June 1, 1864, ibid.; Meade to Burnside, 9:40 P.M., June 1, 1864, ibid., 462–3. William Marvel, in his *Burnside* (Chapel Hill, 1991), 375–6, suggests that Meade's propensity to find fault with Burnside stemmed from his view of the 9th Corps's commander as a "potential competitor."

8. Lockwood to Williams, June 10, 1864, in *OR,* Vol. 36, Pt. 3, pp. 727–8; Roebling's report, in Warren Collection, NYSLA; Nevins, ed., *Diary of Battle,* 398; George Breck, "From Battery L," *Rochester Daily Union and Advertiser,* June 23, 1864.

9. Warren to Meade, 5:00 A.M., June 2, 1864, in *OR,* Vol. 36, Pt. 3, pp. 486–7; Roebling's report, in Warren Collection, NYSLA.

10. Humphreys to Burnside, 7:45 A.M., June 2, 1864, and 9:15 A.M., June 2, 1864, in *OR,* Vol. 36, Pt. 3, p. 399; Humphreys to Warren, 7:00 A.M., June 2, 1864, ibid., 487–8.

11. Circular, 9:30 A.M., June 2, 1864, ibid., 504; Potter to Lewis Richmond, 10:30 A.M., June 2, 1864, ibid., 504.

12. West, *30th Battalion Virginia Sharpshooters,* 101.

13. H. B. McClellan manuscript, paraphrased in Freeman, *R. E. Lee,* 3, pp. 381–2; J. W. Thomas diary, June 2, 1864, in Book 79, FSNMP.

14. Caldwell, *Brigade of South Carolinians,* 157; William S. Stewart, *A Pair of Blankets: War-Time History in Letters to the Young People of the South* (New York, 1914), 138–9. For

the time of Mahone's departure, see "Letter from Virginia," *Mobile Advertiser and Register,* June 17, 1864.

15. Lee to Seddon, 8:00 P.M., June 2, 1864, in *OR,* Vol. 36, Pt. 3, p. 867; Heth's report, in MC; T. J. Watkins memoir, in FSNMP.

16. Tobie, *First Maine Cavalry,* 279; Breathed's report, in SHC; R. P. Chew's report, in USAMHI; Martin L. Smith's diary, June 2, 1864, in Maryland Historical Society.

17. Isaac J. Ressler diary, June 2, 1864, in *Civil War Times Illustrated* Collection, USAMHI; Tobie, *First Maine Cavalry,* 279–80; Woodall diary, June 2, 1864, in FSNMP. According to Alfred Young's count, Lee lost no more than 23 troopers on June 2. Lee noted only that he skirmished "heavily all day with the enemy's infantry and cavalry" (Fitzhugh Lee's report, in MC).

18. Agassiz, ed., *Meade's Headquarters,* 140; Sparks, ed., *Inside Lincoln's Army,* 379–80.

19. Alanson A. Haines, *Fifteenth Regiment New Jersey Volunteers,* 207–8.

20. Charles W. Cowtan, *Service of the Tenth New York Volunteers (National Zouaves) in the War of the Rebellion* (New York, 1882), 278; Newell M. Smith, "The Story of the 155th New York Volunteers," n.p., quoted in Kevin M. O'Beirne, "Into the Valley of the Shadow of Death: The Corcoran Legion at Cold Harbor," *North and South* 3 (2000), 71.

21. Smyth's report, in *OR,* Vol. 36, Pt. 1, p. 452; Benedict, *Vermont in the Civil War,* 1, pp. 463–4; Fisk diary, June 1, 1864, in LC.

22. Barlow to Walker, 12:15 P.M., June 2, 1864, in *OR,* Vol. 36, Pt. 3, p. 484; Walker to Barlow, 1:10 P.M., June 2, 1864, ibid.

23. Grant to Meade, 2:00 P.M., June 2, 1864, ibid., 478; Humphreys, *Virginia Campaign,* 178–9; Agassiz, ed., *Meade's Headquarters,* 140.

24. Circular, June 2, 1864, in *OR,* Vol. 36, Pt. 3, p. 483; Walker to Birney, 2:00 P.M., June 2, 1864, ibid., 487; Mulholland, *Story of the 116th Regiment Pennsylvania,* 253; J. Noonan, "Unpublished History of 69th New York," in Powers Collection, USAMHI.

25. West, *30th Battalion Virginia Sharpshooters,* 101–2

26. Morton, "Skirmish at Totopotomoy Creek," 55; B. Welch Owens, "The Maryland Boys," *Richmond Dispatch,* March 9, 1902.

27. George M. Edgar to Colonel Johnston, July 24, 1902, in Edgar Collection, SHC; John W. F. Hatton Memoir, in LC.

28. Morton, "Skirmish at Totopotomoy Creek," 55; Edgar, "When Grant Advanced Against a Wall," 5–6; Alexander, *Fighting for the Confederacy,* 404; "Another Account of Breckinridge's Brigade at Cold Harbor," *Atlanta Journal,* February 22, 1902.

29. Wilcox's report, in VSL; James S. Harris, *Historical Sketches of the Seventh Regiment North Carolina Troops* (Mooresville, N.C., 1893), 50; "From 45th Georgia Infantry Regiment," in Antoinette Smith Jenkins Collection, Eastern Carolina University Library; Caldwell, *Brigade of South Carolinians,* 158; James H. Lane, "History of Lane's North Carolina Brigade," in *SHSP* 9, p. 244.

30. Zack C. Waters, "Tell Them I Died Like a Confederate Soldier: Finegan's Florida Brigade at Cold Harbor," in *Florida Historical Quarterly* 69 (1990), 157–63; D. L. Greer, "Memoir of the War," *Lake City (Fla.) Index,* February 2, 1906; D. H. Dorman, *Fifty Years Ago: Reminiscences of '61–5* (Tallahassee, n.d.), 7.

31. Barlow to Walker, 5:00 P.M., June 2, 1864, in *OR,* Vol. 36, Pt. 3, pp. 484–5; William Y. W. Ripley, *Vermont Riflemen in the War for the Union, 1861–1865: A History of Company F, First United States Sharpshooters* (Rutland, Vt., 1883), 173.

32. Thomas Henry's report, in *OR,* Vol. 36, Pt. 1, pp. 384–6; Nathan Church's report, ibid., 375; J. M. Ray, "Cold Harbor," *National Tribune,* December 31, 1891.

33. Barlow to Walker, 7:50 P.M., June 2, 1864, in *OR,* Vol. 36, Pt. 3, p. 485.

34. Thompson, *Thirteenth Regiment of New Hampshire Volunteer Infantry,* 355–6.

35. °Stephen Weld to father, June 2, 1864, in Massachusetts Historical Society, *War Diary and Letters,* 302; James W. Cartwright to Mother, June 2, 1864, in *Civil War Times Illustrated Collection,* USAMHI; Arthur B. Wyman to sister, June 5, 1864, in Civil War Miscellaneous Collection, USAMHI; Philip Cheek and Mair Pointon, *History of the Sauk County Riflemen, Known as Company A, Sixth Wisconsin Veteran Volunteer Infantry, 1861–1865* (Madison, Wisc., 1909), 106.

36. Hawkes's Morning Report Book, June 2, 1864, in Coco Collection, USAMHI.

37. Charles F. Walcott, *History of the Twenty-First Regiment Massachusetts Volunteers in the War for the Preservation of the Union* (Boston, 1882), 330–1; Gregory A. Coco, ed., *Through Blood and Fire: The Civil War Letters of Major Charles J. Mills, 1862–1865* (Lanham, Md., 1982), 98; S. G. Leasure letter, June 6, 1864, in M. Gyla McDowell Collection, Pennsylvania State University Library; Hawkes's Morning Report Book, June 2, 1864, in Coco Collection, USAMHI; Stone, *Personal Recollections of the Civil War,* 171; Elisha G. Marshall's report, in *OR,* Vol. 36, Pt. 1, p. 926; Willcox's report, ibid., 942.

38. Clarence Wilson, "At Cold Harbor," *National Tribune,* August 17, 1893.

39. Hopkins, *Seventh Regiment Rhode Island Volunteers,* 182.

40. Marshall's report, in *OR,* Vol. 36, Pt. 1, p. 926.

41. Cutcheon's report, ibid., 971; Joseph Jones to Editor, June 3, 1864, *Detroit Advertiser and Tribune,* June 8, 1864; "From the Twentieth Infantry," *Detroit Free Press,* June 16, 1864.

42. Watson, *From Ashby to Andersonville,* 213; Hamilton Dunlap diary, in M. Gyla McDowell Collection, Pennsylvania State University Library; Marshall's report, in *OR,* Vol. 36, Pt. 1, pp. 926–7.

43. Bingham F. Junkin diary, June 2, 1864, <www.iwaynet.net/~lsci/junkin/>, accessed June 19, 1999; Gavin, *Campaigning with the Roundheads,* 454; Committee of the Regiment, *Thirty-Fifth Regiment Massachusetts,* 245; Massachusetts Historical Society, *War Diary and Letters,* 301.

44. "Diary of a Confederate Officer," in *Our Living and Our Dead,* February 11, 1874.

45. Jackman and Hadley, eds., *Sixth New Hampshire,* 274–5.

46. Heth's report, in MC; James L. Morrison Jr., ed., *The Memoirs of Henry Heth* (Westport, Conn., 1974), 189; Charles B. Jones, "Historical Sketch of 55th North Carolina Infantry," in *Our Living and Our Dead,* April 22, 1874; H. C. Kearney, "Fifteenth Regiment," in *Histories of the Several Regiments,* ed. Walter Clark, 1, p. 745; Joseph Mullen Jr. diary, June 2, 1864, in MC; Alfred H. Belo, *Memoirs of Alfred H. Belo* (Boston, 1902), 41.

47. Committee of the Regiment, *Thirty-Sixth Regiment Massachusetts,* 188–9; Risden T. Bennett, "Fourteenth Regiment," 727; "City Intelligence: Death of Brigadier General George E. Doles," *Richmond Daily Examiner,* June 4, 1864; Henry W. Thomas, *History of the Doles-Cook Brigade, Army of Northern Virginia, CSA* (Atlanta, 1903), 77; John West, "Sharpshooter Kildee," in *Camp-Fire Sketches and Battle-Field Echoes,* comp. William C. King and W. P. Derby (Springfield, Mass., 1888), 273–4.

48. Spear, *Civil War Recollections,* 116; J. L. Smith, *Corn Exchange Regiment,* 454–7. The 118th Pennsylvania lost 92 soldiers in the action.

49. Roebling's report, in Warren Collection, NYSLA; Warren to Humphreys, 4:30 P.M., June 2, 1864, in *OR,* Vol. 36, Pt. 3, p. 491.

50. Tilney, *My Life in the Army,* 82–3.

51. I. G. Bradwell, "Cold Harbor, Lynchburg, Valley Campaign, Etc., 1864," *Confederate Veteran* 28 (1920), 138; "Flag of 12th Georgia Artillery,"ibid., 16 (1908), 113; George W.

Nichols, *A Soldier's Story of His Regiment and Incidentally of the Lawton, Gordon, Evans Brigade* (Jesup, Ga., 1898), 162.

52. Mary G. Brainard, *Campaigns of the One Hundred and Forty-Sixth Regiment New York State Volunteers* (New York, 1915), 216.

53. D. P. Marshall, *Company K, 115th Pennsylvania Volunteer Zouaves* (N.p., 1888), 67; Brainard, *Campaigns of the One Hundred and Forty-Sixth Regiment New York,* 216.

54. Bradwell, "Cold Harbor, Lynchburg, Valley Campaign, Etc.," 138; Sigma to editor, June 3, 1864, *Raleigh Daily Confederate,* June 7, 1864; Henry Nordhaus, "How Colonel Winslow Died," *National Tribune,* April 1, 1897; Tilney, *My Life in the Army,* 83.

55. *Memorials of William Fowler* (New York, 1875), 86; White journal, 83, in LC; J. Clayton Youker, ed., *The Military Memoirs of Captain Henry Cribben of the 140th New York Volunteers* (N.p., n.d.), 72–6.

56. Bradwell, "Cold Harbor, Lynchburg, Valley Campaign, Etc.," 138; Roster of Company F (Hopps) and Roster of Field Staff and Band (Baker, Hanvey), 12th Georgia Battalion, <http://www.pollette.com/12thbat/staff.htm>, accessed January 15, 2002; Nordhaus, "How Colonel Winslow Died"; *Memorials of William Fowler,* 86–7.

57. Nevins, ed., *Diary of Battle,* 400.

58. Warren to Meade, June 2, 1864, in *OR,* Vol. 36, Pt. 3, p. 493; Roebling's report, in Warren Collection, NYSLA.

59. "General Lee's Army," *Daily Richmond Examiner,* June 4, 1864.

60. Early, *Autobiographical Sketch,* 363; Lee to Seddon, 8:00 P.M., June 2, 1864, in *OR,* Vol. 36, Pt. 3, p. 867; George W. Nichols, *Soldier's Story,* 163.

61. I am indebted to Alfred Young for helping me calculate Confederate casualties.

62. J. H. Patterson, "Eleventh Regiment of Infantry," *Journal of the Military Service Institution of the United States,* 12 (1891), 376; Thomas H. Anderson, "Fourteenth Regiment of Infantry," ibid., 11 (July 1890), 688; *Memorials of William Fowler,* 87.

63. Coco, ed., *Through Blood and Fire,* 98; Gavin, *Campaigning with the Roundheads,* 454; Nevins, ed., *Diary of Battle,* 401.

64. Agassiz, ed., *Meade's Headquarters,* 141; Grant, *Personal Memoirs,* 1, p. 266.

65. Agassiz, ed., *Meade's Headquarters,* 100.

66. Law, "From the Wilderness to Cold Harbor," 139; Jeffrey D. Stocker, ed., *From Huntsville to Appomattox* (Knoxville, Tenn., 1996), 73–4; Thomas A. Nicoll to Editor, June 3, 1864, *Selma Daily Reporter,* June 29, 1864; James P. Simms's report, in *OR,* Vol. 36, Pt. 1, p. 1064; Alexander, *Military Memoirs,* 539. An excellent description of Law's handiwork appears in Laine and Penny, *Law's Alabama Brigade,* 270.

67. Best, *121st New York,* 157; Luckenbill diary, June 3, 1864, in Historical Society of Schuylkill County.

68. Smith's report, in *OR,* Vol. 36, Pt. 1, p. 1002; D.L.C. to editor, June 4, 1864, *Pittsburgh Evening Chronicle,* June 11, 1864.

69. Law, "From the Wilderness to Cold Harbor," 139; Dame, *From the Rapidan to Richmond,* 199–200; Edgar, "When Grant Advanced Against a Wall," 6, in SHC; Edgar to Colonel Johnston, July 24, 1902, in Edgar Collection, SHC.

70. Lee to Seddon, 8:00 P.M., June 2, 1864, in *OR,* Vol. 36, Pt. 3, p. 867.

71. Freeman, *R. E. Lee,* 3, p. 383.

72. Grant, *Personal Memoirs,* 2, pp. 269–70; Grant's report, in *OR,* Vol. 36, Pt. 1, pp. 21–2.

73. Horace Porter, *Campaigning with Grant,* 174–5; Wilbur R. Dunn, *Full Measure of Devotion: The Eighth New York Volunteer Heavy Artillery* (2 vols.; Kearney, Nebr., 1997), 2, p.

56; Wilkeson, *Recollections of a Private Soldier,* 127. Porter's *Campaigning with Grant* must be approached with care. Published more than thirty years after the war, it contains much information that is useful. Unfortunately for historians, however, Porter embellished his accounts for dramatic effect, invented dialogue, and often got his facts confused. For example, he wrote a lengthy account of Grant's pause at Bethesda Church on June 2, during which pews were removed from the church and placed outside, where photographs were taken. Such an incident indeed took place, but it occurred on May 21, not June 2, and the site was Massaponax Church in Spotsylvania County, not Bethesda Church near Richmond. In short, while Porter's narrative has value, it is dangerous to rely on it in the absence of corroborating evidence.

74. Horace Porter, *Campaigning with Grant,* 172.

75. Ibid., 173.

76. Warren to Humphreys, 8:00 A.M., May 30, 1864, in *OR,* Vol. 36, Pt. 3, p. 637; Hancock to Humphreys, May 31, 1864, ibid., 380; S. R. Smith Letter, June 1, 1864, in Delaware Public Archives.

77. Horace Porter, *Campaigning with Grant,* 173; Humphreys, *Virginia Campaign,* 181.

78. Horace Porter, *Campaigning with Grant,* 172.

79. Walker, *Second Army Corps,* 463; Nevins, ed., *Diary of Battle,* 363.

80. Nevins, ed., *Diary of Battle,* 363; Agassiz, ed., *Meade's Headquarters,* 143; John D. Smith, *Nineteenth Regiment of Maine Volunteer Infantry,* 188.

81. Warren to Meade, June 2, 1864, in *OR,* Vol. 36, Pt. 3, p. 493; Warren to Humphreys, ibid.

82. Roebling's report, in Warren Collection, NYSLA. Meade's dispatch to Warren, which appears in the official records, stresses that "harmony and cooperation on the part of General Burnside and yourself are earnestly enjoined" (Humphreys to Warren, in *OR,* Vol. 36, Pt. 3, p. 494).

X   JUNE 3 4:30–5:30 A.M.: *Hancock, Wright, and Smith Attack at Cold Harbor*

1. John D. Smith, *Nineteenth Regiment of Maine Volunteer Infantry,* 188–9.

2. Meade to wife, June 4, 1864, in Meade, *Life and Letters,* 200; Badeau, *Military History of General Ulysses S. Grant,* 2, p. 184.

3. Smith's report, in *OR,* Vol. 36, Pt. 1, p. 1002.

4. Circular, 8:30 P.M., June 2, 1864, ibid., 484; J. W. Muffly, *The Story of Our Regiment: A History of the 148th Pennsylvania Volunteers* (Des Moines, Iowa, 1904), 268.

5. Nathan Church's report, in *OR,* Vol. 36, Pt. 1, p. 375; George W. Scott's report, ibid., 381; Thomas Henry's report, ibid., 383; Brooke's report, ibid., 414; Muffly, *Story of Our Regiment,* 268.

6. Wilkeson, *Recollections of a Private Soldier,* 130–1.

7. Billings, *Tenth Massachusetts Battery,* 200.

8. Muffly, *Story of Our Regiment,* 268.

9. George M. Edgar, "Studies of the Campaign of the Wilderness, May 4–June 12, 1864," in Edgar Collection, SHC; Goldsborough, *Maryland Line,* 268; Hatton memoir, LC; O. G. Wright letter, June 6, 1864, *Wilmington (N.C.) Daily Journal,* June 20, 1864.

10. Frederick Mather recollections, *Albany (N.Y.) Evening Journal,* October 23, 1895; Wilkeson, *Recollections of a Private Soldier,* 131; A. Du Bois, "Cold Harbor Salient," in *SHSP* 30, p. 277; Edgar, "Studies of the Campaign of the Wilderness, May 4–June 12, 1864," in

Edgar Collection, SHC. An excellent recounting of the attack of the 7th New York Heavy Artillery is in Keating, *Carnival of Blood,* 116–28.

11. W. T. Baldwin, "In a Federal Prison," in *SHSP* 29, p. 231; Du Bois, "Cold Harbor Salient," 277.

12. T. C. Morton, "Gave His Life for His Flag," *Confederate Veteran* 12 (1904), 70–1.

13. Ibid.; "Another Account of Breckinridge's Brigade at Cold Harbor Battle," *Atlanta Journal,* February 22, 1902; Keating, *Carnival of Blood,* 118, 121, 375; Edgar to Johnson, July 24, 1902, in Edgar Papers, SHC; Mather recollections, in *Albany (N.Y.) Evening Journal,* October 23, 1895; Edgar, "When Grant Advanced Against a Wall," 8, in SHC.

14. Wright letter, June 6, 1864, *Wilmington (N.C.) Daily Journal,* June 20, 1864; Owens, "The Maryland Boys," *Richmond Dispatch,* March 9, 1902.

15. S.M.T., "Cold Harbor," in *National Tribune,* November 19, 1891; William Child, *A History of the Fifth Regiment, New Hampshire Volunteers, in the American Civil War, 1861–1865* (Bristol, N.H., 1893), 254.

16. S.M.T., "Cold Harbor."

17. Charles E. Hapgood's report, in Child, *Fifth Regiment, New Hampshire,* 257; John K. Thompson to George M. Edgar, July 22, 1902, in Edgar Collection, SHC.

18. Wright letter, June 6, 1864, *Wilmington (N.C.) Daily Journal,* June 20, 1864; Owens, "The Maryland Boys," *Richmond Dispatch,* March 9, 1902.

19. Dorman, *Fifty Years Ago,* 7; Bryan to wife, June 3, 1864, in Bryan Papers, Florida State Archives, Tallahassee. A fine recounting of the Floridians' performance on June 3 is in Don Hillhouse, *Heavy Artillery and Light Infantry: A History of the 1st Florida Special Battalion and 10th Infantry Regiment, C.S.A.* (Jacksonville, Fla., 1992), 79–82.

20. Thomas diary, June 3, 1864, in Book 79, FSNMP.

21. Goldsborough, *Maryland Line,* 126–7; Owens, "The Maryland Boys," *Richmond Dispatch,* March 9, 1902; S.M.T., "Cold Harbor"; Wright letter, June 6, 1864, *Wilmington (N.C.) Daily Journal,* June 20, 1864.

22. Keating, *Carnival of Blood,* 122; Du Bois, "Cold Harbor Salient," 277–8.

23. Goldsborough, *Maryland Line,* 127–9; Owens, "The Maryland Boys," *Richmond Dispatch,* March 9, 1902; Keating, *Carnival of Blood,* 1221; Samuel T. McCullough diary, June 3, 1864, in Hotchkiss-McCullough Papers, UV.

24. S.M.T., "Cold Harbor"; Hapgood's report, in Child, *Fifth Regiment, New Hampshire,* 257; James E. Larkin's report, ibid., 270; Clarence Derrick to George M. Edgar, July 5, 1902, in Edgar Papers, SHC.

25. Wilkeson, *Recollections of a Private Soldier,* 131.

26. Muffly, *Story of Our Regiment,* 269; Frank A. Burr, *Life and Achievements of James Addams Beaver* (Philadelphia, 1882), 141–2; Brooke's report, in *OR,* Vol. 36, Pt. 1, p. 414; W. A. Clark, "At Cold Harbor," in *National Tribune,* October 27, 1887; Stevens, *Berdan's United States Sharpshooters,* 446.

27. Noonan, "Unpublished History of 69th New York," in Powers Collection, USAMHI; Menge and Shimrak, eds., *Civil War Notebook of Daniel Chisholm,* 118; Mulholland, *Story of the 116th Regiment Pennsylvania Volunteers,* 255–6.

28. Elliott, "Martin's Brigade," 193; Wilkeson, *Recollections of a Private Soldier,* 132; Brooke's report, in *OR,* Vol. 36, Pt. 1, p. 414.

29. A. F. G. to Dear Friend Roger, June 7, 1864, quoted in Waters, "Tell Them I Died Like a Confederate Soldier," 171; Dorman, *Fifty Years Ago,* 8; Keating, *Carnival of Blood,* 127–8; Mather recollections, *Albany (N.Y.) Evening Journal,* October 23, 1895.

30. Edgar, "When Grant Advanced Against a Wall," 8; Edgar to Johnston, July 24, 1902, in Edgar Papers, SHC; Derrick to Edgar, July 5, 1902, in Edgar Papers, SHC; Edgar, "Studies of the Campaign of the Wilderness, May 4–June 12, 1864," in Edgar Papers, SHC.

31. Keating, *Carnival of Blood,* 131; Larkin's report, in Child, *Fifth Regiment, New Hampshire,* 270.

32. "Historical Album of Orleans County, New York," 105, quoted in Dunn, *Full Measure of Devotion,* 2, p. 309; James P. McIvor's report, in *OR,* Vol. 36, Pt. 1, p 465. Spaulding of the 2nd Battalion was sick on June 3. Captain James Maginnis commanded in his place.

33. John Hoffman diary, June 2, 1864, in RNBP, Book 24; Alanson A. Haines, *Fifteenth Regiment New Jersey Volunteers,* 206.

34. Smyth's report, in *OR,* Vol. 36, Pt. 1, p. 452; Gibbon's report, ibid., 432–3.

35. Thomas W. Higginson, *Harvard Memorial Biographies* (2 vols.; Cambridge, 1867), 1, p. 93.

36. Eli Nichols to family, June 6, 1864, *Niagara Falls (N.Y.) Gazette,* August 23, 1938; Nelson Armstrong, *Nuggets of Experience* (San Bernardino, Calif., 1904), 48.

37. William Smith diary, June 3, 1864, in Zack C. Waters Private Collection; Army Correspondence, June 7, 1964, *Augusta (Ga.) Telegraph,* June 15, 1864.

38. Higginson, *Harvard Memorial Biographies,* 1, p. 93; *Lockport (N.Y.) Daily Journal and Courier,* July 29, 1864.

39. Alanson A. Haines, *Fifteenth Regiment New Jersey Volunteers,* 208.

40. *Lockport (N.Y.) Daily Journal and Courier,* July 29, 1864; Nichols to family, June 6, 1864, *Niagara Falls (N.Y.) Gazette,* August 23, 1938; Joseph Willett letter, June 5, 1864, quoted in Dunn, *Full Measure of Devotion,* 2, p. 312.

41. Willett letter, June 5, 1864, quoted in Dunn, *Full Measure of Devotion,* 2, p. 312; "Historical Album of Orleans County, N.Y.," 105, quoted in Dunn, *Full Measure of Devotion,* 2, p. 316; John Hoffman diary, June 3, 1864, in Book 24, RNBP; *Batavia (N.Y.) Daily News and Batavian,* August 19, 1899; Dunn diary, June 3, 1864, in RNBP, Book 23.

42. W. W. Bates to John T. Sprague, June 6, 1864, *Albany (N.Y.) Angus,* June 13, 1864; Higginson, *Harvard Memorial Biographies,* 1, p. 94; Frederick S. Cozzens, *Colonel Peter A. Porter: A Memorial* (New York, 1865), 46–7; McIvor's report, in *OR,* Vol. 36, Pt. 1, p. 460.

43. Armstrong, *Nuggets of Experience,* 50; Henry R. Swan to Abbie, June 4, 1864, in *Civil War Times Illustrated* 9 (1972), 43.

44. Swan to Abbie, June 4, 1864, in *Civil War Times Illustrated* 9 (1972), 43; W. I. Hallock to Editor, *American Tribune,* August 24, 1893; Alanson A. Haines, *Fifteenth Regiment New Jersey Volunteers,* 208; Bibb to Clisby, June 4, 1864, *Macon Daily Telegraph,* June 14, 1864; Wendell D. Croom, *The War History of Company C, 6th Georgia Regiment* (Fort Valley, Ga., 1879), 24–5.

45. O'Beirne, "Into the Valley of the Shadow of Death" 76–7; Newell M. Smith, "The Story of the 155th New York," in *The Courier,* 5, p. 46; John Russell Winterbotham to Folks at Home, June 4, 1864, and June 10, 1864, in Kevin O'Beirne, "Our Boys Stood Up Like Heroes," *Irish Volunteer* 5 (2000).

46. John Beattie's report, in *OR,* Vol. 36, Pt. 1, p. 464; Elliott, "Martin's Brigade," 193; Winterbotham to Folks, June 10, 1864, in O'Beirne, "Our Boys Stood Up Like Heroes," *Irish Volunteer* 5 (2000), 1; McMahon, "Cold Harbor," 217; "Col. M'Mahon Dead," *Rochester Daily Union and Advertiser,* June 13, 1864; Wilson G. Lamb, "Seventeenth Regiment," in *Histories of the Several Regiments,* ed. Walter Clark, 2, p. 5. Kevin O'Beirne, the foremost modern student of the Corcoran Legion, doubts Winterbotham's account, noting that Winterbotham's

social background made it unlikely that he would have hobnobbed with McMahon, and that he was not a witness to McMahon's death.

47. Theodore G. Ellis's report, in *OR,* Vol. 36, Pt. 1, p. 458; Charles D. Page, *History of the Fourteenth Regiment Connecticut Volunteer Infantry,* 283; Kepler, *Fourth Regiment Ohio Volunteer Infantry,* 179–81

48. William P. Haines, *Men of Company F,* 67; Bowen diary, June 3, 1864, in FSNMP; Timothy Bateman diary, June 3, 1864, in RNBP, Book 24; Edward G. Longacre, *To Gettysburg and Beyond: The Twelfth New Jersey Volunteer Infantry, II Corps, Army of the Potomac, 1862–1865* (Heightstown, N.J., 1988), 217–9.

49. Cowtan, *Services of the Tenth New York,* 282–3.

50. Smyth's diary, June 3, 1864, in Delaware Public Archives, Dover; Smyth's report, in *OR,* Vol. 36, Pt. 1, p. 452; Elliott, "Martin's Brigade," 193.

51. John D. Smith, *Nineteenth Regiment of Maine Volunteer Infantry,* 189.

52. Ibid., 189–90; Turino, *Civil War Diary of Lieutenant J. E. Hodgkins,* 91.

53. Aubery, *Thirty-Sixth Wisconsin Volunteer Infantry,* 68–9; Alanson A. Haines, *Fifteenth Regiment New Jersey Volunteers,* 208.

54. Aubery, *Thirty-Sixth Wisconsin Volunteer Infantry,* 68–9; John Gibbon to family, June 4, 1864, in Maryland Historical Society, Baltimore; John D. Smith, *Nineteenth Regiment of Maine Volunteer Infantry,* 189–90; Turino, *Civil War Diary of Lieutenant J. E. Hodgkins,* 91.

55. "Charges and Specifications Preferred Against Brigadier General J. T. Owen, U.S. Volunteers," in *OR,* Vol. 36, Pt. 1, pp. 435–6; Gibbon, *Recollections of the Civil War,* 231–2. Gibbon wrote in his report: "At daylight I rode to the line and found Owen's brigade not even under arms, and, of course, not in the advanced position I had assigned it the night before" (*OR,* Vol. 36, Pt. 1, p. 433).

56. "Charges and Specifications Preferred Against Brigadier General J. T. Owen, U.S. Volunteers," in *OR,* Vol. 36, Pt. 1, pp. 435–6; Ward, *One Hundred and Sixth Regiment Pennsylvania,* 265; Henry Roback, *The Veteran Volunteers of Herkimer and Otsego Counties in the War of the Rebellion, Being a History of the 152nd New York* (Little Falls, N.Y., 1888), 91.

57. Roback, *Veteran Volunteers of Herkimer and Otsego Counties,* 91; Ward, *One Hundred and Sixth Regiment Pennsylvania,* 265.

58. Gibbon's report, in *OR,* Vol. 36, Pt. 1, p. 433.

59. Elliott, "Martin's Brigade," 193.

60. Brainerd, *Bridge Building in Wartime,* 233.

61. Morse, *Personal Experiences,* 102–3.

62. Best, *121st New York,* 157–8.

63. William J. Wray, *History of the Twenty-Third Pennsylvania Volunteer Infantry, Birney's Zouaves* (Philadelphia, 1904), 115–6.

64. Westbrook, *49th Pennsylvania,* 205–6; David A. Stohl to Col. H. C. Eyer, June 5, 1864, in Susan Boardman Collection, USAMHI; James S. Anderson to family, June 4, 1864, in State Historical Society of Wisconsin, Madison.

65. Luckenbill diary, June 3, 1864, in Historical Society of Schuylkill County; Keiser diary, June 3, 1864, in USAMHI; Britton and Reed, eds., *To My Beloved Wife and Boy at Home,* 236; Upton's report, in *OR,* Vol. 36, Pt. 1, p. 671; Vaill, *Second Connecticut,* 66–7.

66. Hagood, *Memoirs,* 260; Brigade return, June 4, 1864, in Fred Sanborn Papers, LC.

67. Horn's report, in *OR,* Vol. 36, Pt. 1, p. 789.

68. "Hunton's Brigade," *Richmond Whig,* June 8, 1864; Abbott, *Personal Recollections,* 74–5; Russell diary, June 3, 1864, in Niagara County Historical Society, Lockport, N.Y.

69. Prowell, *Eighty-Seventh Regiment, Pennsylvania,* 152; George J. Oaks to Frederick Schoen, June 4, 1864, *Rochester Daily Union and Advertiser,* June 13, 1864; Truex's report, in *OR,* Vol. 36, Pt. 1, p. 727; Edwin M. Haynes, *Tenth Regiment, Vermont,* 145; *Letters of Major Peter Vredenburgh,* N.p., n.d., 23.

70. Horn's report, in *OR,* Vol. 36, Pt. 1, p. 739; Binkley's report, ibid., 744; William H. Ball's report, ibid., 747; Myers diary, June 3, 1864, in RNBP; Davidson, ed., *Civil War Letters of the Late 1st Lieut. James J. Hartley,* 97; Roe, *Ninth New York Heavy Artillery,* 101. The historian of the 126th Ohio thought the division advanced about 200 yards: John H. Gilson, *History of the 126th Ohio Volunteer Infantry, from the Date of Organization Until the End of the Rebellion* (Salem, Ohio, 1883), 63.

71. Fisk diary, June 2, 1864, in LC; Rhodes, ed., *All for the Union,* 158.

72. Joseph B. Polley, *Hood's Texas Brigade: Its Marches, Its Battles, Its Achievements* (New York, 1910), 242; D. H. Hamilton, *History of Company M, First Texas Volunteer Infantry, Hood's Brigade* (Waco, 1962), 60; J. H. Cosgrove, "About the Attack at Cold Harbor," *Confederate Veteran* 20 (1912), 511.

73. Wheaton's report, in *OR,* Vol. 36, Pt. 1, p. 699; Thomas McLaughlin's report, ibid., 693; C.A.B. to editor, June 7, 1864, *Pittsburgh Evening Chronicle,* June 14, 1864; Hoon diary, June 3, 1864, in Lord, ed., "Diary of a Soldier—1864," *North South Trader* 4 (1976), 13. The 93rd Pennsylvania of Wheaton's division remained in the rear guarding ambulance trains. "From the 93rd Regiment," *Lebanon (Pa.) Courier,* June 16, 1864.

74. Fisk diary, June 3, 1864, in LC.

75. Lewis Grant's report, in *OR,* Vol. 36, Pt. 1, p. 708.

76. Benedict, *Vermont in the Civil War,* 1, pp. 466–7; R. W. B., "From the Tenth Regiment," *Springfield (Mass.) Daily Republican,* June 22, 1864; Benton's report, in *OR,* Vol. 36, Pt. 1, p. 718; D.L.C. to editor, June 4, 1864, *Pittsburgh Evening Chronicle,* June 11, 1864.

77. Smith's report, in *OR,* Vol. 36, Pt. 1, p. 1002.

78. Nicolas Bowen to J. H. Martindale, June 2, 1864, ibid., Pt. 3, p. 508; Nicolas Bowen to Brooks, June 2, 1864, ibid., 508; Smith's report, ibid., Pt. 1, p. 1002.

79. John H. Mahon "Civil War Assault Tactics," in *Military Analysis of the Civil War: An Anthology* (Millwood, N.Y., 1977), 262–3; Marston's report, in *OR,* Vol. 36, Pt. 1, p. 1006; Henry's report, ibid., 1012–3; Derby, *Bearing Arms,* 304. The 9th New Jersey of Stannard's brigade did not participate in the charge, having been delayed when its transport grounded coming up the Pamunkey.

80. George E. Place narrative, in Bartlett, *Twelfth Regiment, New Hampshire,* 207.

81. William C. Oates, *The War Between the Union and the Confederacy and Its Lost Opportunities* (New York, 1905), 366; Stocker, ed., *From Huntsville to Appomattox,* 174–5; William C. Jordan, *Some Events and Incidents During the Civil War* (Montgomery, 1909), 82; Laine, *Law's Alabama Brigade,* 270.

82. Marston's report, in *OR,* Vol. 36, Pt. 1, p. 1006; Burnham's report, ibid., 1009.

83. Stocker, ed., *From Huntsville to Appomattox,* 174; William C. Jordan, *Some Events,* 83.

84. Stocker, ed., *From Huntsville to Appomattox,* 174; Oates, *War Between the Union and the Confederacy,* 174.

85. Kreutzer, *Notes and Observations,* 201–2; "The Costly Charge of the 81st New York," *National Tribune,* September 20, 1883.

86. Bartlett, *Twelfth Regiment, New Hampshire,* 202, 206; William G. Moegling's report, in *OR,* Vol. 36, Pt. 1, p. 1017.

87. Derby, *Bearing Arms,* 308.

88. Smith's report, in *OR,* Vol. 36, Pt. 1, p. 1002.

89. Martin A. Haynes, *Second Regiment, New Hampshire,* 235–7; Smith's report, in *OR,* Vol. 36, Pt. 1, p. 1003. A set of maps in the Charles Chase Collection, UV, depicts Stedman immediately north of the middle ravine and Stannard on the ravine's south bank.

90. Bartlett, *Twelfth Regiment, New Hampshire,* 207.

91. Ibid., 202–3, 208; Stocker, ed., *From Huntsville to Appomattox,* 174.

92. Bartlett, *Twelfth Regiment, New Hampshire,* 204–5.

93. Ibid., 208; Moegling's report, in *OR,* Vol. 36, Pt. 1, p. 1017; Martin A. Haynes, *Second Regiment, New Hampshire,* 176.

94. William P. Derby, "Charge of the Star Brigade at Cold Harbor," *Springfield (Mass.) Daily Republican,* July 4, 1886.

95. Samuel H. Putnam, *The Story of Company A, Twenty-Fifth Regiment, Mass. Vols, in the War of the Rebellion* (Worcester, Mass., 1886), 287; Derby, *Bearing Arms,* 302, 308.

96. William P. Derby, "Charge of the Star Brigade," in *Camp-Fire Sketches,* comp. King and Derby, 322–4.

97. Stocker, ed., *From Huntsville to Appomattox,* 174–5; Pinckney D. Bowles, "Battle of Cold Harbor," *Philadelphia Weekly Times,* January 31, 1885; Josiah Pickett's report, in *OR,* Vol. 36, Pt. 1, p. 1016.

98. Oates, *War Between the Union and the Confederacy,* 366–7; Putnam, *Story of Company A,* 288–9; Dame, *From the Rapidan to Richmond,* 203–4.

99. J. Waldo Denny, *Wearing the Blue in the 25th Massachusetts Volunteer Infantry, with Burnside's Coast Division, 18th Army Corps, and Army of the James* (Worcester, Mass., 1879), 318–9; J. Waldo Denny, *Address Delivered at Second Reunion K Association, 25th Massachusetts Volunteers, at Worcester, Mass., September 26, 1870* (Boston, 1871), 23.

100. Derby, *Bearing Arms,* 302–5; "Gave Up His Canteen," *Boston Morning Journal,* May 30, 1893; Thomas A. Nicoll to Williams, June 3, 1864, *Selma (Alabama) Daily Reporter,* June 20, 1864.

101. Stannard's report, in *OR,* Vol. 51, Pt. 1, p. 1261.

102. Derby, *Bearing Arms,* 306–7; Emmerton, *Record of the Twenty-Third Regiment Massachusetts,* 208–9; Law, "From the Wilderness to Cold Harbor," 141.

103. Smith's report, in *OR,* Vol. 36, Pt. 1, p. 1003; L'Hommedieu journal, June 3, 1864, in RNBP.

104. Guy V. Henry's report, in *OR,* Vol. 36, Pt. 1, p. 1013; Hiram B. Crosby's report, ibid., 1013–14; Members of the Regiment. *Story of the Twenty-First Regiment,* 238.

105. Cunningham, *Three Years with the Adirondack Regiment,* 129.

106. Smith's report, in OR, Vol. 36, Pt. 1, p. 1003.

107. Kershaw to Sorrel, 7:50 A.M., June 3, 1864, in Alexander Papers, SHC.

108. Return of Casualties in the Union forces, June 2–15, 1864, in *OR,* Vol. 36, Pt. 1, pp. 166–80.

109. Read, "Diary of the Movements of the 3rd Division, 6th Army Corps," 51, in Manassas National Battlefield Park; Return of Casualties, in *OR,* Vol. 36, Pt. 1, p. 173; Martindale's report, ibid., Vol. 51, Pt. 1, p. 1255; Stannard's report, ibid., 1262; Elwell's report, ibid., Vol. 36, Pt. 1, p. 1015; Derby, *Bearing Arms,* 309; Putnam, *Story of Company A,* 289; Denny, *Wearing the Blue,* 336; Derby, "Charge of the Star Brigade," 324; Entry 652, Record Group 94, NA; Martin A. Haynes, *Second Regiment, New Hampshire,* 239; "The Costly Charge of the 81st New York, *National Tribune,"* September 20, 1883; Barthalomeu S. De Forest, *Random Sketches and Wandering Thoughts* (Albany, N.Y., 1866) 224

110. 2nd Corps Addenda, in *OR,* Vol. 36, Pt. 1, p. 367; Walker, *Second Army Corps,* 513–5; Humphreys, *Virginia Campaign,* 184. The Return of Casualties for the period June 2 through June 15 shows a total of 1,561 casualties for Barlow and 1,674 for Gibbon, totaling 3,215 for the twelve-day period. The 2nd Corps was under fire almost that entire time, rendering losses between 2,000 and 2,500 a reasonable estimate for June 3.

111. Keating, *Carnival of Blood,* 131–2; Report of Casualties, in *OR,* Vol. 36, Pt., 1, p. 166; James E. Larkin's report, ibid., 376; Return of Casualties, 2nd N.Y.H.A., Entry 652, Record Group 94, LC. Humphreys puts Barlow's total losses for June 3 through June 12 at about 1,100 men (*Virginia Campaign,* 183).

112. Gibbon's report, in *OR,* Vol. 36, Pt. 1, p. 433; Return of Casualties, ibid., 167; John Byrne's report, ibid., 163; John Beattie's report, ibid., 464; John Coonan's report, ibid., 466; James M. Hudnut, *Casualties by Battles and by Names in the Eight New York Heavy Artillery, August 22, 1862–June 5, 1865* (New York, 1913); Aubery, *Thirty-Sixth Wisconsin Volunteer Infantry,* 69; Gibbon, *Personal Recollections,* 233. Gibbon's amended figure seems high, as the official returns for the period June 2–June 15 place his total losses at 1,674. For somewhat different figures in the Corcoran Legion, see O'Beirne, "Into the Valley of the Shadow of Death," 77.

113. I am indebted to Bruce Trinque of Niantic, Connecticut, for pointing out to me the contrast in losses between these two regiments that charged across comparable ground.

114. I thank Alfred Young for helping me calculate Confederate losses. Figures cannot be exact, as some units reported casualties for several days. Also, some units, such as Finegan's and Martin's brigades, made attacks later on June 3, incurring additional losses.

115. John H. Reagan, *Memoirs, With Special Reference to Secession and the Civil War,* ed. Walter Flavius McCaleb (New York, 1906), 191–3.

116. Law, "From the Wilderness to Cold Harbor," 141; William S. Dunlop, *Lee's Sharp-shooters; or, The Forefront of Battle: A Story of Southern Valor That Never Has Been Told* (Little Rock, Ark., 1899), 94.

117. George A. Armes, *Ups and Downs of an Army Officer* (Washington, D.C., 1900), 94–5; 2nd Corps Daily Addenda, in *OR,* Vol. 36, Pt. 1, p. 366; Menge and Shimrak, eds., *Civil War Notebook of Daniel Chisholm,* 118.

118. Thomas W. Hyde, *Following the Greek Cross,* 211; William F. Smith, "Eighteenth Corps at Cold Harbor," 225; Grant, *Personal Memoirs,* 2, p. 276. Porter, in his *Campaigning with Grant,* 179, has Grant making a speech to his staff in words almost identical to those Grant used in his *Personal Memoirs* two decades later. One cannot help questioning the authenticity of Porter's reporting.

XI　JUNE 3 *Lee Stalemates Grant Again*

1. Agassiz, ed., *Meade's Headquarters,* 143–4.

2. Rose memorandum, June 3, 1864, in LC; Meade to Grant, 5:15 A.M., June 3, 1864, in *OR,* Vol. 36, Pt. 3, p. 524; Meade to Grant, 5:30 A.M., June 3, 1864, ibid., 525; Hancock to Meade, 6:00 A.M., June 3, 1864, ibid., 525.

3. Hancock to Meade, 6:45 A.M., June 3, 1864, ibid., 530; Grant to Meade, 7:00 A.M., June 3, 1864, ibid., 526; Badeau, *Military History of General Ulysses S. Grant,* 2, p. 296.

4. Dickert, *Kershaw's Brigade,* 375.

5. Armstrong, *Nuggets of Experience,* 51; I. Richard Reed, "100 Years Ago Today," *Niagara Falls (N.Y.) Gazette Weekly,* June, 1964.

6. Roback, *Veteran Volunteers of Herkimer and Otsego Counties,* 92; Kepler, *Fourth Regiment Ohio,* 179–80; Bowen diary, June 3, 1864, in FSNMP; Thomas D. Cockrell and Michael B. Ballard, eds., *A Mississippi Rebel in the Army of Northern Virginia: The Civil War Memoirs of Private David Holt* (Baton Rouge, 1995), 276.

7. J.F.T., "Some Florida Heroes," *Confederate Veteran* 11 (1903), 363; W. A. Hunter to wife, June 5, 1864, in Zack C. Waters Private Collection, Rome, Georgia.

8. Newspaper clipping in Dunham File, St. Augustine Historical Society, St. Augustine, Florida.

9. Humphreys to Warren, June 2, 1864, in *OR,* Vol. 36, Pt. 3, p. 494; L. O. Merriam recollections, 41, in FSNMP; John L. Parker, *Twenty-Second Massachusetts Infantry,* 460; Warren to Meade, 6:00 A.M., June 3, 1864, in *OR,* Vol. 36, Pt. 3, p. 536; Roebling's report, in Warren Collection, NYSLA.

10. Monroe F. Cockrell, ed., *Gunner with Stonewall: Reminiscences of William Thomas Poague* (Jackson, Tenn., 1957), 96–7; John A. Sloan, *Reminiscences of the Guilford Grays, Co. B, 27th N.C. Regiment* (Washington, D.C., 1883), 96; Heth's report, in MC.

11. Percy Daniels's report, in *OR,* Vol. 36, Pt. 1, pp. 932–3; Hopkins, *Seventh Regiment Rhode Island Volunteers,* 184; Letter, June 4, 1864, *Providence (R.I.) Daily Journal,* June 20, 1864; Henry S. Burrage Reminiscences, 16, in MOLLUS Unpublished Files, USAMHI.

12. Committee of the Regiment, *Thirty-Sixth Regiment Massachusetts,* 192; H. H. Lawhon, "Forty-Eighth Regiment," in *Histories of the Several Regiments,* ed. Walter Clark, 3, p. 120; Frederick E. Cushman, *History of the 58th Regiment Massachusetts Volunteers* (Washington, D.C., 1865), 9.

13. *Our Living and Our Dead,* April 15, 1874.

14. Thomas H. Parker, *History of the 51st Regiment of Pennsylvania Volunteers and Veteran Volunteers* (Philadelphia, 1869), 560–1; David Benfer diary, June 3, 1864, in USAMHI; A. H. to editor, June 10, 1864, *Detroit Advertiser and Tribune,* June 22, 1864. Willcox later claimed that Hartranft advanced before Curtin. Hartranft, however, stated that he and Curtin advanced at the same time (Willcox's report, in *OR,* Vol. 36, Pt. 1, p. 946; Hartranft's report, ibid., 952).

15. Hartranft's report, in *OR,* Vol. 36, Pt. 1, p. 952; Willcox's report, ibid., 946.

16. John L. Parker, *Twenty-Second Massachusetts,* 460–1; Henry B. James, *Memories of the Civil War* (New Bedford, Mass., 1898), 79–80; Francis J. Parker, *Story of the Thirty-Second Regiment Massachusetts,* 219–20.

17. John L. Parker, *Twenty-Second Massachusetts,* 461; Jack to editor, June 8, 1864, *Boston Evening Journal,* June 21, 1864; Carter, comp., *Four Brothers in Blue,* 418; Edwin C. Bennett, *Musket and Sword,* 265–6.

18. Nevins, ed., *Diary of Battle,* 403–4.

19. James H. Wilson, *Under the Old Flag,* 1, p. 431.

20. Wilson to Humphreys, 5:00 P.M., June 2, 1864, in *OR,* Vol. 36, Pt. 3, p. 512; James H. Wilson, *Under the Old Flag,* 1, pp. 431–2; Manaton to editor, June 10, 1864, *Newark Daily Advertiser,* June 18, 1864.

21. Wilson to Humphreys, 8:10 A.M., June 3, 1864, in *OR,* Vol. 36, Pt. 3, pp. 559–60.

22. Humphreys to Burnside, 10:15 A.M., June 3, 1864, ibid., 548; Burnside to Humphreys, 11:05 A.M., June 3, 1864, ibid.

23. Burnside to Humphreys, 7:35 A.M., June 3, 1864, ibid., 547; Wright to Humphreys, 7:45 A.M., June 3, 1864, ibid., 544; Smith to Meade, June 3, 1864, ibid., 553.

24. Humphreys to Smith, 8:00 A.M., June 3, 1864, ibid., 553; Nevins, ed., *Diary of Battle,* 405–6.

25. Smith to Meade, June 3, 1864, in OR, Vol. 36, Pt. 3, p. 554; Hancock to Meade, 8:25 A.M., June 3, 1864, ibid., 530–1.

26. Meade to Hancock, 8:45 A.M., June 3, 1864, ibid., 531; Hancock to Meade, ibid.

27. Swinton, *Campaigns of the Army of the Potomac,* 487; *New York Times,* June 7, 1864; McMahon, "Cold Harbor," 227. George A. Bowen of the 12th New Jersey of Smyth's brigade wrote in a memorandum transcribed from his diary in 1889 that after the regiment had entrenched, "the order was again given to charge but the men positively refused to attempt another assault, notwithstanding all we could do in the way of driving or exhortation." Bowen's memorandum, however, incorporates considerable postwar material and is suspect as a contemporaneous recounting.

28. Grant to *Toledo Blade,* February 7, 1884, in *New York Times,* February 12, 1884; Walker, *Second Army Corps,* 516 n. 1; Benedict, *Vermont in the Civil War,* 1, pp. 466–7; Houston, *Thirty-Second Maine Regiment,* 221–2; Augustus Woodbury, *Major General Ambrose E. Burnside and the Ninth Army Corps* (Providence, R.I., 1867), 399 n; Thomas L. Livermore, "Grant's Campaign Against Lee," in *PMHSM* 4, p. 446. Wilkeson, in his *Recollections of a Private Soldier,* claimed to have observed troops refusing to charge and was roundly denounced as "unprincipled" by Hancock's aide Walker (Francis Walker, *General Hancock* [New York, 1894], 224). Writers of subsequent regimental histories sometimes alluded to men refusing to attack, parroting Swinton's claim but providing no corroborating circumstances.

29. Zack C. Waters, "All That Brave Men Could Do: Joseph Finegan's Florida Brigade at Cold Harbor," in *Civil War Regiments* 3 (1994), 19–20; H. W. Long, "Reminiscences of the Battle of Cold Harbor," in United Daughters of the Confederacy Scrapbook, Florida Department of Archives and History, Tallahassee; J.F.J., "Some Florida Heroes," 365; Waters, "Tell Them I Died Like a Confederate Soldier," 172–3.

30. Warren to Meade, 9:00 A.M., June 3, 1864, in *OR,* Vol. 36, Pt. 3, p. 538; Warren to Meade, 9:30 P.M., June 3, 1864, ibid; Meade to Warren, 10:00 A.M., June 3, 1864, ibid., 539; Hancock to Humphreys, 10:30 A.M., June 3, 1864, ibid., 532; Charles H. Morgan to Birney, 10:40 A.M., June 3, 1864, ibid., 535; Warren to Meade, 11:20 A.M., June 3, 1864, ibid., 539–40.

31. William F. Smith, "Eighteenth Corps at Cold Harbor," 227.

32. Grant, *Personal Memoirs,* 2, p. 272.

33. Grant to Meade, 12:30 P.M., June 3, 1864, in *OR,* Vol. 36, Pt. 3, p. 526.

34. Hampton Connected Narrative, 39; James H. Wilson, *Under the Old Flag,* 1, pp. 432–3.

35. "The Recent Cavalry Operations," *Atlanta Daily Intelligencer,* June 14, 1864.

36. Chapman's report, in *OR,* Vol. 36, Pt. 1, p. 901; Ide, *First Vermont Cavalry,* 176–7; Benedict, *Vermont in the Civil War,* 2, p. 644; Tenney, *War Diary,* 118.

37. Wilson diary, June 3, 1864, in LC; "The Recent Cavalry Operations," *Atlanta Daily Intelligencer,* June 14, 1864.

38. Raymond Herek, *These Men Have Seen Hard Service: The First Michigan Sharpshooters in the Civil War* (Detroit, 1998), 169–70; Burnside's report, in *OR,* Vol. 36, Pt. 1, p. 914; Willcox's report, ibid., 946.

39. Edward Rogers's report, ibid., 940; Charles Cummings's report, ibid., 937.

40. Merriam recollections, 42, in FSNMP.

41. Willcox's report, in *OR,* Vol. 36, Pt. 1, p. 946; Hartranft's report, ibid., 952; Roebling's report, in Warren Collection.

42. Wilson diary, June 3, 1864, in LC; Gerard A. Patterson, "In a Most Disgraceful Man-

ner," *Civil War Times Illustrated* (1990), 46–7; Early, *Autobiographical Sketch,* 363; Thomas J. Luttrell diary, June 3, 1864, in RNBP; Wilson's report, 11:00 P.M., June 3, 1864, in *OR,* Vol. 36, Pt. 1, p. 875; Chapman's report, ibid., 901.

43. Humphreys, *Virginia Campaign,* 188; Charles A. Page, *Letters of a War Correspondent* (Boston, 1899), 91; Willcox's report, in *OR,* Vol. 36, Pt. 1, p. 946; Burnside to Meade, 6:05 A.M., June 4, 1864, *OR,* Vol. 36, Pt. 3, p. 583.

44. As always, I am indebted to Alfred Young for helping me calculate Confederate losses. Alexander, *Military Memoirs,* 542, estimated Lee's losses for June 3 between 1,200 and 1,500. See also Humphreys, *Virginia Campaign,* 192–3.

45. J.F.T., "Some Florida Heroes," 364.

46. Ibid.; Francis P. Fleming, *Memoir of Captain C. Seton Fleming, of the Second Florida Infantry, C.S.A.* (Jacksonville, Fla.,1881) 85–7.

47. Waters, "All That Brave Men Could Do,"21; Long, "Reminiscence"; Fleming, *Memoir of Captain C. Seton Fleming,* 87.

48. Smyth's diary, June 3, 1864, Delaware Public Archives; Banes, *Philadelphia Brigade,* 273; Cowtan, *Services of the Tenth New York,* 285–6; Ward, *One Hundred and Sixth Regiment Pennsylvania,* 267; Kepler, *Fourth Regiment Ohio,* 180.

49. Aaron Geiger to wife, June 17, 1864, in Clippings File, Florida Department of Archives and History, Tallahassee; H. M. Hammill, "A Boy's First Battle," *Confederate Veteran* 12 (1904), 540; D. L. Greer, "Memoirs of the War," *Lake City (Fla.) Index,* February 2, 1902.

50. Lyman to family, June 3, 1864, in Agassiz, ed., *Meade's Headquarters,* 148.

51. Ibid.

52. Grant to Halleck, 2:00 P.M., June 3, 1864, in *OR,* Vol. 36, Pt. 3, p. 524; Dana to Stanton, June 3, 1864, ibid., Pt. 1, pp. 87–8.

53. Dana to Stanton, 8:30 A.M., June 4, 1864, ibid., 88–9; "The Loss Around Cold Harbor," *New York Herald,* June 6, 1864; *New York Times,* June 7, 1864. For an interpretation more critical of Grant, see David E. Long, *The Jewel of Liberty* (Mechanicsburg, Pa., 1994), 201–4.

54. William L. Fox, *Regimental Losses in the American Civil War, 1861–1865* (Albany, N.Y., 1898), 541–51. I am indebted to Scott Hartwig of the Gettysburg National Battlefield Park for information on Confederate losses at Gettysburg.

55. Martha Derby Perry, comp., *Letters from a Surgeon of the Civil War* (Boston, 1906), 187.

56. Lyman to family, June 3, 1864, in Agassiz, ed., *Meade's Headquarters,* 148; Biddle to wife, June 4, 1864, in Meade Papers, HSP; Lyman's journal, June 4, 1864, in Lyman Collection, MHS; Higgenbotham to folks, June 4, 1864, in *Irish Volunteer Journal.*

57. Meade to wife, 8:00 A.M., June 4, 1864, in Meade, *Life and Letters of George Gordon Meade,* 2, pp. 200–1; Biddle to wife, June 4, 1864, in Meade Collection, HSP.

58. Private in Company E to Editor, June 6, 1864, *Winsted (Conn.) Herald,* June 10, 1864; Simon B. Cummins to Lute, June 4, 1864, in Melvin Jones, ed., *Give God the Glory: Memoirs of a Civil War Soldier* (N.p., 1979), 61; Peter Vredenburgh to family, June 4, 1864, in *Letters of Major Peter Vredenburgh,* 23.

59. Brainerd, *Bridge Building in Wartime,* 232.

60. Meade to wife, June 4, 1864, in Meade, *Life and Letters,* 2, p. 200. Meade's aide Biddle wrote home on June 5 that Meade had managed all of the army's operations except for the North Anna campaign, which he viewed as bungled by Grant (Biddle to wife, June 5, 1864, in Meade Collection, HSP).

61. Nevins, ed., *Diary of Battle,* 405; Upton to sister, June 4, 1864, in Peter S. Michie, *Life and Letters of Emory Upton* (New York, 1885), 108.

62. Lee to Davis, 1:00 P.M., June 3, 1864, in Douglas Southall Freeman, *Lee's Dispatches to Jefferson Davis* (New York, 1957), 212–4; Lee to Seddon, 8:45 P.M., June 3, 1864, in *OR,* Vol. 36, Pt. 3, p. 869.

63. Bibb to Clisby, June 4, 1864, *Macon Daily Telegraph,* June 4, 1864; Simms to sister, June 4, 1864, in Peacock, "Georgian's View of the War in Virginia," 107–8; A. T. Nicholson to niece, June 16, 1864, quoted in J. Tracy Power, *Lee's Miserables: Life in the Army of Northern Virginia from the Wilderness to Appomattox* (Chapel Hill, 1998), 77; Tower, *Lee's Adjutant,* 167; Venable, "Campaign from the Wilderness to Petersburg," 536.

64. J. William Jones, *Personal Recollections of Robert E. Lee* (New York, 1874), 40.

65. Samuel H. Walkup to family, May 29, 1864, in SHC; Special Orders No. 138, in *OR,* Vol. 36, Pt. 3, pp. 873–4. The most recent and most accurate count of Confederate casualties during the Overland campaign are in Alfred C. Young, "Numbers and Losses in the Army of Northern Virginia" *North and South* 3 (2000), 15–29. Young documents almost 6,900 casualties in the Army of Northern Virginia from May 27 through June 12. The actual number was probably higher.

66. LeGrand J. Wilson, *The Confederate Soldier* (Fayetteville, Ark., 1902), 177–8.

67. Grant to Halleck, June 5, 1864, in *OR,* Vol. 36, Pt. 3, p. 598.

Bibliography

MANUSCRIPTS

Auburn University Libraries, Special Collections

James H. Lane Collection
    James H. Lane's Report

Central Michigan University, Clarke Historical Library

Dexter McComber Diary

Cincinnati Historical Society

Rogers Hanneford Memoir

Civil War Library and Museum, Philadelphia

William Brooke Rawle Diary and Letters

Connecticut Historical Society, Hartford

Josiah Corban Letter
James Deane Memoir

Cornell University, John M. Olin Library

John S. Crocker Diary

Dartmouth University Library

Eri Davidson Woodbury Letter

Delaware Public Archives, Dover

S. R. Smith Letter
Thomas Smyth's Diary

Duke University, William R. Perkins Library

Richard H. Anderson's Report
John N. Cumming Letter
J. D. Ferguson Memoranda
Bradley T. Johnson Letter
Lawrence M. Keitt Letter
J. L. Sperry Letter
James S. Wingard Letter

Eastern Carolina University

Antoinette Smith Jenkins Collection
   "From 45th Georgia Infantry Regiment"

Florida Department of Archives and History, Tallahassee

Council Bryan Letter
Aaron Geiger Letter
H. W. Long Reminiscences

Fredericksburg and Spotsylvania National Military Park Library

Alfred M. Apted Diary
George A. Bowen Diary
Daniel Sayre Brewster Letter
Stephen D. Burger and George P. Bouton Memoir
James M. Cadwallader Diary
L. Calhoun Cooper Letter
Samuel Cormany Diary
Benjamin Y. Draper Diary
Lestor Hildreth Diary
William Judkins Memoir
L. O. Merriam Recollections
William A. Miller Letter
William H. Moody Memorandum
Milton H. Myers Diary
Allen Parker Diary
Alexander B. Pattison Diary
F. F. Robbins Diary

Robert S. Robertson Letter
J. William Thomas Diary
Francis Gardner Walter Diary
J. T. Watkins Memoir
John James Woodall Diary

Georgia Department of Archives and History, Atlanta

W. W. Abercrombie Letter
Joseph P. Fuller Diary
Charles P. Hansell Memorandum, "History of the 20th Georgia Battalion of Cavalry"
Henry F. Jones Letter
J. M. Reynolds Letter
Charles Sanders Letter

Rutherford B. Hayes Presidential Center, Fremont, Ohio

John R. Rhoades Letter

Historical Society of Pennsylvania, Philadelphia

E. C. Gardiner Collection
    Henry C. Baird Papers
George G. Meade Collection
    James C. Biddle Letters
    George G. Meade Letters

Historical Society of Schuylkill County, Pottsville, Pennsylvania

Lewis Luckenbill Diary

Indiana University, Lilly Library

64th New York Memoir

Library of Congress, Manuscript Division

William O. Bourne Papers
    Alonzo Ansden Manuscript
David Coon Letter
Wilbur Fisk Diary
George M. Gilchrist Letter
J. B. V. Gilpin Diary
William G. Halls Diary
John W. F. Hatton Memoir

Luther A. Rose Diary
Fred Sanborn Memoirs
Gilbert Thompson Memoirs
John Chester White Journal
James H. Wilson Diary and Memorandum

Manassas National Battlefield Park Library

James B. Ricketts Papers
    James M. Read, "Diary of Movements of the 3rd Division 6th Army Corps"

Mary Ball Washington Library, Lancaster, Virginia

John W. Chowning Diary

Maryland Historical Society, Baltimore

John Gibbon Letter
Charles E. Phelps Collection
    Martin L. Smith Diary
Lewis H. Steiner Diary

Massachusetts Historical Society, Boston

Theodore Lyman Journal

Michigan State University Libraries

John E. Irwin Diary

Minnesota Historical Society, Minneapolis

Harrison B. George Diary

Mississippi Department of Archives and History, Jackson

B. L. Wynn Diary

Museum of the Confederacy, Eleanor S. Brockenbrough Library, Richmond

Robert A. Hardaway Extract
Henry Heth's Report
Fitzhugh Lee's Report
Joseph Mullen Jr. Diary
G. Moxley Sorrel Journal

National Archives, Washington, D.C.

Holmes Conrad Combined Service Record, Roll 61
James H. Kidd's Report
Record Group 94 (Casualty Returns)

New York Historical Society, New York

Isaac C. Hadden Letter
William A. Paine Diary

New York State Library and Archives, Albany

Gouverneur K. Warren Collection
    Washington A. Roebling's Report
    Gouverneur K. Warren Letters

Niagara County Historical Society, Lockport, New York

Edward E. Russell Diary

Ohio Historical Society, Columbus

William McVey Diary

Scott C. Patchen Private Collection, Centreville, Virginia

Francis Cordrey Manuscript

Pennsylvania State University Library

M. Gyla McDowell Collection
    Hamilton Dunlap Diary
    S. G. Leasure Letters

Richmond National Battlefield Park

Timothy Bateman Diary
Glenn Brasher, "'Hell's Half Acre': The Battles around Bethesda Church, May–June
    1864"
Charles H. Crawford, "Flying Pontoons with Grant's Army"
Washington L. Dunn Diary
W. C. Hall Diary
John Hoffman Diary
Richard W. L'Hommedieu Journal
Thomas J. Luttrell Diary

Milton Myers Diary
J. W. Reardon Letter
Bryce A. Suderow, "May 28, 1864: Haw's Shop, Virginia"
Eugene A. Thompson Letter

Michael T. Russert Private Collection, Cambridge, New York

George Perkins Diary

Rutgers University Library

Civil War Diaries and Journals Collection
    Dwight Kilbourn Diary

St. Augustine Historical Society, St. Augustine, Florida

Dunham File
    Newspaper clipping

Rosanne Groat Shalf Private Collection

"Macmurdo House Paper—1994," unpublished manuscript

State Historical Society of Wisconsin, Madison

James S. Anderson Letter

South Carolina Historical Society, Charleston

Middleton Family Papers
    William S. R. Brockenbrough Letter
    Henry W. Richardson Letter
    M. E. L. Letter
Thomas L. Pinckney Diary
Benjamin H. Rutledge Memorandum

United States Army Military History Institute, Carlisle, Pennsylvania

Alonzo Alden, "169th New York: A Brilliant Record"
David Benfer Diary
Susan Boardman Collection
    David A. Stohl Letter
Civil War Miscellaneous Collection
    James W. Cartwright Letter
    Paul Lounsbury Manuscript

Orlando P. Sawtelle Letter
James B. Thompson Memoir
Charles E. Wood Diary
Arthur B. Wyman Letter
Civil War Times Illustrated Collection
Abraham Harshberger Memoir
Isaac H. Ressler Diary
J. N. Jones Diary
Thomas Clemens Collection
James L. Rea Letter
Gregory A. Coco Collection
George P. Hawkes Diary and Morning Report Book
William J. Dailey Diary
Edmund D. Halsey Diary and Report
Avery Harris Memoir
Harrisburg Civil War Round Table Collection
Henry Keiser Diary
Maurus Oestreich Diary
Lewis Leigh Collection
R. Preston Chew's Report
Daniel Godkin Letter
Jay Luvaas Collection
Alfred Thompson Letter
MOLLUS Unpublished Files
Henry S. Burrage Reminiscences
Powers Collection
J. Noonan, "Unpublished History of 69th New York"
Save the Flags Collection
Charles H. Minnemeyer Diary
Lewis C. White Reminiscences
Murray J. Smith Collection
Charles R. Paul Diary
Michael Winey Collection
Isaac R. Dunkelberger Memoir

University of Michigan, Bentley Historical Library

John Bancroft Diary
John E. Irwin Diary
William Bradford Irwin Journal
Military Order of the Loyal Legion of the United States Collection
George G. Hopper Memoir

University of Michigan, William L. Clements Library

James S. Schoff Collection
   Martin L. Smith Letter

University of North Carolina, Chapel Hill, Southern Historical Collection

Edward P. Alexander Collection
   Edward P. Alexander Letter
   Joseph B. Kershaw Dispatches and Letter
Rufus Barringer Letter
James Breathed Report
Noah J. Brooks Diary
George M. Edgar Collection
   Clarence Derrick Letter
   George M. Edgar Letters
   George M. Edgar, "Studies of the Campaign of the Wilderness, May 4–June 12, 1864"
   ———, "When Grant Advanced Against a Wall"
John S. Henderson Papers
   John E. Dugger Letter
Kenneth Rayner Jones Diary
Cornelia McGimsey Collection
   Lewis Warlick Letter
Joseph Fred Waring Diary

University of South Carolina, South Caroliniana Library

Wade Hampton Connected Narrative
Gabriel E. Manigault Manuscript

University of Vermont, Special Collections

Chester K. Leach Letter
William Wells Letter

University of Virginia, Alderman Library

George S. Bernard Diary
Charles Chase Maps
Hotchkiss-McCullough Papers
   Samuel T. McCullough Diary

Virginia Historical Society, Richmond

Buckner McGill Randolph Diary
Ella Moore Bassett Washington Diary

Virginia Military Institute Library

John J. Shoemaker's Report

Virginia State Library, Richmond

St. George Tucker Brooke Autobiography
James F. Wood Diary
Cadmus M. Wilcox Report

Zack C. Waters Private Collection, Rome, Georgia

W. A. Hunter Letter
William Smith Diary

Western Reserve Historical Society, Cleveland

Palmer Regimental Papers
   Well A. Bushnell Memoirs
   Walter H. Farwell Memoirs

Yale University Library

Brinecke Barnitz Papers
   Albert Barnitz's Field Notes

NEWSPAPERS

Albany (N.Y.) Angus, June 13, 1864
Albany (N.Y.) Evening Journal, October 23, 1895
American Tribune (Indianapolis), August 24, 1893
Atlanta Daily Constitutionalist, June 5, 1864
Atlanta Daily Intelligencer, June 14, 1864
Atlanta Journal, February 22, 1902
Augusta (Ga.) Constitutionalist, June 16, 1864
Augusta (Ga.) Telegraph, June 15, 1864
Batavia (N.Y.) Daily News and Batavian, August 19, 1899
Boston Daily Advertiser, June 2, 1864
Boston Evening Journal, June 7, 21, 1864
Canaan Connecticut Western News, August 24, 1911
Charleston (S.C.) Daily Courier, June 3, 1864, September 21, 1864
Charleston (S.C.) Mercury, June 4, 1864
Cincinnati Daily Commercial, March 31, 1865
Columbia (S.C.) Daily South Carolinian, May 29, June 3, September 25, 1864
Detroit Advertiser and Tribune, June 8, 16, 22, 1864

Detroit Free Press, June 15, 16, 1864
Harper's Weekly, June 25, 1864
Lake City (Fla.) Index, February 2, 1902
Lebanon (Pa.) Courier, June 16, 1864
Litchfield (Conn.) Enquirer, July 7, 9, 1864
Lockport (N.Y.) Daily Journal and Courier, July 29, 1864
Macon (Ga.) Daily Telegraph, June 14, 1864
Mobile (Ala.) Daily Advertiser and Register, June 2, 7, 17,1864
New Haven (Conn.) Daily Morning Journal, June 27, 1864
New Haven (Conn.) Daily Palladium, June 21, 1864
New York Daily Tribune, June 3, 8, 1864
New York Herald, June 2, 3, 6, 1864
New York Times, June 7, 1864, February 12, 1884, August 19, 1928
Newark (N.J.) Daily Advertiser, June 18, 1864
Niagara Falls (N.Y.) Gazette, August 23, 1938
Our Living and Our Dead (New Bern, N.C.), February 11, April 15, 22, 1874
Painesville (Ohio) Telegraph, June 23, 1864
Philadelphia Inquirer, June 3, 6, 1864
Philadelphia Weekly Times, April 19, 1884
Pittsburgh Evening Chronicle, June 11, 14, 1864
Providence (R.I.) Daily Journal, June 20, 1864
Raleigh (N.C.). Daily Confederate, June 7, 1864, February 22, 1865
Richmond Daily Chronicle, July 24, 1864
Richmond Dispatch, March 9, 1902
Richmond Enquirer, May 21, June 2, 1864
Richmond Examiner, May 30, June 1, 4, 1864
Richmond Sentinel, June 1, 1864
Richmond Whig, June 8, 1864
Rochester (N.Y.) Union and Observer, June 21, 23, July 21,1864
Savannah (Ga.) Morning News, July 20, 1864
Selma (Ala.) Daily Reporter, June 20, 1864
Springfield (Mass.) Daily Republican, June 22, 1864
Washington, D.C., Daily Morning Chronicle, June 2, 7, 1864
Wilmington (N.C.) Daily Journal, July 4, 20, 1864
Windham County (Conn.) Transcript, June 16, 1864
Winsted (Conn.) Herald, June 10, 1864
Winston-Salem (N.C.) Daily Sentinel, January 9, 1915
Xenia (Ohio) Torchlight, June 19, 1864

OFFICIAL COMPILATIONS

Annual Report of the Adjutant-General of the State of Connecticut for the Year End-ing March 31, 1865. New Haven, 1865.

The War of the Rebellion: A Compilation of the Official Records of the Union and Confederate Armies. 130 vols. Washington, D.C., 1880–1901.

BIOGRAPHIES, MEMOIRS, AND NARRATIVES

Abbott, Lemuel A. *Personal Recollections and Civil War Diary, 1864.* Burlington, Vt., 1908.

Adamson, Alberta R., et al., eds. *Recollections of the War of the Rebellion: A Story of the Second Ohio Volunteer Cavalry.* Wheaton, Ill., 1996.

Agassiz, George R., ed. *Meade's Headquarters, 1863–1865: Letters of Colonel Theodore Lyman from the Wilderness to Appomattox.* Boston, 1922.

Alexander, Edward P. *Military Memoirs of a Confederate.* New York, 1907.

Allen, Stanton P. *Down in Dixie: Life in a Cavalry Regiment in the War Days.* Boston, 1888.

Armes, George A. *Ups and Downs of an Army Officer.* Washington, D.C., 1900.

Armstrong, Nelson. *Nuggets of Experience.* San Bernardino, Calif., 1904.

Athearn, Robert G., ed. "The Civil War Diary of John Wilson Phillips." *Virginia Magazine of History and Biography* 62 (1954), 98–104.

Atkinson, Dorothy F. *King William County in the Civil War: Along Mangohick Byways.* Lynchburg, Va., 1990.

Badeau, Adam. *Military History of General Ulysses S. Grant, from April, 1861, to April, 1865.* 3 vols. New York, 1881.

Baylor, George. *Bull Run to Bull Run: Four Years in the Army of Northern Virginia.* Richmond, 1900.

Barber, E. "The Gallant Part Taken in the Fight by Drake's Brigade." *National Tribune,* April 8, 1886.

Beale, G. W. *A Lieutenant of Cavalry in Lee's Army.* Boston, 1918.

Beaudry, Paul S. *The Forgotten Regiment: History of the 151st New York Volunteer Infantry Regiment.* N.p., 1995.

Beaudry, Richard E., ed. *War Journal of Louis N. Beaudry, Fifth New York Cavalry.* Jefferson, N.C., 1996.

Belo, Alfred H. *Memoirs of Alfred H. Belo.* Boston, 1902.

Bennett, Edwin C. *Musket and Sword; or, The Camp, March, and Firing Line in the Army of the Potomac.* Boston, 1900.

Beyer, F. F., and O. F. Keydel. *Deeds of Valor: How America's Civil War Heroes Won the Congressional Medal of Honor.* Stamford, Conn., 1992.

Blackford, Susan Leigh, comp. *Letters from Lee's Army; or, Memories of Life In and Out of the Army in Virginia During the War Between the States.* New York, 1947.

Blight, David W., ed. *When This Cruel War Is Over: The Civil War Letters of Charles Harvey Brewster.* Amherst, Mass., 1992.

Bloodgood, J. D. *Personal Reminiscences of the War.* Cincinnati, 1893.

Booth, George W. *Personal Reminiscences of a Maryland Soldier in the War Between the States, 1861–1865.* Baltimore, 1898.

Bradwell, I. G. "Cold Harbor, Lynchburg, Valley Campaign, Etc., 1864." *Confederate Veteran* 28 (1920), 138–9.

Britton, Ann H., and Thomas J. Reed, eds. *To My Beloved Wife and Boy at Home: The Letters and Diaries of Orderly Sergeant John F. L. Hartwell.* Madison, N.J., 1997.

Brooks, Ulysses R. *Butler and His Cavalry.* Columbia, S.C., 1909.

Buel, Clarence C., and Robert U. Johnson, eds. *Battles and Leaders of the Civil War.* 4 vols. New York, 1884–1888.

Burr, Frank A. *Life and Achievements of James Addams Beaver.* Philadelphia, 1882.

Calhoun, C. M. *Liberty Dethroned.* N.p., n.d.

Cardwell, David. "When the Gallant Lieutenant Ford Was Killed." *Confederate Veteran* 26 (1918), 207–8.

Carpenter, Francis B. *Six Months at the White House with Abraham Lincoln.* New York, 1866.

Carter, Robert G., comp. *Four Brothers in Blue; or, Sunshine and Shadows of the War of the Rebellion.* Austin, Tex., 1978.

Casler, John O. *Four Years in the Stonewall Brigade.* Girard, Kans., 1906.

Chipman, Donald. "An Essex County Soldier in the Civil War: The Diary of Cyrille Fountain." *New York History* 66 (July 1985), 281–98.

Christian, Charles B. "The Battle at Bethesda Church." In *SHSP* 33, pp. 57–64.

Clark, Rufus W. *The Heroes of Albany: A Memorial of the Patriot-Martyrs of the City and County of Albany.* Albany, N.Y., 1866.

Clark, W. A. "At Cold Harbor." *National Tribune,* October 27, 1887.

Clingman, Thomas L. "Second Cold Harbor." In *Histories of the Several Regiments and Battalions from North Carolina in the Great War, 1861–65,* edited by Walter Clark, 5, pp. 197–205. Goldsboro, N.C., 1901.

Cockrell, Monroe F., ed. *Gunner with Stonewall: Reminiscences of William Thomas Poague.* Jackson, Tenn., 1957.

Cockrell, Thomas D., and Michael B. Ballard, eds. *A Mississippi Rebel in the Army of Northern Virginia: The Civil War Memoirs of Private David Holt.* Baton Rouge, 1995.

Coco, Gregory A., ed. *Through Blood and Fire: The Civil War Letters of Major Charles J. Mills, 1862–1865.* Lanham, Md., 1982.

Coffin, Charles C. *Redeeming the Republic: The Third Period of the Rebellion in the Year 1864.* New York, 1890.

Coffin, George H. *Three Years in the Army.* N.p., 1925.

"Col. Elisha S. Kellogg." *Connecticut War Record* 2 (September 1864), 261–3.

Comstock, Cyrus B. *The Diary of Cyrus B. Comstock.* Edited by Merlin E. Sumner. Dayton, 1987.

Cone, A. J. "A Close Call." *Confederate Veteran* 27 (1919), 372.

Cosgrove, J. H. "About the Attack at Cold Harbor." *Confederate Veteran* 20 (1912), 511.

"The Costly Charge of the 81st New York." *National Tribune,* September 20, 1883.

Cowper, Pulaski, comp. *Extracts of Letters of Major General Bryan Grimes to His Wife.* Raleigh, N.C., 1884.

Cozzens, Frederick S. *Colonel Peter A. Porter: A Memorial.* New York, 1865.

Croner, Barbara M. *A Sergeant's Story: Civil War Diary of Jacob J. Zorn, 1862–1865.* Apollo, Pa., 1999.

Crotty, D. G. *Four Years Campaigning in the Army of the Potomac.* Grand Rapids, Mich., 1874.

Dame, William M. *From the Rapidan to Richmond and the Spotsylvania Campaign.* Baltimore, 1920.

Dana, Charles A. *Recollections of the Civil War.* New York, 1899.

Davidson, Garber A., ed. *The Civil War Letters of the Late 1st Lieut. James J. Hartley, 122 Ohio Infantry Regiment.* Jefferson, N.C., n.d.

Davies, Henry E. *General Sheridan.* New York, 1895.

De Forest, Barthalomeu S. *Random Sketches and Wandering Thoughts.* Albany, N.Y., 1866.

DeMay, Jessica H., ed. *The Civil War Diary of Berea M. Willsey.* Bowie, Md., 1995.

Dennett, Tyler, ed. *Lincoln and the Civil War in the Diaries and Letters of John Hay.* New York, 1939.

Derby, William P. "Charge of the Star Brigade." In *Camp-Fire Sketches and Battle-Field Echoes,* compiled by William C. King and W. P. Derby (Springfield, Mass., 1888), 321–4.

"Diary of a Confederate Officer." *Our Living and Our Dead,* February 11, 1874.

Dorman, D. H. *Fifty Years Ago: Reminiscences of '61–65.* Tallahassee, n.d.

Dowdey, Clifford, ed. *The Wartime Papers of R. E. Lee.* New York, 1961.

DuBois, A. "Cold Harbor Salient," In *SHSP* 30, pp. 276–9.

Early, Jubal A. *Autobiographical Sketch and Narrative of the War Between the States.* Bloomington, Ind., 1960.

Elliott, Charles G. "Martin's Brigade, of Hoke's Division." In *SHSP* 23, pp. 189–98.

Elmore, Albert Rhett. "Incidents of Service with the Charleston Light Dragoons." *Confederate Veteran* 24 (1916), 541.

Field, Charles W. "Campaign of 1864 and 1865." In *SHSP* 14, pp. 542–63.

Fleming, Francis P. *Memoir of Capt. C. Seton Fleming, of the Second Florida Infantry, C.S.A.* Jacksonville, Fla., 1881.

Fox, William L. *Regimental Losses in the American Civil War, 1861–1865.* Albany, N.Y., 1898.

Freeman, Douglas Southall, *R. E. Lee.* 4 vols. New York, 1934–35.

———, ed. *Lee's Dispatches to Jefferson Davis.* New York, 1957.

Gallagher, Gary W., ed. *Fighting for the Confederacy: The Personal Recollections of General Edward Porter Alexander.* Chapel Hill, 1989.

Galwey, Thomas F. *The Valiant Hours: An Irishman in the Civil War.* Harrisburg, Pa., 1961.

Gause, Isaac. *Four Years with Five Armies.* New York, 1908.

George, W. W. "In a Federal Prison." In *SHSP* 29, pp. 229–39.

"Gen. John Irvin Gregg." *National Tribune,* January 26, 1892.

Gerrish, Theodore. *Army Life: A Private's Reminiscences of the Civil War.* Portland, Me., 1882.

Gibbon, John. *Personal Recollections of the Civil War.* New York, 1928.

Gill, John. *Reminiscences of Four Years as a Private Soldier in the Confederate Army 1861–1865.* Baltimore, 1905.

Goss, Warren L. *Recollections of a Private: A Story of the Army of the Potomac.* New York, 1890.

Grant, Ulysses S. *Personal Memoirs of U. S. Grant.* 2 vols. New York, 1885.

———. "Preparing for the Campaign of '64." In *B&L* 4, pp. 97–117.

Gray, Richard A., Jr., ed. *1864 Pocket Diary of Pvt. George R. Imler, Co. E, 138th Regiment Pennsylvania Volunteers.* N.p., 1963.

Greiner, James M., et al., eds. *A Surgeon's Civil War: The Letters and Diary of Daniel M. Holt, M.D.* Kent, Ohio, 1994.

Hagood, Johnson. *Memoirs of the War of Secession.* Columbia, S.C., 1910.

Hall, Harry H. *A Johnny Reb Band from Salem: The Pride of Tarheelia.* Raleigh, N.C., 1963.

Halliburton, Lloyd. *Saddle Soldiers: The Civil War Correspondence of General William Stokes of the 4th South Carolina Cavalry.* Orangeburg, S.C., 1993.

Hamil, John W. *The Story of a Confederate Soldier.* N.p., n.d.

Hammill, H. M. "A Boy's First Battle." *Confederate Veteran* 12 (1904), 540–1.

Hammock, Henry M., ed. *Letters to Amanda from Sergeant Arion Hill Fitzpatrick, 45th Georgia Regiment, Thomas' Brigade, Wilcox' Division, Hill's Corps CSA to His Wife Amanda Olive Elizabeth Fitzpatrick, 1862–1865.* Culloden, Ga., n.d.

Hanover County Historical Society. *Old Homes of Hanover County, Virginia.* Hanover, Va., 1983.

Harris, Malcolm H. "The Port Towns of the Pamunkey." *William and Mary Quarterly* 23 (October 1943), 493–516.

Harrold, John. *Libby, Andersonville, Florence: The Capture, Imprisonment, Escape, and Rescue of John Harrold.* Philadelphia 1870.

Hatton, Robert W., ed. "Just a Little Bit of the Civil War, as Seen by W[illiam] J. Smith, Company M, 2nd O. V. Cavalry." *Ohio History* 84 (1975), 113–4.

Haw, Joseph R. "The Battle of Haw's Shop" *Confederate Veteran* 33 (1925), 373–6.

———. "Haw's Shop Community, of Virginia." *Confederate Veteran* 33 (1925), 340–1.

Higginson, Thomas W. *Harvard Memorial Biographies.* 2. vols. Cambridge, Mass., 1867.

Himan, Michael I. "The Charge at Cold Harbor." *National Tribune,* April 24, 1884.

Houghton, Henry. "The Ordeal of Civil War: A Recollection." *Vermont History* 41 (1973), 31–49.

House, Charles J. "How the First Maine Heavy Artillery Lost 1179 Men in 30 Days." *Rockland, Me. Bugle* 2 (1895), 87–95.

Howard, Harold E., ed. *"If I Am Killed on This Trip, I Want My Horse Kept for My Brothers."* Manassas, Va., 1980.

Howe, Mark De Wolfe, ed. *Touched with Fire: Civil War Letters and Diary of Oliver Wendell Holmes, Jr., 1861–1864.* New York, 1969.

Humphreys, Henry H. *Andrew Atkinson Humphreys: A Biography.* Philadelphia, 1924.

Hunter, William A., ed. "The Civil War Diaries of Leonard C. Ferguson." *Pennsylvania History* 14 (1947), 196–213.

Hunton, Eppa. *Autobiography of Eppa Hunton.* Richmond, 1933.

Hursh, Warren C. "Battle of Hawes's Shop." *National Tribune,* November 11, 1886.

Husby, Karla Jean, comp., and Eric J. Wittenberg, ed. *Under Custer's Command: The Civil War Journal of James Henry Avery.* Washington, D.C., 2000.

Hyde, Thomas W. *Following the Greek Cross; or, Memories of the Sixth Army Corps.* Boston, 1894.

Irving, Theodore. *"More Than Conqueror"; or, Memorials of Col. J. Howard Kitching.* New York, 1873.

James, Henry B. *Memories of the Civil War.* New Bedford, Mass., 1898.

J.F.T. "Some Florida Heroes." *Confederate Veteran* 11 (1903), 363–5.

Jones, Charles B. "Historical Sketch of 55th North Carolina Infantry." *Our Living and Our Dead,* April 22, 1874.

Jones, J. William. *Personal Recollections of Robert E. Lee.* New York, 1874.

Jones, Melvin, ed. *Give God the Glory: Memoirs of a Civil War Soldier.* N.p., 1979.

Jones, Terry L., ed. *The Civil War Memoirs of Captain William J. Seymour: Reminiscences of a Louisiana Tiger.* Baton Rouge, 1991.

Jordan, David M. *"Happiness Is Not My Companion": The Life of General G. K. Warren.* Bloomington, Ind., 2001.

Jordan, William C. *Some Events and Incidents During the Civil War.* Montgomery, 1909.

Kent, Arthur A., ed. *Three Years with Company K: Sergt. Austin C. Stearns, Company K, 13th Massachusetts Infantry.* Rutherford, N.J., 1976.

Kidd, James H. *Personal Recollections of a Cavalryman with Custer's Michigan Cavalry Brigade in the Civil War.* Ionia, Mich., 1908.

King, William C., and W. P. Derby, comps. *Camp-Fire Sketches and Battle-Field Echoes.* Springfield, Mass., 1888.

Krick, Robert K. *Lee's Colonels: A Biographical Register of the Field Officers of the Army of Northern Virginia.* Dayton, Ohio, 1992.

Lane, Mills, ed. *Dear Mother, Don't Grieve About Me, If I Get Killed, I'll Only Be Dead: Letters from Georgia Soldiers in the Civil War.* Savannah, Ga., 1977.

Law, Evander McI. "From the Wilderness to Cold Harbor." In *B&L* 4, pp. 118–44.

Letters of Major Peter Vredenburgh. Privately printed, N.p. n.d.

Long, David E. *The Jewel of Liberty.* Mechanicsburg, Pa., 1994.

Long, E. B. "Ulysses S. Grant for Today." In *Ulysses S. Grant: Essays and Documents,* edited by David L. Wilson and John Y. Simon. Carbondale, Ill., 1981.

Longacre, Edward G. *From Union Stars to Top Hat.* Harrisburg, Pa., 1972.

———. "From the Wilderness to Cold Harbor in the Union Artillery." *Manuscripts* 35 (1983), 202–13.

Lord, Francis A., ed. "Diary of a Soldier—1864," *North South Trader* 4 (1976), 12–4.

Lowry, George E. "Cold Harbor: The Story of the Slaughter as Told by an Indiana Veteran." *National Tribune,* November 25, 1886.

Lynch, John W., ed. *The Dorman-Marshbourne Letters.* Senoia, Ga., 1995.

McBride, A. J. "Some War Experiences." In Book 20, RNBP

McBride, R. E. *In the Ranks: From the Wilderness to Appomattox Court House.* Cincinnati, 1881.

McElfresh, Earl B. *Maps and Mapmakers of the Civil War.* New York, 1999.

McGuire, Judith White [Brockenbrough]. *Diary of a Southern Refugee, During the War.* New York, 1867.

McIlwaine, H. R., ed. "Diary of Captain H. W. Wingfield." *Bulletin of the Virginia State Library* 16 (July 1927), 9–47.

McLauchlin, A. A. "The 115th New York." *National Tribune,* December 13, 1886.

McMahon, Martin T. "From Gettysburg to the Coming of Grant." In *B&L* 4, pp. 81–94.

———. "Cold Harbor." In *B&L* 4, pp. 213–20.

Mahon, John H. "Civil War Assault Tactics." In *Military Analysis of the Civil War: An Anthology.* Millwood, N.Y., 1977.

Manarin, Louis H., ed. "The Civil War Diary of Rufus J. Woolwine." *Virginia Magazine of History and Biography* 71 (October 1963), 432–48.

Massachusetts Historical Society. *War Diary and Letters of Stephen Minot Weld, 1861–1865.* Boston, 1979.

Mather, Fred. "A 7th N.Y.H.A. Man Gives Some Experiences." *National Tribune,* January 30, 1896.

———. "Under Old Glory." *National Tribune,* January 30, 1896.

Meade, George, ed. *Life and Letters of George Gordon Meade.* 2 vols. New York, 1913.

Meier, Heinz K., ed. *Memoirs of a Swiss Officer in the American Civil War.* Bern, 1972.

Memorials of William Fowler. New York, 1875.

Menge, W. Springer, and J. August Shimrak, eds. *The Civil War Notebook of Daniel Chisholm.* New York, 1989.

Michie, Peter S. *Life and Letters of Emory Upton.* New York, 1885.

Miers, Earl Schenck, ed. *Wash Roebling's War.* Newark, 1961.

Miller, Delavan S. *Drum Taps in Dixie: Memories of a Drummer Boy, 1861–1865.* Watertown, N.Y., 1905.

Miller, Richard F., and Robert F. Mooney, comps. *The Civil War: The Nantucket Experience, Including the Memoirs of Josiah Fitch Murphey.* Nantucket, Mass., 1994.

Milling, James A. "Recollections." *Confederate Veteran* 6 (1997), 6–18.

Morrison, James L., Jr., ed. *The Memoirs of Henry Heth*. Westport, Conn., 1974.

Morse, Francis W. *Personal Experiences in the War of the Great Rebellion, from December, 1862, to July, 1865*. Albany, N.Y., 1866.

Morton, T. C. "Gave His Life for His Flag." *Confederate Veteran* 12 (1904), 70–1.

———. "Incidents of the Skirmish at Totopotomoy Creek, Hanover County, Virginia, May 30, 1864." In *SHSP* 16, pp. 47–56.

Mulholland, St. Clair A. *Military Order Congressional Medal of Honor Legion of the United States*. Philadelphia, 1905.

The National Tribune Scrap Book. Washington, D.C., n.d.

Neese, George. *Three Years in the Confederate Horse Artillery*. New York, 1911.

Nevins, Allan, ed. *Diary of Battle: The Personal Journals of Colonel Charles S. Wainwright, 1861–1865*. New York, 1962.

Nichols, George W. *A Soldier's Story of His Regiment and Incidentally of the Lawton, Gordon, Evans Brigade*. Jesup, Ga., 1898.

Nordhaus, Henry. "How Colonel Winslow Died." *National Tribune*, April 1, 1897.

Oates, William C. *The War Between the Union and the Confederacy and Its Lost Opportunities*. New York, 1905.

O'Beirne, Kevin M. "Into the Valley of the Shadow of Death: The Corcoran Legion at Cold Harbor." *North and South* 3 (2000), 68–81.

———. "Our Boys Stood Up Like Heroes," *Irish Volunteer* 5 (2000), 1.

Olcott, Mark, comp. *The Civil War Letters of Lewis Bissell*. Washington, D.C., 1981.

Olsen, Bernard A., ed. *Upon the Tented Field*. Red Bank, N.J., 1993.

Page, Charles A. *Letters of a War Correspondent*. Boston, 1899.

Parker, Ezra K. *From the Rapidan to the James Under Grant*. Providence, R.I., 1909.

Patterson, Gerard A. "In a Most Disgraceful Manner." *Civil War Times Illustrated* (March/April 1990), 46–7.

Peacock, Jane B., ed. "A Georgian's View of the War in Virginia: The Civil War Letters of A. B. Simms." *Atlanta Historical Journal* 23 (1979), 102–18.

Perry, Martha Derby, comp. *Letters from a Surgeon of the Civil War*. Boston, 1906.

Peyton, George Q. *A Civil War Record for 1864–1865*. Edited by Robert A. Hodge. Fredericksburg, Va., 1981.

Pfanz, Donald C. *Richard S. Ewell: A Soldier's Life*. Chapel Hill, 1998.

Pollard, Edward A. *The Lost Cause*. New York, 1867.

Pollard, Harry T. "Some War Events in Hanover County." *Hanover County Historical Society Bulletin* 52 (1995), 2–5.

Porter, C. "Did Soldiers Refuse to Charge!" *National Tribune*, March 7, 1889.

Porter, Horace. *Campaigning with Grant*. New York, 1897.

Power, J. Tracy. *Lee's Miserables: Life in the Army of Northern Virginia from the Wilderness to Appomattox*. Chapel Hill, 1998.

Preston, Noble D. "Hawes's Shop." *National Tribune*, April 21, 1887.

Ray, J. M. "Cold Harbor." *National Tribune*, December 31, 1891.

Reagan, John H. *Memoirs, With Special Reference to Secession and the Civil War*. Edited by Walter Flavius McCaleb. New York, 1906.

Rhea, Gordon C. "The Testing of a Corps Commander: Gouverneur Kemble Warren at the Wilderness and Spotsylvania." In *The Spotsylvania Campaign,* edited by Gary W. Gallagher, 61–79. Chapel Hill, 1998.

―――. "Union Cavalry in the Wilderness: The Education of Philip H. Sheridan and James H. Wilson." In *The Wilderness Campaign,* edited by Gary W. Gallagher, 106–35. Chapel Hill, 1997.

Rhodes, Robert Hunt, ed. *All for the Union: The Civil War Diary and Letters of Elisha Hunt Rhodes.* New York, 1991.

Ritchie, David F. *Four Years in the First New York Light Artillery.* Edited by Norman L. Ritchie. New York, 1997.

Robbins, Walter R. *War Record and Personal Experiences.* N.p., n.d.

Robertson, James I., Jr., ed. *The Civil War Letters of General Robert McAllister.* New Brunswick, N.J., 1965.

Robertson, P. "A Reminiscence of Cold Harbor." *National Tribune,* March 30, 1884.

Robertson, Robert S. "Diary of the War." Edited by Charles N. and Rosemary Walker. In *Ft. Wayne (Ind.) Old Fort News* 28 (1965), 156–207.

―――. "From Spotsylvania Onward." In *War Papers Read Before the Indiana Commandery Military Order of the Loyal Legion of the United States,* 344–58. Indianapolis, 1898.

―――. *Personal Recollections of the War.* Milwaukee, 1895.

Rodenbough, Theophilus F., comp. *From Everglade to Cañon with the Second Dragoons.* New York, 1875.

Rosenblatt, Emil, and Ruth Rosenblatt, eds. *Hard Marching Every Day: The Civil War Letters of Wilbur Fisk, 1861–1865.* Lawrence, Kans., 1992.

Rosser, Thomas L. "Promotion for Extraordinary Skill." In *Lost Cause* 1 (1898), 53–4.

Sanford, George B. *Fighting Rebels and Redskins: Experiences in Army Life of Colonel George B. Sanford, 1861–1892.* Edited by E. R. Hagemann. Norman, Okla., 1969.

Scharff, Charles W. "The Battle of Cold Harbor." *National Tribune,* May 20, 1886.

Schiller, Herbert M., ed. *A Captain's War: The Letters and Diaries of William H. S. Burgwyn, 1861–1865.* Shippensburg, Pa., 1994.

Schoyer, William T., ed. *The Road to Cold Harbor: Field Diary, January 1–June 12, 1864, of Samuel L. Schoyer, Captain, Company G, 139th Pennsylvania Volunteer Regiment.* Pittsburgh, 1986.

Sheridan, Philip H. *Personal Memoirs of P. H. Sheridan.* 2 vols. New York, 1888.

Silliker, Ruth L., ed. *The Rebel Yell and the Yankee Hurrah: The Civil War Journal of a Maine Volunteer, Private John W. Haley, 17th Maine Regiment.* Camden, Me., 1985.

Simon, John Y., ed. *The Papers of Ulysses S. Grant.* 20 vols. Carbondale, Ill. 1967–1999.

Small, Harold A., ed. *The Road to Richmond: The Civil War Memoirs of Major Abner R. Small of the 16th Maine Vols.; With His Diary as a Prisoner of War.* Berkeley, Calif., 1957.

Smith, William F. "The Eighteenth Corps at Cold Harbor." In *B&L* 4, pp. 221–30.

S.M.T. "Cold Harbor." *National Tribune,* November 19, 1891.

Sorrel, G. Moxley. *Recollections of a Confederate Staff Officer.* New York, 1917.

Sparks, David S., ed. *Inside Lincoln's Army: The Diary of Marsena Rudolph Patrick, Provost Marshal General, Army of the Potomac.* New York, 1964.

Spear, Ellis. *Civil War Recollections of General Ellis Spear.* Edited by Abbott Spear. Orono, Me., 1997.

Stevens, George T. *Three Years in the Sixth Corps.* Albany, N.Y., 1866.

Stewart, William S. *A Pair of Blankets: War-Time History in Letters to the Young People of the South.* New York, 1914.

Stiles, Robert. *Four Years Under Marse Robert.* New York, 1903.

Stocker, Jeffrey D., ed. *From Huntsville to Appomattox.* Knoxville, Tenn., 1996.

Stone, James M. *Personal Recollections of the Civil War, by One Who Took Part in It as a Private Soldier in the 21st Volunteer Regiment of Infantry from Massachusetts.* Boston, 1918.

Sumner, Merlin E., ed. *The Diary of Cyrus B. Comstock.* Dayton, Ohio, 1987.

Swank, Walbrook D., ed. *Confederate Letters and Diaries, 1861–1865.* Mineral, Va., 1988.

Taylor, Gray Nelson. *Saddle and Saber: Civil War Letters of Corporal Nelson Taylor.* N.p., n.d.

Taylor, Walter H. *General Lee: His Campaigns in Virginia, 1861–1865, with Personal Reminiscences.* Norfolk, Va. 1906.

Temple, Wayne C., ed. "A Signal Officer with Grant: Letters of Captain Charles L. Davis." In *Civil War History* 7 (1961), 428–37.

Tenney, Luman Harris. *War Diary, 1861–1865.* Cleveland, 1914.

Thomas, Mary Warner, and Richard A. Sauers, eds. *"I Never Want to Witness Such Sights": The Civil War Letters of First Lieutenant James B. Thomas, Adjutant, 107th Pennsylvania Volunteers.* Baltimore, 1995.

Thorpe, James S. *Reminiscences of Army Life During the Civil War.* N.p., n.d.

Tilney, Robert. *My Life in the Army: Three Years and a Half with the Fifth Army Corps, Army of the Potomac, 1862–1865.* Philadelphia, 1912.

Tower, R. Lockwood, ed. *Lee's Adjutant: The Wartime Letters of Colonel Walter Herron Taylor, 1862–1865.* Columbia, S.C., 1995.

Trout, Robert J., ed. *Riding with Stuart: Reminiscences of an Aide-de-Camp, by Captain Theodore S. Garnett.* Shippensburg, Pa., 1994.

Turino, Kenneth C. *The Civil War Diary of Lieut. J. E. Hodgkins, 19th Massachusetts Volunteers.* Camden, Me., 1994.

Tyler, William S., ed. *Recollections of the Civil War by Mason Whiting Tyler.* New York, 1912.

Urwin, Gregory J. W. *Custer Victorious: The Civil War Battles of General George Armstrong Custer.* Rutherford, N.J., 1983.

Venable, Charles S. "General Lee in the Wilderness Campaign." In *B&L* 4, pp. 240–6.

————. "The Campaign from the Wilderness to Petersburg." In *SHSP* 14, pp. 522–42.

Walker, Francis A. *General Hancock*. New York, 1895.

Waring, Joseph Ioor. "The Diary of William G. Hinson During the War of Secession." *South Carolina Historical Magazine* 75 (1974), 14–23.

Warner, Ezra J. *Generals in Blue: Lives of the Union Commanders*. Baton Rouge, 1964.

————. *Generals in Gray: Lives of the Confederate Commanders*. Baton Rouge, 1964.

Waters, Zack C. "All That Brave Men Could Do: Joseph Finegan's Florida Brigade at Cold Harbor." *Civil War Regiments* 3 (1994), pp. 1–23.

————. "Tell Them I Died Like a Confederate Soldier: Finegan's Florida Brigade at Cold Harbor." *Florida Historical Quarterly* 69 (October 1990), 156–75.

Watson, Ronald G. *From Ashby to Andersonville: The Civil War Diary and Reminiscences of George A. Hitchcock*. N.p., 1997.

West, John. "Sharpshooter Kildee." In *Camp-Fire Sketches and Battle-Field Echoes*, compiled by William C. King and W. P. Derby (Springfield, Mass., 1888), 273–4.

White, John C. "A Review of the Services of the Regular Army During the Civil War." *Journal of the Military Service Institution of the United States* (December 1912), 64–9.

White, Russell C., ed. *The Civil War Diary of Wyman S. White, First Sergeant of Company F, 2nd United States Sharpshooter Regiment, 1861–1865*. Baltimore, 1991.

White, William S. "A Diary of the War, or What I Saw of It." In *Contributions to a History of the Richmond Howitzer Battalion*, 2, pp. 89–286.

Wilkeson, Frank. *Recollections of a Private Soldier in the Army of the Potomac*. New York, 1887.

Wilson, Clarence. "At Cold Harbor." *National Tribune*, August 17, 1893.

Wilson, James H. *Under the Old Flag*. 2 vols. New York, 1912.

Wilson, LeGrand J. *The Confederate Soldier*. Fayetteville, Ark., 1902.

Wilson, Paul E., and Harriett S. Wilson, eds. *The Civil War Diary of Thomas White Stephens, Sergeant, Company K, 20th Indiana Regiment of Volunteers*. Lawrence, Kans., 1985.

Wittenberg, Eric J., ed. *One of Custer's Wolverines: The Civil War Letters of Brevet Brigadier General James H. Kidd, 6th Michigan Cavalry*. Kent, Ohio, 2000.

Wolcott, Charles F. "Army Story." In *Report of the Proceedings of the Sixth Ohio Cavalry* (1911), 40–1.

Worsham, John H. *One of Jackson's Foot Cavalry*. Jackson, Tenn., 1964.

Youker, J. Clayton. *The Military Memoirs of Captain Henry Cribben of the 140th New York*. N.p., n.d.

Young, Alfred C. "Numbers and Losses in the Army of Northern Virginia" *North and South* 3 (March 2000), 14–29.

Unit Histories

Adams, John G. B. *Reminiscences of the Nineteenth Massachusetts Regiment.* Boston, 1899.

Aldrich, Thomas M. *The History of Battery A, First Regiment Rhode Island Light Artillery in the War to Preserve the Union, 1861–1865.* Providence, 1904.

Ames, Nelson. *History of Battery G.* Marshalltown, Iowa, 1900.

Anderson, Thomas H. "Fourteenth Regiment of Infantry." In *Journal of the Military Service Institution of the United States* 11 (1890), 673–95.

Aubery, James M. *The Thirty-Sixth Wisconsin Volunteer Infantry.* Milwaukee, 1900.

Banes, Charles H. *History of the Philadelphia Brigade.* Philadelphia, 1876.

Bartlett, Asa W. *History of the Twelfth Regiment, New Hampshire Volunteers, in the War of the Rebellion.* Concord, N.H., 1897.

Beale, R. L. T. *History of the Ninth Virginia Cavalry in the War Between the States.* Richmond, 1899.

Benedict, George G. *Vermont in the Civil War: A History of the Part Taken by the Vermont Soldiers and Sailors in the War for the Union, 1861–5.* 2 vols. Burlington, Vt., 1888.

Bennett, Brian A. *Sons of Old Monroe: A Regimental History of Patrick O'Rorke's 140th New York Volunteer Infantry.* Dayton, Ohio, 1992.

Bennett, Risden T. "Fourteenth Regiment." In *Histories of the Several Regiments and Battalions from North Carolina in the Great War, 1861–65,* edited by Walter Clark, 1, pp. 705–32. Goldsboro, N.C., 1901.

Best, Isaac O. *History of the 121st New York State Infantry.* Chicago, 1921.

Billings, John D. *The History of the Tenth Massachusetts Battery of Light Artillery in the War of the Rebellion.* Boston, 1881.

Bobbyshell, Oliver C. *The 48th in the War, Being a Narrative of the 48th Regiment, Infantry, Pennsylvania Veteran Volunteers, During the War of the Rebellion.* Philadelphia, 1895.

Boudrye, Louis N. *Historic Records of the Fifth New York Cavalry, First Ira Harris Guard.* Albany, N.Y., 1874.

Bowen, James L. *History of the Thirty-Seventh Regiment Massachusetts Volunteers in the Civil War of 1861–1865.* Holyoke, Mass., 1884.

Bowen, James R. *History of the First New York Dragoons During Three Years of Active Service in the Great Civil War.* Lyons, Mich., 1900.

Brainard, Mary G. *Campaigns of the One Hundred and Forty-Sixth Regiment New York State Volunteers.* New York, 1915.

Brainerd, Wesley. *Bridge Building in Wartime.* Edited by Ed Malles. Knoxville, Tenn., 1997.

Bruce, George A. *The Twentieth Regiment of Massachusetts Volunteer Infantry, 1861–1865.* Boston, 1906.

Caldwell, J. F. J. *The History of a Brigade of South Carolinians, First Known as Gregg's, and Subsequently as McGowan's Brigade.* Philadelphia, 1866.

Camper, Charles, and J. W. Kirkley. *Historical Record of the First Regiment Maryland Infantry.* Washington, D.C., 1871.

Chamberlin, Thomas. *History of the One Hundred and Fiftieth Regiment Pennsylvania Volunteers, Second Regiment, Bucktail Brigade.* Philadelphia, 1905.

Cheek, Philip, and Mair Pointon. *History of the Sauk County Riflemen, Known as Company A, Sixth Wisconsin Veteran Volunteer Infantry, 1861–1865.* Madison, Wisc., 1909.

Child, William. *A History of the Fifth Regiment, New Hampshire Volunteers, in the American Civil War, 1861–1865.* Bristol, N.H., 1893.

Clark, James H. *The Iron Hearted Regiment.* Albany, 1865.

Clark, Walter, ed. *Histories of the Several Regiments and Battalions from North Carolina in the Great War, 1861–65.* 5 vols. Goldsboro, N.C., 1901.

Clayton, W. W. *History of Onondaga County New York.* Syracuse, 1878.

Committee of the Regiment. *History of the Thirty-Fifth Regiment Massachusetts Volunteers.* Boston, 1884.

Committee of the Regiment. *History of the Thirty-Sixth Regiment Massachusetts Volunteers.* Boston, 1884.

Contributions to a History of the Richmond Howitzer Battalion. 3 vols. Richmond, 1883–86.

Cowtan, Charles W. *Services of the Tenth New York Volunteers (National Zouaves) in the War of the Rebellion.* New York, 1882.

Craft, David. *History of the One Hundred Forty-First Regiment Pennsylvania Volunteers, 1862–1865.* Towanda, Pa., 1885.

Croom, Wendell D. *The War History of Company C, 6th Georgia Regiment.* Fort Valley, Ga., 1879.

Crowninshield, Benjamin W. *A History of the First Regiment of Massachusetts Cavalry Volunteers.* Boston, 1891.

Cunningham, John L. *Three Years with the Adirondack Regiment: 118th New York Volunteer Infantry.* Norwood, Mass., 1920.

Cushman, Frederick E. *History of the 58th Regiment Massachusetts Volunteers.* Washington, D.C., 1865.

Cutcheon, Byron M., comp. *The Story of the Twentieth Michigan Infantry.* Lansing, Mich., 1904.

Dalton, Peter P. *With Our Faces to the Foe: A History of the 4th Maine Infantry in the War of the Rebellion.* Union, Me., 1998.

Davis, Charles E. *Three Years in the Army: The Story of the Thirteenth Massachusetts Volunteers from July 16, 1861, to August 1, 1863.* Boston, 1894.

Dawes, Rufus R. *Service with the Sixth Wisconsin Volunteers.* Marietta, Ohio, 1890.

Denny, J. Waldo. *Address Delivered at Second Reunion K Association, 25th Massachusetts Volunteers, at Worcester, Mass., September 26, 1870.* Boston, 1871.

———. *Wearing the Blue in the 25th Massachusetts Volunteer Infantry, with Burnside's Coast Division, 18th Army Corps, and Army of the James.* Worcester, Mass., 1879.

Derby, William P. *Bearing Arms in the Twenty-seventh Massachusetts Regiment of Volunteer Infantry During the Civil War.* Boston, 1883.

Dickert, D. Augustus. *History of Kershaw's Brigade.* Newberry, S.C., 1899.

Driver, Robert J., Jr. *52nd Virginia Infantry.* Lynchburg, Va., 1986.

————. *First and Second Maryland Cavalry C.S.A.* Charlottesville, Va., 1999.

Dunlop, William S. *Lee's Sharpshooters; or, The Forefront of Battle: A Story of Southern Valor That Never Has Been Told.* Little Rock, Ark., 1899.

Dunn, Wilbur R. *Full Measure of Devotion: The Eighth New York Volunteer Heavy Artillery.* 2 vols. Kearney, Nebr., 1997.

Emmerton, James A. *Record of the Twenty-Third Regiment Massachusetts Volunteer Infantry in the War of the Rebellion, 1861–1865.* Boston, 1886.

Everts, Hermann. *A Complete and Comprehensive History of the Ninth Regiment New Jersey Volunteers Infantry.* Newark, N.J., 1865.

Fields, Frank E., Jr. *28th Virginia Infantry.* Lynchburg, Va., 1985.

Fortieth Annual Reunion of the Sixth Ohio Volunteer Veteran Cavalry. N.p., 1905.

Gavin, William G. *Campaigning with the Roundheads: The History of the Hundredth Pennsylvania Veteran Volunteer Infantry Regiment in the American Civil War, 1861–1865.* Dayton, Ohio, 1989.

Gilson, John H. *History of the 126th Ohio Volunteer Infantry, from the Date of Organization Until the End of the Rebellion.* Salem, Ohio, 1883.

Goldsborough, William W. *The Maryland Line in the Confederate States Army.* Baltimore, 1900.

Gould, Joseph. *The Story of the Forty-Eighth, a Record of the Campaigns of the Forty-Eighth Regiment Pennsylvania Veteran Volunteer Infantry.* Philadelphia, 1908.

Gracey, Samuel L. *Annals of the Sixth Pennsylvania Cavalry.* Philadelphia, 1868.

Haines, Alanson A. *History of the Fifteenth Regiment New Jersey Volunteers.* New York, 1883.

Haines, William P. *History of the Men of Company F, with Description of the Marches and Battles of the 12th New Jersey Volunteers.* Mickleton, N.J., 1897.

Hall, Isaac. *History of the Ninety-Seventh Regiment New York Volunteers (Conkling Rifles) in the War for the Union.* Utica, N.Y., 1890.

Hamilton, D. H. *History of Company M, First Texas Volunteer Infantry, Hood's Brigade.* Waco, 1962.

Hardin, Martin D. *Twelfth Pennsylvania Reserves.* New York, 1891.

Harris, James S. *Historical Sketches of the Seventh Regiment North Carolina Troops.* Mooresville, N.C., 1893.

Haskin, William L. *The History of the First Regiment of Artillery.* Portland, Me., 1879.

Haynes, Edwin M. *A History of the Tenth Regiment, Vermont Volunteers, with Biographical Sketches of the Officers Who Fell in Battle.* Lewiston, Me., 1870.

Haynes, Martin A. *History of the Second Regiment, New Hampshire Volunteers.* Manchester, N.H., 1865.

Hays, Gilbert Adams, comp. *Under the Red Patch: Story of the Sixty-Third Regiment Pennsylvania Volunteers, 1861–1864.* Pittsburgh, 1908.

Herek, Raymond J. *These Men Have Seen Hard Service: The First Michigan Sharpshooters in the Civil War.* Detroit, 1998.

Hillhouse, Don. *Heavy Artillery and Light Infantry: A History of the 1st Florida Special Battalion and 10th Infantry Regiment, C.S.A.* Jacksonville, Fla., 1992.

History of the Fourth Maine Battery Light Artillery in the Civil War, 1861–1865. Augusta, Me.,1905.

Hopkins, William P. *The Seventh Regiment Rhode Island Volunteers in the Civil War.* Providence, R.I., 1903.

Houghton, Edwin B. *Campaigns of the Seventeenth Maine.* Portland, Me., 1866.

Houston, Henry C. *The Thirty-Second Maine Regiment of Infantry Volunteers.* Portland, Me., 1903.

Hudnut, James M. *Casualties by Battles and by Names in the Eighth New York Heavy Artillery, August 22, 1862–June 5, 1865.* New York, 1913.

Hutchinson, Nelson V. *History of the Seventh Massachusetts Volunteer Infantry in the War of the Rebellion.* Taunton, Mass., 1890.

Hyde, William L. *History of the One Hundred and Twelfth Regiment N.Y. Volunteers.* Fredonia, N.Y., 1866.

Ide, Horace K. *History of the First Vermont Cavalry Volunteers in the War of the Great Rebellion.* Baltimore, 2000.

Isham, Asa B. *An Historical Sketch of the Seventh Regiment Michigan Volunteer Cavalry.* New York, 1893.

Izlar, William V. *A Sketch of the War Record of the Edisto Rifles, 1861–1865.* Columbia, S.C., 1914.

Jackman, Lyman, and Amos Hadley, eds. *History of the Sixth New Hampshire Regiment in the War for the Union.* Concord, N.H., 1891.

James, Henry B. *Memories of the Civil War.* New Milford, Conn., 1898.

Judson, Amos M. *History of the Eighty-Third Regiment Pennsylvania Volunteers.* Erie, Pa., 1865.

Kearney, H. C. "Fifteenth Regiment." In *Histories of the Several Regiments and Battalions from North Carolina in the Great War, 1861–65,* edited by Walter Clark, 1, pp. 733–49. Goldsboro, N.C., 1901.

Keating, Robert. *Carnival of Blood: The Civil War Ordeal of the Seventh New York Heavy Artillery.* Baltimore, 1998.

Kepler, William. *History of the Fourth Regiment Ohio Volunteer Infantry.* Cleveland, 1886.

Kirk, Hyland C. *Heavy Guns and Light: A History of the 4th New York Heavy Artillery.* New York, 1890.

Kreutzer, William. *Notes and Observations Made During Four Years of Service with the Ninety-Eighth New York Volunteers, in the War of 1861.* Philadelphia, 1878.

Laine, J. Gary, and Morris M. Penny. *Law's Alabama Brigade in the War Between the Union and the Confederacy.* Shippensburg, Pa., 1996.

Lamb, Wilson G. "Seventeenth Regiment." In *Histories of the Several Regiments and Battalions from North Carolina in the Great War, 1861–65,* edited by Walter Clark, 2, pp. 1–13. Goldsboro, N.C., 1901.

Lane, James H. "History of Lane's North Carolina Brigade." In *SHSP* 9, pp. 241–5.

Lawhon, H. H. "Forty-Eighth Regiment." In *Histories of the Several Regiments and Battalions from North Carolina in the Great War, 1861–65,* edited by Walter Clark, 3, pp. 114–24. Goldsboro, N.C., 1901.

Lewis, George. *The History of Battery E, First Regiment Rhode Island Light Artillery.* Providence, R.I., 1892.

Lewis, Osceola. *History of the One Hundred and Thirty-Eighth Regiment Pennsylvania Volunteer Infantry.* Norristown, Pa., 1866.

Lloyd, William P. *History of the First Regiment Pennsylvania Reserve Cavalry.* Philadelphia, 1864.

Longacre, Edward G. *To Gettysburg and Beyond: The Twelfth New Jersey Volunteer Infantry, II Corps, Army of the Potomac, 1862–1865.* Heightstown, N.J., 1988.

Ludwig, H. T. J. "Eighth Regiment." In *Histories of the Several Regiments and Battalions from North Carolina in the Great War, 1861–65,* edited by Walter Clark, 1, pp. 387–415. Goldsboro, N.C., 1901.

McDermott, Anthony W. *A Brief History of the 69th Regiment Pennsylvania Veteran Volunteers.* Philadelphia, 1889.

McDonald, Archie P. *Make Me a Map of the Valley: The Civil War Journal of Stonewall Jackson's Topographer.* Dallas, 1973.

McDonald, William N. *A History of the Laurel Brigade, Originally the Ashby Cavalry of the Army of Northern Virginia and Chew's Battery.* Baltimore, 1907.

McKethan, A. A. "Fifty-First Regiment." In *Histories of the Several Regiments and Battalions from North Carolina in the Great War, 1861–65,* edited by Walter Clark, 3, pp. 207–21. Goldsboro, N.C., 1901.

Maier, Larry B. *Rough and Regular: A History of Philadelphia's 119th Regiment of Pennsylvania Volunteer Infantry, The Gray Reserves.* N.p., 1997.

Marbaker, Thomas D. *History of the Eleventh New Jersey Volunteers.* Trenton, N.J., 1898.

Marshall, D. P. *Company K, 155th Pa. Volunteer Zouaves.* N.p., 1888.

Marvel, William. *Burnside.* Chapel Hill, 1991.

Means, Paul B. "Additional Sketch, Sixty-Third Regiment." In *Histories of the Several Regiments and Battalions from North Carolina in the Great War, 1861–65,* edited by Walter Clark, 3, pp. 545–657. Goldsboro, N.C., 1901.

Members of the Regiment. *The Story of the Twenty-First Regiment, Connecticut Volunteer Infantry.* Middletown, Conn., 1900.

Merrill, Catherine. *The Soldiers of Indiana in the War for the Union.* Indianapolis, 1869.

Miller, Samuel H., ed. "The Civil War Memoirs of the First Maryland Cavalry, C.S.A., by Henry Clay Mettam." *Maryland Historical Magazine* 63 (1963), 137–69.

Minnigh, H. N. *History of Company K, 1st Infantry, Pennsylvania Reserves.* Duncansville, Pa., 1891.

Moyer, Henry P. *History of the Seventeenth Regiment Pennsylvania Volunteer Cavalry.* Lebanon,. Pa., 1911.

Muffly, J. W., ed. *The Story of Our Regiment: A History of the 148th Pennsylvania Volunteers.* Des Moines, 1904.

Mulholland, St. Clair A. *The Story of the 116th Regiment Pennsylvania Volunteers in the War of the Rebellion: The Record of a Gallant Command.* Philadelphia, 1899.

Myers, Frank M. *The Comanches: A History of White's Battalion, Virginia Cavalry, Laurel Brigade, Hampton Division, A.N.V., C.S.A.* Baltimore, 1871.

Newell, Joseph K. *Ours: Annals of 10th Regiment, Massachusetts Volunteers in the Rebellion.* Springfield, Mass., 1875.

Nichols, James M. *Perry's Saints; or, The Fighting Parson's Regiment in the War of the Rebellion.* Boston, 1886.

One Hundred and Fifty-Fifth Pennsylvania Association. *Under the Maltese Cross: Antietam to Appomattox, the Loyal Uprising in Western Pennsylvania, 1861–1865, Campaigns 155th Pennsylvania Regiment.* Pittsburgh, 1910.

William H. Osborne, *The History of the Twenty-Ninth Regiment of Massachusetts Volunteer Infantry, in the Late War of the Rebellion.* Boston, 1877.

Page, Charles D. *History of the Fourteenth Regiment Connecticut Volunteer Infantry.* Meriden, Conn., 1906.

Palmer, Abraham J. *The History of the Forty-Eighth Regiment, New York State Volunteers.* Brooklyn, N.Y., 1885.

Parker, Francis J. *The Story of the Thirty-Second Regiment Massachusetts Infantry.* Boston, 1880.

Parker, John L. *History of the Twenty-Second Massachusetts Infantry, the Second Company Sharpshooters, and the Third Light Battery, in the War of the Rebellion.* Boston, 1887.

Parker, Thomas H. *History of the 51st Regiment of Pennsylvania Volunteers and Veteran Volunteers.* Philadelphia, 1869.

Patterson, J. H. "Eleventh Regiment of Infantry." *Journal of the Military Service Institution of the United States* 12 (1891), 371–9.

Polley, Joseph B. *Hood's Texas Brigade: Its Marches, Its Battles, Its Achievements.* New York, 1910.

Powell, William H. *History of the Fifth Army Corps.* New York, 1896.

Powelson, Benjamin F. *History of Company K of the 140th Regiment Pennsylvania Volunteers.* Steubenville, Ohio, 1906.

Preston, Noble D. *History of the Tenth Regiment of Cavalry, New York State Volunteers.* New York, 1892.

Prowell, George R. *History of the Eighty-Seventh Regiment, Pennsylvania Volunteers.* York, Pa., 1901.

Publication Committee of the Regiment, *History of the Eighteenth Pennsylvania Cavalry.* New York, 1909.

Pullen, John J. *The Twentieth Maine: A Volunteer Regiment in the Civil War.* Philadelphia, 1957.

Putnam, Samuel H. *The Story of Company A, Twenty-Fifth Regiment, Mass. Vols, in the War of the Rebellion.* Worcester, Mass., 1886.

Pyne, Henry R. *Ride to War: The History of the First New Jersey Cavalry.* New Brunswick, N.J., 1961.

Rawle, William B. *History of the Third Pennsylvania Cavalry, Sixtieth Regiment Pennsylvania Volunteers, in the American Civil War.* Philadelphia, 1905.

Ray, Neill W. *Sketch of the 6th Regiment N.C. State Troops.* N.p., n.d.

Ripley, William Y. W. *Vermont Riflemen in the War for the Union, 1861–1865: A History of Company F, First United States Sharpshooters.* Rutland, Vt., 1883.

Roback, Henry. *The Veteran Volunteers of Herkimer and Otsego Counties in the War of the Rebellion, Being a History of the 152nd New York.* Little Falls, N.Y., 1888.

Roberts, William P. "Additional Sketch Nineteenth Regiment." In *Histories of the Several Regiments and Battalions from North Carolina in the Great War, 1861–65,* edited by Walter Clark, 2, pp. 99–109. Goldsboro, N.C., 1901.

Roe, Alfred S. *The Ninth New York Heavy Artillery.* Worcester, Mass., 1899.

———. *The Tenth Regiment Massachusetts Volunteer Infantry, 1861–1864.* Springfield, Mass., 1909.

———. *The Thirty-Ninth Regiment Massachusetts Volunteers, 1862–1865.* Worcester, Mass., 1914.

Rose, George M. "Sixty-Sixth Regiment." In *Histories of the Several Regiments and Battalions from North Carolina in the Great War, 1861–65,* edited by Walter Clark, 3, pp. 685–701. Goldsboro, N.C., 1901.

Santvoord, Cornelius Van. *The One Hundred and Twentieth Regiment New York State Volunteers.* Roundout, N.Y., 1894.

Scott, Kate M. *History of the One Hundred and Fifth Regiment of Pennsylvania Volunteers.* Philadelphia, 1877.

Simons, Ezra D. *A Regimental History of the One Hundred and Twenty-Fifth New York State Volunteers.* New York, 1888.

Sloan, John A. *Reminiscences of the Guilford Grays, Co. B, 27th N.C. Regiment.* Washington, D.C., 1883.

Smith, John D. *The History of the Nineteenth Regiment of Maine Volunteer Infantry 1862–1865.* Minneapolis, 1909.

Smith, J. L. *History of the Corn Exchange Regiment: 118th Pennsylvania Volunteers, from Their First Engagement at Antietam to Appomattox.* Philadelphia, 1888.

Stevens, C.A. *Berdan's United States Sharpshooters in the Army of the Potomac, 1861–1865.* St. Paul, Minn., 1892.

Stewart, Robert L. *History of the One Hundred and Fortieth Regiment Pennsylvania Volunteers.* Philadelphia, 1912.

Survivors Association. *Twenty-Third Pennsylvania Volunteers.* Philadelphia, 1882.

Sypher, J. R. *History of the Pennsylvania Reserve Corps.* Lancaster, Pa., 1865.

Terrill, J. Newton. *Campaign of the Fourteenth Regiment New Jersey Volunteers.* New Brunswick, N.J., 1884.

Thomas, Henry W. *History of the Doles-Cook Brigade, Army of Northern Virginia, CSA.* Atlanta, 1903.

Thompson, Millett S. *Thirteenth Regiment of New Hampshire Volunteer Infantry in the War of the Rebellion, 1861–1865.* Boston, 1888.

Thomson, O. R. Howard, and William H. Rauch. *History of the Bucktails: Kane Rifle Regiment of the Pennsylvania Reserve Corps.* Philadelphia, 1906.

Thorp, John H. "Forty-Seventh Regiment." In *Histories of the Several Regiments and Battalions from North Carolina in the Great War, 1861–65,* edited by Walter Clark, 3, pp. 85–101. Goldsboro, N.C., 1901.

Tobie, Edward P. *History of the First Maine Cavalry.* Boston, 1887.

Vaill, Theodore F. *History of the Second Connecticut Volunteer Heavy Artillery, Originally the Nineteenth Connecticut Volunteers.* Winsted, Conn., 1868.

Vautier, John D. *History of the 88th Pennsylvania Volunteers in the War for the Union, 1861–1865.* Philadelphia, 1894.

Waitt, Ernest L. *History of the Nineteenth Regiment Massachusetts Volunteer Infantry.* Salem, Mass., 1906.

Walcott, Charles F. *History of the Twenty-First Massachusetts Volunteers in the War for the Preservation of the Union.* Boston, 1882.

Walker, Francis A. *History of the Second Army Corps in the Army of the Potomac.* New York, 1887.

Ward, Joseph R. C. *History of the One Hundred and Sixth Regiment Pennsylvania Volunteers.* Philadelphia, 1883.

Wells, Edward L. *A Sketch of the Charleston Light Dragoons.* Charleston, S.C., 1888.

———. *Hampton and His Cavalry in '64.* Richmond, 1899.

West, Michael. *30th Battalion Virginia Sharpshooters.* Lynchburg, Va., 1995.

Westbrook, Robert S. *History of the 49th Pennsylvania Volunteers.* Altoona, Pa., 1898.

Weygant, Charles H. *History of the One Hundred and Twenty-Fourth Regiment New York State Volunteers.* Newburgh, N.Y., 1877.

Wilkinson, Warren. *Mother, May You Never See the Sights I Have Seen: The Fifty-Seventh Massachusetts Veteran Volunteers in the Last Year of the Civil War.* New York, 1990.

Wilson, Arabella M. *Disaster, Struggle, Triumph: The Adventures of 1,000 "Boys in Blue."* Albany, N.Y., 1870.

Wise, Jennings C. *The Long Arm of Lee; or, The History of the Artillery of the Army of Northern Virginia.* 2 vols. Lynchburg, Va., 1915.

Woodbury, Augustus. *Major General Ambrose E. Burnside and the Ninth Army Corps.* Providence, R. I., 1867.

Woodward, Evan M. *Our Campaigns: The Second Regiment Pennsylvania Reserve Volunteers.* Philadelphia, 1865.

Wray, William J. *History of the Twenty-Third Pennsylvania Volunteer Infantry, Birney's Zouaves.* Philadelphia, 1904.

Wyckoff, Mac. *A History of the 2nd South Carolina Infantry: 1861–65.* Fredericksburg, Va., 1994.

CAMPAIGN STUDIES

Anderson, J. H. *Grant's Campaign in Virginia: May 1–June 30, 1864.* London, 1908.

Atkinson, C. F. *Grant's Campaigns of 1864 and 1865: The Wilderness and Cold Harbor.* London, 1908.

Baltz, Louis J., III. *The Battle of Cold Harbor: May 27–June 13, 1864.* Lynchburg, Va., 1994.

Calrow, Charles J. "Cold Harbor: A Study of the Operations of the Army of Northern Virginia and the Army of the Potomac from May 26 to June 13, 1864." Typescript in RNBP.

Dowdey, Clifford. *Lee's Last Campaign: The Story of Lee and His Men Against Grant, 1864.* New York, 1960.

Frassanito, William. *Grant and Lee: The Virginia Campaigns.* New York, 1983.

Furgurson, Ernest B. *Not War But Murder: Cold Harbor, 1864.* New York, 2000.

Hotchkiss, Jedediah. *Confederate Military History: Virginia.* Atlanta, 1899.

Humphreys, Andrew A. *The Virginia Campaign of '64 and '65.* New York, 1883.

Livermore, Thomas L. "Grant's Campaign Against Lee." In *PMHSM* 4, pp. 407–59.

Miller, J. Michael. *The North Anna Campaign: "Even to Hell Itself," May 21–26, 1864.* Lynchburg, Va., 1989.

Porter, Charles H. "The Battle of Cold Harbor." In *PMHSM* 4, pp. 321–62.

Rhea, Gordon C. *The Battle of the Wilderness: May 5–6, 1864.* Baton Rouge, 1994.

———. *The Battles for Spotsylvania Court House and the Road to Yellow Tavern: May 7–12, 1864.* Baton Rouge, 1997.

———. *To the North Anna River: Grant and Lee, May 13–25, 1864.* Baton Rouge, 2000.

Ropes, John C. "Grant's Campaign in Virginia in 1864." In *PMHSM* 4, pp. 363–405.

Schaff, Morris. *The Battle of the Wilderness.* Boston, 1910.

Shreve, William P. "The Operations of the Army of the Potomac May 13–June 2 1864." In *PMHSM* 4, pp. 289–318.

Swinton, William. *Campaigns of the Army of the Potomac.* New York, 1866.

Trudeau, Noah Andre. *Bloody Roads South: The Wilderness to Cold Harbor, May–June 1864.* Boston, 1989.

Index

Page numbers in italics refer to illustrations and maps.

514 INDEX